COMMUNIST PENETRATION OF
THE THIRD WORLD

COMMUNIST PENETRATION
OF THE
THIRD WORLD

Edward Taborsky

Robert Speller & Sons Publishers, Inc.
New York, New York 10010

© 1973 by Edward Taborsky

CIP
Taborsky, Edward
Communist Penetration of the Third World

Includes bibliographies
1. Communism-1945   2. Communist strategy.
3. Underdeveloped areas.   I. Title
HX44.T26   329'.078   72-13724
ISBN 0-8315-0137-5

First edition

Printed in the United States of America

To
VACLAV BENES

CONTENTS

Preface

When Lenin became disappointed in his expectations of a forthcoming proletarian upsurge in Germany and the advanced capitalist countries of Western Europe following the First World War, he began to look to the East as a possible alternate route toward fostering and eventually bringing about the coveted communist World Revolution. In much the same vein, when Stalin's heirs realized their inability to advance the cause of communism in Europe beyond the line reached at the end and in the aftermath of the Second World War, they began turning their attention increasingly to the less developed countries of Asia, Africa and, more recently, Latin America. The Soviet example was promptly followed by Soviet Russia's East European communist associates and Communist China.

As documented by the increasing body of literature on the subject, this notable shift in communist strategy attracted and continues to attract the attention of the students of world communism. In addition to numerous articles in scholarly journals and chapters in collections of readings and books on Soviet and Chinese foreign policies, communist strategy in what is now referred to as the "Third World" has been explored in a number of book-length studies. Some of them concern themselves only with one or several developing countries while others examine communist activities pertaining to one continent or subcontinent, or concentrate only upon one aspect of strategy, such as economic penetration. Nearly all of the books on communist strategy relative to the Third World published in the West cover pertinent Soviet activities and a number of them scrutinize also those of native communists. A few pay attention also to the Third World ventures of Communist China and fewer still touch upon the contributions made by communist East Europe. However, none of these studies covers the communist strategy vis-a-vis the Third World in its entirety.

It is the purpose of the present volume to fill this gap and present an overall exposition and analysis of communist strategy in and toward the Third World without limiting the examination to a particular geographic target area or a particular aspect of strategy, and irrespective of the communist country or party involved in its pursuit. Hence, our study purports to encompass all of the significant aspects of communist strategy. In illustrating and documenting them, it draws on pertinent activities in all of the four main areas into which the Third World is usually subdivided, i.e., Africa, the Middle East, non-communist Asia and Latin America. While emphasizing the Soviet strategic doctrine and practice, it pays attention also to corresponding contributions of the communists of the Third World, Communist China, Eastern Europe and, wherever appropriate, Tito's Yugoslavia and Castro's Cuba. Not only does such a multilateral approach permit the communist strategy to be viewed and grasped as a whole, but it also affords ample opportunity for meaningful comparison and contrast.

Finally, a few words should be said about the organization of the volume. The first two chapters, which serve also as a sort of general introduction, are devoted to a discussion of the basic communist ideological dicta relative to the Third World. In substance, they attempt to identify the rationale underlying and explaining the communist interest in the developing areas of the World at the present stage of the East-West struggle. The ensuing chapters seek to describe, analyze and evaluate the communist strategy in and vis-a-vis the Third World. Drawing on both communist statements and actual behavior, each chapter concentrates on a major aspect of strategy, dealing first with its Soviet version and comparing it with the corresponding attitudes and conduct of the other countries of the "world socialist system" as well as the communists of the Third World itself. In addition to examining the theoretical underpinning, the devices, methods and techniques constituting the respective aspect of strategy, each chapter endeavors to determine the factors promoting and/or impeding the pursuit of communist goals through that particular strategy component and to evaluate the results obtained so far. The final chapter seeks to sum up the main findings of the preceding chapters, to draw an overall balance sheet of communist successes and failures and, on this basis, to venture a tentative estimate of communist prospects in the Third World in the near future.

In concluding this preface I wish to express my gratitude to the Social Science Foundation of the Denver University and Research Institute of the University of Texas at Austin for their generous grants which enabled me to complete this study. Also, I would like to thank the editors of the *Review of Politics, Orbis, Social Science Quarterly, Canadian Slavic Studies, Central European Federalist,* and *East Europe* for allowing me to use some of the materials from my articles previously published in the said journals.

Edward Taborsky.

CHAPTER I

THE LESS DEVELOPED COUNTRIES — THE "WEAKEST LINK IN THE CHAIN OF IMPERIALISM"

"It is perfectly clear that in the impending decisive battles in the world revolution the movement of the majority of the population of the globe, initially directed toward national liberation, will turn against capitalism and imperialism and will, perhaps, play a much more revolutionary part than we expect," said Lenin addressing the Third Congress of the Communist International.[1] "Lenin had profound faith in the creative powers of the peoples of the East," asserts *Fundamentals of Marxism-Leninism,* the present official Soviet manual of ideology and strategy, "and he foresaw that the great day would come when they would break the fetters of colonial enslavement."[2] As stressed in Leonid Brezhnev's message to a 1969 international symposium of "leaders of national liberation movement" and Soviet specialists on the affairs of the Third World, "Lenin's theory of the national liberation movement and his strategy of durable alliance between the international proletariat and the oppressed peoples charted the way to victory in the struggle against colonialism, for the independence, freedom and social progress of the peoples.... True to the behests of the great Lenin, the Soviet people stand, as always, in fraternal solidarity with the peoples of the newly-emerged independent states, with the national liberation movement, rendering them all-around political, moral and material assistance. . ."[3]

Judging by their statements about, and their involvement in, the world's less developed areas in recent years Lenin's heirs have evidently concluded that their teacher's prophesy has at long last come true. "The disintegration of the imperialist colonial system now taking place is a postwar development of history-making significance," reported Nikita S. Khrushchev to the Twentieth Congress of the Soviet Communist party in February 1956 in his very first major official pronouncement as the new leader of world communism. In an extensive chapter devoted specifically to the national-liberation movement, the 1961 *Program of the Soviet Communist Party* proclaims the Party's "fraternal alliance with the people who have thrown off the colonial or semi-colonial yoke" to be "the corner-stone" of its internationalist policy. The *Program* also makes it the Party's "internationalist duty to assist the peoples who have set out to win and strengthen their national independence, all people who are fighting for the complete abolition of the colonial system."[5] One of the basic aims of Soviet foreign policy, restates once again the editorial in *Pravda* of June 2, 1971, "is to support the national-liberation movement and to realize an all-embracing cooperation with the young developing states."

The East European Communist regimes subscribe *in toto* to this new communist emphasis on the less developed areas of the world; and also, despite her ideological tug-of-war with the Soviet Union, does Communist China. Alongside the representatives of other communist parties of the world, the leaders of the ruling communist parties of both China and East Europe (except Yugoslavia) appended their signatures to the 1960 Moscow *Declaration of Eighty-One Communist Parties,* meant to serve as an official international code of communist policy and strategy. This code designates "the breakdown of the system of colonial slavery under the impact of the national-liberation movement" as "a development ranking second in historic importance only to the formation of the world socialist system." It gives extensive directives for the "building of socialism in new nations," declares "the socialist countries" to be "true and sincere friends of the peoples fighting for liberation and those who have thrown off the imperialist yoke," and offers them help "in strengthening their independence."[6]

Why are the communist regimes interested so much today in the less developed areas of the world? What are their motivations, purposes, and objectives? Why, at the present stage of the East-West struggle, do communists view the developing nations of Asia, Africa and Latin America as an especially promising arena in which to advance the cause of ultimate communist victory on the global scale?

The reasons that have prompted the communist regimes to focus their international attention on what is today generally labeled as the Third World, may be divided into two somewhat overlapping categories:

1. reasons of an ideological nature based on postulates of communist ideology and anticipations predicated on the Marxist-Leninist "world outlook";

2. reasons of primarily strategic and tactical nature, based on the practical necessities and opportunities of the present stage of the anti-capitalist struggle.

It is the purpose of this and the following chapter to discuss the first-named category while the remaining chapters are devoted primarily to matters falling under the second-named category. However, as students of communist affairs well know, there is no sharp and well-defined dividing line between ideology and strategy in the teaching and practice of Marxism-Leninism. Rather, the boundaries between the two are vague and precepts of Marxist-Leninist ideology and strategy are more often than not so intertwined that a clean-out separation is almost impossible. Hence, while the first two chapters of the present volume concentrate mainly upon considerations of an ideological nature, they cannot avoid touching occasionally on matters of strategy as well. Vice-versa, pertinent aspects of ideology have to be mentioned again in later chapters even though these chapters are concerned first and foremost with precepts and devices of strategy, its actual uses in various countries of the Third World, and an analysis of the resulting communist successes and failures. In fact, the principal purpose of the first two chapters is to lay out the main ideological dicta advanced by Soviet, East

European, and Chinese communist leaders and ideologues in support and justification of the major role assigned to the less developed countries in the communist designs for the ultimate global victory. This sets the stage for the ensuing exploration of the major facets of communist strategy vis-a-vis the Third World.

Communist Ideology and Its Role

Before entering into the discussion of major communist ideological dicta relative to the Third World, a few words ought to be said about the role of ideology in communist foreign policy and strategy. How important is it? To what extent, if any, is communist decision-making and behavior in world affairs influenced by tenets of ideology? What input into communist foreign policy and strategy determination does Marxism-Leninism represent? Does ideology serve as a guide to action or is it used as a mere pretext or *ex-post facto* justification of acts prompted solely or primarily by considerations of non-ideological nature? (Obviously, if the latter were the case, there would be little purpose in exploring communist ideology in the context of this study.)

As can be expected, the official communist stand amounts to a resounding affirmation of Marxism-Leninism's paramount importance as a virtually infallible guide in, and a decisive input into, every phase of decision-making from the initial cognition, analysis and evaluation of factors involved to the last step in policy or strategy execution. "Without a revolutionary theory there can be no revolutionary movement...," reads Lenin's famous statement on the subject written in *What is To Be Done?* in 1902. "...the role of vanguard can be fulfilled only by a party that is guided by the most advanced theory," meaning, of course, Marxism as understood and interpreted by Lenin himself.[7] Marxist-Leninist theory, held Lenin's successor, Joseph Stalin, "gives the Party the possibility... to understand the international connections of the surrounding occurrences, to foresee the course of events and to recognize not only how and where the events will develop at the present time but also how and where they should develop in the future."[8] Repeating Lenin's dictum on the importance of theory, Stalin's successor, Nikita S. Khrushchev, though certainly the least orthodox leader Soviet Russia has ever had, spoke up against those who "would ever think of belittling the importance of revolutionary theory," reaffirmed the role of Marxism-Leninism as "a guide to practical revolutionary action," and dwelled upon "the common way shown by Marxism-Leninism" as the only way in which socialism could be attained anywhere.[9] The 1960 Moscow *Declaration* proclaims Marxism-Leninism to be "the lodestar of the working people of the whole world at all stages of their great battle for peace, freedom and better life, for the establishment of the most just society, communism."[10] Speaking at an international symposium on the topic of *The 50th Anniversary of the October Revolution and the International Working Class* in Moscow in November 1967, Michail Suslov, the chief theoretician of the Soviet topmost hierarchy, declared all communist victories and achievements to have been "unseparably associated with Marxism-Leninism, its creative development. . ."[11]

Other recent Soviet statements on the role of Marxist-Leninist ideology refer to it as "the mighty ideological weapon of cognition and revolutionary transformation of society along communist lines";[12] "the revolutionary weapon in the struggle for overthrow of the exploiting system and for the construction of Communism";[13] a *"guide to action,"* "a scientific basis for revolutionary policy," and a "time telescope" enabling communists "not only to chart a correct path through the labyrinth of social contradictions, but to predict the course events will take, the direction of historical progress and the next stages of social advance:"[14] the "theoretical foundation under the edifice of the great union of socialist forces and the national liberation."[15]

Western views are, of course, vastly different and much more varied, ranging from opinions regarding ideological tenets as major determinants of communist strategy to convictions that the ideology's role as guide to actual behavior is altogether negligible. Although the matter has been much debated and written about over the years, no consensus has been reached, and probably never will. However, a substantial majority of Western students of communism consider the Marxist-Leninist ideology as a major conditioner of communist decision-making.[16] Nor does the controversy seem to have been brought any closer to resolution by the quantitative content-analysis techniques, such as are undertaken in Triska-Finley's *Soviet Foreign Policy* (even though the authors' findings tend to confirm the relevance of Marxist-Leninist ideology in Soviet foreign policy and strategy determination).[17] After all, the frequency of "doctrinally stereotyped words or phrases," or ideologically conditioned premise-conclusion relationships in statements by members of the Soviet ruling elite, do not necessarily correspond to the degree to which ideological precepts actually serve as policy or strategy determinants or co-determinants. It does not and cannot reveal which of these precepts are, in Lowenthal's words, "truly operative" and which are "merely traditional scholastic ballast."[18]

Hence, in the last resort, the answer to the question as to whether, and to what extent, Marxist-Leninist ideology is relevant to communist conduct is up to each analyst's own interpretation, and his more or less educated guess. As for the author of the present study, he sides with those students of communist, and especially Soviet, behavior who continue to view the Marxist-Leninist ideology as being a major and multi-functional input into the process of communist foreign policy and strategy formulation and execution. The Marxist-Leninist "world outlook" serves the communist strategy-makers as a tool of cognition and analysis so that they tend to comprehend reality and to perceive all factors and correlations of events and forces entering into their decision-making process through the distorting lenses of their one-sided ideology and interpret and evaluate them accordingly. It lends a measure of credibility, in the eyes of communists and good many of their unsophisticated followers in the Third World, to the extravagant promises of communist eschatology, buttresses the myth of the inevitability of communist victory and thus helps communists to absorb failures and snap back from setbacks.

Despite the Sino-Soviet dissension and the inroads and growing inner and outer pressures of revisionism, the official Soviet version of Marxism-Leninism still prevails. It operates as a medium of communication and a unifying bond between Soviet communists and most of the communists of the Third World who unlike some of their European comrades, continue mostly to defer to Moscow's doctrinal *ukases*. It purports to justify and rationalize communist actions, legitimize, as Aspaturian puts it, "Moscow's behavior as a global power," and validate Soviet Russia's "self-appointed role as the guardian and spokesman of the oppressed masses of the world against international imperialism."[19] As shown below and in subsequent chapters of this study, considerations of Marxist-Leninist ideology account directly or indirectly for such communist definitions and decisions as which countries qualify as "imperialist," "socialist" or "national-democratic"; which social classes or strata should be considered as enemies, collaborators, allies or "potential" allies; which group is entitled to act as vanguard and what must be its qualification; what activities constitute "neo-colonialism" and what attaches "strings" to economic aid offers; whether a "revolutionary situation" exists and what stage or sub-stage of the revolution obtains in a given country; whether a certain state sector of the economy, a certain brand of nationalism or a given ruling junta has a "progressive" or "reactionary" character; etc.

Since ideology thus appears to perform a number of important functions in the formulation and execution of communist foreign policy and strategy, it must certainly be considered in a study devoted to communist strategy in the less developed countries. As suggested by Triska and Finley, "the tenacity of programmatic Soviet foreign policy may be understood as a function of persistent definitions of the elements and process of the international system, for which Marxist-Leninist doctrine is the only logical originator."[20]

Developing Nations in Soviet Ideology

The ideological foundation for the present communist emphasis on the world's less developed areas has been devised in Moscow. While the post-Stalin leaders of the Soviet Union have allowed their East European partners a certain latitude in some aspects of practical politics, they have by no means loosened their tight grip in the matters of ideology. As far as Soviet Russia's East European partners are concerned, the monopoly of doctrinal wisdom, the exclusive prerogative of authentic interpretation and, if need be, adaptation of the teaching of Marxism-Leninism, still belongs to Moscow. Pressed on one side by the "dogmatist" challenge on the part of Communist China and, on the other side, by the "revisionist" menace of Tito's Yugoslavia, persistent deviationist tendencies elsewhere in Eastern Europe and West European communists' flirtations with polycentrism, the Soviet leadership seeks even more assiduously to preserve ideological supremacy over its remaining domains in Eastern Europe. This is especially evident in matters pertaining to the communist stand vis-a-vis the non-communist part of the world. Thus, as shown in Chapter II, East European communist theoreticians have not developed any new theories on the place and role of the less developed countries in the world-wide contest between communism and capitalism. Instead, they have tended to follow the ideological precepts made in Moscow. A similar claim of Soviet primacy in the elaboration of communist ideology has been insisted upon, though lately with little success, with regard to Communist China.

Hence, an enquiry into the ideological reasons behind communist interest in the less developed areas must necessarily begin with Moscow. And if it begins with Moscow, it must inevitably start with Lenin, for every elaboration and every turn of ideology must be justified, even today, by an appropriate reference to the Master and by a "creative" interpretation of his teaching. "Lenin worked out the theory of the national-liberation revolution, a theory that became a leading star for the revolutionary fighters of the colonial world," wrote the Soviet reviewer of a recent volume on *Lenin On Friendship with the Peoples of the East*.[21]

Indeed, the Soviet theoreticians of Marxism-Leninism have been going through the Master's prolific writings with a fine-toothed comb in an endeavor to provide a solidly founded Leninist justification for the current communist emphasis on the less developed parts of the world as the main zone of communist operations.[22] However, in so doing, they have had to overcome a major problem, namely, Lenin's well-nigh all-inclusive preoccupation with Europe in contrast to his rather cursory and definitely quite secondary interest in other continents beyond the immediate periphery of Soviet boundaries.[23] It is true that, after his early hopes in a forthcoming proletarian revolution in Europe have gone sour, Lenin became somewhat more interested in Asia, as is indicated by some of his pronouncements of late 1919 and 1920, such as his address at the opening of the Second All-Union Congress of Communist Organizations of the Peoples of the East in November 1919[24] and his statement at the Second Congress of the Comintern in July-August 1920.[25] But even in such instances Lenin unmistakably demonstrated his low regard for non-European areas of the world as a route toward the international proletarian revolution. For instance, Lenin resolutely opposed the efforts of the Indian communist M. N. Roy at the Second Congress of the Comintern to convince it to accept as a fundamental principle the complete dependence of the revolutionary movement in Europe upon the triumph of revolutions in Asia.[26] A few weeks later he failed to address the First Congress of the Peoples of the East which met at Baku and thus allowed a unique opportunity to slip by of displaying before two thousand Asian delegates his interest in Asia. By 1922, with the Genoa Conference, the Soviet-German deal at Rapallo, and the effort to secure western trade and technical know-how, his attention shifted once again to Europe where it remained until his death. Moreover, it should be stressed that Lenin's *vostok* (the East) meant Asia, in the first place China, Turkey, Persia and Afghanistan, the traditional targets of Russia's Asian aspirations, and in the second place India. Elsewhere, especially in Africa and Latin America, Lenin's interests were practically nil, although, as suggested in his *Imperialism, the Highest Stage of Capitalism,* and by his 1920 interview with the Japanese newspaperman K. Fuse, he believed that, by spreading capitalism to their colonies and "arming their colonials," the West was "digging itself a grave in the East."[27]

Nonetheless, enough references to the non-European peoples could be culled from Lenin's extensive writings and speeches to enable the Soviet leninologists to show how Lenin's predictions of the forthcoming collapse of imperialism made half a century ago are presumably coming true before our very eyes, and thus produce an updated Leninist or, rather, neo-Leninist theory of present developments.

What is, then, the body of ideological dicta advanced by Soviet theoreticians of Marxism-Leninism to explain the current communist shift of emphasis from capitalism's "heartlands" in the West to its "preserve" in Asia, Africa and Latin America?

These dicta may be summed as follows:

1. A major conclusion reached by Lenin in his analysis of imperialism was that the export of capital from imperialist countries to their colonial possessions, which he considered to be one of the decisive hallmarks of the final stage of capitalism before its collapse, "greatly affects and accelerates the development of capitalism" in the world's backward areas. This leaves them bare to the ever sharpening contradictions inherent in the capitalist system and plants there the same seeds of decay that Marx had uncovered in European capitalism.[28] As revealed by their numerous pronouncements, the Soviet leaders hold that the above developments referred to by Lenin have now culminated and the time has come for the Soviet Bloc, as Khrushchev put it in his 1962 address on "Vital Question of the Development of the Socialist World System," to contribute to "the acceleration of those internal processes which may take these [economically underdeveloped] countries onto the highway leading to socialism.[29]

2. One of the most important contradictions that capitalism is said to have transplanted from its traditional habitat in Western Europe and North America into the other continents is the class struggle. Developing their industries and plantations in Asia, Africa and Latin America, and exploiting more and more cheap native labor to reap ever larger "super profits," the western capitalists inevitably brought about the emergence of a proletarian working class that was bound to rise in due time against its foreign exploiters and their native henchmen. A basis was thus laid for a gradually sharpening class struggle coupled, since the capitalist exploiters were mostly foreign, with an eventual struggle for national liberation. According to the Soviet belief, this formidable combination of social and national revolutions has by now materialized. "A new contingent of the world proletariat - young working class movement of the newly free, independent and colonial countries of Asia, Africa and Latin America," claims jubilantly the 1961 *Program of the Soviet Communist Party,* "has entered the world arena."[30] It is this "new contingent of the world proletariat," led by its vanguard,

the communist parties of the respective countries, that is counted upon by the Soviet leaders to assume sooner or later the leadership of the masses in the "decisive battle for the overthrow of capitalism, for the victory of socialist revolution."[31] As restated forcefully by one of the foremost Soviet theoreticians, Alexander Rumiantsev, one-time editor-in-chief of *Pravda* and the *World Marxist Review,* "a class approach to social pheno-mena and processes has always been an axiom of Marxism. Without it neither Marxist-Leninist theory nor successful prac-tical activity of the communist and workers' parties to change the world in the interests of the working masses is conceivable. . . . Any assessment of the epoch and its basic contradiction which ignores and repudiates the substance of Marxism-Leninism - the theory of the class struggle and the inevitable victory of the working class, of all working people, as its end result - lacks scientific validity."[32]

While the Leninist teaching of the transplantation of the class struggle carries with it a good deal of credibility when applied to Asia, Latin America and, to a certain degree, North Africa, it has encountered trouble in what is today called Sub-Sahara or Black Africa. Claiming that the black African society is essen-tially a society without classes, even the African socialists of pronouncedly Marxian leanings deny that conditions under which a class struggle develops are present in their countries. Since such a claim vitiates the communist ideological analysis of the African situation in one of its most sensitive aspects, the communist theoreticians, led by the foremost Soviet Africano-logist, the late Professor I. I. Potekhin, launched a resolute campaign against such heretical viewpoints. While conceding that there are many peculiarities setting Africa apart from other areas, Potekhin criticized time and again the "African social-ism" and its erroneous denial of the necessity of class struggle, and maintained that "the only guiding star [on the way to socialism in Africa] can be the scientific [i.e. Marxist-Leninist] theory of socialism."[33]

The same theme has been stressed repeatedly in the *World Marxist Review,* the official mouthpiece of the Soviet-led part of the world communist movement. Sharply attacking the ar-guments of President Senghor of Senegal that there were no classes in Africa, one of the articles in a series devoted to the problems of the national-liberation struggle in the less developed countries asserts that in Senegal and elsewhere in Africa "the bourgeoisie already plays the same role as the bourgeoisie in all capitalist countries," "may well be likened to a confidential agent of foreign monopolies," "serves as a screen for neo-colonialism," and that its interests are "diametrically opposed to the interests of the peasants, the workers."[34] "The African working class appeared on the political scene before the African national bourgeoisie," holds another article in the same series and, re-writing recent history in the typical communist fashion, its author continues: "There is no doubt that just as the African working class acted as the decisive fighting force and pace-setter in the battle for political independence, so now, in the new stage facing the new states, the working class is coming forward as the decisive force in the struggle to destroy the remnants of colonialism and neo-colonialism and to build the new Africa."[35] Whereas the native bourgeoisie in tropical Africa is numerically and economically very weak, Potekhin asserts, the native working class is numerically relatively strong. Furthermore, since the working class of Sub-Sahara Africa consists mostly of migrant laborers, their continuous migration from countryside to town and back to countryside brings with it a heightening of class consciousness. This "cycle of movement" thus is said to perform the same function observed by Lenin in 1905 in Russia where the striking workers deported from Petersburg often returned to their native villages, told the peasants about the conflagration in the cities, explained to them the meaning of political demands, and thereby helped to create a new type of class-conscious young peasants.[36] Summing up the Soviet case against the African socialism, a 1965 volume on *Independent Countries of Africa* views the doctrines of African socialism as being "shot through with bourgeois illusions," such as denial of the existence of classes and class struggle in African society, idealization of the existing social structure and patriarchal relationships, and exaggeration of the role of religion.[37]

Alongside with the "African socialism" the "Arab socialism" has also been taken repeatedly to task, primarily because of its denial of the necessity of class struggle. "Ideologically, Egyptian

'Arab socialism' is a conglomeration of scientific and utopian socialism, petty-bourgeois ideas, narrow nationalism, religious prejudices and subjective idealism," wrote *World Marxist Review* in an exchange of views on the Problems of the National Liberation Movement of the Arab Peoples.[38] "It does not aim at abolishing the exploitation of man by man which is the object of socialist revolution. It does not clearly and definitely recognize class struggle to be an objective law of development of a society divided into exploiters and the exploited." Indeed, Colonel Nasser's persistent exclusion of the concept of class struggle from his "Arab socialism" was the main ideological fault found with the late Egyptian leader by Soviet theoreticians and Middle Eastern specialists.

Hence, in the official communist viewpoint, the class struggle, the classical Marxist-Leninist weapon and foremost method of the proletarian revolution, is fully applicable to the less developed areas of the world, including the Middle East, and Black Africa, greatly enhancing the possibilities for solutions along the Marxist-Leninist pattern.

3. Besides creating conditions for the emergence of the working class, the capitalists are also credited with having unwittingly contributed to the rise of national consciousness among the colonial peoples as well as the knowledge of the ways and means as how best to fight for their freedom. In his *Imperialism, The Highest Stage of Capitalism,* Lenin cites with full approval Hilferding's statement on how the import of capital into the colonies "excites constantly growing resistance against the intruders of the peoples who are awakening to national consciousness" and how "capitalism itself gradually procures for the vanquished the means and resources for their emancipation."[39] In his report to the Second Congress of the Comintern in July 1920 Lenin took up the same theme: "The imperialist war has helped the revolution; the bourgeoisie tore soldiers out of their colonies, out of backward countries, out of isolation. . . . [Thus] the imperialist war has drawn the dependent peoples into world history."[40] If the First World War did that much even though, against Lenin's fervent hopes, it ended with a victory of "imperialism," how much more telling has been, in communist opinion, the impact of the Second World War from which the

"forces of socialism" emerged victorious and which ushered the era of the "socialist world system"?

In order to fit the "newly awakened national consciousness" of the emerging nations into the proper model of Marxism-Leninism, reconcile it with the time-honored principle of proletarian internationalism, and lay a respectable ideological basis for its utilization in promoting communism, the Soviet ideologues have updated and slightly adjusted the Marxist-Leninist teaching on nationalism. Noting that in many countries "the liberation movement of the peoples that have awakened proceeds under the flag of nationalism," the 1961 *Soviet Communist Party Program* directs the Marxists-Leninists to "draw a distinction between the nationalism of oppressed nations and that of the oppressor nations."[41] While the latter is, of course, all bad, the nationalism of the oppressed nations is possessed of a sort of dual, Jekyll-Hyde character. Its evil Hydean face is represented by that aspect of the Third World nationalism "expressing the ideology and interests of the reactionary exploiting top stratum," which presumably endeavors to utilize nationalist slogans for its own selfish interests. But its better part "contains a *general democratic element* directed against oppression," an element that "finds expression in the striving of the oppressed peoples to free themselves from imperialist oppression, to gain national independence and bring about a national renascence,"[42] It is this latter element that communists are asked to support "because they consider it historically justified at a given stage." They can support it, they are told by the *Fundamentals,* "with a clear conscience" and "without relinquishing an iota of the principle of proletarian internationalism."[43] After all, as avers a recent authoritative Soviet work on the Third World, "in conditions of foreign imperialist domination and a weak local bourgeoisie, the *national* consciousness of an oppressed, impoverished and illiterate populace in a liberated or emerging country constitutes to all intents and purposes an inchoate form of *class* consciousness and growing stronger, heightens the latter."[44]

4. Having been forced to grant their colonies political independence, the imperialists seek to retain and perpetuate their control through economic ties. While gaining national freedom in a formal sense, the ex-colonies continue to be denied the

genuine and full independence that comes only with economic independence. This is the most frequent of all the themes advanced today by communist ideologists when dealing with the less developed countries. Mindful of Lenin's 1920 warning against "the deception which the imperialist powers systematically practice by creating, in the guise of politically independent states, states which are absolutely dependent upon them economically, financially, and militarily,"[45] Khrushchev used the occasion of his very first report as First Party Secretary to the Twentieth Congress of the Soviet Communist party in 1956, to label the winning of political freedom by the peoples of the former colonies and semi-colonies as only "the first" prerequisite of their "full independence, that is, of the achievement of economic independence."[46] Although the post-Stalin era of smiles and the "Geneva spirit" vis-a-vis the West was supposedly still in effect when Khrushchev delivered his report, the Party's new leader accused "the imperialists" of turning their economic relations with underdeveloped countries into the object of blackmail and extortion, "imposing military and political conditions on them" and resorting, under United States leadership, to "new forms of enslavement under the guise of the so-called 'aid' to underdeveloped countries."

This revived Leninist teaching on the imperialist nullification of political independence through economic stranglehold and the imperative necessity to expose and counteract this "deception" has become one of the fundamental articles of the communist ideology relative to the less developed countries. As such, it has been duly embodied in the Moscow *Declaration of Eighty-One Communist Parties:* "The imperialists headed by the U. S. A. make desperate efforts to preserve colonial exploitation of the peoples of the former colonies by new methods and in new forms. The monopolies try to retain their hold on the levers of economic control and political influence in Asian, African, and Latin American countries. These efforts are aimed at preserving their positions in the economy of the countries which have gained freedom and at capturing new positions under the guise of economic 'aid' drawing them into military blocs, implanting military dictatorships and setting up war bases there."[47] It has been included in much the same phrasing in the new *Program of the Soviet Communist Party*[48] and the *Declaration* adopted by the 1969 International Conference of Communist and Workers' Parties.[49] And it has become an ever-recurrent topic of Soviet propaganda seeking to castigate the West for its neo-colonialism and for allegedly "robbing" the Third World through various neo-colonialist devices of huge sums averaging some 6.5 billion dollars annually in the sixties and expected to reach as much as 15 billion dollars in the seventies.[50] "The struggle for economic independence constitutes the basic contents of the present stage of the national-liberation movement," proclaimed Suslov in a major speech at the 1968 commemoration of the 150th anniversary of Karl Marx's birth.[51] Hence, far from being ended by the winning of political independence, the struggle and the contradictions between ex-colonies and the "imperialists" only enter a new stage; and this new stage is seen as offering very good chances for dislodging the Western powers from their positions and registering further gains for communism.

5. The acquisition of economic independence will put an end to imperialist exploitation of the ex-colonial countries. Foreign monopolies will be chased out, their assets nationalized and the immense values sucked out previously by the vampires of foreign monopoly-capitalism will go instead to the benefit of the ex-colonial peoples. Among other things, this will eliminate what the communist writers consider today to be "one of the main present forms of imperialist exploitation" and "plundering" of ex-colonial countries, namely, the so-called "non-equivalent exchange" (*neekvivalentnii obmen*), i.e., trading overpriced manufactured goods for underpriced primary commodities and footdstuffs.[52]

The liquidation of these devious forms of neo-colonialism is supposed not only to cut the economic hold of capitalist powers on the less developed countries, but also to cause serious repercussions in the imperialist countries themselves. As pointed out by Lenin in his *Imperialism, The Highest Stage of Capitalism,* "the receipts of big monopoly profits" by the capitalists from their colonial investments enable them to "corrupt certain sections of the working class" and thus delay the collapse of the capitalist systems in their home countries.[53] Although this teaching about the capitalist "bribing" of their "labor aristocracy" belongs among the least credible of all the Marxist-Leninist tenets, the Soviet leaders nevertheless resort to it as a means of explaining both the failure of the workers of capitalist countries to rise against their oppressors and the West's high living standards. "Even the relatively high standard of living in the small group of capitalistically developed countries," asserts the *Program of the Soviet Communist Party,* "rests upon the plunder of the Asian, African and Latin American peoples. . ."[54] Hence, by helping the less developed countries in their struggle against these new forms of imperialist exploitation, the socialist countries are contributing to the downfall of capitalism in the economically advanced countries as well.

6. Besides eliminating capitalist exploitation, the pursuit of economic independence is expected to pave the way for the transformation of the ex-colonial countries into states of national democracy (*natsional'naia demokratiia*), a new pattern of government designed specifically for the emerging nations of Asia, Africa and Latin America. "In the present historical situation," states the 1960 *Declaration of Eighty-One Communist Parties,* "favorable domestic and international conditions arise in many countries for the establishment of an independent national democracy; that is, a state which consistently upholds its political and economic independence, fights against imperialism and its military blocs, against the new forms of colonialism and the penetration of imperialist capital, a state which rejects dictatorial and despotic methods of government, a state in which the people are insured broad democratic rights and freedoms (freedom of speech, press, association, demonstration, establishment of political parties and social organizations), the opportunity to work for the enactment of an agrarian reform and other democratic and social changes and for participation in shaping government policy."[55] Confirming this semantic novelty and stressing the "vast prospects" it opens for the peoples of economically underdeveloped countries, the new *Program of the Soviet Communist Party* designates as its political basis "a bloc of all the progressive, patriotic forces fighting to win complete national independence and broad democracy, and to consummate the anti-imperialist, anti-feudal, democratic revolution."[56]

Although the concept of national democracy has emerged officially only recently, a good case for its Leninist origin can be made by a reference to Lenin's 1920 authorization that the label "national-revolutionary" be substituted for "bourgeois-democratic" to describe the Asian revolutionary movement.[57] Both of these terminological adaptations, Lenin's of 1920 and Khrushchev's of 1960-61, imply a more advanced level of political consciousness on the part of the masses in those less developed countries which already are, or are in the process of becoming, national democracies. In that sense, national democracy, being by its definition militantly anti-western, anti-capitalist, and politically as well as economically pro-communist, represents a new sub-stage of progression beginning with the "formal" political independence from the imperialist camp and ending eventually with the membership in the world socialist system. "There is no doubt," stresses B. Ponomarev, one of the foremost ideologists of the Soviet Communist Party, "that a national democratic state makes it possible to open up prospects - as the objective and subjective prerequisites ripen depending on the struggle of the peoples of these countries - for a transition to a higher form of social structure."[58] Or, as another Soviet writer puts it, "national democracy is an amalgam of genuine national independence, broad democracy in social life and rapid development of progressive forms of production along non-capitalist lines, which lead, through struggle, to the victory of socialism."[59] Having previously conceived of a specific developmental sub-stage of the "people's democracy" (narodnaia demokratiia) for the benefit of Eastern Europe, China, North Korea and Northern Vietnam, Soviet theoreticians have now devised a somewhat different and, on purpose, rather loosely defined sub-stage of national democracy to meet the conditions prevalent in the Third World. "The concrete shape and contours of national democracy cannot be determined in advance for a particular country," explains a Soviet specialist in the affairs of the Third World, "...it will emerge on the scene in a distinctive national garb."[60]

The main attraction of such a national democracy rests undoubtedly in its usefulness in exploiting to communist advantage the concept of the "bloc of all progressive patriotic forces" which is supposed to be its class basis and in facilitating the work of native communists in countries governed by non-communist majorities. "A feature of national democracy ... is that it is not a state of a single class, of even two classes - workers and peasants; nor will it be a dictatorship of a single class or even two classes. It will be a state representing the interests of the entire patriotic section of the nation vis-a-vis the deposed reactionary classes. The political tenor of the life of society will be determined not by one class or by one party but by all the patriotic classes, by a bloc of the democratic parties."[61] Another Soviet writer is even more specific: "Such a state [of national democracy] from the very outset contains in itself a germ of democratic dictatorship of a revolutionary bloc of the proletariat, peasantry and urban petty bourgeoisie."[62]

As shown by the deft communist use of a similar device of "national", "fatherland", "popular" or "united" fronts in Eastern Europe in 1944-48, the creation of such "democratic" and "patriotic" blocs makes it easier for communist strategists to prevent the rise of an independently organized anti-communist movement, or at least make it more difficult. Within such a bloc of "patriotic" forces, which comprises the working class, the peasants, national bourgeoisie and democratic intelligentsia, and even "revolutionary army officers," a further subdivision takes place and an alliance of the working class and the peasantry is established as the bloc's inner core. Such an alliance, specifically prescribed both by the 1960 *Declaration of Eighty-One Communist Parties* and the new *Program of the Soviet Communist Party,* is in an excellent position to gain the upper hand within the bloc. And since the alliance itself is to be guided by its politically most conscious part, the working class, which in its turn is led by its vanguard, the Communist party, optimum conditions arise for the eventual communist control of the entire bloc and, through it, its political super-structure, the national democracy. Thus "the creation of national democratic states makes possible the full use of the revolutionary and anti-imperialist potential of the national bourgeoisie in the general interests of the liberation movement."[63] Writing in the September 1969 issue of the *World Marxist Review,* the noted Soviet specialist in the affairs of the Third World, Professor R. Ulianovskii, opines that national democracy, which he describes as "essentially the revolutionary dictatorship of the non-proleta-rian toiling masses," "does not clash with the socialist democra-cy to come nor does it rule out the possibility, under certain conditions, of political power passing into the hands of the working class."[64]

7. Foremost among the favorable prospects connected with the establishment of a state of national democracy is a transition to a "non-capitalist path of development" (*nekapitalisticheskii put' razvitiia*). Suggested previously in the Comintern's 1928 *Thesis on the Revolutionary Movement in the Colonies* as a possible course for "the backward colonies,"[65] it has now become one of the most discussed concepts among the Soviet theoreticians dealing with the developing nations. "One of the basic questions confronting these [emergent] nations is," states the 1961 *Program of the Soviet Communist Party*, "which road of development the countries that have freed themselves from colonial tyranny are to take, whether the capitalist road or the non-capitalist."[66] Answering this rhetoric question, the *Program* advises them, as also does the *Declaration of Eighty-One Communist Parties* and the 1969 *Moscow Declaration*, to reject capitalism, which "is the road of suffering" and take instead the non-capitalist path leading them to socialism which "is the road of freedom and happiness." "It is clear to Communists and they try to bring it home to the broad masses," asserts the *Fundamen-tals*, "that only by the path of non-capitalist development is it possible to put a speedy end to age-old backwardness, to raise the living standards of the whole people, and to consolidate properly the independence of the country."[67]

Judging by the consistent uniformity with which the Soviet ideologists have been using the concept in their writings and the meticulous care with which they differentiate it from socialism, the non-capitalist path of development is evidently meant to serve as a distinct transitional stage or sub-stage in the "complex multi-stage process" from capitalism to socialism and commu-nism. "The non-capitalist way is a transition form in social relationships," explains Sobolev. "It is neither capitalism nor socialism; at the same time it contains elements of capitalism and of socialism and also of pre-capitalist relations."[68]

The Soviet theoreticians visualize the non-capitalist path of development as a "complex and many-sided phenomenon" containing a "plurality of sectors." [69] As stressed in an authoritative article in the *World Marxist Review,* "the non-capitalist road can differ greatly from country to country," depending on the prevailing "combination and interaction of the modes of production." [70] It may even involve "the co-existence of contradictory trends over a lengthy period of time. [71] It can and should be adapted to the needs of individual countries. Although national democracy is considered to be the type of state best suited for the non-capitalist path, the latter can nonetheless be embarked upon in other state forms as well. However, one thing is prescribed as a *sine qua non:* a relentless class struggle must be waged by the forces of "nascent socialism" against the "domestic reaction" and "the still existing capitalism" which must be gradually dislodged from one position after another to clear the way for the eventual construction of socialism. [72] The non-capitalist path is "the stage of the social and economic development of the liberated countries in which the necessary prerequisites for the building of socialism are created by non-capitalist methods." [73] As restated in no uncertain terms by A. Sobolev at a 1967 Cairo seminar on "Africa: National and Social Revolution," "the ultimate aim of the non-capitalist stage, which is a continuation of the national-democratic revolution, is to ensure the development of this revolution into a socialist revolution, to prepare conditions for the direct building of socialism." [74] The non-capitalist way "is manifestly not in contrast with socialism or the socialist way," holds another Soviet specialist on the Third World. "On the contrary, given a multi-structured and under-developed economy, the non-capitalist way is the embryo of the socialist way." [75] Indeed, "the adoption of the path of non-capitalist development by emergent national states is part of the world-wide transition from capitalism to socialism." [76] By no means should the non-capitalist path of development be considered as a "third way" or a midway stage, a sort of a permanent alternative to both socialism and capitalism. "The idea that the non-capitalist path of development is a special formation, so to speak, something intermediate between capitalism and socialism, is unscientific." [77]

This description and interpretation of the non-capitalist path of development suggests why the Soviet theoreticians have revived and expanded this almost forgotten concept of the Comintern days, and why some of them now boast that future historians will rank the adoption of the non-capitalist path by a group of ex-colonies as "the third most important development of our age" (the first two being the rise of the socialist world system and the break-up of the colonial system).[78] Reckoning in the less developed countries with a fairly prolonged period of mixed "multi-level" economy that could be termed neither capitalist nor socialist, Soviet theoreticians felt the need for an interim sub-stage of development specifically devised for countries where capitalism had not been fully developed. As stressed once again by Ulianovskii's article on "Leninism, Soviet Experience and the Newly-Free Countries," "the non-capitalist path is the road to socialism for peoples and countries still largely at the pre-capitalist stage or in transition to capitalism, and with a weak and numerically small working class."[79]

8. A major factor contributing to the non-capitalist path of development is the state sector of the economy. "The creation and extension on a democratic basis of the state sector in the national economy, particularly in industry, a sector independent of foreign monopolies and gradually becoming a determining factor in the country's economy," stresses the *Declaration of Eighty-One Communist Parties*, "is of great importance in these [ex-colonial] countries." "The state sector alone ... is in a position to resist the monopoly grip, to break the colonial structure of the economy .... it is an objective factor spearheaded against imperialism and the anarchy of private capitalism."[80] If used "progressively", i.e., as "an effective means of struggle against foreign monopolies;"[81] it not only strengthens economic independence from foreign capitalism but, in so doing, creates "objective prerequisites for the overgrowth of the given stage of the national-liberation struggle into another, higher stage of its development able to bring about, in particular, the formation of the government of national democracy."[82]

Calling for "the backing of all the progressive forces in the former colonies and semi-colonies for measures aimed at strengthening of the state sector" during a 1962 exchange of views on the socialist world system and the national-liberation movement, the Soviet participant, Academician Arzumianian, enumerated the following benefits that derive from the state sector:

it "is the logical continuation of the anti-imperialist struggle and, in many cases, a direct attack on the position of the imperialist monopolies;

can be and often is an effective means of accumulating national resources and channelling them into the basic sectors of the national economy;

restricts the area of private capitalism;

safeguards (especially if there is a monopoly of foreign trade) the country against the pernicious influence of the capitalist world market;

creates and develops productive forces in a manner best suited to their transition to socialist ownership;

facilitates utilization of the experience gained by the socialist countries in planning, industrialization and peasant cooperation, etc."[83]

In stressing the "progressive role" of the state sector of the economy in less developed countries, Soviet ideologists take great pains to differentiate it from the "reactionary" role that state capitalism plays in the West. "The state-capitalist forms of economic life developing in the young national states," urges the *Fundamentals,* "should not be confused with what is now observed in the developed capitalist countries of the West." In these countries "*state-monopoly* capitalism prevails;" and this means "an overall reactionary rule of the monopolies, which fully subordinate the state machine to themselves." On the other hand, in the countries of Asia and Africa, state capitalism in its present form is not an instrument of the imperialist monopolies; on the contrary, it was called into existence in the endeavour to find "a defence against the attack of the capitalist monopolies of the West and is objectively aimed against their expansion."[84]

9. Taking the political road of national democracy, and embarking on the non-capitalist path of economic development, assures presumably the less developed countries of yet another alluring benefit: they can by-pass capitalism, move fast through the stage of socialist construction, and eventually reach the utopia of communist society at about the same time as the Soviet

Union. "The most important aspect of the non-capitalist way is the socio-economic and class development leading from colonial, feudal or semi-feudal economy, by-passing the capitalist stage, to socialism."[85] Mentioned first by Lenin, who had previously ridiculed similar hopes cherished by Sun Yat-sen, at the Second Congress of the Comintern in 1920, and adopted subsequently by the Sixth World Congress of the Comintern in 1928,[86] the precept was emphatically re-affirmed by Khrushchev in 1956: "...life has confirmed Lenin's proposition that, with the support of the advanced socialist states, some formerly backward countries could go over to the socialist system and advance through definite stages of development to communism, by-passing the capitalist stage."[87] That would save such countries, as Khrushchev promised in another speech in 1962, "from the burdens and torment associated with the capitalist stage of development" and create there "real possibilities for building socialism . . . irrespective of the level of economic and social development reached by them at the time of their revolutions."[88] As Sobolev assured his audience in his address at the 1967 Cairo seminar on *Africa: National and Social Revolution,* "the non-capitalist path of development makes possible a grand historical leap from primitive, semi-slave-owning, semi-feudal, semi-capitalist relations, by-passing advanced capitalism, to a democratically organized society and, eventually, to socialism."[89] Extolling the paramount importance of Lenin's ideas for present day national liberation movement in a special issue of *New Times* devoted to Lenin's Centenary, Ulianovskii lays special emphasis precisely upon the by-passing-of-capitalism precept: "Lenin's conclusion that the newly-free peoples could make the transition from economic backwardness to the path leading to socialism while by-passing or sharply reducing the capitalist stage of development, is one of the greatest contributions to the cause of working humanity."[90]

Since this unique feat of skipping an entire stage of development can be accomplished only with the "fraternal help" of the countries of the socialist world system, it can be easily understood why Soviet ideologists hope that the promise of by-passing capitalism should help the communist designs in the less developed countries.

10. Important though it is by itself, the by-passing of capital-

ism is but a part of a broader thesis of the alleged overall relevance and beneficence of Soviet experience as contrasted with the irrelevance and outright harmfulness of the western example. While serving as the main plank in the communist propaganda beamed round-the-clock at the peoples of the developing countries, this self-praising assertion has been provided with what Lenin used to call "theoretical grounds," and has been elevated to a major tenet of communist ideology. Its substance lies, of course, in the claim that the Soviet Union itself had once been a backward, semi-feudal, underdeveloped country exploited by foreign capitalists working in connivance with native upper classes. Yet, by following the infallible teaching of Marx and Lenin, it could emerge in the course of a few decades as the world's second largest industrial power destined soon to overtake the first one, the United States. It has thus uncovered a shortcut from economic backwardness to industrial greatness, a foolproof recipe which "transformed a backward country into an industrial country within the lifetime of one generation and not in the course of centuries," and which it is prepared selflessly to share with all the ex-colonial countries willing to take the road of socialism.[91] Pointing to the low rates of economic growth registered by the developing countries under bourgeois rule, Soviet spokesmen assert that it would take the new states centuries to catch up even with the present levels of the advanced capitalist countries. On the other hand, if they take the road of "scientific socialism," their economic advancement will promptly attain a fast rate of growth characteristic of the socialist countries. Thus, in the words of the late Professor Potekhin, "the experience of the radical transformation of economically and culturally backward Russia into a great, advanced socialist power cannot but stir the Africans," and, in so doing, make them follow the Soviet example.[92] Belaboring the same theme at some length in the second part of his article on "Leninism, Soviet Experience and the Newly-Free Countries," Ulianovskii sums it up as follows: "One can hardly point to a single essential socio-economic problem confronting the 'third world' in the solution of which the study of Soviet experience and Lenin's legacy and their application in conformity with the specific national, economic, cultural and historical conditions and the contemporary international situation would not be of utmost value."[93]

The claim of relevance of the Soviet model for developing nations is supported, in particular, by references to the experience of Soviet Central Asia. Backward and primitive in 1917 as are many of the ex-colonial countries of today, and inhabited largely by non-Russian peoples related ethnically and religiously to groups across the border in non-communist regions of Central Asia, the Soviet Central Asian Republics seem to be especially well suited for this purpose. Hence, the Soviet ideologists and propagandists cite quite frequently the example of Soviet Central Asia's economic modernization under the Soviet rule, when pressing home their thesis of the superiority of the Marxist-Leninist model of economic development over other alternatives.[94]

Nor is the Soviet thesis of the relevance of the Soviet way limited to economics alone. As pointed out by Brzezinski, several other features of communism, such as centralization of power, revolutionary rejection of the past, collectivism and mobilization of the masses by the political elite utilizing indoctrination and terror, "have a great deal of direct pertinence to the developing nations."[95] In order to develop the sense of national identity that is often lacking in ex-colonial countries, and to keep them from disintegrating under the impact of various centrifugal and separatist forces, their ruling groups have to stress and practice centralization. To be able to modernize as rapidly as possible, they have to get rid of the dead weight of the past. In mobilizing the masses, endeavoring to make them shed the old ways of behavior, and conditioning them to their new role, they have to develop a radical and rather one-sided ideology and perhaps even resort to terror to enforce compliance. And they feel that their countries cannot afford the luxury of individualism and pluralism, but must use power-monopolistic and collectivist approaches.

Since all these are features present in abundance in communist systems and mostly absent in western democracies, it is small wonder that the Soviet ideologists have made the relevance of "scientific socialism" a major plank in their ideological appeal to the developing nations.

11. The communist interest in the less developed countries is explained and ideologically justified also in terms of the struggle for peace. While "the abolition of war and establishment of ever-lasting peace on earth is a historical mission of communism," imperialism "regards wars of aggression as natural means of settling international issues" and is even "making preparations for the most terrible crime against mankind - a world thermonu-clear war."[96] It seeks to involve the ex-colonial countries in these criminal ventures by "drawing them into military blocs, im-planting military dictatorships and setting up war bases there."[97] However, these "peace-loving non-socialist countries" are most anxious to "safeguard themselves against the hazards of partici-pation in aggressive military blocs."[98] The socialist system which strives to "prevent world war and provide conditions for the complete banishment of war from the life of society" is, therefore, "a natural center of attraction" for the emergent nations.[99] "Life shows that the policy of peace, of strengthening peaceful coexistence, does not impede but promotes an upsurge of the national-liberation movement."[100] Thus an excellent opportunity arises for the joining of the efforts of the newly-free peoples and the peoples of the socialist countries in the struggle against the war danger; such a "mighty front which expresses the will and struggle of two thirds of mankind, can force the imperialist aggressors to retreat."[101]

The paramount issue of the "struggle for peace" makes the less developed countries attractive as a most promising zone of operations. Lenin's teaching of the inevitability of a war between the capitalist and socialist camps has been abandoned and Khrushchev and his successors have elevated the necessity to avoid such a war to a foremost article of communist faith. Therefore, the communist strategy of "peaceful coexistence" at the current stage of the East-West struggle calls for the use of such methods and techniques as would minimize the risk of a global thermo-nuclear war. Foremost among them are sub-version, exploitation cf chaos, playing social strata against one another, fostering internal strife and preparing revolutions, infiltrating the state apparatus and various organized groups, anti-western propaganda, cultural diplomacy and economic pen-etration. For obvious reasons, such techniques are not likely to bring decisive results in politically and industrially advanced countries which have had a lot of experience with such communist tactics. But they seem to offer a better chance of success in the young ex-colonial nations that are as yet unstable, politically and economically weak, and where the masses, and in some instances even the leaders, are inexperienced, emotional, and lack the necessary degree of political sophistication to promptly spot the danger of such devious maneuvers.

12. To facilitate the communist designs aimed at luring the developing nations away from the West and making them more vulnerable to communist influence, Soviet theoreticians have worked out their own *sui generis* concept of non-alignment. Grossly distorting the normal meaning of the term, they have taken great pains in defining non-alignment in a strictly anti-western and pro-communist sense. As perceived by Soviet theoreticians, non-alignment "is the embodiment of the anti-colonial foreign policy of the newly developing countries."[102] It "bears a distinctly anti-imperialist character" and "is in substance one of the forms of the anti-imperialist struggle."[103] It is "the policy of continuing the anti-imperialist struggle in the new historical circumstances..."[104] and has nothing to do with "the fetishism of 'non-bloc' policy."[105] It must be understood as "rejection of diktat by the West, as refusal to co-operate with imperialism, as an expression of [the non-aligned countries'] resolve to break with the entire system of relations of domination and subordination on which imperialism rests, and, lastly, as condemnation of the aggressive military blocs into which the 'free world' seeks to inveigle the developing countries." It presupposes active participation in the struggle against the U. S. aggressive policy in Vietnam and Southeast Asia as a whole, against the expansionist aspirations of Tel-Aviv in the Middle East, against racist and fascist colonial regimes in Southern Africa, which rely on the support of U. S. imperialism and the NATO bloc.[106] On the other hand, "cooperation of non-aligned states with countries of the socialist community, the Soviet Union included, in no way runs counter to the non-alignment concept."[107]

Hence, implicit in the Soviet concept of non-alignment is the adoption of a friendly attitude toward and cooperation with Soviet Russia and her socialist allies, coupled with coolness and down right enmity toward the West, especially the United States; support of, or at least no opposition against, the Soviet stand on all major international issues; and non-participation in any form of Western-controlled or Western-oriented regional associations. "To regard non-alignment as meaning merely non-participation in military blocs," warns a Soviet analyst, "is to present a distorted picture of its present state and prospects."[108] Nor should the non-aligned countries keep "at an equal distance" from both the East and the West. Such a stand would force them presumably "into the Procrustean bed of self-isolation," prevent them from playing "an important progressive role in international affairs," and "bring grist to the imperialist mill."[109]

13. Finally, the communist thrust into the Third World is ideologically underpinned by Lenin's teaching on the "revolutionary situation." In his *Against Revisionism,* Lenin singled out three "objective" conditions that he deemed indispensable for a "revolutionary situation" to develop: 1. the inability of the ruling classes to maintain their rule in an unchanged form; 2. an acute want and suffering of the oppressed classes; 3. a resulting sharp increase in the activities of the masses able to utilize "fissures" caused by the "national crisis" involving the ruling classes for breaking into the open with their discontent and indignation. "Without these objective changes, which are independent not only of the will of separate groups and parties, but even of separate classes, a revolution, as a general rule, is impossible."[110]

As indicated by their statements and analyses of conditions in the Third World since the middle fifties, Soviet leninologists have evidently concluded that, while receding somewhat in the advanced countries of Europe and North America, Lenin's "objective" requisites of a "revolutionary situation" have begun to materialize in the developing nations of Asia, Africa and Latin America. "...the Marxist thesis concerning the existence of conditions for a socialist revolution only in the countries of a developed capitalism has lost its validity in the era of imperialism. Leninism has concluded that the proletariat wins in the first place in such countries which are the weak links in the chain of imperialism." Hence, the "leninist theory of the socialist revolution has opened wide vistas for the struggle for democracy and socialism in the colonial and dependent countries."[111]

Such are the main elements of the ideological justification

advanced by Soviet interpreters of Marxism-Leninism in support of the present communist interest in the less developed countries. Such are the theoretical grounds that are supposed to make it good Marxism-Leninism to give the developing areas of the world the first priority among the current targets of the communist strategy of "peaceful coexistence." The common denominator of these ideological efforts, embodied officially in the 1960 *Declaration of Eighty-One Communist Parties* and the new *Program of the Soviet Communist Party,* is obviously the Soviet conviction that, as viewed through the lenses of a "creatively" interpreted Marxism-Leninism, conditions have now been created in the less developed countries of Asia, Africa and Latin America that make them truly the "weakest link in the chain of imperialism."

Although Lenin himself is dutifully given credit for this discovery, it would be more in accord with historical truth to assign it to a much less known figure, namely, the Soviet communist of Tatar origin, Mirza Sultan Galiev, a high ranking official in Stalin's Commissariat of Nationalities. Writing as co-editor of *Zhizn' Natsional'nostei* (Life of Nationalities), an official organ of the Soviet Commissariat of Nationalities, Sultan Galiev criticized the strategic blunder which the communist leaders had committed by centering their attention on West Europe and by neglecting the capitalism's weakest link in the East.[112] By a twist of irony, by no means unusual in things communistic, Sultan Galiev was expelled from the Party in 1923 as a nationalist deviationist and subsequently vanished in Stalin's purges in 1929, while his ideas were posthumously ascribed to Lenin.

Notes for Chapter I

[1] V. I. Lenin, *Collected Works,* Vol. 32, p. 482.

[2] *Fundamentals of Marxism-Leninism,* Second Revised Edition, Moscow, 1963 (cited further as *Fundamentals*), p. 399; see also R. Ulyanovsky, "Lenin and the National Liberation Movement," *New Times,* No. 16, 1970, pp. 8 ff.

[3] "Lenin Symposium," *New Times,* No. 41, 1969, p. 5.

[4] *XX siezd kommunisticheskoi partii Sovetskogo Soiuza,* (XXth Congress of the Communist Party of the Soviet Union), further cited as *XX siezd.*

[5] English translation of the *Program* as edited and annotated by Herbert Ritvo, *The New Soviet Society*, New York, 1962, p. 93 (further cited as *Ritvo*).

[6] English text as published in Dan N. Jacobs, ed., *The New Communist Manifesto and Related Documents*, Evanston, 1961, pp. 11-47, (cited further as *Jacobs*)

[7] *Selected Works*, New York (no date), Vol. II, pp. 47 and 48; *Collected Works*, New York, 1927, vol. 5, p. 342.

[8] A. J. Vyshinskii and S. A. Lozovskii, *Diplomaticheskii Slovar*, (Diplomatic Dictionary), Moscow, 1948, Vol. I, pp. 591-92.

[9] "For a Close Tie Between Literature and Art and the Life of the People," *Pravda*, August 28, 1957, as cited in DeVere E. Pentony, ed. *Soviet Behavior in World Affairs*, San Francisco, 1962, p. 131; and Khrushchev's report to the 21st Congress of the Soviet Communist party in 1959. English text in the *Current Digest of the Soviet Press*, Vol. 11, Nos. 2-5 (further cited as *Digest*).

[10] *Jacobs*, p. 47.

[11] "October and the World Revolutionary Process," *New Times*, No. 50, 1967, p. 1.

[12] Frol Kozlov's speech at the Twenty-Second Congress of the Soviet Communist party in 1961, *Pravda*, October 29, 1961.

[13] B. N. Ponomarev, ed., *Politicheskii Slovar* (Political Dictionary), 2nd ed., Moscow, 1958, pp. 199-200.

[14] *Fundamentals*, pp. 18, 17.

[15] R. Ul'ianovskii, "*O edinstve sil sotsializma i natsional'no-osvoboditel 'nogo dvizheniia*" (On the Unity of the Forces of Socialism and the National-Liberation Movement), *Pravda*, October 14, 1968.

[16] For a sampling of western views see, for instance: Vernon V. Aspaturian, "Foreign Policy Perspectives in the Sixties" in Alexander Dallin and Thomas B. Larson, eds. *Soviet Politics Since Khrushchev*, Englewood Cliffs, 1968, p. 132; R. N. Carew Hunt, "The Importance of Doctrine," *Problems of Communism*, VII, 1, 1958, pp. 10-15; Samuel Sharp, "National Interest; Key to Soviet Politics," *ibid.*, pp. 15-21; Richard Lowenthal, "The Logic of One-Party Rule," *ibid.*, pp. 21-30; Donald Zagoria, *The Sino-Soviet Conflict, 1956-1961*, Princeton, 1962, p. 225; Francois Guillaume, "*La Doctrine Soviétique du sous-développement*," *Politique Etrangere*, Vol. 36, 4, 1962, pp. 360 ff.; Bertram Wolfe, "Communist Ideology and Foreign Policy," *Foreign Affairs*, Vol. 41, 1962, pp. 152-170; Robert V. Daniels, *The Nature of Communism*, New York, 1962; Chester Bowles, "Is Communist Ideology Becoming Irrelevant?" *Foreign Affairs*, Vol. 40, 1962, pp. 553-565; Jan F. Triska and David D. Finley, *Soviet Foreign Policy*, New York, 1968, pp. 107-148.

[17] cited in note 16.

[18] Richard Lowenthal, *op. cit.*

[19] *Soviet Politics Since Khrushchev*, p. 133.

[20] *op. cit.*, p. 146.

[21] *Lenin o druzhbe s narodami Vostoka, Kommunist*, No. 1, 1962, p. 117.

[22] See, for instance: V. I. Lenin, *The National-Liberation Movement in the East*, Moscow, 1957; *Lenin o druzhbe s narodami Vostoka* (Lenin on Friendship with the Peoples of the East), Moscow, 1961; *Fundamentals*, Chapter 16: The National-Liberation Movement of the Peoples Against Imperialism, pp. 394 ff; and numerous articles in *Kommunist, World Marxist Review, New Times, Mirovaia Ekonomika i Mezhdunarodnye Otnosheniia, Mezhdunarodnaia Zhizn'*, etc.

32 *Communist Penetration of the Third World*

[23] See Stanley Page, *Lenin and World Revolution*, New York, 1959; Allen S. Whiting, *Soviet Policies in China, 1917-1924*, New York, 1954.

[24] *Sochineniia*, 3rd ed. 1935, XXIV, p. 542 ff. and Page, *op. cit.*

[25] *Sochineniia*, 3rd ed., 1935, XXV, pp. 331 ff.

[26] Allen S. Whiting, *op. cit.*, p. 54. See also A. Kartunova, "Lenin and the National Liberation Movement," *New Times*, No. 33, 1969, pp. 13 ff.

[27] *Lenin i Vostok, Sbornik Statei*, Moscow, 1925, pp. 60-64.

[28] V. Lenin, *Imperialism, The Highest Stage of Capitalism*, New York, 1939, p. 79.

[29] *World Marxist Review*, 5, 9, 1962, pp. 3 ff.

[30] Ritvo, p. 70.

[31] The 1960 *Declaration*, Jacobs, p. 35.

[32] A. Rumiantsev, "Concerning the Basic Contradiction of Our Time," *World Marxist Review*, 7, 7, 1964, p. 3.

[33] *"Ob afrikanskom sotsializme, Otviet moim opponentam,"* (About the African Socialism. A Reply to My Opponents). *Mezhdunarodnaia Zhizn*, No. 1, 1963. See also I. I. Potekhin's *African Problems, Analysis of Eminent Soviet Scientist*, Moscow, 1969, especially pp. 35-40, and Y. Zhukov et al., *The Third World*, Moscow, 1970 (further cited as *Third World*), pp. 207 ff.

[34] Will McLorin, "The Bourgeoisie in Senegal and Neo-Colonialism," *World Marxist Review*, 5, 10, 1962, pp. 114 ff; also, "Socialist World System and the National-Liberation Movement. Exchange of Views," *ibid.*, 6, 3, March 1963, p. 64.

[35] Jack Woddis, "Role of the African Working Class in the National-Liberation Movement," *World Marxist Review*, 5, 7, 1962, pp. 44 ff.

[36] Jack Woddis, *op. cit.*, referring to Lenin's lectures on the 1905 revolution.

[37] I. N. Gavrilov, ed., *Nezavisimye Strany Afriki: Ekonomicheskie i Sotsial' nye Problemy* (The Independent Countries of Africa: Economic and Social Problems), Moscow, 1965. For an extensive review of the book see "An Objective Soviet View of Independent Africa," *Mizan*, 7, 9, 1966, pp. 1-8. See also "Afro-Asian Concepts of Socialism," *World Marxist Review*, 14, 6, 1971, pp. 163 ff.

[38] 7, 9, 1964, pp. 54 ff.

[39] p. 146.

[40] V. I. Lenin, "The International Situation and the Fundamental Tasks of the Communist International," *Selected Works*, London, 1946, Vol. X, pp. 197-98.

[41] Ritvo, p. 88; also see *Fundamentals*, pp. 400-402.

[42] Italics in the original. See also a discussion of "two trends of nationalism" in *Third World*, pp. 223-234, and E. Bagramov, *"Natsional'nye voprosy v ideologicheskoi borbe"* (National Questions in the Ideological Struggle), *Pravda*, April 7, 1969.

[43] p. 402.

[44] *Third World*, pp. 227-28.

[45] "Preliminary Draft of Theses on the National and Colonial Question," *Selected Works*, X, p. 237.

[46] *XX siezd.*

[47] *Jacobs*, p. 31.

[48] Part VII: The National-Liberation Movement.

[49] Published in *Pravda*, June 18, 1969; English translation in *Information Bulletin*, 12, 1969, pp. 9-68, and *World Marxist Review*, 12, 7, pp. 19 ff (cited further as 1969 *Moscow Declaration*).

[50] Soviet literatûre denouncing alleged Western and, in particular, American economic exploitation of the developing nations and denigrating capitalist economic aid to them is virtually inexhaustible. Here are a few typical samples: Yurii, Bokharyov, "Africa: Anatomy of the Military Coups," *New Times*, No. 14, 1966; R. A. Ulianovskii, *The Dollar and Asia, U. S. Neo-Colonialist Policy in Action*, Moscow, 1965, F. Tarasov, *"Tsena Assotsiatsii* (The Cost of the Association), *Pravda*, February 24, 1968; Y. Gvozdev, "Latin America, Wall Street's New Tactics," *New Times*, No. 36, September 6, 1967; pp. 18-20; Yu. Eliutin, *"Za schet chuzhogo Karmana, Valiutno-finansovyi krizis v SSHA i Latinskaia Amerika* (On the Account of the Foreign Pocket. The Currency and Financial Crisis in the U. S. A. and Latin America), *Pravda*, December 13, 1968; K. Tarasov, *"Eksport kapitala i imperialisticheskaia 'pomoshch' Latinskoi Amerike,"* (The Export of Capital and Imperialist 'Aid' to Latin America), *Mirovaia Ekonomika i mezhdunarodnye othosheniia*, (cited further as MEIMO), No. 1, 1965, pp. 38 ff; Z. Romanova, *"Bitva monopolii,"* (The Battle of the Monopolies), *Pravda*, February 6, 1969, p. 4; R. Ul'ianovskii, *"Na novykh rubezhakh,"* (On New Boundaries), *Pravda*, January 3, 1968, pp. 3-4; *Third World*, pp. *107-124, A. Barinov, "Enlarged Common Market - No Smooth Sailing,"* *New Times*, No. 51, December 1971, pp. 18 ff. See also Chapter IX of this volume.

[51] *Karl Marks -genial'nyi uchitel' i vozhd' rabochego klassa,"* (Karl Marx - The Ingenious Teacher and Leader of the Working Class), *Pravda*, May 6, 1968, pp. 1-3. See also *Third World*, pp. 120 ff.

[52] See articles cited in note 50.

[53] p. 151.

[54] Chapter IV: The Crisis of World Capitalism.

[55] For an early authoritative elaboration of the concept of national democracy see B. Ponomarev, *"O gosudarstve natsional'noi demokratii,"* (On the State of National Democracy) *Kommunist*, No. 8, May 1961, pp. 33 ff. However, Ponomarev merely belabors the main points of the 1960 *Declaration* without adding anything new or significant. See also Leland Stauber, *Recent Soviet Policy in the Underdeveloped Countries. The Significance of the 'National Democracy' Doctrine*. An unpublished doctoral dissertation, Harvard University, 1964.

[56] Part I, Chapter VI.

[57] Whiting, *op. cit.*, pp. 51-52.

[58] *op. cit.*

[59] A. Sobolev, "National Democracy, the Way to Social Progress," *World Marxist Review*, 6, 2, 1963, p. 42; see also the same author's "Some Problems of Social Progress," *ibid.*, 10, 1, 1967, p. 21-29.

[60] Sobolev, *op. cit.* For a discussion of the concept of national democracy see also William T. Shinn, "The 'National Democratic' State", *World Politics*, XV, 3, 1963, pp. 377 ff.

[61] Sobolev, *op. cit.; Fundamentals*, pp. 421-22; Peter Keuneman, "New Features of the National-Liberation Movement," *World Marxist Review*, 7, 12, 1964, pp. 3 ff.

[62] V. Tiagunenko in *Krasnaia Zvezda* (Red Star), November 11, 1964, cited in *Mizan*, 6, 11, 1964, p. 10.

[63] *"Natsional'no-osvoboditel'noe dvizhenie - neotemlemaia chast mirovogo revoliutsionnogo protsesa,"* (National-liberation Movement - An Inalienable Part of the World Revolutionary Process), editorial in *Kommunist*, No. 2, 1962, pp. 15 ff.

[64] "Some Aspects of Non-Capitalist Way for Asian and African Countries," *World Marxist Review*, 12, 9, 1969, pp. 86 ff.

[65] London, 1929, p. 8. It was also mentioned by V. Kuchumov, *"K desiatiletiiu mongolskoi revoliutsii,"* (To the tenth Anniversary of the Mongolian Revolution) KI, June 30, 1931, p. 15, cited in Kermit McKenzie, *Comintern and World Revolution, 1928-1943*, New York, 1964, p. 262.

[66] Part VI.

[67] p. 422.

[68] Sobolev's speech at the International Seminar in Berlin, *World Marxist Review*, 7, 11, 1964, pp. 77-78.

[69] *ibid.*

[70] "Lenin and the National-Liberation Movement," *World Marxist Review*," 12, 12, 1969, pp. 20 ff.

[71] R. A. Ulyanovsky, "Leninism, Soviet Experience and the Newly-Free Countries," *New Times*, No. 1, 1971, pp. 8 ff.

[72] Sobolev, *op. cit.;* also, Keuneman, *op. cit.*

[73] R. Ul'ianovskii, *"Sotsializm i Natsional'no-osvoboditel'noe dvizhenie"* (Socialism and the National-Liberation Movement), *Pravda*, April 15, 1966; also the same author's *"Na novykh rubezhakh"* (On the New Boundaries), *Pravda*, January 3, 1968.

[74] *op. cit.* in *World Marxist Review*, 10, 1, 1967, p. 27; also, Tiagunenko, *op. cit.*, and *Third World*, pp. 176-185.

[75] R. Ulyanovsky, *op. cit.*, in note 64 and the same author's "Once More about the Non-capitalist Way," *World Marxist Review*, 13, 6, 1970, pp. 85 ff.

[76] Yuri Sumbalyan, "Lenin on the Non-Capitalist Path of Development," *New Times*, No. 42, 1969, pp. 14 ff.

[77] Ul'ianovskii, *op. cit., Pravda*, April 15, 1966; see also a report by E. M. Zhukov at a conference at Baku on September 19, 1967, cited in *"Friedliche Koexistenz und Weltrevolution", Ost-Probleme*, 19, 26, 1967, pp. 709-11.

[78] G. Mirsky, "Developing Countries at the Crossroads," *New Times*, No. 1, 1971, pp. 18 ff.

[79] *New Times*, No. 1, 1971, pp. 18 ff.

[80] *Jacobs*, p. 42, and *World Marxist Review*, 6, 3, 1963, p. 58.

[81] P. Avakov and P. Andreasian, *"Progresivnaia rol' gosudarstvennogo sektora,"* (The Progressive Role of the State Sector), *Kommunist*, No. 13, 1963, pp. 92 ff.

[82] R. Ul'ianovskii, *"Ekonomicheskaia nezavisimost' - blizhaishaia zadacha osvoboditel'nogo dvizheniia v Azii,"* (Economic Independence - The Next Task of the National-Liberation Movement in Asia), *Kommunist*, No. 1, 1962, p. 107; also K. Ivanov, *"Natsional'no-osvoboditel'noe dvizhenie i nekapitalisticheskii put',"* (The National-Liberation Movement and the Non-Capitalist Path), *Mezhdunarodnaia Zhizn'*, No. 5, 1965.

[83] *World Marxist Review*, 6, 3, 1963, p. 58.

[84] p. 419. See also *Third World*, pp. 160-163.

[85] Sobolev, *op. cit., World Marxist Review*, 6, 2, 1963, p. 42.

[86] *Revolutionary Movement in the Colonies*, New York, 1932. Also McKenzie, *op. cit.*

[87] *XX siezd.*

[88] *World Marxist Review*, 5, 9, 1962, pp. 18-19.

[89] "Some Problems of Social Progress," *World Marxist Review*, 10, 1, p. 26.

[90] *op. cit.* in note 2. See also the same writer's "Leninism, Soviet Experience and the Newly-Free Countries," cited above.

[91] *Program of the Soviet Communist party,* Chapter VI.

[92] *Kommunist,* No. 1, 1966, pp. 104-113.

[93] *New Times,* No. 2, January 13, 1971, pp. 20 ff.

[94] See, for instance: Alexander Vladin, "Africa: The Outlook for Industrialization," *New Times,* No. 20, 1966, pp. 11-13; Alec Nove and J. A. Newth, *The Soviet Middle East. A Communist Model of Development,* London, 1967; B. Khomklov, *"Sila Leninskoi Natsional ' noi politiki i bessilie ee kritikov"* (The Force of the Leninist National Policy and the Helplessness of its Critics), *Pravda,* February 19, 1969. "Soviet Central Asia and the Developing Countries," *New Times,* No. 37, 1971, pp. 10 ff.; *Third World,* pp. 258-59.

[95] "Communism and the Emerging Nations," in J. Roland Pennock, ed., *Self-government in Modernizing Nations,* Englewood Cliffs, 1964, pp, 81-99.

[96] *Program of the Soviet Communist Party,* Chapter VIII.

[97] *Declaration of Eighty-One Communist Parties.*

[98] *Program of the Soviet Communist Party.*

[99] *ibid.*

[100] A Soviet government statement justifying the conclusion of the nuclear test ban treaty with the United States, *Pravda,* September 21, 1961; also, *"Mirnoe suschestvovanie i revoliutsionnaia bor'ba"* (Peaceful Coexistence and Revolutionary Struggle), *Kommunist,* No. 3, 1963, pp. 24 ff.

[101] *Program of the Soviet Communist Party,* Chapter VI. In his article "The Meaning of Peaceful Coexistence" *Problems of Communism,* X, 1, 1961, pp. 11 ff, Henry Pachter asserts that Khrushchev's "real contribution is the discovery of neutralism, its legitimization and use by Soviet propaganda and diplomacy, its amplification into a new theory of Soviet foreign policy."

[102] Lev Stepanov, "Non-Alignment Today," *New Times,* No. 46, 1966, pp 9-11.

[103] Mikhail Kremnyov, "The Non-Aligned Countries and World Politics," *World Marxist Review,* 6, 4, 1963, p. 30.

[104] Ye. I. Selezneva, "Characteristics of the Foreign Policy of the Neutralist States of Asia and Africa," *Narody Azii i Afriki,* No. 4, 1963, p. 3; see also Ea. Etinger and O. Milikyan, *Neitralizm i Mir* (Neutralism and Peace), Moscow, 1964, and the book's review in *Mizan,* 6, 8, 1964, pp. 10-14, "Neutralism and Non-Alignment: The Soviet View."

[105] Kremnyov, *op. cit.*

[106] V. Sidenko, "Non-Alignment: The Prospects," *New Times,* No. 36, 1970, pp. 18 ff.

[107] *ibid.*

[108] Stepanov, *op. cit.*

[109] Sidenko, *op. cit.*

[110] V. I. Lenin, *Against Revisionism,* Moscow, 1959, p. 228; *Fundamentals,* pp. 494-495.

[111] N. V. Tropkin, *Ob Osnovakh Strategii i Taktiki Leninizma* (On the Foundations of the Strategy and Tactics of Leninism), Moscow, 1955, p. 14.

[112] R. Pipes, *The Formation of the Soviet Union, Communism and Nationalism, 1917-23,* Cambridge, 1954, p. 169. Stanley Page (op. cit. p. 144) thinks that Sultan Galiev's article could not have appeared without Lenin's approval and even encouragement. However, that is not necessarily so. Certainly there is nothing in Lenin's writings to suggest that he shared this view.

CHAPTER II

THE THIRD WORLD IN EAST EUROPEAN AND CHINESE COMMUNIST IDEOLOGY

As shown in subsequent chapters of the present study, the communist controlled countries of Eastern Europe, as well as communist China, have been engaged for a number of years in various activities designed to foster the cause of communism in the developing areas of Asia, Africa and Latin America. Using such devices as trade, credits and other forms of economic aid, agreements on technical and scientific cooperation, cultural exchanges, offers of scholarships for native students to study at communist institutions of higher learning as well as through more or less subtle methods of propaganda, infiltration and subversion, the communist regimes of Eastern Europe and mainland China have been paralleling and supplementing similar endeavors of the Soviet Union.

Being communist, they are supposed as a matter of course to be guided in all such endeavors by the never failing lodestar of "scientific socialism." Hence, whatever may be its real reasons, their countries' involvement in the affairs of the Third World must be officially explained and justified in terms of the Marxist-Leninist "world outlook."

What are, then, the main dicta serving as the ideological

rationalization of the communist East European and Chinese concern with the developing areas of Asia, Africa and Latin America? How do they compare to the corresponding Soviet dicta? Are they identical with the Soviet version as they are supposed to be in deference to the sacrosanct Marxist-Leninist canon of doctrinal unity? Or do they differ, at least in some aspects, from the Soviet prototype?

The East European Position

In contrast to extensive Soviet literature devoted to the ideological substantiation of the communist thrust into the developing countries of the Third World, East European writings on the subject have been relatively meager and sketchy. Evidently, East European communist theoreticians have left the doctrinal elaboration of the communist stand vis-a-vis the Third World largely to their Soviet colleagues. Nonetheless, enough materials have accumulated over the years, mainly in the form of articles in East European periodicals and statements by East European spokesmen at various communist conferences devoted to the questions of the national-liberation movement, to allow an evaluation of East European communist thought on the subject.

In substance, the East European communist theoreticians, with the exception of the Yugoslavs and (since the sixties) the Albanians, have followed faithfully the Soviet line. Having formally committed their parties and regimes to the Soviet-prescribed ideological *fiats* by signing the 1960 *Declaration of Eighty-One Communist Parties* as well as the 1969 *Declaration of the Communist and Workers' Parties,* East European communists have missed no suitable opportunity to place on the record publicly their unreserved endorsement of Soviet Russia's current emphasis on the less developed areas of the world as the most promising arena of communist operations as well as her evaluation of the part that the ex-colonial countries are expected to play in the East-West struggle.

Each and every one of the congresses held by the communist parties of East Europe since the adoption of the 1960 *Declaration* and the 1961 *Program of the Soviet Communist Party* has become a scene of repetitive professions of loyalty to the Soviet edicts and the ideology and policy they prescribe for the relations between the world socialist system and the national-liberation movement of the Third World. "The documents marking the outcome of the Moscow consultations of the leaders of the Communist and Workers' parties and the CPSU Program accepted by the 22nd Congress," reads a typical statement published in the main theoretical organ of the Czechoslovak Communist party *Nová mysl* in March 1963, "are effective weapons in the struggle for Leninist truth in theory and they represent the correct political line in practice. This line was the ideological blueprint of the 12th Congress of our Party and for the recent congresses of the fraternal parties in Bulgaria, Hungary, Italy and the GDR, whose conclusions also assume an exceptional international importance as a result."[1] Four years later, the official monthly of the Central Committee of the Hungarian Communist party chanted much the same tune: "The common main guideline of the Communist and Workers' parties fixed at the 1957 and 1960 Moscow conferences has proved its vitality in the course of being put into practice, and the Parties following this line have achieved great success."[2]

A similar pattern of ideological sycophancy has also pervaded the various international meetings convoked from time to time under Soviet or pro-Soviet sponsorship for the specific purpose of discussing the "paths of development of newly emergent countries" and other matters pertaining to the Third World.[3] Whenever and wherever delegates from communist East Europe took the rostrum they have kept their statements strictly within the ideological framework devised by their Soviet mentors. And the same lack of originality has been documented time after time by articles on the affairs of the Third World in Bulgarian, Czechoslovak, East German, Hungarian, Polish and Rumanian periodicals and newspapers.[4]

It is true that most of the countries of communist East Europe have managed in the sixties to reduce somewhat the degree of their subordination to Moscow and some of their theoreticians have even begun expressing doubts about a few aspects of the Soviet version of Marxism-Leninism. However, none of this seems to apply to ideological precepts governing the communist relations with the national-liberation movement. This has been so even in the case of Rumania, the *"enfant terrible"* of the Warsaw Pact system, which pushed her quest for independence from the Kremlin farther than any other member of the Soviet Bloc. While adopting a stand directly opposite to the Soviet-recommended line in such important foreign policy matters as the establishment of diplomatic relations with West Germany and the refusal to break-off diplomatic relations with Israel, the leaders of communist Rumania and their ideologists have taken no exception to the Soviet precepts concerning the developing nations.

A similar situation developed in Czechoslovakia during her short-lived independence stance prior to the Soviet invasion of the country in August 1968. While Dubček's "new model of socialist democracy" comprised several significant departures from Soviet-style communism, it stayed well within the ideological bounds prescribed by Moscow for communist relationship to the national-liberation movement. Addressing the Seventh Congress of Czechoslovakia's agricultural cooperatives soon after Novotný's ouster from the Party's First Secretaryship that triggered the liberalization process of the "Czechoslovak spring" of 1968, Dubček reasserted his regime's resolve to continue giving, "in the spirit of the principles of proletarian internationalism," all possible aid to the "revolutionary democratic national-liberation movements that actively oppose the imperialist expansion, colonialism and neo-colonialism."[5] A major article on Czechoslovakia's foreign policy written in the midst of the liberalization process by the country's Foreign Minister, Jiří Hájek, restated Czechoslovakia's interest in the developing nations as a "permanent factor" of her foreign policy and based it squarely upon "the Marxist idea regarding the natural union of the revolutionary workers' movement of the industrial countries with the liberation movement of the colonial nations."[6] The Czechoslovak Communist party's Action Program of April 1968 continued to pledge Czechoslovakia's support for "the further unfolding of the anti-imperialist front" in the Third World.[7]

Since the East European ideological dicta on the place and role of the Third World in the East-West struggle merely paraphrase and regurgitate the official Soviet version, their discussion in full can be dispensed with in favor of just a few typical samples illustrating the degree of East European ideological conformity in this respect.

As their Soviet comrades, communist spokesmen of Eastern Europe have persisted in emphasizing the importance of the national-liberation movement and the opportunities which the revolutionary process in the developing nations offers for an effective struggle against western imperialism and for a "peaceful" victory of communism. They have pinpointed Asia, Africa and Latin America as "one of the most important arenas in the worldwide struggle between the forces of progress and those of reaction."[8] They have subscribed to the slanted Soviet concept of non-alignment and rejected the "false idea" conceiving of the Third World as a sort of a buffer zone between socialism and capitalism.[9] They have characterized "a firm alliance and solidarity of socialism with the national-liberation movement" as "the highest guarantee and a decisive requisite of a common victory."[10] They have hailed "Lenin's thesis that the liberation struggle of nations oppressed by imperialism and the international proletarian revolution would merge into a united world revolutionary process."[11] They have praised the Soviet Communist party's "bold line of creative Leninism," its analysis of the situation in the less developed countries, and promised to help such countries "in every possible way in their struggle for a full national and social liberation."[12] They have proclaimed assistance to the less developed countries to be their parties' "internationalist duty" and "the very substance of proletarian internationalism."[13]

They have stressed "The decisive role of the world socialist system in the struggle of nations for the removal of all forms of colonialism and the liquidation of imperialist influence in these [ex-colonial] countries."[14] They have thrown their support behind the post-Stalin Soviet thesis of the evitability of the war between the socialist and capitalist countries and the determination to defeat imperialism without a thermonuclear war by concentrating on the less developed countries as the "weakest point in the capitalist system."[15] They have embraced wholeheartedly the Soviet-sponsored idea of the setting up of systems of national democracy in Asia, Africa and Latin America as a suitable stepping stone and a new sub-stage in the process of transition from capitalism or pre-capitalism to socialism.[16] They have shared the ambivalent attitude of their Soviet colleagues toward the various forms of native socialism in the developing countries, praising them for rejecting capitalism but criticizing them for denying the need of class struggle and for other deviations from "scientific socialism."[17] They have dwelled upon the inadequacy and incompleteness of mere political independence and the need to continue the struggle until full economic independence has been won. They have stressed the Soviet-conceived non-capitalist path of development as "the only way to solve the basic economic problems and thus to achieve genuine economic independence." They have adopted without reservations the Soviet view extolling the "progressive" role of the state sector of the economy in the developing countries and contrasting it with the "reactionary" role of state capitalism in the industrially developed countries. Considering state capitalism in developing areas as "an objective necessity" in the struggle against foreign economic domination, they have referred to it as "an important means of freeing the less developed areas from the fetters of foreign monopoly capital."

They have emphasized industrialization as "the surest way to complete national liberation," for it brings about the desired growth of the working class and thus affords welcome opportunities for the proper alignment of class forces. They have taken great pains to denigrate the exploitative designs of neo-colonialism, especially American and West German, as well as "collective colonialism" allegedly pursued by the European Common Market countries in their relations to Africa, and to stress the relevance and attractiveness of the example of the Soviet Union and the other socialist countries showing that "economic backwardness can be abolished in a brief space of time" if socialism is chosen over capitalism.[18] In particular, the Bulgarian and Rumanian theoreticians, representing the two least industrialized East European countries falling to communism (not counting Albania), have done their utmost to prove by reference to their own countries that "the experience of small socialist countries which were economically backward in the past and now have an up-to-date industry and agriculture is of particular significance for the underdeveloped countries" and how socialist production helps to "solve one of the fundamental problems of eliminating backwardness - that of the rapid accumulation of capital." [19]

The Yugoslav Stand

Having been expelled from the Cominform and ejected from the Soviet Bloc in 1948, the Yugoslav communists were thereby released also from Moscow's ideological tutelage. And indeed, after a few years of ideological foot-dragging, they began slowly to develop their own version of Marxism-Leninism. This loosening of ideological ties with Moscow gathered momentum, in particular, in the late fifties, after the failure of Khrushchev's attempt to lure Tito back into the Soviet fold in 1955-1956. It became even more pronounced in the sixties after the 1960 *Declaration of Eighty-One Communist Parties* condemned "the Yugoslav variety of international opportunism, a variety of modern revisionist 'theories' in concentrated form," accused the Yugoslav communist leaders of a "betrayal of Marxism-Leninism" and "subversive work against the Socialist camp and the World Communist Movement." [20]

However, while putting their freedom from Moscow's tutelage to good use in challenging several important aspects of the Soviet version of Marxism-Leninism, Yugoslav ideologists do not appear to have departed in any significant way from the basic Soviet-approved ideological dicta relative to the developing nations. Though they have refrained increasingly from expressing themselves in the trite jargon encountered in customary Soviet and East European communist statements, they seem to adhere essentially to ideological attitudes closely resembling those of the Soviet Bloc countries. [21] Thus they concur in the communist-held emphasis on developing nations as the most promising arena for promoting the communist cause at the present time. They look at the national-liberation movement as an integral part of the world revolutionary process that would eventually pave the way to socialism. In a major article in Moscow's *Pravda* on April 7, 1970, Tito fully endorsed Lenin's view that the national-liberation struggle and the anti-colonial movement was "an integral part of socialist revolutions." [22] The Yugoslav analysts' evaluation of conditions and opportunities in the Third World runs much along the Soviet lines. They subscribe to the standard communist view of western imperialism and neo-colonialism as the chief exploiter and a continued threat to the independence of the emerging nations and regard aiding the latter as the socialist countries' hallowed internationalist duty. "The help for the nations fighting against colonialism and against neo-colonialist attempts is one of the basic principles of the Yugoslav policy of active and friendly coexistence," wrote Antun Vratuša, the then Yugoslav Undersecretary of State in 1962. [23] Outlining Yugoslavia's foreign policy in his report to the Federal Assembly in 1969, the then Yugoslav Secretary of State for Foreign Affairs, Mirko Tepavać, describes his country's non-alignment policy as a form of struggle waged by Yugoslavia against "imperialism and hegemony". [24] The communique on Brezhnev's talks with Tito in September 1971 stressed Soviet Russia's and Yugoslavia's "decisive support of the peoples of Asia, Africa, and Latin America, defending their freedom and independence in the struggle against the forces of imperialism and neo-colonialism." [25]

Yugoslav spokesmen have embraced the general communist thesis that the non-capitalist path of development is more suited to the needs of the nations of Asia, Africa and Latin America than western capitalism and that expropriation of foreign monopolies is a political and economic *sine qua non* for the gaining of genuine independence. Much like their Soviet colleagues, they believe that "even the forms of state capitalism [in the developing nations] can play - and do play in certain given periods - a progressive role." [26] They share the Soviet view that the underdeveloped countries might be able to "by-pass the specific stages of capitalist development and build directly the necessary economic foundations for the development of socialism." [27] They hope that industrialization and the "growth of productive forces" in the developing nations will strengthen the native working class which they, too, regard as the main driving force of the socialist revolution. Finally, the Yugoslav theoreticians have been just as adamant as their Soviet and East European counterparts in rejecting most of the Chinese communist dicta on the Third World, especially those downgrading the principle of peaceful coexistence, minimizing the importance of economic aid, and encouraging recourse to violence and armed struggle.

Thus, in so far as the ideological justification of the communist

interest in the Third World is concerned, the Yugoslav communists seem to differ from their Soviet comrades in only two
respects: the issue of the relevance of the Soviet model and the
meaning of non-alignment.

On the issue of relevance, the Yugoslav communists agree, of
course, with the basic communist contention that the socialist
path of development is infinitely worthier of following than the
capitalist model. However, keenly aware of what happened to
Yugoslavia when she adopted the Soviet pattern after World
War II, they do not consider the Soviet model (and even less so
the Chinese model), as suitable for developing nations. Although
they are careful enough and politic enough not to say it openly,
they imply that the Yugoslav way of constant adaptation of
socialism to the changing realities holds more relevance for the
nations willing to embrace socialism than any other model thus
far tried. Indeed, as Alvin Rubinstein points out in his *Yugoslavia and the Non-Aligned World,* "for many Afro-Asian leaders,
Yugoslavia is an example of a relatively new nation that is
nurturing national cohesion, maintaining its political independence and making economic and social progress."[28] Nor can
they fail being impressed by Yugoslavia's success in balancing
her relations with both the East and the West. Also, being much
more broad-minded and less orthodox than the Soviet theoreticians, Yugoslav communists seem ready to approve of almost
any one from the great variety of ways along which a country
may march toward socialism in accordance with its own specific
conditions. Hence, they show sympathy with even such forms of
native socialism of the developing nations that the Soviet and
other East European communist ideologists have been watching
with jaundiced eyes.

With regard to the concept of non-alignment, Yugoslav
communists, jealous of their country's independent status vis-
a-vis the Soviet Bloc, insist, above all, on independence as the
main element of their "dynamic definition," of non-alignment.[29]
To be sure, the Yugoslav concept of "positive," "active" or
"dynamic" non-alignment is basically anti-western and was
never meant to be a policy of mere neutrality between the blocs.
"The policy of non-alignment never was or ever could be a policy
of passive resistance to the division of the world, or a policy of

equidistance," said Tito in his speech to the Cairo Conference of Non-Aligned Countries in 1964.[30] As restated in 1969 by Yugoslavia's Secretary of State for Foreign Affairs, it "by no means implies the adoption of some sort of middle-of-the-road course between the blocs..."[31] Perhaps nothing bares the predominantly anti-western nature of the Yugoslav understanding of non-alignment more blatantly than the Yugoslav reference to Prince Sihanouk of Cambodia and the late President Sokarno of Indonesia as "distinguished leaders of non-alignment," not to speak of Yugoslavia's recognition of the Vietcong as the Provisional revolutionary government of South Vietnam.[32]

Nonetheless, the Yugoslav concept of non-alignment does postulate not only "the sovereign right of all countries to choose the systems and forms of development that suit them best," but also full freedom of action in the field of foreign relations even if that means acting contrary to Soviet or Chinese wishes and interests.[33] In rejecting, alongside with imperialism, colonialism and neo-colonialism, "all other forms of foreign domination which increasingly resort to policies of force and pressure, including armed intervention, subversive activities and interference in internal affairs of other countries," the Yugoslav concept of non-alignment reveals itself to be anti-Soviet as well.[34] Even more outspoken in this respect has been Gavro Altman, one of Yugoslavia's foremost journalists and member of the editorial board of *Komunist,* the Yugoslav communists' main theoretical journal. In a major article on "Lasting values of Non-Alignment" published in the 1969 volume of *Socialist Thought and Practice,* he criticizes the unnamed but easily identifiable advocates of "forcible intervention for the purpose of safeguarding 'the interests of socialism'" for approving non-alignment "in relation to the other bloc" and for being "willing to praise it as a means of struggle against American domination, but not as a general principle."[35] Moreover, a tendency has lately evolved in Yugoslavia to broaden the definition of non-alignment so as to cover "a much wider circle of countries than was the case during the Belgrade [1961] or the Cairo [1964] non-alignment meetings." i.e., including some countries that do not qualify as non-aligned according to Soviet standards.[36]

The extent to which the Yugoslav deviation from the Soviet-sponsored concept of non-alignment has angered the Soviet leaders has been clearly revealed in a sharp "Reply to Our Critics" published in the 1969 volume of *New Times*.[37] Its author, V. Kudryavtsev, Political commentator of the Soviet government paper *Izvestiia,* takes the Yugoslavs to task for evading the class criterion and basing their policy of non-alignment "on an anti-Marxist geopolitical division of the world into big and small countries." This approach, he claims, reduces the concept of non-alignment to that of a "movement of all the small and medium-sized countries," attempts "to isolate the national-liberation movement from its great and reliable ally, the Soviet Union," and blunts its "anti-imperialist orientation."

The Chinese View

Since the Sino-Soviet rift burst wide open in the early sixties, the two communist giants have been bombarding one another with bitter accusations of all sorts of ideological heresies. In the acrimonious exchange of open letters between the Central Committees of the Soviet and Chinese Communist parties in 1963-1964 and the subsequent avalanche of mutually vituperative statements by their spokesmen and condemnatory articles in their respective press media, they have produced an entire list of impermissible doctrinal errors and departures from "correct" Marxism-Leninism, presumably committed by the other side. However, a careful perusal of the pertinent Soviet and Chinese materials reveals that the difference in the respective ideological positions of the two parties has been less pronounced than their strident quarrel would lead one to believe. That is true of the stand taken with regard to the Third World as well. As shown in subsequent chapters, the Russians and the Chinese appear to be in genuine disagreement on some aspects of communist strategy deemed best at the present stage of the Third World's development. But their fundamental ideological assessment of the place and role of the developing nations in the East-West struggle is much the same; and the few Chinese departures that can be detected are only of slight ideological significance.[38]

Thus the leaders of communist China fully endorse the present communist view regarding the less developed areas of the world as the weakest link in the chain of imperialism. Indeed, they go further in that respect than the Russians, contending that the Soviet leaders underestimate the role the nations of the Third World are going to play in the anti-imperialist struggle. "Certain persons," asserts the letter sent by the Central Committee of the Chinese Communist party to the Central Committee of the Soviet Communist party on June 14, 1963, "go so far as to deny the great international significance of the anti-imperialist revolutionary struggles of the Asian, African and Latin-American peoples and, on the pretext of breaking down the barriers of nationality, color and geographical location, are trying their best to efface the line of demarcation between oppressed and oppressor nations and between oppressed and oppressor countries, and to hold down the revolutionary struggle of the peoples in these areas."[39]

Invoking Lenin's thesis that "the revolutionary movement in the advanced countries would actually be a sheer fraud if, in their struggle against capitalism, the workers of Europe and America were not closely and completely united with the hundreds of millions of colonial slaves who are oppressed by the capital,"[40] the Chinese statement accuses those same "certain persons" of "taking a passive or scornful or negative attitude toward the struggle of the oppressed nations for liberation" and thus "in fact protecting the interest of monopoly capital, betraying those of the proletariat and degenerating into Social Democrats."[41] With vicious sarcasm it denounces those "certain persons" of seeking to "create a new 'theory' to justify the rule of imperialism in these [ex-colonial] areas, the promotion of its policies of old and new colonialism"; and it serves an ominous warning that "the attitude taken toward the revolutionary struggles of the people in Asian, African and Latin American countries is an important criterion for differentiating those who want revolution from those who do not and those who are truly defending world peace from those who are abetting the forces of aggression and war."[42]

In a long article published on September 6, 1963, in the Chinese Communist party organ *Jenmin Jih-Pao,* devoted to an extensive explanation of the origins and growth of the Chinese-

Soviet differences, the Chinese communist leaders have claimed credit for having caused "many of the wrong theses", included in the original draft of the 1960 *Declaration of Eighty-One Communist Parties* by its Soviet drafters, especially those pertaining to the national-liberation movement, to be rejected and replaced by the "correct views" set forth by the Chinese delegation. And the Chinese summary of "bad things" perpetrated by Khrushchev, published after the Soviet leader's demotion, includes the accusation that "under the signboard of 'peaceful coexistence' he did his utmost to oppose and sabotage the national-liberation movement and went so far as to work hand in glove with U. S. imperialism, suppressing the revolutionary struggles of the oppressed nations."[43]

In contrast to the Soviet "fraudulent 'theory' pretending friendship and support for the less developed countries but in reality downgrading their importance and thus "catering to the needs of imperialism," the Chinese communist leadership affirms in most emphatic terms the decisive role that the peoples of Asia, Africa and Latin America are destined to play in the anti-imperialist crusade. "The various types of contradictions in the contemporary world," asserts the Chinese letter of June 14, 1963, "are concentrated in the vast areas of Asia, Africa and Latin America; these are the most vulnerable areas under imperialist rule and the storm-centers of world revolution dealing direct blows at imperialism. The national democratic revolutionary movement in these areas and the international Socialist revolutionary movement are the two great historical currents of our time." In a sense, therefore, the Chinese letter goes on, "the whole cause of the international proletarian revolution hinges on the outcome of the revolutionary struggles of the peoples of these areas who constitute the overwhelming majority of the world's population," for "it is impossible for the working class in the European and American capitalist countries to liberate itself unless it unites with the oppressed nations and unless those nations are liberated."[44]

Thus a bitter Sino-Soviet dialogue has developed over the entire issue of the developing areas of the world. Whereas the Chinese communists have indicted the Soviet leaders for an outright betrayal of the just cause of the ex-colonial peoples, the latter have countered by accusing the Chinese of falsely posing "as the most consistent champions of the oppressed peoples."[45] In their endeavor "to win in the easiest way popularity among the peoples of Asia, Africa and Latin America" they have gone so far as to pervert the Marxist-Leninist teaching on contradictions. As asserted by the Soviet theoreticians, the Chinese hold that the main contradiction of our time is the contradiction "not between socialism and imperialism, but between the national-liberation movement and imperialism" and that the decisive force in the struggle against imperialism "is not the world system of socialism, not the struggle of the international working class, but again the national-liberation movement."[46] Grossly overstating their case just as the Chinese have overstated theirs, the Soviet spokesmen have denounced the Chinese for "ignoring the effective role of the world socialist system," "downgrading the historical role of the struggle of the working class in the developed capitalist countries,"[47] and "preaching a regrouping of revolutionary forces in which the vanguard role of the international working class is eliminated."[48] They have lashed out at them for "granting to the working class of those areas of the world where the main production forces of modern capitalism are concentrated only the role of an 'auxiliary' to the national-liberation movement," thus "crossing out with a single flourish the revolutionary potential of the proletariat of Western Europe, the United States, Canada and Japan" and "ignoring the contribution of the working class of the capitalist countries to the united cause of the world revolutionary process ..."[49] They have condemned the Chinese for "inflaming national and even racial prejudices,"[50] basing their foreign policy on "petty-bourgeois belligerent nationalism" rather than proletarian internationalism,[51] "confusing the basic contradiction with that of the weakest link," vulgarizing and perverting communism's most fundamental concept, the Marxist dialectics.[52]

While the Chinese-Soviet exchange of views does reveal a certain difference in the ideological assessment of the role of ex-colonial countries in the East-West struggle, it appears to be only one of degree rather than substance. Despite the harsh overtones of the debate, both sides evidently agree that the developing countries represent today "the weakest link of the capitalist chain" and, logically, should be viewed as the prime target of communist penetration. Both agree that the communization of "imperialism's one-time preserve" in Asia, Africa and Latin America is a necessary prerequisite for the coveted victory of communism on the global scale. Hence, apart from the basic argument over what constitutes "the main contradiction of our time," the Chinese ideologists appear to differ from their Soviet colleagues in their interpretation and assessment of several ideological propositions advanced by the Soviet theoreticians in support of the current communist preoccupation with the developing areas: the concept of national democracy; the usefulness of the non-capitalist path of development; the value of state capitalism; the relevance of the Soviet example; the role of developing areas in the struggle for peace; and the function of the working class.

National democracy. By signing the 1960 Moscow *Declaration* the Chinese communists gave their approval, reluctant though it may have been, to the concept of national democracy as therein defined. Indeed, the concept is somewhat reminiscent of the "New Democracy" worked out by Mao in 1939-40 as the most desirable type of government for countries emerging from the era of colonialism.[53] Discarding "the capitalist republic under bourgeois dictatorship" and "the socialist republic of the Soviet type" as being both unsuitable for the emerging nations, Mao asserts that "the form of state to be adopted by the revolutions in colonial and semi-colonial countries during a given historical period can only be a third one, namely, the new-democratic republic. This is the form for a given historical period and therefore a transitional form, but an unalterable and necessary form."[54] However, Mao's "New Democracy" comprises, as its most essential political ingredient, "the joint dictatorship of several revolutionary classes" (workers, peasants, petty bourgeoisie and the leftwing progressive part of the national bourgeoisie). Moreover, as Mao has stressed on a number of occasions, such a "New Democracy" must be led by the proletariat as "only under the leadership of the proletariat can such a republic be completely realized."[55]

Although this "joint-dictatorship" feature has been left out of the 1960 Moscow *Declaration,* the Chinese communists, as

indicated by their various recent statements, evidently continue
to imply it in their understanding of the concept of national
democracy and thus virtually equate national democracy *(natsional'naia demokratiia)* with what in Soviet terminology goes
under the designation of a people's democracy *(narodnaia
demokratiia).*[56] While calling for a "broad united front against
imperialism and its lackeys" and willing to include in such a front
"not only the workers, peasants, intellectuals and petty bourgeoisie, but also the patriotic national bourgeoisie and even
certain kings, princes and aristocrats who are patriotic," the
Chinese open letter of June 14, 1963, makes it clear that the
proletarian parties in the respective less developed countries must
"insist on the leadership of the revolution." On the other hand,
the Soviet ideologists do not hold the leadership by the proletarian party, or even the working class, necessary at the national
democratic stage of development. "National democracy can be
established under the leadership of any democratic class - the
working class, the peasantry, the small urban bourgeoisie. In
some countries the leading force may be the intelligentsia,
including the revolutionary army officers."[57] According to the
Fundamentals, a mere "prospect" of "participation of the
working classes and their parties in the management of the state"
seems to suffice to qualify a developing country as a state of
national democracy.[58] The leadership of the proletariat becomes
necessary, in Soviet view, only for the further transition from the
national democratic stage to socialism and communism.[59]

Whereas the Soviet communists are thus inclined to consider
as national democracies, or at least as well on the way toward
this type, ex-colonial countries where communist parties are
merely allowed the freedom to operate and possibly participate
in government even without having much actual power (let alone
holding the reins of leadership), the Chinese communists view
such countries as bourgeois dictatorships. They reserve the
designation of national democracy only for those countries where
the native Communist party actually leads a coalition of several
"revolutionary" classes. Cuba qualified as such in Chinese eyes
after Castro's takeover (before she advanced still further to
become a member of the world socialist system) but not such
countries as Ghana (prior to Nkrumah's ouster), Guinea,

Brazzaville Congo, Algeria, Tanzania or Indonesia (prior to the eclipse of Sukarno), all of which have been commended at one time or another by various Soviet spokesmen for being on the verge of becoming national democracies.

The Non-Capitalist Path of Development and the State Sector. This difference of views on the concept of national democracy is necessarily reflected also in the respective Chinese and Soviet stands on national democracy's economic foundation, namely, the non-capitalist path of development and the state sector of the economy. In substance, the Chinese communists are considerably less optimistic than their Soviet comrades about the advantages that the communist cause supposedly derives from the non-capitalist path of development if it is embarked upon prematurely. "The Chinese leaders virtually reject the possibility of a non-capitalist path . . ." asserts G. I. Mirskii, a noted Soviet specialist on the Third World. "The leaders of the CPR do not admit that the new situation in the world resulting from the emergence of the world socialist system enables even those liberated countries in which immediate conditions for the construction of socialism do not yet exist to start already now along the non-capitalist path."[60] If one can believe Suslov, Teng Hsiao-Peng, Secretary General of the Chinese communist party, went so far as to dismiss the entire thesis of the non-capitalist path as "idle chatter."[61] As the Chinese see it, in those countries that are still led by non-proletarian groups the development of the state sector of the economy, far from being a "progressive factor" as claimed by the Soviet theoreticians, tends rather to become a regressive "monopoly state capitalism" which merely strengthens the national bourgeoisie and the "monopoly capitalists" and weakens the proletariat.[62] Relying on Engels's statement that transformation into state ownership does not do away with the capitalist nature of productive forces,[63] they view nationalization undertaken while non-proletarian strata are still in command as "a fraud of the bourgeoisie" meant merely to "line the pockets of monopoly capitalists."[64] Only after the proletariat has taken over the reins of power in a given country can the enlargement of the state sector of the economy be depended upon to contribute to the advancement of socialism.

Thus, unlike the Soviet theoreticians, the Chinese communists believe that, from the standpoint of the Marxist-Leninist revolution, private capitalism may even be preferable to state capitalism at an initial stage of ex-colonial independence. In holding such a belief the Chinese ideologists can fall back on Mao's earlier thesis unfolded before the Seventh National Congress of the Chinese Communist party in April 1945. "Some people fail to understand," Mao then said, "why the Communists should advocate the development of capitalism under given conditions instead of fearing it. Our answer is simple: to replace the oppression of foreign capitalism and native feudalism with capitalism developed to a certain degree is not only an advance but also an unavoidable process. Such a development is beneficial not only to the bourgeoisie, but also, or even more, to the proletariat."[65]

The Relevance of the Chinese Model. While the Soviet theoreticians consider the Soviet experience to be more suited to the needs of the developing countries than that of the capitalist West, the Chinese in their turn look at their own example to be more relevant in this respect than the Soviet. Even when the chances of victory seemed quite remote, Mao held that the Chinese revolution was "pregnant with significance for world revolution" and that "the eyes of the revolutionary masses throughout the world" were upon China.[66] After victory had been won in 1949, Liu Shao-Ch'i, then Red China's Number Two man, proclaimed that "the path taken by the Chinese people in defeating imperialism and its lackeys and in founding the People's Republic of China is the path that should be taken by the peoples of the various colonial and semi-colonial countries in their fight for national independence and people's democracy."[67]

This Chinese belief that their country can serve better than Russia as a developmental model in Asia and Africa, and possibly even in Latin America, a belief implicit in the recent Chinese pronouncements on the matter, belongs probably among the Chinese communists' most firmly rooted convictions; and it may well be the one Chinese claim that has a most credible ring in the ears of the most impatient and the most leftist of Asian, African and Latin American revolutionaries. After all, unlike Russia, China is a non-European, non-white country of formerly semi-colonial status. At the time of the communist victory she was economically, educationally and socially more backward, less industrialized, and more dominated by foreign capital than Tsarist Russia had been when the Bolsheviks took over in 1917.[68] Nor are Communist China's "anti-imperialist" endeavors in the developing countries hampered by any need to play the peaceful co-existence game with the "imperialist West" such as tends to inconvenience at times Soviet Russia and makes perhaps the most radical segment of the colonial and ex-colonial communist movement doubt the depth and the genuineness of Soviet commitment to its revolutionary cause.

The "Struggle for Peace." The Chinese communists take also a strong exception to the Soviet thesis seeking to justify communist interest in, and concentration on, the developing areas of the world in terms of the "struggle for peace." Adamantly opposed to any thought that "the contradiction between the oppressed nations and imperialism can be resolved without revolution by the oppressed nations," the Chinese ideologists scornfully reject what they describe, not quite so accurately, as the Soviet "attempt to substitute peaceful competition for the revolutionary struggles of the oppressed peoples and nations." In their view, the victory over imperialism can be attained only by non-peaceful methods, mainly through armed revolutionary struggle and wars of national liberation."[69] Deeply conscious of their own revolutionary experience replete with reliance on armed struggle and guided by Mao's famous dictum that "political power grows out of the barrel of a gun", the Chinese communist spokesmen have spared no ammunition in an incessant verbal bombardment of the Soviet leaders' "brazen betrayal" of Marxism-Leninism through their alleged reliance on peaceful methods.[70] "Extreme philistine stupidity"; "Arabian night tale"; "downright deception"; "the embellishment of capitalist wage slavery"; "robbing Marxism-Leninism of its revolutionary soul"; its "mutilation beyond recognition"; these have been but a few of the many Chinese vituperative descriptions of the Soviet post-Stalin theory and practice of peaceful co-existence.[71]

The Function of the Working Class. Finally, one can discern a certain difference between the Soviet and Chinese assessments of the role of the working class in the developing countries.

While both the Soviet and Chinese ideologists dutifully parrot the traditional Marxist-Leninist dicta on the necessity of class struggle and the importance of the working class in the Third World, the Chinese spokesmen seem to be less obsessed with the idea than their Soviet colleagues. They certainly do not appear to share the professed Soviet enthusiasm for the "young working class of the newly free, independent and colonial countries of Asia, Africa and Latin America" hailed so exuberantly in the 1961 *Soviet Communist Party Program.* Noting that the peasants constitute by far the largest population group in the Third World and aware of the overwhelmingly peasant character of the Chinese revolution, the Chinese communist ideologists tend to view the Third World's peasantry rather than its industrial proletariat as the main and most decisive force of the national-liberation movement and the socialist revolution. Thus the above-mentioned Soviet accusations that the Chinese communists have downgraded the role of the working class in their analysis of the revolutionary process in the Third World and that "Mao inherited from petty-bourgeois doctrines the idea of the special revolutionary character of the peasants"[72] do have some substance.

As could be expected, the East European communist regimes (with the obvious exception of Albania) and their ideologists have thrown their support behind the Soviet stand in the Sino-Soviet argument concerning the less developed countries.[73] They have joined their Soviet colleagues in denouncing the Chinese leaders for their endeavors to curry favor with the less developed countries by proclaiming the national-liberation movement to be "the most revolutionary and most decisive force fighting against imperialism[74] and assigning the world socialist system only "a secondary, strictly auxiliary place."[75] They have accused them of rejecting "the thesis of the international Communist movement which proclaims that the contradiction between socialism and imperialism is the main contradiction of our time" and asserting, instead, that the main contradiction today is the one between imperialism and the national-liberation movement.[76] They have censured them for "retreating from the positions of Marxism-Leninism and proletarian internationalism" and trying "to create their own kind of 'Marxism-Leninism' which should answer to their great Chinese nationalist aspirations ... and which is to be determined by geographical, racial, national and other traits. . . ."[77] They have taken them to task for "sliding into positions of national communism and replacing the class-political viewpoint in foreign policy matters by an Asiatic, Eastern, racist and anti-European standpoint."[78] They have reproached them for taking a "negative approach to the strategic principle of peaceful coexistence" and minimizing the revolutionary role of the working class in the national-liberation movement.[79] They have found the Chinese guilty of an unwarranted "schematic" overemphasis on armed struggle to the exclusion of other important forms of fighting imperialism; of "equating social revolution with war";[80] of "subjective strategy . . . supplemented by a notion of imperialism in a sort of ridiculous toothless shape."[81] Contrary to the Chinese skepticism on the matter, the East European theoreticians have endorsed the Soviet views that victory over imperialism, especially in the less developed areas, can be achieved through a successful economic competition with the West.[82]

*

Thus, in spite of the growing disunity within the communist camp, the ideological rationale underlying the communist endeavors in the Third World reveals a high degree of uniformity. The regimes of Soviet Russia's East European Warsaw Pact partners and their official spokesmen have so far merely echoed and belabored the Soviet-approved precepts. Nor have the Yugoslav communists deviated significantly from the fundamentals of the Soviet doctrine on the place and role of the developing nations in world affairs. In that particular respect one finds little of the innovation that has characterized some other aspects of Yugoslav communism. As for communist China, the pyrotechnics accompanying the Sino-Soviet accusations and counter-accusations in which the two communist giants have been trying their utmost to portray one another as a hopeless ignoramus in matters of Marxism-Leninism create an impression of a truly abysmal ideological disagreement. However, when the thick veneer of propagandistic verbiage is removed, the Sino-Soviet differences show themselves to be only of secondary nature and seem to relate much more to matters of strategy, tactics and timing than the basic ideological outlook.

Notes for Chapter II

[1] D. Rozehnal, "The Leninist Road of World Communism," *Nová mysl*, No. 3, March 1963. English translation in the *Czechoslovak Press Survey*, No. 1223(71), Radio Free Europe, New York. See also, "The Guiding Principles Prepared by the Central Committee of the Hungarian Socialist Workers' Party for the Congress, *Nepszabadsag*, August 19, 1962, English translation in the *Hungarian Press Survey*, No. 1211, Radio Free Europe, New York; Harsanyi J., "The Universality of Marxism-Leninism and the Uniform Strategy of the International Working Class," *Tarsadalni Szemle*, February 1965, English translation in the *Hungarian Press Survey*, No. 1572, February 1965; editorial on "The Ideas of Marxism-Leninism and the Principles of Proletarian Internationalism Are Invincible", *Rudé právo*, January 15, 1963, English translation in *Czechoslovak Press Survey*, No. 1185, January 1963.

[2] An interview with Friguyes Puja, Head of the Central Committee's foreign department, published in *Partelet*, February 1967, English translation in the *Hungarian Press Survey*, No. 1792, 1967.

[3] A number of such conferences have been held throughout the sixties under the auspices of the *World Marxist Review*, such as the 1961 Prague conference on the Path of Development of Newly Emergent Countries whose proceedings were published in the *World Marxist Review*, Vol. 5, 1962, beginning with No. 5.

[4] For a few early samples see: editorial in *Novo Vreme*, Vol. 2, February 1963, English translation in the *Bulgarian Press Survey*, No. 408, Radio Free Europe, New York; V. Koucký, "For Further Development of Socialism and the Task of Social Sciences," *Nová mysl*, No. 8, August 1, 1962, English translation in the *Czechoslovak Press Survey*, No. 1139 (195); *Rudé právo*, August 4, 1963; F. Havlíček, "Topical Questions of the Revolutionary Movement," *Mezinárodní politika*, No. 2, February 1963, English translation in the *Czechoslovak Press Survey*, No. 1214 (56); Václav Mandous, "Our Relations to the Economically Less Developed Countries," *Práce*, November 22, 1962, English translation in the *Czechoslovak Press Survey*, No. 1167 (281).

[5] *Pravda* (Bratislava), February 2, 1968.

[6] Jiří Hájek, "Konstanty a nové prvky v zahraniční politice" (The Constant and the New Elements in Foreign Policy), *Nová mysl*, No. 8, August 1968, pp. 984-99.

[7] "*Akční program komunistické strany Československa,*" (The Action Program of the Communist Party of Czechoslovakia), *Rudé právo*, April 10, 1968, pp. 2-31; See also Edward Taborsky, "The New Era in Czechoslovakia," *East Europe*, 17, 11, 1968, pp. 19-29.

[8] Janos Kadar's report to the Ninth Congress of the Hungarian Socialist Workers' Party in November 1966, *Nepszabadsag*, November 29, 1966, English translation in the *Hungarian Press Survey*, No. 1770, December 1966.

[9] See Jan Prazsky, "The Non-Alignment Movement," *World Marxist Review*, 13, 11, November 1970, pp. 78 ff.

[10] Vladimír Koucký in a leading article on *Mezinárodní význam října*, (The International Meaning of October), *Život strany*, No. 18, August 1967, pp. 1-4.

[11] Miroslav Novotný, "*ČSSR a Afrika,*" (CSSR and Africa), *Nová mysl*, No. 7, 1967, pp. 81-86. See also, Václav Pleskot, "*Zahraničná politika:*

58   *Communist Penetration of the Third World*

bilancia a perspektivy" (Foreign Policy; the Balance and the Perspectives), *Predvoj,* No. 1, January 4, 1968, pp. 12-13; Jaroslav Šedivý, *"Sovětský svaz a třetí svět"* (The Soviet Union and the Third World), *Praha-Moskva,* No. 5, 1966, pp. 15-21.

[12] V. Koucký, "For Further Development of Socialism and the Task of Social Sciences," *Nová mysl, op. cit.*

[13] Jan Janoušek and Josef Dusek, "Why We Assist the Underdeveloped Countries," *Pochodeň,* September 25, 1962, English translation in the *Czechoslovak Press Survey,* No. 1159; also, Václav Mandous, "The Socialist Countries and their Attitude to the Movement for National Liberation in the Colonial Countries", *Pravda* (Plzen), July 4, 1963; The resolution of the XIIIth Congress of the Communist Party of Czechoslovakia, Special Supplement to *Rudé právo,* June 7 and 8, 1966. The duty to "support the nations fighting for their liberation from under the imperialists' and colonialists' rule" was even included in the preamble to the Czechoslovak Communist Party Rules adopted in 1962. See also an interview with the Head of the International Department of the Central Committee of the Czechoslovak Communist party. *"O mezinarodním postavení CSSR"* (Concerning the International Position of the CSSR), *Mladá fronta,* May 5, 1970.

[14] Evžen Paloncy, *"Komunismus a národne osvobozenecké hnutí"* (Communism and the National-Liberation Movement), *Nová mysl,* No. 8, August 1963, pp. 897 ff.

[15] Vaclav Mandous, "Our Relations to the Economically Less Developed Nations," *op. cit.*

[16] See the various statements made by East European representatives at the above-mentioned conference on, the developing nations published in the *World Marxist Review,* Vol. 5 beginning with No. 5, 1962, pp. 62 ff.

[17] See, for instance, Miroslav Novotný, *"ČSSR a Afrika,"* op. cit.

[18] See for instance, Paul Friedlaender, Harmut Schilling, "West German Imperialism - Bulwark of Colonialism," *World Marxist Review,* 5, 4, 1962, pp. 18 ff; Bohumil Šimon, *"Diskuse a činy"* (Discussion and Action), *Hospodářské noviny,* April 29, 1966, pp. 1-3; Alois Volf, *"ČSSR a rozvojové země"* (CSSR and the Developing Countries), *Rudé právo,* August 1, 1965; Bronislaw Rudowicz, *"Kraje socjalistyczne Trzeciemu światu,"* (The Socialist Countries to the Third World), *Glos Pracy,* May 5, 1965. Dr. Ladislav Balcar, *"Komplexní program a rozvojové země"* (The Complex Program and the Developing Countries), *Tribuna,* No. 1, January 26, 1972, p. 17.

[19] B. Zacharescu in *World Marxist Review,* 5, 7, 1962, pp. 70 ff, and K. Dobrev, *ibid.,* No. 5, pp. 66 ff.

[20] *Jacobs,* pp. 43-44.

[21] Information on the Yugoslav attitude has been drawn from various Yugoslav statements and publications. See for instance: Nijaz Dizdarevic's article in *Nedeljne informativne novine,* Belgrade, August 27, 1967, English text in Radio Free Europe *Release on Yugoslavia,* August 31, 1967; chapter on Yugoslavia in *Südosteuropa und die Entwicklungsländer* (Southeast Europe and the Developing Countries), München, 1963, pp. 9-73; A report on the "Significance of the October Revolution" delivered by Rato Dugonjić, President of the Federal Conference of the Socialist Alliance of Working People of Yugoslavia, at a Belgrade meeting held in commemoration of the 50th anniversary of the Bolshevik revolution. "Lenin's October Has Changed the Course of History," *Socialist Thought and Practice,* no. 28, 1967, pp. 68-79;

"Yugoslav View on Assistance to Economically Under-developed Countries," *Yugoslav Survey,* Vol. 1, No. 2, 1960, pp. 265-273; Tito's speech during his 1965 visit to Algeria, *"La co-existence est la seule alternative a une guerre nucléaire mondiale,"* *Questions Actuelles du Socialisme* No. 77, 1965, pp. 3-17; "Conclusions of the Federal Conference of the Socialist Alliance on the Position of Newly Liberated Countries and on the Relations of Yugoslavia with Those Countries," *Socialist Thought and Practice,* No. 26, 1967, pp. 148-151; "Yugoslav Cooperation with Developing Countries," *Yugoslav Life,* X, 2, 1965, p. 2; Tito's speech at Pristina, *Yugoslav Facts and Views,* No. 21, 1967; Edward Kardelj, "Present-day Policy of Non-Alignment," *Yugoslav Facts and Life,* No. 38, 1968; "Non-Alignment Means Independence and Peace," *Yugoslav Life,* XIV, 2, 1969; Gavro Altmant, "Lasting Values of Non-Alignment," *Socialist Thought and Practice,* No. 34, 1969, pp. 52 ff.; *The Policy of Non-Alignment in the Contemporary World,* Institute for International Politics and Economics, Belgrade, 1969. See also Alvin Rubinstein, *Yugoslavia and the Non-Aligned World.*

[22] *"Lenin 'Myslitel' i Strateg Sotsialisticheskoi revoliutsii,"* (Lenin - The Thinker and the Strategist of Socialist Revolution).

[23] *Borba,* March 26, 1962, cited in *Südosteuropa und die Entwicklungsländer,* p. 13.

[24] "Non-Aligned Yugoslavia's Policy not Tactics," *Yugoslav Life,* XV, 1, 1970.

[25] *"Sovetsko-jugoslavskoe zaiavlenie,"* (The Soviet-Yugoslav Declaration), *Pravda,* September 22, 1971.

[26] "Yugoslav View on Assistance to Economically Underdeveloped Countries," *op. cit.,* pp. 265-273.

[27] Programme of the League of Communists of Yugoslavia (cited in the article mentioned in note 26).

[28] p. 196.

[29] See for instance M. Gavrilovič's discussion of the First World Symposium on the Policy of Non-Alignment in *Yugoslav Life,* XIV, 2, 1969, p. 1; Tito's statement at the Cairo Conference of Non-aligned Nations in October 1964, *Politika,* October 7, 1964; N. Dizdarevič, *op. cit.;* "The Policy of Non-Alignment Today: Its Consolidation on a Broader Basis," *Borba,* June 1, 1967; Tito's speech at the Sixth Congress of the Socialist Alliance of the Working People of Yugoslavia, *Socialist Thought and Practice,* No. 22, 1966, pp. 45-52; "Non-Alignment Gains Momentum," *Yugoslav Life,* XII, 3, 1968, pp. 1-2.

[30] Special Supplement to *Yugoslav Life,* IX, 11, November 1964. See also Edward Kardelj, "Present-day Policy of Non-Alignment," *op. cit.*

[31] *op. cit.* in note 24.

[32] See S. Dolanc, "Non-Alignment Is a Struggle Against All Kinds of Subjection," *Socialist Thought and Practice,* No. 40, 1970, pp. 28 ff., and Leo Mates, "Non-Alignment and the Great Powers," *Foreign Affairs,* 48, 3, April 1970, pp.

[33] "Widening Gap Between the Developed and Underdeveloped," (Tito's speech at the Zagreb University), *Socialist Thought and Practice,* No. 38, 1970, pp. 3 ff.

[34] Final communique of the Consultative meeting of non-aligned countries, *Yugoslav Facts and Views,* No. 57, 1969.

[35] No. 34, April-June 1969, pp. 52 ff.; see also the same author's undated brochure *Standing Clear of Blocs,* published by *Socialist Thought and Practice,*

and Radivoj Uvalic, "New Meeting of Non-Aligned Nations," *Review of International Affairs*, No. 461, 1969, pp. 1 ff.

[36] *Yugoslav Life*, XIV, 2, 1969.

[37] "Let's Be Objective," *New Times*, No. 31, 1969, pp. 22 ff.

[38] As Richard Lowenthal cautions, both the Chinese and the Russians tend to minimize their own departures from communist orthodoxy and maximize the departures debited to the opponent. See Richard Lowenthal, "Soviet and Chinese Communist World Views" in Donald W. Treadgold, ed., *Soviet and Chinese Communism, Similarities and Differences*, Seattle, 1967, pp. 374-404.

[39] English text in *Peking Review*, No. 25, 1963.

[40] "The Second Congress of the Communist International," *Selected Works*, Moscow, 1952, Vol. II, part 2, 11472-73.

[41] *Peking Review*, No. 25, 1963

[42] *Ibid.*

[43] "Why Khrushchev Fell," *Peking Review*, No. 48, 1964.

[44] A good discussion of the contrasting Chinese and Soviet views on the importance of developing nations in the context of communist policy and strategy may be found in Donald W. Treadgold, *op. cit.*, Part Six "Russia and China in International Affairs" pp. 267 ff.

[45] V. Shelepin, "Maoist Intrigues in the Third World," *New Times*, No. 26, 1969, pp. 6 ff. See also L. Kirichenko, "Peking's Diplomatic Game, *ibid.*, No. 17, 1971, pp. 4 ff.

[46] An open letter to the Central Committee of the Chinese Communist party published in *Pravda*, July 14, 1963. See also A. Rumyantsev, "Concerning the Basic Contradiction of Our Time," *World Marxist Review*, 7, 7, 1964, p. 3, and *Third World*, pp. 24 ff.

[47] *"Za general'nuiu liniiu mirovogo kommunistiches-kogo divizheniia, protiv levogo opportunizma, natsionalizma i avantiurizma"*, (For the General Line of the World Communist Movement. Against Leftwing Opportunism, Nationalism and Adventurism) an editorial in *Kommunist*, No. 14, 1963, pp. 3 ff; T. Timofeev, *"Veduschchaia revoliutsionnaia sila"* (The Leading Revolutionary Force), *Pravda*, December 24, 1969.

[48] "Marxism-Leninism Is the International Doctrine of the Communists of All Countries," *Pravda*, May 11 and 12, 1964; English text in the *Current Digest of the Soviet Press*, XVI, 19, 1964.

[49] V. Nekrasov, "Working Class on the Offensive Against Imperialism," *Pravda*, August 18, 1963; English text in the *Current Digest*, XV, 33, 1963; also see M. Suslov's report at the plenary session of the Central Committee of the Soviet Communist party, *Pravda*, April 3, 1964; A. Kartunova, "Lenin and the National Liberation Movement," *New Times*, No. 33, 1969, pp. 13 ff.

[50] Nekrasov, *op. cit.*

[51] Irina Trofimova, "Great-Power Chauvinism - Basis of Peking Foreign Policy," *New Times*, No. 23, 1971, pp. 22 ff., reviewing the monograph *Foreign Policy of the People's Republic of China*, published in 1971 by the Far East Institute of the USSR Academy of Sciences.

[52] A. Rumyantsev, *op. cit.*, and A. Sobolev, "The Universality of Contradiction and the Concreteness of the Truth," *World Marxist Review*, 7, 6, 1964, pp. 28 ff.; F. Timofeev, *"Leninskii kurs mirovogo kommunisticheskogo dvizhenia i ego protivniki"* (The Leninist Course of the World Communist Movement and Its Adversaries), *Kommunist*, No. 13, 1963, pp. 33 ff.

[53] See "On New Democracy" and "The Chinese Revolution and the Chinese

Communist Party," *Selected Works of Mao Tse-tung,* London, 1954, III pp. 106 ff and 73 ff.

[54] "On New Democracy" *op. cit.* See also Richard Lowenthal, "'National Democracy' and the Post-Colonial Revolution," in Kurt London, ed. *New Nations in a Divided World,* New York, 1963, p. 66.

[55] "The Chinese Revolution and the Chinese Communist Party," *op. cit.;* see also Mao's political report at the Seventh National Congress of the Communist Party of China in April 1945, *op. cit.,* IV, pp. 271 ff, where he stressed again the leadership of the proletariat which he distinguished, however, from a "one-class dictatorship."

[56] See Donald S. Zagoria, "Sino-Soviet Friction in Underdeveloped Areas," *Problems of Communism,* X, 2, 1961, pp. 1 ff.

[57] A. Sobolev, "National Democracy, The Way to Social Progress," *World Marxist Review,* 6, 2, 1963, p. 46. Similar views were expressed by Soviet theoreticians on many different occasions. See, for instance, *World Marxist Review,* 6, 3, 1963, pp. 52 ff, and 7, 10, 1964, and G. Mirsky's article in *New Times* No. 18, 1964. More on the question of the working class leadership in Chapter V.

[58] p. 421.

[59] A. Sobolev, *op. cit.* in note 57, stressing that transition to socialism can be effected "only under the leadership of the working class allied with the peasantry headed by the Marxist-Leninist vanguard." See also an editorial in *Kommunist* No. 14, September 1963, p. 28. However, in 1964 some of the Soviet theoreticians began to allow for possibilities of a transition to socialism or "socialist construction" even without proletarian leadership. More about it in Chapter V.

[60] "*Sotsializm, Kapitalizm i Slaborozvitye Strany*" (Socialism, Capitalism and the Less Developed Countries), *MEIMO,* No. 6, 1964, p. 65.

[61] *Pravda,* April 3, 1964.

[62] See, for instance, "More on Differences Between Comrade Togliatti and Us," *Peking Review,* No. 10-11, 1963, pp. 8 ff.; William T. Shinn, Jr., "The 'National Democratic' State," *World Politics,* XV, 3, 1963, pp. 377 ff.

[63] Marx and Engels, *Selected Works,* Moscow, 1958, Vol. II, pp. 148-49.

[64] *Peking Review,* No. 10-11, 1963, pursuing a discussion with Togliatti's views, and *Peking Review,* No. 17, 1963.

[65] "On Coalition, On Government," *Selected Works of Mao Tse-tung,* Vol. IV, pp. 275-76.

[66] "Strategic Problems of China's Revolutionary War," December 1936, *Chinese Communist World Outlook,* Washington, 1962, p. 6.

[67] A speech at the Trade Union Conference of Asian and Australian countries, November 16, 1949. *Chinese Communist World Outlook,* p. 7.

[68] For a discussion of the advantages which China seems to offer to ex-colonial countries see Peter S. H. Tang, *Communist China As a Developmental Model for Underdeveloped Countries.* The Research Institute on the Sino-Soviet Bloc, Washington, Monographic Series No. 1; Alexander Eckstein, "A Study in Economic Strategy," *Survey,* No. 38, 1961; A. M. Halpern, "The Foreign Policy Uses of the Chinese Revolutionary Model," *The China Quarterly,* Vol. 5-8, No. 7, 1961, pp. 1-6; Thomas P. Thornton, "Peking, Moscow, and the Underdeveloped," *World Politics,* XIII, 4, pp. 491 ff; Kurt London, "The Role of China," *Problems of Communism,* XI, 4, 1962, pp. 22-27; Richard Lowenthal, *World Communism, The Disintegration of a Secular*

Faith, p. 128. A somewhat different view of the Chinese claim of relevance as a model for developing nations is held by Roderick MacFarquhar, "The Chinese Model and The Underdeveloped World," *International Affairs,* 39, 3, 1963, pp. 372 ff.

[69] Theses 5 and 13 of the Chinese letter of June 14, 1963. See also Donald Treadgold, *op. cit.*

[70] See, for instance, "Peaceful Coexistence — Two Diametrically Opposed Policies," *Peking Review,* No. 51, 1963, pp. 6 ff; "The Proletarian Revolution and Khrushchev's Revisionism. Comment on the Open Letter of the C. C. of CPSU," *ibid.,* No. 14, 1964, pp. 5 ff., etc. More about the Chinese stand on armed struggle in Chapter XIII.

[71] *Ibid.*

[72] "Pseudo-revolutionaries Unmasked," a long anti-Chinese article of *Pravda,* June 18, 1970, reprinted in English in the *Information Bulletin,* No. 11, 1970, pp. 34 ff. More about the Chinese view of the proletariat's role in Chapter V.

[73] See, for instance: Janos Nemes, "The Word of Truth," *Nepszabadsag,* July 18, 1963, English text in the *Hungarian Press Survey,* No. 1353; editorial in *Nowe Drogi,* September 1963, English text in the *Polish Press Survey,* No. 1589; Evzen Paloncy, *op. cit.;* D. Horodyński, *"Polityka i Ideologia 1963 - Jeszcze o stanowisku chinskim"* (Politics and Ideology 1963 - Once Again Concerning the Chinese Attitude), *Zycie Warszawy,* September 8 and 9, 1963; Viaczyslaw F. Rakowski, "Contrary to Most Vital Interests," *Polityka,* September 28, 1963, English text in the *Polish Press Survey,* No. 1600; Zdeněk Bradáč, *"Proletárský internacionalismus a politika KS Činy"* (Proletarian Internationalism and the Policy of the Chinese Communist Party), *Nová mysl,* No. 9, 1963, pp. 1052 ff.; Vasil Ivanov, "The Creative Development of Marxism-Leninism and the Dogmatism of the Chinese Rulers," *Rabotnichesko Delo,* September 26, 1963, English text in the *Bulgarian Press Survey,* No. 486; Karel Kára, *"Některé základní problémy charakteru současné epochy"* (Some Basic Problems of the Character of the Contemporary Epoch), *Filosofický časopis,* No. 3, 1964, pp. 294 ff.; I. Harsanyi, *op. cit.;* Fugyes Puja, "Some Conflicting International Issues," *Partelet,* February 1967, English text in the *Hungarian Press Survey,* No. 1792; Jaroslav Jakubec and Vladimir Wacker, *"Ekonomická propaganda a naše vnějši hospodářské vztahy"* (Economic Propaganda and Our External Economic Relations), *Život strany,* No. 7, 1967, pp. 49-52; Vladimir Janku, "Zásadovost v politice mirového soužiti" (Regard for Principles in the Policy of Peaceful Coexistence), *Život strany,* No. 20, 1967, pp. 50-55.

[74] Evžen Paloncy, *op. cit.*

[75] Todor Zhivkov's contribution to the special issue the *World Marxist Review* dedicated to the Centenary of the First International, *World Marxist Review,* 7, 8, 1964, pp. 12 ff.

[76] *Nowe Drogi, op. cit.,* Karel Kára, *op. cit.*

[77] Vasil Ivanov, *op. cit.*

[78] František Havlíček, *"Nacionálni komunismus - ideologie čínských vedoucich"* (National Communism - Ideology of the Chinese Leaders), *Mezinárodni politika,* No. 101, 1963, pp. 436-38.

[79] *Nowe drogi, op. cit.,* Horodyński, *op. cit.* See also *"Antysocjalisticzna i Nacjonalisticzna Treśč Maoizmu"* (The Anti-Socialist and Nationalist Essence of Maoism), *Trybuna Ludu,* January 23, 1972.

[80] Todor Zhivkov, *op. cit.*
[81] D. Rozehnal, *op. cit.*
[82] *Rudé právo*, August 4, 1963; D. Rozehnal, *op. cit.*

CHAPTER III

COMMUNIST STRATEGY VIS-A-VIS THE DEVELOPING NATIONS A FEW PRELIMINARY OBSERVATIONS

While the tenets of Marxist-Leninist ideology go a long way toward explaining the current communist concentration on the less developed areas of the world, they are not its only reasons. As stated in Chapter I, along with motivations based on ideology proper, determinants other than strictly ideological have also played an important (and probably even predominant) part in encouraging communist policy-makers to rearrange their schedule of priorities by shifting, at least for a while, their main thrust from Europe to Asia, Africa and Latin America. Undoubtedly, foremost among them are considerations of strategy and tactics.

In earlier Leninist terminology little distinction was made between the two terms. Lenin himself seldom used the word strategy and spoke of tactics in terms that would also comprise strategy as generally understood. Thus in his *Two Tactics of Social-Democracy in a Democratic Revolution* he defined tactics as "the character, direction, and methods of [the Party's] *current policy* of the Party and is worked out for shorter periods on the basis of the Party's general line ..."[2] However, the boundary dividing strategy and tactics is necessarily vague, especially in the highly flexible Marxist-Leninist operational pattern which puts the highest premium on the ability and readiness to change the forms of the struggle "most swiftly and unexpectedly."[3] Therefore, no attempt will be made in our discussion of communist operations in the developing areas to distinguish between strategy and tactics, though our attention will be focused primarily on such devices, methods and techniques as are of a more fundamental nature and thus qualify more as strategy than tactics.

Nor is it always possible to differentiate between ideology and strategy, as has already been explained in Chapter I. Since the doctrine of Marxism-Leninism is supposed to guide the communists in all their actions and the unity of theory and practice is proclaimed to be the foremost axiom, communist strategy is presumably based on a "scientific [i.e., Marxist-Leninist] analysis of the given stage of the struggle in the given situation."[4] Hence, concepts of communist ideology and strategy are closely interlocked. Moreover, Lenin, whose contribution to Marxism-Leninism lay much more in the elaboration of revolutionary strategy and tactics than in the development of theoretical tenets, virtually incorporated a number of predominantly strategic concepts into ideology itself. "The strategy and tactics of Leninism," asserts a recent Soviet volume on communist strategy, "are one of the most important component parts of the great Marxist-Leninist teaching regarding the transformation of the world according to the new communist principles...."[5] Thus, even though this and the following chapters concern themselves with major aspects of strategy, occasional references to such tenets of ideology as are correlated to the respective devices of strategy cannot be avoided.

The Basic Rationale Underlying the Communist Strategy Shift

There are several telling reasons of strategic or tactical nature why the less developed countries of Asia, Africa and Latin

America rather than the advanced industrialized countries of Europe and North America figure today as prime areas of communist operations.

The massive postwar consolidation of non-communist Europe and the impressive vigor of the West European and North American free enterprise system, which has belied the recurrent Marxist-Leninist predictions of its impending and inevitable collapse, make the chances of communist victory in Europe and North America more remote than ever. So do the American military commitments in Europe and the presence of United States forces, as they imply a constant danger of a head-on confrontation with Communism's most potent adversary, a confrontation which communist strategists seek to avoid. Aware of its well-being, prosperity and ways of life vastly superior to those of the communist orbit, Western Europe and North America can gain little and lose much by following the communist example. Moreover, the Europeans have by now behind them decades of experience with various communist stratagems and machinations so that most of them harbor few illusions as to the communists' ulterior motives.

On the other hand, in contrast to the relatively high level of political, economic and social stability prevalent in Europe and North America, instability, flux and even outright chaos plagues much of Asia, Africa and Latin America; and the history of communist expansion clearly reveals that chaos is the *sine qua non* of communist takeovers. Memories of Western colonialism and the high-handed practices used, in not too distant past, by some segments of western capitalism in Africa, Asia and Latin America afford the Russians, whose imperialism had till now been limited mostly to areas adjacent to Russia, and even more so to the Chinese who had themselves been a victim to colonialist designs, a golden opportunity for anti-western propaganda among the highly emotional Asian, African and Latin American masses. Having to operate in a political atmosphere slanted thus in communist favor, even those native politicians who are aware of real communist intentions often find it necessary to flirt with communism and pro-communism, engage in public anti-western tirades and thereby concede new openings to communist maneuvering. Moreover, to many Asians and Africans, and even some

Latin Americans, searching for a shortcut from backwardness to modernity and painfully aware of their peoples' unpreparedness for the intricate democratic processes, the communist developmental model based on regimentation from above does often seem more suited to conditions prevailing in their countries than the example of the democratic West.

Thus the developing countries of Asia, Africa and Latin America appear to be much more vulnerable than Western Europe and North America to the current communist strategy of "peaceful coexistence" with its abandonment of global thermonuclear war as a road to communist victory and its main concentration on psychological warfare, economic penetration, political subversion, deft exploitation of colonial legacies and the many difficulties of early statehood, fomenting of civil strife and localized "wars of national liberation." If, as the communist strategic doctrine maintains, the decisive battle with the strongest adversary is to be avoided until such an adversary, i.e., the United States, has been isolated and encircled by overwhelming forces of communism, then Asia, Africa and Latin America are precisely the areas where, in communist view, such a strategy can best be applied at this stage of the East-West struggle. "The new period in world history which Lenin predicted has arrived," opined Khrushchev in his report to the Twentieth Congress of the Soviet Communist Party in 1956, "the peoples of the East are playing an active part in deciding the destinies of the whole world and are becoming a new and mighty factor in international relations."[6]

The Sino-Soviet Split

In the middle fifties when the communist foreign policy-makers began shifting emphasis from Europe and the Asian borderlands of the Sino-Soviet Bloc and formulating a new strategy for the penetration of the non-contiguous zones of the Third World, there was only one communist strategy-making center, namely, Moscow. It is true that even then the Chinese communist leadership held certain strategic views that were not in full accord with those of the Kremlin and, in particular, saw in the Chinese march to power rather than the Soviet a model better suited to the needs of colonial and ex-colonial nations. However, since the Chinese leaders were at that time in no position to become actively involved in the fortunes of other countries beyond the immediate periphery of China, their views on the subject did not much matter even had they cared to press for their acceptance. As for communist East Europe, the minute measures of lesser dependence conceded Soviet Russia's satellites in the first years after the death of Stalin did not extend to matters of international relations and global strategy whose elaboration remained a monopoly of Moscow. Nor were Yugoslavia's activities and pronouncements at the early phase of her independence from Moscow such as to constitute a distinctive enough pattern of strategy to be counterposed to that of Moscow.

This Soviet monopoly of determining strategy for the entire world socialist system has, of course, been broken in the sixties when the Chinese communists publicly rejected the Soviet leadership and denounced the whole Soviet strategy of "peaceful coexistence" as a virtual sell-out of communist interests, especially in the developing areas, to the United States imperialism. Hence, the world socialist system no longer has any united strategic doctrine, but at least two of them: one elaborated by Soviet Russia and followed, in substance, by East European communist regimes (save Albania and Yugoslavia) and by Outer Mongolia; and the other conceived by Communist China and favored by Albania, North Korea and, it seems, North Vietnam. Moreover, in the sixties Yugoslavia became far more outspoken and more active in her relations with the developing nations and Tito registered a measure of success in his endeavors to become a major spokesman for the cause of the Third World and the strategy of "active non-alignment." Thus emerged a third pattern or, rather, mini-pattern of strategy relative to the developing nations. Finally, yet another kind of strategy was developed by Castro's Cuba, for the Castroite strategy seems to combine in a maverick fashion Soviet and Chinese elements and add a few adaptations of its own.

The diversity that has afflicted the communist strategic doctrine as a result of the Sino-Soviet split requires that the respective strategies of Soviet Russia and China be treated separately. Nonetheless, in spite of the furore of the Sino-Soviet accusations and counter-accusations, it appears that a substantial body of communist strategic concepts, including those applicable to the emerging nations, is shared by the two communist giants; the disagreement between them concerns only matters of less fundamental strategic importance. That is even truer in case of Yugoslavia whose strategy, save on one or two aspects, amounts virtually to a milder variation of the Soviet pattern. As for Castroite Cuba, her strategy is concerned almost exclusively with Latin America, though a few instances of Cuban meddling in African affairs have occurred.

Therefore, the most practical and least overlapping way of dealing with the subject in the chapters to follow seems to be to consider first the essential aspects of the Soviet strategy, indicate briefly the near-total East European concurrence therein, and then single out those significant elements (if any) in which the Chinese, Yugoslav or Castroite strategies differ from the Soviet.

The Sources of Communist Strategy

However, before proceeding with our examination of communist strategy, mention ought to be made of its sources. Where is one to look to ascertain and identify the various elements and components of communist strategy? There are, in substance, two such sources:

a. First, there is a publicly stated body of strategy contained in a steady stream of official and semi-official communist pronouncements expounding the strategy and tactics which communists and their allies are supposed to follow. Foremost among them are such high-level documents as the 1960 *Declaration of Eighty-One Communist Parties;* and the 1969 *Moscow Declaration;* the 1961 *Program of the Soviet Communist Party; Fundamentals of Marxism-Leninism,* the previously mentioned official Soviet manual of communist ideology and strategy; statements issued by highest Communist party organs of the leading communist countries, such as the letters on the Sino-Soviet disagreements exchanged between the Central Committees of the Soviet and Chinese Communist parties; and numerous articles in leading communist periodicals and newspapers, such as *Pravda, Izvestiia, Kommunist, Mezhdunarodnaiia Zhizn', Novoie*

Vremia, Mirovaia Ekonomika i Mezhdunarodnye Otnosheniia, Jenmin Jih Pao, Peking Review, World Marxist Review, etc.

b. Second, close attention must be paid to the actual communist conduct relative to the developing countries. Since all communist activities are supposed to be "concrete expressions" of the general political line worked out "on the basis of a scientific analysis of the given stage of the struggle in the given situation,"[7] communist actions in various countries must be viewed as a component part and a reflection of an overall strategic design. Much like pieces of a jig-saw puzzle, the individual communist actions begin, when properly placed and related, to reveal soon enough the basic pattern.

To gain the best possible understanding of communist strategy both of these sources, one of which is explicit and the other implicit, must be used jointly and checked against each other. If too much weight were given to official pronouncements, to what the communist leaders *say* their strategy is, a distorted picture would easily result. While top-level official declarations, meant to serve as guidelines for communist operations in various parts of the world, do reflect fairly accurately communist thinking on the main aspects of strategy, they also contain many embellishing propaganda frills and many ambiguous terms as well as a good deal of the customary communist double-talk and "Aesopian" language. Hence, the true meaning of many communist pronouncements can be grasped only when they are considered in the light of their application in actual practice.

On the other hand, an unduly disdainful attitude toward the publicly stated body of communist strategy and a one-sided emphasis on actual behavior might cause one to overlook the close correlation and interdependence of various communist strategic and tactical devices and operations. Thus one could easily be misled by a seeming occasional contradiction of communist conduct in different geographical locales and psychological settings, and fail to see the full dimensions of the overall communist strategic design in its entirety and in all its ramifications.

Therefore, our examination of communist strategy and tactics will draw on both the above-mentioned sources, for this seems to be the best available way how to offset the one-sidedness of either source and to arrive, if at all possible, at a balanced evaluation.

Main Tasks of Communist Strategy.

The choice of the various methods, devices and techniques that go into a given strategy is governed primarily by the principal purposes or, to use the official Marxist-Leninist terminology, "the main tasks of a given historical stage"[8] that such a strategy is meant to accomplish. What are, then, these "main tasks" that communist strategists plan to fulfill in the world's developing areas at the present "third [and presumably final] stage of the general crisis of capitalism" which the non-communist world has recently entered upon according to official Marxist-Leninist findings?[9] Judging both by official statements and actual behavior, the paramount communist objective evidently is to induce the developing countries of Asia, Africa and Latin America to defect from the West and eventually join the East, the world socialist system. "The transition from capitalism to socialism is not an act of simultaneous liberation of all countries from the rule of capitalism, but a gradual process of defection of individual countries from the world capitalist system."[10] The attainment of this fundamental objective is viewed as a gradual process which involves the following main steps:

1. Elimination of Western influence, especially in the military, political, economic and cultural field.

2. Introduction of the anti-Western and pro-communist version of non-alignment as outlined in Chapter I.

3. A step-by step transition to non-capitalist and socialist forms in political, economic, cultural and social life.

4. Steady growth and deepening of cooperation with the communist countries and its gradual expansion into an ever closer association in one field after the other, leading ultimately to an associate and then full membership in the world socialist system.

Thus, if all went according to communist plans, the United States and its Western allies would ultimately end in isolation and, confronted with the overwhelming odds of a united Soviet-led communist bloc of the whole of Asia, Africa, Latin America and Eastern Europe, would presumably surrender without a fight.

Quite an array of strategic and tactical precepts, methods and techniques are employed by communist strategists to advance this ambitious objective and thereby to pave the way for the hoped-for eventual communist victory on a global scale, a victory without which the countries of the world socialist system itself admittedly would be unable to complete the final phase of their own communist construction. Some of these precepts have been devised especially or primarily for conditions and situations likely to arise in the developing areas. Others are of a more general nature intended both for developing and industrially advanced countries. However, the latter devices are the concern of this study only in so far as they have been used, or are likely to be used, in Asia, Africa or Latin America. The order in which the various precepts and devices are considered in the ensuing chapters is not meant to indicate the degree of their importance or any sort of priority, although an attempt has been made to arrange them in inter-related groups.

Notes for Chapter III

[1] *Collected Works*, Vol. 9, p. 22. Cited also in *Fundamentals*, p. 345.
[2] *Fundamentals*, p. 345.
[3] *Ibid.*, p. 349.
[4] *Ibid.*, p. 345.
[5] Tropkin, *op. cit.*, pp. 3-4.
[6] *Pravda*, February 7, 1956.
[7] *Fundamentals*, p. 345.
[8] *Ibid.*
[9] *Declaration of Eighty-One Communist Parties.*
[10] *Fundamentals*, p. 492.

CHAPTER IV

PARTICIPATION IN NATIONAL DEMOCRATIC REVOLUTIONS AND NATIONAL DEMOCRATIC FRONTS

Perhaps none of the tenets of communist strategy is more fundamental for the early phases of communist operations in the developing countries than the twin devices of participation in national-democratic revolutions and National Democratic Fronts. And none seems to be of a more general application throughout the Third World.

Participation in the National-Democratic Revolution

It has been a long-standing axiom of the Marxist-Leninist teaching that a genuine, i.e., Marxist-Leninist, socialist revolution can occur only under the leadership of a class-conscious and well-organized proletariat guided by its vanguard, the Communist party. Since a proletariat of this type was rather scarce in the newly emerging countries at the time of their liberation from the "imperialist yoke" and the native communist parties there were weak and in many instances virtually non-existent, the Soviet theoreticians have ruled out any chance of an immediate or early transition to socialism of the Marxist-Leninist variety. Hence, in

Soviet view, the emerging countries of the Third World have entered what communist theoreticians term the bourgeois-demo-cratic or, in a more recent version, national-democratic revolu-tion. "Brilliantly grasped"[1] and advanced for Russia by Lenin in his *Two Tactics of Social Democracy in the Democratic Revolu-tion* and subsequently for colonial and ex-colonial countries as well,[2] the thesis that a bourgeois or national democratic revolu-tion should be regarded as the first step in the inevitable progression from capitalism or pre-capitalism to socialism has become an integral part of communist teaching, especially with regard to what Lenin called the "more backward states and nations in which feudal or patriarchal or patriarchal-peasant relations predominate."[3] It figured prominently in the Com-intern's *Thesis on the Revolutionary Movement in the Colonies and Semi-Colonies*[4] and even more so during the popular-front era of 1934-1938.[5] After Stalin's death, it has been reiterated in an authoritative Soviet study *On the Fundamentals of the Strategy and Tactics of Leninism* which refers to the bourgeois democratic revolution as "a gigantic step toward the socialist revolution."[6] It has been stressed in the latest official *History of the Communist Party of the Soviet Union* which praises Lenin for having "developed Marx's idea of permanent revolution into the consistent theory of the bourgeois-democratic revolution developing into a Socialist Revolution" and claims that "a skipping of the bourgeois-democratic stage of the revolution would only have led to the isolation of the proletariat . . ."[7] And it is reaffirmed most emphatically in the *Fundamentals of Marxism-Leninism* which views the democratic and socialist revolutions as "in general" constituting "two phases of a single revolutionary process" rather than two separate and independent revolutions.[8] Speaking for Soviet Russia at a major communist-sponsored conference on The Socialist World System and the National-Liberation Movement, the Soviet Academician Ar-zumanian declared approvingly that the national revolution "does not set as its immediate aim the task of establishing the dictatorship of the proletariat."[9] The same view appears to be entertained also by the veteran pro-Soviet leaders of most of the Communist parties of the Third World.[10]

What stand are, then, the Marxist-Leninists directed to take during the initial democratic phase of the revolution? What is to be their *modus operandi?*

Again, it is Lenin who is credited by his past and present successors for having formulated and "brilliantly substantiated" the fundamental principles of communist tactics at the bourgeois-democratic stage of the struggle. Having sharply condemned "the attempt of the Mensheviks to belittle the significance of the bourgeois revolution for the proletariat" and "to keep the proletariat away from it,"[11] Lenin urged his comrades and all the proletarians as early as 1905 "not to keep aloof from the bourgeois revolution" but rather "to take a most energetic part in it."[12] Similarly, in 1920 he called in his *Draft Theses* upon the communist parties to assist the bourgeois-democratic movement in colonial and semi-colonial areas.[13]

Thus the well-known communist concept of the participation in the bourgeois or national democratic revolutions was born to be applied wherever direct and immediate communist seizure of power and the establishment of a dictatorship of the proletariat was not feasible or desirable. As such, the concept has been since then reaffirmed, explicitly and implicitly, in all the major communist strategy pronouncements of the Comintern era as well as the present days, such as the new *Soviet Communist Party Program, The Declaration of Eighty-One Communist Parties,* and the *Fundamentals.* Indeed, the necessity for such a communist participation in the democratic revolutions of today is deemed to be even more justifiable than in Lenin's days, because nowadays "the elements of the democratic and socialist revolutions are interwoven as a result of which the fulfillment of a number of tasks of the socialist revolution is possible in the initial, democratic, stage."[14]

Since the fundamental rationale of the communist participation in national democratic revolutions is to convert them eventually into socialist revolutions of a Marxist-Leninist type, the "tasks" to be attained at the democratic phase of the revolution and the main tactical devices and techniques to be used in the process have been set with that overriding objective in mind. Culled from the latest Soviet statements and deduced from the basic ideological tenets discussed in the first chapter as well as from actual communist behavior, they comprise:

a. consolidation of political independence which is to be achieved mainly through the elimination of all Western influences, refusal to participate in any western-controlled regional blocs and associations, military, political, economic or other, the uprooting of imperialist economic domination and its main instrument of "neo-colonialism", and the ejection of foreign monopolies;

b. an all-out struggle against the United States which is branded as "the mainstay of colonialism today" engaged in "desperate efforts to preserve colonial exploitation of the former colonies by new methods and in new forms";[15]

c. nationalization of key branches of national economy and "democratization of their management"[16] as a way toward dislodging and weakening both foreign and native capitalists and embarking upon the desirable non-capitalist path of development;

d. fostering industralization not merely for strictly economic reasons but also for bettering the class structure through a gradual increase of the native working class and a resulting sharpening of the class struggle;

e. enactment of radical agrarian reforms so as to gain the favor and support of broad masses of small and poor peasants;

f. a forceful advancement of a pleasing program of political, economic and social reform urging improved living standards, better working conditions, "broad democratic rights and freedoms" and other popular demands likely to appeal to the broad masses, while doing the utmost to portray western imperialists as opponents and communists and their associates as proponents of such desirable improvements;

g. the pursuance of "an independent and peaceful foreign policy" coupled with an economic and cultural cooperation with the socialist countries;

h. cooperation of native communists and working class with other "progressive forces, especially the peasantry, and branding as reactionary each and every group or party unwilling to go along while at the same time guarding jealously the communist party's organizational and operational independence;

i. penetration of labor unions, cooperatives, peasant associations, sport organizations and even "unorganized sections of the population" with a purpose of steering them first along a "non-aligned," yet anti-Western, course, and then gradually make them slide under communist controls;

j. gaining positions on various levels of government, both legally and illegally, particularly in the military establishment, police and agencies supervising communications media, education and agrarian matters;

k. utilizing every opportunity to strengthen the position of the communist parties and the proletariat at the expense of other groups and classes resulting in due time in the hegemony of the proletariat led by the Communist party;

l. finally, as the culmination of all these "tasks", a "peaceful assumption of power" which is said to be "more in keeping with the whole world outlook of the working class,"[17] resorting to non-peaceful methods such as armed struggle and "wars of national liberation" only in extreme instances, notably in countries "fettered to imperialist powers by military and other onerous agreements," and this only if and when conditions are such as to offer a good prospect of victory.

While communists should by no means waste time in pushing for the desired conversion of the democratic revolution into a socialist revolution, they are to proceed cautiously and avoid "unjustified over-zeal" and "undue haste." Even though the two types of the revolution, democratic and socialist, are said to have now drawn so close as to constitute "two phases of a single revolutionary process,"[18] the proper course for the developing countries is to pass through a preparatory stage of "general democratic development" before qualifying for socialism. Otherwise, "neglect of general democratic problems and undue haste may narrow the popular basis of socialist revolution and compromise the noble idea of socialism in the eyes of the masses."[19] Thus the Soviet strategists evidently envisage a fairly prolonged period of national-democratic revolution and an active communist participation therein, which will gradually make it "over-grow" into a socialist revolution of the Marxist-Leninist type.

The National Democratic Fronts

As the Third World's proletariat is generally weak in numbers

and in "class-revolutionary consciousness" at the initial phases
of the national democratic revolution, it needs help of non-proletarian strata to accomplish the tasks called for by the Soviet
strategists for the particular stage of the struggle. "Soviet
experience has shown," asserts the *Soviet Communist Party
Program* of 1961, "that the working class can fulfill its historic
mission as the builder of a new society only in a firm *alliance with
the non-proletarian masses,* primarily the peasantry."[20] Hence,
wherever, and whenever the communists do not feel strong
enough to seize power single-handed, they invariably endeavor to
overcome their weakness by seeking out, and entering into
cooperative arrangements with, allies from among non-proletarian and even certain bourgeois groups. That is what Lenin had
preached and practised in Russia and that is what he had
recommended in 1920 also for "colonial and backward countries."[21] Affirmed rather cautiously and unenthusiastically by the
Comintern in its 1928 *Thesis on the Revolutionary Movement in
the Colonies and Semi-Colonies*[22] and more zestfully during the
1934-1938 popular-front era,[23] this Leninist precept suits perfectly the conditions obtaining in the emerging countries of the
Third World. It is, therefore, hardly surprising that the necessity
and desirability of communist collaboration with all "progressive" and "patriotic" forces of the new nations is urged by all the
current authoritative documents and statements on communist
strategy and tactics.[24]

"The question of creating a broad alliance of anti-imperialist
forces has risen today with particular sharpness," asserts an
article in *Pravda* on May 27, 1965, commemorating the 45th
anniversary of Lenin's *Left-wing Communism, an Infantile
Disorder.* "It would be a serious mistake to appraise the
participation of the working class and its party in the broad anti-
imperialist alliance as some kind of 'dispersion', as loss of face by
the communists or perhaps a transition to the ruinous path of
conciliation."[25] The "revolutionary-democratic dictatorship" accompanying the victory in the national-liberation revolution,
holds R. Ulianovskii, should rest on "the non-proletarian, semi-
proletarian and, where they have already formed, proletarian
masses of the working people in a kind of coalition with the
patriotic strata of the small bourgeoisie and part of the middle

bourgeoisie if the latter is not sabotaging social transformations." The Marxists, he goes on, should be "flexible and
perspicacious enough not to alienate the masses, and should
constantly seek allies in those social strata and groups who, while
at a given moment not fully accepting the theory of scientific
socialism, nevertheless do partially use it today and may embrace
it tomorrow." [26]

If the non-proletarian allies are to be utilized to the best
communist advantage, their collaboration must be properly
coordinated and organized. "It is important not only to achieve
political accord," stresses the *Fundamentals,* but "agreement on
united action needs to be consolidated *organisationally.* A united
front becomes a powerful force only when the allies do not
confine themselves to declaring their community of aims, but
necessarily reach agreement on setting up a united organization
(such as a National Front, a Front of National-Democratic
Unity, etc.), and on joint action within the framework of this
organization." [27]

Thus the National Democratic Front has become the officially
prescribed organizational form for the communist participation
in the national-democratic revolutions of the Third World.
Fashioned somewhat after the popular fronts of the latter thirties
and the united, fatherland and other such fronts set up at
communist behest in Eastern Europe after World War II, they
are promoted in Africa, Asia and Latin America on substantially
the same alluring grounds as their ill-fated predecessors, namely,
the importance of national unity in the face of extreme danger
and a pressing need of national reconstruction. "The urgent tasks
of national rebirth facing the countries that have shaken off the
colonial yoke," pontificates the *Declaration of Eighty-One
Communist Parties,* "cannot be effectively accomplished unless a
determined struggle is waged against imperialism and the remnants of feudalism by all the patriotic forces of the nations united
in a single national-democratic front." [28] The United-Front
approach has become especially alluring after its successful
application in Chile, resulting in the 1970 election of the
communist-backed Marxist socialist, Salvador Allende, to
Chile's Presidency. Since the victory of the Popular Unity Front
the Chilean example has been hailed and commended repeatedly

both by Soviet writers and the Soviet-oriented communists of the Third World. "The Chilean experience confirms in the most convincing fashion," states an article in *Pravda* on September 25, 1971, that "the unity of popular anti-imperialist forces, cemented by the unity of the proletariat . . . is the guarantee of a successful advancement of the liberation movement."[29] Also, the Chilean example has inspired the communists of Uruguay to try, though with little success, a similar approach in the 1971 elections in that country.

While a call for a concerted united effort of "all the patriotic forces" at a time when a newly born country seeks to build its very foundations has a strong emotional appeal and makes good sense, the advantages which Soviet strategists hope to derive from the establishment of National Democratic Fronts have little in common with a genuine national rebirth. As bared by relevant Soviet documents and borne out by actual communist behavior, the application of the National-Front concept serves the following essential purposes: [30]

a. it makes it much harder to fight communism because any party or group so doing exposes itself at once to accusations of splitting up the "national democratic unity" which is deemed so essential for the new countries;

b. it divides the non-communists into the "ins," praised as "progressive", and the "outs," denounced as "reactionaries," precludes an establishment of a common front against communism and thus fits admirably into the favorite communist divide-and-conquer strategy;

c. it allows communists to subdivide further their "progressive" National-Front partners into those having greater and those having lesser "revolutionary potential," favor one over the other as required by the given situation and the problems to be solved, and discard one after the other those whose "revolutionary potential" has already been "exhausted";

d. it lifts communists out of isolation, allows them to conceal better their real nature and intentions, and thus confers upon them a measure of respectability in the eyes of unwitting non-communists;

e. it provides communists with a legitimate platform and a subtle disguise for their propaganda so that the National Front can be made to serve sometimes as a virtual communist Front organization;

f. it affords them an excellent opportunity to gain popularity at the expense of their National-Front partners as communists can usually outbid all their competitors in demagoguery and advocacy of most radical solutions likely to attract the restive underprivileged masses even though they might not be the correct and lasting solutions in the long run;

g. it facilitates the gradual infiltration of associated parties by communists disguised as *bona fide* members and thus contributes to the communist Trojan-horse tactics of subversion from within;

h. it brings them all these tactical advantages of the National-Front cooperation, yet makes it possible for them to preserve their Party's organizational and operational independence which communists under no circumstances are supposed to give up;

i. it is expected to enable the Communist party to secure eventually the leadership of the entire National Front and change the national-democratic revolution into a Marxist-Leninist revolution without incurring the grave risks and the heavy sacrifices of a civil war.

As aptly put by Richard Lowenthal, "the struggle for 'national democracy' is a struggle for communist leadership within the united national front for the extension of Communist influence on the nationalist government and the Communist occupation of key positions in the political, military and economic state machine; it is, however, conducted wherever possible within the framework of the existing nationalist regimes without aiming at the overthrow of popular nationalist leaders *at this stage.*"[31]

Since the main *raison d'etre* of communist associations with non-proletarian groups and parties is to pave the way for an eventual seizure of power by the communists acting as a self-styled vanguard of the proletariat, the National Democratic Front is evidently a mere temporary arrangement, a sort of matrimony of convenience that is to be dropped when it has served its basic purpose. Such was clearly the attitude of Lenin who dwelled upon the strictly temporary nature of any such alliances with bourgeois or semi-bourgeois groupings, was for supporting them only as "the rope supports the hanged man"[32] and proved right by his actual behavior Trotsky's dictum concerning Lenin's readiness to discard allies as squeezed-out lemons when no longer needed. Such seemed to be also the view of the Comintern which insisted in its *Thesis on the Revolutionary Movement in the Colonies and Semi-Colonies* on the attainment of the hegemony of the proletariat and the leadership of the communist party as the foremost task of the bourgeois-democratic revolution, a postulate that could hardly be compatible with a genuine united-front partnership of proletarian and non-proletarian parties.[33] As late as 1950 I. I. Potekhin maintained that "the stage of the common national front is possible only when and where the proletariat has not yet emerged as an independent and decisive force, as the antipode to the national bourgeoisie, where the proletariat is still not in a condition to lead the struggle of the non-proletariat working masses."[34]

However, since the death of Stalin the Soviet strategists, feeling more than ever the necessity of attracting non-proletarian allies in the less developed countries, have taken great pains to create the impression that communist cooperation with non-communists on a footing of equality and mutuality is a lasting proposition. Thus Khrushchev scornfully rejected as a "fabrication" assertions that the communists would "swallow up" their allies after they have won power and stressed that "in actual fact, communists consider it not only possible, but desirable to maintain cooperation with non-communist parties after coming to power."[35] Similarly, the *Fundamentals* proclaims that the "communists are not interested in making temporary use of their partners in the democratic front and then discarding them, as reactionary propaganda claims. On the contrary, they want to advance further together with them so as to reach a real solution of all democratic problems and to satisfy in the best possible manner the just demands of the broadest sections of the people . . ."[36]

Do these more recent statements suggest that the Soviet strategists have modified the earlier Leninist-Stalinist precept that non-proletarian allies be dropped after a successful transition from the national-democratic to the socialist phase of the revolution? Not by any means. When stating that the communists "want to advance further together" with their allies, they do so on the explicit assumption that the communists would succeed in persuading their National-Front partners to shed their bourgeois and petty-bourgeois biases and go over to the positions of "scientific socialism" and "creative Marxism." Those unwilling to yield to such persuasive efforts would be ejected as "right-wing opportunists" and "enemies of unity." Thus the former allies can be retained only on the condition that, as Ulianovskii puts it, they are "uplifted" to "the level where they can understand the fundamentals of scientific socialism," i.e., become obedient puppets of the victorious communist party.[37] That was precisely the fate of the parties and groups that had joined the communists in such united-front arrangements in Eastern Europe and China.[38] The National Democratic Front may indeed remain, but only in name, as an empty shell and a façade for the communist dictatorship.

The Chinese Version

The twin concepts of communist participation in the national democratic revolution and the National Democratic Fronts in the developing countries have been fully endorsed not only by the communist regimes of Eastern Europe and by pro-Soviet Communists of the Third World but by the Chinese communist leaders as well. As for the latter, they have continued to adhere to the two concepts even after having publicly broken with their Soviet comrades in the early sixties. Indeed, the Chinese eagerness to participate in national democratic revolutions in the emerging ex-colonial nations and to collaborate with non-proletarian masses, including even the "progressive" part of the national bourgeoisie, has been as great as that of Soviet Russia. And the Chinese Twenty-Five Theses of June 1963 indicate that their concept of the united front is at least as broad as its Soviet version and that they are possibly even less choosy than their Soviet comrades in picking their allies.[39]

Nonetheless, several significant nuances may be noted in the way in which the two devices are understood and practised by the two regimes.

To begin with, the Chinese approach appears to be less gradualist and more impatient than the Soviet. Like their Soviet counterparts, the Chinese strategy-makers reckon generally with a rather prolonged phase of national democratic revolution to precede its conversion into a socialist revolution. However, considering the armed struggle as the best technique of anti-imperialist strategy in the Third World, they do seem to have a tendency "to jump adventurously across stages of the revolution" and to push for a forcible transition to socialism even when conditions therefor do not obtain.[40] It is true that the Chinese Twenty-Five Theses themselves state that "it would be 'Left' adventurism if the proletarian party should rashly launch a revolution before the objective conditions are ripe," whereas "it would be Right opportunism" should the proletarian party fail to lead the revolution and "seize state power" when the objective conditions are ripe.[41] Yet, their behavior and pronouncements to-date suggest that the Chinese leaders tend more to run the risk of the former than the latter. Thus, they are guilty precisely of that "undue haste" which Soviet spokesmen caution against.

A slight difference can also be noted in the respective Chinese and Soviet attitudes concerning the united fronts. The Chinese communists seem to stress quite heavily what is called in the communist jargon a united front "from below," i.e., seeking and attaining the desired unity of action and promote the communist leadership of the national-liberation movement by appealing to the masses over the heads of the nationalist leaders, thus undercutting the latter's power base and confronting them with a *fait accompli.*[42] By the same token, they frown at united fronts "from above" formed by agreements with nationalist leaders as they consider such coalition-type arrangements as leaving the nationalist positions intact and even possibly strengthening them.

On the other hand, the Soviet communists have taken a more balanced and more tolerant stand, both in theory and in actual practice. They, too, prefer a united front "from below." "A solid and effective (*deesposobnyi*) united front cannot be created through mere agreements at the top," stressed V. Tiagunenko in summarizing the previously mentioned MEIMO discussion on "Socialism, Capitalism, the Less Developed Nations." "It must be supported by joint action, that is, it must be forged through mass action from below resulting from joint action of various class and social groups."[43] However, as borne out by actual practice in a number of developing nations, Soviet strategists and their native communist associates are by no means loath to settle for cooperative arrangements tantamount to a united front "from above" if and when resort to a united front "from below" is not feasible or advisable.[44]

Yet another strategy matter about which the Chinese and the Soviet communists have differed in recent years has been the delicate issue of the communist party's independence within the framework of the united front. Theoretically the Soviet and Chinese views are virtually identical. The gist of their numerous official and semi-official pronouncements, both before and after the Sino-Soviet split, is that participation in the united front must not lead to the loss of communist ideological, political and organizational independence.[45] But in actual practice the Soviet strategy-makers appear not to insist on the application of this particular aspect of communist united-front strategy as much as do their Chinese colleagues. As shown in Chapter VI, Soviet spokesmen have condoned, or at least tolerated, a demise of communist independence in several African one-party states. On the other hand, the Chinese communist leaders, reminiscent no doubt of their party's 1927 debacle brought about by the communist fusion with the Kuomintang, reject most resolutely any united-front approach that would jeopardize communist independence.

Finally, the Soviet and the Chinese communists do not see eye to eye when it comes to the issue of the leadership of the national-liberation revolution and the National Democratic Front. As discussed more fully in Chapter VI, when absolutely necessary, Soviet strategists are prepared to concede the leadership of the united front, at least at the early stages of the revolution, to "national" or "revolutionary" democrats or some other such group rather than pushing for communist leadership at all cost. On the other hand, the Chinese leaders are adamant in insisting that, to be acceptable for them, a united front must from the beginning be led by communists.

Notes for Chapter IV

[1] *Fundamentals*, p. 485.

[2]"Preliminary Draft Theses on the National and Colonial Question," *Selected Works,* Vol. 10, p. 231.

[3]*Ibid.*

[4]pp. 21 ff. See also Kermit E. McKenzie, *Comintern and World Revolution, 1928-1943,* pp. 71 ff.

[5]McKenzie, *op. cit.,* pp. 135 ff and 159 ff.

[6]N. V. Tropkin, *op. cit.,* p. 23.

[7]Moscow, 1960, p. 103.

[8]p. 487.

[9]"The Socialist World System and the National-Liberation Movement, Exchange of Views," *World Marxist Review,* 6, 3, 1963, pp. 52 ff.

[10]See, for instance, a major article by the veteran Brazilian Communist party leader Luis Carlos Prestes on "Political line and tactics of Brazilian communists in the New Conditions," *World Marxist Review,* 11, 6, 1968, pp. 31-38.

[11]*History of the Communist Party of the Soviet Union,* Moscow, 1939, p. 65-66.

[12]"Two Tactics of Social Democracy in the Democratic Revolution," *Selected Works,* Vol. III, p. 77.

[13]*Selected Works,* Vol. 10, p. 231.

[14]*Fundamentals,* p. 487.

[15]*Declaration of Eighty-One Communist Parties, Jacobs,* p. 31 and the 1969 *Moscow Declaration.*

[16]*Fundamentals,* p. 483.

[17]*Ibid.,* p. 500.

[18]*Fundamentals,* p. 487.

[19]*Kommunist,* September 1962.

[20]*Ritvo,* p. 43.

[21]*"Detskaia bolezn' levizny v kommunizme."* (Leftwing Communism: An Infantile Disorder) *Sochineniia,* xxxi, p. 52; Preliminary Draft, *Selected Works,* 10, p. 231.

[22]pp. 33-35.

[23]McKenzie, *op. cit.,* pp. 159 ff.

[24]See the *Soviet Communist Party Program,* especially Chapter VI, the *Declaration of Eighty-One Communist Parties,* the 1969 *Moscow Declaration, Fundamentals,* Chapters 13, 14 and 16; Tropkin, *Ob osnovakh,* p. 28, and *"Ob strategii i taktike Leninizma,"* (About the Strategy and Tactics of Leninism), *Kommunist,* No. 1, January 1955, p. 108; *The Third World,* p. 188; and B. N. Ponomaryev's speech at the International Symposium held in Moscow on "The 50th Anniversary of the October Revolution and the International Working Class," *New Times,* No. 50, 1967, pp. 3-9.

[25]See also R. Ulianovskii, "Socialism and the National-Liberation Movement," *Pravda,* April 15, 1966.

[26]R. Ul'ianovskii, *"Nekotorye voprosy nekapitalisticheskogo razvitiia osvobodivshikhsia stran"* (Some Questions of the Non-Capitalist Development of the Liberated Countries), *Kommunist,* No. 1, January 1966, pp. 113 ff. English text in the *Yearbook of Communist Affairs,* 1967, pp. 547 ff.

[27]p. 380.

[28]*Jacobs,* p. 31.

[29]Vitalii Korionov, *"Latinskaia America v ostroi bor'be,"* (Latin America in a Sharp Struggle), *Pravda,* September 25, 1971, p. 4. See also, L. Rybalkin, "Chile: Gains, Problems and Prespectives," *New Times,* No. 31, 1971, pp. 6 ff.;

Luis Corvalan, *"Chili: k vlasti prokhodit narod,"* (Chile: The People Comes to Power), *Pravda,* December 1, 1970; a round table conference held at Santiago, Chile, under the sponsorship of the Editorial Board of the *World Marxist Review* and the Central Committee of the Communist party of Chile: "Latin America: Liberation Struggle and the Working Class," *World Marxist Review,* 14, 7, 1971, pp. 72 ff; "Communists and the Masses," *World Marxist Review,* 14, 9, 1971, pp. 39 ff.; *"Latinskaia Amerika: vazhnye peremeny,"* (Latin America: Serious Changes), *Pravda,* May 11, 1972.

[30] A good recent illustration how communists can and do exploit their membership in such united fronts for partisan purposes is offered by their behavior in Chile and in the Indian state of Kerala. See, for instance, Luis Corvalan, *op. cit.,* and B. Shurygin, *"Kerala: uspekhi i problemy."* (Kerala: Successes and Problems), *Pravda,* September 25, 1971.

[31] Richard Lowenthal, "'National Democracy' and the Post-Colonial Revolution," in Kurt London (ed.), *New Nations in a Divided World,* pp. 56 ff. Italics added.

[32] *Detskaia bolezn,* p. 69.

[33] p. 26.

[34] "Stalin's Theory of Colonial Revolution and the National-Liberation Movement in Tropical and South Africa," in Thomas P. Thorton, ed. *The Third World in Soviet Perspective,* Princeton, 1964, p. 36.

[35] Nikita S. Khrushchev, *For Victory in Peaceful Competition with Capitalism,* New York, 1960.

[36] p. 381.

[37] R. Ul'ianovskii, *"Nekotorie voprosy",* *op. cit.;* see also W. Sheppard, "The One-Party System and Democracy in Africa," *World Marxist Review,* 7, 3, 1964, pp. 86 ff., in which the author argues that "the revolutionary democrats will gradually go over to the positions of creative Marxism, convinced that the Marxian doctrine is omnipotent because it is true."

[38] On the pitiful fate of such parties in Eastern Europe see, for instance, Edward Taborsky, "The 'Non-Communist' Parties in Czechoslovakia," *Problems of Communism,* VIII, 2, 1958, pp. 20 ff.

[39] See especially Thesis 9 of the letter sent by the Central Committee of the Chinese Communist party to the Central Committee of the Soviet Communist party on June 14, 1963.

[40] G. Mirskii's statement in *"Sotsialism, Kapitalizm, Slaborozvitye Strany,"* *MEIMO,* No. 6, 1964, p. 65.

[41] Thesis 12.

[42] See also Donald S. Zagoria, "Russia, China, and the New States," in Donald W. Treadgold, ed., *Soviet and Chinese Communism,* pp. 405 ff.

[43] *MEIMO,* No. 6, 1964, p. 81.

[44] For instance, at one time or another in Syria, Sudan, Iraq, Ceylon, etc.

[45] See, for instance, Thesis 9 of the Chinese letter of June 14, 1963; Lin Piao, "Long Live the Victory of the People's War," *Peking Review,* September 3, 1965; Akopian's statement in the *MEIMO* discussion of "Socialism, Capitalism, the Less Developed Nations," *MEIMO,* No. 6, 1964, p. 74; Zagoria in Treadgold, *op. cit.,* pp. 408 and 413.

CHAPTER V

FOSTERING THE CLASS STRUGGLE AND BUILDING-UP
A CLASS-CONSCIOUS PROLETARIAT

As noted in Chapter I, the concept of class struggle and the role of the working class figure high among the Marxist-Leninist tenets deemed applicable to the developing areas of the world. Despite the obvious fact that the social structure of the newly emerging nations is vastly different from the situation in the capitalist countries of nineteenth-century Europe upon which Karl Marx based his class-struggle theory, the Soviet theoreticians nevertheless insist upon the necessity and desirability of class struggle for economically underdeveloped areas as well. Thus the promotion of class struggle and the leadership of the proletariat have become a major concern of communist strategy and tactics in the Third World.

The Class Struggle - A Sine Qua Non

Since the days of Lenin it has been a standard article of communist creed that no socialist revolution can be brought about anywhere without a resolute class struggle spearheaded by the "most revolutionary class in history," the proletariat. "The main thing in the doctrine of Marx," said Lenin, "is that it brings out the historic role of the proletariat as the builder of a socialist society."[1] The class struggle is the "driving force of development of society."[2] "... no matter what form the proletarian revolution takes, it is always the highest stage of development of the class struggle."[3] "For the working class this theory [of the class struggle] provides the scientific basis of the tactics of its struggle for emancipation."[4] Recent authoritative Soviet statements on theory and strategy take great pains to stress the compatibility of the policy of "peaceful coexistence" with the class struggle and even go so far as to define peaceful coexistence as "a specific form of class struggle, a new form of the class struggle of the working class and the socialist countries in the world arena."[5] The *Declaration* adopted by the 1969 Moscow Conference of Communist Parties claims that the policy of peaceful coexistence actually "helps to promote the class struggle against imperialism on a national and worldwide scale." These communist documents discuss at length the various forms of class struggle - economic, ideological and political - and make it amply clear that they consider the emerging nations of the Third World as the proper arena in which it is to be waged.[6] "In the highest imperialist stage of capitalism," asserts the *Fundamentals,* "the socialist revolution may occur first in the less developed countries if the social and political contradictions there have become sufficiently acute."[7]

Nor should the intensity of the class struggle be weakened in any way because of considerations for the proletariat's partners in the National Democratic Fronts. On the contrary, it is to be waged with relentless vigor even against the proletariat's *ad hoc* allies, especially the national bourgeoisie, so as to expose their vacillations, make them lose the confidence of the masses, and thus produce a shift in the alignment of class forces in favor of the proletariat. Addressing an international seminar held in Berlin in September, 1964, in commemoration of the centenary of the First International, A Sobolev envisaged "a bitter class struggle" during the non-capitalist stage of development.[8] And, as pointed out by the Secretary General of the Soviet-oriented Ceylonese Communist party, writing in the same volume of the *World Marxist Review,* the class struggle is to continue unabated even at the more advanced level of national democracy, the new interim developmental stage immediately preceding, and over-growing into, the socialist stage.[9]

The Third World's Proletariat and Its Weaknesses

To succeed in its ultimate purpose of converting the national democratic revolution into a socialist revolution, the class struggle must be waged by and led by the working class, the proletariat. "The main tactical principle, one that runs through Lenin's whole book," states the official *History of the Communist Party of the Soviet Union* referring to Lenin's *Two Tactics of Social Democracy in the Democratic Revolution,* "is that the proletariat can and must be the *leader* of the bourgeois-democratic revolution. . . ."[10] According to the *Fundamentals,* "transition from capitalism to socialism can take place only through the setting up of working-class power"; and the democratic revolution can grow into a socialist revolution only if "the working class is able to take the leadership in it."[11] As stressed by Academician Arzumanian, speaking at an international seminar concerned with "The Socialist System and the National-Liberation Movement," "the tasks of the revolution find their fullest and most consistent solution when the most revolutionary class of society - the working class - becomes its leading force."[12] Even the least doctrinaire among Soviet scholars working in the field of Asian, African and Latin American studies, such as R. Avakov and G. Mirskii, hold that "in the final analysis, the choice of a path depends on which class becomes the leading force of society."[13]

Indeed, the present Soviet strategists have fully endorsed Lenin's teaching that even an existing revolutionary situation would not lead to an actual revolution unless the necessary "objective conditions" are supplemented by "subjective conditions," of which the primary one is the existence of a "revolutionary class" able and ready "to carry out decisive action strong enough to smash or impair the existing power . . ."[14] Soviet writers from Lenin to the present have left no doubt that such a class can only be the "wage-workers," the proletariat.[15] The necessity of working-class leadership has been reaffirmed most emphatically after the Soviet invasion of Czechoslovakia. Since then, Soviet writers have repeatedly pointed to Czechoslovakia as an abhorrent example of what could happen when the sacrosanct Marxist-Leninist imperative of proletarian leadership and the principle of class struggle are downgraded. [16]

It is true that in countries where the native working class is especially weak, allowance has been made by some of the Soviet theoreticians for "elements close to the working class," the so-called "revolutionary democrats," the "international working class" or the "socialist world system" to perform the leading role ordinarily assigned to the respective country's proletariat. [17] But these are only temporary concessions meant to meet the momentary tactical needs. As such, they do not in any way invalidate the general official Marxist-Leninist thesis on the supremacy of the working class and do not "cancel its historic mission of being the vanguard and principal motive force of the revolution." [18] "The claim that the working class is incapable of taking the lead in the revolutionary process holds no water," asserts a 1967 editorial in *New Times*. [19] While pressing home his thesis that developing countries can move toward socialism even without proletarian leadership, Ulianovskii hastens to add that "none of this . . . does away with the self-evident proposition that in all countries, including those just starting to bypass capitalism, socialism can triumph only on the basis of scientific socialism, under the leadership of the working class closely allied with the working peasantry." [20] In the same vein, discussing the victory of the communist-backed Popular Unity Front in Chile in his long report at Moscow's Institute of Marxism-Leninism, B. Ponomaryov, Secretary of the Central Committee of the Soviet Communist party, singled out as the first "basic lesson" of the Chilean experience its confirmation of "the role of the working class . . . as the main motive and leading force of the revolution" and its refutation of "the opportunist contentions that this role is now being taken over by the intelligentsia, urban middle strata, students or other social groups." [21] Moreover, as is evident from their statements and writings, not even the Third World communists of pro-Soviet leanings seem to relish the idea of foregoing the traditional Marxist concept of the necessity of working-class leadership. [22] As the veteran Syrian communist leader, Khaled Bagdash, puts it: "Be the objective conditions in one or another country what they may, and no matter how weak numerically and poorly organized its working class, no other social group, no other class and no individual can take over the historic mission of the working class. A policy which does not take cognizance of this is doomed to fail." [23]

This being so, it can be easily understood why the Soviet theoreticians and their native associates have been paying so much attention to matters pertaining specifically to the working class in emerging nations and why they have been striving so hard to overcome the various difficulties confronting them in that crucial sector of the anti-imperialist front. Obsessed as they are with the class-struggle dogma, communist writers have produced a number of studies analyzing the social structure of the various regions and countries of Asia, Africa and Latin America. Not at all surprisingly, they have found the class structure in such societies to be very uneven and "extremely complex." [24] While noting with pleasure a gradual increase in the size of the African, Asian, and Latin American working class, they have, nevertheless, concluded that the situation leaves much to be desired from a Marxist-Leninist viewpoint and that "the movement of the working class is lagging behind the rhythm and requirement of the revolutionary process." [25] The gist of their findings may be summarized as follows:

1. The number of persons qualifying as proletarians in the Marxist-Leninist meaning of the term remains rather small throughout the Third World. Although the working class in non-communist Asia, Africa and Latin America has increased fourfold since the Second World War, according to communist estimates, and exceeded 130 million by the middle sixties, [26] this seemingly impressive overall figure sounds much more modest when it is spelled out in proportional terms. Thus, the estimated 85 million workers of non-communist Asia represent only some 8 per cent of the population, with corresponding ratios of some 5.5-7 and 12-14 per cent, respectively, for Africa and Latin America. [27] Indeed, "the fact that in many young states [of the Third World] there is no working class or else it is only forming and has not yet asserted itself as an independent political force" is advanced as the primary reason why the "tried and tested road of people's democracy" could not be used there. [28] Moreover, the

genuine Marxist-Leninist prototypes of proletarians, the industrial workers at the bench, constitute only a small part of the above total, namely, by communist-accepted figures, 14 million in Asia, 7 million in Latin America and 4 million in Africa, the balance consisting of agricultural laborers, part-time and migratory workers.[29]

2. The social origin and background of the Asian, African and Latin American working class also do not always meet the communist criteria. A large proportion of workers employed in industrial enterprises of the less developed nations is made up of the first generation of rural migrants.[30] Thus, most of the workers are actually peasants who have only recently left their rural habitat. Many of them are migratory or seasonal laborers who periodically return to their native villages after having worked temporarily in the cities.[31] Because of their primitive rural background, continued ties to the folks back home and deeply imbedded traditionalist or tribal attitudes, people like these are viewed by Marxist-Leninist writers as a lower species of workers, less dependable, lacking "a solid working-class tradition" and open to "wide-spread penetration of petty-bourgeois ideology...."[32] In Asia, as a Soviet analyst ruefully reports, even many second and third-generation proletarians are "closely connected with the villages and through them with their community and caste."[33] Even in Latin America, where the industrial working class is more developed than in Africa and Asia, communist analysts complain that the rapid flow of manpower from the countryside "diluted the working class" and that these "new workers often fell under the influence of the pro-American agents in the labour movement."[34]

3. Another weakness that Soviet theoreticians and their native associates have uncovered in the evolving class structure of emerging nations lies in the tendency to create an elitist "labor aristocracy." Noting that certain small groups of skilled workers, especially those employed in some of the high-priority state-owned enterprises, enjoy considerably higher wages and other benefits than the poorly-paid bulk of the working class, they are worried lest "a stratum of a workers' aristocracy" be formed which would "gravitate toward bourgeois ideology." Such a stratum was identified by communist analysts as existing espe-

cially in Latin America, mainly among workers in the "monopo-
ly-owned enterprises" who are said to "live in an atmosphere
steeped in North American way of life and thinking."[35]

Since the emergence of such a "labor aristocracy," allegedly
"bribed" by the capitalists into accepting capitalism, is advanced
by communist spokesmen as a major reason why the working
class has not as yet managed to overthrow capitalism in the
highly industrialized countries of Europe and North America,
the threat implicit in such a tendency cannot be taken lightly.

4. Nor are communist analysts pleased with the fact that in
most of the developing countries far too many workers are
employed in "the non-productive" sectors and in relatively small
enterprises which often constitute "small islands set in the ocean
of a peasant economy."[36] The communist strategists know from
past experience that workers can be influenced and manipulated
more successfully when they are massed together in great
numbers, live in close quarters in congested areas, have no direct
personal contact with their employers, and feel depersonalized,
alienated and lost in a huge collective mass. Considering "the
level of concentration of the proletariat" as "the principal factor
determining its role in the socio-political development of a
country,"[37] communist analysts feel that the dispersion of
workers among many smaller units makes the work of communist agitators more difficult. Such workers are deemed more
susceptible to bourgeois, petty-bourgeois and reformist influences than the workers employed in large industrial establishments.[38]

5. But the most vexing problem that Soviet observers have
encountered in their studies of the class structure in developing
countries has been the working class's low level of class consciousness. To Marxist-Leninists, this is a fundamental issue, for
they view class consciousness as the main catalyst in the
revolutionary process. "The probability of a socialist revolution
and its success directly depend on the scope of the class struggle
waged by the proletariat and on its class-consciousness and
organisation."[39] Only if it is endowed with an adequate level of
class-consciousness can the proletariat assume its rightful role as
"the advanced detachment of the working people" and "the
shock force" of the socialist revolution "storming the ramparts

of the old society."[40] In the Soviet official view, a high level of class-consciousness can overcome the proletariat's numerical weakness and enable it to attain leadership "even in the countries of weakly developed capitalism where the working class is a minority of the population."[41]

What are the ingredients of this all-important requisite for proletarian success? As defined by Lenin and affirmed by Soviet interpreters of today, class consciousness implies three main elements:[42]

a. "the workers' understanding that the only way to improve their conditions and to achieve their emancipation is to conduct a struggle against the capitalist factory-owner class";

b. their awareness that "they all constitute one class, separate from all the other classes in society";

c. their realization "that to achieve their aims they have to work to influence affairs of state" and, more specifically, that they must become conscious of, and "act up to," their role as the hegemon in the struggle of *all* the toilers and exploited against the oppressors and exploiters." For "the proletarian who is not conscious of the idea that his class must be the hegemon . . . is a slave who does not realize his slavish position."

Such a Leninist-style class consciousness as comprising all these elements is hard to come by even under conditions of developed capitalism; and Soviet strategists readily concede that "the formation of the class-consciousness of the proletariat is therefore a complex process."[43] Hence, it is hardly surprising that "the young working-class movement of the newly-free, dependent and colonial countries of Asia, Africa, and Latin America" is found wanting in this respect.[44]

According to communist writers, the proletariat of emerging nations is not yet fully conscious of its status as a distinctive class or of its class interests, let alone its predestined role of revolutionary leadership. In many areas it is not even aware of the necessity of class struggle, and succumbs to "dangerous illusions," fostered by the "corroding influence of bourgeois ideologies," that the workers' lot can be improved without it. In Africa, Asia and the Middle East, in particular, workers have been led astray by their national leaders' promotion of native forms of socialism founded on national unity rather than class conflict.[45]

The deeply rooted tribal, clan, family, and religious ties and loyalties also impede the rise of sharp class barriers and the awakening of revolutionary class-consciousness. Nor do Soviet observers hold much hope that the situation will improve very soon. "... in the early stages of an industrialization the proportion of experienced and class-conscious workers who are connected with traditions of class struggle may temporarily decrease," admit two Soviet scholars writing on the "Peculiarities in the Composition and Structure of the Working Class in the Economically Under-Developed Countries of Asia and Africa"; and this "to a certain extent facilitates the penetration of bourgeois influences among the workers."[46] Nor does the situation seem much better in Latin America where, as an editorial in *New Times* puts it, "the old core of the working class had been swamped ... by the rapid influx of new contingents of workers in 1940-55."[47] "Lacking experience in class struggle," laments the editorial, "these newcomers to the working class have been prone to fall under the influence of the reactionaries and social demagogues and have shied away from the road of struggle, of genuine revolution." Also, as another Latin American communist complains, the addition of former peasant and petty-bourgeois elements "had a negative effect on the Latin American labor movement because non-proletarian elements naturally gravitated toward anarcho-syndicalism, Right opportunism and ultra-Left extremism."[48]

Overcoming the Problems

Proceeding from this general analysis of the class structure in less developed countries, Soviet strategists have set forth two basic high-priority tasks, one quantitative and one qualitative: to increase the Third World's proletariat in numbers and to enhance its political maturity and revolutionary class consciousness. They hope to accomplish these tasks in three main ways: 1. economic, 2. ideological, and 3. organizational.

The Class Function of Industrialization

In line with the Marxist-Leninist emphasis on the decisive role of economic factors in shaping man's destinies, Soviet strategists expect the class picture to gradually brighten with progressive industrialization. As industries develop, asserts the 1961 *Soviet Communist Party Program,* the ranks of the working class "will swell and its role on the socio-political scene will increase."[49] The construction of hundreds of industrial enterprises in the developing countries is more than just the creation of important branches of economy," states an authoritative article in *Pravda* on "The USSR and the National-Liberation Struggle"; "it also means the formation of a working class."[50] Besides augmenting the proletariat's numerical strength, industrialization is relied upon to improve its composition and cohesiveness as well as its ideological level.[51] As the workers of Asia, Africa and Latin America are gradually transferred from small workshops to larger plants, they "overcome the disunion and isolation that was the curse of the other mass movements of the working people."[52] Daily work at such large enterprises presumably "instills in the workers such qualities as the spirit of collectivism, capacity for strict discipline, united action, and mutual aid and support," which are qualities "invaluable not only in labour but also in struggle."[53] Moreover, large-scale industry requires better educated workers and such workers are supposedly better able to grasp the virtues of Marxism-Leninism, especially the meaning and the necessity of class struggle. "Skilled industrial and agricultural workers are exerting great influence on the workers who were employed in the old, often semi-primitive enterprises."[54]

Hence, in helping the developing countries economically, industrially and technologically, the Soviet Union is also guided by the desire to produce an alignment of class forces more favorable to the communist cause.

Raising the Level of Class Consciousness

The growing concentration of workers brought about by the industrialization process is also counted upon to facilitate indoctrination of workers in the essentials of Marxism-Leninism which alone can raise class consciousness to the desired level. "To play its part in the liberation struggle the scientific world outlook of the working class must become the possession of the masses of the workers."[55] As workers gather by thousands "under the roofs of plants and factories which are, as a rule, located in large cities,"[56] they can be reached by communist agitators and propagandists much more easily than when they are scattered in isolated small units throughout the countryside. It becomes simpler for well-trained communist activists to establish contacts, convene meetings, and incite workers to "day-to-day struggle" which the Soviet strategists consider "the best school of class-consciousness for the workers."[57] Most importantly, demagogy, emotional appeals and advocacy of the most extremist solutions to real or imaginary ills, all of which are time-honored communist devices, ordinarily necessitate massive audiences in order to succeed.

The creation of optimum conditions for workers' indoctrination and their fullest utilization is all the more important because the level of class consciousness among the workers of Asia, Africa, and Latin America has been so low. As noted above, communist activists have to contend with various undesirable "bourgeois" and "idealistic" concepts and attitudes, such as "petty-bourgeois" varieties of native "non-scientific" socialism, "leftist liberalism," "economism," "bourgeois nationalism," "patriarchalism," Pan-Africanism and Pan-Arabism, communalism and tribalism, "religious obscurantism," "fetishism" and various notions of "negritude," not to mention the more recent "revisionist" and "dogmatist" deviations from the Soviet-prescribed line of Marxism-Leninism.

Thus, raising the revolutionary class consciousness of the Asian, African and Latin American proletariat through intensive indoctrination in the necessity of class struggle and other crucial aspects of Marxist-Leninist ideology and strategy commands a high priority on the agenda of Soviet strategy-makers.

Penetration of the Labor Movement

Along with the size of the working class and its ideological maturity and class consciousness, the attainment of the highest possible degree of the proletariat's organization is considered to be an essential postulate of the communist strategy of class struggle and a prerequisite of communist victory. The Comintern's 1928 *Thesis on the Revolutionary Movement in the*

Colonies and Semi-Colonies listed "the degree of organization of the working class" among factors of "decisive significance for the immediate growing over of the revolution from one stage to another higher stage"; and it warned against the grave danger of "an insufficiently accurate political and organizational delimitation of the proletariat from the bourgeoisie."[58]

The recent Soviet official pronouncements on strategy and tactics talk in much the same vein. The *Fundamentals, the Declaration of Eighty-One Communist Parties* as well as the 1969 *Moscow Declaration* dwell upon the organization of the proletariat as one of the main determinants of the course and the outcome of the revolution.[59] In spite of the setbacks which they have suffered thus far in their bid to lure the workers to the communist side the Soviet strategists nevertheless continue to profess their undiminished confidence in the proletariat's unique organizational ability. "Marx and Engels divined in the working class such capacity for organization as no other class possesses," asserts the *Fundamentals*, and it points to the proletariat's "more highly developed organization" (when coupled with a high degree of class consciousness) as the main reason why the working class is "the most militant and revolutionary class of society."[60]

To utilize the proletariat's alleged superior capacity for organization has thus become one of the most pressing tasks of communist strategy in the developing countries. This is reflected, in particular, in strenuous communist efforts to gain control of the Third World organized labor movement.

The communist strategy-makers became aware of the revolutionary potential of the non-European labor movement long before the collapse of the colonial system after the Second World War. As early as 1928 the Comintern included "the wide-spread development of trade union organisation of the working class" among the "general basic tasks" of communist strategy in colonial and semi-colonial countries during the "bourgeois-democratic" stage of the revolution.[61] It listed "a certain definite level of development" in trade union organization of the proletariat among the "minimum prerequisites" for the transition of the revolution from its democratic to its socialist stage. Also, it urged communists in the colonies to organize the unorganized workers, to convert existing workers' organizations into "real class trade unions," and to wrest the leadership of trade unions from the hands of "the national-reformist and reactionary trade union leaders."

While colonies were in firm control of colonial powers, the prospects of accomplishing these "basic tasks" were rather remote. But the mass emancipation of former colonies in the wake of the Second World War and the late fifties seemed to offer a long awaited breakthrough. Emotional anti-Westernism, resentment against one-time foreign masters and supervisors, chaotic conditions characteristic of the post-emancipation era, lack of experience and sophistication on the part of native labor, personal ambitions of local would-be labor leaders, and other such factors created favorable conditions for the activities of communist and pro-communist labor organizers. With their appetite whetted by communist successes in dominating organized labor in Eastern Europe during the early post-war era, Soviet strategists stepped up their endeavors to gain ascendancy over the labor movement in the developing nations and thus to implement Lenin's injunction to transform labor unions into "a very useful auxiliary to the political, agitational and revolutionary organizations."[62] "One of the most important tactical forms of struggle is the work of Communists in the labor unions and other mass organizations of the toilers ..." stresses and authoritative Soviet study of Leninist strategy and tactics.[63] The *Declaration of Eighty-One Communist Parties* directs the communists to "extend their work in trade unions," which it designates as a work of "the utmost importance."[64] Other communist pronouncements contain similar exhortations.[65] Although these directives are addressed to communists in all parts of the non-communist world, the current Soviet emphasis on the Third World makes them applicable, first and foremost, to Asia, Africa and Latin America. "We see our obligation and internationalist duty," said the Soviet Trade Unions boss, Alexander Shelepin, addressing the 14th Soviet Trade Union Congress in February 1968, "in intensifying contacts with the trade unions of these countries [Asia, Africa and Latin America] and giving them aid."[66] The 1969 *Moscow Declaration* dwells specifically on the growing importance of "international ties between the young proletariat of Asia and Africa and the working class of the socialist countries." As restated most emphatically by P. Pimenov, Secretary of the USSR Central Council of Trade Unions in his article in the 1971 volume of *New Times,* "the Soviet trade unions consider it their task to contribute in every possible way to the strengthening and development of progressive trade unions in the developing countries and to help to bring them closer to the world progressive labour movement."[67]

The ultimate goal of communist strategy relative to the labor movement of developing areas is, of course, to place it under communist control and use it, when the right moment comes, as the main lever for establishing the coveted dictatorship of the proletariat. That is the role the communist-controlled labor unions were assigned in the process of "peaceful" transition to socialism in Eastern Europe in 1945-48; and communist strategists evidently hope that the organized labor movement will eventually perform a similarly important function in the Third World. However, realizing that conditions suitable for the attainment of this ambitious ultimate goal may take quite some time to mature, they concentrate presently on several intermediate goals that are designed to:

a. sever the labor unions of the developing countries from Western contacts;

b. unify them nationally and internationally on a basis of "independence";

c. indoctrinate them with Marxist-Leninist ideology;

d. utilize them to coerce native governments unwilling to do so on their own to move toward communist-sponsored goals.

a. Foremost priority has been assigned to the task of isolating the Third World labor from the labor movement in the Western world and "liberating" it "from the grip which the *International Confederation of Free Trade Unions* sought to lay on it."[68] No effort has been spared in this respect. Asian, African and Latin American labor unions affiliated with the *International Confederation of the Free Trade Unions* (ICFTU) have been urged to drop their affiliation. To attain this all-important objective a massive propaganda campaign has been unleashed by all the propaganda media at communist disposal, especially via the communist-controlled *World Federation of Trade Unions* (WFTU) and its agents, against the ICFTU and any and all regional groupings associating or cooperating with it. They have been portrayed as American-controlled tools of neo-colonialism, "yellow syndicalism," lackeys of monopoly capitalism, agents of the CIA, contemptible splitters of the unity of the labor movement sending delegates "with pockets packed with dollars" to sabotage the native labor movement's drive for independence.[69]

To prove the "genuineness' of the professed communist concern for the independence of the Third World's labor movement the WFTU has slowed and in some areas even suspended its own efforts to induce native labor unions of emerging nations to join its own ranks. (This tactical shift from earlier efforts to make the native labor unions affiliate with the WFTU has been caused, at least in part, by the fact that the WFTU's recruitment drive was losing ground in competition with similar efforts of the ICFTU.)[70]

b. Another major intermediate goal of Soviet strategy vis-a-vis the labor movement of Asia, Africa and Latin America has been to encourage by all means its unity, both within the respective nations and on the continental scale. "The restoration of unity within the trade union movement in countries where it is split, as well as on the international scale, is essential for heightening the role of the working class in political life and for the successful defense of its interests."[71] "Overcoming the split [in the working-class movement] is an important condition for the fulfillment by the working class of its historic mission."[72] Hence, communists must be "consistent champions of trade union unity within the framework of each country and in the international arena."[73]

Again, these official directives are addressed to communists of all countries, but their primary target today is the Third World where emphasis on working class unity has become an ever recurrent theme in speeches and writings of native communists.[74] "To win the workers' vital demands," reads an authoritative article in the 1969 volume of *New Times,* "the trade unions of developing countries must above all maintain and strengthen their independence and class character and ensure trade union unity in each country."[75] It is also in Asia, Africa and Latin America where communist organizers have since the late concentrated their efforts to induce native trade unions to merge into single national units which would then join together in independent continental associations unaffiliated with any outside labor confederations.

This communist insistence on the unity of the labor movement can be understood only if viewed against its ideological background. Since capitalist masters can increase their profits and "super profits" primarily by underpaying their workers and misappropriating the "surplus value" of their labor, capitalism, even in less developed forms, is tantamount, in Marxist-Leninist view, to the exploitation of workers. Therefore, save for a small number of the previously-mentioned "labor aristocracy" and "the top section of trade-union bureaucracy," genuine workers must necessarily be procommunist, for only the abolition of capitalism and the advent of Marxist-Leninist "scientific" socialism can do away with their exploitation. This applies even more fully to ex-colonial nations where the exploitation of cheap native labor has been more marked than in the mother-countries of imperialism. A major device with which the bourgeois-capitalist or semi-feudal ruling classes have thus far managed to preserve their supremacy over the working class is to keep the latter divided and disunited. "The lack of unity enables the bourgeoisie to counterpose one section of the working class to another and even to use certain groups of workers under its influence for a struggle not against the enemies of the proletariat but against their class brothers, against the revolutionary working-class movement."[76] Therefore, the establishment of a united workers' organization is the appropriate strategic answer to these disruptive bourgeois-capitalist machinations. Imbued with the spirit of class solidarity and proletarian internationalism, such an organization is bound, in the Marxist-Leninist view, to become procommunist. Moreover, a call for workers' unity in order to enhance their chances in the struggle for better working conditions and higher wages is both plausible and popular; and communists are accomplished masters in embracing popular causes and diverting them to their own uses. Needless to add, it must be a unity slanted to communist goals. If and when the resulting unification turns against communist interests, it is promptly denounced as "reactionary" and "anti-worker."

The endeavors of communist strategists to unify the Third World labor movement under communist or at least procommunist aegis have encountered both success and failure.

In Latin America, where organized labor is larger than elsewhere in the Third World and the syndicalist tradition is fairly well-established, a substantial number of labor unions have fallen under communist or procommunist control and communist-directed "United" or "Single Workers'" Centres have been created in various Latin American countries. These are, for example: the *Bolivian Miners' Federation* and the *Bolivian Labor Center;* the *Single Centre of Chilean Workers* (CUTCH), the *United Workers' Centre of Venezuela,* the *Confederation of the Workers of Colombia* (CSTC), the *Confederation of Ecuadorian Workers,* the *Single Centre of Uruguayan Workers* (CUTU) and Uruguay's *National Convention of Workers* (CNT), the *Unitary Salvadorian Labor Federation* and the recently revived *General Labor Confederation of Peru.*[77] Communist organizers have also registered some success in their long-standing efforts to organize the procommunist Latin American trade unions on a continental scale. A procommunist Latin American Congress of Trade Union Unity held in Brazil at the beginning of 1964 resolved to constitute itself into a permanent body and a Secretariat of the *Latin American Permanent Congress for Trade Union Unity* was set up in 1967. Two years later, in February 1969, a committee for Trade Union Unity in Central America was founded in Costa-Rica to foster communist-oriented labor unity throughout Central America.

On the other hand, communist organizers have encountered setbacks in a number of Latin American countries, including the three largest ones, Brazil, Argentina and Mexico. Thus the communist-controlled Argentinian *Movement for Trade Union Unity and Coordination* (MUCS) has virtually disintegrated and communists have been removed from the offices they held in Argentina's *General Confederation of Labor* (CGT).[78] In Mexico, the Communist party was bitterly disappointed at the formation of a single *Mexican Congress of Labor* under non-communist control in 1966 and felt compelled to denounce it as representing "bourgeois movements and ideology" rather than the working class. Reporting on the state of the trade union movement at the plenary meeting of the Central Committee of the Communist party of Venezuela in September 1970, the Party's National Secretary in charge of trade union matters complained bitterly that the trade union movement in Venezuela was badly split and "dominated by reformists who strip the unions of their class and revolutionary character even in the sphere of economic struggle."[79] Communist hold on the Chilean organized labor was weakened when Christian democratic candidates made substantial gains in the 1972 election of the Chilean Central Workers' Confederation.[80]

In Africa, the communist unification endeavors have met with recurrent difficulties. "United action is perhaps the most important and the most difficult problem confronting the labor movement in Africa," wrote Ibrahim Zakharia, the African Secretary of the WFTU, in a major article on "The Trade Unions and the Political Scene in Africa" in 1964.[81] Among the factors causing difficulties, the author cited the "extraordinarily diffused nature of the unions inherited from the colonial period," "the large number of small unions and of rival trade union centers in one country" and "the extremely heterogenous nature of the African proletariat." In 1961 communist operators scored their first major break-through when some fifteen native labor unions comprising some two million members formed an *All-African Trade Union Federation* (AATUF) along the "independent" lines advocated by the WFTU.[82] At the time of its second congress held at Bamako in June 1964, the AATUF claimed the membership of thirty-seven unions from thirty-six countries.[83] However, the communists admit that the new Federation left much to be desired. "... the work of the [*All-African Trade Union*] Federation on all-African problems has been practically at a standstill," complained Ali-Yata, First Secretary of the Communist party of Morocco, in 1967.[84] He also found the labor movement in a number of African countries to be still "insufficiently independent." The work of communist (and any other) organizers has been further complicated by the tendency, prevalent in a growing number of African countries, for strict government controls of labor unions.[85] Thus, ironically, the tendency of African one-party regimes to resort to the Soviet-style practice of converting labor unions to instruments of the ruling party works against its inventors. As long as the respective country's regime appears to be willing to go along with communist designs, that is not too bad. But when the regime changes, the investment goes down the drain. A classical illustration has been Ghana whose Soviet-oriented *Trade Union Congress* was meant, prior to Nkrumah's ouster, to spearhead the communist drive to push the ICFTU from Africa and to unite African trade unions under pro-communist aegis.

Yet another obstacle to communist endeavors to win over the African labor has been the *African Trade Union Confederation* established in 1962 with the help of the *International Confederation of the Free Trade Unions* as a Western-sponsored rival to the AATUF. Although the representatives of the two rival African associations agreed in March 1969 to proceed with the formation of a united African trade union movement and to set up "an independent anti-colonial and anti-imperalist *All-African Trade Union Center*," it remains to be seen to what extent, if any, communist hopes may be realized.[86] Meanwhile, the labor movement in most of the African countries remains split into many rival unions competing with one another for a relatively few members. Nonetheless, labor unions in several African countries, such as Nigeria, Brazzaville Congo, Dahomey and Gambia have joined the communist-controlled *World Federation of Trade Unions* in recent years.[87]

A somewhat similar pattern of multiple labor union rivalry and infighting seems to exist in the developing nations of Asia. Communist organizers have registered some success, especially in India and Ceylon. In India they control the large *All-India Trade Union Congress* (AITUC), the main rival of the *Indian National Trade Union Congress* (INTUC) affiliated with India's ruling Congress Party.[88] In Ceylon they are in charge of the strong *Ceylon Trade Union Federation* and several unaffiliated government employees' unions.[89] They also hold key positions in the *National Trades Union Congress of Singapore* and the *Trade Union of Khmer Workers of Cambodia*.[90] Prior to the abortive communist coup in Indonesia, they dominated much of the Indonesian labor movement and the communist leader Aidit went so far as to boast in 1965 of "no less than 5 million organized workers. . . ready to take up arms."[91] In the Middle

East, trade union centers in Syria, Iraq and South Yemen have become members of the WFTU and a close cooperation is maintained with the *Confederation of Arab Trade Unions.*[92] Elsewhere in underdeveloped parts of non-communist Asia, communist strategists have made little headway considering the effort put into their ambitious schemes. ". . . it is patent that the degree of organization of the proletariat in South and Southeast Asia is still inadequate" and "working class solidarity is retarded by the absence of trade union unity at all levels."[93] And in Asia's one-party states communists appear to encounter much the same problem as in African one-party states mentioned above.

　　c. Organizing the workers and, if possible, uniting them all in a single huge communist-controlled labor federation is also expected to provide improved facilities for spreading the teaching of Marxism-Leninism. A permanent workers' organization with a steady membership, regular meetings, an established apparatus of functionaries, and readily available funds can be utilized much more efficiently and much more consistently for indoctrination purposes than unorganized *ad hoc* assemblies, especially when membership consists, as it does in most of the emerging nations, predominantly of persons lacking in political sophistication and short on experience with the communist *modus operandi.* As Lenin wrote, communists "must learn to approach the most backward, the most undeveloped members of this [working] class, those who are least influenced by our science and the science of life, so as to be able to speak to them, to draw them closer to them, raise them steadily and patiently to the level of Social Democratic consciousness, without making a dry dogma out of our doctrine - to teach them not only from books, but through participation in the daily struggle for existence of these backward and undeveloped strata of the proletariat."[94]

　　The Soviet strategists have striven hard indeed to "educate" the Third World's labor in the spirit of "scientific" socialism and bring closer the day when the trade unions there could develop into "schools of communism" as Lenin had hoped.[95] "To trade unions of the countries of Asia, Africa and Latin America," reported Shelepin to the 14th Congress of the Soviet Trade Unions in February 1968, "we give the diverse moral and material support and assistance necessary for them to strengthen their ranks and to develop actively among the working people."[96] In the pursuit of this "internationalist duty" the Soviet Union has been supplying the Third World's cooperating trade unions with expert organizers and instructors.[97] It has been offering appropriate indoctrination and training courses and seminars to African, Asian and Latin American trade union functionaries or would-be-functionaries.[98] It has set up, at the Higher Trade Union School in Moscow, an international department specifically designed to train trade unionists from Asian, African and Latin American countries.[99] Soviet Trade Unions have served over the years as obliging hosts and willing consultants to untold numbers of trade union officials and delegations from developing nations invited to Russia to see how trade union matters should be handled. Soviet trade union functionaries have been paying good will visits to their counterparts in the developing nations bringing them free advice, encouragement, ideological and organizational knowhow, and other forms of that "diverse moral and material support" referred to by Shelepin.

d. As directed by their Soviet mentors, communists in labor unions are to "show themselves consistent fighters for the economic interests of the workers" and "the staunchest and most energetic organisers on the strike committees."[100] However, unlike the ordinary trade union members, they are led to view economic objectives and achievements not as an end in itself, but as a means contributing toward the attainment of an altogether different political end, namely, the advancement of communism. By displaying zeal and vigor in the pursuit of workers' economic interests and helping them to secure certain tangible improvements in working conditions and wages, communists expect to win the workers' confidence and gradually gain key functions and leading positions. When this happens, it enables them to direct rank-and-file members to communist purposes, such as: throwing the labor support behind those native politicians willing to promote or, at least, not to impede pro-communist policies; staging massive protest meetings and street demonstrations against anti-communist forces; resorting to politically motivated strikes to force adoption of procommunist attitudes, policies and programs and the abandonment of those which the communists find objectionable; and organizing, wherever feasible, workers' militia or other such units allegedly required for security and order in and around industrial establishment, but in reality meant to serve as an armed force at communist disposal. That is the way in which communists have striven, at Soviet behest and under Soviet guidance, to divert the labor unions' mission to pro-Soviet political objectives in Eastern Europe. Judging by their statements and behavior relative to Asia, Africa and Latin America, the same strategy for the utilization of organized labor to promote the cause of communism has been planned for, and is being attempted, in the countries of the Third World.

Probably the best illustration to-date of the communist labor unions' manipulation for purposes of political power in the Third World was offered by Sudan in 1964. Taking fullest advantage of the unsettled political situation in the country and their status of legality (meanwhile lost, regained and lost again), the Sudanese communists managed to infiltrate, and to secure key positions in, a number of Sudanese trade and professional unions. Thereupon, they organized a *National Front of Professional Organizations* and, following the stratagem used by East European communists in 1945-48, succeeded in obtaining for it three seats in the Sudanese coalition cabinet — one for the bar association, one for the labor federation and one for tenant farmers. Thus, under the pretense of trade union representation, the communists and their fellow travelers gained three more seats in addition to the one that the communists were assigned in their own right.[101] The leadership of the communist-controlled *Sudanese Federation of Trade Unions* was also involved in the 1971 abortive coup against Numeiry's government and its President, Shafi Ahmed El Sheikh (who was also Vice-President of the WFTU) was executed for his part in the revolt.[102]

In a somewhat different fashion, communist controlled labor unions helped also to raise to power the pro-communist regime of President Alphonse Massamba-Debat in Brazzaville Congo in 1964.[103] And the support of the communist-led segment of the Chilean organized labor contributed substantially to the election of Salvador Allende to Chile's Presidency.[104]

But the stratagem most widely used in the Third World to promote communist interest through the labor movement has been the time-honored device of fomenting strikes, exploiting

them for their own purposes, and then converting them into full-
scale anti-capitalist and anti-Western class warfare. That has
occurred especially in Latin America where the massive United
States' economic presence enables communist agitators to capitalize on the ubiquitous *anti-yanquismo.* "The class battles of the
proletariat acting as the vanguard of the national liberation
movement are aimed above all against the American imperialism," stressed the *Pravda* editorial of August 26, 1970.
Indeed, Soviet spokesmen and their Latin American associates
have repeatedly expressed satisfaction with "the dynamics of the
growth of the strikers' movement," citing that the workers'
participation in Latin American strikes rose from nine million in
1955 to twenty million in 1960 and twenty-five million in 1965,
and crediting these "successes" to "the communist and workers'
parties."[105] It is interesting to note, however, that, as of 1967,
B. N. Ponomarev appeared less enthusiastic about "the strike
movement" of Latin America. Claiming that participation in
Latin American strikes actually declined from a total of 20-24
million in 1959-61 to 13-15 million "in subsequent years," he saw
in it "a certain ebb in the strike movement."[106]

Yet another way in which communist strategists seek to utilize
the labor movement in the Third World for their anti-Western
and anti-U.S. crusade has been well illustrated by the Latin
American Trade Union Conference held in August 28-30, 1969,
in Lima. As the *New Times* itself has admitted, a "sharply anti-
imperialist" unanimity was achieved at the conference "thanks
to the inclusion in the agenda of two issues which the overwhelming majority of Latin American workers regard as vitally
important: solidarity with Peru, which has nationalized the
U.S.-owned International Petroleum Company, and with the
struggle for the return to the Latin Americans of the natural
riches exploited by foreign companies.[107] Thus the "Lima
Declaration" adopted at the conference could be brandished as
yet another of the Latin American labor's continued "assaults on
the U.S. imperialists' positions south of the Rio Grande."[108]

In their assessment of the role of labor unions in the Third
World some communist spokesmen have gone so far as to
concede to them, under certain conditions, even the function of
"vanguard" of the working class, a function which is supposed

ordinarily to be filled by the Communist party. Writing in the *World Marxist Review,* A. Sobolev took the stand that in countries where Marxist-Leninist parties do not yet exist "the role of revolutionary vanguard may to some extent be played by the trade unions."[109] Similar statements have been made by other Soviet Orientalists and Africanists.[110] Some communist writers, however, have taken a more cautious attitude toward this delicate issue. While considering the trade union movement in the less developed nations to be "the component part of the revolutionary international movement of the working class," Ibrahim Zakharia, the then Secretary of the communist-controlled WFTU, warned against exaggerating the role of labor unions in Africa and contended that the "vanguard theory" was causing an artificial isolation of unions from other forces participating in the national revolution and thus was engendering "sectarianism."[111]

The East European Concurrence and Contribution

Since the communist regimes of East Europe subscribe to the Soviet ideological dicta relative to the developing nations, it is hardly surprising that they also concur and take active part in the Soviet-prescribed strategy of fostering the class struggle and promoting the growth of a class-conscious proletariat throughout the Third World. Thus the official spokesmen of East Europe's communist regimes stress the imperative necessity of a relentless class struggle as a prime aspect of communist strategy in the developing areas of the world. They frown at any notions that conditions obtaining in many parts of the Third World are not conducive to this form of struggle.[112] They view the class struggle as "the Archimedian point" (*archimedesowy punkt*) and "central tenet" of Marxist-Leninist strategy.[113] Rejecting Chinese accusations that the Soviet-advanced concept of peaceful co-existence implies any weakening of the class struggle, the East European theoreticians regard peaceful co-existence as just a "new original form of the class struggle,"[114] a "new stage in the singular form of class struggle between the proletariat and the imperialist bourgeoisie on the international arena,"[115] They have gone along both with the Soviet analysis of the class structure in the developing areas and the Soviet prescriptions for correcting the uncovered weaknesses, such as promoting industrialization to increase the inadequate size of the native working class, stepping up efforts to heighten its class-consciousness, driving as many wedges as possible between the labor movement of the developing nations and its counterpart in the West, and thus facilitating its conversion into a pliable tool of communist subversion.

While the burden of the actual implementation of the class-struggle strategy has been borne primarily by the Soviet Union, the East European communist contribution in this regard has been by no means negligible. In particular, Soviet Russia's East European partners have played a major role in the persistent communist endeavors to induce the labor unions of the Third World to steer away from cooperation with the *International Confederation of Free Trade Unions* and the non-communist trade unions of the West, and to establish instead closer relations with the WFTU and the trade unions of the communist countries. Through the years, there has been continuous exchange of visits of trade union functionaries between the countries of the Third World and communist East Europe. Since the latter fifties when the communist vying of the developing countries began, untold numbers of African, Asian and Latin American trade union officials deemed likely to be influenced in the desired direction have been treated to generous all-expense-paid junkets in one or more countries of communist East Europe so as to enable them "to draw from the rich experiences" of the revolutionary trade unions of the communist countries.[116] The Confederation of Yugoslav Trade Unions has also been quite active in this respect.[117] Year after year, courses and seminars have been organized by the trade unions of the various countries of communist East Europe, independently or in cooperation with the *World Federation of Trade Unions,* to train and indoctrinate trade union officials of the Third World.[118] At the same time, trade union delegations from communist countries of East Europe, including Yugoslavia, have been touring the various countries of the Third World in a concerted effort to "strengthen mutual collaboration" and "deepen the solidarity" with the labor movement of the developing nations.[119] Nor did the East European communist rulers allow the occasions of such mutual visits to pass by without persuading their Third World hosts or guests to adopt appropriate communiques lambasting Western imperialism, denouncing the "disruptive work" of the ICFTU and its native "lackeys," and giving approval to policies and causes favored by Soviet Russia and her associates. Occasionally, the East European labor unions would also help in the financing of procommunist activities in the Third World.[120]

In one particular respect, however, the East European contribution to Soviet strategy of exploiting the labor movement of the Third World has become somewhat moot, and one might even say dysfunctional, in recent years: namely, the utilization of the WFTU. Encouraged by the Chinese, Albanian, Italian and Yugoslav challenges to Soviet leadership, the Rumanian trade union delegates to the Sixth Congress of the WFTU held in October 1965 suddenly abandoned their earlier subservience and insisted, together with the Chinese and Albanian delegates, that all decisions be henceforth reached by unanimous consensus, and that the affiliated unions be granted the right of not having to carry out decisions to which they have not agreed.[121] Such demands could not, of course, but weaken the use of this well-known communist Front organization as a tool of Soviet strategy, especially when coupled with the growing conviction of many delegates that the WFTU should not involve itself so much in strictly political aspects of international affairs, but ought to concern itself primarily with *bona fide* labor questions. The situation was further compounded by the Soviet invasion and occupation of Czechoslovakia in August 1968 which was promptly condemned by the WFTU's Secretariat as being "in conflict with all the fundamental principles on which the very existence of the WFTU rests."[122] Thus the role that the WFTU was originally assigned in Soviet strategic schemes has been gravely impaired.

The Chinese Stand

As noted in Chapter II, the question of the class struggle and the role of the working class has become one of the major bones of Sino-Soviet contention. The Chinese criticism of Soviet behavior turns mainly around their claim that the Russians pay only lip service to the cause of the class struggle but do not practice it as it ought to be practiced. Opposed as they are to the Soviet version of peaceful co-existence, the Chinese leaders consider the Soviet and communist East European description of peaceful co-existence as a specific form of class struggle to be nothing less than a cover-up for a shameful retreat from the genuine and resolute class struggle in the Leninist meaning of the term. Also, as has already been pointed out earlier, the Chinese strategists insist on the assumption of the leadership by the proletariat and its vanguard party at an early phase of the national democratic revolution, accuse the Russians of ambivalence concerning this important strategic issue, and suspect them of an untoward tendency to compromise with bourgeois elements at the expense of the proletariat.

On the other hand, there is a good deal of truth in the Soviet assertions (discussed in Chapter II) that the Chinese leaders have downgraded the "historical role" of the working class of the developed countries and that they have refused to go along with the Soviet proposition that, in the absence of an adequate native proletariat, the role of the revolutionary vanguard in the Third World should accrue to the "international working class." Evidently, and for very good reasons, the Chinese strategists do not believe that the rather mythical entity dubbed "international working class" and presumably embracing (in addition to the workers of the communist countries) the workers of the United States, Great Britain, West Germany, Japan, Sweden and other economically advanced countries could or would do the job assigned them (against their will and desire) in the Soviet pronouncements. Rather, the Chinese tend to rely more on the native proletariat of the respective developing countries. However, they do not visualize and conceptualize it along the official Soviet lines. Deeply influenced by their own revolutionary experience in China, they view the proletariat of the developing nations not so much in terms of the industrial workers and urban working class, but more in terms of agricultural laborers, landless and quasi-landless peasants, small tenant farmers and artisans as well as tribesmen and feudalist and semifeudalist servants. Consequently, the social base of the proletariat of the Third World as conceived by the Chinese seems to be considerably broader and much more rustic than the corresponding

Soviet formula, for it comprises also groups that the Soviet theoreticians usually include in the poor-peasant segment of the peasantry and the petty bourgeoisie rather than in the working class proper.[123] Even though this Chinese version of the proletariat will not in all likelihood be any more successful than its Soviet version in performing its hoped-for revolutionary vanguard function, it appears at least to be more germane to the actual conditions prevailing in the Third World than the rather artificial Soviet construct.

It is necessary to note, however, that the Chinese communists have not lost interest in the industrial working class of the Third World. Nor is there much truth in Soviet accusations that the Chinese leaders have substituted "unscientific, geopolitical interpretation for the class approach" in their relations toward the developing countries.[124] While being less excited about the revolutionary potential of the Asian, African and Latin American urban proletariat than their Soviet colleagues, they have nonetheless striven hard in recent years to gain its allegiance and to lure it away both from the West and from the Soviet camp. Ever since they split openly with the Soviets in the early sixties, the Chinese have been active in a number of developing countries offering aid and advice to native labor unions, denouncing the machinations of "Soviet revisionists," inviting good native prospects to visit China, etc. A typical sample of such communist infighting has been the tug-of-war between the Moscow-oriented Communist Party of India (KPI) and its pro-Peking rival KPI (M) over the control of the strong All-India Trade Union Federation. The Chinese delegates have stood up recurrently to Soviet communists in the sessions of the WFTU and have thus been instrumental in undercutting its effectiveness as an instrument of communist strategy in the Third World labor movement. In 1964 they went so far as to denounce the official report of the General Council of the WFTU as a "policy of capitulationism and division which works to the advantage of the imperialist forces."[125] Similarly, they have used the conferences of the Afro-Asian Solidarity, beginning with the one held at Moshi in February 1963, to press for separate Afro-Asian trade union conferences from which the Soviet and East European communist delegates would be excluded.

Notes for Chapter V

[1] *Against Revisionism,* Moscow, 1959, p. 140.

[2] *Fundamentals,* p. 160

[3] *Ibid.,* p. 172.

[4] *Ibid.,* p. 149.

[5] The 1961 *Program of the Soviet Communist Party,* Ritvo, p. 105; *Declaration of Eighty-One Communist Parties,* Jacobs, *op. cit.,* pp. 28-29; *Fundamentals,* p. 471; M. Sidorov, *"Lenin o meprimirimosti sotsialisticheskoi i burzhuaznoi ideologii,"* (Lenin About the Incompatibility of the Socialist and Bourgeois Ideologies) *Pravda,* August 1, 1969.

[6] *Fundamentals,* p. 164.

[7] *Ibid.,* p. 162.

[8] *World Marxist Review,* 7, 11, 1964, pp. 77-78.

[9] *Ibid.,* 7, 12, 1964, pp. 3 ff.

[10] Moscow, 1939, p. 66

[11] *Fundamentals,* p. 171 and 486.

[12] *World Marxist Review,* 6, 3, 1963, p. 64.

[13] *"O klassovoi strukture v slaborazvitykh stranakh"* (On Class Structure in Less Developed Countries), *MEIMO,* No. 4, 1962, pp. 68-72. English text in Thornton, *op. cit.,* p. 277.

[14] *Fundamentals,* p. 496.

[15] *Ibid.,* p. 172 and 154.

[16] See, for instance T. Timofeev, *"Vedushchaia revoliutsionnaia sila,"* (The Leading Revolutionary Force), *Pravda,* December 24, 1968, and the same author's *"Vedushchaia revoliutsionnaia sila epokhi,"* (The Leading Revolutionary Force of the Epoch), *Pravda,* July 31, 1971; N. Bikkenin, *"Lenin ob istoricheskoi missii rabochego klassa i partii kommunistov"* (Lenin on the Historical Mission of the Working Class and the Party of the Communists), *Pravda,* February 19, 1969.

[17] G. Mirsky, "Proletariat and National Liberation," *New Times,* No. 18, 1964, pp. 6 ff; Uri Ra'anan, "Moscow and the 'Third World'"; *Problems of Communism,* XIV, 1, 1966, pp. 109 ff.; R. Ul'ianovskii, "Some Questions of the Non-Capitalist Development of the Liberated Countries," *Kommunist,* No. 1, 1966, pp. 109 ff., discussed also in "An Alternative to Communist Parties" in *Mizan,* 8, 2, 1966, pp. 53 ff.; Alexander Sobolev, "Some Problems of Social Progress," *World Marxist Review,* 10, 1, January 1967, p. 23; Vl. Li, "The Role of the National Liberation Movement in the Anti-Imperialist Struggle," *International Affairs* (Moscow), No. 12, 1971, pp. 69 ff. More about the question of leadership of non-proletarian groups see in Chapter IX.

[18] R. Iscaro, *op. cit.* See also Vadim Korfunov, "The Working Class—the Leading Revolutionary Force of Our Time," *New Times,* No. 11, 1972, pp. 18 ff.

[19] "The Latin American Working Class—Its Strength and Weakness," *New Times,* No. 54, 1967, p. 3. See also B. Ladygin, M. Lebedev, "A Weapon in Our Struggle," *World Marxist Review,* 11, 3, 1968, pp. 51-58, reaffirming Lenin's proposition on the leading role of the working class in the battle for socialist revolution.

[20] Rotislav Ulyanovsky, "Some Aspects of Non-Capitalist Way for Asian and African Countries," *World Marxist Review,* 12, 9, 1969, pp. 86 ff.

[21] P. Ponomaryov, "Topical Theoretical Problems of World Revolutionary

Process," *Information Bulletin,* 23-24, 1971, pp. 65 ff. (An abridged English text of an article published in the *Kommunist,* No. 15, 1971).

[22] See, for instance, Luis Figueroa, "Some Problems of the Working-Class Movement in Latin America," *World Marxist Review, 9, 3, 1966, pp. 62-68; Luis Carlos Prestes, "Political Line and Tactics of Brazilian Communists in the New Conditions,"* World Marxist Review, 11 6, 1968, p. 38; Haled Bagdash, "Problems of the National Liberation in Syria, *ibid.,* p. 43; Alvaro Delgado, "The Working Class and Labor Movement in Colombia," *World Marxist Review,* 9, 9, 1966, pp. 51 ff.; Ramiro Otero, "Some Problems of the Working Class and Trade Union Movement in Latin America," *Information Bulletin,* 2, 1968, p. 25; "Political Resolution of the Sixth Congress of the Brazilian Communist Party," *ibid.,* 3, 1969, p. 19; "Once More about the Non-Capitalist Way," *World Marxist Review,* 13, 6, 1970, pp. 85 ff.; M. Chaoui, "Leninism and Problems of Revolutionary Movement in Arab Countries," *World Marxist Review,* 13, 5, 1970, pp. 60 ff.

[23] "The National-Liberation Movement and the Communists," *World Marxist Review,* 8, 12, 1965, pp. 16 ff., and "Lenin and Struggle against Opportunism and Revisionism in National Liberation Movement," *ibid.,* 13, 4, 1970, pp. 92 ff.

[24] R. Avakov and G. Mirskii, *op. cit.,* in Thornton, *op. cit.,* p. 277. See also V. Jordansky, *Tupiki i perspektivy tropicheskoi Afriki (Blind Alleys and Perspectives of Tropical Africa),* Moscow, 1970, which contains a section on "The Strength and Weakness of the Proletariat." Review of the book was published under the title "Social Portrait of Africa" in *New Times,* No. 9, 1971, p. 34.

[25] *World Marxist Review,* 10, 5, 1967, p. 54.

[26] Pieter Keuneman, "New Features of the National-Liberation Movement," *World Marxist Review,* 7, 12, 1964, pp. 3 ff.

[27] *Ibid.,* The Venezuelan communist economist F. Mieres, cited in *New Times,* No. 34, 1967, p. 1, estimates that some 30 million of the total Latin American population of 250 million are wage and salary earners in towns. However, he considers only 15 million of them as being "urban proletarians" while another 15 million "proletarians and semi-proletarians" are engaged in agriculture. Much the same figures are given by Ramiro Otero, member of the Central Committee of the Communist Party of Bolivia in his "Some Problems of the Working-Class and Trade Union Movement in Latin America," *World Marxist Review,* 10, 7, 1967, pp. 56-65. Ota Lev, a Czechoslovak communist writer, estimates the number of wage-earners in Africa at 20 million, i. e., less than 7 percent of the population. "Wage-Labor in Africa; Heritage of Colonialism and Prospects," *World Marxist Review,* 12, 1, 1969, pp. 51-56. Writing specifically about South and Southeast Asia in November 1966, Vladimir Lukin puts the number of factory workers only at three to six percent of the population of the region, "Some Aspects of Class Structure in South and Southeast Asia," *World Marxist Review, 9, 11, 1966, pp. 47 ff.*

[28] G. B. Starushenko, "The Social Content and Political Form of the Non-Capitalist Development in Young States," *Sovetskoie Gosudarstvo i Pravo,* No. 4, 1966, p. 105. See also G. F. Kim, "The Theory and Practice of the Non-Capitalist Road," *Narody Azii i Afriki,* No. 4, 1966, p. 57.

[29] Zakharia, *op. cit.,* Otero, *op. cit.,* B. N. Ponomarev's speech at the Moscow symposium "The 50th Anniversary of the October Revolution and the International Working Class," *New Times,* No. 50, 1967, pp. 3-9. Moreover, as pointed out regretfully by a Latin American communist, the ratio of the

industrial proletariat, "the core of the working class," to the proletariat as a whole has actually decreased "in recent years" as compared to the situation in 1950. Otero, *op. cit.*

[30] L. A. Gordon's and L. A. Fridman's article in *Narody Azii i Afriki,* No. 2, 1963, pp. 2-22, English text in Thornton, *op. cit.*, p. 185; R. Avakov and G. Mirskii, *op. cit.,* Thornton, *op. cit.*, p. 287; Figueroa, *op. cit.; Third World,* p. 46.

[31] Jack Woddis, "Role of the African Working Class in the National Liberation Movement," *World Marxist Review,* 5, 7, 1962, pp. 44 ff.; V. P. Verin, *Prezidentskie Respubliki v Afrike,* (Presidential Republics in Africa) Moscow, 1963.

[32] R. Avakov and G. Mirskii, *op. cit.,* in Thornton, *op. cit.,* p. 287; also, Verin, *op. cit.,* Lukin, *op. cit.,* Delgado, *op. cit.,* Jordansky, *op. cit.*

[33] Vladimir Lukin, "Some Aspects of Class Structure in Southeast Asia," *World Marxist Review,* 9, 11, 1966, p. 49.

[34] Juan Cobo, "Latin America: Workers on the March," *New Times,* No. 37, 1969, pp. 28-29. See also Nicolas Chaoui, *op. cit.*, where the author bewails the weakness of the working class in Arab countries.

[35] Otero, *op. cit.*

[36] Figueroa, *op. cit.,* Lukin, *op. cit.,* Ibrahim Zakharia, in *World Marxist Review,* 7, 12, 1964, pp. 19 ff.; *Third World,* p. 46.

[37] R. Avakov and G. Mirskii, *op. cit.,* in Thornton, *op. cit.,* p. 287.

[38] Otero, *op. cit.*

[39] *Fundamentals,* p. 477.

[40] *Ibid.,* p. 477.

[41] *Ibid.*

[42] V. I. Lenin, *"Proiekt i obiasnenie programmy sotsial demokraticheskoi partii,"* (The Project and the Clarification of the Program of the Social Democratic Party), *Sochineniia,* I, 1964, pp. 439-40; and V. I. Lenin, *Marx-Engels-Marxism,* Moscow, 1953, pp. 333-34; *Fundamentals,* p. 304

[43] *Fundamentals,* p. 167.

[44] See Lukin, *op. cit.;* I. I. Potekhin, *"Panafrikanizm i Bor'ba Dvukh idelogii"* (Pan-Africanism and the Struggle of Two Ideologies), *Kommunist,* No. 1, 1964, pp. 104-113; Jack Woddis, *op. cit.;* Avakov-Mirskii, *op. cit.*

[45] See I. I. Potekhin, *"Afrika smotrit v budushchee,"* op. cit.; I. I. Potekhin, *"Ob 'afrikanskom sotsializme': Otvet moim opponentam,"* (About 'African Socialism': A Reply to My Opponents), *Mezhdunarodnaia zhizn,* No. 1, 1963; "Problems of the National-Liberation Movement of the Arab Peoples," *World Marxist Review,* 7, 9, 1964, pp. 54 ff.; Ibrahim Zakharia, "The Trade Unions and the Political Scene in Africa," *World Marxist Review,* 7, 12, 1964, pp. 19 ff.; Lukin, *op. cit.*

[46] L. A. Gordon and L. A. Fridman, *op. cit.,* Figueroa, *op. cit.;* Jordansky, *op. cit.*

[47] "The Latin-American Working Class—Its Strength and Weakness," No. 34, 1967, p. 2. See also Roque Dalton and Victor Miranda, "Present phase of the revolutionary movement in Latin America," *World Marxist Review,* 10, 5, 1967, pp. 48-57, and Cobo, *op. cit.*

[48] "Latin America: Liberation Struggle and the Working Class," *World Marxist Review,* 14, 7, 1971, pp. 72 ff.

[49] *Ritvo,* p. 187.

[50] June 28, 1965. English text in the *Current Digest,* No. 26, 1965. In particular, communist strategists look with anticipation toward a rapid growth

of the working class in Latin America. See Iscaro, *op. cit.*, Delgado, *op. cit.*, Figueroa, *op. cit.*

[51] *Fundamentals*, p. 297; L. A. Gordon and L. A. Fridman, *op. cit.*

[52] *Fundamentals*, p. 297.

[53] *Ibid.*

[54] *Pravda*, June 28, 1965; L. A. Gordon and L. A. Fridman, *op. cit.*

[55] *Fundamentals*, p. 167.

[56] *Fundamentals*, p. 297.

[57] *Ibid.*, p. 167; *Declaration of Eighty-One Communist Parties*, Jacobs, p. 37.

[58] pp. 36 and 26. The Communist Party of China was rebuked in the same document for having committed this "fundamental mistake" in 1925-27.

[59] *Fundamentals*, p. 477; *Declaration of Eighty-One Communist Parties*, Jacobs, *op. cit.*, p. 40.

[60] *Fundamentals*, pp. 300 and 298; also Lukin, *op. cit.*, Delgado, *op. cit.*, Figueroa, *op. cit.*

[61] *Ibid.*, pp. 21-22, 44.

[62] *What is to be done? Collected Works: The Iskra Period*, New York, 1929, p. 191; see also Thomas Taylor Hammond, *Lenin on Trade Unions and Revolution*, New York, 1957, and John Hutchinson, "Trade Unionism and the Communists: American and International Experiences," in William Peterson, ed., *The Realities of World Communism*, Englewood Cliffs, 1963.

[63] N. V. Tropkin, *Ob Osnovakh Strategii i Taktiki Leninizma*, pp. 33-34.

[64] Jacobs, *op. cit.*, p. 37.

[65] *Fundamentals*, p. 342; Ibrahim Zakharia and Cuthbert Magigwana, *op. cit.*; Margaret Roberts, "African Trade Unionism in Transition," *World Today*, 17, 10, 1961, pp. 447 ff.; the 1969 *Moscow Declaration*.

[66] *Pravda*, February 28, 1968.

[67] "The Soviet Trade Unions' International Ties," *New Times*, No. 28, 1971, pp. 13 ff.

[68] Ali Yata, First Secretary of the Communist Party of Morocco, addressing the 1966 Cairo seminar on Africa, *World Marxist Review*, 10, 1, 1967, p. 11.

[69] Zakharia, *op. cit.*; A. Bykhovsky, "George Meany's Subversion," *New Times*, No. 31, 1965, pp. 21-22; "Cold Warrior," *ibid.*, No. 9, 1966, pp. 21-22; "Trade Unions in Africa," *World Marxist Review*, 9, 1, 1966, pp. 64 ff.; Jack Woddis, "British Trade Union Leaders in Africa," *New Times*, No. 6, 1966, pp. 16-17; I. Lebedev, *"Kar'era Mistera Brauna,"* (The Career of Mr. Brown), *Pravda*, February 5, 1969, p. 4; Pierre Gensous, "An Act for Unity," *World Marxist Review*, 13, 1, 1970, pp. 38 ff.; Juan Cobo, "Before the Lima Conference," *New Times*, No. 34, 1969, p. 28.

[70] See Margaret Roberts, *op. cit.*

[71] *Declaration of Eighty-One Communist Parties*, Jacobs, *op. cit.*, pp. 37-38. See also Gensous, *op. cit.*, and the same author's "Toward Anti-Imperialist Unity," *World Marxist Review*, 12, 7, 1969, pp. 89 ff.

[72] *Fundamentals*, p. 310; see also Delgado, *op. cit.*, Iscaro, *op. cit.*

[73] 1969 *Moscow Declaration*.

[74] See, for instance, Delgado, *op. cit.*; Orlando Millas, "Splachivat anti-imperialisticheskie sily," (To Join Together the Anti-Imperialist Forces), *Pravda*, May 19, 1969.

[75] "World Trade Union Congress," *New Times*, No. 44, 1969, pp. 3-4. See also the editorial "Proletariat Latinskoi Ameriki boretsia," (The Proletariat of Latin America Fights), *Pravda*, August 16, 1970.

[76] *Fundamentals*, p. 310; also, Lukin, *op. cit.*

[77] Information gathered from various sources, such as *Este y Oeste, Communism in Latin America, New Times, Pravda, World Marxist Review*, etc.

[78] A bitter complaint about the trade union situation in Argentina was raised by the Argentinian communist Paulino Gonzales Alberdi in an article on "Anti-Imperialist Struggle in Argentina and the Communist Party," *World Marxist Review*, 11, 10-11, 1968, pp. 77-84.

[79] "Report on the Trade Unions," *Information Bulletin*, 21, 1970, pp. 6 ff.

[80] AP report from Santiago: "Anti-Marxist Forces Gain in Chilean Elections," *Austin American Statesman*, June 3, 1972.

[81] *World Marxist Review*, 7, 12, 1964, pp. 19 ff.

[82] Margaret Roberts, *op. cit.;* Zakharia, *op. cit.;* Yu. Popov. *"Trudovaia Afrika Ob'edinaetsia"* (Working Africa Is Uniting), *Azia i Afrika Segodnia*, No. 5, 1961; S. Valiev, *"Sozdanie Vseafrikanskoi Federatsii Profsoiuzov"* (The Creation of the All-African Federation of Trade Unions), *ibid.*, No. 7, 1961.

[83] Zakharia, *op. cit.*

[84] Ali Yata, "Neo-colonialism in Africa," *World Marxist Review*, 10, 1, 1967, pp. 1-12. See also G. Ye. Kanaev, *Prof-soiuznoe dvizhenie v Marokko* (The Trade Union Movement in Morocco), Moscow, 1962; *Profsoiuzy Stran Zapadnoi Afriki* (The Trade Unions of the Countries of West Africa), Moscow, 1962; "Soviet Approaches to African Trade Unions," *Mizan*, 7, 7, 1965, indicating that the "Soviet observers have been far from satisfied with the trade union situation in Africa in the early sixties.

[85] See, for instance, Morton A. Reichek, "Labor in Africa," *New Leader*, July 5, 1965, pp. 9-11.

[86] See, for instance, Yu Potemkin, *"Trudovaia Afrika"* (The Working Africa), *Pravda*, April 16, 1969, p. 4.

[87] See P. Pimenov, "World Trade Union Congress," *New Times*, No. 42, October 22, 1969, pp. 1 ff. Another African Workers organization getting the Soviet nod is the *Federation of Workers' Trade Unions of Malagasy* (FISEMA), lauded highly in Kumalov and V. Tvertsev, "Madagascar at the Crossroads," *New Times*, No. 22, 2, 1972, pp. 22 ff.

[88] Sharokh Sabavala, "Communism and India's Unions," *New Leader*, January 23, 1961, pp. 15-16.

[89] See Robert Scalapino, ed., *The Communist Revolution in Asia*, 1965, p. 379.

[90] "Singapore's Trade Unions," *New Times*, No. 23, 1966, pp. 23-24, and *USSR and Third World*, I, 2, 1971.

[91] Scalapino, *op. cit.*, p. 268.

[92] Gensous, "An Act for Unity," *op. cit.*, Pimenov, *op. cit.*, in note 87.

[93] Lukin, *op. cit.*, pp. 49-50.

[94] *"O smeshenii politiki s pedagogikoi* (About Mixing Politics and Pedagogy), *Sochineniia*, 7, 1935, p. 307.

[95] *Left-wing Communism: An Infantile Disorder*, Moscow, 1952, p. 57.

[96] *Pravda*, February 28, 1968. English text in the *Current Digest*, XXI, 9, 1968.

[97] See, for instance, A. Sanchez Madariaga, "The Communist Drive against Latin American Unions," *Free Labour World*, June 1961.

[98] As revealed by Shelepin in 1968, about 500 persons have graduated by 1967 from courses given in Moscow alone "for activists of the trade union movement" from the Third World.

[99] Pimenov, *op. cit.* in note 67.

[100] *Fundamentals*, p. 342.

[101] See Hedrick Smith, "Islamic Parties Fight Sudan Reds," *New York Times*, November 18, 1964, and John Howell and M. Beshir Hamid, "Sudan and the Outside World," *African Affairs*, 68, 2, 1969, pp. 299-315.

[102] See Eric Rouleau, "Sudan Communists: Routed by Arabism," *Le Monde Weekly*, English edition, No. 123, 1971, pp. 11 and 13.

[103] "Leftward Trend in Brazzaville Worries West," *New York Times*, May 26, 1964.

[104] Juan Cobo, "Chile after the Election," *New Times*, No. 38, 1970, pp. 6-7.

[105] V. Borisov, *"Shiritsia Front Klassovykh Bitv"* (The Front of Class Struggles Spreads), *Pravda*, August 28, 1967. See also R. Iscaro, "The Working Class in the Struggle for the Liberation of Latin America," *World Marxist Review*, 9, 3, 1966, pp. 49 ff.

[106] B. N. Ponomarev, *op. cit.*

[107] Juan Cobo, "Latin America: Workers on the March," *New Times, op. cit.*

[108] *Ibid.*

[109] "National Democracy: The Way to Social Progress," 6, 2, 1963, pp. 39 ff.

[110] I. I. Potekhin, *"Vozrastaiushchee znachenie Afriki v mirovoi ekonomike"* (The Growing Importance of Africa in World Economies), *Kommunist*, No. 6, 1957, pp. 110-11.

[111] Zakharia, *op. cit.*

[112] See, for instance, Miroslav Novotný, "CSSR a Afrika" (CSSR and Africa), *Nová mysl*, No. 7, 1967, pp. 81-86; E. Kamenov, "Our Policy of Peaceful Co-existence," *Rabotnichesko Delo*, December 20, 1962, English text in *Bulgarian Press Survey*, No. 384, Radio Free Europe Release of January 16, 1963, pp. 2-7; "Under the Banner of Marxism-Leninism Toward New Conquests in the Fight for Peace and Socialism," and editorial in *Novo Vreme*, Vol. 2, February 1963, English text in *Bulgarian Press Survey* No. 408, March 8, 1963, pp. 2-6; D. Rozehnal, "The Leninist Road of World Communism," *Nová mysl*, No. 3, March 1963, English text in *Czechoslovak Press Survey*, No. 1223 (71), March 29, 1963, pp. 2-16; Juliusz Waclawek, "Internacjonalizm-suwerennosc-nacjonalizm" (Internationalism, Sovereignty, Nationalism), *Argumenty*, December 1, 1968.

[113] Waclawek, *op. cit.*

[114] Kamenov, *op. cit.*

[115] *Novo Vreme*, editorial cited in note 112 above. See also Rozehnal, *op. cit.*

[116] *Odborář*, August 1967, No. 17, p. 918. Such visits have been well publicized in the trade union newspapers and journals of the respective countries.

[117] See, for instance, "Confederation of Yugoslav Trade Unions," *Socialist Thought and Practice*, No. 34, 1969, pp. 90-92; also, Rubinstein, *Yugoslavia and the Non-Aligned World*, pp. 193 ff.

[118] Brzezinski mentions in his *Africa and the Communist World* (p. 105) that first such training center for African trade union officials was established under the WFTU sponsorship in Budapest in September 1959. Since then such schoolings have been held in all countries of communist East Europe, even in tiny Albania.

[119] *Odborář*, August 1962, No. 17, p. 918.

[120] See, for instance, Brzezinski, *op. cit.*, p. 107, citing East German financial support for such activities in Guinea. East German and Czechoslovak trade unions have been reported as supporting with money Ghana's TUC in

Nkhrumah's days. Czechoslovakia's *Revolutionary Trade Unions* provided, together with the Soviet Trade Unions, complete equipment for the main conference hall of Algeria's House of Trade Unions. See *Práce,* September 29, 1966.

[121] William McLaughlin, "Fresh Air in the WFTU," *East Europe,* 14, 12, 1965, pp. 9 ff. See also Kevin Devlin, "Workers of the World Disunite," *Orbis,* Vol. X, Fall 1966, pp. 782-802.

[122] See Radio Free Europe paper of September 27, 1968, on 'WFTU: Arena for Pro-Czechoslovak Struggle."

[123] The "Chinese proletariat is largely made up of bankrupt peasants," wrote Mao and his associates in "The Chinese Revolution and Party," *Selected Works of Mao,* London, 1954, Vol. III, p. 93.

[124] See Evgeny Tarabrin, "Peking's Maneuvers in Africa," *New Times,* No. 6, 1972, pp. 18 ff.

[125] Cited after *Avanti* (Rome), October 25, 1964.

CHAPTER VI

THE MISSION OF THE COMMUNIST PARTIES

Closely related to the endeavor to expand, organize and indoctrinate the Asian, African and Latin American working class are the efforts to establish viable Communist parties in developing countries where none existed before and to strengthen those already in operation. As shown in Chapter I, from Lenin's time to the present, Communist party leadership has been considered as indispensable for the victory of socialism; and the current Soviet ideological pronouncements not only make this thesis fully applicable to the developing nations, but also go so far as to claim that even the success of the national liberation struggle itself is "unthinkable in any country" without an active communist participation.[1]

While stressing the importance of the proletariat and the peasantry, the Soviet dicta, past and present, make it amply clear that neither can accomplish the tasks assigned them by communist strategy-makers unless they are guided by the Communist party as the working class's enlightened revolutionary vanguard. "Only a political party of the working class, i.e., a Communist Party," said Lenin, "is capable of uniting, educating and organising such a vanguard of the proletariat and the whole mass of the working people, a vanguard which is alone able to resist the inevitable petty-bourgeois vacillations of this mass, the inevitable traditions and relapses of trade-union narrowness or trade-unionist prejudices amidst the proletariat, and to lead the proletariat politically and through it to lead all the masses of the working people."[2]

Although Lenin was willing, if need be, to concede the leadership temporarily to non-proletarian elements at the initial phase of the national-democratic revolution, he insisted that the bourgeois-democratic movement be aided "only on the condition that the elements of future proletariat parties existing in all backward countries, which are not merely communist in name, shall be grouped together."[3] Citing these and other pertinent statements of Lenin, the *Fundamentals* holds that "with the aid of trade unions, mutual aid societies and other similar organisations alone the workers will never be able to put an end to capitalism and build a socialist society."[4] The 1961 *Program of the Soviet Communist Party* proclaims "the leadership of the Marxist-Leninist party" to be an "indispensable condition" for "the triumph of the socialist revolution and the building of socialism."[5] "Historical experience convincingly shows that the leadership by a Marxist-Leninist Party is the decisive factor in the revolutionary remaking of society," stressed I.V. Kapitonov, Secretary of the Central Committee of the Soviet Communist Party, delivering the main speech at the festive anniversary meeting on Lenin's 99th birthday in Moscow on April 22, 1969.[6] While allowing the leadership of "revolutionary democratic strata" at the early phase of national-democratic revolution, V. Volskii, Director of the Institute for Latin America of the USSR Academy of Sciences, insists that the attainment of the "much more complex- goals and tasks of the socialist revolution" necessitate "the leadership of the avantguard party of the working class armed with the Marxist-Leninist theory."[7]

Hence, efforts to establish viable Communist parties in developing countries where none existed before and to strengthen those already in operation figure among the most pressing tasks of present-day communist strategy in the Third World. How successful have the communist strategy-makers been in these efforts? How prepared are the Communist parties of developing nations for the crucial role they are supposed to play in communist revolutionary strategy in Asia, Africa and Latin America?

Understandably, the situation varies considerably from one region to another and from country to country. The Communist parties of the Third World range in size from the once huge Communist Party of Indonesia which claimed as many as two-and-one-half or even three million members prior to its 1965 demise, to minute groupings of "like-minded Marxists" or "Marxists-Leninists" in some areas of sub-Sahara Africa. They differ greatly in the degree of organization, cohesiveness, class composition, prestige, fighting spirit, leadership qualities and ideological maturity. Nor are circumstances under which they have to operate and to which they have to react always similar. This being so, no full-fledged generalization is possible. Nonetheless, certain prevailing characteristics can be traced, though all of them do not apply to each and every Communist party of the Third World. They have been duly noted by Soviet and other communist analysts and some of the flaws they have uncovered cause them no small concern. "Speaking of the Communist movement on the threshold of the seventies," conceded V. Zagladin, assistant Head of the International Department of the Central Committee of the Soviet Communist party, "one can hardly bypass the serious difficulties it has encountered in recent years."[8]

The Size

A major problem for communist strategists lies in a woefully small Party membership throughout most of the Third World. The 1960 *Declaration of Eighty-One Communist Parties* referred to Communist parties in 87 countries with a total membership in excess of 36 million and hailed this as a "signal victory for Marxism-Leninism and a tremendous achievement of the working class." *The Fundamentals*, published two years later, mentioned 88 parties with more than 40 million members.[9] In his speech at the Twenty-Third Congress of the Soviet Communist party in March 1966, L. Brezhnev claimed almost fifty million members organized in 88 parties.[10] A 1969 article in *Pravda* listed the number of communists throughout the world as "more than 40 million," while the 1970 volume of *New Times* spoke of 89 "communist and workers' parties" with a membership "approaching 50 million."[11]

However, the bulk of this impressive total (over 94 percent) consists of ruling parties of the world socialist system. As for the Third World, the Soviet release about the numerical strength of the "communist and workers parties" published in *Pravda* in January 1967 claimed (as of 1966) a sum total of 4,203,000 members in all of non-communist Asia, Africa and America.[12] But this includes also communist and "workers" parties of countries that do not fall in the category of less developed nations, such as Japan, South Africa, Israel, Canada and the United States, as well as some three million members claimed by the Communist Party of Indonesia prior to its 1965 collapse. Moreover, there is little doubt that the *Pravda* article, designed as it was to stress "the dynamics of the development" of world communism, errs on the optimistic side. A more realistic calculation would cut the figure to less than 2 1/2 to 3 1/2 million even if the membership of the Indonesian Communist Party were taken at its grossly inflated pre-1965 total. However, it stands to reason that the reprisals taken against the Indonesian Communist Party after its attempted coup must have resulted in a very substantial reduction of its membership, quite possibly to a mere 150,000 estimated by the U.S. Department of State.[13] That would leave approximately one-half million Communist party members scattered over all of Africa, Latin America and the neutral belt of mainland Asia, a thin spread indeed.

As revealed in table I above, the situation has been worst in Africa. Prior to the Second World War Communist parties existed only in the Northern Arab belt of Africa, and were woefully inadequate even there. New communist parties have begun cropping up in other parts of the continent in the late fifties and the sixties. However, their membership is extremely small and, worse still, seems to be in a state of stagnation. Not even the Soviet sources claim (as of 1969) more than some 60,000 Party members in all of Africa, including South Africa and the Portuguese colonies. Modest as this claim is, it is contested by Western analysts whose estimates run from a low of around ten

TABLE I

The Communist Parties of the Third World (as of 1972)

Country	Membership Western estimate	Membership Communist claim	Status legal	Status illegal	Sino-Soviet split pro-Soviet	Sino-Soviet split pro-Chinese	Attended the 1969 Moscow Conference
Africa							
Algeria	9,800	60,000[1]		x	x		x
Congo (Zaire)	400			x	x		
Egypt	negligible			x	x		
Lesotho	negligible			x			x
Libya	negligible			x			
Malagasy	negligible			x			
Mauritius	negligible		x				
Morocco	300			x		neutral	x
Nigeria	less than 1,000			x	x		x[2]
Senegal	negligible						
Sierra Leone	very small[3]			x			
Sudan	7,500			x	x		x
Tunisia	100			x			x
Zanzibar (Tanzania)	very small			x		x	
The Middle East							
Iran	7,500			x	x		x
Iraq	500		x		split		x
Jordan	2,000			x	split		x
Kuwait	500			x		x	
Lebanon	negligible		x		split		x
Persian Gulf States	1,500			x			
Saudi Arabia	negligible			x	split		
Syria	negligible		x			x	
Yemen	3,000		semi-legal			x	x

TABLE I (Cont.)

Country	Membership		Status		Stand on the Sino-Soviet split			Attended the 1969 Moscow Conference
	Western estimate	Communist claim	legal	illegal	pro-Soviet	pro-Chinese		
Non-Communist Asia (except the Middle East)	302,200							
Afghanistan	400			x	x			
Bangladesh			x		x			
Burma	5,000			x			split	
Cambodia	1,000	1,400		x			split	
Ceylon	4,000	6,000	x				split	x
India	162,000	300,000[4]	x				split	x
Indonesia	100,000[5]			x			split	
Laos	13,000			x			neutral	
Malaysia	2,000			x		x		
Nepal	10,000	18,000		x			split	x[6]
Pakistan	1,750			x			split	
Philippines	1,850			x				x
Singapore	200			x		x		
Thailand	1,000			x				
Latin America	222,575	350,000[7]						
Argentina	60,000			x	x			x
Bolivia	2,800			x			split	x
Brazil	13,000			x			split	x
Chile	90,000	117,000	x		x			x
Colombia	11,000	20,000	semi-legal				split	x
Costa-Rica	1,000		x				split	x
Dominican Republic	1,400			x			split	x
Ecuador	1,200	2,000		x			split	x
El Salvador	100	400		x			split	x
Guatemala	750			x	x			x
Guyana	100[8]			x	x			x[8]
Haiti	unknown			x	x			x
Honduras	300			x	x			x

TABLE I (Cont.)

Country	Membership		Status		Stand on the Sino-Soviet split		Attended the 1969 Moscow Conference
	Western estimate	Communist claim	legal	illegal	pro-Soviet	pro-Chinese	
Jamaica	negligible			x	x		
Mexico	5,000	8,000	x		split		x
Nicaragua	100	250		x	x		x
Panama	125	500		x	x		x
Paraguay	4,500			x	split		x
Peru	3,200		x		split		x
Trinidad and Tobago	negligible						
Uruguay	20,000		x		x		x
Venezuela	8,000	13,000	x		x		x

Notes:

1. Including communists of South Africa and the Portuguese Colonies; 2. Referred to in the official communique about the Conference as "Nigerian Marxists-Leninists"; 3. According to the State Department reports there is no organized communist party in Sierra Leone. However, the Communist Party of Sierra Leone is listed as having sent greetings to the 9th Congress of the League of Yugoslav Communists in 1969. See *Socialist Thought and Practice*, No. 33, 1969. 4. The pro-Soviet Communist Party of India claims a membership of 250,000. *Pravda*, March 18, 1972. 5. The U.S. State Department estimates that there are some 5,000 Indonesian communists still active and at large, while some 150,000 may be in jail or on parole; 6. The Moscow communique mentioned the Communist Party of East Pakistan in attendance; 7. This figure includes also Communist party members from the French overseas departments of Martinique and Guadeloupe and also the Cuban Communists; 8. The People's Progressive Party led by Cheddi Jagan considers itself "Marxist-Leninist" and it took part in the 1969 Moscow World Conference of Communist and Workers' parties.

Sources: World Strength of the Communist Party Organization. An Annual Report issued by the Bureau of Intelligence and Research of the U.S. Department of State. Publication No. 8526 of May 1971 and No. 8658 of June 1972: various Soviet, Communist East European and other communist publications. Not included in the statistics are the Communist parties existing in the remaining colonial dependencies and in French overseas departments.

thousand to a high of some 30,000 out of a population of some 350 million.

On the other hand, this sorry state of affairs is eased somewhat by the presence in Africa of a number of pro-communist leftist parties, such as the Sudanese Union Party of Mali, the Democratic Party of Guinea, the Socialist Workers' and Peasants' Party of Nigeria, the African Party of Independence of Senegal, the Afro-Shirazi Party of Tanzania, the People's Union of Cameroon and the Arab Socialist Union. These parties, labeled as "workers, national-democratic, and left-wing socialist parties" in the official communist terminology,[14] sent delegations to attend the Twenty-Third Congress of the Soviet Communist Party in March 1966.[15] The delegations of the Democratic Party of Guinea, the Afro-Shirazi Party and the Arab Socialist Union of Egypt attended also the 24th Congress of the Soviet Communist party in March 1971 and were joined on that occasion by delegates of TANU, the ruling party of Tanzania, the Congolese Party of Labor (from Brazza-ville Congo) and the Revolutionary Council of the Democratic Republic of Sudan.[16] The most recent addition to the list of Africa's "militant revolutionary parties" that has earned warm Soviet approval appears to be the Independence Congress Party of Madagaskar (AKFM).[17] The leaders of these parties are referred to sometimes in Soviet and East European communist quarters as "comrades" and some of them have committed themselves publicly to "scientific socialism," the well-known Soviet alias for Marxism-Leninism, though their understanding of the term is by no means identical with its Soviet interpretation. Since they pursue policies that are in most instances favorable to the Soviet Union and unfavorable to the West, and cooperate ordinarily with Soviet Russia in the arena of international relations, they are considered by Soviet strategists as the next best thing to full-fledged Communist parties. As explained in an article in *Izvestiia*, "unlike the bourgeois-nationalist parties which represent the interests of the national bourgeoisie and feudal circles" and "press for conciliation with the imperialists," the African national-democratic parties "are closely linked with the laboring strata."[18] Although their conception of the ways of transition to socialism is said to differ from Marxism-Leninism, the "growing anti-imperialist alliance of Communist and national-democratic parties" presumably "rests not on temporary and transitional political situations or factors, but on the profound share of vital interests of the peoples of socialist countries and of peoples fighting for national independence."[19]

Nonetheless, despite communist optimism, such a loose relationship is inherently unstable. This was documented in an especially striking fashion by the behavior of the Convention People's Party of Ghana and Mali's Sudanese Union, two of the African "revolutionary democratic" parties most cherished and counted upon by Soviet strategists. Both of them were declared guilty of not having prevented, in 1966 and 1968, respectively, the overthrow of pro-Soviet regimes, thus "evoking jubilation in imperialist quarters."[20]

Nor can the communist strategy-makers feel happy about the size of Communist parties' membership throughout the rest of the Third World, although it is better there than in Black Africa. The approximately 8,000 Party members in the Middle East represent, of course, a higher Party-population ratio than is the case in Africa. Yet, it is still an infinitesimal figure of considerably less than one tenth of one percent. As in Africa, the Soviet communists strive to cultivate several "revolutionary democratic" parties in the Middle East, such as the Democratic Party of Kurdistan, the Syrian and Iraqi parties of "Arab Socialist Rebirth" and the party of the "National Front of the Democratic Republic of Yemen" all of which sent delegates to the 24th Congress of the Soviet Communist Party. But the benefit the Soviet strategists derive from such groupings have thus far been rather marginal.

In the remainder of non-communist Asia the ratio would rise above three tenths of one percent provided one could still credit the Communist Party of Indonesia with the three million members once claimed.[21] However, were Indonesia left out of the computations, the Party-population ratio immediately plummets to a ratio even lower than that of the Middle East. As for Latin America, the 222,000 Party members represent only a negligible fraction of a population of almost 300 million. Even if one accepted at its face value the Soviet claim of some 300,000 Party members in Latin America listed in *Pravda* in November 1968 or even 350,000 mentioned in the *World Marxist Review* in 1971 (both of which evidently include also some 120,000 members of the Cuban Communist party), the ratio would still remain pitifully low.[22]

These meager results in Party recruitment can be explained and excused in Africa, especially below the Sahara, where national independence is a recent phenomenon and industrial proletariat, the class presumed to be the most rewarding hunting-ground for communist recruiters, is rather scarce. But they can hardly be discounted without painful soul-searching on mainland Asia and in Latin America where the collapse of colonialism occurred much earlier, and where communist parties have existed since the twenties and progressive industrialization has given birth to a sizable working class in a number of areas. Indeed, somber voices have at times broken through the crust of the customary official optimism and found their way into communist and communist-controlled publications. Analysing conditions in Latin America in an article in the *World Marxist Review*, a communist writer has regretfully concluded that "the revolutionary parties of the working class" have been "lagging behind" and that "even though the Communists have sound programs and are waging a valiant struggle on behalf of the working class and the entire people, most of the Communist parties of Latin America evidently still do not exert a *constant and effective* political influence on the basic sections of the working people."[23]

The Status of Illegality

Matters are further complicated by the status of illegality or semi-legality in which Communist parties find themselves in all but a few countries of the Third World. As of 1971, there was no Communist Party enjoying the status of legality in all of Africa, except perhaps the miniscule and utterly insignificant Communist Party of Mauritius. Similar conditions prevailed until recently in the developing countries of the Middle East where all the Communist parties were gradually proscribed. However, the trend was broken in 1966 in Syria where the ban on the Communist Party was tacitly eased by the new regime of the leftist wing of the Baath Socialist Party and the Party was subsequently allowed to join the newly formed Progressive National Front.[24] The Lebanese Communist party was legalized in 1970, and the Iraqi Communist party in 1971 when it was also admitted to the new United Front set up by the Baath Party of Iraq.[25] As for the rest of non-communist Asia, after the outlawing of the Communist Party of Indonesia (and disregarding the unclear situation in Laos), only two Communist parties in the developing nations of non-communist Asia continued to cling to the status of legality by 1972, namely, those of India and Ceylon; and the once illegal Communist party of East Pakistan emerged as a legalized Communist Party of Bangladesh. In Latin America, the Communist parties of Chile, Uruguay, Mexico, Peru, Venezuela, and (since 1970) the People's Vanguard Party of Costa-Rica could be said to have a status of legality as of 1971.[26] Another Latin American Communist party, that of Colombia, appears to be operating in a sort of twilight zone of semi-legality circumscribed by various restrictions, such as the denial of the right to participate in elections.[27]

While the status of illegality or semi-legality does not preclude the Communist parties concerned from existing and operating, it certainly renders the pursuit of their objectives more difficult. Denied access to authorized media of communications, deprived of the right of assembly and organization, barred from legitimate participation in public life, with their leaders often forced into hiding or exile and subject to arrest if and when the ruling regimes choose to do so, the native communists must operate under many restraints which make recruitment of new members much more difficult and gravely impair the Parties' effectiveness. Confronted with such adverse circumstances, how can they meet, in particular, their obligation to "explain the ideas of socialism to the masses, to educate the working people in a revolutionary spirit, to develop their revolutionary class consciousness and to show all the working people the superiority of Socialist society"?[28]

Since many communist parties of the developing nations went through varying periods and cycles of legality, semi-legality, and illegality, there is a substantial body of evidence indicative of how they have been affected by their changing status. It suggests that the status of illegality has been detrimental to them whereas the status of legality has been ordinarily to their advantage. Almost invariably, it has been during periods of their legality that the Communist parties concerned made their main advances, gained more followers, had better success in proselytizing, infiltrating labor unions, student associations, youth groups and other desirable targets, and even securing valuable footholds in the government apparatus.

Thus the Argentinian Communist party registered substantial gains during 1954-59 and again after 1964 when previous prohibitions of communist activities were lifted. The Brazilian Communist party, though outlawed since 1947, could take full advantage of the lenient attitudes of the Goulart regime, but suffered a severe setback when the new regime of Castello Branco began to enforce vigorously anti-communist measures. The Chilean Communist party has scored heavily since it regained legality in 1958, so much so that the Party gained 14.8 percent of the votes cast in the municipal elections of 1967 and 17.4 percent in the municipal elections of 1971. The communist-backed Popular Unity Front gained the plurality in the 1970 presidential elections and the communists got three seats in President Allende's cabinet. The People's Vanguard Party of Costa-Rica claimed a fourfold increase in its membership in two years since its legalization in 1970.[29] The Communist party of Iraq benefited greatly from the relative freedom of operations granted it by the Quasim regime, rose to a membership of 40,000[30] and managed to place a number of its members in the Iraqui state apparatus. However, it lost again many of its gains after Quasim's fall. The Syrian Communist party advanced greatly between 1954 and 1957 when it was allowed to operate openly. It was pushed back severely by the repressive measures applied to it after Syria merged with Egypt in the UAR in 1958. But it rebounded again in 1966 when the new regime lifted the ban on the Party's activities and two Syrian communists were subsequently appointed to posts in the new cabinet of Hafez-el-Assad. The Guatemalan Communist party had its heydays in 1951-54 during the Arbenz regime, but went quickly into eclipse when it was outlawed in 1956. The Communist Party of Sudan made its greatest thrust and obtained four cabinet seats after it emerged from illegality following the overthrow of General

Abboud's military regime in 1964. It promptly lost most of its gains when pushed back into illegality in 1965, only to recoup the losses and obtain at least five cabinet seats after regaining legality following the leftist coup of May 1969.[31] But it lost it all in 1971 when it was outlawed again following the coup attempted against Numeiry's regime. A similarly spectacular illustration of what a shift from legality to illegality means was offered by the 1965 collapse of the huge Communist Party of Indonesia which had once been virtually within the reach of supreme state power under the permissive regime of Sokarno.

Needless to say, the status of legality *per se* can by no means be considered as the primary cause of communist advancements which usually result from a multiplicity of factors, political, economic, social, psychological and other. However, where such factors conducive to communist advancement exist, they can be exploited much better by a Communist party allowed to operate freely, recruit members openly, secure fullest publicity for the propagation of communist and pro-communist courses and causes, and avail itself to the fullest extent of all the facilities to which legality gives access, than by a Communist party restrained by a status of illegality with all the harrassments, obstacles and impediments that such a status entails.

The predicament of the proscribed Communist parties of many countries of the Third World is made worse still by the prevailing Soviet policy of maintaining at all costs friendly official relations even with such non-aligned countries as disallow native communist parties and suppress their activities. Whatever advantages Soviet policy-makers hope to gain through their ambivalent behavior, it tends to exasperate native communists and undermine their efforts. One can well imagine the quandary of devout native communists languishing in local jails, running from local police or forced into banishment from their own countries while their persecutors are praised by Soviet and East European Communist leaders as fine "revolutionary democrats", dined and wined in the Kremlin or even awarded titles of Heroes of Socialist Labor and made Honorary Doctors by Soviet and East European universities.

Typical of the displeasures felt by the Afro-Asian communists for such Soviet behavior was a speech made by the leading, and traditionally pro-Soviet, Arab Communist Khaled Bagdash on the occasion of the 30th anniversary of the Seventh Congress of the Comintern held in Prague in October 1966. In what amounted to an open disapproval of the Soviet policy of cooperation with the Afro-Asian nationalist regimes which ban and persecute native Communist parties, Bagdash rebuked those who pursue a "policy of alliance" with their persecutors.[32]

Aware of this dilemma, the Soviet strategists have striven hard to promote conditions under which their comrades in the Third World could engage in their work in full legality and without molestation. As mentioned earlier, this is one of the main reasons for the Soviet advocacy of National Democratic Fronts in which weak native communist parties can expect to find a safe haven in their years of childhood and adolescence. That is why communist pronouncements, such as the 1960 and 1969 *Declarations*, harp so strongly on the necessity of "broad democratic rights and freedoms," especially the freedom of speech, press, assembly, demonstrations and establishment of political parties and social organizations. That is why they dwell so much on the alleged resolve to use only peaceful, non-violent means to promote their cause wherever conditions of freedom exist and to take the road of "non-peaceful transition" only "where the exploiting classes resort to violence against the people." Nor have Soviet endeavors been limited to ideological pronouncements alone. Wherever feasible, various forms of pressure have been employed to better the lot of native communist parties, ranging from private expressions of displeasure to public criticism in the Soviet press and tightening of economic aid.

Thus, to cite just a few examples, an editorial in *Pravda* of October 26, 1965, condemned "the wholesale arrests and searches of communists" in Indonesia.[33] Another article in *Pravda* on November 13, 1965, carried, under the expressive title "The Soviet Public is Concerned," an article on the protest made by the Soviet Red Cross against the arrests of Algerian communists. On February 24, 1966, *Pravda* published a statement by the Soviet Communist Party's Central Committee criticizing the sentencing of the Indonesian communist Njono. When the Moroccan government took in August 1969 into custody the Moroccan communist Ali-Yata, the Soviet Communist Party's daily demanded his immediate release and the *Union of Soviet Journalists* as well as the *Soviet Committee for the Solidarity With the Countries of Asia and Africa* sent sharp protests to the Moroccan Minister of the Interior.[34] The ruthless reprisals taken by the Numeiry regime against the Sudanese communists for their involvement in the coup of 1971 led to an avalanche of angry protests in Soviet papers and other communications media.[35] The Chairman of the Presidium of the Supreme Soviet of the USSR, N.B. Podgorny, even went so far as to appeal directly to General Nimeiry that the lives of the Sudanese communist leaders condemned to death be spared.[36]

While the Soviet expressions of concern for the sad fate of the Indonesian, Moroccan and Sudanese communists brought no results, it seems that in two instances, those of Syria and Algeria, they did help. As asserted by *Le Monde* on April 12, 1966, the Soviet Union is said to have made its aid in financing a giant hydro-electric project on the Euphrates River conditional on Syrian permission for Khaled Bagdash to return from his exile in East Europe, for the Syrian communist party to publish its paper, and for communist participation in the government coalition. Nonetheless, as revealed by communist complaints, persecution of Syrian communists, said to involve arrests, beating and even torture, was evidently resumed in 1970.[37] As for Algeria, most of the prominent communists arrested in 1965 were released in 1968 and placed under "residence surveillance."[38]

The Defective Social Structure

Another matter that causes communist observers concern is the faulty social composition of the Third World's Communist parties. Being by definition "the vanguard of the working class, i.e., its advanced, class-conscious part capable of leading the masses in the struggle for the overthrow of capitalism and the building of socialism,"[39] a communist party should ideally have a membership consisting predominantly of industrial workers. However, in actuality, communist parties of the developing nations generally fall far short of this proletarian ideal. In most instances their membership is a social hodge-podge with a strong middle-class admixture, a sampling of proletarian and semi-proletarian rural strata, a sizable dose of "young angry men" recruited mainly from radical elements of the native student body, a smattering of professional revolutionaries, but with no genuine working class majority.[40] Only the Communist parties of Uruguay, Chile and Argentine, with workers making up, as of 1971, between 63 and 78 percent of party members, deem to satisfy communist criteria.[41]

This defective class composition of communist parties of Asia, the Middle East, Africa and even Latin America has disturbed the communist leaders for a long time. Analysing the situation in the colonies and semi-colonies in 1928, the Sixth World Congress of the *Comintern* drew attention to the difficulty "that party membership in the first stage of the movement is recruited from petty-bourgeoisie, especially revolutionarily inclined intelligentsia and frequently students." Feeling that such elements find it difficult to "free themselves from their petty-bourgeois attitudes," it directed the communist parties in the colonies to become "genuinely proletarian also in their social composition."

Evidently, the results attained in the ensuing four decades have not been good enough, for calls for improvements in the class structure of the communist parties of the Third World are not less urgent today than they were more than forty years ago.

However, the official emphasis on making the communist parties of developing nations genuinely proletarian by concentrating primarily upon the recruitment of industrial workers has not gone unchallenged. Thus the communist parties of Latin America were criticized by a pro-Soviet Latin American communist for having been orientated "solely on the urban working class," for neglecting agricultural laborers and not paying sufficient attention to "the middle sections which grew in numbers and importance" and "to the radical circles of the petty bourgeoisie and the student body..."[42] A similar call for the communist parties of Asia to concern themselves more with the "political organization of the rural proletarians and semi-proletarians" was made by "a group of staff members of the Institute of Asian Peoples under the USSR Academy of Sciences."[43]

The Low Ideological Level

The unsatisfactory class composition of the communist parties of developing nations is held responsible, at least in part, for their relatively low ideological level. In that respect, the communist parties of Asia, the Middle East, Africa and Latin America seem to suffer from much the same ills that afflict their countries' working class whose vanguard they are supposed to be. While their leading figures, most of whom are the veterans of the communist movement, are evidently well versed in Marxist-Leninist theory and strategy, most of the parties' rank-and-file members appear to have at best only a rudimentary notion of the doctrine and its implications. They have been drawn into the Party fold more by emotional anti-westernism, dislike of colonial-style capitalism, the lure of Marxism-Leninism's revolutionary slogans and promises rather than a cool-headed acceptance of the overall Marxist-Leninist world outlook and a thorough understanding of the doctrine's fundamental tenets. For a good many of them the adoption of Marxism-Leninism results from a search for a new authoritarian creed to replace the earlier faith in the old ways and values shattered by the break-up of traditional society taking place today in so many parts of the Third World.[44] Even the more sophisticated among this new species of converts hardly qualify as genuine Marxists-Leninists, for theirs is an eclectic philosophy combining certain aspects of Marxism with selected elements of non-Marxian socialism, cooperativism, communalism, nationalism, and even religious spiritualism. This is especially true of Africa. "There are probably no more than a handful of Communists in the whole African continent," wrote a noted student of African and Middle Eastern communism in 1961, "whose political education and judgment come up to Moscow's requirement."[45] As ably expressed by the late Walter Kolarz, the Afro-Marxists do not seem to have any use for Marxism as a universal material ideology governing all aspects of life, but confine its validity only to the sphere of economics and the problems of state, while attempting to satisfy their spiritual needs by drawing from the storehouse of their own, indigenous culture.[46] The situation is undoubtedly better, from Moscow's standpoint, among the higher echelons in Asia and

Latin America, but probably hardly so among the rank-and-file members.[47] Lacking in "ideological steadfastness," one of the most important qualities of a good communist, the communists of developing nations are all the more vulnerable to various "petty-bourgeois", "reformist," "revisionist," "Rightist," nationalist and other undesirable influences. To overcome this grave danger by raising substantially the ideological level of the Asian, African and Latin American communists has thus become one of the major aspects of Soviet operations in the Third World. As stated in the *Fundamentals*, "the struggle for the purity of the Marxist-Leninist world outlook is an immutable law of the existence and development of the Communist Parties."[48]

Poor Discipline

The penetration of adverse influences has been facilitated by the loose discipline characteristic of most of the communist parties of the Third World. Problems of discipline plague, of course, every political movement, especially in its initial years, and are inevitably bound to afflict even more a movement laying such an extreme emphasis on absolute subordination and obedience as do Marxist-Leninists. But in most parts of Africa, the Middle East, Asia and Latin America it is more than that. The peoples of these areas seem to possess a highly excitable mentality oriented toward emotionalism, inclined more toward anarchism than strict discipline, lacking in balance and consistency, and prone to abrupt changes of mood and direction. Their behavioral pattern tends to be unstable, subject to vacillations and sudden jolts, wanting in persistence and abounding in factionalism, based on personalism rather than institutionalism and on caudillism rather than collective guidance. Such a temperament and behavior is ill-suited for the kind of iron discipline and centralised collective leadership the communist strategists insist upon. It is hardly conducive to the "absolute centralization and strictest discipline" demanded by Lenin,[49] and it makes well-nigh impossible the creation of "stable groups of experienced authoritative and influential leaders" deemed indispensable for communist success. As pointed out by various studies of Asian, African and Latin American communism, major psychological hurdles lie in the way of fashioning the communist parties of the developing nations into disciplined cohorts obediently following the orders of their collective leadership organs.[50] It is highly unlikely that a sizable communist party of this kind could be produced from below, i.e., as a progressively growing "voluntary union of like-minded persons united for the purpose of applying the Marxist-Leninist world outlook and carrying out the historic mission of the working class"[51] anywhere in the Third World in the foreseeable future. The only way this could be done would be from above, i.e., through a forcible seizure of power by a group which would then impose involuntary regimentation from above. Furthermore, both such a seizure of power and the imposition of discipline would probably have to be aided from outside to be successful.

The Impact of the Sino-Soviet Split

The difficulties encountered by the communist strategists in developing native communist parties and guiding them along the tortuous path toward fulfillment of their vanguard mission are further aggravated by the Sino-Soviet split. In so far as communist parties of the developing countries are concerned, the quarrel of the two communist giants has had at least two far-reaching consequences:

1. First, it has destroyed the unity of the communist movement of the Third World by cleaving it into two mutually hostile camps, each looking for inspiration and guidance in a different direction. As a result, there is today hardly a communist party in the Middle East, Africa, Latin America and non-communist Asia that has managed to steer clear of the fracas. In a number of instances the pro-Soviet and pro-Chinese wings have parted company and established their own pro-Soviet or pro-Chinese communist parties. By the latest count, such separate parties exist in Argentine, Bolivia, Brazil, Burma, Ceylon, Chile, Colombia, the Dominican Republic, Ecuador, Egypt, India, Lebanon, Malyasia, Mexico, Nepal, Paraguay, Peru and Syria. According to the *Peking Review* of January, 1968, there were ten pro-Peking Communist parties in Latin America as of 1968.[52]

Writing in *New Times* in June 1969, V. Shelepin complains that
"organizations which style themselves 'Communist parties'"
have been set up by Peking in Ceylon, Madagascar, Somalia,
Kenya, Kinshasa Congo "and other countries."[53] He accuses
"the Peking leaders and their agents" of conducting "a persistent
offensive against the politically most conscious detachment of
the Asian and African revolutionary movement — the Communists." In some countries of the Third World, such as Burma,
Bolivia, Dominican Republic, Colombia, Mexico and India,
there is a three or even four-way split resulting from the rise of
Trotskyite and Castroite factions. Elsewhere, the pro-Soviet and
pro-Chinese wings have avoided a formal rupture, but are locked
in a bitter struggle that has reduced the apparent unity to a sham.
Moreover, if the pro-Chinese elements carry out the Peking
directives "to discard these decaying old revisionist groups and
build new revolutionary parties" and "draw a clear line of
demarcation both politically and organizationally between themselves and the revisionists,"[54] more open splits are bound to occur
before the process is completed. An especially bad case of
"splitism" plagues the communists in India, the country that has
become the foremost target of Soviet wooing. There the Maoist
Communist Party (Marxist) of India (CPM) and the pro-Soviet
Communist Party of India (CPI) have been locked for years in a
continued struggle which seems to have reached the highest level
of bitterness during the 1971 elections. While the pro-Chinese
communists have denounced their pro-Soviet comrades as "enemies of the people" and "agents of the bourgeoisie," the latter
have countered by accusing the pro-Chinese communists of
making "surreptitious adjustments and an understanding with
the Parties of the Rightist alliance in Kerala, Tamilnad, West
Bengal and other states."[55]

Furthermore, the Sino-Soviet tug-of-war has been instrumental in encouraging a trend toward greater measure of self-
assertion among the Third World's communists. Being weak and
mostly unable to stand on their own feet, the Communist parties
of developing nations could hardly afford to insist on their right
to independence as have some of the Communist parties of
Western Europe. Nonetheless, some of them have begun recently
to flirt with revisionist ideas and display a tendency toward more
independence.

Foremost among the parties bitten by the polycentrist bug is the Communist Party of Sudan which has been, until its virtual annihilation by General Numeiry's regime in 1971, the most successful of all communist parties of Africa. In interviews with the Cairo paper *Al-Jumhuriyya*, the Italian Communist party's daily *L'Unità*, and the Yugoslav Press Agency *Tanjug*, the Party's Secretary General, late Abdel Khalig Mahgoub, rejected "the transference or results arrived at by sections of the socialist movement to another country," repudiated "centralism in the world communist movement," declared himself against "the imposition of a single political line on the Communist movement," and called for communists "to take up an independent position in applying the general concepts of Marxism in accordance with their countries' circumstances."[56]

A somewhat similar polycentrist stand, though spelled out more cautiously, was taken by Syria's Khaled Bagdash in his above-mentioned speech at the 30th anniversary of the Seventh Congress of the *Comintern*. While disagreeing with those who "would subordinate the tactics of the Soviet Union and its entire foreign policy to the tactical requirements of the other Communist parties," Bagdash chastised those holding the "erroneous" and "dangerous" view that "all the Communist parties should take exactly the same attitude as the Soviet Union."[57] Although the leading organs of most of the communist parties of the Third World endorsed the 1968 Soviet action against Czechoslovakia, their stand did not go unopposed among their rank-and-file; and several otherwise Soviet-oriented communist parties of the developing nations, such as those of Ceylon, India, Mexico, the Dominican Republic and Morocco, mustered enough courage to express some form of disapproval or at least dismay. Worst affected of all the Communist parties of the Third World by the Soviet invasion of Czechoslovakia has been the Communist party of Venezuela which split wide open over the issue. A number of prominent Venezuelan communists, including the former Party leader, Pompeyo Marquez, and Teodoro Petkoff, author of a book praising the Czechoslovak experiment, were expelled from the Party and formed a dissident group "Movement for Socialism" (MAS).[58] As shown in the Table I, a number of communist parties of the Third World (other than those listed as pro-Chinese) failed to send representatives to the 1969 Moscow World Communist Conference, though two of these may be the "two parties working underground" whose

names were presumably omitted "for considerations of security."[59] And the Dominican Communist Party refused to sign the
Declaration adopted by the Conference.[60]

Thus the unity which communists were directed by the 1960
Declaration to cherish "like the apple of their eyes,"[61] and which
the 1969 *Declaration* cited as "the most important factor in
rallying together all the anti-imperialist forces,"[62] is gone. So is
"the internationalist solidarity of all Marxist-Leninist parties"
without which "the success of the working class cause in any
country is unthinkable."[63] And with the unity of the world
communist movement in such disarray, the Soviet Communist
Party can no longer perform the role of "the universally
recognized vanguard of the world Communist movement" assigned to it officially by the 1960 *Declaration*, but no longer
mentioned in the 1969 *Declaration*.

2. Second, the Sino-Soviet conflict interferes with the communist strategy and tactics relative to communist cooperation with
non-proletarian groups and the assumption of the leadership. As
mentioned earlier, Soviet strategists envisage a comparatively
long period of cooperation between the native communists and
the non-communist segments of the national-liberation movement. Aware of the many weaknesses plaguing communist
parties in most parts of the Third World, they counsel against
premature attempts to seize the leadership and advocate rather a
cautious gradualist approach in that respect. On the other hand,
the Chinese communist leaders, bent on pushing for revolutions
at all cost and scornful of Soviet procrastination, urge the
communists of the developing nations to wrest the leadership of
the national-liberation movement from the unworthy hands of
the vacillating bourgeois nationalists even if it means resorting to
armed struggle and risking defeat. Thus the Sino-Soviet split has
rendered more difficult the avoidance of the two notorious
communist vices of *khvostism* ("Tailism") and sectarianism
identified earlier by Lenin and subsequently noted by the 1928
Comintern Thesis on the Colonies and Semi-Colonies.[64] Should
communists be too dilatory, too deferential vis-a-vis the national
bourgeoisie and their other temporary allies, too slow in stepping
into their rightful position of the vanguard, they would be
committing the heresy of *khvostism*. If they acted too hastily,

sought to assume the leadership prematurely and thereby alienated their partners and became isolated from the masses, they
would be guilty of sectarianism. However, sailing safely through
the narrow straits between the Scylla of *khvostism* and the
Charybdis of sectarianism, none too easy under any circumstances, has become almost impossible as a result of the Sino-
Soviet quarrel. Whatever the native communists may do, the
chances are slim that it will please both Moscow and Peking.
Moreover, the understandable desire of Soviet and pro-Soviet
communists to disprove the Chinese charge that they lack
revolutionary zeal involves a grave risk of rash and premature
tours de force that are likely to harm the communist cause
throughout the Third World even when they may occasionally
lead to momentary local gains.

The dilemma was brought into sharp focus by the proceedings
and resolutions of the Tri-Continental Solidarity Conference
held at Havana in January 3-15, 1966. Convened with an obvious
Soviet blessing and an equally obvious Chinese displeasure, the
Havana gathering of the leading representatives, of Asian,
African and Latin American Communist and "revolutionary"
parties was evidently expected by its Soviet backers and well-
wishers to confirm the correctness of the Soviet version of the
strategy of "peaceful coexistence" and to administer a rebuff to
the impetuous, saber-rattling Chinese "sectarianism." However,
the Conference, whose insignia depicted symbolically a hand
clasping a machinegun, turned out to be much more belligerent
than the Russians had bargained for.[65] Worse still, the belea-
guered Soviet delegate, Sharif Rashidov, alternate member of
the Soviet Party's Politbureau, eager not to appear less resolutely
anti-imperialist than others, felt obligated to "howl with the
wolves" and to sign the conference's fiery and overly militant
resolutions calling for armed revolutions and assailing as agents
of neo-colonialism a number of governments with which the
Soviet Union was striving hard to maintain good and friendly
relations. Thus, in order to score against the Chinese, the Soviet
Union had to allow itself to be maneuvered into a rather
embarrassing position vis-a-vis the very regimes it seeks to
entice. Illustrative of this embarrassment was the protest against
Rashidov's conduct at Havana reportedly made by the Uru-

guayan government As revealed by Uruguayan sources, the Soviet Ambassador to Uruguay, pressed for an explanation, had to fall back on the typical Soviet tongue-in-cheek statement that Rashidov spoke "privately" and not for the Soviet government.[66]

The Troubles with the Fidelistas

In addition to the disruptive impact of the Sino-Soviet schism Soviet strategists and their associates and collaborators in the Third World are confronted also with the parallel and somewhat similar challenge on the part of Fidel Castro and the Castroites. For obvious reasons, Latin America has been by far the foremost target of Cuban strategy. While Castro's agents have been also active in some parts of Africa, such as Algeria, Brazzaville Congo, Tanzania, Guinea and (prior to Nkrumah's ouster) Ghana, their impact there has been very slight.[67] Moreover, apart from usual propaganda, the Cuban operations in Africa have been limited mainly to the training of guerrilla fighters, as bodyguards to some of the African leaders, providing study facilities in Cuba for a modest number of African students and some negligible economic aid. In so far as the African Communist parties are concerned, Castroite influence seems to have been virtually nil. On the other hand, the Communist parties of Latin America have been cast in the role of Castro's whipping boys and have suffered much from Castroite inroads.

Somewhat ironically, the most exasperating problem that Fidelismo poses for the Latin American communists stems from the very fact that Castro chose, soon after seizing power, to proclaim himself a communist, to convert his revolutionary movement into a self-styled Communist Party of Cuba and to enroll Cuba, with Soviet blessing and support, as a member of the world socialist system. If he were truly a Marxist-Leninist in the Soviet meaning of the term, or at least behaved as such, all would have been well. A Castro willing to follow the Soviet line and to abide by Soviet directives would have become an invaluable asset for communist strategy in the Third World, especially Latin America. He would have been cited as a shining example of what a man guided by the infallible wisdom of Marxism-Leninism and given fraternal Soviet aid can accomplish; and other communists in the Third World would have been urged to follow and emulate him. Indeed, Soviet strategists expected that, willy-nilly, Castro would do substantially as told, for Cuba's isolation in the Western hemisphere and her near-total dependence on the Soviet Bloc, especially in economic matters, would leave him with little choice. Furthermore, after the Sino-Soviet conflict broke into the open and disagreements arose subsequently between Cuba and communist China over their sugar-for-rice deal in 1964, Soviet leaders seem to have hoped that Castro would side with them against China and would thus become an important tool in helping them counter the Chinese menace.[68]

However, things have not turned out that way. Far from becoming a loyal and obedient ally of the Soviets, Castro has sought to evolve and promote a strategy and tactics of his own fashioned much more along the Chinese than Soviet line, stressing armed struggle and guerrilla operations as "the fundamental line" of revolutionary action rather than the Soviet-preferred *"via pacifica"* and looking for support among radical students, land-hungry peasants and disgruntled petty-bourgeois elements rather than the classical industrial working class.[69] Worse still, Castro's agents and followers throughout Latin America have been hard at work propagating their idol's ideas among both the communists and the non-communist left, and organizing Castroite groups to put them into effect.

Their work has been greatly aided by the Castroites' assumption of control in 1966 and 1967 of two international organizations designed to foster anti-imperialist revolution in the Third World. As noted above, Castro and his associates succeeded in maneuvering the Tricontinental Solidarity Conference held in Havana in January 1966 into subscribing to a strategy that was essentially Castroist. The *Organization of the Solidarity of the Peoples of Asia, Africa, and Latin America* (O.S.P.A.A.A.L.) created by the Conference, domiciled at Havana and headed by a Castroite communist as its Secretary General, became a convenient vehicle for the propagation of Fidelismo. Yet another and even more useful tool fell into Castro's hands when the "First Latin American Solidarity Conference" that met at Havana from July 31 to August 10,

1967, set up a permanent *Organization of Latin American Solidarity* (O. L. A. S.), again with headquarters at Havana and with Castroites in firm control of its general secretariat.[70]

Thus, instead of helping the Russians overcome the breach in the world communist movement, Castro has become yet another factor contributing to its disintegration. In Latin America, in particular, his maverick brand of Fidelist "communism" has emerged as an appealing alternative and a dangerous competitor to the Soviet, Chinese, Trotskyite and Yugoslav revisionist versions. Castroite factions exist today virtually in all countries of Latin America [71] and are engaged everywhere in a bitter struggle not only against the "Yankee imperialism" and its "native lackeys" but also against orthodox communist establishments in their respective countries. The Fidelistas and, above all, their *"Jefe Maximo"* have heaped abuse on the heads of the pro-Soviet communist party leaders. They have branded them as "pseudo-revolutionaries" and rigid schematists guided by an antiquated doctrine and using shop-worn and ineffective methods "having characteristics of a church."[72] They have been referring to them derisively as "illustrious revolutionary thinkers" and *"los super-maduros"* (the "over-mature ones") who have "matured in such a way that they have rotted." They have portrayed them as superannuated, foot-dragging, irresolute procrastinators and hypocrites who talk revolution but lack the guts to pursue it. The Communist Party of Venezuela, which has stood up to the Castroites probably most resolutely of all the Communist parties of Latin America, has been contemptuously denounced as a "mafia" and its leaders as "reactionary gentlemen" (*senores reaccionarios*).[73] The leaders of the Communist parties of Argentina, Brazil and Colombia have also figured high on the list of Castro's favorite targets. Bloody confrontations between Castroite "ultra-leftists" and orthodox pro-Soviet Communists have also occurred in various countries of Latin America, such as the Dominican Republic, Venzuela, Colombia, and even Chile.[74]

Nor has Moscow, Cuba's main benefactor, been spared Castroite criticism, even though it has been couched in much milder terms than the invectives hurled at Moscow's associates in Latin America. Much like the Chinese communists, the Fidelistas have expressed unhappiness over the Soviet Union's peaceful co-existence policy and its concomitant coolness toward reliance on guerrillas and armed struggle. They have taken exception to Soviet efforts to develop economic relations with the countries of Latin America (other than Cuba and, more recently, Chile), viewing such efforts as a help to socialist Cuba's sworn enemies and weakening the cause of the socialist revolution in the Western hemisphere.[75] Castro's displeasure with Moscow's strategy undoubtedly lay behind his decision to send only a low-level functionary, Jose R. Machado-Ventura, Minister of Health, to represent Cuba at so solemn an occasion as the 50th anniversary of the Bolshevik revolution held in Moscow in November 1967. The same reason probably explains why the delegation of the Cuban Communist Party to the International Conference of Communist and Workers' Parties held in Moscow in 1969 attended solely in the capacity of an observer.

The vicious Castroite offensive against the orthodox communist parties of Latin America has certainly complicated the work of pro-Soviet communist parties. It has interfered with the recruitment of new party members as many potential prospects, especially the younger ones, tend to jump on the more glamorous Castroite bandwagon rather than join the dull and sluggish-looking establishments of the orthodox communist parties. It has rendered even more difficult than would otherwise be the case the communist efforts to indoctrinate their own ranks with the "correct," i.e., Muscovite, kind of Marxism-Leninism and to achieve and maintain the desired level of inner-party discipline. It has fostered the spreading of the very vices whose pernicious influences orthodox communists are to avoid and combat, such as "sectarianism," "ultra-leftism" and "adventurism." It has led to deep dissensions and cleavages within the Latin American communist movement and in a number of instances to censure and even expulsion of functionaries found guilty of pro-Castro leanings, "ultra-leftism" and advocacy of guerilla warfare as the main method of revolutionary action. Such have been the cases, to cite a few outstanding examples, of:

Diego Montana Cuellar, high-ranking functionary of the Colombian Communist party censured and expelled from the Party in 1968;

Douglas Bravo and Luben Petkoff, prominent members of the

leadership of the Communist party of Venezuela, expelled in 1967;

a group of dissident functionaries of the Communist party of Brazil expelled in 1967.[76]

Smarting under the continuous Castroite barrage, the belabored pro-Soviet leaders of Latin American Communist parties have fought back. In various statements and articles published in their parties' national organs, in the *World Marxist Review*, *New Times* and in Russian periodicals and newspapers, such as *Pravda* itself, they and their Soviet mentors have come out in defense of the correctness and efficacy of their policies and strategy against the Castroite accusations.[77] Without mentioning Castro by name, they have lashed out at irresponsible "adventurist" and "ultra-leftist" groups existing in many parts of Latin America. They have denounced their political platform as having "nothing in common with communism" and "forcing" upon the masses subjectivist pseudo-revolutionary methods of struggle. They have rejected their contention that "the armed struggle can be called artifically at any time and in any country irrespective of the existing conditions." They have taken them to task for ignoring the leading role of the working class in the national-liberation struggle, repudiating the worker-peasant alliance as well as the role of the Communist party as the revolutionary vanguard.

Not at all surprisingly, the sharpest anti-Castro declarations, and ones pointing the finger directly at the leadership of the Cuban Communist party, came from the Communist party of Venezuela, Castro's favorite villan. In an official statement explaining the reasons why the Venezuelan communists would not participate in the 1967 O.L.A.S. Conference, the Political Bureau of the Party's Central Committee accused the Cuban Communist party leaders of having launched a "systematic campaign of distortions and infamies" against the Communist parties of Latin America and created a "diversionist center stimulating fractionalism and masking trotskyite and anti-communist tendencies under a pseudo-Marxist and ultra-radical phraseology that sows confusion among the masses and in the very bosom of the revolutionary camp."[78]

The continued tug-of-war between the Castroites and the

orthodox communists characterized also the O.L.A.S. Conference of 1967 where the delegates of Latin American Communist parties, although greatly outnumbered by Castroites, put up a stiff fight, though mostly unsuccessful, on behalf of the orthodox Soviet strategy.[79] The struggle became at times so bitter and tempers rose so high that some of the communist delegates considered walking out altogether. According to reliable reports, the communist exodus was prevented only thanks to the strenuous conciliation efforts of Rodney Arismendi, the First Secretary of the Communist party of Uruguay, who had gone for consultations to Moscow prior to the Conference and evidently brought back the Soviet advice and directives not to allow the anticipated controversy to be pushed to the breaking point.[80]

The unusually mild Soviet reactions to Castro's behavior attest more than anything else to the delicate nature of the dilemma that Castroism has inflicted upon the Soviet strategists. Knowing that the United States would not tolerate a Soviet invasion and occupation of Cuba, Soviet leaders feel precluded from using there the ultimate weapon they were able to deploy against Czechoslovakia in 1968 and Hungary in 1956 when other methods of "comradely persuasion" had failed. Hence, they have at their disposal against Castro only sanctions of a political and economic nature. They could move from oblique criticism and nameless innuendos they have been using in the past to naming the culprits and indicting Castro and his followers, formally and publicly, as sectarian deviationists, thus giving them the treatment meted out to the Maoists and the Trotskyites. They could cut off the massive Soviet economic aid to Cuba and thereby wreak havoc on the island's economy that has become so dependent on the Soviet Bloc.

However, whatever might be the damage inflicted upon Castro and Cuba by such drastic measures, they would do much more harm than good to Soviet designs in Latin America and the entire Third World. After all, the main political and strategic assets that the Russians gained from Cuban developments since Castro's take-over have been: a). the extension of the world socialist system to the Western hemisphere; b). the creation of a living example of what a developing country allegedly can do for itself if it accepts selfless Soviet help and joins the socialist camp; c). the availability of highly desirable port and other facilities for the Soviet fleet. All these Soviet advantages would, of course, go down the drain should the Russians attempt to push the hot-blooded and quick-tempered Castro beyond the bounds of his endurance. Moreover, should the Soviet leaders ever decide to go as far as declaring Castro to be actually a pseudo-communist and a nationalist using communism merely as a disguise, they would jettison yet another major dividend derived from Castro's labeling himself and his movement as communist: namely, using Cuba to expose the United States' inability to make good on its oft-repeated assurances that communism would not be allowed to establish itself anywhere in the Western hemisphere.

It would thus seem that there is not much that the Soviet strategists can really do about the Castroite dilemma which is likely to plague them and the orthodox Latin American communist parties in one way or another and in varying degrees of intensity as long as Castro remains at the helm in Cuba.

The Yugoslav Alternative

Compared to the Chinese and Castroite threats, Yugoslav communism does not appear as yet to constitute a serious challenge to the pro-Soviet Communist parties of the Third World. Indeed, the Yugoslav brand of socialism and Yugoslavia's version of non-alignment have more appeal for the Third World's "revolutionary democrats" and socialists of non-Leninist variety than for the overwhelmingly orthodox-minded leaders of the traditional communist parties. Nor have there been any attempts on the part of Yugoslav communists to emulate the Chinese and Cuban example in setting up competitive communist splinter groups committed to the Yugoslav way.

In their turn, the leaders of the Communist parties of the Third World are no longer under the anti-Yugoslav injunction of the 1960 *Declaration* which had officially condemned the "Yugoslav variety of international opportunism, a variety of modern revisionist 'theories' in concentrated form" and denounced the leaders of the League of the Communists of Yugoslavia for "betraying Marxism-Leninism" and carrying on "subversive work against the Socialist camp and the world Communist movement."[81] Since the injunction has been omitted from the *Declaration* adopted by the Moscow Conference of 1969, there is no longer any formal bar to the establishment of friendly relations between the League of Yugoslav Communists and the Communist parties of the developing nations. However, knowing well that Yugoslav communists are still intensely disliked by Moscow, the Soviet-oriented leaders of most of the Communist parties of the Third World have tended to play it safe and keep their contacts with Yugoslav communists in a low key. For instance, only four Communist parties of the Third World, those of Chile, Sudan, Venezuela and Mauritius, sent delegates to attend the 9th Congress of the League of the Communists of Yugoslavia held in March 1969 and boycotted by the Soviet and East European Communist parties (except the Rumanian) because of the Yugoslav continued criticism of the 1968 Soviet invasion of Czechoslovakia.[82]

While the Chinese and Castroite communism (dubbed left-wing sectarianism" in Soviet terminology) has so far affected the Communist parties of the Third World much more than has its Yugoslav version (often referred to by the Soviet ideologists as "revisionism" and "right-wing opportunism"), the latter may eventually develop into as tough a competitor of Soviet-style communism in the developing areas as it has already become in some parts of Europe. After all, revisionist alternatives of modernized communism, such as those of presentday Yugoslavia or Dubček's Czechoslovakia prior to the Soviet invasion of the country, can hardly fail in the long run to look more attractive to most rank-and-file Communist party members of the Third World than the stale neo-Stalinist version continued to be offered by Stalin's heirs.[83] Moreover, the revisionist "socialism with human face" is certainly more suited than the orthodox Soviet communism to serve as a platform from which the Third World's communists could work out cooperative arrangements with non-Marxist socialists and other leftist groups, or with which they might try to appeal to their countries' public in general.

The Competition of Native Socialists

Finally, one of the most delicate issues confronting the communist parties and their Soviet strategists in the developing areas is the competition of native socialist and other leftist parties and groupings. With conservative and other right-of-the-center parties there is no problem. Since they oppose socialism in any form and seek essentially to preserve the economic and social *status quo*, the issues between them and the communists are clear-cut and they can be treated as enemies without causing any confusion. With bourgeois parties of the center matters are somewhat more complicated as some of their objectives are similar to the interim goals pursued by the communists at the initial national-liberation stage. But the real dilemma arises when communists are confronted with the presence of active parties of the left. Such parties in developing countries stand for radical changes in the social and economic *status quo*, including a sweeping land reform and a struggle against the vested interests of the native aristocracy and the upper classes: they are generally in favor of socialism (albeit not of a Marxist-Leninist variety), and critical of capitalism; many of them are anti-Western and the remainder neutralist. As they are for socialism and pursue certain major goals similar to those sponsored by communist propaganda, they cannot very well be denounced as reactionary. At the same time they pose a more serious long-term menace to the communist cause than do bourgeois parties for two reasons: 1.) Unlike the bourgeois parties, they are in a position to recruit followers in the same social groups upon which the communists count as their main reservoir, namely, the workers, poorer peasants and the radically inclined intelligentsia. 2.) Unlike the parties guided by Marxism-Leninism, they view their political, economic and social objectives as ends in themselves, not merely as a means to another, altogether different end, i.e., the establishment of the dictatorship of the proletariat. They strive for their own native type of "socialism-in-one-state" as a final stage of the process and for its own sake rather than an interim step meant to advance the ultimate global victory of communism coveted by genuine Marxists-Leninists. As Tanzania's President, Julius Nyerere, said in his speech at the official banquet in the Kremlin during his 1969 visit to Moscow: "[Our] choice of socialism . . . emanates from the communal traditions of Africa. We are building on the foundation of these traditions. . . . We are endeavoring to build socialism on the bases responding to our past, our present conditions and our striving for equality among people and human dignity in all spheres of life."[84] But such a proposition is miles apart from the "scientific socialism" in the Marxist-Leninist meaning of the word.

Hence, in fulfilling their crucial task of determining "the *chief enemy* against which the shock forces of the masses have to be concentrated,"[85] the communist parties of the developing countries should really point their finger at the parties of the democratic and socialist left wherever these parties are active and have some measure of success.[86] However, to do this would bare the communist insincerity and thus undermine their own propaganda. It would offend the ordinary rank-and-file members of the criticized leftist parties and impair communist chances of enticing them to switch to communism. And it would run afoul of the very purpose of the communist-favored stratagem of the National Democratic Front conceived specifically as a device of cooperation between the communists and the parties of the non-communist left and other "progressive" groupings.

The communist strategists have thus far attempted to handle this thorny dilemma of communist relationship with the Third World's leftist parties with considerable caution and flexibility. In essence, they have fallen back on the tactics employed over many years vis-a-vis the socialist parties of the West, namely, drawing a distinction between the leaders and the led.[87] While only kind words are said publicly about the latter, the treatment reserved for the leaders varies widely, depending on the specific conditions and developmental stage in each country and the tactical needs thereby created. Wherever the leaders of native leftist parties are anti-Western and side mostly or frequently with the communist camp on important political issues, they are treated with a correct to kind consideration commensurate to the merit earned and the degree of cooperation deemed necessary to benefit the communist cause. At times kindness is even proffered in advance in anticipation of, and as an inducement to, forthcoming pro-communist behavior. But when such leaders shed the pro-communist bias or fail to live up to communist expectations, and when hope is abandoned that they could be brought back to the desired course, all considerations are set aside and replaced by rebuke apportioned in accordance with the magnitude of the sins committed and with the measure of communist disillusionment.

The best known examples of the leftist non-communist and socialist leaders exposed to the soft treatement have been Egypt's Gamal A. Nasser, Algeria's Ben Bella, Ghana's Nkrumah, Tanzania's Nyerere, Chile's Salvador Allende, and, at least initially, Mali's Modibo Keita. Khrushchev went so far as to refer to Ben Bella and Nasser as "comrades."[88] And, as mentioned earlier, the heads of the delegations of the Third World's "workers', national-democratic and left-wing socialist parties" in attendance at the 23rd Congress of the Soviet Communist party in March 1966 were invariably spoken of as "comrades." Representative samples of the opposite treatment are supplied by the former Venezuelan President, Romulo Betancourt, and the leader of the Peruvian Aprista party, Haya de la Torre, hailed initially as progressive leaders but subsequently condemned as "servants of imperialism," subverters of Marxism-Leninism, "docile tools directed against the interests of the people," "stooges and agents of the oligarchy" and worse.[89]

In some instances, however, the communist strategy-makers are faced with a veritable Hobson's choice, offering no prospect of gain no matter what attitude they may take. That is especially true in countries where their leftist competitors are in control of the government and are in the process of carrying out social and economic reforms appealing to the broad masses. A good illustration of this sort of a communist cul-de-sac was provided by Eduardo Frei's Christian Democratic regime in Chile. Since Frei refused to invite communists to cooperation, they were duty-bound to criticize him. Unable to pin on him the label of a reactionary, they complained that reactionary forces had taken advantage of "the inertia, blunders and the inconsistencies of the Christian Democratic government."[90] On the other hand, they could not very well repudiate completely a government that reestablished diplomatic relations with the USSR and committed itself to a breaking-up of large landholdings, a more equitable land redistribution and the "cheleniazation" of the copper industry. Hence, they took refuge in obscure equivocations, such as the following cryptic sentence from an authoritative communist statement: "To the reformist policy of the government, the vanguard of the proletariat must respond by acting flexibly without the slightest manifestation of sectarianism, displaying broadmindedness and at the same time firmly upholding the revolutionary position in debates and mass actions."[91] As for Frei himself, a high-ranking Chilean communist, Jose Gonzales, speaking at the 13th Congress of the Chilean Communist party in October 1965, went so far as to praise the then Chilean President as "a manly and honorable fellow able to respect the ideas of opponents and look truth in the eyes." This flattering description evidently met with Soviet approval as Gonzales' statement was also reprinted in Moscow's *Pravda*.[92]

Frei's successor, Salvador Allende, being a Marxist socialist who has given the communists 3 seats in his administration and pushed through such communist-desired measures as the nationalization of Chile's mineral resources, stepped-up distribution of big land holdings and the restoration of diplomatic relations with Cuba, has thus far been *persona grata* for both the Chilean communists and their Soviet mentors. Whether, and how long, this will last is impossible to say. As is indicated by past experience with similar coalitions with the communists elsewhere, sooner or later the non-communist partners in the coalition are likely to refuse going along with communist *desiderata*, for their notion of socialism is vastly different from the Marxist-Leninist variety of their communist associates. When that point is reached, and provided Allende remains faithful to his promise to build socialism in Chile in a constitutional way, the communist-socialist honeymoon is bound to suffer and eventually grind to a halt. Indeed, the Chilean communists may have already had some second thoughts about the beneficence of their cooperation with Allende after they had analyzed the results of the 1971 municipal elections. While the communists increased their representation by less than 3 percent (from 14.8 to 17.4) above the result of the municipal elections of 1967, their socialists allies increased their hold on the electorate by 9 percent (from 13.9 to 22.9). So it may well be that the communist image of Allende will gradually worsen with the passage of time.

The Vanguard Role in Abeyance?

Thus the frantic communist endeavors to develop and

strengthen the right kind of "revolutionary workers' parties" in the developing areas and preserving their unity have so far yielded only very mediocre results. Numerically, organizationally, structurally, as well as ideologically, the Communist parties of non-communist Asia, the Middle East, Africa and Latin America remain, as a whole, rather weak and are ill-prepared for the exacting vanguard role assigned them in communist strategic plans. "Unfortunately we very often forget," laments a prominent Latin American communist writing in the *World Marxist Review*, "that the role which the Party is called upon to play as the vanguard of the revolution is one thing in theory and quite another in practice . . ."[93] Although he refers specifically to the communist parties of Latin America, the same holds true of Africa and, with the exception of South Vietnam and Laos, non-communist Asia.

In discussing the developments of communist parties, the *Fundamentals* concedes that "before become real vanguards the revolutionary parties usually pass through a number of stages of political and organisational development."[94] In the initial stage they are little more than "propagandistic groups" conducting their work mainly within their own ranks. Next they move to the second stage where they "go to the masses", begin "merging of the spontaneous working-class movement with the ideas of socialism" and transform it "into a class conscious organised movement." Only then can come the third stage in which "the party becomes a real political force capable of leading." Evidently, most of the communist parties of the developing nations seem today to be no further than the initial phase of the second stage and still have a long way to go if they are ever to reach the above-described third stage. That does not mean, of course, that they pose no menace. In the climate laden with emotionalism, frustration and feelings of social injustice, and in the unsettled and near-chaotic political and economic conditions existing in so many of the emerging nations, even small communist groups represent a greater threat than do communist parties many times larger in well-established, politically, economically and socially progressive countries of the West.

However, as suggested by the self-critical and rather despondent statements by some of the more sincere communist writers, the chances of a communist assumption of leadership in the developing countries in the near future are rated as rather dim. Despairing over the ability to build effective communist parties in some portions of the Third World, some of the communist spokesmen, among them the well-known Soviet theoretician A. Sobolev, have suggested (as noted in Chapter V) that in countries where Marxist-Leninist parties do not yet exist, "the role of revolutionary vanguard may to some extent be played by the trade unions."[95] A few have even gone so far as to express doubts concerning the feasibility of preserving the organizational independence of native communist parties in certain emerging nations.

This delicate issue has emerged mainly in connection with the establishment of anti-Western one-party states in Africa where, as one communist writer puts it, "the working class and its Marxist-Leninist vanguard" are confronted with the problem "whether to join the mass party or to build an independent working class party." The writer's suggestion seems to be that in countries "where the state directed by a single mass party represents the revolutionary dictatorship of the people and seeks to suppress anti-national elements," the communists should join this "new type of mass revolutionary party." But they must retain their "ideological independence," for the main rationale for their membership in such parties is to "spread ideas of Marxism-Leninism in these parties, gradually bringing their ideological platform closer to scientific socialism."[96] A similar view maintaining that in one-party states of Africa, such as Ghana (prior to Nkrumah's ouster), Algeria, and the United Arab Republic, "it is not necessary to found purely Marxist-Leninist parties" was expressed by a Nigerian communist at a conference on the Centenary of the First International held in Moscow in September 1964.[97] Although the above-mentioned statements were made by non-Soviet communists, the fact that they were allowed to appear in the Soviet-sponsored and Soviet-edited *World Marxist Review* indicated, if not Soviet agreement with such theses, at least their toleration. This was further corroborated by a 1970 Soviet volume on *Political Parties of*

Africa which recommends that the communists enter the ranks of such ruling parties so as to revolutionize them and raise them "to the level of a conscious socialist vanguard."[98]

The vague and ambivalent Soviet attitude on such a fundamental issue of communist strategy is borne out also by actual Soviet behavior. After Ben Bella banned the Algerian Communist party in 1962, Moscow swallowed the affront and began to act as if the Party had ceased to exist. Larbi Bouhali, the First Secretary of the Central Committee of the Algerian Communist party, began to be referred to simply as "Algerian."[99] The outlawed Egyptian Communist party became virtually a non-party after Khrushchev elevated Nasser to the status of a meritorious "comrade." As noted by the monitoring service of the *Radio Free Europe*, a program produced on May 11, 1964, by the "Voice of Iraqi People," a clandestine communist station operating from East Germany, to commemorate Khrushchev's seventieth birthday, broadcast greetings to the Soviet ruler from every Middle Eastern Communist party except the Egyptian party.[100] Nor were the Algerian and Egyptian Communist parties, two of the largest Communist parties in the Northern Arab tier of Africa, represented at the 23rd Congress of the Soviet Communist party by a formal official delegation. A few "representatives of the Algerian Communists and other comrades" were said to be present as individuals, but a mere mention of the fact by Brezhnev in his opening speech caused the delegation of the Algerian National Liberation Front to walk out in protest. And the once-largest Communist party of the Third World, the Communist party of Indonesia, sent neither a delegation nor was it mentioned among the "fraternal parties" whose representatives were in attendance at the Congress.[101] As far as the Algerian Communist party is concerned, its existence ceased to be ignored when it was listed, under its new name of the Socialist Vanguard Party of Algeria, as having attended the 1969 Moscow Conference. But the Egyptian Communist party remained relegated to the limbo though, of course, it might have been one of the "two parties working in the underground" whose names were said by the official communique of the Conference to have been withheld for considerations of security.[102]

Such a stand betraying a willingness to sacrifice the sacrosanct principle of Communist party independence in certain one-party states is, of course, in flagrant contradiction not only to Lenin's teaching on the subject, but also to the long-standing directives of the international communist movement. While permitting temporary cooperation and "in certain circumstances even a temporary union between the Communist Party and the national revolutionary movement," the *Thesis on the Revolutionary Movement in the Colonies and Semi-Colonies*, adopted by the Sixth World Congress of the Comintern in 1928, cautioned that such a union must by no means "degenerate into a fusion of the Communist movement with the bourgeois-revolutionary movement."[103] Rather, the *Thesis* prescribed that the Communist parties must "from the very beginning *demarcate themselves in the most clear-cut fashion*, both politically and organizationally, from all the petty-bourgeois groups and parties" and that the "Communist movement in all circumstances must unconditionally preserve the independence of the proletarian movement and its own independence in agitation, in organization and in demonstrations."

Hence, it is hardly surprising that the recurring suggestions hinting at a possible abandonment of communist organizational independence dismayed and alarmed some of the Third World's communists. A most forceful objection to such heretical behavior was voiced by Khaled Bagdash in his above-mentioned talk on the 30th anniversary of the Comintern. While conceding that communists should recognize the role of other revolutionary groups, the veteran Arab communist leader cautioned that "the unity cannot be based on the disbandment of the Communist parties or their being dissolved in other parties."[104] "Is there anyone today," he asked indignantly, "who would venture to claim that proletarian parties have no place in the conditions prevailing in the newly-free African and Asian countries? Five years later, writing in the *World Marxist Review*, the Syrian communist leader remained just as adamant: "....even in the early formative years of the national liberation movement it is necessary, Lenin taught us, to build an independent revolutionary proletarian-organization, if only a small core or embryo to borrow Lenin's expression. And this applies even to the most economically backward countries."[105]

The harshness of Bagdash's criticism is not perhaps fully justified for, as far as the communists are concerned, their joining of the 'revolutionary mass parties" is much more in the manner of a Trojan Horse style operation of infiltration and attempt of conquest from within than a genuine disbandment and dissolution. Already, Soviet spokesmen have begun criticizing the national mass parties of the developing nations as being "highly unwieldly," ideologically weak, unable to be "the people's leader and educator" and in no position to "act as a politically conscious vanguard." [106] To correct the situation, they have called for a "reconstruction" of these mass parties into "vanguard parties" that would be "organizationally and ideologically monolithic" and would unite in their ranks "the most progressive democratic forces." [107]

The preferred communist stratagem to effect such a transformation is the creation, within the existing mass parties, of tightly organized inner cores of trained and devout "activists" who would assume the role of the real vanguard. [108] To Soviet satisfaction, steps toward such a two-level reorganization have already been taken in some of Africa's "revolutionary mass parties," such as Egypt's Arab Socialist Union and Algeria's FLN, and native communists have managed to secure certain vantage positions in these "parties within the parties." However, it is doubtful whether the stratagem will work in today's developing nations any better than it did in China in the 1920's when a somewhat similar strategy ended in a dismal failure. The steps taken by Egypt's President, Anvar Sadat, against pro-Soviet elements in the Arab Socialist Union in 1971 indicate that it will not.

It would thus appear that the ghost that has haunted communist consciences ever since the fiasco of the Kuomintang experiment may have come back to plague them once again.

Notes for Chapter VI

[1] *Fundamentals of Marxism-Leninism*, p. 425.
[2] *Collected Works*, 4th Russian edition, Vol. 32, p. 222.
[3] Preliminary Draft, *Selected Works*, 10, p. 231.
[4] p. 333.
[5] *Ritvo*, p. 29.
[6] *Moscow News*, Supplement to No. 17, 1969. See also N. Lomakin, "O

rukovodiashchei roli kommunisticheskoi partii v stroitel'stve sotsializma," (On the Leading Role of the Communist Party in the Construction of Socialism), *Pravda,* September 19, 1968.

[7] V. Vol'skii, *"Novyi etap bor'by narodov,"* (A New Stage in the Struggle of the People), *Pravda,* March 19, 1968. See also V. V. Zagladin, ed., *Mezhdunarodnoe kommunisticheskoe dvizhenie,* (The International Communist Movement), Moscow, 1971, and *Third World,* p. 220.

[8] "World Communism on the Threshold of the Seventies," *New Times,* No. 1, 1970, pp. 17 ff.

[9] p. 360.

[10] *Pravda,* March 30, 1966.

[11] *"Pod znamenem edinstva kommunisticheskogo dvizheniia,"* (Under the Banner of the Unity of the Communist Movement), *Pravda,* March 4, 1969 and *New Times, op. cit.* in note 8.

[12] F. Burlatskii and E. Kuskov, *"V bor'be za splochennost kommunisticheskikh sil,"* (In the Struggle for the Unity of Communist Forces), *Pravda,* January 20, 1966.

[13] *World Strength of the Communist Party Organizations,* 23rd Annual Report, Bureau of Intelligence Research, Department of State, Washington, 1971, Publication No. 8526, cited hereafter as *World Strength.*

[14] *Pravda,* March 30, 1966.

[15] *Ibid.* The Sudanese Union Party and the Democratic Party of Guinea had previously despatched delegations also to the 22nd Congress of the Soviet Communist Party; and a delegation of the Soviet Communist Party attended the Sixth Congress of the Sudanese Union Party in 1962. Theodore Shabad, "Soviet Party Sets Tie to Mali Group," *New York Times,* September 11, 1962.

[16] Culled from *Pravda,* March 28-31, 1971.

[17] See K. Kamalov and V. Tsvetskov, "Madagaskar at the Crossroads," *New Times,* No. 2, 1972, pp. 22 ff.

[18] V. Midtsev, "You Wanted to Know: Alliance of Fighters Against Imperialism," *Izvestiia,* May 17, 1966, English text in the *Current Digest of the Soviet Press,* XVIII, 20, 1966, p. 20.

[19] *ibid.*

[20] R. Domenger, A. Letnev, "Tropical Africa: Its Parties and the Problems of Democracy," *World Marxist Review,* 13, 10, 1970, pp. 58 ff., and Tunji Otegbeye, "Leninism and the African Revolution," *ibid.,* 13, 8, 1970, pp. 78 ff.

[21] The *Pravda* article quoted above speaks of 3.8 million Party members in "non-socialist" Asia. But this figure is evidently based on the largely hypothetical estimate of the size of the Indonesian Communist party. Moreover, it includes such countries as Japan as well as the Asiatic portions of the Middle East. The *Pravda* article cited in note 11 lists a much more modest claim of 650 thousand communists in all of non-socialist Asia, including Japan.

[22] N. Mostovets, *"Boevoi front kommunisticheskogo dvizheniia,"* (The Battle Front of the Communist Movement), *Pravda,* November 20, 1968, speaks of some 300,000 Communist party members in Latin America. An article on "Latin America: Liberation Struggle and the Working Class," *World Marxist Review,* 14, 7, 1971, estimates the number of Communists in Latin America as "over 350,000," counting also Cuban Communists.

[23] Jose Manuel Fortung, "Has The Revolution Become More Difficult in Latin America?" *World Marxist Review,* 8, 8, 1965, pp. 38 ff.

[24] See about this a laudatory article by R. Petrov, "Syria's Democratic Forces Unite," *New Times,* No. 12, March 1972, p. 21.

[25] "Communists Hail Sudan's Delegate," *New York Times,* January 9, 1972.

[26] Cheddi Jagan's People's Progressive Party should be added to the list if it is deemed to be communist. As stated by Jagan in an article in the 1969 volume of the *World Marxist Review,* the PPP was "in the process of transforming itself from a loose mass party to a Marxist-Leninist type of party." "What the Future Holds for Guyana," *World Marxist Review,* 12, 10, 1969, pp. 42 ff. The People's Vanguard Party of Costa-Rica could participate in elections in 1970 for the first time in the last 22 years.

[27] The Communist party of Colombia was able to hold legally its Party Congress in December 1971.

[28] *Jacobs,* p. 42.

[29] Arnoldo Ferreto, "For a Militant Working-Class Party," *World Marxist Review,* 14, 11, 1971, pp. 53 ff.

[30] *Život strany,* No. 33, 1968, p. 10.

[31] See David Hurst, "Sudan Military Coup Strengthens Local Reds," *The Washington Post,* May 27, 1969, and the congratulatory article of N. Pozdnyakov, "Path of the Sudan Revolution," *New Times,* No. 32, 1969, pp. 21-22.

[32] *World Marxist Review,* 8, 12, 1965.

[33] See also I. Antonov, "Black Days for Indonesia," *New Times,* No. 10, 1966, pp. 4 ff.; B. Belin and V. Tumanov, *"Sud ili bezzakonie?"* (Judgment or Lawlessness?) *Pravda,* August 5, 1967.

[34] *"V zashchitu Ali Iata,"* (In Defense of Ali Yata) *Pravda,* August 26, 1969; *"Svobodu Ali Iata,"* (Freedom for Ali Yata), *ibid.,* August 27, 1969; *"Prekratit' repressiuu,"* (Stop the Repression) *ibid.,* Oct. 9, 1969; *"Svobodu patriotam Marokko,"* (Freedom for the Patriots of Morocco) *ibid.,* Dec. 2, 1969. For a protest against the treatment of Iraqi communists see "Who profits from Persecution of Communists in Iraq," *World Marxist Review,* 14, 4, 1971, pp. 146-148, and "End Persecution of Communists in Iraq," *World Marxist Review,* 13, 8, 70, p. 93.

[35] See, for instance, *"Krovavyi proizvol v Sudane,"* (Bloody Arbitration in Sudan), *Pravda,* July 30, 1971; "The Repression in Sudan," *New Times,* No. 32, 71, pp. 8-9; "Terror in Sudan," *ibid.,* No. 31, 71, p. 15.

[36] *"K sobytiiam v Sudane,"* (About the Events in Sudan), *Pravda,* July 31, 1971.

[37] "Death of Ahmad Al-Zuibi," *Information Bulletin,* No. 15-16, 1970, pp. 25 ff.

[38] *World Strength.*

[39] *Fundamentals,* p. 335.

[40] See, for instance, Lucian W. Pye, *Guerrilla Communism in Malaya,* Princeton, 1956, and Walter Laqueur, *Communism and Nationalism in the Middle East,* Melbourne, 1956, showing that most Asian and Middle Eastern parties originated as study groups set up mainly by intellectuals without political experience and that Arab Communist parties consist essentially of intelligentsia and middle class groups. See also "Certain Fundamental Problems of the Mexican Communist Party," *Information Bulletin,* No. 3-4, 1971, pp. 63 ff.

[41] "Latin America: Liberation Struggle and the Working Class," *World Marxist Review,* 14, 7, 1971, pp. 72 ff., and "Communists and the Masses," *ibid.,* 14, 9, 1971, pp. 38 ff.

[42] Jose Manuel Fortuny, *op. cit.,* p. 43. The 1966 Congress of the Uruguayan Communist Party also stressed the need of more attention to be paid to agricultural workers and small and medium peasants. See *"El Partido Communist Uruguayo despues Las Elecciones,"* (The Uruguayan Communist Party After the Elections) *Este y Oeste,* March 1967.

[43] "The Agrarian Question and the Developing Countries of Asia," *World Marxist Review,* 8, 9, 1965, pp. 38 ff.

[44] See, for instance, Lucian W. Pye, *op. cit.;* Walter Laqueur, "Communism and Nationalism in Tropical Africa," *Foreign Affairs,* 3, 9, 1961, p. 611; Walter Kolarz, "The West African Scene," *Problems of Communism,* X, 6, 1961, p. 234.

[45] Walter Laqueur, "Communism and Nationalism in Tropical Africa," *op. cit.*

[46] "The West African Scene," *op. cit.,* p. 23.

[47] The lack of ideological maturity is often cited in customary self-criticism in which the organs of these parties periodically engage. See, for instance, "Peru: *El P.C. y Las Guerrillas,"* (Peru: The C. P. and Guerrillas) *Este y Oeste,* January 1967, pp. 13 ff.; "Certain Fundamental Problems of the Mexican Communist Party," *op. cit.;* B. Ponomaryov, "Topical Theoretical Problems of World Revolutionary Process," *op. cit.;* "Advancing Under the Banner of Marxism-Leninism," *Information Bulletin,* 4-5, 1972, pp. 65 ff., a reprint of the self-critical editorial article of the English- language edition of the Indonesian Communist Journal *Tekad Rakjat,* No. 1, 1972.

[48] p. 351.

[49] *Selected Works,* 1952, Vol. II, Part 2, p. 344.

[50] See, for instance, Ernst Halperin, *Communism in Mexico,* Cambridge, 1963, and Lufti El Kohli, "Current Phase of the Anti-Imperialist Struggle in Africa," *World Marxist Review,* 10, 1, 1967 pp. 13 ff.

[51] *Fundamentals,* p. 334.

[52] See also Robert J. Alexander, "The Communist Parties of Latin America," *Problems of Communism,* XIX, 4, 1970, pp. 37 ff.

[53] "Maoist Intrigues in the Third World," *New Times,* No. 26, 1969, pp. 6 ff.

[54] *People's Daily and Red Flag,* November 10, 1965.

[55] "Success for India's Democratic Forces," *World Marxist Review,* 15, 5, 1971, pp. 139 ff; see also "Rout of Rightists: Massive Gain for Democratic Forces," *Information Bulletin,* 12-13, 1971, pp. 95 ff.

[56] *Al Jumhuriyya,* Cairo, February 3, 1965; *L'Unità,* January 11, 1965; Tanjug release, March 4, 1965; all cited in the *Free Europe Radio Release* of April 27, 1965.

[57] *World Marxist Review,* 8, 12, 1965, pp. 16 ff. 44a. See, for instance, *"Problemas Doctrinales y Crisis de Direccion en el Partido Comunista de Chile,"* (Doctrinal Problems and the Crisis of Direction in the Communist Party of Chile) *Este y Oeste,* Vol. VII, No. 123, February 1969, pp. 1-7, showing how many party members, especially the youth and the intellectuals, were dismayed by the sycophantic stand of their Party's leaders who first praised Dubček and his "socialism with a human face" but switched subsequently to support the Soviet intervention.

[58] See *"Na IV. s'ezde kompartii Venezuely,"* (At the IVth Congress of the Communist Party of Venezuela) *Pravda,* Jan. 27, 1971; *Nakanune IV. s'ezda venezuel'skikh kommunistov,* (On the Eve of the IVth Congress of Venezuela's

Communists) *ibid.* Oct. 20, 1970; "Unite the Party Around A Program," *Information Bulletin,* 10, 1970, pp. 43 ff. Having endorsed the Czechoslovak experiment in his book *Checoeslovaquia: El Socialismo Como Problema,* (Czechoslovakia: Socialism As a Problem) Petkoff published as follow-up a revisionist volume entitled *Socialismo para Venezuela* (Socialism for Venezuela). See also an attack on Petkoff's "mixture of neo-Trotskyism and Marcuseanism with a dash of liberal opportunism" in "Latin America: Liberation Struggle and The Working Class," *op. cit.*

[59] See the official communique published in *Pravda,* June 18, 1969, and *World Marxist Review,* 12, 7, 1969, pp. 3-4.

[60] *ibid.*

[61] *Jacobs,* p. 43.

[62] *World Marxist Review,* 12, 7, 1969, pp. 5-25.

[63] *Jacobs,* p. 45.

[64] p. 26.

[65] For a discussion of the Conference and its background see D. Bruce Jackson, "Whose Men in Havana?" *Problems of Communism,* XV, 3, 1966, pp. 1 ff.

[66] Richard Eder, "Russians Clarify Statement on Latin American Revolts," a *New York Times* News Service release, February 18, 1966. More about the confrontation between the Soviet oriented Communists of the Third World and their Maoist and Castroite opponents in Ch. XIII.

[67] For a good discussion of Cuban activities in Africa see Nicolas Lang, *"Los Cubanos en Africa Negra,"* (The Cubans in Black Africa) *Este y Oeste.* VI, 121, 1968, pp. 106.

[68] See, for instance, *"La Conferencia de la O. L. A. S.,* (The OLAS Conference)" *Este y Oeste,* VI, 108, 1967, pp. 1 ff.

[69] More on the Castroite attitudes in such matters in chapters concerned with the respective aspects of the communist strategy. See also Luis E. Aguilar, "Fragmentation of the Marxist Left," *Problems of Communism,* XIX, 4, 1970, pp. 1 ff., and Robert Alexander, *op. cit.*

[70] For an excellent discussion of the proceedings and results of the Conference see *"La Conferencia de la O. L. A. S., op. cit.,* and Edward Gonzales, "Castro: The Limits of Charisma," *Problems of Communism,* XIX, 4, 1970, pp. 12 ff.

[71] *World Strength,* various issues of *Este y Oeste, Communism in Latin America,* Alexander, *op. cit.*

[72] See Fidel Castro's speech at the O. L. A. S. Conference, cited in *"La Conferencia de La O. L. A. S.," op. cit.*

[73] *ibid.*

[74] See the AP correspondent's report from Chile on the clashes between young communists and "ultra-leftist extremists" at the University of Concepcion: "Chile Clash Leaves one Student Dead," *Austin American,* December 4, 1970; J. Texier, "Petty-bourgeois Revolutionism in Chile," *World Marxist Review,* 15, 7, 1972, pp. 85 ff.

[75] See Castro's interview with Herbert L. Matthews, *Washington Post,* December 25, 1967; *"La Conferencia de La O. L. A. S," op. cit.*

[76] "Pro-Castroite Leanings in Latin America," *Communism in Latin America,* November 1967: *"Situacion de los Movimientos Communistas en Venezuela,"* (The Situation of the Communist Movements in Venezuela), *Este y Oeste,* X VII, 125, 1969, pp. 1 ff.; *Voz Proletaria,* May 9, 1968; Luis Carlos

Prestes, "Battle of Brazil's Communists," *World Marxist Review*, 15, 2, 1972, pp. 16 ff.

[77] See R. Ghioldi (high-ranking member of the Executive Committee of the Central Committee of the Argentinian Communist Party), *Zaria chelovechestva,"* (The Dawn of Mankind), *Pravda*, October 25, 1967; Luis Corvalan, (secretary General of the Chilean Communist Party), *"Nemerknushchii svet idei oktiabria,"* (The Never Disappearing Light of the Idea of October), *ibid.*, October 27, 1967; N. Mostovets, *"Boevoi front kommunisticheskogo dvizheniia,"* (The Battle Front of the Communist Movement), *ibid.*, November 20, 1968; V. Volskii, *"Latinskaia Amerika: Problemy osvoboditel'noi bor'by,"* (Latin America: The Problems of the Liberation Struggle), *ibid.*, June 27, 1970; *Voz Proletaria*, May 9, 1968; also various articles in *New Times* and *World Marxist Review.*

[78] *Este y Oeste*, Vol. VI, No. 108, 1967, pp. 31-32.

[79] The Communist parties of Venezuela, Argentina and Brazil did not send any delegates.

[80] *"La Conferencia de La O. L. A. S.",*, *op. cit.*

[81] *Jacobs*, pp. 43-44.

[82] *Socialist Thought and Practice*, No. 33, 1969.

[83] See also Rubinstein, *Yugoslavia and the Non-Aligned World*, holding much the same view.

[84] *"Druzhestvennoe sotrudnichestvo"* (Friendly Cooperation), *Pravda*, Oct. 9, 1969. See also H. Boumedienne's emphasis on Algeria's resolve to build "a socialist community corresponding to its specific situation and experience" in the speech welcoming Kosygin on his visit to Algeria in October 1971, *Pravda*, Oct. 7, 71.

[85] *Fundamentals*, p. 482.

[86] See, for instance, Rollie E. Poppino, *Communism in Latin America*, New York, 1964, and Robert Alexander's article on "Communism in Latin America" in Jean Kirkpatrick, ed., *The Strategy of Deception: A Study in World-wide Communist Tactics*, New York, 1963.

[87] See a long explanation of these tactics in *Fundamentals*, pp. 358 ff.

[88] *Pravda*, May 2, 1964, and Associated Press release from Aswan, May 14, 1964, cited in Uri Ra'anan, "Moscow and the Third World," *Problems of Communism*, XIV, 1, 1965, pp. 23 ff.

[89] V. Volskii, *"Latinskaia America,"* *op. cit.*; "For an Early Agrarian Reform," *Information Bulletin*, 15, 1969, pp. 38 ff. V. Andrianov, "Venezuela' the Lesson of Recent Events," *International Affairs*, No. 6, 1960, pp. 83-84, and *Krasnaia Zvezda*, June 22, 1962, both quoted in Cyril E. Black and Thomas P. Thornton, eds., *Communism and Revolution*, Princeton, 1964, p. 354. See also the Soviet condemnation of "Malagasy socialism" of the ruling Social Democratic Party of Madagascar, K. Kamalov and V. Tsvetkov, *op. cit.*

[90] Orlando Millas, "Christian Democratic Reformism," *World Marxist Review*, 8, 11, 1965, pp. 65 ff; Also, "The Revolutionary Line of the Chilean Communists," *ibid.*, 8, 12, 1965, pp. 104 ff.

[91] *World Marxist Review*, Vol. 8, No. 11, 1965, p. 69, citing from the periodical *Principios.*

[92] October 19, 1965.

[93] Jose Manuel Fortuny, *op. cit.*

[94] p. 335. See also "the main criteria of the maturity of the workers

revolutionary vanguard" stressed by B. Ponomaryov in his above-cited 1971 report at the Institute of Marxism-Leninism.

[95] "National Democracy - The Way to Social Progress," *World Marxist Review,* 6, 2, 1963, pp. 39 ff.

[96] W. Sheppard, "The One-Party System and Democracy in Africa," *World Marxist Review,* 7, 4, 1964, pp. 86 ff.

[97] Philip Mosely, "Communist Policy and the Third World," *Review of Politics,* 28, 2, 1966, pp. 210 ff. See also Lufti El Kholi, "Perspectives of Cooperation and Unity of the Progressive Forces of the Arab Countries," *World Marxist Review,* 9, 10, 1966, pp. 49 ff. While stating that Egypt's "Communist and other progressive and national organizations have voluntarily relinquished independent existence," the author cautions that "the Egyptian revolutionary experience cannot be extended to the other Arab countries."

[98] V. S. Solodovnikov, ed. *Politicheskie Partii Afriki* (The Political Parties of Africa), Moscow, 1970. See also the reference to the book in *U. S. S. R. and Third World,* 1, 3, 1971, pp. 131.

[99] *Pravda,* June 2, 1964.

[100] A Free Europe Radio release of June 24, 1964: "Communists in Egypt: The Lost Tribe."

[101] *Pravda,* March 30, 1966.

[102] However, "press reports" suggest that the two unnamed Communist parties in attendance at the Conference were those of Nepal and the Phillippines. See "The International Communist Conference," *The World Today,* 25, 7, 1969, p. 282.

[103] p. 26. See also Kermit McKenzie, *Comintern and World Revolution, 1928-1943,* p. 135.

[104] *World Marxist Review,* Vol. 8, No. 12, 1965, pp. 16 ff.

[105] "Lenin and Struggle Against Opportunism and Revisionism in National-Liberation Movement," *World Marxist Review,* 13, 4, 1970, pp. 92 ff.

[106] See N. Gavrilov in *International Affairs,* No. 7, 1966, p. 42, and G. Mirskii in *New Times,* No. 48, 1965; also, N. Prozhogin, "The Choice of Algeria: Socialism," *Kommunist,* No. 10, 1965, pp. 102 ff.

[107] Gavrilov, *op. cit.;* A. Iskenderov and G. Starushenko, in *Pravda,* August 14, 1966.

[108] Prozhogin, *op. cit.,* Mirskii, *op. cit.,* Gavrilov, *op. cit.,* Iskenderov, *op. cit.* See also "Algeria: United Front or One Party?" *Information Bulletin,* No. 4, 1970, pp. 30 ff.

CHAPTER VII

UTILIZING THE PEASANTRY

From the days of Lenin one of the most fundamental tenets of communist strategy has been that, to be victorious, the proletariat and its communist vanguard must gain the support and cooperation of peasant masses. Hence, as shown in Chapter IV, the communists consider the peasantry their most desirable ally and assign them a prominent place in the National Democratic Fronts.

This communist preference for the peasantry over any other non-proletarian class or stratum is firmly rooted in Lenin's teaching. It constitutes one of the most fundamental aspects of Leninist strategy of the revolution, especially for countries of predominantly agrarian character. Lenin believed that, before the proletariat could assume revolutionary leadership, it had first to form an alliance with the peasantry. The proletariat, he held, could "become a victorious fighter for democracy only if the peasant masses join its revolutionary struggle."[1] He considered the worker-peasant alliance to be the guarantee of our successes and our ultimate victory."[2] "The supreme principle of proletarian dictatorship, Lenin teaches, is working-class alliance with the toiling peasantry," stressed the Soviet Communist Party's leading theoretician, M. Suslov.[3] When Lenin drafted his *Theses on the National and Colonial Questions* in 1920, he extended his precept on the role of the peasantry to the underdeveloped countries of the East as well. He urged communists to "render special assistance to the peasant movement in the backward countries," "to strive to give the peasant movement the most revolutionary character and to establish the closest possible alliance between the West European communist proletariat and the revolutionary peasant movement in the East, in the colonies and backward countries."[4]

Lenin's *ukase* on the worker-peasant alliance continued to govern communist strategy even after the Master's death. "The peasantry, along with the proletariat and in the character of its ally, represents a driving force of the revolution," proclaimed the 1928 Comintern *Thesis on the Revolutionary Movement in the Colonies and Semi-Colonies*. As Lenin had done in 1920, it exhorted communists "to give a revolutionary character to the existing peasant movement," wage propaganda for "a fighting bloc" of proletariat and peasantry, to organize new revolutionary peasant unions and committees. It referred to the agrarian revolution in colonies and semi-colonies as "the axis of the bourgeois-democratic revolution" and urged communists to take advantage of the intensification of class contradictions in the village and to "give a consciously revolutionary direction" to the dissatisfaction of the peasants.[5]

These long-standing communist precepts on the role of the peasantry in the bourgeois-democratic revolution seemed to be ideally suited to the conditions prevailing in the less developed countries of Asia, Africa and Latin America during the postwar era of the "collapse of the colonial system." In all these countries agriculture predominated over industry and rural population greatly exceeded the urban dwellers. Most of the agricultural holdings were concentrated in the hands of a small minority of wealthy landowners contrasting sharply with an overwhelming number of landless or quasi landless peasants, tenants and sharecroppers barely able to eke out miserable hand-to-mouth existence from their toil. The inevitable result was a feeling of exploitation and social injustice intensified by the growing awareness of better alternatives and the quickening pace of social change. Such factors could only convince contemporary communist strategists that the victory of their cause in Asia, Africa and Latin America depended upon the support of the peasant masses. "The alliance of the working class and the peasantry is the most important force in winning and defending national independence, accomplishing far-reaching democratic transformations and insuring social progress," asserted the 1960 *Declaration of Eighty-One Communist Parties*.[6] Using virtually the same language and referring specifically to the national-liberation movement of Asia, Africa and Latin America, the 1961 *Program of the Soviet Communist Party* proclaimed the worker-peasant alliance to be "the fundamental condition for the success of the struggle to carry out far-reaching democratic changes and achieve economic and social progress."[7] The *Fundamentals* devotes an entire chapter to a fervent advocacy of the alliance of the working class and the peasantry which it designates as "one of the principal ideas of Leninism." It pronounces the peasantry to be closest to the proletariat of all the non-proletarian classes of bourgeois society and claims that "of all the political parties known to history only the Communists have waged a consistent struggle for strengthening the alliance of workers and peasants." Noting that the peasants constitute the majority of the population in "the colonial and dependent countries," it concludes that "only through a close alliance with the peasantry can the working class become the leader of the national-liberation movement."[8]

This official Soviet thesis has been echoed in recent communist statements and writings. The Third World's peasantry is referred to as "a component part in the general revolutionary process" and "the most mass base of the national-liberation revolutions" which "determines the force and the scope of these revolutions."[9] It is said to constitute "the most active revolutionary force of the national-liberation movement."[10] "The object of non-capitalist development is to win to the side of socialism the peasantry," states Ulianovskii in a major article on "Leninism, Soviet Experience and the Newly-Free Countries" in the 1971 volume of *New Times*.[11] Addressing the 1969 International Conference of Communist and Workers Parties, Brezhnev labeled "the question of the position of the peasantry" to be "today the central question of the revolutionary process" in Asia and

Africa."[12] The *Declaration* adopted by the Conference describes
the "toiling peasantry" of the Third World as having "great
revolutionary potential" and "taking an active part in the
struggle against imperialism, for the national liberation of
peoples and for consolidating the independence of the young
states."[13] In the same vein some of the Third World's communists of pro-Soviet leanings invariably insist upon the necessity of
the worker-peasant alliance as a *sine qua non* of their success;
and some of them designate the peasantry (rather than the
working class) as "the main motive force of the national-
liberation revolution."[14] Moreover, the idea has begun to crop
up in communist writings that "the most 'proletarianized' section
of the peasantry, the agricultural workers," might perhaps be
acceptable as the forefront of the social revolution pending the
emergence of an adequate industrial working class.[15]

Thus the struggle for the allegiance of broad peasant masses
and their subordination to communist leadership has become one
of the most important tasks of communist strategy and tactics in
the Third World and it has been discussed as such extensively in
recent communist writings.[16] "It is sometimes contended,"
states a prominent Soviet specialist in the Third World's affairs,
"that the greatest discovery of Marxism in the twentieth century
is the theory of the peasantry as the principal motive force of the
revolution."[17]

Bringing About the Worker-Peasant Alliance

How do communist strategists propose to bring about the
worker-peasant alliance and to induce the peasantry to accept
communist leadership? Several major techniques have been
devised for this all-important purpose, mostly by adapting earlier
stratagems to present circumstances.

1. Reminiscent of the familiar Leninist divide-and-conquer
approach, communist theorists subdivide the peasantry into
several strata ranging from landless agricultural laborers to
agricultural capitalists and "latifundists." However, as Lenin
had done when he was in dire need of Russian peasant support,
for practical operational purposes they use a crude dichotomous
formula counterposing against each other the exploited peasant

masses and the exploiting uppermost stratum of big landowners. Among the exploited strata they tend to lump together, at least temporarily, four of the five categories of rural population discerned by Lenin,[18] namely the poor, landless agricultural proletariat earning their livelihood by working for capitalist landlords; the semi-proletarian "dwarf" peasants forced to supplement through wage-labor the meager income obtained from their own or rented miniscule plots of land; the small peasants able to till their own or rented small holdings without having to use outside help; and even the middle peasants who use hired labor "fairly frequently" and who are able to secure "a certain surplus" that may be converted, "at least in good years," into capital. Added to these four categories in the emerging countries with inherited communal property systems are tribesmen working within such systems as they are deemed to be exploited by their tribal chiefs.

On the other hand, the exploiting rural stratum is limited, at the national democratic phase of the revolution, to the numerically minute group consisting of semi-feudal latifundists, plantation owners, autocratic tribal chieftains and the "big peasants," i.e., in Lenin's definition, "capitalist entrepreneurs in agriculture" employing regularly hired labor and "connected with the peasantry only by their low cultural level, habits of life and the manual labour they themselves perform on their farms."[19] Since the categories classified as exploited represent an overwhelming majority of the rural population of the Third World, communists hope to be able to pose all the more as true champions of the peasant cause while securing at the same time a highly suitable target against which to direct the pent-up anger of the masses.

2. To be attracted to the cause of the revolution peasants must be made fully aware of the depth of their exploitation and the responsibility therefore must be placed squarely on the shoulders of the "imperialists" and their "lackeys." In this respect, the hapless poverty in which rural masses find themselves in most areas of the Third World provides communist propagandists with a veritable bonanza. "The imperialist bourgeoisie of Europe and North America," claims the *Fundamentals*, "has done all it could to preserve the feudal forms of exploitation in the colonial and semi-colonial countries. Owing to its efforts almost the same

forms of feudal landownership and servitude that existed in the Middle Ages have persisted up to now, in the second half of the twentieth century, in Asia, Africa, Latin America and even parts of Europe, such as Spain and south of Italy."[20] Lashing out time and again at these "feudal survivals," Soviet propagandists draw the bleakest possible picture of this sad legacy of the colonial era consisting presumably of: ownership of most agricultural land by the "landlord class"; inability of the poor peasants to buy land and a resulting necessity "to rent it from the landlords on enslaving terms" and accept disadvantageous share-cropping arrangements; the imposition of obligations to till the landlord's land and thus making the peasants "virtually serfs performing corvee labour for the feudal lord"; "a dense web of debts entangling most of the peasants," making them increasingly dependent on the landlords and usurers; peasants' oppression by local officials, magistrates and policemen acting on behalf of the big landowners.[21]

Nor are the peasant masses of the emerging nations given any hope that their lot may be alleviated if and when semi-feudal conditions give way to capitalism. Communist writers do concede that the semi-feudal system in many of the developing nations is being gradually replaced by agricultural capitalism, "growing in breadth and depth,"[22] and that the reforms undertaken in most of the ex-colonial countries "have curtailed the economic power and political influence of the privileged and traditional parasitic elements among the landlord class."[23] But they claim that such a development only "brings the peasantry new deprivations," "exacerbates the problem of agrarian over-population" and increases the "pauperization and proletarianization" of the peasant masses.[24] Just as "the fruits of the bourgeois revolution" in Europe "were reaped mainly by kulaks, usurers and merchants" who "became the bulwark of the bourgeois state,"[25] so the benefits of the national democratic revolution in many countries of the Third World are being allegedly grabbed by the "rich peasants" who are thus gradually taking over the role of the chief villains alongside the "reactionary top section of the bourgeoisie" in the communist analysis of social forces in the developing nations.

3. Besides being made aware of their exploitation by their native class enemies, the semi-feudal landlords, the emerging capitalist "village rich" and the imperialist bourgeoisie, the peasant masses must be convinced that their only hope for genuine and lasting improvement of their situation lies in the victory of the proletarian revolution and that therefore they are promoting their own interests when they join the worker-peasant alliance under communist leadership. Consequently, the emphasis on the identity of interests of workers and peasants has become a recurrent theme of communist agitation and propaganda.

The workers and peasants are said to be "closely related" both by their origin and their position in capitalist society. The working class was formed historically as a result of peasants being "ruined and dispossessed of their lands." They are both toilers "who earn their bread in the sweat of their brow." They have a common class enemy. Their alliance is "dictated by the vital interests of both classes." The peasants "cannot achieve their emancipation from the yoke of the landlords and monopoly capital without the support of the working class."[26] As stressed by the spokesmen at a 1971 round-table conference on Latin America sponsored in Chile by the editorial board of the *World Marxist Review*, "the only way the peasants can satisfy their hunger for land is by alliance with, and under the guidance of, the working class."[27] While capitalism is blamed for "ruthlessly reducing to nought the efforts of the peasants to become independent farmers on their own land," and thus ruining small peasant farms and forcing "enormous masses of peasants to abandon their homes," communists are portrayed as zealous "defenders of the vital interests of peasant masses."[28] Rejecting "the slander that the proletarian revolution gives the peasants nothing and is hostile to them," the communist spokesmen portray the tremendous advantages that the victory of the working class offers to the peasants. They point to the results of communist victories in Russia, Eastern Europe and China to claim that peasants there were helped "to realise their most cherished hopes," the landlords' ownership of land was abolished, the principle the "land belongs to those who till it" was put into effect, and peasants were given possession of millions after millions of hectares of arable land and freed from previous burdens and requisitions.[29]

Since the peasants are meant to be only a junior partner in the worker-peasant alliance, even though they have an overwhelming numerical superiority over the workers in all developing countries of the Third World, communist writers are at pains to justify this obvious iniquity. The main official argument is that, "because of the very conditions of their life, the workers are much better organised than the peasants" and have more experience in fighting the exploiting classes.[30] Since "the colonial peasantry" cannot, because of "its illiteracy and backwardness," take the lead in the national-liberation struggle, the class-conscious workers are expected to "take upon themselves the main brunt of the struggle" and make "the greatest sacrifices."[31] As put quite bluntly in a recent volume on the *Third World*, "the peasantry may be said to be an army that can win only if it is under a competent command, which is generally provided by a different social milieu," i.e., preferably the workers.[32]

A similar view regarding the peasantry of the less developed countries as incapable of assuming political leadership has been advanced in the Soviet journal *International Affairs*. Speaking of Africa, a Soviet author dismisses as erroneous the ideas that the peasants might become "the guiding force of African society," mainly because they "are incapable of elaborating a consistent and truly revolutionary ideology."[33] This attitude seems to be shared by native communists of pro-Soviet leanings. While referring to the peasantry as "the main motive force of the national-liberation revolution and most numerous class of African society," the Sudanese communist quoted earlier in this chapter concedes that the African peasantry "cannot itself exercise political leadership of the revolutionary movement because of its position which is aggravated by the onerous aftermath of colonial rule."[34]

Thus the leading position in the alliance is assigned the working class "not for the sake of any advantage or privileges compared to the peasants," but in order to achieve success in the common struggle. However, to lessen the adverse psychological impact of conferring officially a status of inferiority on their peasant partners, communist spokesmen profess publicly "profound faith in the intelligence of the working peasants," belief in their "creative powers." They accuse "the enemies of socialism" of their "contempt and disdain for the peasantry and their flagrant under-estimation of the common sense and creative abilities inherent in the peasantry as a class."[35]

4. A major lure that communist strategists dangle before the peasantry of the developing nations is the insistence on a radical agrarian reform. Believing that "the failure to solve the agrarian question is one of the most burning social-economic problems of the non-socialist countries of Asia, Africa and Latin America,"[36] and capitalizing on the grossly unjust land distribution existing in much of the Third World, communist propagandists have spared no effort to persuade the land-hungry rural masses of communist determination to set things right. The 1960 *Declaration of Eighty-One Communist Parties* lists the "carrying out of agrarian reforms in the interest of the peasantry" as second only to the consolidation of political independence among "the national democratic tasks" to be accomplished by "the progressive forces" of the countries that have shaken off "the colonial yoke."[37] Such importance is attached to this particular aspect of communist strategy that the urgency of agrarian reforms is reaffirmed twice more in the same document. Similarly, the 1961 *Program of the Soviet Communist Party* stresses in its chapter on the national-liberation movement "the implementation of radical land reforms with the participation of the entire peasantry and in its interests."[38] So do, of course, the *Fundamentals*, the 1969 *Moscow Declaration* and other communist writings.[39]

The emphasis in the communist approach to agrarian reforms in the developing countries is on radicalism. Indeed, the word radical appears virtually as a constant epithet whenever communist spokesmen address themselves to the matter of land distribution. Their radicalism pertains both to the extent of the reform and to the method of carrying it out. As for its extent, communist strategists urge as sweeping an expropriation of agricultural land and as low a maximum permissible private landholding as is politically feasible in the countries concerned. As for the method of the reform, they prefer outright confiscation over expropriation coupled with compensation, particularly of latifundia and other large estates. In this respect the *Fundamentals* supports "the agrarian reforms proposed by the Communist Parties of the Latin American countries" envisaging "the confiscation of lands from landlords who own great estates."[40] However, exceptions may be made for lesser landowners, especially those belonging to groups that constitute the National Democratic Front. For the sake of "democratic unity" and in line with the well-known Leninist stratagem of making temporary concessions to vacillating middle strata at the early stages of the revolution, such landowners may be either provisionally exempted from expropriation or paid some compensation for the land they have surrendered. The *Fundamentals* mentions concessions of this kind in connection with privately owned capitalist industry which may be exempt from nationalization or nationalized only gradually and for a "certain compensation."[41] But Leninist flexibility permits such exceptions in agriculture as well. Indeed, the agrarian reform enacted recently by Velasco's regime of Peru has been warmly commended both by the Soviet and Peruvian communists even though it promises compensation to the owners of the expropriated land.[42]

The communist strategists have three overwhelming reasons for their radicalism in handling the agrarian question in less developed countries. First, they see in the existing system of landownership the worst imaginable kind of exploitation. Consequently, as Marxists-Leninists, they believe that they must take a firm stand for drastic surgery in correcting the evil, and where possible, oppose any form of compensation to former exploiters.

Second, advocating extreme measures against the wealthier segment of the rural population whips up the belligerence of the poorer masses and thus serves to sharpen the class struggle in the countryside. This aggravation of "the internal antagonisms of the peasantry may make it more difficult," as a group of Soviet orientologists says, "to maintain a united front on the fundamental issues of the peasant struggle for land, more favourable terms of lease and hire, against usurer exploitation."[43] At the same time, however, it enables communists to become more popular among the predominant poorer strata and it contributes to a realignment of class forces that the communists consider advantageous for their cause.

Third, communist strategists must be radical in order to discredit the various alternatives proposed by their non-communist opponents. Keenly cognizant of the extent to which the chances of the eventual communist victory would be impaired by agrarian reforms undertaken by "bourgeois-national" governments, they feel compelled to denounce as inadequate or even harmful any redistribution of land for which communists cannot claim credit.[44] In no field, asserts the *Fundamentals,* does the inconsistency of the national bourgeoisie manifest itself so clearly as in the agrarian problem. Here more than anywhere else it makes concessions to the feudal-landlord elements by sacrificing to them the interests of the many millions of the peasants who bore the brunt of colonial oppression."[45] The national bourgeoisie of the developing nations is often accused of giving the landlords "enormous" compensation for land taken from them. While being given some credit for its interest in destroying feudal relations, it is blamed for being "afraid to encroach on the property of the landlords," preferring "to let the landlords retain their large landholding" and only helping them in changing to a capitalist type of enterprise. "Being caught between the powerful class of feudal lords and landowners on the one hand, and the multimillion peasant masses demanding radical agrarian reforms on the other, the national bourgeoisie, as a rule, has tended to compromise with the former at the expense of the peasant interests."[46] Far from solving the land question to the benefit of the working peasantry, the "half-baked reforms" undertaken by the national bourgeoisie merely "modernize the economic role of the landlord in the countryside," "give rise to a strong stratum of peasant entrepreneurs" and tend to enhance the position of the national bourgeoisie.[47] Hence, "only people's power based on alliance of the working class and peasantry is capable of abolishing completely all the survivals of feudalism and of transferring the land to the peasants without compensation."[48]

However, this generally skeptical, and often negative, attitude toward agrarian reforms adopted without communist participation has undergone more recently a notable modification. The "national-democratic" regimes of several countries of the Third

World, such as those of Algeria, the UAR, Peru, and, since
Allende's assumption of the Presidency, Chile, have lately earned
the Communists' commendation for the agrarian reforms they
have embarked upon even though, with the exception of Chile,
the communists themselves could claim no credit for them. The
most interesting of these unusual instances of communist praise
appears to have been that of Peru whose 1969 agrarian reform
elicited highly favorable comments in the Soviet press, including
Pravda itself. Singling out the agrarian reform as the most
important of all the measures adopted by Velasco's military
regime, the author of the *Pravda* article, Alfredo Abarka,
member of the Political Commission of the Central Committee
of the Peruvian Communist Party, lauds the reform for its
"progressive, anti-feudal and anti-imperialist contents."[49] In
particular, he applauds its thrust against the Peruvian
"oligarchy" and the foreign-owned "agrarian-industrial complexes on the coast" and its provisions for the creation of
agricultural cooperatives. Also, he is pleased with the low level of
promised compensation which is to be determined according to
the land value assessments for tax purposes rather than by the
much higher actual market value Hence, "its limited bourgeois-
democratic character notwithstanding," the Peruvian reform is
said to "correspond to the life-long hopes of the Peruvian
peasantry in its struggle for land."[50]

5. In vying for the allegiance of the peasant masses of the less
developed nations communist strategists seek to assure them that
the paramount communist concern is an equitable redistribution
of land among the peasants, not its collectivization. All they
allegedly want to do is to realize their time-honored slogan "the
land belongs to those who till it." Addressing themselves
specifically to Latin America, where the maldistribution of
agricultural land is perhaps worse than anywhere else, they cite
with approval the documents of Latin American Communist
parties declaring that "the democratic state which will be created
in the course of the national-liberation struggle will recognise the
peasants' right to the ownership of land seized by them from the
landlords and will issue them appropriate title deeds."[51] Thus
"the continuous and consistent struggle of the Marxist parties for
turning the land over to those who till it gives the lie to the

bourgeois propaganda that tries to persuade the peasants that the communists want to deprive them of land." On the contrary, "the communists guarantee the peasants not only the retention of the land they own, but also a reasonable increase in the land they farm."

Despite these disclaimers, communist strategists have not abjured agrarian collectivization in the less developed countries. In the same volume from which the above quotations were taken, one reads further that "a division of land alone, a mere transfer of the landed estates to the peasants, does not solve the peasant question and does not deliver the working peasants from poverty, kulak dominance, backwardness and the low productivity of small-scale farming."[52] A solution of these problems can be achieved only through "socialist unification," "cooperative association," "cooperation on a socialist basis," "collective cultivation of land" which alone "can pave the way to a well-to-do life for the peasantry."[53] In lending support to peasant demands communists are cautioned not to "stray into supporting private ownership tendencies within the peasantry."[54]

Perceiving the delicacy of the issue and caught between the divergent postulates of the doctrine and the propaganda, communist strategists apparently have found it necessary to be ambiguous. Lest they confuse their own followers, who presumably believe in the superior virtues of socialized agriculture, they must insist on the collectivization of land as the only way "to improve the life of *all* peasants and to put an end to the exploitation and oppression of man by man."[55] Also, they are quick in praising any steps taken toward agricultural collectivization anywhere in the Third World.[56]

On the other hand, fearing that few Asian, African or Latin American peasants would be lured into the communist fold by a prospect of becoming *kolkhozniki* or *sovkhozniki*, communist statements meant primarily for use in the Third World appeal to the peasants' natural possessive instincts by emphasizing the land-redistribution aspects of communist strategy while minimizing their ulterior collectivization designs. "The nationalization of land would have aroused the discontent and opposition not only of the group of landlords hit by the agrarian reforms, but also of the main mass of the Egyptian peasantry..", asserts a 1965 Soviet book on *The Economy of Africa*, seeking to explain and justify the relatively modest agrarian reform undertaken by Egypt. "It would be shortsighted, to say the least, to carry out an immediate nationalization of land which would lead to conflict with the peasantry who form the overwhelming majority of the population. Making concessions to the age-old aspirations of the fellahin, the government sees its task in gradually and patiently explaining and demonstrating in practice the advantages of the collective form of ownership."[57] Similarly, speaking specifically of tropical Africa, another Soviet study denies the existence of "any acutely felt need for the compulsory redistribution of the stock or land" as "there is a sufficient quantity of unoccupied and undistributed land."[58] It is also interesting to note that Soviet writers have reprimanded "the Maoists" for urging some African countries "to launch out on agricultural collectivization even before the economic and psychological conditions for this are ripe."[59]

Nonetheless, while posing as supporters of individual land distribution among the peasant masses, Soviet strategists do endeavor, in a cautious and subtle manner, to promote the idea of agricultural co-operativism in less developed countries. Soviet propagandists and their East European associates have been distributing propaganda materials depicting the happy life and prosperity of peasants on the cooperative farms of the Soviet Union and communist East Europe. They have been taking dignitaries and farm delegations from developing nations on red carpet tours of carefully selected model farms. They have been sending hand-picked cooperative farm specialists to the less developed countries to make propaganda for, and provide instruction on, cooperative farming in the socialist manner. They have been offering seminars and courses on theoretical and practical aspects of socialist cooperativism specifically designed for students and functionaries from the developing nations.[60] As stated in the official journal of the Czechoslovak Central Council of Cooperatives, courses for cooperative workers of the developing nations have become "the permanent part of the development of international relations."[61]

Yet another favorite communist device employed both to propagate the virtues of socialist cooperativism in the developing nations and to point up the "predatory" agrarian policies of the Western powers and their native associates have been periodic international cooperative conferences organized and backed financially by the communist-controlled *World Federation of Trade Unions*. Convened in turn in various capitals of communist countries and attended by carefully selected delegations and observers from developing countries, such conferences have invariably resulted in fiery resolutions blaming the ex-colonialists and the "neo-colonialists" for all the agrarian and other economic ills encountered by the emerging nations and exhorting peasants and agricultural and plantation workers, "the most oppressed strata of the capitalist world," to step up their struggle for socialism.[62]

6. As ardent believers in the importance of "the organizational weapon," communist strategists have always placed great emphasis on the necessity to organize rural masses. Having determined that he could not win without peasant support, Lenin called in *Two Tactics of Social-Democracy in the Democratic Revolution* for an "immediate organization of revolutionary peasant committees."[63] After the revolution of 1905 was defeated he blamed the failure in part on the peasants' actions being "too unorganized."[64] He again dwelled upon the need to organize the rural masses when he drew the *Theses on the Agrarian Question* in 1920.[65] In drafting its *Thesis on the Revolutionary Movement in the Colonies and Semi-Colonies* in 1928, the Comintern urged in the organization of "revolutionary peasant unions and peasant committees."[66]

More than four decades later, the organization of the rural masses of Asia, Africa and Latin America is still a major endeavor of communist strategy, an endeavor that has become, in communist view, even more urgent as feudal survivals gradually give way to rural capitalism. "In these circumstances," writes a group of Soviet orientologists, "the problem of political organization of the rural proletarians and semi-proletarians, the main force of the peasant movement, is highly important."[67] Discussing the role of the peasant movement in Asia, a Soviet analyst considers "the creation of democratic peasant organizations and the strengthening of them where they exist" as "one of the primary tasks of the progressive movement."[68] He adds that the "enormous responsibility for strengthening the union of the working class and the peasantry rests upon the vanguard of the proletariat, the communist parties."

Hence, communist organizers have been striving hard to organize and unionize rural masses of the Third World, to infiltrate and control from within peasant groups already in existence, to discredit those unwilling to cooperate, and to create new ones under overt or covert communist guidance. In areas where communist-controlled urban labor unions are already in existence, it becomes one of their important functions, as it had been in Russia and Eastern Europe, to help to establish local peasant unions and act as their patrons. Wherever feasible, such grass roots operations are expected to facilitate communist infiltration of the peasant movement and offer a better chance of communist control over worker-peasant alliance built "from below" than does a formation of such an alliance "from above" through political agreement with leading organs of peasant organizations already established.[69]

These strenuous communist efforts have led to the establishment of communist-controlled or communist-influenced peasant groups in some of the developing countries, especially in Latin America. Such have been, to cite several typical examples:

the *Ranquil Peasant Confederation of Chile* [70] and

the *Chilean Federation of Peasants and Indians* affiliated with the communist-controlled *Trade Union Center of Working People;*[71]

the *National Peasant Council* of Chile set up by Allende's regime in December 1970 to help in carrying out the agrarian reform;

the *Confederation of Peruvian Peasants* which, in the words of a Latin American communist, "became the center of the struggle of the colons, tenant farmers, share croppers and members of peasant communities against the Latifundists";[72]

The *National Agrarian Federation of Uruguay;*[73]

The *Independent Peasant Confederation* (Confederacion Campesina Independiente) of Mexico, created in 1963 and seized by a pro-Peking faction in 1964;[74]

the *Confederation of Agricultural Workers of Brazil;*

National Peasants' Federation of Ecuador, organized in 1967 by the communist-controlled *Confederation of Ecuadorean Workers*;

  United Rural Producers' League in Argentina;[75]

two communist-influenced peasant unions organized in Costa Rica with the help of the Costa-Rican Communist party;[76]

  the *Confederation of Peasants and Agricultural Workers* of Nicaragua and the *National Peasant Federation* of Honduras, (both of them meanwhile disbanded);[77]

  the *All-India Kisan Sabba* (a peasant front) led by the pro-Peking Communist Party of India and the *Independent Peasant Central* organized by the pro-Soviet Communist Party of India in 1963 whose members were subsequently expelled from the Central.

Despite the number of organizations and efforts expended, virtually all of the communist-organized or communist-controlled peasant groupings of the Third World are small, loosely organized, and rather ineffective. The only exception seems to be Chile where the Chilean Communist party has been engaged in attempts to organize peasant unions for many years and has registered some gains. In May 1961 it was instrumental in bringing about the First National Campesino Congress held under the auspices of the communist-led *Popular Action Front* (FRAP) and the communist-controlled *United Workers Central.*[78] Communist activities among Chilean peasants registered a further increase after the 1970 electoral victory of the Popular Unity Front. In particular, communist organizers unfolded an ambitious campaign aimed at creating a network of communist-influenced peasant councils throughout rural Chile.

7. Finally, communist strategy-makers seek to capitalize on the peasantry's ethnic and racial differentiations and dissensions. It seems that communists consider the peasant masses of the Third World to have become an especially promising target for this sort of approach. In a number of developing countries of Asia, Africa and Latin America the poorest, the most under-privileged and the most exploited rural strata may often be found among groups ethnically or racially different from the ruling circles. The Kurds of Iraq, the Afro-Shirazis of Zanzibar (prior to the overthrow of the Arab ruling circles), and the Indians of several countries of Latin America are only a few examples. This

being so, it is consistent with the communist *Weltanschauung* to view such underdog ethnic and racial groups as specific targets of communist appeals. Efforts in this direction have been particularly evident in Latin America where a very substantial portion of the peasantry, and certainly the poorest one, consists of Indians, many of whom are illiterate and often speak only their native Indian dialect. According to communist claims, "Indians form the bulwark of the peasant struggle against the latifundists and are also proponents of cooperative forms of tilling the soil."[79]

Factors Impeding Communist Endeavors

As mentioned above, a number of conditions exist in many parts of the Third World that seem to make the peasant masses of those areas vulnerable to communist enticements and maneuvers. On the other hand, there are a number of factors operating against communist interests.

1. A primary obstacle to establishing a viable worker-peasant alliance has been the difficulty in getting peasants properly organized. This had caused concern to Lenin who found peasants "hardest to move" of all the segments of the population and spoke of "the enormous difficulty" in organizing them.[80] The Comintern met with the same predicament and its endeavor to improve matters by establishing a *Peasant International* in 1923, on the assumption that a separate peasant organization would be more effective, proved to be a failure.

Contemporary communist strategists encounter similar difficulties. Scattered throughout the countryside with a woefully inadequate transportation and communications system and living often in remote areas far away from centers of commerce and industry, most peasants·of the Third World are far less accessible than urban dwellers. Their geographical isolation from the mainstream of political life, coupled with the traditionalist way of life, patriarchalism, religious belief, instinctive distrust of outsiders and widespread illiteracy make the work of communist (or any other) organizers extremely difficult. This failure of communist efforts to organize the Third World's peasantry has been duly noted in many western studies of developing nations.[81]

Communist analysts seem to agree. "...The peasantry, with all its tremendous revolutionary potentialities, has yet to awaken in most of the new nations to active political life," laments G. Mirskii. "Practically no third world country has a strong and organized revolutionary movement and the proletarian-peasant alliance is as yet more of a slogan than a reality."[82] While describing the peasantry of Asia and Africa as a "mighty revolutionary force" in his speech at the 1969 International Conference of Communist and Workers' Parties, Brezhnev characterized it as "an elementary force (*stikhiinaia sila*), with all the wavering stemming from this fact, with all the contradictions in ideology and politics...."[83]

The lack of success of their work among the peasants is conceded also by the communists of the Third World. "In some cases the Communist parties have underestimated work in the countryside, and this has undoubtedly impeded the enlistment of the peasants in revolutionary struggle," confesses a Latin American communist. "If the Communists worked more vigorously and systematically among the peasants they would hasten the evolution of this class from a reserve for reaction or reformism into a revolutionary force capable, together with the proletariat and under its leadership, of leading the other exploited classes to the conquest of power."[84] Writing in the November 1971 issue of the *World Marxist Review*, L. Padilla, member of the Central Committee of the Communist party of Bolivia, complained that, despite the facilities gained under the regime of General Torres, "peasant participation in the activities of the [communist-controlled] Labor Center was limited" and "only a small proportion of the peasants adopted Marxist-Leninist ideas."[85] The political resolution adopted by the Ninth Congress of the Communist party of India in October 1971 called for "urgent and effective measures to overcome the weaknesses of the peasant movement which is one of the most serious failures of the democratic movement in the country today."[86] Perhaps nowhere has the weakness of the communist hold over the peasantry been illustrated more dramatically and more convincingly than in Indonesia. As late as January 17, 1965, the leader of Indonesia's communists, Aidit, boasted publicly that "ten million organized peasants are ready to take up arms."[87] But those ten million peasant supporters failed to materialize when the Party needed them in its attempted coup.

Conditions, however, have been changing lately to communist advantage in this respect. The advancement of technology is slowly but continually loosening the barriers of geographical isolation in many countries of the Third World, exposing more and more areas to modern influences. This not only affords communist organizers an easier physical access to the rural masses, but also makes the masses temporarily more susceptible to communist appeals. Demagogy and extremism have their best chances at times of transition when traditional attitudes and values have begun to recede, but before new patterns and attitudes have taken roots. Moreover, lured by exaggerated hopes of a better life in the cities, poor peasants of Latin America, Asia and some parts of Africa have been moving in recent years from rural areas to the already congested metropolitan complexes. Unable to find adequately paying jobs or to afford decent accommodation, they settle in squalid shantytowns on the outskirts. While their living conditions may not be worse than what they have left behind in the countryside, the sharp contrast between their own misery and the glamor of high city life they can daily observe deepens their sense of injustice. Compressed into huge ghettoes many such one-time peasants come, physically as well as psychologically, within a much easier reach of communist agitators than they had ever been back in their rural village shacks, becoming thus "the inflammable material" of the revolution.[88]

2. Another factor making communist work among the peasants more difficult is the peasant attachment to religion. Though this is by no means an exclusive trait of the peasantry alone, rural people are usually more religious than urban dwellers. In this sense, when dealing with the peasants, communist strategists must take religion more fully into account than in their handling of other classes or population strata. That is especially so in the developing countries where the peasantry constitutes by far the largest segment of the population and continues to be strongly influenced by religious beliefs, whether it be Christianity, Islam, Buddhism, or some other. "In the liberated countries, where the religious factor is an important aspect of the real existing

situation," writes a prominent Soviet specialist in the affairs of the Third World, "it would be adventurism to ignore it. Opposing the practice of religious rites in these conditions means insulting the religious feeling of believers, completely isolating oneself from the masses and discrediting the ideas of social liberation."[89] As pointed out by R. Ulyanovsky in a 1971 article in *International Affairs*, "...in the specific conditions prevailing in the developing countries, the proclamation of a struggle against religious philosophy would inevitably doom any political force seeking the trust of the middle strata, the urban population and the peasant masses."[90]

Faced with such a dilemma, communist strategists have been forced to temporize. On the one hand, they try to avoid hurting the peasants' religious feelings. Anti-religious bias is meticulously excluded from statements and materials directed toward the general public of the Third World. Anyone asserting that no genuine religious freedom exists in communist countries is dismissed as a malicious slanderer or a victim of imperialist propaganda. Native religious leaders deemed favorably inclined toward the Soviet Bloc countries, or at least potentially so, are occasionally invited to the Soviet Union and to the communist countries of Eastern Europe and given the opportunity to talk to carefully selected religious dignitaries and to visit the best-preserved places of worship. Soviet and East European church delegations are sent on goodwill missions to various developing countries and a few Soviet Moslems are regularly allowed to undertake pilgrimages to Mecca and other holy places of Islam. Among the dignitaries welcoming the Pope during his 1970 visit to Ceylon was also the Ceylonese Communist party chief, Pieter Keuneman.

On the other hand, communist analyses of religious and church relations in the Third World directed primarily to Marxist audiences point to religion and church as bulwark of reaction and one of the chief impediments to communist success. They consider religious "obscurantism" and "prejudices" as the primary cause of peasants' ignorance and backwardness and a major factor retarding "the maturing of class consciousness."[91] They view all major churches and sects, whatever their denomination, as foes of communism and tools of imperialism.[92] In particular, communist strategists concentrate their denunciations on those religions, churches and sects that are linked to the Western world and which therefore can more easily be labeled as "stooges" of Western imperialism. Foremost among their targets has traditionally been the Catholic Church which is deemed most dangerous of all, mainly because of its highly efficient world-wide organization, its militancy, its dominant position in Latin America and substantial penetration into Africa.

In an effort to cover up the discrepancy between their own fundamental hostility to religion and the necessity to avoid antagonizing the predominantly God-loving peasant masses of the developing nations, communist policy-makers fall back on stratagems employed in their own countries. Even though communists themselves do not believe in God, the standard communist argument goes, they recognize and respect religious convictions of others. What they are against, they assert, is not an honestly held belief in God, but religious obscurantism and clericalism, i.e., misuse of religion for political purposes, for keeping the masses in ignorance and prejudice, for opposing social progress and especially for the perpetuation of exploitation of man by man, such as church support of rich landholders against poor peasants and the church's alleged support for imperialism, colonialism and neo-colonialism.

In particular, communist propagandists differentiate between the church hierarchy composed allegedly of despotic bishops, aided and abetted by their reactionary clergy and, on the other side, ordinary God-fearing parishioners, mostly poor and small peasants, with an occasional smattering of "progressive" or "patriotic" priests who have remained "loyal to the people" in spite of harassment by their anti-people church superiors. In this fashion communist strategists seek to drive a wedge between the believers of the less developed countries and their religious leaders, while dissimulating their commitment to the ultimate destruction of religion and pretending that what is at stake is not religious freedom, but an elementary requirement of political, economic and social justice.

As church hierarchies in some areas of the Third World, particularly in Latin America, have traditionally supported the *status quo* favoring vested land interests against the broad peasant masses, these communist allegations have carried with them a certain measure of credibility. However, due to changing church attitudes, this is becoming less true today than formerly. For some years the church and the clergy of the developing countries have become much more concerned with social issues, and in many instances have even thrown their support behind land reform programs and other postulates of social justice for the poor and underprivileged. This changing image of the church is of special significance primarily in Latin America where Catholicism had long figured among impediments to social progress. Thus the standard communist anti-church cliches are likely to become gradually more and more obsolete and their utilization in communist strategy vis-a-vis the peasant masses less effective.

Aware of this, communist spokesmen, Soviet and other, have recently begun to tone down the atheist element in communist doctrine and to call for a "creative dialogue" that would pave the way for a measure of cooperation between the communists and religious believers.[93] Soviet writers have been citing with approval statements made by the Third World's communists warning that "the building of socialism would be endangered" if it appeared in the eyes of the people as an enemy of religion. Some of them have even cautioned against "militant anti-clericalism" which "would inevitably separate the believing and the non-believing supporters of socialism, to the profit and satisfaction of its enemies."[94] All the same, communist strategists are fully aware of the magnitude of their problem in this respect. "Overcoming the religious beliefs of the working masses," write the authors of a recent Soviet volume on *The Political Parties of Africa*, "is a very complex task. It is not a matter of years but of decades."[95]

3. Yet another dilemma lies in the difficulty of convincing the peasants that the communists are their natural allies and that the fulfillment of peasant aspirations is best served by giving support to the communist cause. To be sure, both the communists and the peasant masses of the developing nations are in agreement on one of the major tasks prescribed by the communist scenarios for the national-democratic state of the revolution, namely, the liquidation of big estates and an equitable redistribution of land among

those who till it. However, once this is attained, the identity of communist and peasant interests comes to an abrupt end. The communists view such a redistribution of land merely as an initial stage of a process leading ultimately to agricultural collectivization. The overwhelming majority of the peasants, having at long last gained possession of the land, want to keep it permanently for themselves and are unwilling to accept voluntarily any collectivization scheme, no matter how glamorized it might be by its communist promoters. That has been the case in all the countries that have already succumbed to communism and in which collectivization had to be brought about through coercion rather than voluntary acceptance by the peasantry. There is no reason to think that the bulk of the peasantry in the developing countries would behave differently. A dramatic illustration of the communist failure to gain the confidence of the peasants has been provided by Che Guevara's abortive attempt to foment a revolutionary uprising in Bolivia. As bared by his diary, the Bolivian peasants refused to cooperate, and even reported the presence of Guevara's band to the authorities. "The mass of peasants," reads one of Guevara's entries, "does not help us at all and has become informers."[96]

The anti-communist attitudes of the Bolivian peasantry came to the fore again in 1971 when some 2,000 *campesinos* invaded the city of Santa Cruz, threw the mayor out of office and demanded the resignation of several members of General Torres's cabinet to prevent what they believed were communist attempts to take over the government. [97] Nor do the Chilean peasants appear to be in favor of a collective cultivation of the land involved in Allende's agrarian reform. As reports from Chile indicate, peasants would rather subdivide the land among themselves than work as "salaried employees" of the envisaged "agrarian reform centers."[98]

Consequently, the communist chances of persuading the peasant masses of Asia, Africa and Latin America of the identity of peasant and communist interests can at best be only short-lived. While communist agitators might occasionally manage, as Lenin had ordained, "to give the peasant movement the most revolutionary character"[99] at the initial phase of the national-democratic revolution, the peasants' revolutionary elan is likely to yield quickly to "petty-bourgeois" ideas once their worst hunger for land has been satisfied. How soon this happens, will depend primarily on the extent of the land redistribution, the speed with which it is carried out, and on the degree to which non-communists may be credited with its accomplishment. Wherever agrarian reforms are carried out without undue delays, with substantial help from non-communist quarters and result in such an apportionment of land as to provide the *bona fide* peasants with enough land and tools to assure those of them willing to work hard a modest existence or at least some improvement over the previous state of affairs, communist efforts to entice the peasants will have been dealt a serious blow.

4. Communist operations among the rural population suffer also from the dearth of peasants in the membership of the Communist parties in the developing areas. Although even approximate figures are hard to come by, estimates made both by Western students of communist affairs and occasionally by communist spokesmen indicate that the number of peasants in Communist parties of non-communist Asia, Africa and Latin America is negligible. "Peasants still account for only an insignificant minority in Latin American communist movements," writes a Western observer of communism in Latin America.[100] Since the Latin American communist parties have been based "solely on the urban working class," laments a prominent Latin American communist, "the important role which...the agricultural laborers can play in the countries concerned was not fully appreciated."[101] He complains that "this section of the working class was often classified as part of the peasantry and its role was reduced to that of an ally of the working class," implying thus that the Latin American communists have been rather remiss in recruiting the rural proletariat of Latin America. Finding fault somewhat along the same lines with the once huge Communist party of Indonesia, an Indonesian communist writer urged his Party "to integrate itself with the peasants". He referred to such an integration as "a fundamental task today of the revolutionary movement against imperialism...."[102] In the same vein, as mentioned in Chapter VI, an authoritative statement prepared by a group of staff members of the Institute of Asian Peoples under the Soviet

Academy of Sciences strongly urged the Asian Communist parties to pay more attention to "the problem of political organization of the rural proletarians and semi-proletarians, the main force of the peasant movement.[103] If the above criticisms are applicable to Latin America and Asia where Communist parties have existed for several decades, they are not less valid for Africa where the native communist movement is of a more recent origin.

This scarcity of peasants in Communist party ranks results in a serious handicap for communist agitation in rural areas. Habitually country folk are rather diffident of city people. A typical peasant would prefer to listen to a fellow peasant rather than to a stranger from the city. Hence, the low level of peasant membership in the Communist parties, itself a consequence of the lack of communist appeal for the peasantry, tends in its turn to undercut even more the efficacy of communist campaigning in rural areas of the developing nations.

5. Yet another obstacle impeding the communist wooing of peasant masses in Africa and, to a somewhat lesser extent, Asia is communalism. Essentially a form of primitive agrarian cooperativism and collective tribal or extended-family landholding, communalism is less vulnerable to the standard communist attacks than feudalism or capitalism. Being of indigenous origin, it cannot be denounced very convincingly as a "vicious by-product" of colonialism and imperialism. Nor is communalism suited to the application of the favorite communist bipolar class analysis, as it is hardly conducive to the emergence of the two antagonistic classes of exploiters and exploited pitted against each other in a merciless life-and-death class struggle in traditional Marxist-Leninist meaning of the term. Rather, it nurtures precisely those "harmful illusions" of class and social harmony which communist strategists decry and detest. Moreover, the strong tribal and family loyalties and patriarchal authoritarianism inherent in the communal pattern tend to strengthen social cohesiveness and thus hamper the penetration of extraneous influences. Speaking of "tribal, communal relations" as a specific feature of Africa, Alexander Sobolev finds that "most of the people did not experience hunger and exploitation was mainly practised by non-economic methods."[104]

In spite of all this, succumbing to an initial flush of optimism triggered by the quick collapse of colonialism in Africa in the late fifties and early sixties, Soviet Africanists seem to have at first developed a rather sanguine view of communalism. "Under certain conditions the village commune can become the starting point for the non-capitalist development of a country and for the construction of socialism," argued I. I. Potekhin in 1960.[105] Drawing a rather questionable parallel between the peasant *obshchina* of 19th-century Russia and the village commune of 20th-century tropical Africa, the late dean of Soviet Africanists believed that the prevalence of agrarian communalism in Africa could facilitate the transition to "scientific socialism."[106] Similar ideas have been expressed in the early sixties by other Soviet students of African affairs. Noting certain "positive" factors characteristic of the African communes, such as "the habits of collectivism in work," "the popular custom of mutual aid," and "communal outlook toward life," they have concluded that communalism offers the rural population "a possibility of moving comparatively painlessly on the rails of cooperation" and a chance of "bypassing the agonizing capitalist stage and moving from communal-tribal organization directly to organization of a socialist type."[107] One Soviet writer has even spelled out at some detail the progressive stages through which the process of transition might move, beginning with a modest collective utilization of the simplest agricultural techniques and ending with a fully collectivized agriculture.[108]

However, the growing disappointment with the evident lack of response to communist wooing among the peasantry of the Third World has led recently to a notable cooling-off in the Soviet attitude toward the "peasant communes," both African and Asian. Thus the previously mentioned 1965 Soviet volume on *The Independent Countries of Africa: Economic and Social Problems* has this to say about the communal system of Africa: "In spite of the special features of patriarchal 'democracy' (*demokratizm*), the African commune not only does not prevent, but on the contrary fosters the development of feudal relations, serving as a kind of nutrient medium for them. The tribal and aristocratic upper crust, sheltering behind ancient customs and traditions, has wide opportunities for exploiting the tribesmen of

the commune, and enriching itself at their expense." Without
discarding altogether the remote chance that communal landholding might "under certain conditions" facilitate the formation
of cooperatives, the author does not strike a very hopeful note
when he says: "It is quite clear that the land commune has
outlived its function and acts as a brake on the progress of the
African countryside."[109] Writing in the *New Times*, another
Soviet writer advises that it is time to "discard certain fairly
widespread illusions about the African commune."[110] Asian
communalism seems to fare no better. Taking Asian peasants to
task for "clinging tenaciously" to "communal survivals often
resulting in weird illusions concerning eternal equality, broth-
erhood and justice, coupled with a narrow outlook and group
egoism," yet another Soviet analyst cautions that these "negative
aspects of peasant psychology" and notions of "empirical
'peasant socialism'" might be used by "reactionary and political
adventurers."[111]

6. Finally, the communist cause among the Third World's
peasants has been damaged by the controversy about the
peasantry's role that has arisen between the Soviet and pro-
Soviet communists on one hand, and the Chinese and pro-
Chinese communists as well as Castroites on the other. As has
already been mentioned in Chapter II, Mao Tse-Tung and the
Chinese communists tend to lean upon the peasant elements
much more than do the Soviet strategy-planners. The "poor
peasants" are "the biggest motive force of the Chinese revolution" and "the main contingent of China's revolutionary forces,"
wrote Mao and his associates in 1939 in their jointly written
textbook *The Chinese Revolution and the Chinese Communist
Party*.[112] Applying their own revolutionary experience from
China to the predominantly peasant countries of Africa, Latin
America and non-communist Asia, the Chinese communist
leaders count primarily upon the poor peasant masses and the
vast rural areas of the Third World to play a decisive role in their
revolutionary schemes.[113] "It must be emphasized," held Lin
Piao, Mao's one-time heir apparent, "that Comrade Mao Tse-
Tung's theory of the establishment of rural revolutionary base
areas and the encirclement of the cities from the countryside is of
outstanding and universal practical importance for the present

revolutionary struggles of all the oppressed nations and peoples and particularly for the revolutionary struggles of the oppressed nations and peoples in Asia, Africa, and Latin America against imperialism and its lackeys...."[114] Similarly, Castro has been quite critical of the Third World's pro-Soviet communists, especially those of Latin America, for their "underestimation of the peasantry as a revolutionary force."[115] Evidently, the Chinese communists and the Castroites seem to share to some extent the attitude advanced by the well-known communist writer Frantz Fanin who held that in colonial countries "the peasants alone are revolutionary" while the working class has been "most pampered by the colonial regime" and is therefore incapable of playing a major role in the revolution.[116]

As mentioned earlier, Soviet strategists and their associates among the communists of the Third World disagree with the Chinese over-reliance on the peasantry of the Third World. They reject the cherished Chinese concept pitting against one another the developing countries as "the world village" and the economically advanced countries as "the world city." They accuse the Chinese communists of exploiting "the political immaturity of the peasant masses" for the purpose of establishing the Chinese hegemony over the Third World.[117]

The sino-Soviet disagreement is also reflected in the respective Chinese and Soviet stands on the all-important issue of revolutionary leadership. Even though they are formally committed to the principle of proletarian leadership, the Chinese communists seem nonetheless to be willing to concede the leadership of the national-democratic revolution to the "revolutionary" peasantry. Moreover, as pointed out in Chapter V, the Chinese notion of the proletarian comprises primarily rural proletarians so that, to the Chinese, the leadership of the proletariat is virtually tantamount to the leadership of the poorest peasant strata rather than the urban working class. On the other hand, while considering the leadership by the working class no longer indispensable during the early stages of the national-democratic revolution, Soviet strategists and the Soviet-oriented communists of the Third World are not prepared to give away the leading role to such a backward class as the peasantry. "All the talk about the leading and vanguard role of the peasantry in the socialist revolution, in the fight for socialism, is not only wrong," asserts the veteran pro-Soviet Arab communist leader Khaled Bagdash, "it reflects a class attitude which officially declares for socialism, but in practice strives toward something else that is not socialism."[118] If some concessions are inevitable, the Soviet strategists prefer, as explained in Chapter IX, to concede a temporary leadership to "revolutionary democrats," the socialist-inclined "progressive" segment of the national bourgeoisie.

Thus the communist effort to utilize the Third World's peasantry so far have met with only meager results. It seems, as a Soviet analyst has pointed out, that "the work of communist parties in winning the peasantry to their side is exceptionally complex and it is the most difficult area of all their activity."[119]

Notes for Chapter VII

[1] *Selected Works,* London, 1936, III, p. 86.

[2] *Polnoe Sobranie* (complete collection), *Sochineniia,* Vol. 45, p. 58.

[3] Leninism and Our Age," *World Marxist Review,* 12, 5, 1969, pp. 3-17.

[4] *Selected Works,* X., p. 236.

[5] pp. 44 and 22.

[6] *Jacobs,* p. 32.

[7] *Ritvo,* p. 87.

[8] pp. 382 and 397.

[9] P. Anen'iev, *"Krest'ianskoe dvizhenie v stranakh Azii,"* (The Peasant Movement in the Countries of Asia), *Politicheskoe samoobrazovanie,* No. 12, 1965, pp. 57 ff.

[10] F. Burlatskii, *"Osvoboditel'noe dvizhenie i i nauchnyi sotsializm,"* (The Liberation Movement and Scientific Socialism), *Pravda,* August 15, 1965, pp. 3-4.

[11] *op. cit.,* pp. 20 ff.

[12] *Pravda,* June 8, 1969.

[13] *op. cit.* See also A. Kurylev, *"Leninskii soiuz rabochego klassa i krestianstva,"* (Leninist Union of the Working Class and the Peasantry) *Pravda,* November 21, 1969.

[14] Osman Babiker, "Anti-Imperialist Unity — An Imperative of Our Time," *World Marxist Review,* 9, 8, 1966, pp. 23 ff.

[15] Yu Potemkin, *"Alzhirskaia revoliutsia: sversheniia i perspektivy"* (The Algerian Revolution: Achievements and Prospects), *MEIMO,* 10, 1964, pp. 26 ff.; Tunji Otegbeye, "Leninism and the African Revolution," *World Marxist Review,* 13, 8, 1970, pp. 78 ff.

[16] See, for instance, Tropkin, *Ob osnovakh ...;* "Agrarian Question in Developing Countries of Asia," *World Marxist Review,* 8, 9, 1965, pp. 38 ff.; R. A. Ul'ianovskii, "Agrarian Reform in the Countries of the Near and Middle East," *Narody Azii i Afriki,* No. 7, 1961, cited in Thornton, *op. cit.,* pp. 189 ff.;

P. Anen'iev, *op. cit.; Agrarno-krest'ianskii vopros na sovremennom etape natsional'-no osvoboditel'nogo dvizheniia v stranakh Azii, i Afriki, i Latinskoi Ameriki* (The Agrarian and Peasant Question at the Contemporary Stage of the National Liberation Movement in Countries of Asia, Africa and Latin America), Moscow, 1965, *Agrarnyi vopros i natsional'no-osvoboditel'noic dvizhenie* (The Agrarian Question and the National Liberation Movement) Moscow, 1962; *Agrarno-krest'ianskii vopros v stranakh Yugovostochnoi Azii (The Agrarian and Peasant Question in Countries of Southeastern Asia),* Moscow, 1963; A. M. Sivovolov, *Ekonomicheskie problemy soiuza rabochego klassa i krest'ianstva v Latinskoi Amerike* (Economic Problems of the Union of the Working Class and the Peasantry in Latin America), Moscow, 1963.

[17] G. Mirskii, "The Proletariat and National Liberation," *New Times,* No. 18, 1964, p. 8.

[18] *The Preliminary Draft of Theses on the Agrarian Question. Alliance of the Working Class and the Peasantry,* Moscow, 1959, pp. 342 ff.

[19] *Ibid.*

[20] pp. 383-4.

[21] *Fundamentals,* p. 386; Anen'iev, *op. cit.; Agrarno-krest'ianskii vopros* ....

[22] "Agrarian Question in Developing Countries of Asia," *op. cit.*

[23] Vladimir Lukin, "Some Aspects of Class Structure in South and Southeast Asia," *World Marxist Review,* 9, 11, 1966, pp. 47 ff.

[24] Anen'iev, *op. cit.;* "Agrarian Question in Developing Countries of Asia," *op. cit.; Agrarno-krest'ianskii vopros....*

[25] *Fundamentals,* p. 383.

[26] *Ibid.,* pp. 382, 383 and 385. See also Kurylev., *op. cit.*

[27] "Latin America: Liberation Struggle and the Working Class," *World Marxist Review,* 14, 7, 1971, pp. 72 ff. See also Ulyanovsky, "Leninism ..." *op. cit.*

[28] *Fundamentals,* pp. 383 and 387.

[29] *Ibid.,* pp. 391 ff.

[30] *Ibid.,* p. 385.

[31] *Ibid.,* p. 385.

[32] *Third World,* pp. 38-40.

[33] Y. Kashin, "Are There Classes in Black Africa?" *International Affairs,* No. 4, 1965, pp. 108-9.

[34] Osman Babiker, *op. cit.,* p. 24.

[35] *Fundamentals,* p. 393.

[36] Review of the book *Lenin o druzhbe s narodami vostoka* in *Kommunist,* No. 1, 1962, pp. 117 ff.

[37] *Jacobs,* p. 32.

[38] *Ritvo,* p. 85.

[39] See, for instance, Tropkin, *Ob osnovakh ...,* R.A. Ul'ianovskii, *op. cit.* in Thornton, *"Agrarnye reformy v stranakh blizhnego i srednego vostoka, Indii i Yugo-vostochnoi Azii"* (Agrarian Reforms in the Countries of the Near and Middle East, India and Southeast Asia), *Narody Azii i Afriki,* No. 2, 1961, pp. 14-30; Nikolai Paklin, "Algeria on the Eve of Agrarian Reform," *New Times,* No. 42, 1966, pp. 14 ff; E. Kovalyov, "Latin America: Agrarian Problems and the Liberation Struggle," *International Affairs,* No. 11, 1971, pp. 44 ff.

[40] *Fundamentals,* p. 390.

[41] *Ibid.,* p. 379.

[42] See, for instance, Juan Cobo, "Agrarian Reform in Peru," *New Times,*

No. 27, 1969, p. 18, and Alfredo Abarka, *"Peru: Glubokie peremeny"* (Peru: Deep Changes), *Pravda,* September 13, 1969, p. 4.

[43]"Agrarian Question . . . ," *op. cit.*

[44]Karl Schmitt considers the Mexican agrarian reform to have been one of the factors accounting for the failure of communist efforts among the Mexican peasants. See his *Communism in Mexico,* p. 223. In the above-mentioned article on Latin America's agrarian problems Kovalyov also cites Mexico as an example of how the bourgeoisie succeeded "in turning land reform onto the path of capitalist reconstruction of agriculture."

[45]*Fundamentals,* pp. 420-21.

[46]Anen'iev, *op. cit.*

[47]R. A. Ul'ianovskii, "Agrarian Reform . . . ," Thornton, *op. cit.,* pp. 189 ff; also *Agrarno-krest'ianskii vopros.* . . .

[48]*Fundamentals,* p. 386.

[49]Alfredo Abarka, *op. cit.,* also Juan Cobo, *op. cit.,* and Kovalyov, *op. cit.*

[50]Abarka, *op. cit.* See also V. Listov, *"Reforma idet vpered"* (The Reform Moves Forward), *Pravda,* June 24, 1970.

[51]*Fundamentals,* pp. 390-91.

[52]*Ibid.,* p. 392.

[53]*Ibid.*

[54]Anen'iev, *op. cit.*

[55]*Fundamentals,* p. 392.

[56]See, for instance, Juan Cobo, *op. cit.;* Michail Pankin, "The USSR and the Developing Countries: Experience of Economic Cooperatives," *World Marxist Review,* 9, 5, 1966, pp. 68 ff.

[57]L. Goncharov, ed., *Ekonomika Afriki* (Africa's Economy), Moscow, 1965. The reference is cited from "The UAR and the 'Proletarian Dictatorship;'" *Mizan,* 8, 2, 1966, pp. 67 ff.

[58]I. I. Gavrilov, ed., *Nezavisimye Strany Afriki: Ekonomicheskie i Sotsialnye Problemy* (The Independent Countries of Africa: Economic and Social Problems), Moscow, 1965. Quotation taken from an extensive review of the book in *Mizan,* 7, 9, 1966, pp. 1 ff.

[59]V. Shelepin, "Maoist Intrigues in the Third World," *New Times,* No. 26, 1969, pp. 6-8.

[60]See, for instance, Vladimír Cihla in *Družstevník,* No. 23, November 16, 1964; *Rudé právo,* March 12, 1966, reporting on the Czechoslovak-Tunisian agreement on cooperation in the cooperative field. A group of Soviet experts visited Brazzaville in the summer of 1966 to discuss Soviet aid for agricultural training schools, according to Radio Moscow, July 6, 1966. An international seminar on agrarian cooperativism was held in Warsaw in September 1966 and was attended by delegates of thirteen countries of Asia and Africa. See *Sztandar Mlodykh* (Warsaw), September 30, 1966. Students from a number of countries of Africa, Asia, and the Middle East have been reported year after year by communist press and radio as studying the organization and methods of cooperative agriculture in various countries of communist East Europe.

[61]Vladimír Cihla, *op. cit.*

[62]See, for instance, *Zemědělské noviny,* September 29, 1962.

[63]*Sochineniia,* Moscow, 1935, VIII, p. 88.

[64]*Ibid.,* XIV, p. 354.

[65]V. L. Lenin, *Alliance of Working Class and Peasantry,* Moscow, 1959.

[66]p. 44.

67 "Agrarian Question in Developing Countries of Asia," *op. cit.*, pp. 38 ff.

68 Anen'iev, *op. cit.*

69 For samples of communist efforts see, for instance, Cesar Levano, "Lessons of the Guerrilla Struggle in Peru," *World Marxist Review,* 9, 9, 1966, pp. 45 ff.; Orlando Millas, "New Conditions of Ideological Struggle of Communists and Catholics," *ibid.,* 9, 5, 1966, pp. 75 ff.; Samuel Mendoza, *"Actividades del Comunismo en Chile en 1962"* (Communist Activities in Chile in 1962), *Estudios Sobre El Comunismo,* No. 39, 1963; Salvador de Madariaga, *Latin America Between the Eagle and the Bear,* New York, 1962, pp. 160 ff.; Rodney Arismendi's article *"Bo'rba za massy"* (Struggle for the Masses), *Pravda,* February 17, 1967; Luis Sanchez, "Nicaraguan Communists in the Van of the Liberation Movement," *World Marxist Review,* 11, 2, 1968, pp. 30 ff.

70 However, according to the statement of a Chilean communist representative at a 1972 seminar the Ranquil organization "has ceased to exist." "Latin America: the Ideological Struggle," *World Marxist Review,* 15, 4, pp. 45 ff.

71 Orlando Millas, *op. cit.* See also *"Reforma agraria y huelgas campesinas en Chile,"* (The Agrarian Reform and Peasant Strikes in Chile), *Este y Oeste,* April 1967, listing a 3-thousand strong *Federacion Campesina* affiliated with the communist-controlled *Central Unica de Trabajadores* and "Communists and the Masses," *World Marxist Review,* 14, 9, 1971, pp. 38 ff.

72 Cesar Levano, *op. cit.*

73 Cited in R. Arismendi, *"Bor'ba za massy," Pravda* February 17, 1967.

74 Karl Schmitt, *Communism in Mexico,* pp. 244-45.

75 Mentioned by an Argentinian Communist in "Latin America: Liberation Struggle," *op. cit.*

76 *World Strength of the Communist Party Organizations,* 21st Annual Report, p. 166.

77 "For Land, Bread and Freedom," *World Marxist Review,* 15, 6, 1972, pp. 81 ff.

78 See Samuel Mendoza, *op. cit.*

79 Cesar Levano, *op. cit.*

80 *Fundamentals,* p. 397.

81 See, for instance, Rollie E. Poppino, *International Communism in Latin America: A History of the Movement 1917-1963, 1964;* Robert A. Scalapino, *The Communist Revolution in Asia,* 1965; Ernst Halperin, *Communism in Mexico,* 1963; Karl Schmitt, *Communism in Mexico,* 1965.

82 "Developing Countries at the Crossroads," *New Times,* No. 48, 1966, pp. 6 ff.

83 *Pravda,* June 8, 1969.

84 Ruben Castellanos, "The October Revolution and the Communist Movement in Latin America," *World Marxist Review,* 10, 6, 1967, pp. 25 ff. See also Roque Dalton and Victor Miranda, "Present Phase of the Revolutionary Movement in Latin America," *World Marxist Review,* 10, 5, 1967, pp. 48 ff., complaining of the "relative slowness" of the process to draw the peasantry into "conscious, active participation in the liberation struggle."

85 "Some Lessons of the Events in Bolivia," *World Marxist Review,* 14, 11, 1971, pp. 23 ff.

86 Reprinted in the *Information Bulletin,* 21-22, 1971, pp. 5 ff. See also Bhabani Sen Gupta, "Indian Communism and the Peasantry," *Problems of Communism,* XXI, 1, 1972, pp. 1 ff., noting communist efforts to mobilize

poorer sections of the Indian peasantry. However, the author notes that "the level of mobilization is still relatively low, except in the state of West Bengal."

[87] Aidit's speech at the meeting of the Indonesian National Front, cited in Scalapino, *op. cit.*, p. 268.

[88] G. Mirsky, "Developing nations at the Crossroads," *op. cit.*

[89] V. Tiagunenko, *"Sotsialisticheskie doktriny obshchestvennogo rezvitiia osvobodivshikhsia stran"* (The Socialist Doctrines of Social Development of the Liberated Countries), *MEIMO,* No. 8, 1965, pp. 83-4. See also R. Ul'ianovskii, *"Nekotorye voprosy nekapitalisticheskogo razvitiia osvobodivshikhsia stran"* (Some Questions of the Non-capitalist Development of the Liberated Countries), *Kommunist,* No. 2, 1966, and V. Zotov, "Socialist Changes in Central Asia and the Religious Question," *Voprosy filosofii,* No. 11, 1967, pp. 60 ff.

[90] "The 'Third World' — Problems of Socialist Orientation," *International Affairs* (Moscow), No. 9, 1971, pp. 26 ff.

[91] Lukin, *op. cit.*

[92] Brzezinski (ed.), *Africa and the Communist World,* p. 36.

[93] See, for instance, Orlando Millas, *op. cit.*

[94] Yu Potemkin, *op. cit.* For a discussion of Soviet attitude on religion in developing nations see "Soviet Views on 'The Religious Factor,'" *Mizan,* 8, 4, 1966, pp. 174 ff.

[95] See a review of the volume in "Anti-Sovieteers: African Excursion," *New Times,* No. 14, 1971, pp. 20 ff.

[96] "Latin America," *Time,* July 12, 1968, pp. 21-22, and Leroy F. Aarons, "Castro Blasts Fellow Reds," *Washington Post,* July 3, 1968.

[97] See the AP report from La Paz, *Austin Statesman,* March 3, 1971.

[98] See AP report from Santiago: "Peasants in Chile Resent State Farm," *Austin Statesman,* October 7, 1971, and Carlos Viejo's report from Santiago "Widespread Opposition Rising to Chile's Marxists," *Austin Statesman,* January 31, 1972.

[99] "Preliminary Draft of Theses on the National and Colonial Questions," *Selected Works,* 10, p. 231.

[100] Rollie Poppino, *op. cit.,* p. 103.

[101] Jose Manuel Fortuny, "Has the Revolution Become More Difficult in Latin America?" *World Marxist Review,* 8, 11, 1965.

[102] Suharjo, "Indonesian Communist Party and the Peasantry," *World Marxist Review,* 8, 7, 1965, pp. 45 ff.

[103] "Agrarian Question in Developing Countries of Asia," *op. cit.*

[104] "Some Problems of Social Progress," *World Marxist Review,* 10, 1, 1967, pp. 21 ff.

[105] *Afrika Smotrit v budushcheie* (Africa Looks to the Future), Moscow, 1960, pp. 24-25.

[106] I. I. Potekhin, *ibid.* Also see his articles in *Aziia i Afrika Segodnia,* No. 10, 1961, and in *Narody Azii i Afriki,* Nos. 1 and 3, 1962.

[107] A. N. Gavrilov, "Tendencies in the Development of Agriculture in Tropical Africa," *Narody Azii i Afriki,* No. 6, 1962, pp. 23 ff., and "The Transformation of the African Countryside," *Aziia i Afrika Segodnia,* No. 12, 1962, pp. 13 ff.; L. Aleksandrovskaia, "The Cooperative Movement in Africa," *MEIMO,* No. 3, 1963, p. 17. For a broader discussion of Soviet views of African communalism see "Soviet Notions about 'The Peasant Commune' in Africa," *The Mizan Newsletter,* 6, 7, 1964, pp. 7 ff.

[108] Aleksandrovskaia, *op. cit.*

[109] Citations taken from an extensive review of the book "An Objective Soviet View of Independent Africa," *Mizan,* 7, 9, 1966, pp. 1 ff.

[110] Vladimir Jordansky, "Problems of Rural Africa," *New Times,* No. 28, 1965, pp. 18 ff.

[111] Lukin, *op. cit.*

[112] *Selected Works of Mao Tse-Tung,* Vol. III, p. 93.

[113] This Chinese emphasis on the peasantry's role is reflected in much of the Chinese writing. See, for instance, Fen Chin-Tan, "The Awakening of Africa," *Peking Review,* No. 37, September 14, 1960, and "The Proletarian Revolution and Khrushchev's Revisionism," *ibid.,* No. 14, April 3, 1964, pp. 5 ff.

[114] Cited in Jay Mallin, *Terror in Vietnam,* 1966, pp. 51 ff. See also Ernst Kux, "Communist Tactics in Non-Aligned Countries and the Ideological Quarrel between Moscow and Peking," in Kurt London, ed., *New Nations in a Divided World,* 1963, pp. 256 ff., and George T. Yu, "China's Failure in Africa," *Asian Survey,* VI, 8, 1960, pp. 46 ff.

[115] See Castro's speech to the students and professors of the Havana University, *Prensa Latina,* March 14, 1967; also, Castellanos' admission of communist neglect of the peasantry, *op. cit.* However, reports have been circulating that, after the dismal failure of Che Guevara's experiment in Bolivia, Castro has begun modifying his earlier ideas that revolutions in Latin America must start in the countryside and with the peasantry. See "Day of the Rural Guerrilla Comes to Quiet End in Venezuela," *Washington Post,* May 4, 1969.

[116] See Jack Woddis's review of *Fanin's book Les damnés de la terre,* in the *Labour Monthly,* 48, 1, 1966, pp. 3 ff.

[117] See an especially bitter attack on the Chinese position in V. Shelepin, "Maoist Intrigues in the Third World," *op. cit.;* also, Haled Bagdash, "Problems of the National-Liberation Movement in Syria," *World Marxist Review,* 11, 6, 1968, pp. 39-44, and "Pseudo-Revolutionaries Unmasked," *Information Bulletin,* No. 11, 1970, pp. 34 ff.

[118] *op. cit.* See also Luis Carlos Prestes, "Political Line and Tactics of Brazilian Communists in the New Conditions," *World Marxist Review,* 11, 6, 1968, pp. 31-38.

[119] Anen'iev, *op. cit.*

CHAPTER VIII

THE BOURGEOISIE AND ITS ROLE IN COMMUNIST STRATEGY

An aspect of strategy that preoccupied communist ideologues and strategists at the early phases of the national liberation struggle has been the Third World's bourgeoisie and the role it is supposed to play in the national-liberation revolution and the hoped-for transition to socialism. Special international conferences have been convened for this very purpose, beginning in 1959 with a "seminar on the national bourgeoisie and the liberation movement in Asia, Africa, and Latin America" held in Leipzig under the auspices of the *World Marxist Review*.[1] The topic has loomed high on the agenda of various communist-convoked sessions and symposia devoted to the affairs of the Third World. [2] It has been a subject of numerous articles in Soviet and other communist periodicals. Also, the question of the communist attitude toward the Third World's bourgeoisie has become one of the bones of contention between Soviet Russia and communist China.

This communist pre-occupation with a class that, in terms of classical Marxism, ought to be branded as the chief enemy of the working class and the concomitant search for an adjustment of bourgeois-communist relations stems, of course, much more from the factual situation prevalent throughout the Third World than any fundamental ideological reassessment. After all, it is the native bourgeoisie that has secured and continues to hold the positions of leadership in the less developed nations of the Third World. As shown earlier in this volume, the Asian, African and Latin American working class is as yet too small, too weak and lacking too much in class consciousness to be able to assume the leadership of the revolution it ought to have according to the canons of Marxism-Leninism. The same defects plague the Communist parties of the Third World — the proletariat's Marxist-Leninist vanguard to be. The proletariat's preferred ally, the peasantry, though by far the largest of all the classes of the Third World, is considered by the communist analysts to be too backward, too passive and too unorganized to play successfully the part of the proletariat's main helper in the communist scheme. Nor can and do communist strategists cherish much hope that the situation in most parts of the Third World might change in the near future so radically as to replace the present rulers with regimes based on the worker-peasant alliances.

Thus "life itself," as the favorite communist phrase goes, has compelled the communist strategists to refashion their earlier precepts, broaden them and adapt them to the new realities. While providing for more flexibility, this refashioning has also contributed an element of uncertainty and confusion, in particular with regard to such matters as how the various segments of the native bourgeoisie differ from one another, which of them are acceptable as allies and which must be viewed as enemies, what is the permissible degree of cooperation, and how long it should last.

The Third World's Bourgeoisie Subdivided

Much time and effort has been spent by communist analysts in recent years on matters of the bourgeoisie's classification, identification and characterization. Complaining that far too little attention had been paid in the past to the proper differentiation of the various strata of the bourgeoisie of the developing nations, and that this in turn had led to erroneous simplifications and "schematic attitudes,"[3] the Soviet and other communist writers have developed lately a tendency of dividing and subdividing the native bourgeoisie into more and more categories, strata and sub-strata. While a substantial measure of consensus has been reached in this effort at a more refined differentiation, doubts and disagreements have also arisen.

To begin with, there is some confusion about the very criteria by which the bourgeoisie and its various segments are to be differentiated.

Most of the communist writers continue to dwell upon the ownership of the means of production and employment of hired labor, going thus by the definition contained in the authoritative *Fundamentals of Marxism-Leninism*.[4] Hence, they exclude from their notion of the bourgeoisie in the classical meaning of the word not only the so-called petty bourgeoisie which possesses only "small means of production" and does not "live by exploiting the labour of others," but also the intelligentsia, small professional men, the middle and lower echelons of the "state bureaucracy" and even the officers corps.[5] A prominent Soviet student of the Third World's class structure has chosen the term of "semi-bourgeoisie" (*poluburzhuaziia*) or "quasi-bourgeoisie" (*kvaziburzhuaziia*) to be applied to the latter groups.[6]

Another criterion by which the native bourgeoisie is classified is its relation to the national economy. Taking into consideration the economic sector in which the bourgeoisie's main activity is concentrated and the nature of this activity, communist analysts distinguish several types or strata, such as:

"bourgeoisified" feudal landlords, latifundists and other rural capitalists;

trading, commercial or "comprador" bourgeoisie engaged mainly in selling imported foreign goods;

the "industrial bourgeoisie" earning profits from native industrial production;

the banking bourgeoisie consisting mainly of native financiers and bank operators;

the usurer bourgeoisie living off money lending and land speculation, especially in rural areas.[7]

But the principal factor that seems to guide the present-day communist strategy-makers in determining to what category the respective groups of the native bourgeoisie should be assigned lies in the manner in which their economic interests are supposed to affect their attitude toward the "imperialists." "What counts is [the bourgeoisie's] attitude toward imperialism," stressed A. Rumiantsev in his concluding remarks at a round-table conference on "Building a United Anti-Imperialist Front" held under the auspices of the *World Marxist Review*.[8] On this basis communist analysts divide the native bourgeoisie of the developing nations into two main categories, the first one frozen into the status of the sworn enemy and the second one cast in the role of a potential though vacillating ally: 1) the pro-imperialist bourgeoisie which consists of those bourgeois segments that are economically tied to foreign enterprises and monopolies and stand thus to lose as foreign economic domination recedes; 2) the "national bourgeoisie" which, suffering as it does economically from the dominance of foreign capital, is "interested in creating and controlling a national market and in defending it against the rapacity of foreign monopolies," and which, therefore, "sees the way of achieving this in the creation of a national state and in liberation from foreign dependence."[9]

These varying criteria, combining both economic and political considerations, allow the communists fairly broad latitude in distinguishing among the different strata of the native bourgeoisie and shuffling them almost at will to fit local situations and tactical necessities. After all, as is affirmed in the *Fundamentals*, the bourgeoisie of the developing nations is "the most contradictory element" and "the various groups of the bourgeoisie have not only different, but frequently diametrically opposite attitudes to the national-liberation struggle."[10] At the same time, however, this latitude leaves the native communists without a reliable ideological guidance on a major aspect of communist strategy.

Foremost among the problems confronting them in this respect in the recent years has been the question concerning those segments of the Third World's bourgeoisie that were and were not eligible for inclusion in the "national bourgeoisie."

One segment of the bourgeoisie about which doubts have developed has been the so-called comprador bourgeoisie. Deriving its profits mainly from trade with foreign capitalists, it had traditionally been considered as "serving directly the interests of imperialist capital" and, for this reason, belonging to the bourgeoisie's pro-imperialist wing.[11] However, this wholly negative attitude began to change in the latter fifties.[12] Several participants in the above-mentioned seminar on the "National Bourgeoisie and the Liberation Movement" took exception to the unduly harsh *Comintern* thesis placing the whole of the colonial trading bourgeoisie in the imperialist camp. Instead, it was held that not all of those who traded with foreign monopolies ought to be "lumped together under the term comprador." Since many of the ex-colonial nations simply have to trade with the West in order to be able to supply their citizens with the necessities of life and to overcome their economic backwardness, some of the trading bourgeoisie engaged in such importation from the West was said to perform in fact a commendable function and should not, therefore, be labeled as an agent of imperialism. Rather, they should be recognized as a legitimate part of the national bourgeoisie.[13]

As for the so-called industrial bourgeoisie, the tendency in classifying it has been to disregard the size of its enterprises as well as the magnitude of its exploitation of labor. Differentiation has been made, rather, according to where its capital is invested. That segment of the industrial bourgeoisie which "fuses its capital with imperialist capital by taking part in mixed enterprises," is deemed to be so dependent on Western monopolies that it is liable to become an agent of imperialism.[14] Again, however, the classification depends primarily on the respective industrialist's attitude in the context of East-West relations. Thus even a native industrial magnate or "monopoly-capitalist" qualifies for membership in the national bourgeoisie provided he is considered sufficiently anti-Western.

Another outgrowth of the recent attempts at a more subtle differentiation is the so-called "bureaucratic bourgeoisie" (*biurokraticheskaia burzhuaziia*), a segment not previously singled out as a separate and distinctive stratum of the Third World's bourgeoisie in official communist pronouncements.[15] In substance, communist writers include in this category such upper and upper-middle echelons of the state apparatus of the developing nations as are considered, rightly or wrongly, as pro-Western or at least as too neutralist for communist liking. However, some go beyond this and extend the term to comprise the lower echelons of all state and public organizations as well, inclusive even of party, trade union and cooperative apparatus.[16]

At first, communist strategists assumed that after the natives had taken over governmental and quasi-governmental positions vacated by the ousted colonial administrations, the new native bureaucracy would gravitate toward "scientific socialism." Although most of these new bureaucrats were of bourgeois or petty-bourgeois origin, they did not own the means of production, did not exploit labor, opposed foreign monopolies and mostly favored nationalization of major sectors of national economy. Hence, they should not have been considered an integral part of the bourgeoisie in the classical Marxist meaning of the term, especially in Africa and Asia, if not in Latin America. For a while, this did indeed appear to be the prevalent communist viewpoint. But disappointment with the attitudes and actions of this new state bureaucracy in an ever increasing number of developing nations has evidently brought about a re-appraisal. Soviet orientologists and Africanologists have begun to speak of "the penetration of bourgeois ideologies into the 'civil service' intelligentsia"[17] and of "the bourgeoisified (*oburzhua-zivaiushchaiasia*) state-party bureaucracy" becoming "the main support of imperialism and neo-colonialism."[18] They have begun to express fears lest the bureaucratic bourgeoisie seek ever closer ties with foreign monopolies and Western imperialism as it has presumably done already in Latin America and in a number of newly emerging countries in Africa, such as Morocco, Senegal, etc.[19] A Soviet author went so far as to denounce the African "bureaucratic bourgeoisie" as the native bourgeoisie's "most parasitic variety,"[20] while another Soviet ideologist has placed the "bureaucratic bourgeoisie" squarely in the category of "main social adversaries of the working people."[21] The bureaucratic bourgeoisie, wrote Mirsky in 1969 "is becoming the chief social mainstay of neo-colonialism, just as the feudal and compradore elements were the bulwark of foreign capital during the period of 'classical' colonialism."[22]

Thus the whole matter of defining the different segments of the Third World's bourgeoisie, gauging the degree of their "revolutionary potential" or "pro-imperialism" and determining on this basis how each of them should be treated seems to be becoming more and more complex.

The Bourgeoisie's Role in Communist Strategy

Although communist theoreticians indulge and sometimes overindulge in classifications, definitions and characterizations of social classes, strata and sub-strata mainly in order to satisfy their doctrinaire bent and semantic predilections, their endeavors to differentiate between the various segments of the Third World's bourgeoisie are motivated primarily by strategic and tactical considerations. What roles should be assigned to the bourgeoisie's various segments? Which of them are to be cast in the part of chief or secondary enemies and to what extent, and which of them should be considered as allies, potential or genuine? Under what circumstances are alliances with bourgeois elements permissible and what should be their principal purpose? What ought to be the position of the proletariat and its Marxist-Leninist vanguard in such alliances? How long should they last and what will become of the allies when the alliance is ended? These and related issues have been argued among communists since Lenin's days; and while consensus has been reached on some of them, others have remained controversial to this day or become so in recent communist interpretations.

One issue on which communist strategy-planners are in agreement is the difference between the bourgeoisie of the "imperialist" countries and that of the developing nations, especially those of Asia and Africa. Whereas Western bourgeoisie is regarded as having lost its "former revolutionary spirit" and become the bulwark of reaction, the ex-colonial bourgeoisie is considered as being, "under certain conditions, still able to play a historically progressive role."[23] Naturally, as communist analysts also agree, this does not apply to the Third World's bourgeoisie in its entirety, but only to its "progressive" section. However, here the agreement ends, for there seems to be no consensus on the all-important question of which strata of the native bourgeoisie should be reviewed as "progressive" and which should not. As noted above, communist spokesmen, Soviet and other, do concur in distinguishing between the "pro-imperialist" bourgeoisie, which is branded as reactionary and as a sworn enemy, and the "national bourgeoisie," which might or might not be progressive. But a good deal of confusion exists as to which portions of the national bourgeoisie belong to its "progressive circles" and thus qualify as an acceptable ally. Nor do official communist sources provide adequate guidance on the matter.

The official communist thesis embodied in the 1960 *Declaration of Eighty-One Communist Parties* credits the national bourgeoisie with a "progressive" character on the ground that it is "objectively interested in the accomplishment of the principal tasks of anti-imperialism, anti-feudal revolution, and therefore retains the capacity of participating in the revolutionary struggle against imperialism and feudalism."[24] Yet, in the same breath it labels the national bourgeoisie as being "unstable" and "inclined to compromise with imperialism and feudalism." Because of "its dual nature, the extent to which the national bourgeoisie participates in revolution differs from country to country," depending "on concrete conditions, on changes in the relationship of class forces, on the sharpness of the contradictions between imperialism, feudalism and the people, and on the depth of the contradictions between imperialism, feudalism and the national bourgeoisie."[25]

The studied ambivalence of this cryptic high-level pronouncement, paraphrased in a similar way in the 1961 *Soviet Communist Party Program* as well as in the *Fundamentals*, leaves the entire question wide-open. Hence, attitudes vary quite substantially throughout the Third World.

Save for a few instances, the Latin American communists generally take a dim view of their countries' national bourgeoisie which, in their opinion, has "lost its revolutionary potential," tends to collaborate with the latifundists, the "big" bourgeoisie and other reactionary groups, defers to American monopolists and is, for these reasons, no longer capable of carrying out urgent reforms, let alone "heading revolutionary processes."[26] Their views are shared, by and large, by Soviet analysts, including even the least orthodox among them, such as Mirskii. Comparing the situation in Latin America with that prevailing in Asia and Africa in his contribution to the 1964 Moscow discussion on

"Socialism, Capitalism, the Less Developed Nations," Mirskii held that the Latin American bourgeoisie did not constitute a serious anti-imperialist force. This was due, he argued, mainly to two "specifically Latin American factors," namely, the reactionary influence of "latifundism" and the bourgeoisie's lopsided dependence on U.S. monopolies.[27] A similarly negative evaluation of the role played by the Latin American national bourgeoisie has been advanced in 1968 by Professor V. Volsky, Director of the Latin American Institute of the Soviet Academy of Sciences.[28] The most notable exception appears to be Chile where at least a portion of the national bourgeoisie associated with the Christian Democratic party is credited somewhat grudgingly with "progressive" ideas, though this is presumably due less to inner convictions than to popular pressure from below.

In Africa and non-communist Asia the situation is seen in a somewhat better light. In a number of countries of both continents the national bourgeoisie is deemed to have not yet "exhausted" its progressive role.[29] This is considered to be so not only in countries led by the "revolutionary democrats," such as Egypt, Algeria, Guinea, Syria and Burma, but also in a number of other countries where governments controlled by representatives of the national bourgeoisie resort to progressive measures, such as nationalization of foreign and large native enterprises, liquidation of large land holdings and establishment of "broad democratic reforms." Having thus switched from the ideology of nationalism to "socialism of the national type" (*sotsializm natsional'nogo tipa*), the national bourgeoisie in such countries willy-nilly moves onto the non-capitalist path of development and thus fulfills unwittingly a "historically progressive" role.[30]

Although communist analysts generally consider the national bourgeoisie of Asia and Africa as more "progressive" than its counterpart in Latin America, they are nevertheless far from enthusiastic about its behavior, especially in recent years. Some of them have been skeptical all along, such as the well-known British communist specializing in African affairs, Jack Woddis.[31] So have been also various Asian and African communists who have traditionally viewed their native bourgeoisie, national or otherwise, as an implacable enemy and have never been happy about Moscow's post-Stalin flirtations with the national bour-geoisie. Others have cooled off subsequently because of the setbacks the strategy of cooperation with the national bour-geoisie has recently sustained in a number of African and Asian countries. Writing in the September 1969 issue of the *World Marxist Review*, a prominent Indian communist complains that "some of the national bourgeoisie" of the newly independent countries "increasingly tend to accept a deal with imperialism," joining thus "the forces of domestic reaction."[32]

An erosion of faith in the revolutionary potential of national bourgeoisie took place also in the Chinese camp. In their public exchange of recriminatory letters with the Soviet Communist party the Chinese leaders had called for a "full appraisal of the progressive role of the patriotic national bourgeoisie and strengthening unity with them,"[33] but have since been shifting more and more to a negative stand.

A similar disenchantment is apparent in Soviet writings of the latter sixties which are more critical of national bourgeoisie of Asia and Africa and in the Third World generally than only a few years previously. "In a number of countries of Asia and Africa," wrote R. Ul'ianovskii in an article on "Socialism and the National-Liberation Movement" the national bourgeoisie "is becoming a force holding back the further development of the liberation struggle while its upper strata are openly collaborating with reaction."[34] He raises a similar complaint in 1968 in another article in *Pravda* where he bewails, in particular, the national bourgeoisie's evident inclination to solve its economic contradictions with foreign capital by mutual accommodation.[35] Much in the same vein, another prominent Soviet theoretician counts the national bourgeoisie "in some cases" among "the main social adversaries of the working people in the various [African] countries."[36]

Native African and Asian communists are even more out-spoken. Writing in the *World Marxist Review*, a Sudanese communist asserts that the national bourgeoisie in Africa is either too closely linked with foreign monopoly capital and has lost its revolutionary potential, or is too weak to play any serious role in revolutionary development.[37] A similar opinion has been voiced by an Egyptian communist claiming that the African national bourgeoisie "has shed the classical revolutionary attributes" and actually has gone into partnership with neo-colonialism.[38] The growing disillusionment with the national bourgeoisie of the Third World was also clearly evident in the discussions of the symposium on "Lenin's Teaching on the National-Liberation Revolution and the Present Phase of Social Progress in the Developing Countries," held in October 1969 at Alma Ata and attended by "200 Soviet specialists and 72 researchers and personalities from 51 Asian, African, Latin American and other countries."[39]

Nonetheless, despite the recent disappointments, cooperation with the "progressive" section of the Third World's national bourgeoisie at the national-democratic phase of the revolution continues to be endorsed by Moscow as an appropriate strategy whenever and wherever the monopoly of power cannot be seized by the proletariat alone or with the sole support of the peasantry. While criticizing the Third World's national bourgeoisie in his above-mentioned 1968 *Pravda* article, Ul'ianovskii asks his readers not to imply that the national bourgeoisie "had everywhere ceased to participate in the anti-imperialist struggle and that it had lost its importance as an anti-imperialist force."[40] Cooperation of communists with the "progressive portion of the national bourgeoisie" in developing countries that have entered upon the non-capitalist path of development has also been included among the theses re-affirmed by the Institute of Marxism-Leninism of the Central Committee of the Soviet Communist party on the solemn occasion of the 150th anniversary of Karl Marx's birth in April 1968.[41]

However, in determining the pattern of their relations to the national bourgeoisie, communists are cautioned, as they had been in the past, about the danger and errors of both left-wing sectarianism and right-wing opportunism.[42] Should they underestimate the national bourgeoisie's anti-imperialist potential and thus become guilty of left-wing sectarianism, they would belittle the national democratic revolution, isolate the proletariat, antagonize a potential anti-imperialist ally, drive the national bourgeoisie into the arms of the feudalists, the big bourgeoisie and other reactionaries, and prevent the formation of a desirable type of a united front. On the other hand, should they overestimate the national bourgeoisie's revolutionary potential and thus commit the heresy of right-wing opportunism, they would tend to capitulate to national bourgeois demands, "slip into the position of bourgeois nationalism," belittle the role of the proletariat, sink into defeatist "khvostism" and foreclose their aspirations to lead the masses.

Such an ideal middle road avoiding both left wing sectarianism and right wing opportunism is, of course, easy to outline and prescribe in theoretical pronouncements. To follow it in the complex and ever-changing conditions prevailing throughout most of the Third World is much harder. Hence, it is hardly surprising that communist treatment of national bourgeoisie varies widely from one country to another, deviations from the foreordained course are a-plenty and disagreements as well as mutual accusations and counter-accusations of left-wing sectarianism and right-wing opportunism abound within communist ranks.

The problem has been aggravated still further as a result of the Sino-Soviet split as well as the impatient mood of Castroites and some of the Third World's socialists with radical anarcho-syndicalist leanings. As noted above, the Chinese communists have by now virtually written off most of the national bourgeoisie of the Third World as a worthwhile ally and switched over to what amounts in communist terminology to a stiff sectarian stand. A somewhat similar attitude laying a greater emphasis on fighting and liquidating the national bourgeoisie rather than associating and cooperating with it has been embraced by the Castroites and certain extremist groups of the Third World's socialists, especially in Latin America. Exposed thus to pressures and denunciations from the extreme left and frustrated by the dearth of tangible results gained from cooperation with the national bourgeoisie, native communists in many parts of the Third World find it ever more difficult to hold to the prescribed middle course and steer clear off both left-wing sectarianism and right-wing opportunism.

Again, as has been the case in the peasant-worker relationship, an especially trying dilemma has arisen in connection with the all-important issue of leadership. Since Lenin's days it has been a fundamental tenet of communist strategy at the bourgeois-democratic or national-democratic stage of the revolution that the leadership of the revolution must be wrested from the hands of the bourgeosie at the earliest possible opportunity and taken over by the proletariat guided by its Marxist-Leninist vanguard party. However, realizing that in many parts of the Third World it may be quite a while before communists could earnestly aspire to their vanguard position, Soviet strategy-makers have toned down their erstwhile insistence on communist-proletarian leadership. Without abandoning the idea of the exclusive communist hegemony as their ultimate goal, they have displayed in the latter fifties and early sixties a willingness to concede, if absolutely necessary, the leadership to the national bourgeoisie, at least at the early stages of the national-democratic revolution. To make the shift less conspicuous and more palatable for orthodox communists, they have referred in this respect to Lenin's views that the bourgeoisie rather than the communists assumes the hegemony "at the beginning of any national movement."[43] The Soviet view seems to have been shared also by a few (but only a few) of the pro-Soviet communists of the Third World willing to accept, in the absence of a strong native proletariat, "other participants in the block of democratic forces" as "the guiding force in the initial stage."[44]

On the other hand, the Chinese communists, mindful of the disaster that had befallen their Party when it conceded leadership to the national bourgeoisie in middle twenties, takes a jaundiced view of any such idea. While they continue to be willing to accept the cooperation of the "progressive" section of the national bourgeoisie and admit it as a junior partner to a united front, they stress that "the wavering and compromising national bourgeoisie" be kept out of leadership which must be firmly grasped, even at the national-democratic phase of the revolution, "by the proletariat through the Communist party."[45] The leadership of the proletariat has, of course, been postulated also by Mao for his "joint dictatorship of several revolutionary classes" designed to rule in his "new democracy."[46] The Third World's "proletarian parties," entrusted by history with "the glorious mission of holding high the banner of struggle against imperialism, against old and new colonialism and for national independence and people's democracy, of standing in the fore-front of the national democratic revolutionary movement and striving for a Socialist future, must insist on the leadership of the revolution," affirms the Central Committee of the Chinese Communist Party in its public letter of June 14, 1963, designed to expose and rebut the revisionist heresies of the Soviet Communist Party leaders. The only association involving the national bourgeoisie that the Chinese communists condone, even at the national-democratic stage of the revolution, is Mao's previously mentioned "joint dictatorship of several revolutionary classes" in which leadership belongs to the communist-led rural and urban proletariat while the anti-imperialist segment of the national bourgeoisie is relegated to an altogether subordinate position.[47]

However, the growing disappointment with the recent behavior of the national bourgeoisie has impelled even the more open-minded among the Soviet and Third World communists to adopt a stiffer stand. While they continue to approve of the participation of national bourgeoisie in the revolutionary struggle, they have by now virtually ruled national-bourgeois leadership as no longer tolerable. "In the period of struggle against the colonial regimes, the national bourgeoisie was often at the head of the struggle," writes Ul'ianovskii in the earlier mentioned 1968 article in *Pravda*. "[But] at the present stage of the national-liberation struggle the national bourgeoisie in many countries has already demonstrated its inability to continue fulfilling this role."[48]

Above all, communist strategists are worried about the grave danger that the national bourgeoisie will gain and maintain the leadership over the peasantry. Should this occur, communist chances would become virtually nil, for a communist-led worker-peasant alliance is deemed indispensable for the communist victory, especially in the Third World with its overwhelming peasant population. "The question of leadership over the peasantry is a basic question of the national-liberation revolution," stresses a Soviet authority. "Who ultimately will win the peasantry — the bourgeoisie or the proletariat — greatly determines the outcome of these revolutions and the paths for the further development of the liberated nations."[49] Hence, the prevention of national-bourgeois hegemony, or its dislodgement wherever it had already materialized, has been one of the major aspects of communist strategy vis-a-vis the national bourgeoisie of the Third World. To attain their objective and to drive a solid wedge between the national bourgeoisie and the peasantry, communists have unleashed in recent years a vigorous defamatory campaign designed to discredit national bourgeoisie in the eyes of peasant masses. In particular, as pointed out in Chapter VII, they have been trying hard to downgrade and disparage the agrarian reforms carried out under national-bourgeois leadership. While conceding that some good has come from such measures, the communist critics dismiss them mostly as inadequate, "half-baked" palliatives incapable of solving the land problem to the benefit of the working peasantry."[50] Moreover, in undertaking these reforms, the national bourgeoisie is said to have been guided not by a genuine concern for the lot of the peasant masses, but by its selfish interest in maintaining its position, "pacifying the countryside," averting the danger of peasant uprisings and containing the peasantry "with the deceptions and social demagoguery engendered by these reforms."[51] Agrarian reforms have allegedly been forced upon the reluctant national bourgeoisie by the fact that "the broad masses of the peasantry in Asia, Africa and Latin America are aware of the just solution of the land question in the Socialist countries..."[52]

Be it as it may, there is no question that the national bourgeoisie did gain favor with much of the Third World's peasantry and undercut communist chances in rural areas wherever it enacted meaningful agrarian reforms. As communist analysts complain, the national bourgeoisie has thus managed to split the peasants, create confusion among them, and cause "a portion of the peasantry which has received actual advantages in the course of the agrarian reforms," to "give up the active struggle."[53]

Thus the fears, expressed in the 1960 *Declaration of Eighty-One Communist Parties*, that, with the growing social contradictions, the national bourgeoisie would "incline more and more to compromising with domestic reaction and imperialism" have been proved justified.[54] With the acquisition of national independence, the gradual improvement of relations with ex-colonial powers and the growing awareness of the communist menace, the national bourgeoisie tends to concentrate on the immediate tasks of national, political, economic and social consolidation and, of course, the preservation of its own leadership against all comers. From the communist perspective, the unwanted characteristics of the national bourgeoisie's "dual nature" have been gaining ascendancy over the traits that communist strategists have been hoping for.

The increasing communist disenchantment with the national bourgeoisie's performance is clearly borne out by the comparison of the 1960 *Declaration of Eighty-One Communist Parties* and the *Declaration* adopted by the Moscow Conference of the Communist and Workers' Parties in 1969. As noted earlier in this chapter, the 1960 *Declaration* emphasized the national bourgeoisie and saw in it a promising (even though unstable) ally. In contrast, the national bourgeoisie is virtually ignored in the 1969 *Declaration*. In calling on "all patriotic and progressive forces" of the Third World to unite with the communists in the struggle against imperialism and its "neo-colonist intrigues," the 1969 *Declaration* addresses itself to several non-proletarian strata, such as the peasantry, working youth, students, intellectuals, urban "middle strata" and "democratic army circles," but fails conspicuously to mention the national bourgeoisie. The only instance in which it alludes to the national bourgeoisie occurs when it cites "the elements of the national bourgeoisie which are increasingly accepting a deal with imperialism" as being, together with "the forces of domestic reaction," in a sharpening conflict with the working class, the peasantry and "other democratic forces, including patriotic-minded sections of the petty bourgeoisie."

Notes for Chapter VIII

[1] For extensive summary of the discussion see "The National Bourgeoisie and the Liberation Movement," *World Marxist Review*, 2, 8, 1959, pp. 61 ff, and 2, 9, 1959, pp. 66 ff.

[2] See, for instance, the discussion on "Socialism, Capitalism, the Less Developed Countries," *MEIMO, op. cit.*, and the round-table conference on

"Building a United Anti-Imperialist Front," *World Marxist Review*, 6, 1, 1963, pp. 69 ff.

[3] See, for instance, V. Tiagunenko's statement in the discussion in *MEIMO*, No. 6, 1964, *op. cit.* in note 2.

[4] p. 154.

[5] See G. Mirsky's statement in the MEIMO discussion mentioned in note 2.

[6] G. Mirsky, *ibid.*

[7] See R. Avakov and G. Mirsky, *'O klassovoi strukture v slaborozvitykh stranakh'' MEIMO*, No. 4, 1962, pp. 68 ff.

[8] *World Marxist Review*, 6, 1, 1963, pp. 69 ff.

[9] *Fundamentals*, p. 398; see also *Third World*, pp. 41 ff.

[10] p. 389.

[11] See *The Thesis on the Revolutionary Movement in the Colonies and Semi-Colonies* and *Selected Works of Mao Tse-tung*, Vol. III, p. 72 ff.

[12] For an early sign of the change see V. Vassil'eva, *"Raspad kolonial'noi sistemy imperializma,"* (The Disintegration of the Colonial System of Imperialism) *Voprosy ekonomiki*, No. 4, April 1956.

[13] *World Marxist Review*, 2, 8, 1959 (especially the contribution by Kia-Nouri) and 2, 8, 1959 (esp. the contribution by Messouak).

[14] *ibid,.* Kai-Nouri's statement.

[15] The distinction between the "classical" bourgeoisie connected with commerce and industry and the "bureaucratic bourgeoisie" is drawn also in a recent book *Les Classes Sociales en Afrique Noire* by French Marxist Raymond Barbé, reviewed with approval in the Soviet journal *International Affairs*. See also Y. Kashin, "Are There Classes in Black Africa?" *International Affairs*, No. 4, 1965, pp. 108-9, and G. Mirsky, "Changes in the Third World," *New Times*, No. 39, 1969, pp. 411.

[16] See G. Aleksandrov's contribution in the MEIMO discussion cited in note 2.

[17] N. Khokhlov in *Literaturnaia Gazeta*, June 2, 1965, cited in "Sense About Africa, Reflection of A Seasoned Soviet Reporter," *Mizan*, 8, 4, 1966, pp. 171 ff.

[18] G. Aleksandrov, *"Bor'ba proletariata v strankakh tropicheskoi Afriki*, (The Struggle of the Proletariat in the Countries of Tropical Africa), MEIMO, No. 3, 1966, pp. 73 ff., and the same author's contribution in the MEIMO discussion cited in note 2. Also, Mirsky, "Changes in the Third World," *op. cit.*

[19] R. I. Ismagilova in I. I. Gavrilov, ed., *Nezavisimye Strany Afriki: Ekonomicheskie i Sotsialnye problemy*, (reviewed in *Mizan*: "An Objective Soviet View of Independent Africa," 7, 9, 1966; also Mirsky's contribution in the MEIMO discussion cited in note 2.

[20] Jurii Bokharyov, "Africa: Anatomy of the Military Coups," *New Times*, No. 14, 1966, pp. 10 ff.

[21] Alexander Sobolyev, "Some Problems of Social Progress," *World Marxist Review*, 10, 1, 1967, pp. 21 ff.

[22] G. Mirsky, "Changes in the Third World," *op. cit.*

[23] *Fundamentals*, p. 401. See also statements to that effect at the discussion sponsored by the *World Marxist Review* and cited in note 1.

[24] *Jacobs*, p. 32. For East European communist endorsement of the desirability of communist cooperation with the national bourgeoisie of the Third World see Evžen Paloncy, *"Komunismus a národně-osvobozenecké hnutí,"* (Communism and the National-Liberation Movement) *Nová mysl*,

No. 8, 1963, pp. 897-907, and F. Havlíček, "Topical Questions of the Revolutionary Movement." *Mezinárodní politika,* No. 2, 1963, English text in *Czechoslovak Press Survey,* No. 1214 (56) March 7, 1963.

[25] *Jacobs,* p. 33. On the dual character of the national bourgeoisie see also Mao's "The Chinese Revolution and the Chinese Communist Party," *Selected Works of Mao Tse-tung,* III. pp. 72 ff.

[26] Louis Corvalan, "Alliance of Anti-imperialist Forces in Latin America," *World Marxist Review,* 10, 7, 1967, pp. 46 ff.; also, R. Iscaro, "The Working Class in the Struggle for the Liberation of Latin America, " *ibid.,* 9, 3, 1966, pp. 49 ff; J. Encarnacio Perez, "Students and Democracy in Mexico, " *ibid.,* 12, 6, 1969, pp.73 ff.; Roque Dalton, *op. cit.;* Rodney Arismendi, *Lenin, La Revolucion y America Latina* (Lenin, Revolution and Latin America) Montevideo, 1970 (praised also in the *World Marxist Review,* 13, 11, 1970, by Victor Gonzalez, "The Relevance of Leninism for Latin America," pp. 101-102.

[27] *Op. cit.,* in note 2.

[28] V. Volskii, *"Latinskaia Amerika: Novyi Etap Bor'by Narodov,"* (Latin America: A New Stage of the Peoples' Struggle), *Pravda,* March 19, 1968.

[29] V. P. Verin, *Presidentskie Respubliki v Afrike,* Moscow, 1963, reviewed in *Mizan,* 6, 7, 1964, pp. 1 ff.; see also the MEIMO discussion cited in note 2.

[30] Avakov and Akopian in the MEIMO discussion cited in note 2.

[31] See his statement in the discussion on "Paths of Development of Newly Emergent Nations," held under the auspices of the *World Marxist Review* in September 1961; Will MacLaurin, "The Bourgeoisie and Neo-Colonialism," *World Marxist Review,* 5, 1, 1962, pp. 14 ff; V. Baryshnikov, *"Natsional'naia burzhuaziia v stranakh vostochnoi Afriki,"* (National Bourgeoisie in the Countries of East Africa) MEIMO, No. 5, 1964, pp. 63 ff.

[32] Strinivas Ganesh Sardesai, "For Unity in Action of World Revolutionary Forces," *World Marxist Review,* 12, 9, 1969, pp. 8 ff.

[33] See point 9 of the June 14, 1963 letter.

[34] *Pravda,* April 15, 1966., English text in the *Current Digest,* XVIII No. 15.

[35] *"Na novykh rubezhakh: O nekotorykh chertakh sovremennogo etapa natsional'no-osvoboditel'nogo dvizheniia,"* (On New Boundaries: Concerning Some Traits of the Contemporary Stage of the National-Liberation Struggle), *Pravda,* January 3, 1968. See also K. Brutens, *"Rastushchaia revoliutsionnaia sila,"* (The Growing Revolutionary Force), *Pravda,* January 23, 1970.

[36] A. Sobolyev, *op. cit.*

[37] Osman Babiker, "Anti-Imperialist Unity — An Imperative of Our Time," *World Marxist Review,* 8, 8, 1966, pp. 23 ff.

[38] Lufti El Kohli, "Current Phase of the Anti-Imperialist Struggle in Africa," *World Marxist Review,* 10, 1, 1967, pp. 13 ff.

[39] "Lenin and the National Liberation Movement," *World Marxist Review,* 12,12, 1969, pp. 20 ff.

[40] *Pravda,* January 3, 1968.

[41] *Ibid.,* April 7, 1968.

[42] *Fundamentals,* p. 380; "The National Bourgeoisie and the National Liberation Movement," *World Marxist Review, op. cit.;* Avakov-Mirsky, *"O klassovoi strukture v slaborazvitykh stranakh,"* *op. cit.*

[43] Y. Zhukov, *"Znamenatel'nyi faktor nashego vremeni,"* (A Significant Factor of Our Time), *Pravda,* August 26, 1960, referred to in Donald Zagoria, op. cit., *Problems of Communism,* X, 2, 1961, pp. 1 ff.

[44] Pieter Keuneman, "New Features of the National Liberation Movement," *World Marxist Review*, 7, 12, 1964, pp. 3 ff.

[45] Statement by Liu Shao-Chi, *World Trade Union Movement*, WFTU, Paris, No. 8, December 1949 and *Ten Glorious Years*, 1949-1959, Peking, 1960. Also, Wang Chia Hsiang's article in *Red Flag*, cited in Zagoria, *op. cit.*, and Mao's address to Shansi Suiyuan, *Liberated Areas Cadres* on April 1, 1948, *Chinese Communist World Outlook*, p. 13.

[46] *Selected Works*, III, pp. 106 ff.

[47] *Selected Works*, III, pp. 72 ff.

[48] *Pravda*, January 3, 1968; also, Ramiro Otero, "Some Problems of the Working-Class and Trade Union Movement in Latin America," *World Marxist Review*, 10, 7, 1967, pp. 56 ff; Luis Corvalan, "Alliance of the Anti-Imperialist Forces in Latin America," *op. cit.'* Jack Woddis, "Role of the African Working Class in the National Liberation Movement," *op. cit.*

[49] Anen'iev, *op. cit.*

[50] Ul'ianovskii, *"Agrarnye reformy v stranakh blizhnego i srednego vostoka. . ." op. cit.'* Anen'iev, *op. cit.' Agrarno-krestianskii vopros, op. cit.;* Kovalyov, *op. cit.*

[51] Ul'ianovskii, *"Agrarnye reformy...," op. cit.*

[52] *ibid.*

[53] Anen'iev, *op. cit.*

[54] *Jacobs*, p. 33.

CHAPTER IX

COURTING THE MIDDLE STRATA

The unwillingness of the national bourgeoisie to play the role assigned to it in the pattern of communist designs vis-a-vis the developing nations has prompted communist strategists to step up their efforts to gain the cooperation of the so-called "middle" or "intermediate" strata (*promezhutochnye sloi*). The greater the disillusionment with the national bourgeoisie, the greater the tendency to stress the role of the Third World's intermediate strata. "When elaborating the strategic line of the Party," states the *Fundamentals*, "...it is necessary to determine correctly the attitude of the Party to the largest *intermediate section* of the population..."[1] Referring evidently to these intermediate strata, G. Mirskii bewailed in 1963 the lack of "any study of those elements of society in the under-developed countries which do not fit into the concept of 'bourgeoisie' but which in many countries play a very large and even leading role."[2] The communist parties of Asian, African and Latin American countries were urged at the previously mentioned 1964 MEIMO discussion on "Capitalism, Socialism, the Less Developed Countries" not to become "fenced off from the nonproletarian strata of the society and their political parties, but to strengthen association with them as much as possible, to pay even greater attention to the intermediate strata, the urban petty bourgeoisie, the intelligentsia, the students, liberal professions, and draw them more boldly into participation in the united national front."[3] Writing in the 1971 volume of *International Affairs*, another Soviet writer stresses the importance of the "intermediate sections (petty proprietors, handicraftsmen, artisans, petty traders, office employees, army officers, intellectuals, persons engaged in free professions, etc.)" who constitute "65 percent of the urban population in the countries of Asia and Africa."[4]

In the same vein, the 1969 International Conference of Communist and Workers' Parties came out wholeheartedly for communist cooperation with the "large masses of middle strata" which were said to be "coming forward in defense of their interests, joining the struggle for general democratic demands, and becoming increasingly conscious of the vital importance of united action with the working class." To smooth the way for this cooperation the *Declaration* adopted by the Conference has even made a subtle terminological adjustment. Whereas the 1960 *Declaration of Eighty-One Communist Parties* spoke of the "urban middle *bourgeoisie*," the 1969 Declaration, referring evidently to the same social grouping, uses consistently the term "urban middle *strata*," a term which has, of course, a better ring for Marxist-Leninist ears.[5]

Just which classes or social groups are supposed to belong to these intermediate strata is not quite clear. Neither the *Fundamentals* nor other Soviet studies of non-communist social systems provide a uniform answer or reliable criteria in this matter. Discussing the classes in "exploiting" societies, the *Fundamentals* distinguishes between two categories, namely: a. the "basic classes," described as "those without which the mode of production prevailing in society could not exist and which have been brought about into being by this very mode of production"; and b. the "non-basic classes" which are not further defined.[6] Dealing specifically with "bourgeois" societies, the official Soviet manual lists "*the capitalists* (bourgeoisie) and "*the wage-earners* (proletariat)" as the only two "basic classes" and, by the same token, relegates all other social groupings to the category of "non-basic" classes. Mentioned among the latter are the landlords, peasantry, the petty bourgeoisie, the intelligentsia and "the declassed elements — the lumpen proletarians — the 'dregs' of capitalist society consisting of bandits, thieves, beggars, prostitutes, and so on."[7] However, when calling the communists' attention to the above-mentioned "largest intermediate section of the population," the *Fundamentals* gives no clue as to what particular group it has in mind. This uncertainty has been compounded further by the 1969 *Declaration* which not only fails to define or even describe what it calls the "urban middle strata," but refers to them as if they did not comprise such segments of the society as the intellectuals, students, petty bourgeoisie or "democratic army circles."[8]

The confused handling of the issue makes it difficult to determine accurately which social groups in the developing nations are actually meant to constitute the said intermediate strata. Perhaps one comes closest to the prevailing view if one should consider as "intermediate" four social strata deemed to be neither proletarian nor bourgeois in most of the communist literature dealing with the subject, namely:

    a. the petty bourgeoisie;

    b. the "progressive" or "revolutionary" intelligentsia;

    c. the "patriotic officers" or "democratically minded army circles";

    d. the "revolutionary democrats."

The Petty Bourgeoisie

The definition and the place of the petty bourgeoisie in the communist analyses of class structure, both Soviet and Chinese, have remained fairly constant over the years. The main criteria distinguishing petty bourgeoisie from bourgeoisie proper have been the small size of the former's holdings and the absence of exploitation of labor. "These are people," states the *Fundamentals*, referring to petty bourgeoisie, "who have possession of smalls means of production, but unlike the big bourgeoisie, do not live by exploiting the labour of others." The bulk of the petty bourgeoisie consists of artisans. craftsmen, small retail merchants and other such small individual self-employers, although small owner-peasants and "petty intellectuals" occasionally also are included in the petty-bourgeois category.[9] The petty bourgeoisie is said to occupy "an intermediate position" in capitalist society. "As owners of private property, they adhere to the bourgeoisie, but as representatives of the strata who live by their own labor and are exploited by the bourgeoisie, they adhere to the workers." However, as the current thesis goes, their economic status progressively worsens as capitalism develops and advances; they suffer more and more from the ruthless competition of big capital and, as a result, they are being increasingly transformed into an enemy of capitalism."[10]

Among the intermediate strata, the petty bourgeoisie, though deemed to be somewhat "unstable and wavering," has since Lenin's days been considered as a "natural ally of the working class."[11] This precept is said to have been violated by Stalin who maintained that "the intermediate strata and forces, in particular, the petty-bourgeois parties," had to be "the object of the 'main blow'" and who thus was guilty of "voluntarily throwing them into the arms of the enemy."[12] The Soviet spokesmen have striven hard in the recent years to correct this strategic blunder. They have been emphasizing Lenin's teaching on how to take advantage of the vacillations of the petty bourgeois elements by making certain concessions to them."[13] They have warned against the tendencies neglecting the petty bourgeoisie's role in the revolution, not differentiating properly between the petty bourgeoisie and bourgeoisie proper, and "displaying an inability or unwillingness' to multiply contacts with the petty urban bourgeoisie.[14] Noting that the petty bourgeoisie has been growing in numbers and importance in the developing countries, and that these countries are, as Ulyanovskii put it, "an ocean of petty-bourgeois trends,"[15] Soviet specialists in the affairs of the Third World, have urged that more attention be paid to it by native communists and that advantage be taken of the fact that the interests of the petty bourgeoisie have begun increasingly to clash with those of the national bourgeoisie and other bourgeois strata.[16] As asserted in the *Declaration* adopted by the 1969 Conference of Communist and Workers' Parties, the "patriotic-minded sections of the petty bourgeoisie" of the Third World are, together with "other democratic forces," in a "sharpening conflict" with "the forces of domestic reaction."[17] Also, communist writers have pointed to the "substantial difference" between "bourgeois-nationalist socialism" aiming at a sort of "abstract just society" and "petty-bourgeois popular socialism" which presumably develops gradually in the desirable direction of the "scientific" socialism.[18]

Similarly, the Chinese strategy-makers have always viewed the petty bourgeoisie as an ally of the proletariat. Analysing the classes in Chinese society in an article written in 1926, Mao Tse-tung referred to the petty bourgeoisie as "our closest friend."[19] Thirteen years later, he pointed out that the petty bourgeoisie, which suffers from the multiple oppression of imperialism, feudalism and big bourgeoisie, forms "one of the motive forces of the revolution and a reliable ally of the proletariat."[20] Thus the positive role of the petty bourgeoisie in the revolutionary process appears to be one of the aspects of communist strategy on which there is no disagreement between the Chinese and the Russians.

This attitude seems also to be shared by native communists of the Third World. Writing in the *World Marxist Review*, Luis Corvalan, Secretary General of the Chilean Communist party, devotes a good deal of attention precisely to the relationship between communists and the petty bourgeoisie.[21] Claiming that "a considerable section of the petty-bourgeoisie are adopting a revolutionary attitude and fighting for the liberation of our continent with the aim of building socialism," he discerns "a distinct bond between the revolutionary trends of the proletariat on the one hand, and those of the petty bourgeoisie, on the other." He warns that this manifestation of the petty-bourgeoisie's "revolutionary mood" should not be regarded as "merely a posture or as an act of desperation." He asserts that the Cuban revolution "has demonstrated that the petty bourgeoisie has a potential of revolutionary courage in battling for national liberation and socialism." Therefore, he insists that "the proletariat must put the accent on unity" with the petty bourgeoisie and he labels the "mutual understanding, cooperation and united action by the proletariat and the revolutionary petty bourgeoisie" to be "a matter of first magnitude." Corvalan goes even so far as to concede, if necessary, the petty bourgeoisie the position of leadership: "While the Latin-American bourgeoisie is no longer capable of heading revolutionary process (though some sections of it may participate in them), the petty bourgeoisie is still a revolutionary force and one that may even play a leading role in countries where the working class is weak numerically and lacks the needed political weight."

Although the petty bourgeoisie's role as an important ally of the proletariat and its vanguard is well established in communist theory and strategy, there are certain problems. Unlike the national bourgeoisie, the petty bourgeoisie is not deemed by communist theoreticians to be possessed of a "dual" character, the notorious Leninist version of the Jekyll-Hyde syndrome. Nonetheless, it too is exposed to certain "vacillations" and is "not infrequently susceptible to the influence of various, often contradictory social forces."[22] It tends "to under-rate the workers and the Communist parties, to gravitate towards nationalism, recklessness, terror and, at times, even anti-communism and anti-Sovietism."[23] It is "susceptible to despair and subjectivism."[24] Due to its "petty-bourgeois consciousness," it succumbs occasionally to "reformist illusions," "pseudo-reformism," "populism," and "economism."[25] A typical petty bourgeois is an "egocentrist" lacking in discipline and organizational ability, prone to succumb to "idealism," "anarchistic individualism" and "nationalistic hysteria."[26] Above all, the petty bourgeoisie of the Third World is considered to be especially vulnerable to the wooing of the national bourgeoisie which is said to be fearful of a possible alliance of the petty bourgeoisie and the proletariat and, therefore, does all it can to prevent such a calamity.[27]

As these and other similar complaints indicate, the strategy of drawing the Third World's petty bourgeoisie toward communism has thus far been rather unsuccessful. While, as Tiagunenko put it with customary Marxist-Leninist euphemism, there have been cases "of the more farsighted representatives of the petty bourgeoisie going over to the positions of the working class,"[28] the bulk of the petty bourgeoisie of the developing countries has been notably cool to the communist wooing. As the Soviet Africanist B. Iordanskii complains in his 1970 volume on *The Blind Alleys and Prespectives of Tropical Africa*, it has proved more difficult to deal successfully with the African petty bourgeoisie than "to curb the activity of two or three Western monopolies or to nationalize the local branches of foreign banks."[29]

It would thus seem that in most instances the petty bourgeoisie has displayed a distinct preference for cooperation with the national bourgeoisie with which it feels a closer affinity than with the proletariat and the communist vanguard. Why that is so can be easily understood. After all, a typical member of the petty bourgeoisie, a handicraftsman, an artisan, a small retail merchant, takes pride in being an independent entrepreneur. He undoubtedly welcomes the nationalization of big enterprises as that does not hurt him and may even ease his situation by relieving him from a stiff competition. But he would resent any steps weakening his status as independent businessman. Although communist propagandists try to do their best to convince him that no such steps are contemplated, the communists' opponents tell him otherwise. Neither side may fully convince him, but the conflicting assertions are usually enough to make him rather mistrustful of communist motives and ulterior designs. Thus it looks as if the communist expectations that the "petty bourgeois popular socialism" will develop toward the Marxist-Leninist "scientific socialism" belonged to the realm of wishful thinking. It is much more likely that the petty bourgeoisie of the Third World will remain under the "pernicious influence of reformism."

The Intelligentsia

Unlike the petty bourgeoisie, the intelligentsia is not deemed to be an independent class in official Marxist-Leninist ideology. Rather, it is defined as "a special social group which exists by selling its mental labour."[30] Since it should not make any difference whether the type of labor one has to sell to earn one's livelihood is physical or mental, the intelligentsia ought to be considered as an integral part of the working class, at least that portion of it which has employee status. However, while adhering in substance to such a view with regard to the "toiling intelligentsia" of Soviet Russia and other communist countries, Marxist-Leninist theoreticians do not follow through when it

comes to the intelligentsia outside of the world socialist system.
Noting that the intelligentsia of the non-communist world,
inclusive of the Third World, is drawn overwhelmingly from
various ranks of the bourgeoisie and petty-bourgeoisie, and only
in very small numbers from the families of manual workers, they
view it not as a single entity, but as a broad composite stratum
consisting of several layers or sub-strata and undergoing a
progressive class differentiation.[31] Mainly, however, they distinguish between the intelligentsia's "upper strata" that are said
to gravitate toward the capitalists and the imperialists, and the
"lower strata", usually referred to as "revolutionary" or "progressive" intelligentsia, that are expected gradually to come
closer to the working class and eventually "go over to the
Marxist-Leninist position."[32] As a prominent Soviet Africanist
puts it, whereas the "progressive representatives" of the Third
World's intelligentsia "realize bold and radical reforms in the
interests of their nations," its other portion, "torn apart from the
masses, threw itself into the political struggle from mercenary
motives, striving after power and personal enrichment."[33]

Mindful of the radical leanings of the Russian intelligentsia in
the latter years of Imperial Russia and the major role it had
played in undermining and eventually toppling Tsarism, communist strategists hope that the intelligentsia may play a somewhat
similar role in the Third World. Being mostly of bourgeois
origin, the Asian, African and Latin American intelligentsia is
thought to be of a rather faulty class provenance. Nonetheless,
there are several factors that lead communists to expect the
"progressive" segments of the Third World's intelligentsia to
cooperate with them not only at the national democratic stage of
the revolution but also in putting it on the road toward socialism.
More than any other group, the Asian, African and Latin
American intelligentsia feels frustrated at the woefully slow pace
of reforms so badly needed to break out from what Richard
Lowenthal calls "the magic circle of stagnation and backwardness."[34] Eager to modernize at almost any cost, it is all the
more easily tempted to listen to assurances that the communist
model of development, which helped to transform Russia in one
generation from a backward agrarian country into an industrial
giant, offers perhaps the coveted miraculous shortcut from

backwardness to modernity, from poverty to prosperity. It sees the diehard conservatism and the vested interests of the ruling circles in many developing countries as a major obstacle of progress and tends to believe that only a radical political, economic and social revolution is capable of bringing about a genuine change for the better. More lax in religious belief than other population strata and searching for a new creed, the intelligentsia has a natural tendency to reach for a ready-made all-embracing "world outlook" offered by the propagators of Marxism-Leninism. Weak in its own political resources and lacking in discipline, it displays an understandable inclination toward hitching its wagon to an aggressive world-wide international movement brandishing confidently an assurance of inescapable victory.[35]

Thus the intelligentsia, tagged by Mirskii in 1969 as "the social stratum which, owing to the weakness of the potential 'basic classes,' has temporarily gained dominance in most developing countries," has become a major target of communist wooing.[36] Aware though they are of certain problems involved, both the Soviet and the native communists seem to be generally optimistic as to the success of their efforts in this respect.[37] "The *intelligentsia* is a social stratum on which the ideas of Marxism-Leninism exert the greatest influence," writes a Latin American communist discussing the intelligentsia's role in communist strategy.[38] Claiming that the achievements of the world socialist system have given the intelligentsia convincing proof that Marxism is "the only scientific pholosophy" and that "socialism releases the creative powers of man," communist strategy-makers feel confident that the "revolutionary" intelligentsia of the Third World will gradually be shifting more and more to the positions of scientific socialism and to ever fuller cooperation with the communists.[39] The intellectuals' "social interests intertwine with those of the working class," asserts the 1969 *Moscow Declaration*, "their creative aspirations clash with the interests of the monopoly employers who place profit above all else." Thus "different groups of intellectuals are coming more and more into conflict with monopolies" and "the alliance of workers by hand and by brain is becoming an increasingly important force in the struggle for peace, democracy and social progress, for the democratic control of production, of cultural institutions and information media and for the development of public education in the interest of the people."

The Students

Students are an important component of the Third World's "revolutionary" intelligentsia which the communist strategists view as especially promising. Although they come predominantly from bourgeois families, there are certain psychological, environmental and other factors that, in communist opinion, help many of them to overcome their bourgeois heritage and background and impel them to join in "the revolutionary movement of the working masses." As suggested in communist analyses of the Third World's student bodies, such are (in addition to the previously mentioned factors influencing the intelligentsia in general): rebelliousness, high-minded idealism and "revolutionary romanticism" traditionally associated with student youth; dissatisfaction with the "semi-feudal" and "semi-colonial" conditions prevalent in many developing countries; impatience with the deficiencies and limited opportunities of their own education which leaves them ill-prepared to cope with the major technological, scientific and economic problems crying for solution in their own countries; realization of the limitations imposed on their own "development potential" by their countries' social, economic and political system dominated by reactionary interests.[40] Moreover, the elemental urge for change and the missionary zeal make them natural opponents of the *status quo,* whatever it may be. While student protests are directed against communist regimes in countries of the world socialist system, they inevitably turn against anti-communist and non-communist governments and become liable to exploitation by communist and pro-communist elements in countries where communists are in opposition. As pointed out by Lipset, university education "is inherently a modernizing force, and hence in underdeveloped countries it will be in conflict with those elements seeking to maintain traditional values and institutions..."[41] Thus it is not surprising that communist agitators have found a fertile soil and a suitable climate for their operations precisely among the restive student bodies of the Third World. This all the more so as their penetration has been greatly facilitated by several additional factors:

a. the ease with which the students, already assembled on the respective campuses, could be organized and converted to ready-made audiences for accomplished communist demagogues;

b. the tradition of university autonomy, making government intervention on academic soil politically difficult and rather unpopular, since it could be interpreted as an unwarranted infringement of freedom even when it was clearly needed to suppress lawlessness and subversion;

c. the habit of wealthy families of sending their children for studies abroad or to private universities at home, reducing thus still further the reservoir of potential non-communist student leadership at native state universities;

d. the highly inflammable anti-Westernism feeding on the memories of Western colonialism and, in case of Latin America in particular, the exaggerated notions of the American "dollar diplomacy" and the dislike of the economic proponderance of the United States in the Western hemisphere;

e. the low participation of non-communist students in campus elections and the lack of unity among democratic student forces, both of which often enable a tightly organized and strongly politically motivated minority of communist and pro-communist activists to gain control of student government.[42]

Communist endeavors among the students seem to have been most successful thus far in Latin America where they have been aided, in addition to the factors just mentioned, by the long-standing Latin American student tradition of political activism and a tendency to resort to violent encounters with government authorities. "...most Latin American universities have become strongholds of the revolutionary struggle," asserts a Latin American communist in an analysis of the student movement in Latin America.[43] He contends that the influence of the "revolutionary Left," as communists customarily designate combinations of communist and pro-communist elements, "is now predominant in the universities of Mexico, Venezuela, Guatemala, the Dominican Republic, El Salvador, Panama, Nicaragua, Brazil, Ecuador, Peru and Uruguay." He goes on to say that "the majority of the students support the revolutionary trends" in Chile and Argentine while "the Left and conservative groups are about equally balanced" in Colombia, Honduras and Bolivia. The Prague-based *International Union of Students* (IUS), one of the most active international communist Front organizations, claims the affiliation of student unions or federations of some fifteen to seventeen Latin American countries.[44] The magnitude of the communist efforts to gain control of Latin American student bodies has been duly noted by Western observers. "Communists have been able to exercise a degree of influence through organizational sophistication which is quite out of proportion to their numerical strength," writes a U.S. student of Latin American affairs. "The efforts of Communists to penetrate, influence and control the student movement are enormous and well-planned undertakings."[45] Meant to describe the situation in Brazil, this statement fits admirably the conditions in most of the other Latin American countries as well.[46]

That communist claims are no idle boasts has been borne out also by actual events. Here are a few illustrations culled from reports by Western analysts and this writer's own on-the-spot observations and interviews.

Probably the most extreme, and most unbelievable, example of what communists could do with a University when allowed a free hand is offered by the Central University of Venezuela at Caracas in the middle sixties. Although no more than 1,500 of the University's student body of over 25,000 were considered to be communists, and of those only some 200 were hard-core stalwarts and "professional revolutionaries," this small but well organized and well-financed minority managed to convert the campus into the main base of communist operations not only in Caracas but also of the countryside.[47] Under the protective shield of academic autonomy barring police from the campus, the University became a sanctuary and recuperation area of communist terrorists, a supply, fund-raising and recruiting center for communist guerrillas—one of the dormitories was even nicknamed Stalingrad — and a convenient cache for stolen cars, police and army uniforms, weapons and explosives of all sorts. It also served as command headquarters for the planning and direction of subversive activities ranging from bank robberies "for the people's cause" to kangaroo court "trials," cold-blooded assassinations and torturing of opponents on university grounds. As bared by evidence pieced together after the government crackdown of December 1966, many non-communist students and faculty members were aware of some of these activities, but kept silent, mainly for fear of reprisals.

A classic illustration of communist exploitation of student discontent has been supplied by the uprising that took place in April 1966 at Mexico's National University in Mexico City, the largest of Latin America's institutions of higher learning. A strike in which some 3,000 of the University's more than 70,000 students participated to protest against the campus police and the tougher entrance examinations was manipulated into a bloody anti-American and pro-Castro riot. The violence was instigated by a hard core of some 400 communist activists and members of the communist-controlled Mexican Movement of National Liberation (MLN), helped by outside agents. Aided by the absence of regular police, who stayed out of the fracas in deference to the principle of university autonomy, the communist-led rioters shouted pro-communist slogans, seized the University radio station and several buildings, ransacked them and brought about the resignation of the University's Rector and 35 professors.[48] Among the outsiders joining and supporting the rioters were reported to have been students from the University of Michoacan in the state of Morelia, considered to be Mexico's most communist-infiltrated campus. Some 25 percent of its 7,500 students are regarded as communists and pro-communists and as ever ready to resort to violence. Its one-time Rector, subsequently dismissed by the State's Governor, declared in 1963 that the philosophical and ideological orientation of the University must be based on the philosophy of dialectical and historical materialism and the doctrine of scientific socialism.[49] He was also reported to have disbursed in 17 months over 50,000 dollars' worth of University funds to pro-communist and anti-U.S. groups and publications.[50] According to reports of Mexican authorities, communist agitators were at work also in the pre-Olympic student riots in Mexico City, which led to the occupation of the campus of the National University by the Mexican army in October 1968. The communist involvement in the student uprisings both in Morelia in 1966 and in Mexico City in 1968 has been proudly recognized by the communists themselves. While denying that the student movement was "an instrument of communist conspiracy," a Mexican communist writing in the *World Marxist Review* stated bluntly that "the Communist Party [of Mexico] supported the student movement without any reservation" and that the communists were "one of the political forces taking part in the fight."[51]

Much the same situation prevailed and still seems to prevail at Uruguay's University in Montevideo. Its Federation of Uruguayan University Students (FEUU), whose secretariat is led by an avowed communist, has a consistent pro-communist record and is known to have close contacts with the huge Soviet Embassy in Montevideo, said to be the headquarters for Soviet operations through South America. The University's journal *Gaceta Universitaria* has become virtually an organ of the Uruguayan Communist party.[52] The FEUU revealed once again its true face during the OAS Conference of the Heads of State at Punta del Este in April 1967. Communist students and their sympathizers battled with police, distributed vitriolic leaflets denouncing "Johnson, the Assassin," and barricaded themselves on the University campus. As this writer could witness in person, small gangs of pro-communist students, who quickly assembled to shout a few vituperative slogans and to break a few windows of American companies, and who promptly dispersed to evade the police, were the only groups that staged anti-American demonstrations in downtown Montevideo during the Punta del Este conference.[53]

Across the La Plata the University of Buenos Aires presented a similar picture. Again, a small minority of communist activists and their sympathizers for years misused the University autonomy, making the University a focal point of pro-communist agitation, interfering with the orderly processes of teaching and discriminating against professors not sharing the minority's extremist views.[54] When the government finally felt compelled to step in and abolish the much abused autonomy, it could establish order only after a pitched battle with some 300 students and at the cost of incurring the wrath of a good many non-communist students and faculty members who felt obligated to protest, partly for fear of becoming unpopular among the students.

This catalogue of illustrations of communist operations among the Latin American students could be continued for several more pages as similar attempts to utilize student dissatisfaction and demonstrations for communist-desired ends have occurred in recent years in Peru, Colombia, Panama, Brazil, Ecuador, the Dominican Republic and elsewhere.[55] But these would be only varied refrains of the same old tune. The story is much the same throughout Africa, non-communist Asia and the Middle East. There, too, many university campuses have become hotbeds of leftist extremism that plays all too frequently into the hands of communist strategists and facilitates their manipulations. Some 25 to 29 student unions of Asian, Middle Eastern and African countries are affiliated with the communist-controlled International Union of Students.[56] Although the communist penetration of the African and Asian student bodies is not quite so pronounced as in Latin America, communists and pro-communists do invariably constitute the best-organized, most active and most vociferous groups on most of the campuses and control, or at least have a strong voice in, a substantial number of student unions and federations, new and old. Thus, to cite a few examples, the *All-India Student Federation* (AISF), the oldest student organization in India founded in 1936, has been under communist control since 1940.[57] Communists dominate the highly enterprising *National Union of Algerian Students* (UNEA), which also brought to Algiers the permanent headquarters for the communist-influenced *Pan-African Student Conference*.[58] Eventually, Col. Boumedienne's regime dissolved the Union in 1972 for becoming a tool of the Avant-Garde Socialist Party, a clandestine group linked to the outlawed Algerian Communist party. Communists, especially those of the pro-Chinese variation, seem to have played also a major role in the recurrent anti-government riots at the Burmese University at Rangoon[59] and the Universities of Ceylon one of which was converted into an arsenal for the abortive insurrection of 1971.[60] Attempts to turn student discontent to communist advantage have also occurred at a number of the universities of Black Africa, such as those of Dakar, Zambia and Madagaskar.[61]

The Problems Encountered

While registering considerable success among the Third World's intelligentsia, especially the students, communist strategists have encountered a number of difficulties.

One of the main faults that the communists find with the "revolutionary intelligentsia" and its student segment is its political and ideological instability. Although considered less unreliable in this respect than the national bourgeoisie and even the petty bourgeoisie, its non-proletarian character is deemed to expose it to "vacillation", one-sided approach to Marxism-Leninism, "nationalism", "reformism", and similar fickle characteristics.[62] This is true, above all, of the students. "Alas, youth and student years are transient," comments ruefully a Latin American communist who discovers that, upon completing their studies, many once revolutionary students tend to "settle down to a measured life within the framework of the existing order."[63] Also, the same emotionalism, "romanticism," and youthful impatience that makes students so receptive to the inflammatory ideology of Marxism-Leninism, easily gives way to disillusionment if and when the initial revolutionary glamor wears off and the doctrine's seemingly infallible guidance and lavish promises begin to lose their credibility.

Nor is it quite as inevitable as communist analysts would like to believe that students of lower class origin should necessarily be drawn to the extreme left. As Lipset suggests, "students from relatively poor families tend to come from that minority within the lower strata which is strongly oriented toward upward mobility and the values of the privileged."[64] Coming from families likely to be "among the more politically conservative of their class" and being usually vocationally oriented they are less interested in extracurricular political activities.

Another problem that causes communist strategists no small concern stems from the Sino-Soviet split and Castro's deviationism. While cutting across other facets of communist strategy in the Third World, the split is most pronounced among younger intellectuals and students. Impatient to attain quick and decisive results, despairing of the slow working of the Soviet-sponsored "peaceful coexistence" strategy, and attracted by the exciting vision of guerrilla heroism, many of them lean toward the strategy of relentless armed struggle at all costs advocated by the Chinese communists and by Castro, a strategy that the Soviet leaders, their East European colleagues and the Third World's pro-Soviet communists denounce as "adventurism" and "blanquism."[65]

The division has become especially sharp in Latin America, where virulent Castroism and the Maoist type of extremism seem to have gained ascendancy among the students and younger intellectuals over the more cautious Soviet approach. An example in point is offered by the *Fourth Latin American Student Congress* that met at Havana in July-August 1966 with an attendance of some 100 representatives of 22 student associations of Latin America and 50 guests and observers. The Congress decided to set up a permanent revolutionary *Student Organization for the Latin American Continent* (OCLAE) with headquarters at Havana. It adopted a militant resolution echoing the Castroite view that "the winning of political power in different countries of Latin America for the benefit of the popular masses cannot be achieved by electoral means but only through revolutionary violence that overthrows the dominating class."[66] The newly established organization also chose to remain independent despite the efforts made by the pro-Soviet *International Union of Students* to get it affiliated with the IUS.

The dissension between the Castroites and the pro-Soviet forces came to the fore also at a Latin American Student Conference held at Merida, Venezuela, in September 1968. Communist presidents of student unions of five Venezuelan Universities, including the Central University at Caracas, walked out in protest against the "divisionist attitudes" of the Castroite-controlled *Universidad de los Andes* which organized the conference in co-operation with the above-mentioned Havana-based *Organizacion Continental Latino Americana de Estudiantes*.[67] Pro-Chinese communists (PCE-ML) managed in their turn to seize control in 1968 of the *Ecuadorean University Student Federation* (FEUE).[68]

A similar parting of the ways occurred among the Afro-Asian writers. The *Afro-Asian Writers' Permanent Bureau*, a communist Front organization originally founded by the Russians in

Tashkent in 1958 and later on moved to Ceylon, was taken over in 1966 by the Chinese communists who convened an "emergency meeting" of the Bureau in Peking in June 1966 with a claimed attendance of delegates from 52 countries and 4 international organizations.[69] On the other hand, the pro-Soviet faction of the Bureau, which held simultaneously an "extraordinary meeting" at Cairo, managed to secure attendance only from six countries (Cameroon, Ceylon, India, Sudan, U.A.R. and USSR).[70]

A major setback for communist operations among the student bodies of the Third World has been the abolition or restriction of University autonomy and the concomitant immunities that has been enacted in a number of countries of the Third World in recent years, such as Venezuela, Panama, Colombia, Argentina, Brazil and Burma. While the curtailment of this relic of the feudal era has given communist and pro-communist agitators a welcome battle slogan, it has been well worth the price as it has denied the communists and their associates privileged sanctuaries in the most desirable strategic locations. Furthermore, it has eased substantially the position of the overwhelming majority both of students who do come to the universities, even in Latin America, to secure an education rather than to engage in politics, and faculty members who prefer the pursuit of knowledge to cultivating demagoguery and catering to the whims of the extremist fringes of the student bodies.

Also, the communist utilization of college campuses has been rendered more difficult wherever the authorities have taken the long overdue steps to get rid of perennial "students" who register not so much for the sake of furthering their education and obtaining a college diploma, but in order to legitimize their presence on the campus for purposes of political activism. Thus, for instance, the resolute enforcement of the rule that a student must take a certain minimum of credit hours and maintain a C or better average resulted in the separation of some 3,000 persons from the student roster of the *National University of Panama*. Coupled with strict control of access to the University campus so as to keep out non-student agitators, this measure seems to have gone a long way toward curbing communist activities.[71] Similarly, more than 2,800 students were reported to have been separated from the Southern University of Bahia Blanca, Brazil, in 1967, for failing examinations.[72] Remedial measures of a similar nature have been taken by the governments of several other countries.

Nor do pro-communist student unions and groups go unchallenged within the student bodies themselves. On many campuses, especially in Latin America, they have recently found competition on the part of Christian democratic student associations. "The growing influence of the *Christian Democrat* trend is another complex and contradictory process characteristic of the student movement on our continent," writes a Latin American communist analyst who considers the "Christian Democratic trend" to be "today the main rival of the revolutionary forces in the student movement."[73] The Christian Democratic influence is especially strong among the Chilean students. In 1968 the Christian Democrats won control for the eighth time in a row of the Student Federation at the University of Chile at Santiago, the largest of Chile's institutions of higher learning, gaining eleven seats on the Federation's Executive Board as against two for pro-Soviet communists and one each for pro-Chinese extremists, the Castroites, and the right wing group. Moreover, in 1968 the Christian Democrats retained control of student bodies of five other Chilean Universities.[74] In 1971, the Chilean communists and their allies suffered another setback in high school student elections in Santiago when Christian Democratic students won ten of the fifteen student offices.[75] Finally, in 1972 communists and their associates registered their worst defeat since Allende's ascension to Chile's Presidency when Eduardo Boeninger, the candidate of the University Front led by the Christian Democrats, was reelected as Rector of the University of Chile. This time Boeninger won the student vote in all but one of the twelve schools of the University's Santiago campus as well as in eight of the University's nine provincial campuses. Moreover, the communist-led People's Union also lost the control of the University Senate.[76]

The divisions within the radical student movement could not but further impair the effectiveness of the *International Union of Students* in its assigned role as a promoter of the Soviet cause among the student bodies of the developing countries. This was well illustrated by the proceedings of the IUS's Tenth Congress held at Bratislava (Czechoslovakia) in February 1971. As revealed by a French delegate to the Congress, strong protests against "the anti-democratic practices and manipulations" by pro-Soviet managers of the Congress were lodged at various stages of the proceedings by student delegations from such countries of the Third World as Argentine, Mexico, El Salvador, the Dominican Republic, Venezuela, Bolivia, the Federation of Black African Students and the Federation of Madagaskar students in France, and even Cuba.[77] Delegates from Guadeloupe and Martinique could not come because they were refused Czechoslovak visas and those from Guatemala and Honduras because the organizers of the Congress "forgot" to send them their air tickets. A sharp controversy developed over the question which of the two rival delegations from Argentina, one pro-Soviet and the other led by adherents of the secessionist "Revolutionary Communist Party," should be seated.

The participation of the intelligentsia and the students in the revolutionary process also has complicated the issue of leadership. Being the best educated stratum of the population and considering itself better qualified than any other social group to know what is good for its respective countries, the intelligentsia and, above all, its radical student segment, aspires to the position of leadership and shows no inclination to yield it to the working class or any other group or class. These aspirations of the Third World's students and intellectuals have been well expressed in Regis Debray's *Revolution in the Revolution*: "The irony of history has willed, by virtue of the social situation of many Latin American countries, the assignment of precisely this vanguard role to students and revolutionary intellectuals, who have had to unleash or rather initiate the highest forms of class struggle."[78] Although Debray refers specifically to Latin America, similar aspirations are entertained by students and intellectuals in other parts of the Third World as well.

A thorny dilemma has thus developed and led to a bitter controversy in which Soviet and pro-Soviet theoreticians condemn unnamed but easily identifiable spokesmen of "ultra-leftism" for considering the Third World's working class as "incapable of taking the lead in the revolutionary process" and urging that the leadership role be assigned to other groups, especially the students.[79] Moreover, doubts about the feasibility of working class leadership in many of the developing countries and queries about the possibility of a substitute leadership from the ranks of the "progressive" intelligentsia and the students have been expressed even by some of the Third World's communists of known pro-Soviet leanings.[80] As stressed by an African participant in the earlier mentioned 1969 Symposium, "where the working class is weak, the transition to non-capitalism can be directed only by a democratic intelligentsia that has absorbed the ideas of Marxism-Leninism and is prepared to create the conditions for a Marxist-Leninist party."[81]

An interesting attempt to reconcile these divergent views has been made by a Latin American communist specialist in student affairs. While adhering to the official Soviet view stressing the desirability and necessity of ultimate working class leadership, the writer asserts that this "should not be taken to imply that in some countries, in some circumstances and at particular moments the student movement cannot *objectively* become a force capable of being in the van of the revolutionary struggle and, in a sense, of·taking the lead in the struggle." The "vacuum of public leadership" created in much of Latin America as well as Asia and Africa by the weakness of the working class, the passivity of the peasantry, and the defection of the national bourgeoisie should, in the author's opinion, be filled by students. He considers the students to be "the most active and mobile section of the revolutionary vanguard," acting as "a kind of social detonator" or "small engine" that sets "the big engine" of mass struggle into motion. Drawing a distinction between the "historical vanguard" and "the real, concrete vanguard," he holds that "situations may arise...where the working class, the 'historical vanguard,' does not lead the 'concrete struggle in a concrete period', in which case the role of the shock force of the movement is assumed by 'the real, concrete vanguard,' i.e., as often as not by one or another contingent of the intellectuals..."[82]

However, the continued communist duelling over the leadership issue suggests that this well-meant attempt of eating one's theoretical cake and having it, too, did not succeed in solving the dilemma.

Finally, Soviet efforts to condition the Third World's intelligentsia and student bodies favorably toward the Soviet-style "scientific socialism" and to make them fulfill the role assigned them in Soviet strategy were damaged by the 1968 Soviet invasion of Czechoslovakia. Soviet Russia's resort to naked force to impose her will upon a small nation whose communist leaders continued to insist on their loyalty to Marxism-Leninism could only tarnish the carefully cultivated image of the Soviet Union as the most trustworthy friend of the national-liberation movement and defender of the national sovereignty of developing countries against the alleged "imperialist" and "neocolonialist" cabals. Matters were made even worse by the clumsy Soviet attempt to justify the invasion by distinguishing between the (wrong) "abstract" and the (right) "concrete" sovereignty, rejecting a "narrowly formal" interpretations of national self-determination and proclaiming officially and publicly the Soviet right of intervention whenever and wherever a "socialist" regime departed from the kind of socialism approved by Soviet leaders.[83] While the Soviet action and the twisted theoretical justification advanced in its support undoubtedly dismayed most of the Third World's Soviet sympathizers irrespective of their social status and occupation, the disillusionment was bound to be deepest precisely among the intellectuals and students, for that is where the degree of idealization of Soviet Russia's intentions ran highest. Even the Federation of African Students in Czechoslovakia issued a fiery protest "sharply condemning" the Soviet intervention and "the chauvinistic and neo-colonialist policy of the USSR that threatens the unity of the internation revolutionary and national-liberation movement." Nor could this disillusionment be but further aggravated by the servile approval of the Soviet action in Czechoslovakia on the part of the Third World's Communist parties, especially those of Latin America, a stand sharply contrasting with the resolute disapproval expressed by the bulk of the non-ruling Communist parties of Europe.[84]

The "Patriotic" Officers

Whereas the petty-bourgeoisie and the "revolutionary" intelligentsia have enjoyed the status of intermediate strata and have been credited with a "revolutionary potential" for many decades, the recent reclassification of the Third World's officers corps represent a significant and intriguing *novum* in communist class analyses. Not so long ago, the military of the non-communist part of the world were invariably considered by communist theorists as the bulwark of reaction and the very antithesis of the revolution. Recruited almost exclusively from upper and middle classes, the officers corps of the non-communist countries of Asia, Africa and Latin America were placed, alongside with the "feudalists," "latifundists" and the "big" bourgeoisie, squarely in the pro-imperialist camp.

However, in line with the recent communist tendency toward a more "creative" interpretation of the complexities of the world situation, communist specialists in Asian, African and Latin American affairs have discarded the one-sided thesis relegating the Third World's military to the status of enemies in favor of a more flexible reevaluation. "The question of the place of the military intelligentsia — the officers — until now almost neglected in Soviet literature, deserves a special study," urged two prominent Soviet students of developing nations in the Soviet journal *Mirovaia Ekonomika i Mezhdunarodnye Otnosheniia* in 1966.[85] Guided undoubtedly much less by ideological considerations than by postulates of bare necessity of having to deal with military regimes in many of the Third World's countries, communist strategists have begun, in the middle sixties, to divide the Third World's officers corps into pro-imperialist and anti-imperialist segments.

Addressing the previously mentioned MEIMO discussion on Socialism, Capitalism, the Less Developed Nations in 1964, G. Mirskii drew a distinction between the "army elite" *(verkhushka armii)* which usually leans to the right and is inclined toward anti-communism and the ordinary officers corps (*riadovoe ofitserstvo*) which constitutes in some countries "the most educated section of the intelligentsia," is "acquainted more than others with progressive ideas" and "strives to modernize their backward countries."[86] An even more forceful plea for a more favorable communist attitude toward the "patriotic" officers of the Third World was advanced in 1965 by K. Ivanov.[87] Arguing that the officers' corps of many countries of the East was chosen nowadays mostly from non-aristocratic and non-feudal elements and that the armies were not "walled off from revolutionary processes under way among the people," the author supported his plea by pointing to "Egypt, Burma, Algeria and some other countries" where "army officers formed the backbone of the revolutionary democratic forces." He even brought in the Decembrists of Imperial Russia whose "historical role" the Marxists fully recognized. Hence, "the noble heart of a patriot may beat beneath an army uniform," he averred in a rare quasi-lyrical outburst.[88]

᾿The sudden spate of military coups that occurred in Africa in 1965 and 1966 and in which the victorious officers in most instances were not exactly of the "revolutionary" variety in the communist meaning of the word, seems to have lowered somewhat the "revolutionary officers" ranking in Soviet classification.[89] Yet, despite their disappointments, the Soviet strategists evidently persist in their dichotomous differentiation of the Third World's military between their "bad" and "good" species. "It should not be thought," explains a Soviet analyst referring to the military coups in Africa in 1965-66, "that military coups are everywhere and always an instrument of reaction. Revolutionary forces also resort to them sometimes, as a means of overthrowing reactionary pro-imperialist regimes that stand in the way of social progress. Under certain conditions such [military] coups can be the start of revolutionary social changes."[90] As stressed in the authoritative Soviet volume on the *Third World*, "an event in the history of the national-liberation struggle in a number of countries has been the prominent role played for the first time by members of military intelligentsia."[91] The communist belief in this thesis could not but be further strengthened by the 1969 military take-overs in Sudan and Libya, both of which resulted in a distinct shift toward the left and toward socialism. Indeed, both coups have been warmly greeted in the Soviet press. "The most important recent events in the Third World are the revolutionary coups in the Sudan and Libya," commented G. Mirskii in *New Times*. "Young officers again, as was the case in Egypt and Syria, acted as a revolutionary force."[92] Subsequently of course, Mirskii and his colleagues had to eat their own words when the military regimes in Sudan as well as Libya failed to fulfill erstwhile Soviet expectations.

Nor have communist strategists given up hope, in spite of so many disappointments in the past, that the right kind of "patriotic" officers and soldiers might yet come to the fore in Latin America. Pointing to the choice that "the sons [of Latin American people] had between "becoming the continuers of the revolutionary traditions of their fathers and grandfathers" and serving as "the Pentagon's pretorian guard," a Soviet analyst writing in *Pravda* in 1967 concluded optimistically: "Life has confirmed that there are in Latin America no few military servicemen of different ranks who do not agree with the shameful role of the Pentagon's hirelings. These patriots are rejecting the cunning (*khitrospleteniia*) of anti-communist slanderers and are taking the road of defending the basic interests of their nations."[93] Again, communist strategists were quick to conclude that their anticipations had been realized when Velasco's and Torres's military regimes seized control of Peru and Bolivia and these "patriotically-minded army officers" began promptly to proceed with the nationalization of foreign economic interests and a substantial agrarian reform.[94] "In Latin America, too, the army ceases to be a reliable bulwark of reaction, as clearly demonstrated by the measures of the military authorities in Peru."[95]

The "Revolutionary Democrats"

Finally, the communist analysts of the Third World's social strata have identified in the middle sixties yet another neither-bourgeois-nor-proletarian element in the guise of the so-called "revolutionary democrats," sometimes also referred to as "national democrats." "This is a select group deemed to stand politically closest to the proletariat of all the intermediate strata and rated definitely the highest among them in "revolutionary potential." The revolutionary democrats presumably "understand the necessity of turning the anti-colonialist revolution into an anti-capitalist one."[96] They "associate the struggle for national independence with radical socio-economic reforms" facilitating thus "the national regeneration of the emergent states along non-capitalist lines."[97] Hopefully, they "will be drawn by the very logic of the class struggle to take their stand on the

positions of the proletariat, on the positions of scientific socialism."[98]

As is apparent from various communist pronouncements,
more than in the case of any other bourgeois, semi-bourgeois or
intermediate stratum, the decisive classification criterion of the
revolutionary democrats appears to be the closeness of their
attitude, real or assumed, to Marxism-Leninism rather than their
class origin, occupation or standing in the social hierarchy.
Although they may thus come from any social group, and may
even be found, according to the Chinese dicta, among "certain
kings, princes and aristocrats who are patriotic,"[99] they are
expected to be drawn mostly from among the most enlightened
segments of the "revolutionary intelligentsia" and "Patriotic
officers."[100] In fact, the most illustrious specimen of revolutionary democrats recognized as such (at one time or another) in
Soviet pronouncements, such as Nasser of Egypt, Ben Bella and
Col. Boumedienne of Algeria, Sukarno of Indonesia, Nkrumah
of Ghana, General Win of Burma, Nyerere of Tanzania and
Sekou Toure of Guinea, have come from the above two groups.

Since the revolutionary democrats are considered by many
communist analysts to be virtually burgeoning Marxists-Leninists who have grasped the necessity of a radical transformation of
their countries to the image of "scientific socialism," they are
ipso facto cast in the role of natural allies of the proletariat and
its communist vanguard. Hence insistence on a close and active
cooperation between communists and revolutionary democrats
has become an important aspect of communist strategy and
tactics in the Third World. The initiative has been taken by
Soviet theoreticians who had invented the new species of revolutionary democrats in the first place. They have come out in
recent years, repeatedly and emphatically, with recommenda-
tions that the Third World's communists should join hands with
the revolutionary democrats and become their "friends and
assistants."[101] Noting, that the revolutionary democrats have
become "a big force in some of the Asian and African countries," they have warned against "underrating the influence of
the national democratic parties" and "taking a haughty attitude
toward them."[102] They have accused those unwilling to collaborate with the revolutionary democrats of "sectarianism" and

unwarranted "ideological purism."[103] They view the revolutionary democrats as "a revolutionary force which is aware that in our time progress is impossible without definite steps toward socialism, which boldly takes those steps. . .and comes close to the positions of scientific socialism on a number of fundamental issues."[104] They consider them to be "naturally prone to ideological evolution" and entertain the belief that "their leftwing espouses Marxist-Leninist views. . ."[105] Thus, as stressed again in 1971 by B. Ponomaryov, "today, when states of a socialist orientation have come into existence, Communists and revolutionary democrats are objectively in one and the same camp, with greater reason than ever."[106]

Some of the Soviet strategists have gone so far as to concede the revolutionary democrats the all-important role of revolutionary leadership, and this not merely at the national democratic stage of the revolution, but also in ushering its "overgrowth" into the socialist revolution. This modification of the Marxist-Leninist teaching seems to have been initiated by G. Mirskii when he wrote in 1964 that "if conditions for proletarian leadership have not yet matured, the historic mission of breaking with capitalism can be carried out by elements close to the working class."[107] The idea was then picked up by another Soviet student of developing nations, N. A. Simonyia, who argued in an article in *Narody Azii i Afriki* in 1966 that, "if the democratic revolution is to develop into a socialist one, there must be a class displacement with the leadership going into the hands of representatives of the working class, the proletariat vanguard, *or revolutionary democrats*."[108] The modification seems to have gained also the support of A. Sobolev, R. Ulianovskii and Vladimir Li. Starting with the assertion that "the forms in which the working class exercises its leading role...are multifarious," Sobolev maintains that "the existence of the socialist world system makes it possible to carry out far-reaching social changes under the leadership of revolutionary democratic parties."[109] Ulianovskii, who is probably the most ardent of Soviet promoters of cooperation between communists and revolutionary democrats, adheres to much the same view. In his 1968 article in *Pravda* he refers with warm approval to the leading role of revolutionary democrats in countries where the proletariat has not yet become an organized class force as "a profoundly positive process."[110] However, in a more recent article in the 1971 volume of *International Affairs,* Ulyanovskii sounds rather cautious about the whole matter. While commending the "Left wing" of the "national democrats" for their work in "preparing conditions for socialist construction in the economically undeveloped countries," he stresses in no uncertain terms that "*it is the working class in the 'Third World' countries that has objectively been assigned the role of vanguard of the socialist forces, and no other class can replace it in that historic function.*"[111]

On the other hand, writing in a later number of the same Soviet journal, Li seems to be leaving the door wide open for what he calls "a gradual advance toward socialism without the immediate leadership of the organized proletariat."[112] Noting that the working class is "for the time being incapable of leading the revolutionary process" in the "overwhelming majority of the Asian and African countries," he likens the insistence on "proletarian hegemony" under these conditions to be "tantamount to advocating the 'Left'-revisionist line of 'leap frog' revolution, which separates the proletarian vanguard from the broad masses of people and other contingents of the national liberation movement, and ultimately alienates them."[113]

Nonetheless, this "profound positive process" of allowing for the leadership of revolutionary democrats is not without negative by-products and dangerous pitfalls. This is readily acknowledged even by those Soviet writers who identify with the most resolute advocates of a close communist cooperation with the revolutionary democrats. "Some representatives of the national democratic movement are rash verbal radicals lacking the persistence to achieve their purpose," cautions Ulianovskii, who finds good many of them to be defective in "capacity for iron discipline," "organization," and "the kind of intensive effort required to build a new society."[113] While "not a few leaders of the national democratic movement conscientiously study Marxist-Leninist theory and use Marxist-Leninist literature in training the national-democratic cadres," others have displayed a regrettable tendency "to restructure scientific socialism — on the pretext of 'adapting' it to local conditions — to fit geographic, historic, cultural, national and racial characteristics." Writing in *Pravda* two years later, Ulianovskii, though upholding the cooperation strategy as forcefully as ever, does admit the continued existence of differences between the communists and the revolutionary democrats on such weighty issues as "the forms and methods of reorganization," "the road of further development of the revolution," "the determination of the role of various social strata and classes" and "above all the determination of the leading role of the working class."[114]

That is, no doubt, why a good number of communist analysts do not quite share to overly optimistic view of the revolutionary democrats entertained by Ulianovskii, Mirskii, Li and their colleagues. This is true, above all, of many prominent communists of the Third World who are willing to collaborate with the revolutionary democrats, and even concede them the status of a temporary vanguard at the national-democratic phase of the revolution, but are not ready to accept the thesis that transition to socialism (as communists understand the term) could truly occur under the revolutionary democratic leadership.

Typical of their attitude is the stern rebuttal expressed by Khaled Bagdash. Conceding that situations might arise when communists should support other social groups or individual leaders "carried to the fore," Bagdash issued a strong *caveat* against any "attempts to justify such alliances by spurious theories repudiating the role of the working class both now and in the future on the pretext of developing Marxism-Leninism to meet the new conditions."[115] Similar views appear to prevail among Latin American communists. While making allowance for the leadership by "such social forces as students, peasantry, revolutionary intelligentsia and petty bourgeoisie" at the initial stages of the revolution, Ramir Otero, member of the Central Committee of the Communist party of Bolivia, stressed that "the *consolidation* of this revolution, is impossible without the *leading role* of the *working class*."[116]

Nor do all Soviet analysts by any means agree with the Mirskii-Sobolev-Li approach. Writing in *Pravda* in 1968 V. Volskii goes along with the idea of the leadership of the "revolutionary democratic strata" in the developing nations at the national anti-imperialist stage of the revolution. But he takes a different attitude when it comes to the socialist phase: "The realization of the far more complex goals and tasks of the socialist revolution...requires the leadership on the part of the vanguard party of the working class, well armed with the Marxist-Leninist theory."[117]

Thus the communist view regarding the proper role of revolutionary democrats in communist strategy vis-a-vis the Third World is far from unanimous, especially when it comes to the delicate issue of revolutionary leadership. This is hardly surprising, for results attained by the communists from cooperation with the revolutionary democrats have so far been rather mixed and inconclusive. As of 1968, seven countries of Asia and Africa were considered by Soviet analysts to be controlled by revolutionary democrats, namely, the U.A.R., Syria, Algeria, Mali, Guinea, Brazzaville Congo and Burma; one other, Tanzania, was said to be "entering upon the same road."[118] Writing three years later, Ulianovskii found revolutionary democrats to be "the ruling parties in the U.A.R., Syria, Somalia, Burma, the People's Republic of the Congo" and possibly also Tanzania.[119] These ruling "revolutionary democrats" have indeed behaved in a number of respects as communists, at least those of Soviet and pro-Soviet variety, would want them to behave. They have been nationalizing foreign-owned and big native-owned enterprises; promoting the state sector of the economy at the expense of the private sector, carrying out agrarian reforms more thorough than those undertaken in most of the other developing nations; establishing friendly relations with the Soviet Union and other countries of the world socialist system and pursuing what Soviet observers acknowledge to be "progressive external policies"; establishing "political structures having the character of one-party regimes" and assuming the forms of "revolutionary, anti-imperialist dictatorship."[120] Since these are actions that communists themselves recommend, the Soviet assertion that, wherever the revolutionary democrats are in control, they "act as Communists would were they in power" and that the communists and the revolutionary democrats go historically in one direction is not without substance.[121]

However, the question is how long will the revolutionary democrats continue doing what communists would like them to do and how far will they go along the path that the communists have marked out for them? No one can be certain, of course, of the final outcome. But the evidence that has accumulated to-date indicates that typical revolutionary democrats have no intention of traveling with the communists all the way and going ultimately over to the positions of "scientific socialism" in the Marxist-Leninist meaning of the term as some of the Soviet theoreticians seem to hope.

That has been amply documented by recent statements and actions of the leaders of most of the countries where, according to Soviet assertions, revolutionary democrats are in power. Ne Win, whose "Burmese way to socialism" had been acclaimed by the Russians, has lately displayed a strong interest in improving relations with the United States and even getting some sorely needed economic and military aid from the West. Evidently, Ne Win was prompted to seek the rapprochement with the West by his increasing problems with communist subversion in Burma.[122] Sekou Toure of Guinea, one of Soviet Russia's earliest favorites in Africa, has time and again kicked over the traces, at one time even ordering the Soviet Ambassador out of the country. Displeased with a number of aspects of communist aid he has been striving hard to get French aid. Colonel Boumedienne of Algeria, his tongue-lashing against Israel notwithstanding, has been displaying a considerable aloofness vis-a-vis the Soviet Union and the socialist world system. While exploiting to the hilt all the Soviet aid he could get, Egypt's Nasser continued until his death to pursue his old game of playing both sides against the middle rather than adopting fully and unequivocally the Soviet version of scientific socialism. To great Soviet dimay, Nasser's successor, Anvar Sadat, got rid of the most pro-Soviet group of the Arab Socialist Union and subsequently dispatched most of the Soviet advisors back to the Soviet Union. Also, the revolutionary democrats in power persist in holding their native communists under close control. Moreover, the sudden fall from power of two "revolutionary democrats" whom communist analysts considered as the most promising for their strategic purposes and whom they used to cite as the most outstanding specimen of the revolutionary democratic species, Indonesia's Sukarno and Ghana's Nkrumah, attests to the uncertainties with which communist strategists have to cope in this respect.

Thus it would seem that, generally speaking, the revolutionary democrats in the countries under their control have by now trodden the path that the communist strategists wanted them to follow about as far as they would go. Although they all believe in socialism, it is a socialism that is vastly different from the *nauchnyi sotsializm* as prescribed by Soviet theoreticians. It is true that the Third World's revolutionary democrats do often refer to "scientific socialism"; but their understanding of the term is quite unlike the Soviet. The way they use it was well explained by Nasser in 1964: "Everyone must employ scientific methods...if we want true socialism, pure and successful, it must follow scientific lines. The opposite of the scientific method is anarchy. Therefore, our socialism is scientific socialism...It is [however] not at all a materialistic socialism, we have not said that our socialism is Marxist, we have not said that we are atheistic..."[123] Nor do the revolutionary democrats recognize "the universal character of class struggle" as some communist theoreticians, such as Ulianovskii, wishfully believe.[124] Taking exception to such optimistic assessments in a letter to the editor of the *World Marxist Review*, two Soviet specialists in the affairs of the Third World ruefully concluded: "A difficult and gradual transition is under way among progressive revolutionary democrats from learning a few isolated tactical slogans and economic principles of Marxism, still a far cry from a scientific understanding of Marxism, to the assimilation of Marxism-Leninism as a complex and indivisible world outlook, a process that may span an entire historical epoch."[125]

Hence, unless they are pushed further by some overwhelming forces beyond their control, the Third World's revolutionary democrats are about to reach, and some of them may have already reached, the crossroads, the fateful parting of the ways, that will take them in due time further away from the road of Marxism-Leninism, both of the Soviet and Chinese version. When that happens, and when communist analysts will have realized that they can no longer be lured back to the "correct" road, the revolutionary democrats are likely in their turn to be declared as having lost their "revolutionary potential" and might well then be reclassified from their present status of allies to that of enemies. "One can hardly remain loyal to the ideals of revolutionary democracy and yet oppose the class-conscious proletariat and its party," opines Ulianovskii in the above-cited 1971 article on "Marxist and Non-Marxist Socialism." But this is precisely what is happening, and has been happening for some time in virtually every country where "revolutionary democrats" have been in power.

Nonetheless, despite all the disappointments, cooperation with the revolutionary democrats remains a legitimate, Soviet-approved postulate of communist strategy in the Third World. As Brezhnev restated in his report to the 24th Congress of the Soviet Communist party in March 1971, "in the struggle against imperialism an ever greater role is being played by the revolutionary democratic parties, many of which have proclaimed socialism as their programme goal. The CPSU has been actively developing its ties with them. We are sure that cooperation between such parties and the Communist parties, including those in their own countries, fully meets the interests of the anti-imperialist movement, the strengthening of national independence and the cause of social progress."[126]

Notes for Chapter IX

[1] p. 346.

[2] See *Mizan,* 6, 4, 1964, p. 5.

[3] See G. Akopian's statement in *"Sotsializm, Kapitalizm, Slaborazvitye Strany,"* MEIMO, No. 6, 1964, pp. 73 ff.

[4] Vl. Li, "The Role of the National Liberation Movement in the Anti-Imperialist Struggle," *International Affairs* (Moscow), No. 12, 1971, pp. 69 ff.

[5] Italics added.

[6] pp. 149 ff.

[7] pp. 154-55.

[8] *op. cit.* An article published in the *World Marxist Review,* 15, 3, 1972, pp. 144 ff, under the title "From National to Socialist Revolution" adds still further to the confusion by lumping together under the term of "so-called intermediate strata" "the peasantry, — urban petty bourgeoisie, and the civilian-military intelligentsia."

[9] *Fundamentals,* p. 155. See also Mao's "Analysis of the Classes in Chinese Society," and his "The Chinese Revolution and the Chinese Communist Party," *Selected Works,* Vol. I, pp. 13 ff. and Vol. III, pp. 72 ff.

[10] *Fundamentals,* pp. 155, 289, 303.

[11] *Ibid.,* p. 289.

[12] *Ibid.,* p. 347.

[13] Tiagunenko's statement in *"Sotsializm, Kapitalizm, Slaborazvitye Strany,"* MEIMO, No. 6, 1964, p. 81.

[14] R. Ulianovsky, "Some Problems of Non-Capitalist Development of the Liberated Countries," *Kommunist*, No. 1, 1966, pp. 109 ff. English translation in the *Yearbook on International Communist Affairs, 1966*, Stanford, 1967.

[15] R. Ulianovsky, "Marxist and Non-Marxist Socialism," *World Marxist Review*, 14, 9, 1971, pp. 119 ff.

[16] Statements by Rastiannikov and Tiagunenko in *"Sotsializm, Kapitalizm, Slaborazvitye Strany,"* op. cit.

[17] op. cit.

[18] R. Ulianovskii's statement in *"Sotsializm, Kapitalizm, Slaborazvitye Strany,"* op. cit., p. 71.

[19] *Selected Works*, Vol. I, p. 20.

[20] *Ibid.*, Vol. III, p. 90. However, Mao's concept of "the petty bourgeoisie other than peasantry" includes not only small merchants, handicraftsmen, petty professionals and lower government functionaries, but also petty intellectuals and students.

[21] "Alliance of Anti-Imperialist Forces in Latin America," *World Marxist Review*, 10, 7, 1967, pp. 44 ff.

[22] *Third World*, pp. 43-43.

[23] Luis Corvalan, *op. cit.*, p. 48.

[24] *Ibid.*

[25] Ramir Otero, "Some Problems of the Working-Class and Trade Union Movement in Latin America," *World Marxist Review*, 10, 7, 1967, pp. 56 ff.

[26] L. Skvortsov, *"Sovremennaia bor'ba idei i kontseptsiia ideologicheskogo razoruzheniia,"* (The Contemporary Struggle of Ideas and the Concept of Ideological Disarmament), *Pravda*, February 7, 1969, pp. 3-4.

[27] Corvalan, *op. cit.*

[28] *Krasnaia zvezda*, November 11, 1964.

[29] *Tupiki i Perspektivy Tropicheskoi Africi*, Moscow, 1970. See also David Morrison, "Tropical Africa: The New Soviet Outlook," *Mizan*, XIII, 1, pp. 48-57.

[30] *Fundamentals*, p. 155.

[31] *Ibid.;* also, Aleksandrov's statement in *"Sotsializm, Kapitalizm, Slaborazvitye Strany,"* op. cit., p. 68.

[32] *Fundamentals*, p. 155; see also V. Kaboshkin and Y. Shchirovskii, "Algeria: From National Liberation to Social Liberation," *Kommunist*, No. 16, 1963, pp. 110 ff.

[33] Aleksandrov, *op. cit.*, p. 68.

[34] *World Communism: The Disintegration of a Secular Faith*, Oxford University Press, 1964, p. 128.

[35] For Western analyses of the attitudes of the Third World's intelligentsia see Robert Alexander, *Communism in LatinAmerica;* Rollie Poppino, *International Communism in Latin America A History of the Movement 1917-1963*, Robert Scalapino, ed., *The Communist Revolution in Asia*.

[36] G. Mirsky, "Changes in the Third World," *New Times*, No. 39, 1969, pp. 4 ff.

[37] See, for instance, Jose Manuel Fortuny, "Has the Revolution Become More Difficult in Latin America?", *World Marxist Review*, 8, 1965, pp. 38 ff.; Ernesto Judis, "The Revolutionary Process in Latin America," *ibid.*, 8, 2, 1965,

pp. 15 ff.; Ruben Castellanos, "The October Revolution and the Communist Movement in Latin America," *ibid.*, 10, 6, 1967, p. 24 ff.

[38] Castellanos, *op. cit.*

[39] quoted from Castellanos, *op. cit.*

[40] See Roque Dalton, "Student Youth and the Latin American Revolution," *World Marxist Review*, 9, 3, 1966, pp. 69 ff.; also, Robert E. Scott, "Student Political Activism in Latin America," *Daedalus*, Vol. 97, Winter 1968, pp. 70-98, and Daniel Goodrich and Edward W. Scott, "Developing Political Orientations of Panamanian Students," *Journal of Politics*, Vol. 23, 1961, pp. 84-107.

[41] Seymour Martin Lipset, "Students and Politics in Comparative Perspective," *Daedalus*, Vol. 97, Winter 1968, pp. 14 ff.

[42] See on this *"Columbia Quiere Reaccionar contra La Subversion en la Universidad,"* (Colombia Wants to React Against Subversion at the University), *Este y Oeste*, No. 102, March 1967, p. 11.

[43] Dalton, *op. cit.;* also, Kevin Lyonette, "Student Organizations in Latin America," *International Affairs*, Vol. 47, 1966, pp. 655 ff.; and *"Latinskaia Amerika: pod'em anti-imperialisticheskoi bor'by*, (Latin America: The Rise of the Anti-imperialistic Struggle), *Pravda*, December 30, 1970, extolling the growing role of Latin American students in the anti-imperialist struggle.

[44] Richard Cornell, *Youth and Communism: An Historical Analysis of International Communist Youth Movements*, New York, 1965, pp. 196 ff. Student organizations of Chile and Guatemala were listed among eight new organizations admitted by the Tenth Congress of the IUS that met at Bratislava in February 1971. See "Students in the Fight Against Imperialism," *New Times*, No. 8, 24, 1971, pp. 13 ff.

[45] Leonard D. Therry, "Dominant Power Components in the Brazilian Student Movement prior to April, 1964," *Journal of Inter-American Studies*, VII, 1, 1965, pp. 27 ff.

[46] For Western analyses of the attitudes of the Latin American students see: Goodrich and Scott, *op. cit.;* Robert E. Scott, *op. cit.;* Therry, *op. cit.;* Robert Alexander, *Communism in Latin America;* Rollie E. Poppino, *International Communism in Latin America;* Luigi Einaudi, "Rebels Without Allies," *Saturday Review*, August 1968, pp. 45 ff.; *World Strength of the Communist Party Organizations;* Edward Taborsky, "Soviet Strategy and Latin American Students," *Social Science Quarterly*, 50, 1, 1969, pp. 116-126.

[47] "How Campus Reds Tried to Take Over a Country," *U.S. News and World Report*, January 16, 1967, pp. 37-38; "Caracas Troops Seize Red Aiders," *New York Times*, December 16, 1966. For the communist confirmation of the important role played by the students in the armed struggle in Venezuela see "Preelection Climate in Venezuela," *World Marxist Review*, 11, 4, 1968, pp. 59 ff.

[48] Behind Student Strike in Mexico," *U.S. News and World Report*, May 16, 1966, p. 55. On MLN's hold over the University of Mexico students see Daniel James, "Rumbles on the Mexican Left," *New Leader*, Vol. 44, October 30, 1961, pp. 16-18.

[49] *"Mexico y la Conferencia Tricontinental de la Habana."* (Mexico and the Three-Continent Conference of Havana), *Este y Oeste*, No. 100, January 1967, pp. 1-9.

[50] *Time*, March 24, 1963, p. 45.

[51] J. Encarnacio Perez, "Students and Democracy in Mexico," *World Marxist Review*, 12, 6, 1969, pp. 73-76. On the events in Morelia see *"Mexico y la Conferencia Tricontinental de la Habana,"* op. cit. For a discussion of communist activities among Mexican students see also Karl M. Schmitt, *Communism in Mexico.*

[52] *"El Communismo en El Uruguay,"* (Communism in Uruguay), *Este y Oeste*, Nos. 126-127, pp. 1-60.

[53] See also "Students Clash with Police," *Buenos Aires Herald*, April 12, 1967. For a discussion of communist influence among Uruguayan students see *"El Comunismo en El Uruguay,"* *Este y Oeste*, VII, Nos. 126 and 127, May and June 1969, pp. 25 ff.

[54] "Where It's Government v. University," *U.S. News and World Report*, August 15, 1966, p. 48.

[55] See: *"Colombia Quiere Reaccionar contra La Subversion en la Universidad, op. cit.;* "Dominican Republic; A Residue of Hate," *Newsweek*, March 11, 1968; *"Los Problemas de la Subversion en el Brasil*, (The Problems of Subversion in Brazil), Part II. *La Posicion de las Fuerzas Estudiantiles,"* (The Position of Student Forces), *Este y Oeste*, No. 124, pp. 16 ff; *Communism in Latin America*, April 1967, reporting the occupation by communist students of the Chemistry Building at the University of San Marcos and a similar occupation of the Liberal Arts and Administration Buildings at the University of San Augustin at Arequipa. In November 1971 bloody clashes occurred between communist and Christian democratic students at the University of Chile at Santiago.

[56] Cornell, *op. cit.* Four Asian and African student unions were admitted by the Tenth Congress of the IUS in 1971: the Students' Federation of the UAR, the Somali Students' Union, the Students' Union of Eastern Pakistan and a student organization from Syria. *New Times, op. cit.;* in note 44. A Sudanese was elected Secretary General of the IUS in 1971.

[57] Philip G. Altbach, "The Transformation of the Indian Student Movement," *Asian Survey*, VI, 8, 1966, pp. 448 ff; the same author's "Student Politics and Higher Education in India," *Daedalus*, Vol. 97, Winter 1968, pp. 254 ff.

[58] "Algerians to Aid Red Youth Forum," *New York Times.* August 25, 1964; also, Clement H. Moore and Arlis R. Hochschild, "Student Unions in North African Politics," *Daedalus*, Vol. 97, Winter 1968, pp. 21 ff.

[59] On Burmese students' activities see Josef Silverstein, "Burmese Student Politics in a Changing Society", *Daedalus*, Vol. 97, Winter 1968, pp. 274 ff.

[60] According to an AP report from Ceylon a three-men royal commission was appointed by the Ceylonese government to investigate the matter.

[61] See F. Tarasov, *"Chto stoit za volneniiami molodezhi,"* (What Is Behind the Emotions of the Youth), *Pravda*, August 30, 1971; "Ways of Anti-Imperialist Struggle in Tropical Africa," *World Marxist Review*, 14, 8, 1971, pp. 83 ff.; "University Crisis," *African Digest*, SVIII, 5, 1971, p. 84; "Malagasy Students Wield Heavy Hand," an AP report from Tananarive, *Austin Statesman*, May 24, 1972; *"K sobytiiam na Madagaskaru,"* (About the Events in Madagaskar), *Pravda*, May 15, 1972.

[62] See Castellanos, *op. cit.*, and Dalton, *op. cit.*

[63] Dalton, *op. cit.* See also Karl Schmitt, *Communism* in Mexico, p. 224. "Once graduated into the business, intellectual or professional ranks," the author notes, "these students seemingly become more conservative."

[64] *Daedalus, op. cit.*

[65] See also Lewis S. Feuer, "The New Marxism of the Intellectuals," *New Leader*, November 4, 1968, pp. 7 ff.

[66] Cited in the *Yearbook of International Communist Affairs*, 1966, pp. 463-64. See also *"A Proposito del IV Congresso de Estudiantes,"* (Concerning the IV Congress of the Students), *Este y Oeste*, No. 101, February 1967.

[67] *Communism in Latin America*, October 1968, Part I, pp. 7-8.

[68] *Ibid.*, June 1968, Part I, p. 14,

[69] *The Yearbook of International Communist Affairs, 1966*, p. 519-22.

[70] *Ibid.*

[71] See the AP release: "Panama's Government Actually Rather Popular," *Austin Statesman*, September 22, 1969

[72] "Latin America Cracks Down on Student-Run Schools," *U.S. News and World Report*, May 27, 1968, pp. 37-38.

[73] Dalton, *op. cit.;* see also Gladys Marin, "The Communists and the Youth," *World Marxist Review*, 9, 3, 1966, p. 69 ff.

[74] *Communism in Latin America*, March 1968, Part I, p. 13, and December 1968, Part I, p. 8.

[75] Chile Under Marxism! Does It Work?" *Newsweek*, November 15, 71, pp. 43 ff.

[76] David Belknapp "Students Surprise Politicians," a report of Los Angeles Times News Service, *Austin American*, June 29, 1972.

[77] Henri Verley, *"Les dessous d'un congrès" Politique Hebdo* (a weekly of communist and leftist dissidents published in Paris), February 25, 1971.

[78] For a discussion of Debray's ideas see Lewis S. Feuer, *op. cit.*

[79] See, for instance, the editorial on "The Latin American Working Class — Its Strength and Weakness," *New Times*, No. 34, 23, 1967, pp. 1 ff. and N. Mostovets, *"Boevoi front kommunisticheskogo dvizheniia,"* (The Battle Front of the Communist Movement), *Pravda*, November 20, 1968

[80] For instance, Jose Manuel Fortuny, "Has the Revolution Become More Difficult in Latin America?" *op. cit.*

[81] "Lenin and the National-Liberation Movement," *World Marxist Review*, 12, 12, 1969, pp. 20 ff.

[82] Dalton, *op. cit.*

[83] Mentioned first in the "Warsaw Letter" sent the Czechoslovak Communist party by the leaders of the Communist parties of the Soviet Union, Poland, East Germany, Bulgaria and Hungary in July 1968 (*Pravda*, July 18, 1968), the new doctrine was fully expounded in a long leading article in *Pravda*, September 28, 1968: S. Kovalev, *"Suverenitet i internatsional'nye obiazanosti sotsialisticheskikh stran,"* (Sovereignty and the International Obligations of Socialist Countries).

[84] According to information gathered from *Pravda* and *Neues Deutschland* for the period of August 22 to September 5, 1968, approval of the Soviet action (although qualified in some instances) was given by the Communist parties of the following Latin American countries: Argentine, Chile, Columbia, Costa-Rica, Cuba, Ecuador, Guiana, Mexico, Panama, Peru, Uruguay and Venezuela.

[85] G. Mirsky and T. Pokataieva, "Classes and Class Struggle in Developing Countries," MEIMO, No. 2, 1966.

[86] MEIMO, No. 6, 1964, p. 64.

[87] *"Natsional'no osvoboditel'noe dvizhenie i nekapitalisticheskii put'"* (The

National-Liberation Movement and the Non-Capitalist Path) *Mezhduna-rodnaia Zhizn,* No. 5, 1965. See also *"Nassers Eigener Weg zum Sozialismus,"* (Nasser's Own Road To Socialism), *Ost-Probleme,* February 11, 1966, pp. 79 ff.

[88] See also a positive evaluation of African officers corps at a seminar at Cairo, *World Marxist Review,* 10, 1, 1967, p. 54.

[89] See Yuri Bokharyov, "Africa: Anatomy of the Military Coups," *New Times,* No. 14, 1966, pp. 10 ff.; also Charles McLane, "Soviet Doctrine and the Military Coups in Africa," *International Journal,* XXI, 3, 1966, pp. 298 ff.

[90] Bokharyov, *op. cit.* See also T. Kolesnichenko, *"Armiia i politika"* (Army and Politics), *Pravda,* November 2, 1966.

[91] *Third World,* p. 50. Italics in the original. See also the sub-chapter "Armed Forces and Politics, *ibid.,* pp. 193 ff.

[92] "Changes in the Third World," *New Times,* No. 39, September 30, 1969, pp. 4-6. See also *"Republikanski przevrot v Libii zmienia uklad sil v Afryce,"* (The Republican Coup in Libya Will Change the Alignment of Forces in Africa), *Zycie Warszawy,* September 3, 1969; A. Usvatov, "The Soviet Union and the Sudan," *New Times,* No. 47, November 26, 1969, p. 19. However, in his 1970 book *Armiia i politka v strankakh Azii i Afriki"* (The Army and Politics in the Countries of Asia and Africa), Mirskii complains of the professional soldiers' lack of sympathy for communists and ruefully concedes (p. 307) that "the psychological mold of military men is not favorable to the development in them of qualities essential for political work." See also Morison, *op. cit.*

[93] Vitalii Korionov, *"V zashchitu svobody i suvereniteta,"* (In Protection of Freedom and Sovereignty), *Pravda,* March 10, 1967; see also the same author's *"Latinskaia Amerika v ostroi bor'be,"* (Latin America in Sharp Struggle), *Pravda,* September 25, 1971, and L. Padilla, J. Laborde, E. Sousa, "Latin America: Anti Imperialist Fight and the Armed Forces," *World Marxist Review,* 14, 3, 1971, pp. 83 ff.

[94] Alfredo Abarka, *op. cit.;* Juan Cobo, "The Peruvian Phenomenon," *New Times,* No. 11, 1970, pp. 21 ff.; V. Borovskii, *"Chto proizoshlo v Bolivii,"* (What Occurred in Bolivia), *Pravda,* October 30, 1970.

[95] G. Mirsky, *op. cit.,* in note 92. See also the same author's "Developing Countries: The Army and Society," *New Times,* No. 48, 1969, pp. 15 ff. and V. Listov, *"Peru: Reformy i Oligarkhiia,"* (Peru: Reforms and the Oligarchy), *Pravda,* February 6, 1972.

[96] G. Mirsky in *MEIMO,* No. 2, 1963, p. 65.

[97] B. N. Ponomarev, "Proletarian Internationalism a Powerful Force in the Revolutionary Transformation of the World," *World Marxist Review,* 7, 8, 1964, pp. 55 ff.

[98] Yu. Potemkin, "The Algerian Revolution — Achievements and Prospects," MEIMO, No. 10, 1964, cited in "Algeria's Difficulties," *Mizan,* 7, 6, 1964, p. 74.

[99] See the letter of the Central Committee of the Communist party of China to the Central Committee of the Communist party of the Soviet Union, June 14, 1963.

[100] See G. Mirsky's statement, *Mizan,* 6, 4, 1964, p. 5; also, Potemkin, *op. cit.*

[101] R. Ul'ianovskii, *"Nekotorie voprosy nekapitalisticheskogo razvitiia os-vobodivshikhsia stran,"* (Some Questions of the Non-capitalist Development of the Liberated Countries), *Kommunist,* No. 1, 1966, p. 113 ff., English text in

the *Yearbook on International Communist Affairs*, 1966, p. 547 ff.; the same author's *"Na novykh rubezhakh,"* (On the New Boundaries), *Pravda*, January 3, 1968, containing an emphatic plea for cooperation between communists and revolutionary democrats; A. Iskenderov and G. Starushenko, "On International-al Themes: Intrigues of Imperialism in Africa," *Pravda*, August 14, 1966; V. Sidenko in *Krasnaia zvezda*, February 8, 1966; G. Mirskii, "Developing Countries at the Crossroads," *New Times*, No. 48, 1966, pp. 6 ff.

[102] Ul'ianovskii, *op. cit.* in *Kommunist* 1966.

[103] Ibid., and also Ul'ianovskii's article in *Pravda* 1968.

[104] "Marxist and Non-Marxist Socialism," *op. cit.*, pp. 119 ff.

[105] R. Domenger, A. Letnov, "Tropical Africa: Its Parties and the Problems of Democracy," *World Marxist Review*, 13, 10, 1970, pp. 58 ff.

[106] B. Ponomaryov, "Tropical Theoretical Problems of World Revolutionary Process," *Information Bulletin*, 23-24, 1971, pp. 63 ff.

[107] *New Times*, No. 18, 1964.

[108] "On the Character of National-Liberation Revolutions," *Narody Azii i Afriki*, No. 6, 1966, pp. 3 ff. English resume in *Mizan*, 9, 2, 1967, pp. 41 ff. Italics added.

[109] "Some Problems of Social Progress," *World Marxist Review*, 10, 1, 1967, pp. 21 ff.

[110] *Pravda*, January 3, 1968.

[111] "The 'Third World' - Problems of Socialist Orientation," *International Affairs*, No. 9, 1971, pp. 26 ff. Italics in the original

[112] Vl. Li, "The Role of the National Liberation Movement in the Anti-Imperialist Struggle," *International Affairs*, No. 12, 1971, pp. 69 ff.

[113] *Kommunist, op. cit.*

[114] *Pravda*, January 3, 1968.

[115] "The National Liberation Movement and the Communists," *World Marxist Review*, 8, 12, 1965, pp. 16 ff.

[116] "Some Problems of the Working Class and Trade Union Movement in Latin America," *op. cit.* Italics are Otero's.

[117] *"Latinskaia Amerika: Novyi Etap bor'by narodov,"* *Pravda*, March 19, 1969.

[118] Ulianovskii, *Pravda*, January 3, 1968; also, G. Mirsky, "Changes in the Third World," *op. cit.*

[119] "Marxist and Non-Marxist Socialism," *op. cit.*

[120] Ulianovskii, *Pravda*, January 3, 1968.

[121] Ulianovskii in *Pravda, op. cit.* 1966 and 1968.

[122] See, for instance, "China Strikes at Burma and Thais Shudder," *National Observer*, April 29, 1968.

[123] *Al-Ahram*, November 13, 1964. Cited after Jaan Pennar, "Moscow and Socialism in Egypt," *Problems of Communism*, XV, 5, 1966, pp. 41 ff.

[124] See Ulianovskii's "Marxist and Non-Marxist Socialism," *op. cit.*

[125] G. Kim and A. Kaufman, "On the Sources of Socialist Conception in Developing Countries," *World Marxist Review*, 14, 12, 1971, pp. 124 ff.

[126] English translation of Brezhnev's report was published as a supplement to *New Times*, No. 15, 1971, pp. 24 ff.

CHAPTER X

WIELDING THE ECONOMIC WEAPON — I

The use and manipulation of economic and financial instruments for the advancement of the communist cause has always been an integral part of communist strategy. As early as December 1917, a mere few weeks after the Bolshevik seizure of power, Soviet Russia's Council of People's Commisars appropriated two million rubles "for the need of the revolutionary internationalist movement" and promised to "render every possible assistance, including financial aid, to the Left internationalist wing of the workers' movement of all countries, whether these countries are at war with Russia, or are allied with her or whether they are remaining neutral."[1]

Yet, in spite of such verbal assurances, in the first three-and-one-half decades of Bolshevik rule, the Soviet economy was clearly in no position to allow any substantial economic involvement abroad. It was only in the middle fifties that the Soviet Union entered the field of foreign aid hitherto virtually pre-empted by the United States, choosing as its main target area the emerging ex-colonial countries of the Third World where Soviet leaders hoped to obtain the best political dividends from their investments. Without delay, Soviet Russia's Comecon partners, one after the other, joined in the undertaking and even Communist China decided to embark on a modest economic offensive of her own.

Thus a fairly substantial communist program of economic aid to the Third World has developed and, coming as a rather unexpected surprise, promptly attracted the attention of Western writers and scholars. Indeed, more has been written about this particular aspect of communist strategy vis-a-vis the Third World than any other. In addition to an abundance of journal articles, there is a growing number of book-length studies, such as, to mention but a few, Henry G. Aubrey's *Co-existence: Economic Challenge and Response*, Joseph Berliner's *Soviet Economic Aid*, Robert L. Allen's *Soviet Economic Warfare*, Alec Nove's *Communist Economic Strategy,* Marshall I. Goldman's *Soviet Foreign Aid*, Jan Wszelaki's *Communist Economic Strategy: The Role of East-Central Europe,* Carol A. Sawyer's *Communist Trade with Developing Countries: 1955-1965*, Leo Tansky's *U.S. and U.S.S.R. Aid to Developing Countries: A Comparative Study of India, Turkey and the U.A.R.* and B.R. Stokke's *Soviet and East European Trade and Aid in Africa.* However, written mostly by economists, these studies dwell primarily upon the economic aspects of the communist foreign aid programs and are concerned less with their political implications. Moreover, some of these works are conceived as more or less detailed case studies of selected individual countries and as such are sometimes lacking in full-fledged overall political evaluation. Nor do most of them pay much attention to the ideological underpinnings of the communist economic offensive or to the role it is meant to play within the overall pattern of communist strategy.

Hence, this and the following chapter are designed to fill the existing gaps and omissions rather than merely to recount in an updated form what has already been said in the above-mentioned studies. While including pertinent economic data on the major facets of communist foreign economic operations, our presentation will concentrate primarily upon the following items:

1. the basic Marxist-Leninist tenets serving as the ideological and political rationale for the communist economic offensive, with particular attention to pinpoint the differences between the

communist and "imperialist" motivations and purposes; or what might perhaps be called the communist theory of foreign aid;

2. the review of the main methods and devices constituting the essence of communist economic strategy, or what might be called its methodology or typology;

3. the main characteristics of communist economic strategy and its relation to politics;

4. the identification of the principal factors favoring and impeding the attainment of the hoped-for objectives of the communist economic policies;

5. the determination, in terms of communist political expectations, of the successes and failures that have thus far resulted from communist economic operations in the Third World.

The Communist Theory of Foreign Aid

The rationale underlying the communist economic offensive in the Third World is firmly rooted in the teaching of Marxism-Leninism. As has been the case with all the other aspects of communist theory and strategy, the communist theory of foreign aid has been worked out by the Soviet theoreticians. True to their habits, the East European communist leaders and most of the Soviet-oriented communists of the Third World have followed the Soviet lead, although some have done so with certain misgivings. Even the Chinese communists initially concurred. Subsequently, however, they began to take issue with some aspects of the matter along with the pro-Chinese elements among the Third World's communists and the Castroites.

The Soviet Version

As developed by today's Soviet interpreters of Marxism-Leninism, the Soviet theory of foreign aid seems to be built around several assumptions, axioms, claims and beliefs.

1. The pivot around which the Soviet theory of foreign aid revolves is the alleged superiority of Marxian socialist economy over the best that capitalism can offer. That has been, of course, the communist credo ever since Karl Marx's devastating critique of capitalism more than a century ago. But it was not until the

late 1950's that, elated over their country's economic and technological achievements and wishfully considering as irreversible the then woefully slow economic growth rate registered by their chief adversary, the United States, the Soviet leaders jumped to the optimistic conclusion that the attainment of Soviet Russia's economic superiority over the United States was within their early reach.[2] So certain did they seem to be of the forthcoming economic victory that they ventured to proclaim in their 1961 *Soviet Communist Party Program* that by 1970 the Soviet Union "would surpass the strongest and richest capitalist country, the U.S.A., in production per head of population," and outstrip it also in the per capita output of "the key agricultural products."[3] "By that time, or possibly sooner," boasted the official *History of the Communist Party of the Soviet Union*, "the Soviet Union will rank first in the world both in the absolute volume of production and production per head of population. This will be *a world historical victory for Socialism* in its peaceful competition with capitalism."[4] Moreover, as added subsequently by the *Fundamentals*, by 1980 "the national income per capita in the Soviet Union will exceed the U.S. future average national income per capita by at least 50 per cent."[5]

The unfailing victory of the Soviet model of economy, governed by the magic "law of balanced, proportional development...never known to mankind in the past,"[6] being thus presumably just around the corner, it is hardly surprising that the Soviet leaders proclaimed the economy to be henceforth the main battlefield between the socialist and "imperialist" camps and Soviet Russia's economic achievements to be the primary weapon with which to tip the scales of the global struggle against imperialism in favor of communism. "The course of social development proves right Lenin's prediction," states the 1960 *Declaration of Eighty-One Communist Parties*, "that the countries of victorious socialism would influence the development of world revolution chiefly by their economic construction.... Capitalism will be defeated in the decisive sphere of human endeavor, the sphere of material production."[7] "We know from history," wrote a Soviet theoretician in an early major article on the economic competition and aid to the underdeveloped countries in the Soviet economic review *Problems of Economics*, "that the outcome of the struggle between different social and economic systems is determined in the final analysis by the system which at the given stage of development offers more favorable conditions for the growth of the productive forces of society."[8] This reliance on the economic weapon has since been repeated time and again on every suitable occasion by Soviet leaders and belabored in innumerable articles by Soviet writers.[9] Although the previously fixed deadlines for the forthcoming communist economic victory over capitalism are conspicuous by their absence from the *Declaration* adopted by the 1969 International Conference of Communist and Workers' Parties, the latest communist manifesto does boast once again of the "swift economic development of the countries belonging to the socialist system at rates outpacing the economic growth of capitalist countries."[10] It promises those willing to jump on the communist bandwagon "the planned, crisis-free development" for their economies and reaffirms the thesis that "the contribution of the world socialist system to the common cause of the anti-imperialist forces is determined primarily by its growing economic potential."

2. While the alleged superiority of the Soviet economic system provides undoubtedly the main plank for the rationale underlying the Soviet theory of foreign aid, its other *raison d-être* appears to stem from the post-Stalinist rejection of war (other than the Soviet-approved "wars of national liberation" and "class-revolutionary" civil wars waged by the "people" against the "oppressors") as a means for the resolution of the capitalist-socialist contradictions. Having declared the prevention of wars as "a historic mission of communism," expressed preference for non-violent methods of transition to socialism, and elevated "peaceful co-existence" to the governing principle of their foreign policy and strategy, the Soviet leaders had to offer a credible "peaceful" alternative for attaining "the victory and consolidation of socialism in the world arena," the officially recognized *sine qua non for* the completion of communism within Soviet Russia herself.[11] In view of the exuberantly optimistic assessment of their country's economic capabilities, they chose, quite logically from their standpoint, economic competition as such an alternative. As Soviet spokesmen see it, economic competition with

capitalism is "one of the most important factors" in the nations' struggle for peace, indeed, the most significant application of peaceful co-existence in international relations, its very translation into practice.[12] It provides "the best foundations for eliminating international tensions and ending the arms race."[13] To fit economic competition with capitalism better into the mold of Marxism-Leninism and to attune it more to the communist way of thinking, the official Soviet documents describe it as a "specific form of class struggle."[14]

3. The presumed excellence of the Soviet economic model is supposed to foster the advancement of communism everywhere. But it is expected to have the greatest impact precisely in the Third World. "A key element in current Soviet world strategy," writes a knowledgeable U.S. student of communist affairs, "is the increasing use of economic and financial aid as a means of weaning the newly independent and uncommitted countries away from western economic influence and thus promoting tendencies toward political neutralism and eventual alignment with the socialist camp."[15] As shown in Chapter I, ever since embarking upon full-fledged operations in the Third World in the later fifties, Soviet policy-makers have been harping continually on the especial relevance of the Soviet model of economic development for the specific conditions and needs of the developing nations and the corresponding unsuitability of the capitalist model.[16]

Thus the benefits that are supposed to accrue to each and every nation accepting Soviet aid and opting for the Soviet-recommended non-capitalist path of economic development presumably makes the Third World by far the most promising locale in which to unfold the communist foreign aid strategy.

4. Another justification advanced in support of Soviet foreign aid to the Third World derives from the communist thesis of the exploitative character of capitalist economic relations with the area. "The objective economic laws of capitalism revealed by Marxism-Leninism" help to "maintain the conditions needed for the economic exploitation of the weak countries by the strong ones, even when the former achieve political independence," asserts a Soviet economist writing in the Soviet review *Voprosy Ekonomiki*. "Merciless suppression and ruthless exploitation of

the weak by the strong has always been and still is the jungle law of capitalism."[17] As Brezhnev told once again the 24th Congress of the Soviet Communist party on March 30, 1971, "the imperialists have been systematically plundering the peoples of dozens of countries in Asia, Africa and Latin America. Every year, they funnel thousands of millions of dollars out of the Third World."[18] Hence, as explained more fully in Chapter I, even after having been granted political independence, the ex-colonial countries remain, in Soviet view, economically in the claws of western imperialists and monopolists who seek to perpetuate their economic stranglehold through "new techniques of neo-colonialist plunder" and "new forms of colonial enslavement under the guise of so-called 'aid' to underdeveloped countries."[19] The only way in which this vicious type of "neo-colonialism" can be broken is to eject western monopolies, uproot all forms of foreign economic domination, decline any type of western aid with "strings attached" and accept instead "the selfless and friendly help" of the Soviet Union and the other socialist countries offered "without any political, military or other conditions whatsoever,"[20] a help that "is an expression of the humane essence of socialism and of its sincere concern for the genuine progress of those underdeveloped nations."[21] Moreover, an expansion of economic ties with communist countries is deemed to protect the developing nations against "the anarchy of the capitalist world market where imperialist monopolies hold sway."[22] Nor did communist propagandists fail quickly to exploit the 1971 U.S. dollar crisis by suggesting that "the discreditable moves made by the U.S. rulers to save the compromised prestige of the dollar" had made the countries of the Third World "the first victims of the monetary disarray caused by the profound and incurable maladies of the capitalist system."[23] Hence, they assert, "there is an ever wider realization in the Third World of the need to curb the appetites of the imperialist monopolies, broaden ties with the socialist states, and adopt a non-capitalist path."

More recently, however, the initial categorical condemnation of all capitalist aid to the Third World has been toned down somewhat and some of the Soviet theoreticians have conceded that even capitalist assistance need not under certain conditions be harmful. These "second thoughts" have obviously been prompted not by a more charitable reassessment of capitalist intentions, but by sheer practical necessity. The Soviet Union has simply found it economically possible to replace from its own resources only a small part of economic losses sustained by many a country of the Third World as a result of anti-Western economic policies undertaken at Soviet behest. "The countries of Asia, Africa and Latin America cannot naturally count on the socialist countries to satisfy all their needs in capital, equipment, technical aid," cautioned V. Tiagunenko, Head of the section for the developing nations of the Soviet Institute of World Economy. "They have to satisfy a considerable part of their needs through the imperialist countries."[24]

5. Even when they accept aid from the West and permit the imperialist monopolies to invest capital in this or that branch of the economy, because of the availability of Soviet aid, the developing nations are now deemed to run less risk of Western exploitation than they once did. As suggested by Khrushchev in his report to the 20th Communist Party Congress, "the very fact that the Soviet Union and the other countries of the socialist camp exist, their readiness to help the underdeveloped countries in advancing their industries on terms of equality and mutual benefit, are a major stumbling block to colonial policy." Therefore, "the imperialists can no longer regard the underdeveloped countries solely as potential sources for making maximum profits," but "are compelled to make concessions to them..."[25] Unlike in the past, "thanks to the support of the socialist countries, [the developing nations] now have the opportunity to act as independent and equal partners in their relations with the imperialist monopolies."[26]

Pushing this line of reasoning still a bit further, the Soviet leaders have tried to claim credit even for the capitalists' own aid to the Third World. Since the Western capitalists would not aid the developing countries if the Soviet Union did not exist, the Soviet argument goes, capitalist aid extended to the developing nations "should also be viewed as a particular kind of Soviet aid to these countries."[27]

6. Earmarked almost exclusively for the public sectors of the Third World's economies, Soviet aid is viewed by Soviet strategy

makers as a major contribution to the realization of one of the most cherished objectives of the communist strategy in the Third World, namely, putting the developing countries onto the "non-capitalist path of development." By strengthening the state sector of national economy at the expense of private business and helping it to become "the determining factor" of the economy, they hope to induce ever deeper structural changes in the economic systems of the recipient countries and pave thus the way for their eventual transition to a fully collectivized system along the lines of the "scientific socialism." As mentioned in Chapter I, the Soviet theoreticians believe that such a course of development may even enable the developing nations to by-pass the capitalist stage of development and thus avoid the "torment" and "suffering" capitalism is said always to bring. Moreover, the Soviet analysts look upon the state sector of the economy not only as the best way to overcome economic backwardness and assure a faster "rhythm of growth", but, above all, as a very effective means of struggle against western monopolies and "a powerful weapon for strengthening national independence."[28] That is also why the Soviet advice to the Third World has dwelt so forcefully upon the imperative necessity of expropriating and nationalizing enterprises and businesses owned by foreign (i.e., western) companies and their native collaborators. Besides increasing and strengthening the desirable state sector of the economy, such measures could be counted upon to exacerbate sill further the relations between the Third World and the West.

However, as has been the case with regard to capitalist aid, a somewhat more pragmatic view has become apparent in recent years also in Soviet attitude concerning private enterprises and nationalization in the Third World. Having observed the economic havoc caused by hasty nationalization of private enterprises in a number of developing countries lacking in trained personnel to run them properly, some Soviet specialists on the affairs of the Third World have begun to caution against "excessive" and untimely nationalization and against "the political harm" that can result from a "total banning of private capital."[29] They have disapproved publicly attempts by unnamed "young, not yet economically strong African states" to "take over the management of all medium and small trade, industrial, handicraft and transport enterprises without having the resources

and cadres necessary for this."[30] Noting that these attempts
"have caused additional economic difficulties and increased the
dissatisfaction of the middle strata," they have warned that "at
the present stage of the liberation revolutions in the African
countries...it would be wrong to attempt an immediate transition from the lower to the higher forms of economy, skipping a
number of intermediary stages."[31] As stressed in an article on
"Neo-Colonialism and Developing Countries," published in the
1971 volume of the *World Marxist Review*, "experience shows
that expropriation of private capital calls for thorough political,
organizational and economic preparations. Hasty and ill-timed
nationalization seriously impairs the productive forces and
becomes an obstacle to the mobilization of internal resources and
further revolutionary reforms."[32]

Also, Soviet theoreticians have taken to task the "Maoists"
for presumably urging several African countries to follow the
"dubious recipe," of "total nationalization at a time when the
state itself is far from having been consolidated and is unable
effectively to manage the economy."[33] Rather, they seem now to
suggest that, for the time being, a measure of private enterprise
ought to be permitted, "given power in the hands of the people,
given a politically alert people, and given contacts with the
socialist world."[35] In particular, as Ulyanovskii puts it, "it is
essential to preserve the small and middle bracket of private
traders (under state control, of course) until the state and the cooperatives are ready to take over the entire distributive system
and handle commodity exchange between the towns and the
countryside."[36]

While continuing to extoll the state sector of the economy in
the developing nations as "progressive" (in contrast to its
"reactionary" nature in advanced capitalist countries), Soviet
analysts have lately become more alive also to the danger that the
state sector may easily acquire a "reactionary" role in the Third
World as well. As a prominent Soviet writer tells it, even in the
developing nations "the nationalization of private property can
lead to socialism only if it is used in the interest of the working
masses, which can be achieved only on the basis of the struggle of
the working class, the toiling peasantry and all progressive
forces."[37]

7. A major aspect of the Soviet theory of foreign aid has been

its lopsided emphasis on industrialization. Reflecting Soviet Russia's own obsession with industrial growth, guided by what Ulam calls a "passion for material improvement and fanaticism in the service of industrialization,"[38] and aware of the magic attraction the very prospect of industrialization holds for the developing countries, the Soviet theoreticians have made of industrialization a virtual panacea for the Third World's economic ills. "The theory and practice of progressive economic development show that industrialization, the installation and development of machine production, is decisive for economic progress," states a Soviet writer in an article on the outlook for industrialization in Africa. "Nothing else can impel it, nothing else can serve as its basis and support. It is industrialization that spurs the development of all productive forces, that raises labour productivity and elevates the standard of living."[39] In particular, Soviet strategists assign the highest priority in their aid programs for the Third World to heavy industry which they consider to be the very foundation not only of economic development, but economic independence as well.[40] As stated by V.A. Sergyeev, the Vice-Chairman of the Foreign Economic Relations Committee of the Soviet Council of Ministers, about 70 percent of the outlay provided in Soviet economic agreements with the developing countries was earmarked for heavy industry[41] whereas, as cited with pride by another Soviet writer, consumer goods account for only five to seven percent of Soviet exports to Asian, African and Latin American countries.[42] In claiming major credit for helping to industrialize the developing nations, Soviet propagandists never tire of stressing that the Soviet Union builds "big economic complexes making for the most effective utilization of their national resources" and representing "the last word in science and technology," and providing the developing nations with "a solid industrial base."[43]

The Soviet emphasis on major industrial projects, preferably in the heavy production field, fits, of course, quite neatly both the Marxist-Leninist conception of desirable economic development and the postulates of communist strategy. Capital goods production and major industrial installations are usually better suited to be run as a public enterprise than smaller units engaged in consumer goods manufacturing. The concentration of aid on such projects is thus all the more likely to promote desirable structural changes in the recipients' economies. Similarly, as shown in Chapter V, the Soviet analysts count on industrialization to effect changes they favor in the Third World's social structure by swelling the ranks of the working class and enhancing thus prospects for a sharper class struggle and proletarian revolutions. By the same token, the growth of larger industrial plants is expected to bring about a higher concentration of workers and place them within an easier reach of communist agitators. Moreover, spectacular projects in the branches considered, rightly or wrongly, as a quintessence of economic virility and a sort of industrial status symbol, such as mammoth dams, huge steel mills and heavy machine-tool works, are likely to yield more propaganda value than would the same investment spread over many smaller units manufacturing prosaic everyday necessities. (Nor should it be overlooked that, after all, heavy industry is Soviet Russia's strongest asset and thus the one in which she can show off better than in other fields of production, let alone agriculture.)

Again, however, the less dogmatic attitudes adopted by some Soviet theoreticians with regard to nationalization and private enterprise have entered also the Soviet thinking on industrialization. To be sure, the emphasis on industrialization and on the priority of heavy industry as the surest way to economic progress and prosperity remains as a general guiding principle of Soviet foreign aid theory and practice. As proudly proclaimed in an article in the 1971 volume of the *World Marxist Review*, as of January 1, 1970, 72 percent of Soviet aid to the Third World went to industry and nine percent to geological prospecting.[44] "This shows," the article goes on, "that Soviet aid is mainly centered on the industrialization of the developing countries, many of which have already been helped in this way to lay the foundations of heavy industry." But there has been a recent tendency toward a more pragmatic attitude. Typical of this modified stand is the following passage contained in a major Soviet study of the economic and social problems of Africa: "In determining ways and means of industrialization in particular countries, it is enormously important to take proper account of the concrete conditions and real possibilities of each country.

There is nothing more harmful than to apply indiscriminately to all independent African countries some kind of universal recipe for economic construction... Industrialization policy, which in itself has universal importance for any African country, must at the same time assess real possibilities — the level of productivity reached, the presence of raw material and power resources and reserves of manpower, and the special features of existing economic relations with the world market..."[45] A similarly pragmatic stand has been taken in 1968 by another Soviet writer who urged that in less developed countries unable to afford to develop heavy industry priority be given to "light and food industry enterprises processing local raw materials."[46]

Whereas Soviet aid is said to aim at helping the developing nations to industrialize and to lift themselves in this way from age-old backwardness to modernity in the shortest possible time, Western imperialists are accused of trying, wherever and whenever they can get away with it, to impede the "real" industrialization of the Third World. Bent on perpetuating the role of developing nations as "agrarian-raw material appendages" of Western capitalist economy and continuing "pumping out raw materials and foodstuffs as cheaply as possible," the imperialist powers are said to be interested in supporting only agriculture and extractive industries, and possibly transportation needed for their "pumping out" and some sectors of light industry, but not in promoting industrial projects of truly major and national importance.[47]

8. In a striking contrast to its emphasis on industrialization the Soviet strategists have shown much less interest in the Third World's agriculture. While professing deep concern for the peasantry of the developing countries, dwelling on the crucial importance of the worker-peasant alliance and advocating radical agrarian reforms, they have treated agriculture rather niggardly in their economic aid programs. Thus, for instance, of the 2,404 projects said to be "completed or being built with the assistance of socialist states in developing countries," (as of 1967) only 147 are listed under the heading of agriculture.[48] Indeed, Soviet aid to agriculture has come mostly as a by-product of projects undertaken primarily for their industrial significance and prestige value, such as the Aswan and Euphrates

river dams, a few tractor assembly plants, and the like. Nor have Soviet spokesmen had anything but abuse and denigration for the West's endeavors to bolster the Third World's agriculture, and this not merely because of their overall negative view of Western aid as such, but also because they regard investments in agriculture as less important for the developing nations than those in industry.

It is true that the sobering process that has somewhat de-dogmatized Soviet thinking in recent years and brought with it a measure of re-appraisal of foreign aid programs, has led to a slightly better appreciation of the role of agriculture in the economies of developing nations. Cautioning against excessive reliance on industrialization in the absence of suitable conditions, some of the Soviet specialists on the Third World have begun to stress the concept of "a simultaneous and balanced development of industry and agriculture" and even to advise against over-hasty abandonment of the single-crop economies where such crops are important earners of needed foreign currencies.[49] However, in spite of its modest upgrading, agriculture still remains the pariah of Soviet foreign aid. As of January 1, 1970, Soviet aid to agriculture represented only 6 percent of the total aid to the developing countries.[50] Evidently, Soviet aid to agriculture appears to be proportionately largest in Africa where, according to a recent Soviet statement, 70 of the 300 construction projects built with Soviet aid are in the field of agriculture.[51]

Why is it that Soviet policy-makers continue to assign the Third World's agriculture such a low priority in their foreign aid program when it has become increasingly recognized by Western experts that agricultural development is truly the key sector of the Third World's overall economic development, at least for some time to come?[52]

Several reasons seem to account for the Soviet lack of support for the Third World's agriculture. Despite the recent updating and streamlining of some of its tenets, the Marxist-Leninist teaching has retained its long-standing anti-agriculture bias. Also, having allowed agriculture in the Soviet Union itself to lag so much behind industrial development, Soviet strategy-makers realize that, whatever they could do, would be a very poor second to what their Western competitors could do. Besides, as they see it, the correct way of helping agriculture lies in industrialization which will eventually improve agriculture by supplying it with machinery, fertilizers, insecticides, etc. But most of all, since only a negligible segment of the agricultural production of the Third World is in public hands, Soviet aid to agriculture would actually tend to strengthen the private sector of the economy and thus bolster rural capitalism that the Soviet strategists fear and despise. Soviet aid to agriculture would be forthcoming more readily if and when Third World agriculture would move toward collectivization. For instance, Soviet writers have proudly pointed to Soviet support for the state-owned mechanized farm at Saratgarh in India and Soviet Russia granted India credit in 1966 for the purchase of equipment for five state farms.[53]

The East European Concurrence

In spite of the revisionist and polycentrist trends that have been at work in communist East Europe in recent years, the East European communist leaders and theoreticians seem to concur wholeheartedly in the Soviet dicta on the role of economic instruments in communist strategy vis-a-vis the Third World. While taking exception to some aspects of Moscow's Marxist-Leninist orthodoxy, they have embraced *in toto* the theory of foreign aid as advanced by the Soviet ideologues.

In unison with their Soviet colleagues, the East European communist spokesmen profess their firm belief in the superiority of the socialist economic model over its capitalist competitor. Although the growing economic problems of recent years have compelled them lately to shed some of their erstwhile illusions, they nevertheless continue to believe that the economic reforms now in progress in their respective countries will correct the "distortions of the personality-cult era" and make the socialist system of economy ever more attractive for the Third World. Hence, they, too, view the communist involvement in the economies of the developing nations as the best way of advancing the cause of communism, proclaim the economy to be presently the "main battlefield" aid to the developing nations as "today's important economic and political slogan," and count on economic competition to bring socialism "an ultimate and decisive victory."[54] "The decisive struggle for communism on the world scale is now being waged on the level of production, technology and scientific progress," asserts *Život strany*, the Czechoslovak Communist Party's journal of party affairs.[55]

Yet, anxious even more than their Soviet mentors to avoid situations that might lead to a war, the East European communist spokesmen have endorsed with enthusiasm the Soviet standpoint presenting economic competition as the main method of struggle for peace and as "a translation into practice" of the principle of peaceful coexistence.[56] In aiding the economies of developing nations the countries of the world socialist system presumably make these "former reserves of imperialism" less dependent on their ex-colonial masters and weaken thereby world capitalism and strengthen "the camp of peace."[57] "Whoever recognizes peaceful co-existence to be the general line of socialist foreign policy and an effective form of the class struggle against imperialism," wrote a Czechoslovak communist in the Party's main theoretical journal, *Nová mysl*, "cannot pass over in silence an indivisible part of this struggle, i.e., a peaceful economic competition between countries with different social systems."[58] This view is shared also by the Yugoslav communists who consider "the help for the nations fighting against colonialism and against neo-colonialist attempts" to be "one of the basic principles of the Yugoslav policy of active and peaceful co-existence."[59]

Similarly, the East European communists have followed the Soviet lead in dwelling upon the relevance of their countries' economic development for the less developed nations. This thesis has been emphasized, in particular, by the Bulgarian and Rumanian communists who could claim, with a measure of justification, the status of economic backwardness at the time of their countries' incorporation in the world socialist system. Addressing a communist-sponsored exchange of views on the *Paths of Development of Newly Emergent Countries*, a Bulgarian communist told the audience how socialism converted his country, "once an agrarian adjunct of the imperialist states with a poverty-stricken population," in a mere seventeen years into a modern nation with "a powerful industry and a mechanized agriculture."[60]

The same lack of originality is apparent in all the other facets of the East European communist theory of foreign aid.[61] Thus the East European communist spokesmen have been rehashing the thesis on the great significance of communist economic aid in helping developing nations to assert their economic independence in the face of continued western efforts at economic domination. They have been echoing Soviet denunciations of the West's "neo-colonialist plundering" of the Third World. They have been claiming credit for having contributed toward the demolition of the monopoly of Western imperialism in the Third World and enabled the developing nations to gain a much better bargaining position in their economic relations with the non-communist countries. They have been vying with Soviet propagandists in extolling the state sector of the economy as the best means of freeing their countries from "the fetters of foreign monopoly capital" and arranging for a "more rational use" of their internal resources.[62] They have been lecturing the developing nations about the virtues of the non-capitalist path of development as the only way in which they could solve their basic economic problems.

Nor have the East European communist ideologues lagged behind their Soviet comrades in praising industrialization as "the surest way to complete national liberation" and to improve the class structure of the population, and in denouncing Western neo-colonialists for favoring the so-called "industrial restraint" theory aimed at obstructing and retarding any genuine industrialization of developing nations and promoting only "handicrafts and small industry."[63] However, while sharing in general the Soviet predilection for heavy industry, the East European communists have never assigned it as lopsided a priority in their foreign aid programs as had the Soviet strategy-makers. Rather, from the very inception of their foreign aid, they have taken a stand in favor of a more balanced ratio between the light and heavy industries, a stand that has subsequently been echoed in the more recent Soviet thinking as well.[64]

The Chinese Exceptions

Unlike the East European communists, who (with the obvious

exception of Albania) have endorsed the Soviet theory of foreign aid in its entirety, the Chinese communists object to several of its aspects.

As has already been mentioned in Chapter II, the Chinese theoreticians do not quite share the Soviet and communist East European confidence that the non-capitalist path of development and the state sector of the economy could be truly relied upon to pave the way for "scientific socialism." If undertaken at a time when the proletariat and its allies are not yet at the helm, such etatization steps tend, in Chinese view, to strengthen rather than weaken the position of the bourgeois and other non-proletarian forces, promote "bureaucratic capitalism which is an ally of imperialism and feudalism", and render thus transition to socialism even more difficult.[65] Hence, the Chinese strategists hold that opportunities for the use of economic instruments in fostering the cause of communism in the Third World are extremely limited.

The Chinese communists contest also Soviet and East European communist claim concerning the relevance of the Soviet and East European economic models for the Third World. Arguing that economic and other conditions prevalent in China at the time of the communist victory in 1949 approximate conditions obtaining in most parts of the Third World, especially in Asia and Africa, more closely than do those of Soviet Russia and Communist East Europe, they believe their own model to be much better suited to the needs of developing nations than anything the European communist countries can offer.

Furthermore, the Chinese communists object to Soviet aid on the ground that such aid, much like that of the imperialist West, jeopardizes the independence of the recipient countries. They have gone so far as branding Soviet economic aid as "filthy lucre" meant to buy adherents and facilitate the Soviet domination of the Third World.[66]

But the main Chinese exception to the Soviet theory of foreign aid stems undoubtedly from the Chinese communists' disagreement with what they consider to be Soviet Russia's exaggeration of the role of peaceful competition. Since the manipulation of economic instruments has been repeatedly stressed by Soviet and communist East European spokesmen as the main ingredient and preferred device of communist strategy of peaceful co-existence, the Chinese rejection of Soviet Russia's alleged "attempt to substitute peaceful competition for the revolutionary struggles of the oppressed peoples" extends, quite logically, to the reliance on economic means of the struggle as well.[67] While conceding in their open letter of June 14, 1963, that "the superiority of the Socialist system and the achievement of the Socialist countries in construction play an exemplary role and are an inspiration to the oppressed peoples and nations," the Chinese leaders have expressed in no uncertain terms their low regard for the strategic value of economic competition: "But this exemplary role and inspiration can never replace the revolutionary struggles of the oppressed peoples and nations. No oppressed people or nation can win liberation except through its own, stanch revolutionary struggle." In yet another portion of their official statement the Chinese leaders attempt to further discredit and ridicule the concept of economic competition by mentioning it with quotation marks and listing the view "that the contradiction between the two world systems will automatically disappear in the course of 'economic competition,'" as one of several "erroneous views" that should be repudiated.

As had been the case with Chinese attacks on other aspects of Soviet strategy, the Soviet leaders did not allow the Chinese sallies to go unchallenged. In an exhaustive report *On the Struggle of the CPSU for the Solidarity of the International Communist Movement* delivered at the plenary session of the Soviet Communist Party's Central Committee in 1964, M. Suslov countered the Chinese accusations by reaffirming resolutely his Party's continued adherence to "the Leninist conclusion that the socialist countries exert their chief influence on the development of the world revolution through their economic successes."[68] Rejecting Peking's contention that economic competition "dooms the masses to passive waiting," Suslov insisted that, quite to the contrary, "the revolutionary importance of the victories of socialism in economic competition" lay "precisely in that they stimulate the class struggle of the working people and make them conscious fighters for socialism."[69] Moreover, by allegedly separating economics and politics and by "absolutizing" the role of politics, the Chinese communists violate, in Soviet view, the all-important Leninist principle of the unity of economics and politics. Such an attitude is said to lead in turn to adventurism, to an excessive reliance on violence and to an unwarranted refusal to recognize "the decisive influence" of the economic achievements of the socialist countries on the development of the "world revolutionary process."[70]

Nonetheless, despite the sharp language used in their public polemics, the Sino-Soviet disagreement regarding the application of economic levers to the Third World is not very substantial. Indeed, it boils down more or less to the differing estimates of the potential recipients' degree of pro-communist and/or anti-communist leanings and their susceptibility to communist manipulations. Moreover, as will be shown below, the Chinese communists have not always followed their own ideological precepts in disbursing foreign aid, granting it even to regimes controlled by non-proletarian strata and to countries not likely to slide down the road of the proletarian revolution in the near future. Thus it seems that the wish to assail the Soviet "revisionists" and "social imperialists" at all cost and China's lack of adequate resources available for foreign aid on a major scale account for the Chinese exceptions to Soviet foreign aid strategy more than any genuine disagreement on the pertinent ideological tenets.

The Ways and Means

The basic economic methods and instrumentalities that the communists use to penetrate and influence the developing countries do not differ in type and format from those traditionally employed in the West's economic relations to the Third World. Their three main forms are trade, credit and technical assistance. The fourth and far less important one is what may be called economic showmanship, meant to impress the Third World with communist economic and technical prowess, such as participation in trade fairs and exhibitions held in developing countries and tours of selected industrial establishments in communist countries by the Third World's V.I.P.'s.

The one method of economic relations (practiced not infrequently by the United States) communist countries rarely use are non-repayable grants, save for occasional and rather small good-will gifts, such as food and drugs for victims of disasters and "imperialist aggressions," mobile ambulances, surplus military hardware or customary special-occasion personal presents to the leaders of various less developed countries. Among the communist countries only China resorts to non-repayable grants on a meaningful scale, having given away a sum total of over 100 million dollars to Cambodia, Ceylon, Nepal, Egypt, Yemen and Guinea.[71] The official explanation of the communist aversion to outright grants is the desire not to offend the dignity of the recipient countries by offering them what would be tantamount to international charity. This is certainly a credible explanation, but there are other plausible reasons for the communist preference for repayable loans over outright donations. While a discreetly offered gift may create a measure of good will, it does not create the kind of continuous ties characteristic for the creditor-debtor relationship. It is precisely this prolonged relationship that offers the best opportunity to steer the recipient country's trade away from its traditional Western markets and make it all the more dependent upon its communist partners.[72] Nor does a gift afford the donor additional opportunities a creditor always has to earn further doses of the debtor's gratitude by recurrent gestures of magnanimity through lightening repayment conditions as a reward for the debtor's friendliness, or gestures of reprisals through stiffened attitudes as a penalty for any display of the debtor's lack of gratitude. Moreover, even if a loan is only partially repaid, it nonetheless returns at least a portion of the original investment and thus makes in the long run this type of economic strategy considerably cheaper than are non-repayable grants.

Trade

Since the beginning of the communist trade offensive in the Third World in 1954, the volume of trade between the communist countries and the developing nations has increased by leaps and bounds. From an overall value of $860 million in 1954 it jumped to over $2.7 billion by 1960 and almost $4 billion by 1965.[73] The growth rate slackened considerably in 1966-67 as the overall increase in that period has been a mere 3.5 percent. But it accelerated again somewhat in 1968, 1969 and 1970, and reached over 5 billion $ in 1970. As for the Soviet Union, her overall trade with the developing countries rose by 25 percent in 1969 and by another 13 percent in 1970 when it reached a total value of over 2.4 billion dollars.[74] Writing in the 1971 volume of *New Times,* a Soviet writer reports that "between 1955 and 1970 the USSR increased trade with developing states by 700 percent, the German Democratic Republic by 370 percent, Poland by 200 percent and Czechoslovakia by 70 percent."[75]

The break-up of imports and exports, the Soviet, East European and Chinese shares as well as those of their less developed trading partners are apparent from table I below.

As Table I reveals, as of 1970, over 47 percent of the communist trade with developing nations falls to Soviet Russia, over 36 percent to communist East Europe, and almost 16 percent to communist China. (The remainder is accounted for by other communist countries, such as North Korea, North Vietnam, Mongolia and Cuba). Asia, including the Middle East, is in the lead with a total 1970 trade volume of $3,650 million representing a whopping 72 percent of the total communist trade with developing nations, while Africa with $964 million and Latin America with $483 million are far behind. If calculated on a per capita basis, communist trade has so far been most intense in the Near East and South Asia, and least intense in Latin America.[76]

In spite of its impressive growth since 1954, communist trade with the developing nations remains nevertheless comparatively low. In 1970, only some 4.5 percent of the exports of developing countries went to communist countries while communist exports accounted only for some 5 percent of the overall imports of developing nations. However, these low overall percentages contrast quite significantly with the high communist share in the trade of several individual developing countries. Thus the communist countries accounted in 1967-70 for 20 percent or more of the total imports of nine developing nations, namely, Afghanistan (63.4 in 1967, 39.1 in 1968, and 42.5 in 1969), Yemen (60.8 in 1967), Mali (38.6 in 1967, 34.7 in 1968, 19.5 in 1969 and 20.9 in 1970), Guinea (35.6 in 1967 and 24.2 in 1968), Egypt (35.1 in

TABLE I

Soviet, East European and Communist Chinese Exports To and From Developing Countries, 1969-1970
(in millions of US $)

Area and Country	USSR Exports 1969	USSR Exports 1970	USSR Imports 1969	USSR Imports 1970	East Europe Exports 1969	East Europe Exports 1970	East Europe Imports 1969	East Europe Imports 1970	Communist China Exports 1969	Communist China Exports 1970	Communist China Imports 1969	Communist China Imports 1970
Africa	178.5	217.0	172.3	226.0	172.0	188.5	135.9	120.8	113.9	136.6	64.5	65.0
Algeria	57.7	69.4	61.6	62.0	26.0	11.2	21.8	23.2	10.8	12.4	9.0	9.0
Cameroon	1.1	0.7	12.0	7.7	1.6	2.6	2.8	0.8	1.3	1.6	...	0.1
Chad	0.3	0.6	...	...	·0.8	0.5	...	...	0.7	0.6	...	...
Congo (Brazzaville)	0.1	0.9	0.8	0.8	...	...	...	...	0.6	1.5	1.4	1.5
Dahomey	0.4	0.8	...	...	...	...	...	...	1.1	1.2	...	...
Ethiopia	2.4	1.4	4.0	0.9	4.6	5.4	2.6	0.4	2.2	2.6	0.5	0.7
Gabon	...	...	...	...	0.2	...	0.8	1.5	...	...	...	...
Ghana	9.3	11.0	15.4	44.2	8.7	8.0	5.3	3.1	4.3	6.7	1.1	2.4
Guinea	8.8	12.4	3.4	3.3	...	...	...	...	...	...	...	...
Ivory Coast	...	0.4	5.8	1.7	2.9	4.2	4.0	2.2	0.8	1.0	...	...
Kenya	0.3	1.6	1.3	0.4	4.8	7.4	1.0	2.7	3.2	3.4	1.3	1.7
Liberia	0.2	0.3	...	...	2.5	2.8	...	...	1.6	1.5	...	...
Libya	10.8	14.3	...	...	28.3	34.0	7.2	0.8	13.2	10.6	...	...
Malagasy Republic	...	...	...	0.7	...	...	...	0.2	...	...	...	...
Malawi	...	...	...	...	...	...	...	...	...	...	...	...
Mali	5.1	5.2	2.0	1.9	0.3	0.6	0.1	0.1	3.1	3.2	...	...
Mauritania	1.6	0.4	...	...	...	...	...	...	...	...	...	...
Mauritius	...	...	...	...	...	...	...	...	...	...	...	...
Morocco	37.1	36.1	17.9	19.6	20.9	28.1	31.3	25.5	13.2	11.0	6.8	7.2
Niger	...	...	...	...	...	...	...	...	0.1	...	...	...
Nigeria	16.7	12.1	24.4	22.6	17.8	31.1	6.4	9.7	15.3	19.7	...	1.2
Senegal	0.2	1.3	0.1	...	1.1	0.7	0.2	0.3	6.7	4.5	...	...
Sierra Leone	1.0	1.8	1.1	...	8.6	8.8	...	0.3	4.2	2.8	...	...
Somalia	2.1	3.1	...	0.4	...	...	...	...	1.1	...	...	0.5
Sudan	16.0	36.1	13.7	14.9	16.8	19.7	18.7	18.0	14.0	11.6	18.5	17.2
Tanzania	0.4											

	1	2	3	4	5	6	7	8	9	10	11	12
Togo	1.1	1.3	0.9	3.1	1.2	1.3	...	...	1.6	1.6	...	1.5
Tunisia	4.2	3.4	3.4	2.9	12.8	16.6	14.6	15.2	...	0.2	...	...
Uganda	1.4	1.2	1.6	3.1	2.3	1.7	9.0	13.7	2.5	2.3	1.2	1.5
Upper Volta	...	...	...	...	0.1	0.1	...	...	...	...	...	...
Zaire (Congo K.)	...	...	...	...	4.3	...	...	...	...	...	...	...
Zambia	...	...	...	...	1.8	...	8.8	...	1.2	1.5	13.8	13.8
East Asia	17.6	21.5	158.4	45.6	45.6	27.3	67.5	54.0	237.5	229.8	106.7	54.0
Burma	2.6	3.3	3.7	1.6	16.2	...	0.9	...	...	1.4	...	...
Cambodia	0.7	0.3	...	1.6	2.7	3.8	1.9	0.3	4.6	8.1	...	3.7
Indonesia	3.6	5.0	23.8	27.8	4.0	...	2.0	...	39.0	40.5	5.0	5.0
Laos	...	2.1	...	...	0.9	...	...	...	...	...	...	...
Malaysia	1.7	1.8	121.8	123.3	3.6	3.9	31.9	22.4	157.1	53.9	44.6	21.6
Singapore	6.2	6.1	1.1	3.2	11.4	12.0	29.4	29.5	136.7	125.9	57.1	22.7
Thailand	2.8	2.9	0.3	0.9	6.8	7.6	1.4	1.8	0.1	...	...	...
Latin America	25.9	9.4	104.4	77.8	136.9	137.7	200.8	251.0	8.1	3.9	0.3	3.8
Argentina	6.8	1.9	25.6	31.3	14.9	18.2	46.0	46.4	0.8	0.9	0.3	2.5
Bolivia	...	...	...	3.4	2.1	...	...	...	...	...	...	1.3
Brazil	12.2	2.7	48.8	23.1	57.0	55.1	85.3	102.3	...	...	...	...
Chile	0.2	0.6	0.1	0.3	5.5	3.3	0.5	0.2	0.2	...	...	...
Colombia	2.6	1.7	4.2	10.4	14.3	16.3	21.6	21.3	...	0.5	...	...
Costa Rica	...	...	5.2	6.9	0.6	1.0	0.2	0.4	...	0.1	...	...
Ecuador	0.2	0.1	13.9	0.8	8.6	6.6	7.9	8.2	...	0.1	...	...
El Salvador	...	...	...	...	0.1	0.1	2.6	6.4	...	...	...	...
Guatemala	...	...	...	...	...	...	0.9	...	...	...	...	...
Guyana	0.7	0.5	...	...	0.7	...	...	...	0.2	0.2	...	...
Honduras	...	...	...	...	0.9	0.8	0.3	1.2	...	...	...	...
Mexico	0.9	0.8	5.6	0.3	14.5	6.0	2.4	3.6	...	...	...	...
Nicaragua	...	...	...	...	0.1	0.1	...	...	...	...	...	...
Peru	1.4	0.1	...	0.2	2.4	1.9	24.1	32.8	4.1	0.2	...	...
Uruguay	0.9	0.9	1.0	1.1	5.7	7.3	9.0	28.0	0.1	0.1	...	...
Venezuela	0.1	0.1	...	...	9.5	21.0	...	0.2	2.7	1.8	...	...

TABLE I (Cont.)

Soviet, East European and Communist Chinese Exports To and From Developing Countries, 1969-1970
(in millions of US $)

Area and Country	USSR Exports 1969	USSR Exports 1970	USSR Imports 1969	USSR Imports 1970	East Europe Exports 1969	East Europe Exports 1970	East Europe Imports 1969	East Europe Imports 1970	Communist China Exports 1969	Communist China Exports 1970	Communist China Imports 1969	Communist China Imports 1970
Near East and South Asia	832.4	936.6	623.3	758.6	573.4	626.6	397.3	441.6	183.7	179.7	105.1	132.1
Afghanistan	44.8	40.0	30.6	34.3	1.7	...	0.5	...	2.4	4.0	...	1.0
Bahrain	...	...	...	...	...	...	...	...	8.0	8.6	...	...
Ceylon	8.3	5.6	14.4	13.3	25.0	19.3	11.3	14.6	47.4	48.6	40.4	42.3
Egypt	238.2	363.2	228.1	310.6	95.5	135.1	131.6	147.9	12.9	15.3	14.0	17.7
India	171.3	135.9	221.4	269.6	142.5	146.9	130.1	138.1	...	...	...	...
Iran	161.6	187.8	56.4	69.1	57.6	74.6	38.0	39.6	1.8	1.7	0.9	4.4
Iraq	67.7	66.0	4.7	4.6	35.5	53.0	5.2	9.5	19.9	20.0	8.0	8.0
Jordan	4.3	7.1	...	...	141.1	10.7	0.5	0.6	4.9	4.2	0.6	0.6
Kuwait	15.3	10.8	...	0.3	12.7	20.8	...	...	25.0	20.4	0.3	2.1
Lebanon	11.6	15.2	3.0	4.2	43.3	45.2	7.6	6.5	10.5	8.8	0.2	0.3
Nepal	0.9	0.8	1.1	0.7	...	...	...	...	2.9	2.0	...	...
Pakistan	39.4	35.7	23.7	31.4	59.5	54.7	47.1	54.6	26.4	27.8	28.9	39.3
Saudi Arabia	4.6	6.0	0.2	...	7.0	8.3	1.0	...	...	...	...	...
Syria	49.8	46.4	37.3	19.2	55.2	48.9	24.4	18.9	17.0	9.8	11.5	15.9
Yemen (Aden)	6.9	4.8	1.0	0.2	3.3	4.1	...	...	4.6	5.0	0.3	0.5
Yemen (Sana)	9.7	11.1	1.4	1.1	0.5	5.0	...	...	...	3.5	...	...
The Third World Total	1,054.4	1,184.5	1,050.7	1,220.8	927.9	980.1	801.5	867.4	543.2	548.0	276.6	254.9

Source: U.S. Department of State, *Communist States and Developing Countries: Aid and Trade in 1971*, Research Study RECS-3 of May 15, 1972.

1967, 39.4 in 1968, 32.9 in 1969 and 31.4 in 1970), Syria (31.1 in
1967, 30.9 in 1969 and 26.3 in 1970), Iraq (21.2 in 1968, 23.2 in
1969 and 26.2 in 1970), Lebanon (28.2 in 1967) and Sudan (21.1
in 1968). Two other countries, Ceylon (19.7 in 1967, 19.4 in 1968,
18.9 in 1969 and 19.1 in 1970) and India (19.7 in 1969) came
close to 20 percent. In the same years the world socialist system
took 20 percent or more of the total exports of six countries of
the Third World, namely, Egypt (48.5 in 1967, 48.6 in 1968, 53.1
in 1969 and 59.1 in 1970), Afghanistan (38.3 in 1967, 40.6 in 1968
and 39.2 in 1969), Syria (29.1 in 1967, 38.3 in 1969 and 27.2 in
1970), Guinea (34 in 1967), Ceylon (20.7 in 1969 and 20.8 in
1970) and Sudan (19.7 in 1968, 19 in 1969 and 28.9 in 1970) while
three other countries, such as Cambodia (18 in 1968 and 22.8 in
1970), India (18.1 in 1967, 18.2 in 1968, 19.2 in 1969 and 20.3 in
1970) and Tunisia (18.9 in 1968), were not far behind. The
biggest trading partners of the communist world among the
developing nations in terms of the overall volume of trade, and
this by quite a substantial margin over others, have been Egypt
and India with respective turnovers of $693 and 645 million in
1965, 722 and 628 million in 1966, 736 and 589 million in 1967,
652 and 639 million in 1968, 726 and 665.4 million in 1969, and
990 and 690 million in 1970.

Finally, with regard to the commodity structure, some 80-85
percent of communist imports from the Third World consist of
foodstuffs and raw materials whereas the main items on the list
of communist exports to the area are machinery and industrial
equipment (over 50 percent in recent years), followed by manufactured goods (about 25-30%) and food products (about 8-13%).

One aspect of communist trade deserving special mention is
transportation. Aware of the economic and political importance
of transportation in general, and air transportation in particular,
and keenly conscious of the prestige value regular air connections
of their capitals with the outside world have for developing
nations, communist countries have sought to strengthen their
influence in the Third World also through an expansion of air
services. Begun on a major scale in the early sixties, the
communist "aerial diplomacy" resulted in a few short years in an
impressive network of regularly scheduled air routes connecting
Moscow and the capitals of the other communist countries of

Eastern Europe with virtually all the capitals and major cities of the developing nations of Asia, the Middle East and Africa. Next to the Soviet *Aeroflot*, the *Czechoslovak Airlines* have been especially enterprising in this respect and have taken an early lead over their East European partners. But the other communist countries of Eastern Europe have also done their share and concluded numerous air agreements with the developing nations of Asia, the Middle East and Africa. That is true even of Bulgaria, technologically the least developed of the East European members of the Comecon. Besides operating a few international lines of their own, such as one between Sofia and Baghdad, the Bulgarians have entered into an agreement with Morocco providing for Bulgarian pilots to fly and the Bulgarian technicians to service *Royal Air Maroc* planes between Rabat and other Moroccan cities.[77]

In addition to air services, Soviet Russia and some of her East European partners have endeavored to develop sea routes serving some countries of the Third World. Thus Poland established as early as 1958 a shipping line from Gdynia and Sczeczin to Accra and subsequently opened in 1961, jointly with East Germany, a shipping route under the name of United West African Service to handle the growing communist trade with Africa. Vessels of the service were to sail regularly three times a month, calling at Casablanca, Dakar, Conakry, Accra and Lagos.[78] China in her turn entered the transportation business with the Third World by assuming in 1967 a major obligation to build a one thousand miles long railway between Zambia and Tanzania, a substantial project deemed to be the third largest foreign aid undertaking in Africa (after the Soviet-sponsored Aswan dam and the U.S. backed Volta river dam in Ghana.) In 1968 China assumed a similar commitment, though on a much smaller scale, to build a 200-mile railway link from the Mali capital, Bamako, to the Guinean railway at Kouroussa.

The Credits

Being advanced strictly for purchases of goods and services from the respective communist countries, and being repayable by subsequent exports to the respective creditor nations, communist credits are actually a form of bilateral trade with postponed deliveries on the part of the debtor nations. It is, of course, this respite in paying for goods and services, coupled with a comparatively low interest charged on the unpaid balance, that makes credit more desirable for the developing nations than the *quid pro quo* of straightforward trading requiring ordinarily a fairly prompt settling of outstanding passive balances. Paralleling the growth of mutual trade, the communist credit commitments to the developing nations have registered a steady, though uneven, increase over the years of the communist economic aid program for the Third World begun in 1954. By 1971 these commitments have reached a cumulative total of 12.74 billion dollars. The distribution pattern is apparent from Table II below.

Soviet Russia is by far the biggest creditor among the communist nations, having accounted, as of 1971, for over 7 billion $ of communist loans, i.e., more than 56 percent of the total. The corresponding figures for communist East Europe and China for the same period have been 3.3 billion and 2.2 billion $, respectively. Duplicating the earlier mentioned trade pattern, the Asian portion of the Third World (inclusive of Egypt) is in the forefront of loan recipients with a total of almost 9 billion $, while Africa with less than 3 billion remains far behind and Latin America is a poor last with a mere 0.8 billion.

Although communist economic credits to the developing nations are by no means an unsubstantial commitment, the figure pales nonetheless when compared to the economic aid granted by the West. Thus in 1967 alone the United States actually spent (not merely committed) 5.6 billion $ in public and private aid to developing countries (of which 3.7 billion was in public funds, [79] while the corresponding communist commitment for the same year was 407 million $ (and 724 million for 1968). As estimated by *Neue Zürcher Zeitung*, communist economic aid to the Third World represented in recent years only about 4 percent of similar aid granted by the West.[80] According to the Organization for Economic Cooperation and Development, economic aid for developing countries from Western nations between 1956 and 1970 totalled 145 billion dollars, which is about 12 times the amount provided by communist countries.

TABLE II

Communist Economic Credits and Grants to Developing Countries — 1954-1971
(In Millions of US $)

Area and Country	1954-1971				1970				1971			
	Total	USSR	East Europe	Com. China	Total	USSR	East Europe	Com. China	Total	USSR	East Europe	Com. China
Africa	2,894	1,236	546	1,112	589	51	84	454	590	192	103	295
Algeria	609	421	96	92	74	—	74	—	229	189	—	40
Cameroon	8	8	—	—	—	—	—	—	—	—	—	—
Central African Republic	6	2	—	4	—	—	—	—	2	2	—	—
Congo (Brazz.)	34	9	—	25	—	—	—	—	1	1	—	—
Equatorial Guinea	1	1	—	—	—	—	—	—	—	—	—	—
Ethiopia	203	102	17	84	—	—	—	—	84	—	—	84
Ghana	231	89	102	40	—	—	—	—	—	—	—	—
Guinea	256	165	25	66	10	—	—	10	—	—	—	—
Kenya	62	44	—	18	—	—	—	—	—	—	—	—
Mali	134	56	23	55	—	—	—	—	—	—	—	—
Mauritania	28	3	—	25	—	—	—	—	20	—	—	20
Morocco	123	88	35	—	44	44	—	—	—	—	—	—
Nigeria	49	7	42	—	7	7	—	—	28	—	28	—
Senegal	7	7	—	—	—	—	—	—	—	—	—	—
Sierra Leone	28	28	—	—	—	—	—	—	—	—	—	—
Somalia	204	66	6	132	—	...	—	—	110	—	—	110
Sudan	269	64	123	82	52	—	10	42	115	—	75	40
Tanzania	282	20	6	256	201	—	—	201	1	—	—	1
Tunisia	105	34	71	—	—	—	—	—	—	—	—	—
Uganda	31	16	—	15	—	—	—	—	—	—	—	—
Zambia	224	6	—	201	201	—	—	201	—	—	—	—
East Asia	741	154	306	281	—	—	—	—	—	—	—	—
Burma	124	14	26	84	—	+	—	—	—	—	—	—

Cambodia	134	25	17	92	—	—	—	—	—	—	—	—
Indonesia	483	115	263	105	—	—	—	—	—	—	—	—
Latin America	816	301	471	44	107	56	51	—	235	38	153	44
Argentina	54	45	9	—	—	—	1	—	27	—	—	—
Bolivia	56	30	26	—	29	28	—	—	—	2	25	—
Brazil	312	85	227	2	—	—	—	—	133	—	—	—
Chile	193	91	100	—	—	—	—	—	—	36	95	2
Colombia	2	2	—	—	—	—	—	—	5	—	—	—
Ecuador	15	—	15	—	—	—	—	—	—	—	5	—
Peru	129	28	59	42	53	28	50	—	70	—	28	42
Uruguay	45	20	25	—	15	—	—	—	—	—	—	—
Venezuela	10	—	10	—	10	—	—	—	—	—	—	—
Near East and South Asia	8,253	5,464	2,032	757	395	87	53	255	868	632	165	71
Afghanistan	745	705	12	28	3	3	—	—	5	9	—	—
Ceylon	175	38	52	85	20	8	—	12	32	—	—	32
Egypt	1,945	1,198	641	106	—	—	—	—	308	192	112	—
India	1,975	1,593	382	—	—	—	—	—	—	—	—	—
Iran	987	562	425	39	54	54	43	—	—	—	—	—
Iraq	807	549	219	62	65	22	—	—	298	222	37	39
Nepal	82	20	—	—	—	—	—	—	—	—	—	—
Pakistan	867	474	74	309	210	—	10	200	209	209	—	—
Syria	443	233	194	16	43	—	—	43	16	—	—	—
Yemen (Aden)	71	—	16	55	—	—	—	—	—	—	16	—
Yemen (Sana)	166	92	17	57	—	—	—	—	—	—	—	—
Third World Total	12,704	7,155	3,355	2,194	1,091	194	188	709	1,693	862	421	410

With regard to their geographical distribution, the communist credit commitments reveal an especially heavy concentration on the same developing countries that also rank high in actual communist trade. Thus, as of 1971, India leads the debtors' list with 1,975 million $, followed by Egypt with 1,945 million, Iran with 987, Pakistan with 867, Iraq with 807 and Afghanistan with 745.

In line with the earlier mentioned communist emphasis on industrialization, the bulk of communist loans to the countries of the Third World have been earmarked for purchases of equipment and machinery for industrial plant installations, such as steel mills and iron foundries, power stations, dams, oil and sugar refineries, plants for the production of cement, textiles, footwear, motorcycles and bicycles, agricultural tools and the like. As a Rumanian economic review boasted in 1966, credits granted by European socialist countries enabled the underdeveloped countries of Asia, Africa and South America to build about 1,200 metallurgical and mining plants, over 80 metal-processing and machine-building enterprises, almost 50 chemical and oil processing plants, 50 electric power stations, over 250 textile and food factories, etc.[81] Going well beyond any previous claims, another Soviet author, writing in the 1970 volume of *New Times*, asserts that "the total number of projects built in the newly emerged states with the assistance of socialist countries is about 2,500."[82] As for the Soviet Union itself, Vasily Sergeyev, Vice-Chairman of the State Committee of the USSR Council of Ministers for Foreign Economic Relations, asserts that, as of 1971, the Soviet Union has helped the developing countries with the construction of "more than 700 industrial enterprises, of which some 340 have already been put into operation."[83] Only seldom has credit been extended for the purchase of consumer goods, except in the form of small swing credits to balance the fluctuations of annual trade. Separate credits have been granted, however, for purchases of military equipment. Soviet military assistance is estimated at 7.95 billion for the period 1955-1971. The largest recipients of such military credits have been Egypt (2,500 million $), Indonesia (1,100), India (1,100) Iraq (1,000), and Syria (580).[84]

Technical Assistance

Technical assistance, the third major aspect of communist

economic aid to the Third World, has been, of course, a logical and inevitable concomitant of the communist trade and credits. The dire shortage, and often virtual non-existence, of adequately trained native personnel has made it impossible for the Third World to advance its coveted goals of industrialization and modernization without direct participation of foreign advisers. Planning and constructing the many industrial plants built and equipped over the years with communist financial help, putting one after the other into operation, and, last but not the least, training natives to take over their operation, has called for the presence of a substantial number of communist managerial and technical personnel, not only in the. key and supervisory positions, but even on lower levels.

Thus, as communist foreign aid programs expanded, the number of economic advisers and technicians from the world socialist system kept increasing throughout the late fifties and early sixties. While some returned home after the completion of their work, others moved in to help in connection with newer projects and to provide services under the growing network of agreements on scientific and technical cooperation concluded between the communist countries and the countries of the Third World.

TABLE III

Communist Economic Technicians in the Developing Countries, 1970-1971 *

	Total		USSR		East Europe		Communist China	
	1970	1971	1970	1971	1970	1971	1970	1971
Total	24,010	35,050	10,600	11,025	5,300	5,425	8,110	18,600
Africa	14,120	24,700	4,010	4,200	3,150	3,300	6,960	17,200
East Asia	310	225	100	150	60	75	150	—
Latin America	175	225	35	75	140	150	—	—
Near East/S. Asia	9,405	9,900	6,455	6,600	1,950	1,900	1,000	1,400

*Minimum estimates of persons present for a period of one month or more.

Source: Same as for Tables I and II.

As shown in Table III, an annual contingent of between 24-35 thousand communist technicians was active in various developing nations in 1970-71, some 10-11 thousand of them from the Soviet Union, between 5-5-½ thousand from communist East Europe and some 5-8 thousand from Communist China. In a significant contrast with the distribution pattern prevalent in communist trade and credits (where Asia ranks first), Africa has been by far the largest beneficiary of communist technical assistance, accounting alone for more than half the communist advisers engaged in the Third World in 1969, 59% in 1970 and more than two thirds in 1971. The Near East and South Asia follows closely behind Africa in this respect, whereas communist technical assistance to Latin America (save Cuba) has been virtually nil. As might be expected the bulk of communist technicians have been deployed mostly in countries which figure high as recipients of communist trade and credits. In 1966, for instance, almost 70 percent of them were employed in Egypt, India, Algeria, Mali, Guinea, Afghanistan, Tunisia, Yemen and Nepal. In 1970, 61 percent of Soviet and 37 percent of East European technicians sent to the Third World were concentrated in Afghanistan, India, Iran, Iraq, Syria and Egypt. Similarly, well over 80% of the Chinese specialists operating in the Third World in 1971 were stationed in Tanzania and Zambia in connection with the Chinese construction of the Tan-Zam railroad. One aspect of their technical assistance programs of which communist countries are especially proud is the training of natives in technical and managerial skills. In addition to the on-the-job training at communist-assisted projects, communist countries have been instrumental in establishing in developing countries numerous centers, schools and institutes for technical and vocational education, both on intermediate and higher level. Thus Soviet Russia, the communist country most active in this field of technical assistance, claims to have helped establish well over ninety such institutions, including college-level technical institutes in India, Burma, Cambodia, Guinea, Algeria and Ethiopia.[85] By 1971 Soviet specialists are said to "have helped to train 250,000 skilled workers and technicians in African and Latin American countries."[86] In Egypt alone the Soviet Union claims to have set up 36 vocational centers which have trained "more than 50,000 skilled workers in the last several years."[87]

Besides developing institutions and courses for technical training and education in the developing nations, facilities for such training of the natives of the Third World have also been provided in communist countries themselves. Various courses of technical and vocational character have been set up in communist countries to minister to these particular needs. Some 2,500 trainees from the Third World attended such courses in 1966, 2,125 in 1967 and 1,700 in 1968, 2,000 in 1969, 1,550 in 1970 and 2,745 in 1971.

TABLE IV

Technical Trainees from the Developing Nations Training
in Communist Countries in 1969-1970

	Total		USSR		East Europe		Communist China	
	1970	1971	1970	1971	1970	1971	1970	1971
Total	1,550	2,745	1,020	1,310	530	1,435	0	0
Africa	210	170	65	90	145	80	0	0
East Africa	15	10	0	0	15	0	0	0
Latin America	0	10	0	10	0	0	0	0
Near East/S. Asia	1,325	2,565	955	1,210	370	1,355	0	0

Sources: Same as for Tables I, II and III.

As shown in Table IV, the bulk of the trainees comes from the Near East and South Asia, some 200 from Africa, and only a negligible number from Latin American and the Far East. Most of them are trained in Soviet Russia and communist East Europe, with only a handful (and none in 69-71) going to communist China. Moreover, the great majority of the Third World's full-time college students who have undertaken academic training at the various communist institutions of higher learning have pursued technically oriented curricula and thus also constitute a part of the communist technical assistance program.

Finally, mention should be made of one aspect of technical assistance that is cherished, rightly or wrongly, by the communists as being conducive to the non-capitalist path of development, namely, the support given to the Third World's coopera-

tive movement. Leaning on her long-standing tradition of cooperative enterprise dating from pre-communist days, not merely in
agriculture but especially in production and trade, Czechoslovakia has been especially active in this respect. Ever since the
late fifties emissaries of the Czechoslovak Central Cooperative
Council have been paying recurrent visits to various parts of the
Third World to establish contacts with the cooperatives of the
developing nations. Representatives of cooperativism from the
developing nations have been invited to Czechoslovakia to be
exposed to and impressed by well organized tours of selected
model cooperatives. Year after year short courses and seminars
on cooperativism have been offered to functionaries and workers
of Asian, African and even Latin American cooperatives.[88]

Economic Showmanship

The three main forms of communist economic strategy —
trade, credits and technical assistance — are supplemented by
consistent and rather spectacular communist participation in
innumerable trade fairs and exhibitions held annually in various
parts of the Third World. Indeed, few (if any) such occasions to
display their economic achievements have been missed in the last
decade; and listing of the fairs attended by communist exhibitors
would be tantamount virtually to a catalogue of the capitals and
other major cities of Asia, Africa and the Middle East, and more
recently even Latin America.[89] While all the communist countries (except Albania and China) have taken a lively part in this
economic showmanship, it seems that, next to Soviet Russia,
Czechoslovakia has been the most active. Capitalizing on her
long-term experience in this type of work and on the prestige
gained through her award-winning exhibits at the New York and
Brussels World Fairs, she has been more successful than her
communist sister-states in impressing the Third World's fair-
goers.

The communist economic showmanship abroad has been
paralleled by similar undertakings at home. Year after year,
communist countries have been serving as generous hosts to
untold numbers of visitors from the less developed countries,
ranging from such prominents as Nehru, Nasser, Haile Sellasie,

Nkrumah, Sekou Toure, Modibo Keita, Nyerere and Prince Sihanouk to sundry delegations of native labor leaders, youth and women groups. Arriving in a steady stream on the invitations of the respective communist countries and organizations, the visitors are given a more or less elaborate red carpet treatment graduated according to their ranking and importance. Even in its most modest version the treatment includes carefully guided tours through the show pieces of communist industry well calculated to create the strongest possible impression of the host country's economic and technological achievements.

Footnotes for Chapter X

[1] *Gazette of the Temporary Workers and Peasants Government,* December 13, 1917. Cited in *The Communist Conspiracy, Strategy and Tactics of World Communism.* Part I, Section B. House report No. 2241, May 29, 1956, p. 14.

[2] Evidently, the Soviet leaders were impressed, in particular, by the high rate of Soviet industrial growth which was claimed to amount to 11.1 percent per annum in 1954-1960 as compared to a mere 2.5 percent for the United States. See, for instance, *Fundamentals,* p. 694, and the *History of the Communist Party of the Soviet Union,* 1960 edition, p. 733.

[3] Ritvo, *op. cit.* pp. 114 and 134.

[4] p. 733. Italics in the original.

[5] *Fundamentals,* p. 694.

[6] *History of the Communist Party of the Soviet Union,* p. 734.

[7] Jacobs, *op. cit.,* p. 12.

[8] V. Rymalov, "Economic Competition — and Aid to Underdeveloped Countries," reprinted in Pentony, *op. cit.* pp. 221 ff.

[9] See, for instance, Podgorny's speech on the 46th anniversary of the October Revolution in 1963; Vadim Zagladin, "Economic Competition Between Socialism and Capitalism: A Perspective View," *World Marxist Review,* 1962, pp. 46 ff.; Alexander Sobolev, "Some Problems of Social Progress," *World Marxist Review,* 10, 1, 1967, pp. 21 ff.; G. Dadashev, *"Marksistskaia politicheskaia ekonomia i razvivaiushchiesia Strany,"* (The Marxist Political Economy and the Developing Countries), *MEIMO,* No. 2, 1965, pp. 84 ff.; A. Alekseev and Yu Shiriaev, *"Ekonomicheskoe sorevnovanie dvukh mirovykh sistem i antikommunizm* (Economic Competition of Two World Economic Systems and Anti-Communism) *MEIMO,* No. 8, 1965, pp. 3 ff.

[10] *op. cit.*

[11] See the *Soviet Communist Party Program,* Ritvo, *op. cit.,* p. 183.

[12] M. Lavrichenko, *"Za razshirenie ekonomicheskikh sviazei, za polnuiu likvidatsiiu kolonializma,* (For the Broadening of Economic Contacts, for a Full Liquidation of Colonialism), *MEIMO,* No. 2, 1964, pp. 60 ff. See also the *Declaration of Eighty-One Communist Parties* and *History,* p. 733.

[13] Rymalov, *op. cit.*

[14] *The Soviet Communist Party Program,* Ritvo, *op. cit.,* p. 105, *Fundamentals,* p. 471.

[15] Donald S. Zagoria, *The Sino-Soviet Conflict, 1956-1961.*

[16] For the reasons given for the suitability of the Soviet model and the unsuitability of the capitalist model, see Chapter I.

[17] Rymalov, *op. cit.* See also the same author's "Western Aid to the 'Third World': Statistics and Reality," *International Affairs* (Moscow), No. 4, 1972, pp. 16 ff.

[18] *New Times,* No. 15, 1971, pp. 24 ff.; "Roots of the Dollar Crisis," *World Marxist Review,* 15, 5, 1972, pp. 83 ff.

[19] Khrushchev at the 20th Party Congress in 1956.

[20] S. Skachkov, *"Bezkoristnaia i druzheskaia pomoshch,"* (The Self - less Friendly Aid), *Ekonomicheskaia Gazeta,* April 20, 1961.

[21] Rymalov, *op. cit.* in note 13. Communist literature denigrating Western economic behavior, past and present, vis-a-vis the developing nations and extolling the "selfless" communist aid to the Third World is virtually inexhaustible. A few samples have been cited in Chapter I. Here are a few more: M. Pankin, "The USSR and the Developing Countries: Experience of Economic Cooperation," *World Marxist Review,* 9, 5, 1966, pp. 68 ff. Yuri Gvozdev, "Common Market for Latin America," *New Times,* 15, 1967, pp. 19-20; V. Listov, *"Marka rvetsia v Latinskuiu Ameriku,"* (The Mark Pushes into Latin America) *Pravda,* September 3, 1969; P. Orlov, "Dialectics of Underdevelopment," *New Times,* No. 15, 1968, pp. 31-32, praising a book by Ramon Losada Aldana, *Dialectica del subdesarrollo* (The Dialectics of Underdevelopment) (Caracas, 1967), in which the author claims that, while the U. S. pledged to aid Latin America with one billion dollars annually, it "siphoned out of Venezuela alone" four billion dollars through non-equivalent exchange from 1958 to 1963; V. B. Rybakov and L. V. Stepanov, *Pomoshch Osvobodivshimsia stranam v politike i strategii imperializma* (The Aid to the Liberated Countries in the Policy and Strategy of Imperialism) *Moskva,* 1964; F. Goryunov, "Anatomy of American 'Aid'", *New Times* No. 25, 1971, pp. 24-25; V. Korionov, *"Imperializm dollara izoschchriaetsia,"* (The Dollar Imperialism Sharpens), *Pravda,* July 31, 1970; Y. Seryogin, "Washington's Latin American Manoeuvres," *New Times,* No. 5, 1970, pp. 24-25; "Indictment of Imperialism," *World Marxist Review,* 12, 7, 1969, pp. 35 ff. A. Atroshenko, "Venezuela vs. the Oil Sharks," *New Times,* No. 32, 1971, pp. 6-7; Teodoro Varela, "Imperialism Continues to Plunder Latin America," *World Marxist Review,* 14, 5, 1971, pp. 96 ff. S. Gionsky, "Washington's Financial Big Stick," *New Times,* No. 10, 1972, pp. 25-26.

[22] Haled Bagdash, "Problems of the National-Liberation Movement in Syria," *World Marxist Review,* 11, 6, 1968, pp. 39 ff.

[23] Y. Osipov, "The Monetary Crisis and the Third World," *New Times,* No. 44, 1971, pp. 27 ff.

[24] *MEIMO,* No. 11, 1964, pp. 16 ff. See also Robert S. Jaster, "Foreign Aid and Development. The Shifting Soviet View," *International Affairs,* 45, 3, pp. 452-464, and Elizabeth Kridl Valkenies, "New Trends in Soviet Economic Relations with the Third World," *World Politics,* XXII, 3, 1970, pp. 415 ff.

[25] English text in Alvin Z. Rubinstein, *The Foreign Policy of the Soviet Union,* 2nd ed., New York, 1966, pp. 404-406.

[26] Tiagunenko, *op. cit.*

[27] Khrushchev in *Pravda,* December 30, 1955, cited in Rymalov, *op. cit.* See

also A. Mikoyan's statement along similar lines cited also in Rymalov, *op. cit.* in note 13.

[28] G. Kim and P. Shastitko, *Pravda*, September 14, 1966.

[29] Tiagunenko in *MEIMO*, No. 6, 1965, p. 79; N. Kuznetsov, "Algeria Chooses Her Way Ahead," *International Affairs*, No. 3, 1964, p. 51.

[30] A. Iskenderov and G. Starushenko, "On International Themes: Intrigues of Imperialism in Africa," *Pravda*, August 14, 1966, p. 4. English text in the *Current Digest*, XVIII, No. 33, 19.

[31] *Ibid.* See also V. Solodovnikov, *"Afrika: Nekapitalisticheskii put',"* (Africa: The Non-Capitalist Path) *Pravda*, August 27, 1970.

[32] Ezekias Papaioannou, "Neocolonialism and Developing Countries," *World Marxist Review*, 14, 5, 1971, pp. 86 ff. See also Valkenies, *op. cit.*

[33] V. Shelepin, "Maoist Intrigues in the Third World," *New Times*, No. 26, 1969, pp. 6-8.

[35] A. Sobolev's statement at the Cairo seminar on "Africa - National and Social Revolution," in October 1966. See *Mizan*, 9, 1967, p. 65.

[36] R. A. Ulyanovsky, "Leninism, Soviet Experience and the Newly Free Countries," *op. cit.*

[37] F. Burlatsky, "The Liberation Movement and Scientific Socialism," *Pravda*, August 15, 1965, English text in *Current Digest*, XVII, No. 34. See also, Jaster, *op. cit.,* and Valkenies, *op. cit.*

[38] Adam B. Ulam, *The Unfinished Revolution, 1960*, pp. 284-5.

[39] Alexander Vladim, "Africa: The Outlook for Industrialization," *New Times*, No. 20, 1966, pp. 11 ff.

[40] See, for inst. an interview on "Business Ties with Developing Nations" of V. A. Sergyeev, Vice-Chairman of the Foreign Economic Relations Committee of the USSR's Council of Ministers, with the editor of *New Times*, No. 12, 1966, pp. 5 ff.

[41] *ibid.,* and in another interview with Sergeyev in *New Times*, No. 3, January 20, 1971 pp. 18 ff.

[42] Mihail Pankin, "The USSR and the Developing Countries: Experience of Economic Cooperation." *World Marxist Review*, 9, 5, 1966, pp. 68 ff.

[43] Pankin, *op. cit.* and V. Shelepin, "The Socialist World and the Developing Countries," *New Times*, No. 9 1970, pp. 20 ff.

[44] Hamid Safari, "Aspects of Struggle for Independence in Asia and Africa," *World Marxist Review*, 14, 4, 1971, pp. 130 ff. In his article "The Soviet Union and the Developing Countries," *International Affairs* (Moscow), No. 5, 1971, 438 pp. 25 ff. V. Sergyeev states that 68.7 percent of Soviet aid went to "industry and power projects."

[45] I. I. Gavrilov, ed., *Nezavisimye Strany Afriki: Ekonomicheskie i Sotsialnye Problemy*, Moscow, 1965. Cited also in "An Objective Soviet View of Independent Africa," *Mizan*, 7, 9, 1966, pp. 1 ff.

[46] M. Semin, CMEA and Africa," *New Times*, No. 23, 1968, p. 23. See also Solodovnikov, *op. cit.,* warning against "excessive industrialization," and Valkenies, *op. cit.*

[47] *Fundamentals*, pp. 423-24; Pankin, *op. cit.* Vladin, *op. cit.,* denouncing the West for efforts to hold the Africans to the level of "semi-starved" 'hewers of wood and drawers of water'"

[48] Shelepin, *op. cit.*

[49] Gavrilov, *op. cit.* See also Valkenies, *op. cit.,* and R. R. Ulyanovsky, "Leninism, Soviet Experience . . ." *op. cit.*

[50] See Safari, *op. cit.* and Sergeyev, *op. cit* in note 44.

[51] V. Gavrilov, "Africa Ten Years After," *New Times,* No. 49, 1970.

[52] See, for instance, Frederick Benham, *Economic Aid to Underdeveloped Countries,* 1961; *Processes and Problems of Industrialization in Under-developed Countries,* a United Nations Publication, New York, 1955.

[53] Pankin, *op. cit.* On December 15, 1970, Tass reported a shipment of Soviet farm machinery for a farm in Kerala. *USSR and Third World,* I, 1, 1971, p. 7.

[54] See for instance, a major article *"ČSSR a Afrika"* (CSSR and Africa) by Miroslav Novotný in *Nová mysl,* No. 7, 1965; *"Revoluce, o ktere se mluví* (A Revolution That is Spoken About) *Zivot strany,* No. 15, August 1966, pp. 11 ff.: Ladislav Dvořák, "National Liberation Movement" in *Nová mysl,* September 1966; *Rudé právo,* August 31, 1962: *"Kde bychom mohli být* (Where Could We Be) *Mladá fronta,* August 9, 1966.

[55] *"Revoluce, o které se mluví"* *op. cit.* See also *"Ekonomická propaganda a naše vnější hospodářské vztahy,"* (Economic propaganda and Our External Economic Relations), *Zivot strany,* No. 7, 1967, pp. 49 ff.

[56] Jaroslav Kohout, "Czechoslovak Economic Relations With Developing Countries," *Czechoslovak Foreign Trade,* No. 6, 1965; František Korbel, "Czechoslovakia's Economic Relations with Industrialized Capitalist Countries," *Czechoslovak Foreign Trade,* No. 6, 1966, pp. 8 ff.: Jaroslav Brabec, *"Mierove spolužitie - ostrý triedný zápas,"* (Peaceful Coexistence - A Tough Class Struggle) *Pravda* (Bratislava) August 7, 1963; *Rudé právo,* April 21, 1962, reporting the speech by Václav Slavik on the 92nd anniversary of Lenin's death.

[57] *Zemědělské noviny,* September 6, 1962; *Z najnovšich dejin československo-sovietských vztahov po roku 1945* (From the Newest History of Czechoslovak-Soviet Relations after 1945) Bratislava, 1962, p. 29; *Práce,* July 7, 1961.

[58] Rozehnal, "The Leninist Road of World Communism," *Nová mysl,* No. 3, 1963. English text in the *Czechoslovak Press Survey,* No. 1223/17.

[59] Statement by the Yugoslav Undersecretary of State Anton Vratuša in *Borba,* March 26, 1972, cited in *Südosteuropa und die Entwicklungsländer,* Munich, 1963, p. 13. See also "Yugoslav Cooperation With Developing Countries," *Yugoslav Life,* X, 2, 1965, p. 2, and "President Tito Visits Asia and Africa," *ibid.,* XIII, 1, 1968, p. 2.

[60] Speech by K. Dobrev, "Paths of Development of Newly Emergent Countries," *World Marxist Review,* 5, 5, 1962, pp. 66 ff; his Rumanian colleague spoke in the same vein, see B. Zacharescu's statement, *ibid.,* 1962, pp. 70 ff.

[61] Information in this paragraph is culled from a long list of various East European statements and articles over a number of years. Here are a few samplings (in addition to sources already mentioned above): Jaroslav Sedivý, *"Sovětský Svaz a Třeti Svět,"* (The Soviet Union and the Third World) *Praha-Moskva,* No. 5, 1966, pp. 15 ff.; Bronislaw Rudowicz, *"Kraje Socja-listyczne Trzeciemu Swiatu"* (Socialist Countries to the Third World) *Glos pracy,* May 5, 1965; *Diskuse a Činy,"* Discussion and Action), *Hos-podářské noviny,* April 29, 1966; Marcel Brožik, *"O hospodářských vztazich s rozvojovými zeměmi,* (Concerning Economic Relations with Developing Countries), *Rudé právo,* May 25, 1965; *"Základni principy mezinárodni sosialistické dělby práce,* (The Fundamental Principles of the International Division of Labor), *Rudé právo,* June 17, 1962; Lubomir Pešl,

"Hospodářské vztahy ČSSR s rozvojovými zeměmi," (Economic Relations of CSSR with Developing Countries), *Hospodářské noviny,* February 18, 1966; Sandor Czeitler, "On Aid for the Underdeveloped Countries," *Kulkereskedelem,* April 1963, English text in *Free Europe's Hungarian Press Survey,* No. 1322; Kohout J. and Wagner R., "The Economic Relations with the Developing Countries," *Mezinárodni politika,* No. 1, January 1963, English text in *Czechoslovak Press Survey,* No. 1198 (30).

[62] Dobrev, *op. cit.*

[63] Zacharescu, *op. cit.* and B. G. Hansen's speech at the exchange of views on the "Paths of Newly Emergent Countries," *World Marxist Review,* 5, 7, 1962, p. 73. Also, Paul Friedlaender and Harmut Schilling, "West German Imperialism. - Bulwark of Colonialism," *World Marxist Review,* 5, 4, 1962, pp. 18 ff; J. Zeman, "Economic and Trade Relations between Czechoslovakia and West Africa," *Czechoslovak Foreign Trade,* No. 12, 1970, pp. 5-6; Tadeusz Gorzkowski, *"Polacy na Bliskim Wschodzie,"* (The Poles in the Near East) *Zolnierz wolnosci,* Dec. 4, 1970; G. Vekshin, *"CMEA and the Developing Countries,"* *New Times,* No. 40, 1971.

[64] See, for instance, the above quoted article by Kohout and Wagner in *Mezinárodni politika* warning that industrialization in the developing countries "cannot be reduced to a building up of heavy industry as an end in itself."

[65] *Red Flag,* October 1, 1959, cited in Richard Lowenthal, "'National Democracy' and the Post-Colonial Revolution," in Kurt London, ed., *New Nations in a Divided World,* p. 67; Donald Zagoria, "Sino-Soviet Friction in Underdeveloped Areas," *Problems of Communism,* X, 2, 1961, pp. 1 ff.

[66] See, for instance, "Peking Says Moscow Is Trying to Buy Support," *New York Times,* September 22, 1964; "China Tells Poor Nations Not to Take Soviet Aid," *ibid.* June 22, 1964.

[67] See point 13 of the Chinese Open Letter of June 14, 1963.

[68] *Pravda,* April 3, 1964, English text in *Current Digest,* XVI, 13, 1964.

[69] *ibid.* See also a long editorial in *Kommunist,* No. 14, September 1963, pp. 4 ff. *"Za general'nuiu liniu mirovogo kommunisticheskogo dvizheniia protiv levogo opportunizma, natsionalizma i avantiurizma,"* (For the General Line of the World Communist Movement against Leftist Opportunism, Nationalism and Adventurism) accusing the Chinese of a failure to recognize the importance of socialist successes in economic competition with capitalism.

[70] G. Glezerman, *"Leninskii printsip sootnosheniia politiki i ekonomiki,"* (The Leninist Principle of the Correlation of Politics and Economics) *Pravda,* January 29, 1969, pp. 3-4.

[71] *Intelligence Report* No. 8426, U. S. Department of State, March 1961, p. 8.

[72] Dealing with the Soviet practice Berliner believes that this, rather than a wish to save money, accounts for the Soviet preference for credits over non-repayable grants. See his *Soviet Economic Aid,* p. 144.

[73] Unless otherwise stated, the data used in this and the following two paragraphs are taken from the U. S. State Department releases: *The Threat of Soviet Economic Policy* Publication No. 7234, 1961; Research Memorandum No. RSB-145 September 18, 1962; Research Memorandum No. RSB-50 of June 17, 1966; Research Memorandum RSB-80 of July 21, 1967; Research Memorandum RSE-120, of August 14, 1968; Research Memorandum RSE-65 of September 5, 1969; Communist States and Developing Countries. Aid and Trade in 1970. Research Study, Bureau of Intelligence and Research, Dept. of

State RECS - 15 of September 22, 1971. Research Study, Bureau of Intelligence and Research, U. S. Department of State, RECS-3 of May 15, 1972.

[74] *ibid.*, see also K. Ivanov, "Founder of Soviet Foreign Policy," *New Times,* No. 16, 1970, pp. 4-7.

[75] Vekshin, *op. cit.*

[76] In the last few years, in spite of Castro's criticism of communist trading with "bourgeois" regimes, Soviet Russia and communist East Europe have stepped up their efforts to increase trade with Latin America. See, for instance, A. Mazin, *"Torgovlia sblizhaet narody,"* (Trade Brings Peoples Together), *Pravda,* December 15, 1967, and A. Nadezhdin and N. Reginin, *"Kogda vygodno vsem partneram,"* (When It is Advantageous for All the Partners), *Pravda,* March 5, 1967.

[77] *Rabotnichesko Delo,* May 24, 1968, *East Europe,* 17, 7, 1968, p. 44.

[78] Radio Warszawa, June 30, 1961, as monitored by *Radio Free Europe.*

[79] OECD figures.

[80] *"Das Janusgesicht der kommunistischen Entwicklungshilfe,"* (Janus' Face of the Communist Development Aid), *Neue Zürcher Zeitung,* October 10, 1967.

[81] Fuiu Al. and Ciulea O., "Trade Development Among Socialist and Non-Socialist Countries," *Probleme Economice,* No. 1, 1966, *Rumanian Press Survey,* No. 618, March 18, 1966.

[82] V. Shelepin, *op. cit.* The author evidently includes in his calculations even all non-economic projects as well.

[83] "The Soviet Union and the Developing Countries," *New Times,* No. 3, 1971, pp. 18 ff., and an article of his under the same title in *International Affairs* (Moscow), No. 5, 1971, pp. 25 ff. The same figure of 700 is also listed in Victor Popov, "Leninist Foreign Policy," *New Times,* No. 13, 1971, pp. 6 ff.

[84] *The State Department Research Memorandum RECS-15,* cited above.

[85] The occasion of the first graduating class turned out in 1968 by Guinea's Polytechnical Institute at Conakry, established with Soviet aid in 1963, has been duly noted in a self-congratulatory article in *Pravda* on August 10, 1968: *"Molodye Kadry Gvinei,"* (Young Cadres of Guinea) by A. Lebedev.

[86] Vekshin, *op. cit.*

[87] R. Petrov, "True Friend of the Arab Peoples," *New Times,* No. 8, 1972, pp. 6-8.

[88] See, for instance, *Družstevník,* November 13, 1961, June 30, 1962, May 20, 1963, January 11, 1964; *Práce,* May 16, 1962; *Rudé právo,* September 24, 1962. See also Chapter VII.

[89] The Latin American fairs have not experienced as much communist participation during the earlier years of the communist economic offensive in the Third World. But more recently there has been an increase in communist attendance there. For instance, Poland held in August 1968 its very first industrial exhibition ever on the Latin American continent in Bogota. *Gos pracy,* June 10, 1968.

CHAPTER XI

WIELDING THE ECONOMIC WEAPON-II

The communist economic strategy vis-a-vis the Third World has been marked by several significant characteristics that implicitly reveal a good deal about communist intentions and purposes.

Main Characteristics of Communist Economic Strategy

First, communist foreign aid appears to be highly selective and is heavily concentrated in comparatively few countries. While United States' aid has been rather broadly spread over some one hundred countries, and as many as eighty of them have shared even in the much smaller West German foreign aid program in 1954-1966, the Soviet Union has given credits in 1954-1971 to only 41 nations of the Third World, communist East Europe to 32 and Communist China to 28.[1] Moreover, great unevenness and disparity prevails among the recipients of communist loans. The fact is that $7.3 billion of 12.7 billion of communist credits extended from 1954 to 1971, i.e., almost 58 percent, went to as few as six countries — India, Egypt, Iran, Pakistan, Iraq and

Afghanistan. On the other hand, the communist credits awarded to twenty-four of the grantees over the entire span of 1954-1971 amounted to less than 150 million dollars each. As shown in the previous chapter, a similar unevenness, though to a somewhat lesser extent, has been apparent also in communist trade with the Third World. Furthermore, communist aid in most instances has been smaller, and often considerably so, than Western grants to the same countries and could, therefore, hardly make most of the developing nations economically too dependent on the world socialist system. However, that has not been so in several cases, such as those of Afghanistan, Syria, Iraq, and Guinea, where communist economic aid has in recent years been higher than credits coming from the West.[2] A somewhat similar situation obtains in Egypt where some 40 percent of the country's industrial projects under Egypt's second five-year plan are said to be underwritten by the Soviet Union, East Germany and Czechoslovakia.[3]

Second, with a few negligible exceptions, the economic relations between the communist countries and their Third World partners have been so far conducted on a strictly bilateral basis. Since both credits extended by a communist country and earnings from trading with it may be used solely for purchases in that particular communist country and nowhere else, such bilateralism ties the developing countries concerned more closely to the world socialist system than would be the case if such credits and earnings could be used elsewhere. Occasionally, there have been tripartite arrangements in which two communist countries participated in projects in one or another developing country, but even these have been quite rare.[4] However, the recent communist willingness to enter into joint production ventures with Western enterprises triggered by recent economic reformism in communist East Europe may well lead gradually to a measure of East-West cooperation in the Third World, at least on the part of the less orthodox of the communist countries. The first instance of such a joint undertaking seems to be a recent Rumanian-French agreement to build jointly a 2.5 million ton oil refinery in India and a consortium of enterprises from Australia, Italy, the United States, Yugoslavia and Rumania formed for the purpose of developing iron ore mining in Guinea.[5] Also, in a number of cases, West German firms constructing enterprises in the Third World, have subcontracted part of the work to nationalized enterprises of one or another country of communist East Europe (other than the Soviet Union).[6]

Communist preference for bilateralism in economic dealings with the developing countries has its logical counterpart in their obvious coolness toward chanelling aid to developing nations, both capitalist and communist, through international agencies. The Soviet Union and the communist countries of Eastern Europe did contribute, after some initial opposition, to the U.N. Expanded Programme of Technical Assistance (EPTA) and lent their support to the Special U.N. Fund for Economic Development (SUNFED), but Soviet and communist participation in such collective aid ventures has remained rather marginal and financially insignificant.[7]

Third, there is often a substantial lag and gap between the targets and commitments expressed in communist aid pledges and trade agreements on the one hand, and their actual fulfillment on the other. Only about 40-45 percent of pledged credits were actually disbursed by 1971. The typical trade and payment agreements concluded between the communist countries and developing nations list usually only general targets (sometimes not even those) and rely on additional executive agreements or protocols to spell out all the pertinent particulars. This procedure often results in a substantial difference between the higher original targets listed in the well publicized general agreements and the more modest figures reached in their subsequent implementation. As estimated by Allen, in 28 percent of the agreements the Soviet Bloc imported one half or less of what it promised to buy and in 36 percent of the agreements it exported one half or less of what it pledged.[8]

Fourth, in trading with the developing nations, the communist countries invariably settle for repayment in local currency. Although eager to secure the best deal possible, they are also more willing than their western competitors to accept in exchange most any merchandise their Third World trading partners can offer.

Fifth, in line with the communist foreign aid theory explained in the previous chapter, communist aid goes to the public sector of the economy, and almost exclusively to its non-agricultural branches, especially those engaged in capital goods production.

Sixth, the communist countries generally charge lower interest rates on their loans to developing nations than do western lenders. As compared to 3.6 percent or more usually charged by the West, typical Soviet credit commitments have been contracted at a 2.5 percent interest and with 12 years to repay. "...Soviet credits, which are granted at 2.5 to 3 percent interest and with payment spread over 10 to 15 years," asserts a Soviet writer, "involve less expenditure than do credits given by the developed capitalist states."[9] China has been even more generous, having granted interest-free loans to several developing countries, such as Ghana in 1964 (22.4 million dollars), Algeria in 1963 (18 million pounds sterling), Zambia and Tanzania in 1970 (400 million dollars) and Pakistan in 1970 (200 million dollars). On the other hand, while granting some loans at 2.5 percent. the countries of communist East Europe have had a tendency to extend loans at a somewhat higher interest. At times their aid is offered at rates as high as 4.5 and even 6 percent, and for shorter periods of 5 to 8 years. Recently, especially since the ouster of Khrushchev, some of the Soviet credit terms have also stiffened somewhat and a larger portion of Soviet economic aid has assumed the form of "trade credits" carrying a higher rate of interest than the traditional 2.5 percent and a shorter amortization period than the habitual 12 years. Yugoslavia's interest charges on her loans to the developing nations have been mostly around 3 percent.[10]

Seventh, whereas the Western imperialists are accused of forcing the developing nations to a non-equivalent exchange by allegedly paying unduly low prices for the Third World's primary commodities and overpricing the manufactured goods they export to it, communist countries claim they do no such thing. Yet, as the recipients' complaints have revealed, communist exports to the developing nations are mostly of poorer quality than similar merchandise from the West; therefore, even when the latter turns out to carry a higher price tag it is often actually less expensive in the long run.[11] Moreover, when communist countries agree to pay higher prices for certain commodities of the Third World, they sometimes make up for the loss by overpricing the goods they export. A 1971 volume on *The Net Cost of Soviet Foreign Aid* estimates that Soviet exports to the developing countries are priced about 15 percent higher and Soviet imports from these countries 15 percent lower than would be the case were these goods bought and sold on the world market.[12]

Eighth, communist aid is advertised by its communist disbursers as being offered with no "strings" attached. In contrast, Western aid is alleged to be contingent upon certain conditions, thus carrying with it an overt or covert interference with the recipient country's internal affairs. Although distorted, this communist claim is not altogether without substance. Indeed, in their economic offensive in the Third World, communist countries have displayed a distinct willingness to go along with the wishes of the receiving country and to extend aid for most any purpose and any project, irrespective of their economic soundness. Consequently, communist credits have often been wasted on various pet or prestige ventures of questionable economic value to the respective developing countries, such as sport stadiums, luxury hotels, airplane purchases for deficit-creating national air services, steel mills where favorable conditions did not obtain. More recently, however, the communist lenders have become more selective. Having over-extended their resources and having occasionally sustained blame when communist-sponsored undertakings turned out to be white elephants, they now seem to attach more importance than previously to the economic viability of the project for which credits are requested.

Ninth, in addition to its legitimate economic function, the technical assistance part of the communist foreign aid program is utilized in yet another, less legitimate, capacity, namely, intelligence-gathering activities. Most of the personnel sent to the Third World within the framework of communist technical assistance appear to be *bona fide* specialists attending to the particular economic tasks they are supposed to handle. However, as borne out by depositions of communist defectors and other sources, concealed among them is an undetermined number of persons who double as agents whose duty it is to collect both economic and non-economic information needed by communist strategists for their operations in the Third World.[13] Among the

Third World countries that have felt compelled to expell members of Soviet trade missions for espionage activities have been Argentine, Brazil, Ceylon, Ethiopia, Ghana, Guinea, India, Iran, Kenya, Lebanon, Mexico, Morocco, Thailand, Uruguay, and others.[14]

Business and Politics

Both the ideological rationale of the communist theory of foreign aid and the main characteristics of communist economic strategy summarized above leave little doubt that the primary purpose of communist economic operations in the Third World is political rather than economic. As restated forcefully in a recent editorial in *Pravda*, "the dialectical conception of the mutual interdependence" and "unity" of politics and economics is one of "the most important principles of Marxism-Leninism" and politics is seen as "a concentrated expression of economics."[15] To be sure, a good portion of communist trade and even some of the credit arrangements with the developing countries can be explained and justified also on economic grounds. There are a number of goods that it is economically advantageous for communist countries to buy from the countries of the Third World, either because they do not have to pay for them in hard currencies or because they can get them more cheaply than elsewhere. Similarly, it makes good economic sense to use the Third World as a disposal for such communist merchandise as can not be sold profitably in the more demanding and much more competitive Western markets. However, as most students of communist strategy seem to concur, economic advantageousness *per se* has thus far played a secondary role in communist economic relations with the Third World, especially those parts of it deemed promising from the communist standpoint.[16] This overwhelmingly political motivation is apparent, in particular, in the cases of the Soviet Union and Communist China whose economic relations with what is today referred to as the Third World used to be negligible (except for Russia's trade with the neighboring Iran and Afghanistan). "The Soviet Union uses all of its foreign economic policies and relations consistently and exclusively to promote the interests of the Soviet state and the philosophy on which it is founded," writes Allen in his *Soviet Economic Warfare.*[17] Although he may have overstated his case, Allen is certainly closer to reality than those who tend to explain Soviet economic ventures in the Third World as being guided, mainly or substantially, by economic rather than political considerations. On the other hand, considerations of economic nature no doubt play a more important role in the dealings between the communist countries of East Europe and the Third World. After all, some of the East European countries, notably Czechoslovakia and East Germany, used to have lively economic contacts with a number of developing countries in the pre-communist era. But even in their case much of what the communist regimes have been doing economically in the Third World has been politically motivated and meant primarily to please and to help Moscow in the attainment of its political objectives.

There is a wealth of evidence substantiating the thesis of the predominance of political over economic considerations in communist economic relations with the Third World.

To begin with, this thesis is amply documented by innumerable communist statements on the matter. As explained in chapters I and X, communist dicta portray economic operations in the Third World as a major device of communist strategy for promoting the cause of communism through peaceful co-existence. They count on such arrangements to change the economic and social structure in the developing nations in the direction they believe to be conducive eventually to "scientific socialism." They see them as potent anti-imperialist weapons aimed at dislodging the West from its position in the Third World and substituting communist influence for that of the West. "...the steady growth of economic relations between the developing countries and the Soviet Union, both in breadth and depth," contends a Soviet economist, "is a natural and irreversible process determined by both the requirements of world economic development and the logic of the anti-imperialist struggle."[18] As illustrated by statements at the 23rd and 24th Congresses of the Soviet Communist Party, foreign aid for the Third World is continually spoken of as an "internationalist duty" that the communists must honor even when it means economic sacrifices on the part of the world socialist system. Similar views have been expressed in various pronouncements of Soviet Russia's communist partners. "It would be incorrect to evaluate our economic relations [with the developing nations] without their complex consideration from a political standpoint," stated an authoritative article on the "Economic Relations of the Czechoslovak Socialist Republic with the Developing Nations." "Through our participation in economic aid we are fulfilling also our international duty...."[19] Thus, as Roger Hilsman rightly points out, "foreign aid is not measured, in the Soviet calculus, on its merits but only as it contributes to policy objectives in recipient countries as a part of a whole complex of official and unofficial bloc activities designed to increase total Soviet power."[20]

The primacy of political motives over purely economic considerations revealed by communist pronouncements is fully corroborated by a closer analysis of actual communist practices.

While, as suggested above, a portion of communist trade with developing nations does make economic sense, most of it does not. Since the bulk of communist exports to the Third World consists of industrial equipment and entire production units, such exports deprive Soviet Russia and the other communist countries precisely of the goods they could well use themselves in their own industrialization programs and the construction of the "material and technical foundations of communism" which is well behind schedule. A machine-tool complex delivered to India, a dam and hydroelectric project built in Egypt or Iraq, an oil or sugar refinery, cement, shoe or tire factory supplied to a developing nation, means that much less for Soviet Russia, Bulgaria, Outer Mongolia, North Korea, China and elsewhere in the socialist world system where shortages of such equipment are commonplace. Moreover, most of these deliveries to the Third World have been on low interest or interest-free credit (and some of them with grace periods free of repayment), thereby representing for many years a net drain on capital resources at a time when a number of ambitious communist projects at home have had to be abandoned or reduced because of insufficient investment funds. Nor are communist leaders unaware of the fact that some of these loans may never be fully repaid.[21] Even when repaid, many of the goods with which the loans are repaid are generally of marginal economic usefulness to the communist creditor-nations.

What has been said of the communist exports of industrial equipment applies equally to communist technical assistance. Due to the shortages of skilled technical personnel prevalent in most of the communist countries, the sending of engineers and technicians to the developing nations constitutes an economic liability (though not a major one as the numbers involved are comparatively small). Hence, unless one is ready to accept at their face value communist professions of pure altruism, the political motivation of communist technical assistance programs is obvious.

Yet another evidence of the secondary importance of strictly economic criteria in the disbursement of communist economic aid lies in the above-mentioned communist tendency (apparent mainly in earlier years of communist economic aid) to grant loans even for projects of only marginal value for the sound economic development of the recipient country. Condonement of such economically fallacious projects can be explained in no other way than by the endeavor of communist strategy-makers to pretend their high regard for the recipient country's national sovereignty in contrast to the West's "spurious" policy of attaching "strings" to its loan commitments.

Even more indicative of the overwhelmingly political character of communist economic relations with the Third World is the pattern of their distribution. A study of the data on communist trade with and economic assistance to the individual nations of the Third World makes it unmistakably clear that political rather than economic benefit figures as the primary criterion in communist choices of respective trade partners and borrowers. "If economic considerations were fundamental to the aid program," writes Berliner, "Afghanistan, Burma, Egypt and Syria would not be the countries that the Soviets would cultivate so diligently."[22] This is equally true of a number of other countries of the Middle East, such as Jordan, Yemen and Lebanon, and even more so of a number of African countries, such as Somalia, Sierra Leone, Mali, Morocco, Guinea, Nigeria and Algeria.

What many of these countries have to offer now and for a long time to come are mostly either raw materials that Soviet Russia and Communist China themselves possess or native products of only marginal economic importance which are more often than not considered as dispensable luxury wares by Soviet and Chinese standards. Hence, there is too little complementarity between the present Soviet and Chinese economies and those of many developing nations to constitute a solid basis of natural and mutually advantageous trade relations. This is not as true in the case of the more advanced countries of communist East Europe. But most of these countries are tied to Soviet Russia as their main supplier of major raw materials so that their purchases of such materials from the Third World have in many, though not all, instances to be kept down.

Finally, the primacy of political considerations behind the communist economic offensive in the Third World seems to be confirmed by its timing. A scrutiny of the communist time-table of economic aid reveals that communist strategy-makers have been timing their economic operations in the respective developing countries so as to take advantage of openings deemed conducive to communist political penetration wherever and whenever they have appeared. In deciding whether or not to aid economically a given developing country at a given time, they have evidently been guided much more by their estimate as to when and where the maximum psychological and political impact could be obtained rather than by a determination as to where and when it would be economically advantageous to buy, sell or invest.

Egypt became all of a sudden worthy of major communist support when her feud with the West reached its climax and made Egypt receptive to communist wooing. It mattered little that the cotton-producing Soviet Union had so little need of the huge quantities of Egyptian cotton that it had to resell a portion of it at cut-rate prices on Western markets. Iraq qualified for communist economic generosity after she had abandoned the Baghdad Pact following the 1958 coup. Even though Russia and communist East Europe are themselves major producers of sugar, Cuban sugar turned out to be desirable after Castro got deep into strife with the United States and had to be bolstered up with massive economic aid so as to maintain a communist foothold in the Western Hemisphere. So did Algerian wine when

France refused in 1968 to purchase as much of this important Algerian cash crop as Algeria needed to sell. Desert-like Somalia, surely one of the economically least viable of the excolonial countries, was promptly found deserving in Moscow's eyes of what was probably the highest per-capita communist credit granted to any nation after the smoldering Somali-Ethiopian conflict erupted into anti-American demonstrations protesting U. S. military aid to Ethiopia. Guinea, Ghana and Mali emerged originally as the main African beneficiaries of substantial communist credits when they had turned stridently anti-Western after acquiring independence. However, both Ghana and Mali began to lose ground in communist calculations when their initial pro-communist bias subsided. Therefore, newer communist loans were switched to such African countries as Algeria and Tanzania where better prospects for communist penetration seemed to develop. In much the same vein, Indonesia, a truly massive recipient of communist aid, was stricken from communist economic aid rolls once Sukarno's flirting with the communist bloc was cut short by the defeat of the abortive communist coup of 1965. On the other hand, Iran, which initially figured near the bottom on the communist list of debtors among developing nations (only 6 million dollars in communist credit was extended to Iran prior to 1962), was granted in 1966 a massive Soviet loan to the tune of 289 million dollars and another Soviet and East European credit of 543 million dollars in 1968-69. All this is designed mainly to induce Iran to proceed further along a course of lesser dependence on the West begun in the middle sixties. Nigeria began to earn Soviet favors, including the underwriting of an iron-and-steel complex on the Niger river, after trouble had developed between her and the West in connection with the Biafra rebellion in 1968. Similarly, Peru, Bolivia and Chile emerged rather suddenly as worthy targets of communist economic and technical assistance when their new regimes became more anti-American in 1969-70. Soviet offers to finance and to build the Aswan dam in Egypt and the Bokaro steel mill in India, two of the most important Soviet foreign aid projects, appeared all the more impressive and scored for Russia so heavily because they came so promptly after the U.S. refusal to sponsor the said projects.

Thus, the conclusion seems to be warranted that the mainspring and fundamental determinant of communist economic policies and operations in the Third World must be sought in the realm of politics rather than economics. Of course, the use of trade, loans and other economic instruments as a device of foreign policy and strategy has not been invented by the communists. The annals of modern diplomacy amply reveal that most nations, especially the Great Powers, have not been loath to manipulate their foreign economic policies to promote political objectives alongside of those of a commercial, financial and economic nature. But no political system of modern times has sought, let alone managed, to make economic relations serve political goals as completely as has the world socialist system. "...we value trade least for economic reasons and most for political purposes," Khrushchev was reported to have once said.[23] What the Soviet strategy-makers and their associates have been trying to accomplish is to rewrite the old imperialist adage *Trade Follows the Flag* so that it reads instead: *Red Flag Follows Communist Trade and Aid.*

The Pros and Cons of Communist Economic Warfare

In pursuing their political objectives in the Third World through economic means communist strategists have, on one hand, been aided by several factors working in their favor. On the other hand, they have also encountered a number of impediments.

The Pros

To begin with, communist economic penetration has been facilitated by the distinct preference for socialism over capitalism that characterizes the economic thinking of leading elites and seems also to have a strong emotional appeal for the broad masses in most of the newly emerging nations. Rightly or wrongly, its past association with colonialism and with the U. S. "dollar diplomacy" in Latin America has given capitalism a bad ring throughout much of the Third World and made socialism appear as a better and more progressive alternative. Moreover, the scarcity of native private capital and the urge to nationalize foreign-owned businesses was bound to weaken private enterprise and strengthen the trend toward one or another form of state socialism. Although Soviet or Chinese-style Marxism-Leninism is not the kind of socialism that the national leaders of the developing nations and most of their followers really want for their countries, communist claims that socialism has been successfully developed throughout the world socialist system and that the developing nations can benefit from its experience gives a definite edge to communist strategy-makers over their non-communist competitors.

Influenced by their anti-capitalist bias, the nationalist leaders of many developing nations have come to regard the communist model of economic development as more relevant for their countries' needs and conditions than the Western economic systems based largely on private enterprise. They seem to have been impressed, in particular, by the industrial development that took place in Soviet Central Asia.[24] It was no coincidence that the international symposium on *Lenin and the National-Liberation Movement* organized to commemorate the centenary or Lenin's birth convened at Alma Ata, the capital of Kazakhstan, one of Soviet Central Asian Republics held as a suitable model of development for the less developed countries of the Third World.[25] Overlooking the massive russification and the tough political, economic, social, religious and cultural regimentation that had accompanied Soviet industrialization of the area, some of the less sophisticated nationalist leaders tend to view the sharp contrast between the economic backwardness of the neighboring non-Soviet areas and the industrial attainment of the Kazakh, Uzbek and Kirghiz Soviet Socialist Republics as living proof of what the adoption of a similar developmental pattern might do for their own countries.

This inclination to try the communist-recommended non-capitalist path is strengthened by the persistent belief, widely spread throughout the less developed countries, that Western capitalism is responsible, wholly or mainly, for most of the Third World's economic woes. While it is true that certain capitalist practices and malpractices did affect adversely the course of economic development in a number of developing countries and instances of ruthless economic exploitation did occur, Western capitalism certainly does not deserve such a blanket condemnation. It can even be argued that in numerous instances the profit-seeking capitalists made, willy-nilly, substantial contributions toward the economic development of the areas where they invested and operated. Nonetheless, the simplicist thesis of the wanton exploitation of the Third World by Western capitalists, colonialists and "neo-colonialists" bleeding the developing countries white and siphoning off their wealth continues to be circulated, fed as it is not only by communist propaganda but also by the non-communist nationalist regimes and the spokesmen of native vested interests seeking to find convenient scapegoats for their own neglect and shortcomings. Having had no part in the colonization of Africa, Latin America and Asia (save for territorial concessions extorted from Iran, Turkey and China), and having been virtually uninvolved economically in the area prior to her recent economic offensive (except for Iran and Afghanistan), Soviet Russia has been able to escape the colonizers' stigma. As a result, her economic activities in the Third World have been less impeded by the legacy of the past than those of her Western competitors.

Another major factor making Soviet trade and aid more desirable than that of its Western counterparts has been the natural endeavor of the countries of Africa, Asia and Latin America to attain a better economic balance between the East and the West. It is not good for any nation to depend economically upon just one country or one group of countries. But such a dependence is felt all the more keenly by ex-colonial nations whose economies have been tied tightly to their one-time colonial masters or, as has been the case with Latin America, subjected to a heavy and continuing influence by the economic interests of one economically and technologically superior power. Overly jealous of their national independence, such countries are all too eager to lessen their lop-sided economic dependence on the West by stepping up their economic intercourse with the countries of the world socialist system.

Nor could the communist economic penetration of the Third World help but be furthered by the above-mentioned willingness of communist countries, especially the Soviet Union, to go along with the recipients' wishes in the choice of economic projects to be supported, irrespective of their economic soundness and viability, to accept repayment in less desirable goods, and even to absorb economic loss should it prove necessary in order to achieve desired political and psychological gains. Of course, Western nations, especially Great Powers, also manipulate at times their foreign economic policies to promote political objectives. Yet they are much more restricted in this respect than their communist rivals. Western democratic regimes, having to account to their taxpayers for the way foreign aid money is used, can seldom subordinate economic aspects of their foreign aid programs to considerations of a political nature to the extent that this is possible for their communist competitors, whose responsibility to their own subjects has thus far been a mere formality. Moreover, a conviction, deeply embedded in the Western democratic ethos, that business and politics should not mix acts as a potent inhibiting factor.

For the same basic reason, communist disbursers of economic assistance have been aided in their work by their unrivaled ability to resort to fast-talking salesmanship in extolling the virtues of what they have to offer. Having to work under constant scrutiny of a free press and political opposition eager to take advantage of any *faux pas*, Western democratic regimes cannot easily feed the developing nations with unrealistic promises, create false hope of speedy economic advancement, and thus bring them what Hans Morgenthau calls "a simple message of salvation."[26] Lest they are subsequently made to eat their own words, they cannot conceal the sad truth that even with foreign aid economic improvement in most countries of the Third World is bound to be painfully slow.[27]

In contrast, as noted earlier, communist foreign aid propagandists can and do make all sorts of extravagant promises of rapid economic growth and an almost miraculous betterment once a less developed country turns away from the West, accepts communist aid and follows communist guidance. They can do so because, in addition to being virtually immune from adverse criticism at home, they expect to secure the same immunity in the target countries once they have attained their ultimate goal of pushing them under communist or at least pro-communist control. Moreover, should communist promises begin to backfire before that final objective is reached, communist strategists hope to be able to disclaim responsibility for failures by blaming them on the vicious cabals of the "imperialists," "reactionaries" and other "dark forces" opposing progress. Thus, they are in a much better position than the West to exploit the "rising expectations" of the emerging nations and the economic and political naiveté still prevalent in some of them; they can even turn disappointment at the slow pace of betterment to communist advantage.

The autocratic nature of the communist political systems that shields the regimes from open criticism at home confers upon them yet another bonus not enjoyed by their democratic rivals; namely, the capability to make quick decisions and thus to utilize with the least possible delay suitable openings for economic penetration whenever they occur. "Quick decision and brisk implementation naturally endows a command economy with a tactical advantage over a pluralistic system that is subject to checks and balances of power," writes Aubrey.[28] As in most other matters, the democratic decision-making process concerning foreign aid is habitually slow and circuitous. Western economic policies are traditionally shaped by a complex interplay of many conflicting attitudes and interests: private versus public, agricultural versus industrial, exporter versus importer, etc. Considering, coordinating, and balancing such diverse interests is necessarily time-consuming; so is the manipulation of public opinion which must be gained or placated. Proposals and counter-proposals have to be written and rewritten to meet all sorts of objections and to satisfy a number of groups and agencies. The legislature must enact appropriate laws and approve and allocate the needed funds, thereby contributing to further protraction of affairs. The Americans "are always studying," complained Guillermo Marguia, Bolivia's Under-Secretary for Mining, to an AP reporter in 1971. "They say, we can't do this or can't do that. We always have problems with the Americans." Hence, "there is a more comfortable atmosphere with the Socialists. They don't ask questions."[29]

None of these considerations bother very much the communist regimes of Soviet Russia, China and communist East Europe.

Being an exclusive prerogative of a narrow oligarchy of top Party leaders, decision-making in communist countries is not hampered by the retarding procedures and considerations encountered in democratic countries. If and when an offer of economic aid to a developing nation is in communist interest, it can be made almost overnight. Since the Party leadership firmly controls all agencies, organized groups, economic and other establishments as well as the communications media, it need not brook any delays, let alone challenges. Once it is reached, the decision can be run through the various "transmission belts" of the formal legislative and administrative machinery just about as fast as the Party bosses want it. Nor is there any danger, as in democratic systems, that foreign aid appropriations would be cut or even rejected or a trade agreement tempered with or disapproved by a hostile or reluctant legislature, that a foreign aid arrangement would be impeded by a labor union strike or a boycott by some powerful business combinations. The worst that can and sometimes does happen in a communist country when an unpopular foreign aid decision is made is some covert grumbling and occasional passive resistance in the form of a sloppier than usual performance at work.

Finally, communist economic efforts in the Third World have been aided, at least in their initial years, by their very novelty. Just as spectators attending a sport event are apt to be especially liberal in sympathizing with an unrated newcomer making a better than anticipated showing against experienced veterans, so were Soviet Russia and other communist countries as new entrants in the economic competition with the West bound to register political and psychological gains far out of proportion to the actual economic value of their contributions.

The Cons

Turning to factors hampering the communists in the pursuit of their aims in the Third World through economic enticements, the most detrimental has been the growing awareness of true communist motives behind the economic offensive. Anxious to secure all the economic aid that they could obtain on the best terms the leaders of the less developed countries have been quite

willing to please their communist benefactors by expressing
publicly their gratitude and signing without qualms the various
communist-sponsored communiques and declarations containing
the customary cliches about Western imperialism, colonialism,
"neo-colonialism," the American intervention in Vietnam, the
"Israeli aggression," peaceful coexistence, disarmament, and
other favorite themes of communist propaganda. But the last
thing they want to do is to barter away their newly gained
independence for economic benefits, however large and however
desirable. Although they have not been saying much about it in
public, the leading circles of developing nations, including even
those having most cordial relations with the world socialist
system, have by no means lost sight of the ulterior designs
lurking behind the apparent economic generosity.[30] Moreover,
the 1968 Soviet invasion of Czechoslovakia and the concomitant
"Brezhnev doctrine" laying an unabashed claim to a right of
intervention in internal affairs of other nations that had embraced socialism has served as an especially strong reminder of
the risk implicit in too great a dependence upon Soviet Russia.

The realization that communist foreign aid objectives are not
as selfless or as business-like as claimed by its communist
promoters has also effected a notable shift of direction in the
Third World's rampant nationalism. Originally directed almost
exclusively against the West and shrewdly exploited by communist strategy-makers posing as the only genuine friends and
supporters of the national-liberation movement, nationalistic
sentiments helped to smooth the way for communist foreign aid
promoters and contributed in no small degree to their initial
successes. However, as erstwhile excessive fears of Western
colonialism and "neo-colonialism" gradually subsided and communist behavior began to give cause for concern, the Third
World's nationalism shed some of its previous anti-Western
onesidedness, acquired a more balanced character, and thus
became operative against the communist countries as well. As
Aubrey put it as early as 1961, "Nationalism is strong medicine,
and the new self-confidence so astutely fostered by the Soviet
bloc and seeming at one time to operate only against the West,
has begun to assert itself in the opposite direction also."[31]

Another obstacle impeding communist economic penetration

of the Third World and its utilization for political purposes has been the dearth of well qualified personnel experienced in matters of foreign aid and trade, and familiar with the specific economic, social and psychological conditions obtaining in the various developing countries. While this presents a problem for all of the communist countries, it affects Soviet Russia's and Communist China's efforts more than those of the communist countries of Eastern Europe. It seems that the Russians and the Chinese, secluded for so long from the outside world and accustomed to the inflexibilities, dogmatism and strict disciplinarianism of their own systems and rigid Marxist-Leninist or Maoist patterns of thought, are having difficulty in understanding the mentality and behavioral pattern prevalent in the Third World and adjusting to the strange, nonchalant, and often chaotic surroundings in which they have to operate. Thus they tend to grow frustrated, unhappy, and often cantankerous. Although they are well paid (though not as well as their Western equivalents) and are materially better off than they were in Russia and China, they quickly became homesick. Living in isolation in their own "ghettoes," they stick mostly together with their own folks and do not mix ordinarily with natives, except when on duty. While this may at times prevent frictions, it also impairs their usefulness as propagandists of the communist cause. Many of them may earn respect as good technicians and engineers, but end by being considered by the natives as unduly reserved, unsociable, and rather unfriendly.[32] The East Europeans have generally fared better in these respects than their Soviet and Chinese colleagues, for they are usually more sociable, more adaptable, more knowledgeable in foreign languages, manners and *savoir-vivre*. However, even they live often in relative isolation from the natives.[33]

Unfamiliarity with conditions in many of the developing countries has accounted also for some of the major communist blunders. To cite but a few examples, there were instances of delivering trucks and agricultural machinery unsuited for tropical climate; sending fishing trawlers with no refrigeration to tropical Zanzibar; a sugar-beet refinery to sugar-cane producing Indonesia, one million screwdrivers to Guinea or a saw mill that could not be transported to its inland destination because of inadequate roads; building a luxury hotel without airconditioning in heat-plagued Burma and without kitchen facilities in Guinea.[34] The blunders resulting from ignorance of local conditions have been further compounded by other none-too-rare malpractices, such as non-observance of agreed deadlines for, and at times even outright cancellation of, deliveries of goods and completion of projects; sending of obsolescent, overpriced or inferior quality goods and machinery without an adequate supply of needed spare parts. According to certain unverifiable sources there may have also been some sabotage of deliveries to developing nations. Thus Soviet tractors shipped to Guinea in 1961 on a Soviet boat arrived reportedly with essential parts of fuel pumps removed and Soviet trucks delivered to Indonesia in 1958 were found with hubcaps missing. As mentioned earlier, there has also been a substantial gap between promises and their fulfillment in the area of communist credit-granting and volume targets set by trade agreements have often remained unattained.

A number of communist-sponsored projects, including some of the much advertised prestige projects, have subsequently turned out to be economic liabilities for the developing nations concerned. That has been the case, for instance, with the Soviet-equipped Ghanaian Airways that ran a huge deficit, the Soviet built luxury hotel at Rangoon remaining near-empty in a country basically hostile to foreign tourism, or the communist-sponsored mammoth heavy-machine building complex at Ranchi in India whose capacity proved to be far in excess of the then Indian demands for its products. Even though much of the communist economic and technical assistance does appear to be adequate and fit to meet the needs of the recipient countries, the blunders and malpractices have been numerous enough and serious enough to cast a shadow on the communist boasts of the excellence of their aid programs. If nothing else, they have made the developing nations more cautious in their economic dealings with the countries of the world socialist system.

Yet another aspect of communist economic relations with the Third World that seemed all right at first, but has subsequently aroused misgivings on the part of developing nations, has been their bilateralism. Since both communist credits extended to developing countries and earnings resulting from their exports to the world socialist system may be spent solely in the respective communist countries, such bilateral arrangements limit their choices of imports and markets, inhibit their overall expansion and diversification of their trade, reduce their chances of earning more hard currency, and make them more vulnerable to communist pressures. Bilateralism has been especially disadvantageous for those countries of the Third World that have built at one time or another positive balances with some of the communist countries such as Brazil, Argentine and Uruguay.[35] Since bilateralism is a *sine qua non* of communist economic dealings, the leaders of developing nations can do little about it if they need communist aid and trade. But their feelings about the matter are probably much like those of the one-time Premier of Burma and foremost advocate of neutralism, U Nu. He is quoted as having said in 1956, after running into difficulties with the Soviets: "A man who takes barter when he can have [convertible] cash must be out of his mind."[36]

Bilateralism has been made even more obnoxious for the developing nations concerned by the communist predilection to dump occasionally goods purchased from one or another of the developing countries on free world markets. In their endeavor to tie the Third World economically to the world socialist system as tightly as possible some of the communist countries have at times become saddled with larger quantities of goods imported from the Third World than they could use themselves. To get rid of such surplus goods, they have on a number of occasions resorted to selling them in Western markets, often at discount prices, thereby competing unfairly with the developing nation or nations from which such goods had been originally purchased and undercutting still further the capabilities of such countries to earn hard currency. Verified instances of such malpractice occurred with Egyptian and Sudanese cotton a portion of which was disposed of by Soviet Russia at reduced prices in Western markets; with India's cashew nuts resold by some of her East European communist partners in spite of no-resale clauses in the respective trade agreements; with Burmese rice re-exported by Soviet Russia and Pakistani rice resold by Bulgaria; and Costarican coffee resold by Poland.[37] Some Indian industrialists expressed a concern lest some of the rolled steel and rolling stock

Soviet Russia agreed to buy from India in 1968 be intended for resale.[38]

Finally, the attainment of political objectives of the communist economic offensive has been hampered in recent years by the inability and/or unwillingness of the world socialist system to satiate the Third World's truly Gargantuan appetite for more and still more aid. Told time and again of the superior virtues of communist economy, the communist selfless desire to help, and the beneficence of the communist model of development for their own countries, leaders of some of the developing nations seem to have come to believe that their countries could indeed advance rapidly to modernity once they befriended communist countries and were given their helping hand. When the initial doses of communist aid, though helpful, have shown themselves to have had a far smaller impact than expected, they have tended to ask for more and more — until their communist benefactors could or would no longer meet all the ever-recurrent demands and became more selective both as to the countries and projects to be supported. Naturally, the recipients whose requests for more aid have been denied or cut were disappointed and their erstwhile enthusiasm for the communist model, gratitude for communist largesse and belief in the economic supremacy of the world socialist system suffered a shock. Thus the lavish promises that had served well the communist strategy-makers in the early phases of their economic offensive have begun to backfire when the initial pace of aid-giving could no longer be sustained.

The Balance Sheet

Having reviewed the factors favoring and impeding communist economic penetration of the Third World it is time to evaluate the results thus far attained. How successful or unsuccessful have communist strategy-makers been in the pursuit of their political objectives through economic means?[39] This is a difficult question to answer, mainly because employment of economic means is an integral part of the overall communist foreign policy and strategy. It is a weapon or vehicle used invariably in conjunction with other strategic and tactical tools and devices, "peaceful" and "non-peaceful," applicable in a given situation and ranging from formal diplomacy and political tourism to subversion, armed uprising and direct military pressures. Hence, it is impossible to determine with any degree of accuracy to what extent, if any, a communist success or failure is attributable to the wielding of the economic weapon alone, such as extending a loan or reneging on a commitment already made, granting or rejecting a trade deal, giving or denying technical assistance, speeding up or slowing down or even stopping work on an important industrial project; and to what extent success or failure should be credited to the utilization of strategic devices of non-economic nature or even to factors having nothing to do with communist activities.

How elusive it can be to try to measure the political impact of economic aid *per se* is borne out by an attempt undertaken to that effect by Triska and Finley in their earlier mentioned *Soviet Foreign Policy*. In order to ascertain the relationship between economic aid and political response the two authors selected a number of Asian and African recipients of communist economic aid and ranked them according to an index indicative of how much more or how much less they had received from communist countries than from the West in 1954-62. Then they examined the voting record of these same countries on "cold-war issues" that came to the vote in the United Nations in 1961 and 1962, arranging the countries according to an index showing the ratio of their voting with communist countries or with the West, (i.e., at least with the United States, Britain and France). Comparing the two indices of "inputs" and "outputs," Triska and Finley found "a strong relationship between a positive index number for economic aid" (awarded countries receiving more economic aid from communist states than from the West) and "a pro-communist voting record in the United Nations." "Obviously," they therefore concluded, "economic assistance is among the principal influences which determine the non-aligned states' political stance in the cold war."[40]

Well, such a conclusion does not seem to be all that obvious, at least not to this writer. Have the Third World countries voting predominantly with the Communist Bloc on those "cold-war issues" in 1961-62 done so principally *because* of the economic aid they received from communist countries? Would they have voted differently had they received less communist aid or none at all? Except for Afghanistan, all of the countries ranked high in Triska and Finley tables as recipients of communist aid and as "strongly supporting the communist doctrines in the UN" are ex-colonies of the West with a record of trouble and conflict with their ex-colonial masters and with an inclination to consider the United States as a bird of the same feather. Being thus strongly anti-Western from the very outset, there is small wonder that they voted against the West, especially on such issues as the Congo, Cuba, Tibet, Korea, China, Mauretania and the nuclear testing which made up seven out of the eight "cold-war issues" considered in the Triska and Finley study. (The eighth issue concerned Hungary). Moreover, the tabulations upon which the authors' thesis of the political importance of economic aid rests contain at least two striking examples clearly contradicting the authors' contention, namely, those of Cambodia and India. Both these countries received almost four times as much aid from the West than from the Communist Bloc in 1954-62. Yet Cambodia's voting record on the above-mentioned issues was 6:2 in favor of the Communist Bloc and that of India 7 to 6. (Another example is Ceylon whose voting record was 9:3 in favor of the Communist Bloc, although Ceylon's economic aid from the West exceeded that from the Communist Bloc for the period concerned.)

Hence, it would appear that the principal determinant of the pro-communist votes tabulated in Triska and Finley was not in all likelihood economic aid, but other factors, above all plain old anti-westernism. That was what caused the said Asian and African countries to vote the way they did on a number of international issues, and that was undoubtedly the main reason why Soviet Russia became so interested in them and offered them economic aid, not the other way round. Moreover, many instances can be cited in which international behavior of African and Asian recipients of communist aid fell short of communist hopes and expectations. Thus the two African members of the United Nations Security Council at the time, Egypt and Ghana, both heavily indebted to the Soviet Union, abstained from voting rather than support the Soviet Union and Rumania in the Security Council vote on the Soviet complaint about the United

Nations policy in Congo in January 1962. Two months later the same two members sided with the United States against the Soviet Union and Rumania in defeating the communist-sponsored Cuban request relative to Cuba's suspension from the Organization of American States. Again, in June 1962, both Ghana and Egypt abstained in the Security Council's vote on the Irish resolution calling for renewed Kashmir talks between Pakistan and India, a resolution hotly contested and eventually vetoed by the Soviet Union. Similarly, the communist endeavors to sabotage the United Nations operations in Congo and to paralyse the Secretariat of the United Nations by the *troika* system was opposed in the General Assembly as well as at the 1961 Belgrade Conference of Non-Aligned Nations by virtually all of the Asian and African countries receiving substantial communist economic assistance. Despite the economic aid extended to the Arab countries, Rumania came under sharp attacks in Egypt, Iraq, Syria, Algeria, and Libya in 1967-1969 because of her refusal to break off diplomatic relations with Israel and subsequently raising them to ambassadorial level.[41] In 1971 virtually all the Third World recipients of Soviet aid parted with the Soviet Union and its East European partners and voted in favor of the U.S.-sponsored General Assembly resolution calling for a cease-fire in the Indian-Pakistani war. Nor did the substantial economic aid received from the Soviet Union prevent Egypt's President from ejecting Soviet advisers in 1972 and Sudan's President from ignoring frantic Soviet pleas to spare the lives of Sudanese communists in 1971.

Therefore, the thesis regarding economic assistance as being "among the principal influences" determining the political behavior of the non-aligned states in the cold war remains unconvincing, statistical data and indices advanced in its support notwithstanding. While the use of economic means certainly is a factor that should be taken into consideration when explaining the nations' political behavior, it is only one of many such factors, and one that has not thus far belonged among the truly major determinants of the attitude of the emerging nations. Rather, their behavior both at home and on the international scene, suggests that they have tended to be swayed at the current stage of their development by predominantly non-economic and often even non-rational influences, considerations and complexes of emotional, nationalistic and, at times, even racist provenance.

Under such circumstances economic instruments *per se* are generally only of limited significance as a vehicle of political influence. In Aubrey's words, "neither aid nor trade can actually be credited with a decisive influence in recent political realignments."[42] Hans Morgenthau seems to hold a similar view when he points out that political results even of successful foreign aid "may be either unpredictable or counterproductive in terms of the political goals of the giving nation" and in any case "are in a large degree uncontrollable."[43] So it is more than likely that the communist leaders and strategy-makers will in the end be disappointed in their political expectations if they really do believe their claims that the economy, especially that of the Third World, is presently the main battlefield of the world revolution and winning there will bring them closer to ultimate communist victory.[44]

While the communist economic offensive in the Third World has thus far failed to achieve its major political goals, it did attain a measure of success in some of its secondary or subsidiary aims.

In providing the developing nations with an alternative source of economic assistance the communist strategy-makers have helped them to become less dependent on the West. By the same token, in extending them long-term loans, having them commit some of their main export crops for repayment of such loans, diverting a portion of their trade from the West to the East through bilateral arrangements, and making many of their industrial establishments dependent on communist-produced spare parts, they have pushed a number of developing countries toward a smaller or larger degree of economic dependence on the Communist Bloc and made them thus more vulnerable to communist political pressures. Furthermore, since communist economic aid is usually contingent upon sizeable commitments of local resources, the communist strategy-makers have thereby gained a measure of influence on the pattern of economic development in the countries concerned.

By encouraging the Third World countries to proceed ever more relentlessly with the nationalization of Western enterprises and assets, communist strategists have contributed to the worsening of relations between developing nations and the West. As Western economic interests and personnel were forced out, additional openings were created for communist advisors and specialists needed to fill the gap, providing the Communist Bloc with still more political leverage.

The communist-fostered industrialization has led to a steady, though rather slow, increase in the size of the Third World's working class, fulfilling thus gradually one of the avowed objectives of the communist economic offensive; namely, the emergence of a "new contingent of the world proletariat — the young working-class movement of the newly-free dependent and colonial countries of Asia, Africa and Latin America."[45] However, as shown in Chapter V, communist expectations that this new Asian, African and Latin American working class would rally *en masse* behind the communist cause and assume the proletariat's "historical role" of spearheading the Marxist-Leninist revolution in its respective countries have so far not materialized. Hence, it is questionable whether changing the class structure of the Third World should be included among the positive achievements in terms of communist strategy.

No such doubt arises in the case of yet another aim of communist economic diplomacy; that is, the aim of projecting in the Third World an image of the Soviet Union as a dynamic industrial giant possessed of superior technology and economic knowhow and willing to share these with its friends. In that respect communist strategy-makers have been quite successful. This has been so partly because, despite the earlier mentioned blunders and malpractices, communist economic performance in the Third World has been, on the whole, good, especially for a novice in the foreign aid field and a newcomer to an unfamiliar part of the world. But mainly it has been the result of careful political planning of the communist economic thrust and its clever exploitation for propaganda purposes. As mentioned above, communist strategists have concentrated from the very beginning on major and often spectacular projects that are especially likely to capture the imagination of the public and stand as eye-catching monuments of the economic virility of their creators. Moreover, they have striven hard to extract the last ounce of propaganda from their economic offerings by giving them lavish publicity on every suitable occasion, from the moment of making the initial offer to the final turning over of the key. Thus, the communists have been getting disproportionately more political mileage than the West from an economic aid program that has amounted year after year to only a fraction of the corresponding but diffused assistance extended to the Third World by the West. As Goldman has correctly pointed out in discussing Soviet foreign aid achievements in the Third World, "it is in the field of public relations that the Russians appear to be at their best."[46]

Thus, measured in terms of its political objectives, the overall balance sheet of the communist economic offensive in the Third World has not been very impressive. After more than fifteen years of concerted efforts, political returns on communist economic investments appear to be rather meager. Gains have alternated with setbacks, and many an initial gain has turned out to be of short duration. In some instances, such as Indonesia, Ghana, Mali and Sudan, the communist investment went politically down the drain with the ouster of those on whom communist strategists pinned their hopes. In several other instances, such as Guinea and Burma, relations toward the Communist Bloc have cooled off in recent years despite substantial communist economic assistance given the said countries. Wherever communist strategists have managed to register a good measure of success, as has been the case in several Arab countries, it seems to have been due more to factors of a non-economic than economic nature.

Nor do communist prospects for effective utilization of economic means for political purposes look more promising for the future. The liberalization trends that have made themselves apparent in communist East Europe and even in Soviet Russia in recent years, and that are likely to become more pronounced (despite temporary setbacks) as time progresses, will make it gradually more difficult for the communist rulers to disregard the interests of their own people in the allocation of their countries' economic resources. That the "internationalist duty" to assist economically the developing nations has struck anything but an enthusiastic response from the populace of the communist countries has been documented by recurrent efforts of communist spokesmen to allay "doubts," "questions," "misunder-standings" and "objections" that evidently keep cropping up regarding the matter. "Occasionally we hear objections on the part of some of our citizens that we ought not to aid the developing countries to such an extent because we cannot then raise the living standards of our people as rapidly as we would wish...."[47] "When there is talk concerning our economic diffi-culties, a question is sometimes posed whether they are not related to our economic cooperation with the developing nations. Aren't our difficulties, it is asked, caused perhaps by our helping others beyond our means....?"[48] While such "questions" have been asked in Czechoslovakia, whose per capita contribution to communist aid to the Third World has been the highest of all of the communist countries involved, more frequently than else-where, the public's negative feelings on the matter seem to be much the same throughout the world socialist system. Hence, as the communist regimes will find it necessary or politic to pay more attention to the attitudes of their subjects, the Third World's aid requests are likely to be scrutinized more closely and commitments are liable to be reduced and additional "strings" attached to them. Such action will inevitably impair the use-fulness of economic instruments for political manipulation.

A somewhat similar situation could also develop in the communist trade with the Third World. As Soviet Russia herself is a major producer of most of the commodities that constitute the main exports of many developing nations and also is the chief supplier of many of these commodities to her Comecon partners, much of the trade between the Communist Bloc and the Third World is not based on natural economic complementariness. Although over time this may change in some instances, the situation will probably worsen in some commodities, such as rubber and cotton, which are being replaced more and more with synthetic materials, and in other raw materials as.new deposits are found and exploited in the Soviet Union and China.[49] The range within which trade between the communist and the Third World countries would be mutually advantageous from a strictly economic viewpoint could, therefore, contract with time rather than expand. As with the loans, it will eventually become harder for communist rulers to pursue such politically motivated and

economically unprofitable trade as internal liberalization progresses and public opinion can no longer be disregarded as much
as used to be the case.

A noteworthy indication of the growing communist realization
that something must be done about the matter has recently come
from Czechoslovakia. Concerned with the unprofitability of his
country's trade with the Third World and the persistently lagging
repayments for Czechoslovakia's exports to developing nations,
a Czechoslovak foreign trade specialist has proposed that the
exports to developing nations be financed from the exporting
enterprises' own resources rather than the state funds.[50] Such a
shift of the economic risk from the state to the enterprises
directly involved in the transaction would probably achieve its
purpose in leading to a more careful evaluation of the economic
advantages or disadvantages of the dealings with developing
countries. At the same time, however, it would undoubtedly
cause the enterprises fearful of sustaining economic loss to reject
as unprofitable or questionable many business transactions that
they would be willing to accept if guaranteed against possible loss
by the state. Thus, if proposals along these lines are ever carried
out, the level of communist trading with the developing countries
would be significantly reduced.

Furthermore, as bad memories of colonialism and foreign
capitalist exploitation become ever dimmer with the march of the
time and illusions about communist aid and trade give way to
soberer second thoughts, even those countries of the Third World
that have not yet done so will gradually become more fully aware
of true communist intentions. As the leaders of the emerging
nations become more experienced and more discerning, they will
undoubtedly find out that the communist model of development
is by no means as suited to the needs and conditions of their
countries as the Soviet and communist propagandists would like
to make them believe. Such a realization is bound to deprive the
use of economic means for political purposes of much of its
effectiveness.

Hence "life itself" will confirm, indeed is already confirming,
that the Soviet leaders and their communist associates in Eastern
Europe and in the developing countries were mistaken in their
beliefs that communist victory in the Third World would be

attained mainly through economic means. Rather. it is much more likely to corroborate the Chinese and Castroite foreboding that communist economic aid extended to non-communist regimes may in the end impede the chances of a communist revolution instead of promoting them.

Footnotes for Chapter XI

[1] See Table II in Chapter X.

[2] See "*Das Janusgesicht....*," *Neue Zürcher Zeitung*, October 10, 1967.

[2] N. Senin, "CMEA and Africa," *New Times, op. cit.*

[4] The earliest one was the Soviet-Czechoslovak-Egyptian deal when the Soviet Union agreed to pay for Czechoslovak arms sent to Egypt.

[5] On the latter see a report in *Ekonomska Politika* (Belgrade), September 1, 1969.

[6] *Christian Science Monitor*, December 4, 1969.

[7] See Alvin Z. Rubinstein, *The Soviets in International Organizations*, Princeton, 1964; also, Robert Loring Allen, *Soviet Economic Warfare*.

[8] Allen, *op. cit.*, p. 164.

[9] Mihail Pankin, "The USSR and the Developing Countries; Experience of Economic Cooperation," *World Marxist Review*, 9, 5, 1966, pp. 68 ff.

[10] "Yugoslav Cooperation with Developing Countries," *Yugoslav Life*, X, 2, 1965, p. 2.

[11] Complaints about the poor quality, defective or unsuited goods sold to various countries of the Third World by the communist countries have been quite numerous. See, for instance, Allen, *op. cit.*, Goldman, *op. cit.*, Berliner, *op. cit.*, Lasky, *op. cit.*

[12] James R. Carter, *The Net Cost of Soviet Foreign Aid*, New York, 1971, p. 96.

[13] See, for instance A. Z. Kaznachaev, *Inside a Soviet Embassy*, New York, 1962, detailing the activities of the Soviet Trade mission in Burma.

[14] *Este y Oeste*, May, 1968. See also "From Scandinavia to Somalia, A Soviet Spy Network Crumbles," *U. S. News and World Report*, April 24, 1967, pp. 44 ff.

[15] G. Glezerman, *"Leninskii printsip sootnosheniia politiki i ekonomiki,"* (The Leninist Principle of the Correlation of Politics and Economics) *Pravda*, January 29, 1969, pp. 3-4.

[16] Berliner, Allen, Aubrey, *op. cit.*; Douglas Dillon, "Realities of Soviet Foreign Economic Policies," *Department of State Bulletin*, February 16, 1959.

[17] p. 4.

[18] Mihail Pankin, *op. cit.*

[19] Lubomír Pešl in *Hospodářské noviny*, February 18, 1966.

[20] State Department Research Memorandum RSB-145.

[21] The then communist boss of Czechoslovakia, *Antonín Novotný*, admitted that some of the loans granted by Czechoslovakia may never be repaid. See his speech to the Party's Central Committee on April 12, 1962, *Usnesení a dokumenty Ú. V. KSČ od celostátní konference KSČ 1960 do XII sjezdu*

KSČ (The Resolutions and Documents of the C. C. of the KSC from the All-state Conference of the KSC in 1960 to the XIIth Congress of the KSC), Praha, 1962; also Zdeněk Krejčí, "Czechoslovak Export-Investment Goods to Underdeveloped Countries," *Zahraniční obchod*, June 1969, pp. 25-26, bewailing the ever growing indebtedness on the part of the developing nations.

[22] *op. cit.*, p. 130.

[23] Arnold Rivkin, "African Problems of Trade and Aid," *Current History*, 43, 25, 1962, p. 29.

[24] See Alec Nove, *The Soviet Middle East, A Communist Model of Development*, and other references cited in Chapter I.

[25] *"Lenin i natsional'no-osvoboditel'noe dvizhenie"* (Lenin and the National-Liberation Movement), *Pravda*, October 2, 1969; R. Ulianovskii, *"Leninizm — znamia svobody i progressa"* (Leninism — The Standard of Freedom and Progress), *Pravda*, October 25, 1969.

[26] "A Political Theory of Foreign Aid," *American Political Science Review*, *op. cit.*

[27] See on this, for instance, Robert L. Heilbroner, "Dynamic Foreign Aid," *New Leader*, September 18, 1961, pp. 18 ff, and Frederic Benham, *op. cit.*

[28] Aubrey, *op. cit.*, p. IX.

[29] AP report from La Paz, *Austin American*, August 17, 1971.

[30] Evidence to this effect is cited in various chapters of the present volume and below in this Chapter.

[31] *op. cit.*, p. 222.

[32] See "In Cairo or Aswan, Ivan Keeps to Himself," *Life*, November 29, 1968, p. 30; "Homesick for Russia in Aswan," *Newsweek*, May 23, 1966; "Russian-Egyptian Friction Quietly Gnawing Alliance," a Cairo report to *Los Angeles Times*, reprinted in *Austin Statesman*, February 14, 1969; "Yemen—'Our Socialist Friends,'" *Newsweek*, May 25, 1970, p. 48.

[33] See, for instance, *"Naši v cizině"* (Our People Abroad), *Kulturní tvorba*, June 1, 1967, an interview with several Czechoslovak specialists working abroad, especially in India, complaining about their isolation and absence of contacts with the natives.

[34] Goldman, Lasky, Allen, *op. cit.*

[35] On the drawbacks of bilateralism see Allen, Aubrey, Sawyers, *op. cit.*

[36] Allen, *op. cit.*, p. 192.

[37] AP report from New Delhi, September 4, 1963; "Pakistani Complaint Against Bulgaria at the U. N.," *New York Times*, March 8, 1967.

[38] I. Temirsky, "USSR-Indian Economic Ties," *New Times*, No. 13, 1968.

[39] As noted earlier, this chapter is concerned solely with political aspects of communist economic operations and is not intended to evaluate them in terms of their strictly economic value, such as, for instance, how well a Soviet-built factory performs and how good an economic asset it represents.

[40] Chapter VII, The Soviet Union and the Developing Areas, pp. 249 ff.

[41] "Arab Break with Rumania," *East Europe*, 18, 10, 1969, p. 54.

[42] p. 222. Similar views are held by Berliner, Nove, Allen. See also John K. Galbraith, "A Positive Approach to Economic Aid," *Foreign Affairs*, 39, No. 3, 1961, pp. 444 ff.

[43] *op. cit.*, p. 307. Though Morgenthau's article is primarily concerned with U. S. foreign aid, his thesis can be applied to communist foreign aid as well.

[44] As noted earlier in the present volume, the Soviet confidence in the potency of economic means in bringing about victory for communism is shared neither

by the Chinese nor the Castroites, both of whom see in it an attempt to downgrade the importance of the armed struggle and suspect that communist economic aid to non-communist regimes may even harm the cause of the revolution.

45 Ritvo, *op. cit.*

46 *op. cit.*, p. 191.

47 Václav Mandous, *"Socialistické země a jejich poměr k národně-osvobozeneckému hnuti koloniálních zemí"* (The Socialist Countries and Their Relationship to the National-Liberation Movement of Colonial Countries), *Pravda* (Plzeň), July 4, 1963.

48 Marcel Brožík, *"O hospodářských vztazích s rozvojovými zeměmi"* (Concerning Economic Relations with Developing Countries), *Rudé právo*, May 25, 1965. Also, Jiří František Kouřil, *"Koho vydržujeme"* (Whom Are We Supporting?), *Rudé právo*, July 5, 1966; *"Kde bychom mohli být"* (Where Could We Be), *Mladá fronta*, August 9, 1966; *"Jak dále v československé vnější hospodářské politice?"* (What Next in Czechoslovak external economic policy?), *Rudé právo*, April 9, 1968.

49 See also Carole A. Sawyer, *op. cit.*, considering the long-run prospects of the Communist Bloc as a market for developing nations as not "altogether encouraging."

50 Zdeněk Krejčí, *op. cit.*

CHAPTER XII

COMMUNIST "CULTURAL DIPLOMACY"

"International cultural relations are as old as the flow of people and ideas across national boundaries. Recently, however, they have gained new dimensions as a result of the increased volume and growing complexity of international exchanges and contacts, the innovations of science and improved communications, the preoccupations of the cold war, the addition of many new states to the international community, and the multiplication of governmental activity."[1]

While being of general validity, this statement fits admirably the communist "cultural diplomacy" vis-a-vis the Third World. Ever since the Soviet Union began to focus its attention upon the developing countries of non-communist Asia, Africa and Latin America after the middle fifties, cultural relations between the countries of the world socialist system and those of the Third World have greatly increased in magnitude, scope and intensity. Within a few years, cultural diplomacy, i.e., as Barghoorn defines the term, "the manipulation of cultural matters and personnel for propaganda purposes,"[2] has emerged as a major device of communist foreign policy and strategy of "peaceful coexistence" throughout the Third World, paralleling and supplementing the communist economic offensive discussed in the preceding two chapters. "Lenin's ideas on the cultural revolution, the experience of the Soviet state and the other fraternal countries in bringing about cultural transformation are of an enormous significance for the developing countries," asserts an authoritative article on "Socialism and Culture" published in the 1970 volume of *Pravda*.[3]

Communist Theory of Cultural Relations

As is the case with other aspects of the communist operational code, the role of cultural relations in communist strategy, their purposes and the results they are expected to yield are explained, defined and justified in terms of the Marxist-Leninist ideology.[4]

1. The very necessity of a forceful communist involvement in international cultural relations derives directly from the long-standing communist thesis concerning the paramount importance of a relentless struggle against "bourgeois and reformist ideologies." According to the 1961 *Program of the Soviet Communist Party*, "a grim struggle is going on between two ideologies — communist and bourgeois — in the world today;"[5] and the Third World is in the very midst of it. This ideological struggle is, in the words of the *Program*, "a most important element of the class struggle" and the victory in the "competition of ideas" is counted upon, together with the concomitant victory in the economic competition between socialism and capitalism, to swing ultimately the balance in favor of communism. Since "the cultural revolution constitutes one of the most important links in the construction of socialism,"[6] and international cultural relations are an integral, and very significant, part of the said "competition of ideas" their cultivation is assigned a high priority among the major instruments of communist foreign policy and strategy.

2. Resort to cultural diplomacy as a means of advancing the communist cause in the Third World is deemed all the more desirable and profitable because the product it has to offer is claimed to be vastly superior to its capitalist equivalent. Just as they have been extolling the unexcelled virtues of the communist economic system and casting aspersions at its capitalist com-

petitor, communist ideologists and propagandists have been even more unabashed in praising the supreme qualities of communist culture and denigrating the "decadent" culture of the capitalist West, especially that of the United States. "Having accomplished the cultural revolution," asserts the *Fundamentals*, "the [Soviet] working class, its Party and state....lay the foundation for an advance of culture unprecedented in history."[7] And the Soviet Party's official manual of communist ideology and strategy goes on describing in superlative terms the achievements of Soviet culture.[8] It lauds the wonderful "spiritual atmosphere" under socialism which "differs radically from that in capitalist society" where "a writer or artist held in the grip of bourgeois ideology has no source from which to draw a positive ideal in life" and where "life often seems to him dark and meaningless, and petty and worthless." It credits socialism with "the conversion of the school from an instrument of class domination of the bourgeoisie into an instrument of socialist reeducation." It depicts socialism as "the first social system which frees culture from the oppression of the money-bags, affording the artist the opportunity to create not in order to pander to the depraved tastes of a small handful of the 'big pots', but for the masses."

It speaks of "the advance to the shining heights" of "communist civilization" which "will always engender in people unusual power of will and intellect, creative impulses, courage, and life-giving energy." It claims that the radical democratization of culture under socialism makes it accessible "not only to a narrow stratum of the intelligentsia, but to the whole of society" and "facilitates the advance of talents in all spheres of scientific and artistic endeavour..." It contrasts the idealized Soviet conditions "for bringing talent to light and supporting it" with those in the capitalist world where "thousands upon thousands of talented people...perish without being able to break their way through poverty, privation and society's indifference." Similar statements averring the superiority of the "truly rich spiritual culture" presumably flourishing under communism over the venal culture of the decaying capitalist society seeking to keep the masses in "bourgeois spiritual bondage" constitute the *leitmotifs* of other Soviet, East European and Chinese communist writings on the subject.[9]

In view of such claims, it is only natural that communist strategy-makers consider cultural diplomacy to be a very important device with which to battle the Western influence and promote the cause of communism. As pointed out in the 1969 *Declaration* adopted by the International Conference of Communist and Workers' Parties, "the political and cultural progress, the superiority of human and moral values [in the socialist countries] enhance the influence of socialism on the working people of the world and reinforce its positions in the struggle against imperialism."

3. The claimed superior quality of communist culture makes also the cultivation of international cultural relations a logical area in which to perform the self-imposed communist mission to help others in obtaining the wonderful benefits enjoyed allegedly by the countries of the world socialist system. That is especially so in the case of the emergent nations of the Third World whom the imperialists are said desperately to endeavor to keep in spiritual bondage and where they seek to "subject educational and cultural institutions and mass media to their influence."[10] Hence, emancipating the masses of the Third World from the "spiritual bondage of all types and forms of bourgeois ideology" and assisting them in their "cultural rebirth" has become a foremost part of the communists' "internationalist duty."[11]

4. While this messianic urge to make communist cultural achievements available to others extends to all parts of the world, today communist strategists evidently consider the underdeveloped countries of the Third World to be the place where their cultural diplomacy is likely to yield the best political dividends. As in the case with other aspects of communist strategy, they rely primarily on the deeply embedded anti-Western bias prevalent throughout most of the Third World to make the Asian, African and Latin American masses, intellectuals and, most of all, semi-intellectuals all the more susceptible to communist cultural wooing. They count on it to lend an additional measure of credibility to standard communist denigration of Western culture, help them to unmask the nefarious motives of imperialist *Kulturträgers* allegedly using culture as a device of domination and neo-colonialism and to convince the developing nations of the selfless character of communist cultural offerings. They expect it to contribute to their success in

implanting in the minds of the peoples of the Third World a lofty and enticing image of the socialist world system as the center (to paraphrase the words of a Soviet writer) of the most advanced culture, the citadel of scientific thought, of revolutionary humanism and of a new, communist morality.[12] As another Soviet writer puts it, referring specifically to the developing nations, "the Soviet Union and the other socialist countries, having achieved great success in the development of science, culture, popular education, etc., have the capability of rendering assistance to the poorly-developed countries of Asia, Africa and Latin America, assisting them in overcoming their old backwardness, the product of colonialism. Cultural cooperation, the construction of institutes, hospitals, schools, of sports facilities, and so on, carried out by the USSR and other socialist countries in the nations of Asia and Africa demonstrates to the working people of these continents the achievements and the power of socialism, its internationalism and humanitarianism."[13]

5. Another reason why communist strategists consider the developing nations to be especially attractive as a target of communist culture offensive lies in their cultural backwardness and low level of sophistication. A given communist cultural offering to a Western, culturally well-developed country is only one of the great multitude of cultural events occurring daily in such a country and constitutes at best an interesting variation yielding usually only a very slight dividend in political terms. On the other hand, in view of the woeful shortages of cultural facilities in most of the Third World, a corresponding offering to an underdeveloped country may become a major cultural event of great significance and political impact. That is true, in particular, of educational offerings where the need of the developing nations appears to be more pressing than in any other area of culture.

By the same token, certain aspects of communist culture, governed as they are by the communist-prescribed populist concept of "socialist realism" with its emphasis on turning out literature and art understandable to the common man, are more attuned to the cultural levels prevailing in the Third World than are the more sophisticated and much more heterogeneous formats of Western culture. As Walter Laqueur points out, "'socialist realism' may not be taken seriously in the West, but it did make more sense than *l' art pour l'art* in countries like Egypt, Syria or Iraq."[14] And Laquer's view that Soviet and communist culture has more appeal in the East than in the West is shared by Barghoorn as well.[15]

6. Also, cultural exchanges with the uncommitted nations of the Third World are not deemed to carry with them as great a risk of contamination for the communist countries as is present whenever bourgeois-capitalist culture is permitted entry into the communist orbit. A product of the "bourgeois" culture of the West that a communist country has to admit as a *quid pro quo* of a cultural exchange program with a Western country, be it a movie, theater performance, book, periodical, exhibition, a visit by a cultural delegation, a group of scholars or students, presents almost always an ideological challenge; for it usually contradicts more or less pronouncedly the official Marxist-Leninist line on Western culture and tends thus to expose the citizens of the communist country in question to a harmful "ideological diversion," and possibly even to a modicum of "bourgeois" acculturation. Undesirable influences may and occasionally do result from communist cultural exchanges with less developed countries as well, mainly in connection with the Third World's students admitted to study at educational institutions of communist countries. But the risk in such cases is rather slight as there is little ideological challenge involved in cultural offerings of the underdeveloped countries consisting of such matters as native folklore, artifacts, and the like.

Communist strategists can thus afford to be much more liberal in granting entry into their respective countries to the culture of the Third World than is the case of the West. Likewise, they can be quite generous in honoring, praising and over-praising the former while criticizing the latter. "The Soviet leaders feel less constrained about expressing admiration for the cultures and folk of India, Iraq, or Indonesia than for Western cultures," says Barghoorn; and this applies to the leaders of other communist countries as well.[16] Hence, communist cultural diplomacy vis-a-vis the Third World, unlike that relative to the West, is in a vantage position to exploit to the fullest extent the most effective tool there is to make it successful, namely, indulging and over-indulging in flattering appreciation, whether deserved or not, of the native culture of the Third World.[17] This, then, provides communist strategists with still more justification for the cultivation and expansion of cultural relations with the developing nations.

7. There is still another important purpose that communist cultural diplomacy aims to accomplish, namely, helping to create in the developing countries a new type of "people's intelligentsia," unflinchingly anti-Western, keenly conscious of the vices of capitalism and the virtues of socialism, and firmly committed to lead the peoples of the developing countries onto the communist-recommended non-capitalist path of development. "To ensure the advance of society's productive forces and culture," states the *Fundamentals*, "the cultural revolution must solve yet another important problem: the development of a new genuine people's intelligentsia, closely linked with the working class and the peasantry."[18] While intended for general use anywhere, this communist directive is especially applicable today to the Third World where conditions seem to be more conducive for the creation of "genuine people's intelligentsia" than in the West.

8. Finally, communist reliance on cultural diplomacy is rationalized in terms of the communist commitment to the cause of peace. Since the present-day version of Marxism-Leninism abjurs war (other than the "wars of national liberation" and "class-revolutionary" civil wars), it is only natural that it lays all the more emphasis on international cultural relations. As an aspect of international relations cultural relations carry intrinsically peaceful connotation and are perfectly suited to conjure up the image of communist peaceableness. "Soviet leaders have always insisted that their professed enthusiasm for international contacts was proof of their devotion to peace," points out Barghoorn. "Soviet exploitation of cultural contacts has usually revolved around the strategy and propaganda of peaceful coexistence."[19]

Thus, alongside with the cultivation of economic relations, the pursuit of cultural diplomacy constitutes one of the foremost devices of communist strategy of peaceful co-existence vis-a-vis the Third World.

The Operational Pattern

Again, as is the case with the communist economic offensive discussed in the preceding two chapters, the methods and instrumentalities of communist cultural diplomacy vis-a-vis the developing countries appear to be rather similar in their format to those used in the West's cultural relations with the countries of the Third World. Much like their Western competitors, the countries of the world socialist system have concluded numerous agreements on cultural and scientific cooperation with individual countries of the Third World and supplemented them from time to time with additional protocols as the need arose. They have been engaging in exchanges of individuals, groups and delegations in many fields of culture, education and science. They have sought to foster the closest possible contacts and ties between the communist and Third World associations of writers, artists, educators and scientific workers. They have established libraries, scientific institutes and cultural centers in many parts of the Third World. They have been taking prominent part in all sorts of cultural exhibitions, festivals and other cultural events held in the Third World. They have made it a point to honor the culture of the developing nations by organizing throughout the world socialist system the respective developing countries' "Days of Culture," displays and performances of indigenous art, music and folklore, as well as publishing books on their history and translations of native literature. They have been printing and exporting to the Third World huge quantities of books and brochures in native languages designed to create a favorable image of communist countries and reflect adversely upon the West. They have been sending professors and scientists to teach at educational institutions in various parts of the Third World and they have been serving as hosts to substantial numbers of students from developing countries studying at colleges in communist countries. They have greatly expanded and intensified their radio broadcasting to developing countries and made it a major instrument of communist cultural penetration. They have been providing the developing countries with Soviet and East European communist films and features, both for movie theaters and television screens, and with touring groups of performing artists and sportsmen. They have established throughout Asia, Africa and Latin America a vast network of "Friendship Societies" intended to serve as local vehicles of communist cultural penetration and matched them with parallel societies in communist countries meant to document the fervent communist desire for friendship and close people-to-people ties with developing nations.

In view of the magnitude and the multiplicity of the communist cultural involvements in the Third World, a full enumeration and description of the manifold cultural relations between the individual developing nations and the various countries of the world socialist system would require a book-length study by itself and would thus be far too long to fit the size of the present volume.[20] Nor would such a detailed description be in accordance with the principal purpose of this study, which is concerned primarily with communist cultural relations with the Third World in terms of their political yield. Hence, what follows is mainly a sampling meant to illustrate some of the major facets and operations of communist cultural diplomacy in the Third World and to provide an adequate factual basis for their political evaluation.

Operations in the Educational Field

Undoubtedly, one of the most important aspects of communist cultural diplomacy vis-a-vis the Third World have been the communist offerings in the field of education. After all, without education and the know-how derived from it, meaningful progress is impossible in virtually every field of significant human endeavor, above all in the all-important area of desirable economic development. Education is thus a foremost requisite and literally a *sine qua non* of economic, social and political modernization that all the developing nations so fervently desire. "It is felt ever more in the whole world that, as far as developmental aid for the new countries is concerned, the foremost priority belongs to 'intellectual' assistance," wrote the President of Prague's University of 17th November, Jaroslav Martinic; "for the basis of any kind of progress in their development lies in the use of new technology, of all the latest achievements of science."[21] Education commands thus a very high place in the scale of the Third World's values. Since it is at the same time precisely *the* commodity that is in a woefully short supply in virtually all the emergent nations, outside help is all the more appreciated and liable to generate much good will toward the donor on the part of the recipients. Also, aid in the field of education can be presented much more easily than other forms of foreign assistance as a selfless contribution devoid of ulterior motives. Moreover, as educational facilities provided through outside aid, particularly studies at educational institutions abroad, can be taken advantage of in most instances only by the brightest segment of the Third World's youth, they afford the providing country an unexcelled opportunity to mold the minds of future elites of the developing nations. Hence, it is hardly surprising that communist strategists have assigned educational offerings a high priority in their cultural relations with the Third World.

Third World Students Studying in Communist Countries

The mainstay of communist aid to the Third World's education and its most publicized part have been the academic facilities provided in the countries of the world socialist system for students from the Third World. Since the inception of the program in 1956, an estimated 48,500 students from developing countries have undertaken academic studies in communist countries.[22] About 55 percent of them studied in the USSR and 45 percent in the various countries of communist East Europe, mainly in Czechoslovakia and East Germany. An undetermined small number of them went to Communist China (where the program was suspended in September 1965 in conjunction with the Chinese "cultural revolution)."[23]

As shown in Table V, most of the Third World students studying in Soviet Russia and Eastern Europe in recent years have come from Africa, with the contingent from the Near East and South East Asia second and that from Latin America third.

Almost all of these students are recipients of scholarships consisting usually of a round trip transportation, free medical care and books, no tuition to be paid, and a monthly allowance

TABLE V

Academic Students from Developing Countries Studying in
Communist Countries in 1970 and 1971

	As of December 1970	As of December 1971
Total	21,415	22,350
Africa	10,990	11,050
East Asia	650	700
Latin America	2,425	2,650
Near East and Southeast Asia	7,350	7,950

Sources: U.S. Department of State Research Studies RSES-34 of August
30, 1971 and RESS-57 of August 31, 1972.

that is notably higher than scholarships awarded to native
students of the respective communist countries.[24] Most of the
scholarships are extended on the basis of a dense network of a
bilateral cultural agreements that communist countries have
concluded over the years with virtually all the countries of the
Third World. Other scholarships for the same purpose are
offered by various international and national communist front
organizations, such as the *International Student Union*, the
World Federation of Democratic Youth and the *World Federation of Trade Unions*, and as awards or prizes in various
communist-sponsored contests.

While the bulk of the Third World students studying in
communist countries go there to pursue college-level courses,
there have also been substantial numbers of students attending
communist secondary schools, mainly those with technical and
vocational curricula.[25] 12,500 Third World students were reported as studying at 300 middle and higher specialized schools in the
USSR in the academic year 1969/70.[26] Occasionally, even some
elementary school pupils from the Third World are admitted to
communist schools. Thus a Czechoslovak paper reported in
October 1962 that the son of Prince Sihanouk was attending the
third grade of one of Prague's 9-year elementary-secondary
schools.[27] The paper added that the young prince was very
popular, liked the food served in the school cafeteria and could
sing five songs in Czech.

In most of the communist countries educational facilities for college-level students from the Third World are provided at, or in conjunction with, the already established institutions of higher learning. However, the administration of the study programs and all matters pertaining to foreign students are handled centrally, usually by special institutes, such as Bulgaria's Institute for the Education of Foreign Students in Sofia or East Germany's Herder Institute of the University of Leipzig. In a few instances new schools have been set up to cater specifically to the needs of students from developing nations. The most outstanding examples of the latter approach are the "Patrice Lumumba People's Friendship University" of Moscow and the "University of 17th November" of Prague.

Moscow's People's Friendship University

Founded in February 1960, "in pursuance of the Leninist policy of helping the emergent nations" and presumably in response to suggestions on the part of "progressive circles of the countries of Asia, Africa and Latin America," Moscow's People's Friendship University has quickly emerged as the Soviet Bloc's largest and most important centre for the "training of national cadres of specialists for the developing nations."[28] According to a recent statement by its President, Sergei V. Rumiantsev, almost 50,000 applications were received in 1960 for the 500 places then available; and more recently some 9 thousand applicants have been vying annually for the 600 vacancies to be filled each year.[29] By 1970 the enrollment reached 4,061 students from 85 countries of whom 834 were from Africa, 964 from Latin America, 770 from the Arab countries, and 524 from Southeast Asia.[30] The remaining 969 were Soviet citizens admitted to serve as companions and a sort of chaperons for foreign students as well as to be trained for future assignments in developing countries. In its first decade of 1960-70 the University graduated 2,335 students of whom 719 were in engineering, 279 in physics, chemistry and mathematics, 460 in medicine and 243 in agronomy. In the same period it awarded 293 Master's degrees and 20 Doctor's degrees.

Upon their admission, foreign students are first assigned to the University's preparatory college (*podgotovitel'nyi fakultet*) designed to teach them the Russian language and fill the gaps in their previous education. Upon having completed these preparatory courses they enter one of the University's six basic colleges or departments: engineering, physico-mathematical and natural sciences, medical, agricultural, historico-philological, economics and law. The University is said to train "specialists of fourteen professions." As revealed in the above quoted statement by the University's President, 40 percent of the enrollees study engineering, agronomy and medicine and 30 percent natural and physico-mathematical sciences, whereas only 30 percent are engaged in the pursuit of the other three fields' of historico-philological, economic and law studies.[31] In line with the Leninist emphasis on the unity of theory and practice, practical on-the-job training constitutes an integral and substantial part of study curricula. For this purpose the University has training facilities in 210 economic enterprises of different kinds in 35 cities and 9 Soviet Republics.

Prague's University of 17th November

Established in 1961, one year after Moscow's People's Friendship University, and named so in commemoration of the uprising of Prague students against the Nazis on November 17, 1939, the University of 17th November serves the same purpose as its Soviet counterpart.[32] As a Czechoslovak paper wrote at the time of its foundation, the new University was a "further proof of the help which our state grants to countries that have freed themselves or are freeing themselves from colonial domination."[33] From 1,254 students from 73 countries registered in the University's first year of operations begun on November 17, 1961,[34] the enrollment rose to over 3,000 foreign students from more than 80 countries of Latin America, Asia and Africa by 1964.[35] Over the years, the annual admission of new students fluctuated between 300-400.[36] The first group of 14 students graduated from the University and were awarded the appropriate diplomas in a solemn session on November 17, 1966, attended also by the President of Moscow's Friendship University.[37] Although the contingent of the graduating students has subsequently increased and reached 85 from 33 countries in 1967,[38] it constitutes only about one fourth of the average annual influx of freshmen, suggesting a high rate of drop-outs or flunk-outs. The above-mentioned report released on the eve of the University's tenth anniversary listed a number of 1,672 students and "post-graduates" from developing countries as having completed their studies by the end of the 1969-70 academic year. 719 of them were from "the Arab area," 351 from Asia, 385 from Africa and 217 from Latin America.

Much like the first-year students of the Moscow institution, foreign students newly admitted to the University of 17th November spend their first year studying the Czech or Slovak language and improving their mostly defective knowledge of basic subjects, such as physics, chemistry, mathematics and biology. This is provided by the University's preparatory college *(fakulta jazykové a odborné připravy)* which operates for this purpose a number of preparatory study centers throughout the country. Upon the successful completion of their preparation students are admitted to the study of their chosen specialties. Until 1966 that meant usually formal enrollment in one or the other of the two colleges of the University of 17th November, namely, the college of natural and technical sciences and the college of social sciences — or, in some instances, assignment to studies at another Czechoslovak University. However, the college of natural and technical sciences was abolished in 1966, so that foreign students in fields other than the social sciences are henceforth assigned to other Czechoslovak institutions offering the desired subjects.[39] Thus, for the majority of its students interested in technical and non-social-science curricula, the University of 17th November has in recent years been cast more and more in the role of an administrative and supervisory center for foreign students rather than being the school that does the actual teaching. Apart from the preparatory chores mentioned above, the University acts now as a teaching institution for foreign students only in general studies of social sciences. As explained by its President, the University's remaining college of social sciences hopes to equip the students with "a broad knowledge of many combined social sciences — economics, law, philosophy, sociology and history — so that they could fulfill, in the concrete conditions of a concrete developmental stage of their country, the tasks entrusted them by the society."[40] Taught in French or English, this broad interdisciplinary social science curriculum, offered primarily to the Third World's elementary and secondary school teachers-to-be and future government employees, is obviously expected to acquaint the students with, and make them receptive to, the Marxist-Leninist world outlook.[41] An important function in this endeavor seems to be assigned to the University's department of "the most recent history of the Czechoslovak Socialist Republic" whose task is said to be to "acquaint foreign students with contemporary life in Czechoslovakia and with the history of the Czech and Slovak nation."[42] Attached to the department is a desk for cultural-educational work designed to make arrangements for the foreign students' extra-curricular "cultural life" and leisure. Also, after the Soviet fashion, class-room instruction is supplemented with practical on-the-job training.

Like its Soviet model, the University of 17th November has been also charged with the task of training Czechoslovakia's own specialists for their assignments in the countries of the Third World. Initially, emphasis was almost exclusively on a variety of language courses enriched with bits of basic information on political, economic and other conditions in pertinent developing countries.[43] These offerings have subsequently been strengthened and reorganized into a two-year curriculum, topped by a comprehensive examination and supervised by a Study and Information Institute for Activities of Czechoslovak Experts Abroad.[44] Over 800 Czechs and Slovaks were registered for such courses in the 1964-65 academic year and 750 for 1967-68. There seems to be a keen interest in these offerings and two thirds of the applicants (who must be recommended by their employers) had to be turned down for the lack of adequate facilities in 1967. Finally, under the above mentioned government ordinance of January 19, 1966, the University of 17th November has been authorized to provide complete college education for Czechoslovak citizens in certain fields designated by the Minister of Education and Culture. Another step in that direction was undertaken in 1971 when an Institute of International Relations was added to the University of 17th November system.[45] Located in Bratislava, the institute offers a four-semester postgraduate program designed to prepare the students "politically, professionally and linguistically" for Czechoslovakia's foreign service as well as "expert activity abroad."

Supporting Educational Endeavors Within the Developing Nations

Another form of communist educational policy and strategy vis-a-vis the Third World has been the assistance extended to a number of non-committed countries of Asia and Africa, and more recently also Latin America, in developing and improving educational facilities within those countries. This type of educational assistance begins ordinarily with invitations addressed to the Minister of Education of the country in question and his chief aids to visit the Soviet Union and/or other communist countries. Upon their arrival the honored guests are taken on a red carpet tour of selected educational institutions well calculated to impress the visitors with the high quality of communist education.[46] This is followed by a generous communist offer to place communist pedagogical experience, free and with no strings attached, at the disposal of the respective developing country. An agreement is then offered providing for such things as groups of professors, teachers and school administrators from the developing country in question to come and observe how the communist school systems work and to attend educational seminars and workshops; professors and teachers from the communist country concerned to teach for a length of time at native institutions of the developing country; communist textbooks translated into the native language and other educational materials to be donated to native schools and school libraries; communist educational exhibits to be shown in the developing countries; and, in a number of instances, new educational institutions and centers to be established with communist aid.

Understandably, the bulk of this aid has come from the Soviet Union. Speaking on the solemn occasion of the festive graduation of the first graduates of Moscow's People's Friendship University, the Soviet Premier, Alexei Kosygin, boasted that "more than 90 educational institutions and centers are being, or have been, built with Soviet assistance in Burma, India, Ethiopia,

Cambodia, Guinea, Indonesia, Mali, Algeria, Kenya, the United
Arab Republic, Afghanistan, Tunisia and other countries."[47]
What seemed to be a somewhat more modest claim was made in
1969 by the Soviet Union's Minister of Higher and Specialized
education, V.P. Eliutin, who mentioned twenty-two educational
establishments "being built and equipped in developing countries
with Soviet assistance and active cooperation of Soviet higher
schools" and seventeen more such projects "to be started
shortly."[48] In the earlier cited article in the 1971 volume of
International Affairs B. Gafurov speaks of "130 higher educational institutions, schools and vocational training centres that
the socialist states have undertaken to build in the developing
countries" and claims that "more than 70 are already function-
ing."[49] The institutions cited as already completed include the
Bombay and Rangoon Technological Institutes, the Higher
Technical Institute of Khmer-Soviet Friendship in Cambodia,
the Polytechnical Institutes in North Vietnam and Guinea, the
African Gas, Oil and Textile Institute in Algeria,[50] a polytechnical institute in Ethiopia, and educational centres in Egypt,
Iraq, and Mali. One of the African countries most favored in this
respect has been Mali where the Soviet Union helped to establish
in 1965 a vocational technical center, an institute to train
administrative personnel, and another one to train nurses and
midwifes.[51] As reported by *Pravda* in December 1965, 289 Soviet
teachers were working in the academic year 1965-66 in Algeria,
Ghana, Guinea, Cambodia, Mali, Somalia and other countries.[52]
According to a Tass release of May 24, 1966, Soviet professors
were scheduled to teach at the Damascus University, while some
330 teachers were to be sent to Algerian schools in 1968.[53] In
1967 the number of Soviet teachers at the above-mentioned
Polytechnical Institute at Conakry was said to have reached 112,
and the number of Soviet instructors at the Polytechnic Institute
at Kabul, Afghanistan, was reported to be approximately 98 in
1970. Some 550 Soviet instructors were said to be preparing
engineers, technicians, doctors and teachers in Guinea, Algeria,
India, Afghanistan and Ethiopia in the academic year 1969-70.
Under a 1970 agreement with Brazzaville Congo, the Soviet
Union will give the African country 20 schools.[54] In Africa a
permanent African student seminar on "The Soviet Union and

the New Africa" has been put into operation in 1969 under the sponsorship of the Soviet Association for Friendship with the Peoples of Africa to "help to spread among the African public the truth about the land of victorious socialism."[55] A Soviet-projected Higher Party School meant to provide appropriate ideological training for functionaries of Mali's national party, The Sudanese Democratic African Assembly, was opened at Bamako in 1967.[56] A Soviet-Chad agreement signed in the same year provided for a number of Russian language teachers to teach at Chad's secondary schools and a protocol concluded between the USSR and the Central African Republic arranged for a despatch of 14 Soviet teachers to the said African country.[57] Under a 1967 Soviet-Indian agreement the publication and distribution of Soviet textbooks, already quite substantial, was to be further increased.[58] The Technical Institute in Bombay, India, established with Soviet assistance, is said to have reached an enrollment of 1,200 students in 1970.[59]

Other communist countries have also taken an active part in this type of educational aid, although on a lesser scale. Agreements on cultural and scientific cooperation concluded over the years between the various countries of the world socialist system and the developing countries of Asia, Africa and Latin America ordinarily contain arrangements for exchanges of delegations of teachers, various forms of cooperation between respective communists and Third World universities, schools and school systems, visiting positions for professors, lecturers and teachers at Third World educational institutions, gifts of diverse educational materials (laboratories, visual aids, films, books and pamphlets). Thus, to cite a few typical instances, over 110 Czechoslovak college and secondary school teachers were reported to be teaching in 13 developing nations of Africa, Asia and Latin America in 1966.[60] Polish teachers were active in Guinea and Hungarian professors have been sent to Kuwait. In a major endeavor to find new openings for communist cultural diplomacy in Latin America, a Czechoslovak cultural delegation headed by the Minister of Education and Culture, toured a number of Latin American countries in 1962, visited their universities and did its best to foster educational exchanges between Czechoslovakia and the countries of Latin America. Three years later, "to broaden cultural cooperation" between Czechoslovak and Latin American universities, a delegation of Czechoslovak universities headed by the former President of Prague's Charles University toured in August and September 1965 the universities of Brazil, Uruguay, Colombia, Chile and Mexico.[61] In 1961 Czechoslovakia agreed to build a technical institute in Somalia and in 1967 over one thousand Bulgarians were building a school at Tripoli in Libya.[62]

Utilization of Mass Communications Media

Not at all surprisingly, a major role in the pursuit of communist cultural diplomacy in the Third World has been assigned to the communications media. Indeed, as Barghoorn wrote in his *Soviet Foreign Propaganda*, "words and pictures have played a more continuous, and perhaps a more vital role than bullets or rubles in Moscow's struggle to undermine the social order of capitalism and to reconstruct society on 'Marxist-Leninist' foundations."[63] While the communications media, especially those most likely to give access to massive audiences, are used for all sorts and types of propaganda, they lend themselves also very well to what Barghoorn considers to be "central to communist cultural diplomacy," namely "the systematic utilization of information, artistic, scientific and other cultural materials, symbols and personnel, and ideas, as instruments of foreign policy."[64]

Radio

For obvious reasons, the one medium most widely used for this purpose has been the radio. Being relatively inexpensive, the modern small transistor sets have cropped up everywhere in the Third World. Even in the isolated hamlets of South America's Andes, the remotest outposts of Asia's Himalayas or in Africa's bush villages, there is someone with a transistor set well capable of pulling in even broadcasts from distant, but powerful transmitters. And, as reported by those who know, even where only few sets are available, villagers get together to listen collectively so that virtually everyone is within the radio's reach. Nor does illiteracy that remains so high throughout much of the Third World prevent the message from getting through to its target as is the case with written words. In fact, the listeners' very illiteracy enhances the radio's impact as it nullifies the influence of other media, such as newspapers.

Taking the fullest advantage of such opportunities, communist countries have been steadily expanding their radio transmissions to the developing countries ever since they began to pay growing attention to the Third World in the middle fifties. As shown in Table VI below, by 1971 the daily output of Soviet broadcasts (in all languages) for Africa reached 64 hours, for Asia 127 hours 20 minutes, and for Latin America 17 hours. At the same time, the other countries of Communist East Europe were pitching in with 15 hours 35 minutes for Africa, 29 hours 45 minutes for Asia and 24 hours 15 minutes for Latin America (See Table VII), while corresponding figures for Communist China's foreign language transmissions were 16 hours for Africa, 97 hours 30 minutes for Asia and 9 hours for Latin America (see Table VIII). Initially, the bulk of these transmissions were in world languages, such as English, French and Spanish. Gradually, broadcasts in native Asian and African languages have been added, programs progressively lengthened and the number of frequencies increased. Thus the Soviet Union initiated broadcasts to Africa in Swahili in January 1959, introducing them with a biographical talk on Lenin, and followed with transmissions in Hausa and Somali languages two years later.[65] By 1971 the Soviet Union's African broadcasts were transmitted in twelve native languages, those for Asia in thirty-four and those for Latin America in four, all this, of course, in addition to broadcasts in Russian, French, English, Spanish and Portuguese. In their turn, the communist countries of Eastern Europe joined in gradually with broadcasts in Arabic, Swahili, Indonesian and Persian, while Communist China included broadcasts in Arabic, Swahili and Hausa to her transmissions for Africa and additional twenty native languages to her broadcasts for Asia.

Added to these totals of communist transmissions via the official government radio stations must be hundreds of additional weekly hours of communist broadcasting by various clandestine or "non-official" transmitters, most of them operating from

TABLE VI

Soviet Broadcasts to Asia, Africa and Latin America — 1967 — 1971
Daily Output

Beamed to	Language	Transm. Time	Language	Transm. Time
AFRICA	Arabic	400 min.	Arabic	570 min.
	Amharic	90 min.	Amharic	90 min.
	Bambara	30 min.	Bambara	30 min.
	English	240 min.	English	270 min.
	French	300 min.	French	230 min.
	Fulani	—	Fulani	10 min.
	Hausa	120 min.	Hausa	150 min.
	Italian	30 min.	Italian	—
	Lingala	30 min.	Lingala	30 min.
	Malagasy	30 min.	Malagasy	60 min.
	Ndebele	—	Ndebele	30 min.
	Portuguese	150 min.	Portuguese	120 min.
	Somali	60 min.	Somali	60 min.
	Shona	—	Shona	30 min.
	Swahili	210 min.	Swahili	210 min.
	Russian	1440 min.	Russian	1920 min.
	Zulu	30 min.	Zulu	30 min.
Total	14	52 hrs. 40 min.	16	64 hrs. 00 min.

TABLE VI (Cont.)

Beamed to:	1967		1971	
	Language	Transm. Time	Language	Transm. Time
ASIA	Arabic	400 min.	Arabic	570 min.
	Armenian	155 min.	Armenian	300 min.
	Adjerbaijan	100 min.	Adjerbaijan	100 min.
	Assamese	—	Assamese	60 min.
	Bengali	150 min.	Bengali	150 min.
	Burmese	90 min.	Burmese	90 min.
	Chinese	660 min.	Chinese	930 min.
	Dari	30 min.	Dari	60 min.
	English	360 min.	English	180 min.
	French	30 min.	French	30 min.
	Gujarati	—	Gujarati	60 min.
	Hindi	165 min.	Hindi	210 min.
	Indonesian	210 min.	Indonesian	210 min.
	Japanese	270 min.	Japanese	310 min.
	Kannada	—	Kannada	60 min.
	Khmer	30 min.	Khmer	60 min.
	Korean	210 min.	Korean	210 min.
	Kurdish	100 min.	Kurdish	100 min.
	Laotian	30 min.	Laotian	60 min.
	Malayalam	60 min.	Malayalam	60 min.
	Marathi	60 min.	Marathi	60 min.
	Nepalese	30 min.	Nepalese	60 min.
	Orija	—	Orija	60 min.
	Persian	405 min.	Persian	405 min.
	Punjabi	60 min.	Punjabi	60 min.

TABLE VI (Cont.)

Beamed to:	1967		1971	
	Language	Transm. Time	Language	Transm. Time
ASIA (Cont.)	Pushtu	90 min.	Pushtu	60 min.
	Russian	1440 min.	Russian	1920 min.
	Sinhalese	60 min.	Sinhalese	60 min.
	Tadjik	120 min.	Tadjik	120 min.
	Tamil	60 min.	Tamil	60 min.
	Telugu	–	Telugu	60 min.
	Thai	60 min.	Thai	60 min.
	Uighur	60 min.	Uighur	60 min.
	Urdu	210 min.	Urdu	210 min.
	Uzbek	30 min.	Uzbek	30 min.
	Vietnamese	300 min.	Vietnamese	300 min.
	Mongolian	155 min.	Mongolian	155 min.
Total	32	103 hrs. 10 min.	37	127 hrs. 20 min.

TABLE VI (Cont.)

Beamed to:	1967 Language	Transm. Time	1971 Language	Transm. Time
LATIN AMERICA	Armenian	30 min.	Armenian	30 min.
	Creole	–	Creole	30 min.
	French	8 min.	French	–
	Guarani	–	Guarani	30 min.
	Portuguese	150 min.	Portuguese	120 min.
	Russian	120 min.	Russian	120 min.
	Spanish	630 min.	Spanish	630 min.
	Quechua	60 min.	Quechua	60 min.
Total	6	16 hr. 38 min.	7	17 hrs. 00 min.
Grand Total for Africa, Asia and Latin America	52	172 hr. 28 min.	60	208 hrs. 20 min.

Source: *Review of East European and Communist Chinese Foreign Broadcasts*, Radio Free Europe Research, Bloc/1 June 28, 1971.

TABLE VII

Communist East Europe's Broadcasts to Asia, Africa and Latin America

TO AFRICA

From:	1967 Language	1967 Transm. Time	1971 Language	1971 Transm. Time
Albania	Arabic	120 min.	Arabic	210 min.
	English	60 min.	English	120 min.
Total	2	2 hr. 00 min.	2	5 hr. 30 min.
Bulgaria	Arabic	150 min.	Arabic	150 min.
	English	60 min.	English	60 min.
	French	60 min.	French	60 min.
Total	3	4 hr. 30 min.	3	4 hr. 30 min.
Czechoslovakia	Arabic	110 min.	Arabic	120 min.
	English	110 min.	English	120 min.
	French	110 min.	French	110 min.
	Swahili	30 min.	Swahili	—
Total	4	6 hr. 00 min.	3	6 hr. 00 min.
East Germany	Arabic	270 min.	Arabic	480 min.
	English	270 min.	English	180 min.
	French	405 min.	French	315 min.
	German	30 min.	German	90 min.
	Swahili	135 min.	Swahili	90 min.
Total	5	18 hr. 30 min.	5	19 hr. 15 min.

Country	Languages	No.	Time	Languages	No.	Time
Hungary	Arabic Hungarian	2	70 min. 90 min.	Arabic Hungarian	—	— —
Total			2 hr. 40 min.			
Poland	English French	2	120 min. 120 min.	English French	2	80 min. 90 min.
Total			4 hr.			2 hr. 50 min.
Rumania	Arabic English French Portuguese	4	90 min. 30 min. 60 min. 30 min.	Arabic English French Portuguese	4	90 min. 30 min. 60 min. 30 min.
Total			3 hr. 30 min.			3 hr. 30 min.
Yugoslavia	Arabic English French	3	60 min. 75 min. 45 min.	Arabic English French	3	60 min. 105 min. 75 min.
Total			3 hr. 00 min.			4 hr. 00 min.
GRAND TOTAL FOR AFRICA						45 hr. 35 min.
TO ASIA						
Albania	Arabic English Indonesian	2	120 min. 60 min. —	Arabic English Indonesian	3	210 min. 30 min. 180 min.
Total			3 hr. 00 min.			7 hr. 00 min.
Bulgaria	Arabic	1	150 min.	Arabic	1	150 min.
Total			150 min.			150 min.

TABLE VII (Cont.)

From:	1967		1971	
	Language	Transm. Time	Language	Transm. Time
Czechoslovakia	Arabic	110 min.	Arabic	120 min.
	English	60 min.	English	60 min.
Total	2	2 hr. 50 min.	2	3 hr. 00 min.
East Germany	Arabic	270 min.	Arabic	480 min.
	English	160 min.	English	180 min.
	German	210 min.	German	45 min.
	Indonesian	30 min.	Indonesian	60 min.
Total	4	11 hr. 10 min.	4	12 hr. 45 min.
Hungary	English	–	English	30 min.
	Arabic	70 min.	Arabic	–
	Hungarian	90 min.	Hungarian	–
Total	2	2 hr. 40 min.	1	0 hr. 30 min.
Poland	–	–	–	–
Total	–	–	–	–
Rumania	Arabic	90 min.	Arabic	90 min.
	English	30 min.	English	30 min.
	Persian	60 min.	Persian	60 min.
Total	3	3 hr. 00 min.	3	3 hrs. 00 min.
Yugoslavia	Arabic	60 min.	Arabic	60 min.
	English	75 min.	English	–
Total	2	2 hr. 15 min.	1	1 hr. 00 min.

TO LATIN AMERICA

Albania	Albanian	60 min.	Albanian	120 min.
	Spanish	60 min.	Spanish	150 min.
	Portuguese	—	Portuguese	180 min.
Total	2	2 hr. 00 min.	3	7 hr. 30 min.
Bulgaria	Bulgarian	60 min.	Bulgarian	90 min.
	Spanish	60 min.	Spanish	120 min.
Total	2	2 hr. 00 min.	2	3 hr. 30 min.
Czechoslovakia	Czech-Slovak	30 min.	Czech-Slovak	30 min.
	Portuguese	110 min.	Portuguese	120 min.
	Spanish	115 min.	Spanish	120 min.
Total	4	4 hr. 15 min.	4	4 hr. 30 min.
East Germany	German	90 min.	German	45 min.
	Portuguese	120 min.	Portuguese	90 min.
	Spanish	120 min.	Spanish	90 min.
Total	3	5 hr. 30 min.	3	3 hr. 45 min.
Hungary	Hungarian	30 min.	Hungarian	30 min.
	Spanish	60 min.	Spanish	60 min.
Total	2	1 hr. 30 min.	2	1 hr. 30 min.
Poland	Polish	120 min.	Polish	—
	Spanish	60 min.	Spanish	—
Total	2	3 hr. 00 min.	—	—

TABLE VII (Cont.)

Beamed to:		1967		1971
	Language	Transm. Time	Language	Transm. Time
Rumania	Spanish	90 min.	Spanish	90 min.
	Portuguese	60 min.	Portuguese	60 min.
Total	2	2 hr. 30 min.	2	2 hr. 30 min.
Yugoslavia	Spanish	90 min.	Spanish	60 min.
Total	1	1 hr. 30 min.	1	1 hr.
GRAND TOTAL FOR LATIN AMERICA . . . . 24 hr. 15 min.
GRAND TOTAL FOR ALL OF EAST EUROPE . . . . 99 hr. 35 min.

Source: Same as for Table VI

TABLE VIII

Chinese Communist Broadcasts to Asia, Africa and Latin America

Beamed to:	1967 Language	Transm. Time	1971 Language	Transm. Time
Africa	Arabic	120 min.	Arabic	120 min.
	Cantonese	60 min.	Cantonese	60 min.
	English	240 min.	English	240 min.
	French	120 min.	French	120 min.
	Hausa	60 min.	Hausa	60 min.
	Italian	30 min.	Italian	30 min.
	Portuguese	120 min.	Portuguese	120 min.
	Chinese-Kuoyou	180 min.	Chinese-Kuoyou	90 min.
Total	9	17 hrs. 00 min.	9	16 hrs. 00 min.
Latin America	Cantonese	120 min.	Cantonese	120 min.
	English	300 min.	English	300 min.
	Chinese-Kuoyou	180 min.	Chinese-Kuoyou	90 min.
	Swahili	90 min.	Swahili	90 min.
Total	3	9 hrs. 00 min.	3	9 hrs. 00 min.
Asia	Arabic	120 min.	Arabic	120 min.
	Amoy	90 min.	Amoy	90 min.
	Bengali	–	Bengali	120 min.
	Burmese	150 min.	Burmese	210 min.
	Cantonese	90 min.	Cantonese	150 min.
	Chaochow	90 min.	Chaochow	90 min.
	English	240 min.	English	300 min.
	Esperanto	–	Esperanto	twice weekly
	Hindi	180 min.	Hindi	240 min.

TABLE VIII (Cont.)

Beamed to:	1967		1971	
	Language	Transm. Time	Language	Transm. Time
ASIA (Cont.)	Hakka	150 min.	Hakka	150 min.
	Indonesian	240 min.	Indonesian	270 min.
	Japanese	420 min.	Japanese	390 min.
	Khmer	120 min.	Khmer	180 min.
	Korean	120 min.	Korean	240 min.
	Laotian	150 min.	Laotian	150 min.
	Malay	120 min.	Malay	120 min.
	Mongolian	180 min.	Mongolian	300 min.
	Persian	60 min.	Persian	60 min.
	Russian	840 min.	Russian	1560 min.
	Standard-Chinese-Kuoyou	150 min.	Standard-Chinese-Kuoyou	360 min.
	Tagalog	60 min.	Tagalog	90 min.
	Thai	180 min.	Thai	180 min.
	Tamil	60 min.	Tamil	60 min.
	Urdu	60 min.	Urdu	60 min.
	Vietnamese	270 min.	Vietnamese	270 min.
	French	–	French	90 min.
Total	23	69 hrs. 00 min.	26	97 hrs. 30 min.
GRAND TOTAL	35	95 hrs. 00 min.	38	122 hrs. 30 min.

Source: Same as for Table VI

TABLE IX

TOTAL TIME ALLOCATED BY COMMUNIST COUNTRIES TO INTERNATIONAL BROADCASTING
(BREAKDOWN BY CONTINENTS)

CONTINENT	ASIA		AFRICA		LATIN AMERICA	
COUNTRY	LA.	TIME	LA.	TIME	LA.	TIME
USSR	37	127:20	16	64:00	7	17:00
CHINA	26	97:30	9	16:00	4	11:30
ALBANIA	3	7:00	2	5:30	3	7:30
E. GERMANY	4	12:45	5	19:15	3	3:45
CSSR	2	3:00	3	6:00	4	4:30
POLAND	0	0:00	2	2:50	0	0:00
RUMANIA	3	3:00	4	3:30	2	2:30
BULGARIA	1	2:30	3	4:30	2	3:30
YUGOSLAVIA	1	1:00	3	4:00	1	1:00
HUNGARY	1	0:30	0	0:00	2	1:30
N. VIETNAM	13	37:10	0	0:00	0	0:00
N. KOREA	5	15:00	3	4:00	2	3:00
CUBA	0	0:00	1	2:25	5	26:00
MONGOLIA	6	3:30	0	0:00	0	0:00
TOTAL	38	310:15	16	132:00	16	81:45

safe locations within the world socialist system. As of 1960, the weekly hours of such broadcasts were estimated at 807 hours to the Far East, 167 hours to Latin America and 244 hours to the Near East and South-east Asia.[66] A more recent Western study of communist foreign broadcasting speaks, as of 1971, of "at least 19 communist controlled 'illegal' or 'clandestine' stations which transmit international broadcasts for at least 80 hours daily."[67] (But not all of such clandestine broadcasts are aimed at the Third World.) One "non-official" communist station especially active in recent years has been Soviet Russia's so-called "Radio Peace and Progress" engaged mainly in vitriolic attacks on the United States beamed in several local languages at the huge population of India. According to Soviet assertions, it is an "unofficial organ of Soviet public opinion" over which the Soviet government allegedly has no control.[68] Among the communist countries most active in this respect have been East Germany and Communist China. Clandestine stations located in East Germany have been said to devote some 25 hours daily to broadcasts in Turkish, Persian, Kurdish and Azerbaijani to Turkey, Iran and Iraq.[69] Communist China maintains or supplies transmitter time and frequencies to the "Patriotic Youth Front Radio" for Burma, "Radio Pathet Lao" and "Radio of the Patriotic Neutralist Forces" for Laos, the "Voice of the Malayan Revolution" for Malaysia, the "Voice of the People of Thailand" and the "Voice of the National United Front of Kampuchea" for Cambodia.[70]

Furthermore, communist countries have managed to obtain a measure of influence and even control over the broadcasting and television programs of some of the countries of the Third World through various agreements on mutual cooperation concluded between communist and native broadcasting and television networks. For instance, arrangements of this sort were made in the sixties by Czechoslovakia with Algeria, Iraq, Indonesia, Lebanon, Tunisia, Burundi and the U.A.R.; by Bulgaria with Iraq and Sudan; by Poland with Ghana, Guinea, and Mali; and by Soviet Russia with Syria, Dahomey, Chad and other countries. Such agreements provide, among other things, for exchanges of staff, experience, radio and television programs. However, a bilaterial arrangement with a communist country puts almost inevitably the much less experienced developing country in a position of a receptive pupil inclined to follow the more experienced communist tutor's directives.

Printed Materials

Next to the spoken word via radio, the printed word is used in a rich variety of forms and on quite a massive scale as a vehicle for communist cultural penetration of the Third World. To be sure, its effectiveness is limited by the widespread illiteracy and semi-literacy prevalent in most of the developing countries. Because of this the printed word cannot very well serve the communist cause among the Third World's masses, save in those countries (mainly in Latin America) where the common man had already acquired the ability and the habit to read. However, everywhere in the Third World it can and does serve the purpose of influencing the educated elites of the developing nations which are, after all, the main target of communist wooing at the current stage of communist strategy vis-a-vis the Third World.

There are several types of printed materials designs to propagandize the communist cause, culture and way of life in the nations of the Third World.

To begin with, there are periodicals, pamphlets, brochures and books published in foreign languages by or on behalf of the Soviet Union and other communist countries and meant for general distribution abroad. To name just a few, these include the Soviet Union's *New Times, Soviet Life, Moscow News, Culture and Life, International Affairs*; Communist China's *Peking Review; China Reconstructs, China Pictorial, Czechoslovak Digest*, Czechoslovakia's *Prague News Letter* and *Czechoslovak Life;* Yugoslavia's *Yugoslav Life* and *Review of International Affairs;* Bulgaria's *Bulgaria Today;* Poland's *Poland* and *Polish Perspectives;* Hungary's *New Hungarian Quarterly* and *Hungarian Review;* Rumania's *Rumania Today;* Albania's *New Albania*; and, last but not the least, the *World Marxist Review*, the official mouthpiece of the Soviet-led portion of the world communist movement. While these materials are designed for propaganda anywhere in the world, a good portion of them are channeled into the countries of the Third World.

Much in the same category are periodicals and other printed materials produced by various international communist Front organizations, such as the *World Federation of Trade Unions, World Peace Council, World Federation of Democratic Youth, International Student Union, Democratic Women's Federation, International Organization of Journalists* and the *Afro-Asian Solidarity Committee.* Although their lopsided dependence on the Soviet Union has been lessened somewhat (and in some cases quite considerably) in recent years, in matters concerning the Third World these Front organizations continue by and large to toe to the Soviet line, and this is reflected in their publications. Also, they produce occasionally issues of their periodicals and other releases prepared specifically for one or another region of the Third World. Moreover, the diplomatic missions of the Soviet Union and some of the other communist countries to the developing nations issue and distribute various information and propaganda sheets, and in some instances even periodical magazines, geared specifically to the propaganda needs of the particular area in which they operate. The most extensive operation of this kind in the Third World is undoubtedly that of the huge Soviet embassy in India whose Information Department publishes several periodicals, such as the *Soviet Review, Soviet Land, Youth Review* and *Sputnik Junior,* all of them carrying materials provided by the Soviet Press Agency *Novosti.*[71] Other examples of the same endeavors are the monthly magazine *Tuluh* (Dawn) published in English, Urdu and Bengali by the Soviet Embassy to Pakistan and the monthly *Polar Star* published in Kampala, Uganda.[72] Finally, added to the list must be the newspapers, magazines and other printed materials published by and on behalf of the communist parties of the Third World and by their local fronts and/or fellow-traveling organizations. According to the Office of Policy and Research of the United States Information Agency, several hundred indigenous communist and fellow-traveling newspapers and periodicals existed in the developing nations as of 1967.[73]

Intended to conjure up the best possible image of communist culture and way of life, periodicals, books and other publications produced by communist countries and communist Front organizations for use abroad are of attractive appearance, printed on good quality paper and often richly adorned with appealing photographs portraying all sorts of communist achievements. They are offered for sale and subscription at very moderate and often nominal cost, mainly through selected bookstores specializing in this type of literature.[74] They are donated in generous quantities to university, school and local libraries and reading rooms. They are displayed in houses of culture and cultural centres built and equipped with communist aid in many of the developing countries. They are available on the shelves of the numerous Societies for the Friendship with the Soviet Union and other communist countries that have cropped up in the Third World since the inception of the communist wooing of the developing nations in the fifties.

However, virtually all of these materials produced by and on behalf of communist countries, parties, Front organizations and fellow-traveling outfits carry with them one major drawback: their communist origin necessarily casts doubts about their objectivity and detracts from their credibility, at least in the minds of those readers who have not yet become emotionally committed to the communist or pro-communist course. To make such readers put aside their doubts, it is crucially important that what they have read in publications of known or suspected communist origin be corroborated by sources that are, or at least appear to be, of non-communist provenance. Hence, communist strategy-makers have striven hard to induce the native non-communist press of the developing nations to carry news and articles deemed desirable from the communist standpoint and to prevent publication of materials considered detrimental for the communist cause.

The main way of attaining this purpose is to supply native press agencies, newspapers and other periodicals of the Third World with all sorts of news items, analyses, commentaries, background and other materials supporting the communist stand. This is the primary reason why communist countries have been so eager to conclude with the developing nations agreements providing for cooperation of their respective press agencies and news services and exchange of information and experiences in the press and publications field. In practice, such "cooperation" and "exchange" turn out to be mostly one-way deals enabling the press agencies of the communist countries, such as the Soviet Union's *Tass* and *Novosti*, Czechoslovakia's *ČTK*, Poland's *PAP*, Communist China's *NCNA* and others, to establish their branch offices in the respective developing countries and obtain thus local bases for their infiltration of the native press.[75] Fully subsidized from state funds, communist press agencies and bureaus have been offering their services for very modest fees and sometimes even without charging anything, underselling thus easily their Western competitors working under the precept of earning their own way.

Naturally, all materials distributed directly or indirectly through communist cultural and information services are carefully selected and edited so that their contents, dictum and interpretation be favorable to the communist causes and reflect adversely upon the West. Whenever this purpose can be served by telling it as it is, so much the better. However, if and when the whole truth would not do the job, half-truths, distortion and innuendos are used instead. Nor are communist strategists above resorting to pure fabrication and downright forgery. A typical early example concerning Africa was a forged document entitled "Annexe to Cabinet Paper on Policy in Africa...Secret, U.K. Eyes Only" and intended to expose the alleged British and U.S. imperialist machinations in Africa.[76] Published in 1960 first in Ghana, it was subsequently distributed throughout Africa in booklet form under the title *The Great Conspiracy Against Africa*. Forged letters, presumably exchanged between Indonesian anti-Sokarno rebel leaders and the U.S. Ambassador to Tokyo and a certain "Admiral Frost" of the U.S. Navy, were planted in Burmese and Indonesian newspapers in 1958 to bare alleged U.S. involvement in anti-Sokarno subversion in Indonesia.[77] A number of forged letters, one purportedly signed by a U.S. Navy official and admitting American bacteriological warfare preparations in Vietnam, were placed in some of India's papers.[78] Similar instances of misusing cultural diplomacy and information service on the part of various communist countries, especially the Soviet Union, have occurred in other parts of the Third World.

Supplying the materials is, of course, only one half of the work. The other half is to see to it that they be actually used, that they appear on the pages of native newspapers and periodicals and be reflected in the editorials and other opinion-forming commentaries. As a matter of course, this requires personal contact with, and assiduous cultivation of, those native publishers, editors, writers, cartoonists and other persons involved in the complex realm of the printed word who are deemed to be malleable through such an approach. As is the case in Western diplomacy, the main on-the-spot role in this respect is assigned to the press and cultural attaches of communist diplomatic missions and their personnel.[79] It falls upon them to establish fruitful relations with natives engaged in publishing and cultural activities by using whatever means may be appropriate and productive in each given case. Such activities involve, among other things, various forms of what Barghoorn calls "psychological bribery,"[80] such as asking promising subjects to dinners, receptions and banquets; getting them invited to cultural events, writers' and journalists' seminars and red-carpet tours in communist countries; arranging for translation and publication of their articles or novels and performance of their plays or compositions in one or another country of the world socialist system; recommending the most deserving collaborators for special honors and decorations; and at times even advance "leaking" of a newsworthy item to a friendly newspaperman.

Outright financial bribery also occurs. Occasionally a direct payment for a communist-sponsored article sneaked into a native newspaper is made or financial remuneration is given a member of the editorial staff who has agreed to become a communist agent. Donations of equipment for publication purposes are sometimes made, such as was the gift of 15 tons of newsprint by the Soviet Communist party to *Etumba*, the paper of the national party of Brazzaville Congo, in 1967,[81] or the outfitting of the headquarters of Mali's Union of Journalists with a rotary press and other equipment by the Union of Czechoslovak Journalists in 1961.[82] Also, substantial portions of book and newspaper editions are at times purchased with communist money as a kind of covert subsidy to cooperative newspaper or book publishers.[83]

Yet another device designed to gain influence over the press and publication business of the developing nations have been communist arrangements for the training of the Third World's journalists. As has been the case with communist educational aid in general, communist assistance in this specific field has comprised both help in developing appropriate schools and courses in the respective developing countries and provision for facilities in communist countries themselves.

Over the years, communist countries have helped in setting up schools, courses or workshops for newspapermen in a number of Asian and African countries, preparing curricula and textbooks, and sending suitable teachers. A good example of this approach has been Guinea's School of Journalism at Conakry staffed mostly by Polish and Czechoslovak journalism teachers and specialists after its establishment in 1961, and a two-month journalism course organized and taught at Kabul by Czechoslovak journalists in 1966.[84] The Czechoslovak Press Agency, ČTK, has been especially active in this respect, mainly in Africa, where it has been instrumental in the sixties in training newspapermen in Guinea, Mali, Algeria and Ghana.[85]

Training facilities provided in the communist countries themselves include mostly various courses, workshops and seminars for journalists and newspaper technicians from Africa and Asia. Organized by the press agencies or Journalists' Unions of the various communist countries, they last usually from a few weeks to six months and give their students a more or less well-rounded training in practical aspects of journalism and newspaper printing and publishing, interspersed with a potent dose of subtle communist indoctrination. Probably the best developed among these facilities is Czechoslovakia's "International School of Agency Journalism and Techniques" (*Mezinárodní škola agenturního novinářství a techniky*), established in 1961 specifically for the training of African newspapermen and claimed to be "the only school of this specialization in the world."[86] Held annually at a lovely Roztěž Castle (placed by the communist regime at the disposal of the Union of Czechoslovak Journalists), the six-month term is taught in French and English by a faculty consisting of experienced editors of the Czechoslovak Press Agency and supplemented usually by a few specialists from the press agencies of other communist countries, such as the Soviet TASS, Polish PAP and East German ADN. A total of 138 students attended the school in the first seven years of its operation (1961-67), most of them from Algeria, Morocco, Mali, Guinea, Ghana, Nigeria, Dahomey, Ethiopia, Kenya, Tanzania and Tunisia.[87]

In its turn, the Prague-based *International Organization of Journalists* (IOJ), one of the major international Communist Front organizations, has also been hard at work over the years in promoting the communist cause in the Third World. "We exerted every effort to explain to people that all roads, however hard they might be, lead to the victory of Lenin's ideas," said the IOJ's Secretary General in his report on the past activities of the organization delivered at the Seventh Congress of the IOJ held in Havana in January 1971.[88] The entire proceedings of the Congress were marked by a continuous stream of attacks on the U.S. imperialism. The main resolution of the Congress expressed solidarity with the national-liberation movement, called upon "progressive" journalists the world over to expose the aggressive plans of U.S. imperialism and declared the community of socialist countries to be the guarantee of peace and security for all the countries of the world.

Use of Other Media of Cultural Diplomacy

While educational exchanges and the utilization of mass communications media via the spoken and printed word must be viewed as the main front of communist cultural offensive, other media have by no means been neglected.

Thus an important role in communist cultural penetration of the Third World is assigned to movies. Almost invariably, cultural and other agreements between communist countries and their less developed partners provide for film "exchanges," which mean in practice that the movie houses and television screens (wherever they already exist) of the respective developing countries are supplied with communist-made films of all sorts, most of them with a more or less pronounced ideological message and a definitely anti-Western bias.[89] "In only eight months of last year," boasted *New Times* in 1969, "the Soviet Cultural Centre at Mogadishu (Somalia) gave 130 film showings attended by 90,000 people."[90] A major target for the communist film diplomacy in Latin America has been Chile.[91] Next to the Soviet

Union, Czechoslovakia has been especially active and successful in this type of "film diplomacy." From time to time, whole festivals or "weeks" of films produced by one or another communist country have been organized in various developing countries. Nor do communist countries miss one opportunity of participating in any international film festivals held in the Third World.

Although live theater and other performing arts and lecturing cannot match the popularity and versatility of the movies, the planners of communist cultural penetration do nonetheless use them throughout the Third World on quite a substantial scale. Dance groups, orchestras, choirs, puppeteers, acrobats and other troupes of performing artists from various communist countries undertake annually extensive tours through many developing nations of Asia, Africa and Latin America.[92] They also participate in the "cultural weeks" of their country that are periodically held in many areas of the Third World, usually under the aegis of the respective native "Friendship Society." Moreover, communist experts sent to developing countries in connection with economic assistance, frequently double as cultural propagandists, delivering talks on their countries, arranging photo exhibitions, etc.[93]

Since sports are rather popular among the populace of the developing nations, sportsmen from communist countries, especially soccer and basketball teams, have also been utilized a good deal for such proselytizing missions. In 1967 the idea emerged of organizing annually a soccer "Friendship Tournament" between teams from Prague, Sofia, Algiers and Tunis.[94]

The "Friendship" Societies and Other Vehicles of Cultural Penetration

As in other aspects of communist strategy, the major characteristic of communist operations in the field of international cultural relations has been the persistent effort to place them, wherever possible, on a full-fledged organizational basis, to institutionalize them and to secure thereby their continuity and permanence as well as better measure of concentration and supervision.

The central role in this organizational scheme in the developing countries belongs to the Societies for Friendship and Cultural Relations with the Soviet Union and similar such societies for "friendship" with other communist countries. By now such societies have been established in most of the countries of the Third World. With a membership recruited mostly from native communists, pro-communists and persons of anti-Western inclinations, these "friendship societies" act usually as organizers, promoters or sponsors of most of the activities and events connected with communist cultural offensive in their respective countries. They serve as hosts to the artists, sportsmen, delegations and other visitors from communist countries. They help to generate good will toward the respective communist countries by organizing exhibitions, film showings, "friendship" or "cultural" weeks and engaging in other communist-desired and communist-suggested activities described on the preceding pages. They recommend and sponsor native students for the study in communist countries. They hold occasionally contests and quizzes on the knowledge about one or another of the communist countries and reward winners with various prizes ranging from free trips to the world socialist system to books and subscriptions to communist foreign-language magazines.[95] Some of the societies for the friendship with the Soviet Union have been instrumental in arranging for Russian language courses and many of them have duly commemorated Lenin's Centenary in 1969-70 with proclamations of the "Lenin Year," appropriate talks and films, and even setting up in their quarters "Lenin Corners."[96] In some instances the friendship societies publish their own magazine, such as the Society for the Friends of Czechoslovakia in Mexico and Bolivia.[97] The headquarters of these friendship societies are, of course, in the capitals of the respective developing countries, but the larger ones have branch offices in other cities and areas. Some of them are quite huge as, for instance, the Nigerian Association for Friendship and Cultural Relations with the USSR which has 60,000 members and 160 branches.[98] All of these societies cooperate very closely with the diplomatic missions of communist countries concerned. In fact, in most instances the initiative appears to lie with the cultural officers of the respective communist country and the friendship society

serves mostly as a willing executor of communist wishes. There
have also been reported cases of communist financial subsidies
for the operations of these friendship societies.

While the main native sponsorship of communist cultural
operations rests on the shoulders of the friendship societies, their
role is by no means exclusive, for there are a number of other
organizations and institutions cooperating with them and supplementing their work. In a number of developing countries there
are more or less elaborate Soviet Cultural Centers as well as
Cultural Centers established by some of the other communist
countries.[99] There are Clubs of Listeners of one or another of the
communist radio stations broadcasting to the respective developing countries.[100] There are Clubs of the native graduates of the
Lumumba University and other communist universities, Clubs of
students of the Russian language, and in Ghana there was at one
time even a Club of the Owners of Czechoslovak Škoda
Automobiles.[101] The earlier cited 1970 *New Times* article on
"The Socialist World and the Developing Nations" mentions 223
"cultural and service institutions" (other than educational institutions) that have been built or are being built with the
assistance of socialist states in developing countries.[102]

The friendship societies located in the developing countries are
paralleled by corresponding friendship societies in the Soviet
Union and other communist countries. Again, as some of their
counterparts in the developing countries, they are set up not only
in the capital cities, but have branches in other areas as well. In
each communist country they are under the overall guidance and
supervision of a central association, such as the Association of
the Soviet Friendship Societies in Moscow, Czechoslovak
Society for International Relations in Prague and other similar
central committees, institutions or associations. In the Soviet
Union they are also grouped along continental lines. For
instance, there has existed since 1959 a Soviet Association for
Friendship with the Peoples of Africa.

As for their functions, the friendship societies operating within
the communist countries attend essentially to the type of work
similar to that performed by their counterparts in the Third
World. However, since cultural relations between the communist
and Third World countries flow mostly in the direction from the

former to the latter, cultural operations of the friendship societies in communist countries are rather limited and, at least from the communist viewpoint, less important than those of the friendship societies operating in the developing nations. It seems that their principal mission is to stay in contact with their counterparts in the Third World, to sponsor occasional performances of native dance and folklore ensembles, participate in organizing from time to time a "day of culture" or "week of culture" of the developing country or region concerned, and to commemorate such country's liberation and birthday.

Communist Cultural Flattery

In so doing, the friendship societies share with other communist agencies involved in foreign policy operations in general and in international cultural relations in particular in what is probably the most potent technique of cultural diplomacy, namely, cultural flattery. Just as a laudatory appreciation of a person's character or achievements, whether deserved or not, usually generates friendly feelings toward the flatterer, so is the praise of a nation's cultural attainments bound to foster positive responses on the part of the praised nation and its nationals.

As mentioned earlier, both the Soviet and other communist leaders and their lieutenants and helpers have been quite prolific in the application of this laudatory technique which has assumed many forms.

Perhaps the most conspicuous and most concentrated manifestations of cultural flattery have been the aforementioned "weeks of culture," sometimes dubbed also as "weeks of friendship" of one or another developing nation or regional grouping of such nations. A typical "week of culture" consists of a number of events intended to honor the cultural and other achievements, past and present, of the Third World country or region so honored. There is usually an exhibition of native art and folkfore, performances by native dancers, singers or other artists, films and lectures on the country or region concerned, etc. The radio, T.V. and the press of the honoring country join in with pertinent programs and articles. High-level officials of the communist host country make ostentatious appearances and deliver flattering talks at the major events of the "cultural week." The attending representatives of the developing country are given the utmost in red-carpet treatment.

The national liberation anniversaries of Asian, African and Latin American countries offer another suitable opportunity for flattery. Besides warm official messages of congratulations sent to the heads and prime ministers of the developing nations, communist countries never fail to commemorate such anniversaries quite prominently in their daily press, on radio and television, and not infrequently also with special theater or other performances in honor of the respective Third World country. The customary receptions held on such occasions by the heads of the diplomatic missions of the celebrating countries are invariably attended by communist VIP's who usually exceed by far, both in rank and number, the officials despatched to similar receptions of Western embassies. Similarly, communist countries take pains to celebrate annually May Twenty-Fifth as the Day of the Liberation of Africa and use it both to extoll Soviet and communist contributions to Africa's liberation and to gratify Africa's self-image.[103]

Other situations that lend themselves admirably for this purpose are, of course, the frequent visits that the leaders and other high-ranking or prominent personalities of the Third World pay to the Soviet Union and other communist countries. Besides being "dined and wined" with the usual communist lavishness and made recipients of high decorations commensurate to their official status, they are told repeatedly, privately and publicly, of their hosts' high appreciation of their country's culture, history and contributions to mankind's progress. The honors heaped on the most prominent visitors include, in particular, awards of honorary Doctor's degrees by various communist universities. Nkrumah of Ghana, Ben Bella of Algeria, Sekou Toure of Guinea, Haile Selassie of Ethiopia and Nasser of Egypt are just a few examples of the Third World leaders so honored.

Much the same kind of cultural flattery is carried by communist leaders and high-level officials directly into the developing countries themselves. Over the years, top Soviet and other communist leaders from Khruschev, Brezhnev and Chou En-lai to Tito, Novotný and Zhivkov have toured an ever growing number of developing nations of the Middle East, Asia, Africa and, more recently, Latin America. The hallmark of all such visits has been a steady stream of praise for the host countries, their culture, history and civilization. Typical of such tactics has been, for instance, the much advertised tour undertaken by China's Chou En-lai to ten African countries in 1963. Next to anti-colonialist tirades and assurances of China's eternal friendship and support, the Chinese Premier's speeches were interspersed with adulatory remarks on Africa's "brilliant ancient civilization," "ancient cultural traditions," glorious history, creation of "a new human civilization" and the like.[104]

Yet another way of cultivating the ego of the developing nations used extensively by communist countries has been to display communist interest in the Third World's culture, history, art and ethnography through research and publications in these fields. Here again the planners of communist strategy vis-a-vis the developing nations have realized better than their Western competitors that few things tickle the pride of a country more, especially a newly emerging one, than seeing its poetry and other literary products translated into foreign languages, studies being made and published by foreign researchers about its history and culture, and the public of other nations being acquainted with its achievements. Acting upon this realization, communist publishing houses have been turning out a steady stream of books, monographs and magazines on the affairs of the Third World. Not only the Soviet Union, but most of the other communist countries have by now established various institutes of African, Asian, Middle Eastern and Latin American studies, usually within the prestigious framework of their Academies of Sciences. They have expanded or newly added university curricula in such studies and created additional departments or chairs for this purpose. Besides including more and more articles on the Third World in the topic-oriented general and specialized magazines, they have begun publishing regular journals earmarked specifically for the discussion of questions of particular continents, subcontinents or major areas of the Third World. "Mention should be made of the great interest our periodical press shows in Africa," said the Director of Soviet Africa Institute and President of the Soviet Association for Friendship with the Peoples of Africa, when interviewed by *New Times* on the occasion of Africa Freedom Day on May 25, 1969.[105] In announcing the latest Soviet addition to these magazines, *Latinskaia Amerika* (Latin America), its editor-in-chief stressed that it will give "considerable space to cultural events and to the literature, the fine arts and architecture of Latin America."[106] Also, communist countries have been busy organizing from time to time ambitious conferences of Africanologists, Orientalists, and other such groups and placing topics relative to the Third World on the agenda of international scholarly congresses. Thus A. Guber, chairman of the Soviet Preparatory Committee for the International Congress of Historians held in Moscow in August 1970, was quick to claim credit for selecting topics pertinent to the Third World. "The choice of problems relating to the history of the African, Asian and Latin American countries shows that the old conception of the history of mankind as being confined solely to the history of Europe and the Afro-Asian territories contiguous with it has definitely been discarded."[107] Much in the same vein, the new (3rd) edition of the *Bol'shaia Sovetskaia Entsiklopedia* (The Large Soviet Encyclopedia) promises a considerably more extensive coverage of Asia, Africa and Latin America than its first two editions.[108]

Naturally, much of the research and publishing on the developing countries is designed primarily to equip the communists themselves with the information and knowledge of the conditions prevalent in various parts of the Third World so that they may be in a better position to carry out communist strategy. All the same, this outpouring of publications on the developing countries of Asia, Africa and Latin America, especially those dealing with their culture, history and ethnography, is well suited to take care of the cultural-flattery mission as well. After all, whatever may be the reasons, it does attest to the strong interest of communist countries in the Third World, which in itself tends to be viewed in the target countries as a form of appreciation.

In order to make the communist interest appear all the more shining, it is contrasted with the lack of interest in, or outright disrespect for, the Third World culture allegedly displayed by the United States and the West. "The Western states mock our

[Egyptian and Chinese] backwardness and boast of their civilization," asserted Chou En-lai during his official visit to Cairo in 1963, "but the Western civilization of the modern age has been achieved to a large extent at the expense of the Afro-Asian countries."[109] Not only do Western imperialists hold native culture of the Third World in contempt, the communists claim, but they are intent upon corrupting and destroying it, "substituting for cherished folk values 'the decadence of Hollywood.'"[110]

Culture and Politics

In the light of the above-discussed dicta that constitute the essence of the communist theory of cultural relations, the overwhelmingly political motivation of communist cultural diplomacy vis-a-vis the Third World is self-evident and needs little further substantiation. Indeed, as one Western student of communist strategy has noted, "cultural assets of the Soviets have been mobilized to make up for the eclipse of Marxist-Leninist ideology...culture as a substitute for ideology is no less of a tool in the strategy of subversion...and can be used to prepare for conquest by other means..."[111] Just as *l'art-pour-l'art* is officially banned as a criterion for all forms of art throughout the world socialist system, so do communist strategists find little use for the slogan of culture-for-culture's sake in their cultural inroads into Asia, Africa or Latin America. Rather, it is culture-for-politics' sake all the way. In communist hands, culture has been made to serve literally as the handmaiden of politics and communist cultural assistance to the developing countries has become a vehicle of "proletarian internationalism." This politicization of cultural relations has been documented time and again by actual operations.

As befits the importance of the aid to education among the devices of communist cultural diplomacy vis-a-vis the developing countries, communist political motivations behind it should be explored first. "Calling any education 'apolitical' or 'nonpolitical' is a bourgeois hypocrisy and nothing but a fraud upon the masses," Lenin once said.[112] Following their Master's precept, Lenin's presentday heirs have missed no opportunity to squeeze out whatever political dividends they can from their aid to the Third World's education.

Their prime target has been, of course, the many thousands of Third World students invited to study in the Soviet Union and other communist countries. The process of politicization begins right at the recruitment stage, for the foremost criterion by which communist selectors are guided has been the applicants' assumed susceptibility to communist influence.[113] Even though the pertinent cultural agreements do authorize the governments of the developing countries in question to recommend applicants for the student quotas assigned them, communist admission authorities have the final word on the matter.[114] As for the vacancies outside of the agreed quotas, there is no problem since suitable applicants are recommended, after careful screening, by various communist Front organizations, native communist leaders, and communist diplomatic and other missions in the respective developing countries. Native politicians of pro-communist leanings are also allowed to share in the selection as this tends to enhance their stature at home and makes them even more indebted to their communist benefactors. A case of this kind that attracted international attention was that of Kenya's Oginga Odinga. After a trip to Moscow and Peking in 1961 Odinga publicly boasted (probably exaggerating quite a bit) that he had at his disposal 2,000 scholarships proferred by the Soviet Union.[115] In any case, he did send a good number of pro-communist Kenyans to study in communist countries in the early and middle sixties.[116]

Another way of finding malleable candidates has been to use recruiters from among the Third World students already studying at communist institutions. Furnished with funds, they are occasionally sent back to their home countries "ostensibly on vacations but actually to recruit 'susceptible' fellow-nationals."[117] Also, communist agents have been reported recruiting among the Third World students who got into trouble in their studies at West European universities. The East Germans and (somewhat less) the Czechs appear to have been especially busy in this respect, seeking out the Asian and African students who failed in their examinations at West German universities.[118] Dismayed by their failure, such students are considered especially prone to listen to communist agents telling them that their failing was due to Western racial bias rather than the students' lack of ability and preparation, and that the color of their skin did not matter in communist countries.

Once they are enrolled at communist universities, the Third World students are exposed to a continuous and many-faceted process of political indoctrination incorporated, more or less subtly, into their prescribed study curricula. As Khrushchev said in his speech opening Moscow's People's Friendship University in 1960: "Of course we shall not impose our views, our ideology, on any of the students.... [though I] am profoundly convinced that the Marxist-Leninist ideology is the most advanced ideology. [But] if any of you arrives at the conclusion that the ideology suits you we shall not take offense."[119] Commemorating the tenth anniversary of the University of 17th November, the author of the earlier-mentioned 1971 article in the Czechoslovak paper *Zemědělské noviny* admitted quite frankly: "We want also to persuade them [i.e., the Third World students] of the correctness of our cause, our socialist order. We want to turn them into educated experts and conscious progressive people."[120]

The first preparatory year, designed to teach new students the language of the host country and acquaint them with its life, lends itself especially well for purposes of indoctrination. Such favorite communist topics and themes as the superior virtues of "scientific socialism," infallible precepts of Marxism-Leninism, devastating critiques of capitalism, imperialism and neo-colonialism coupled with slanted communist interpretation of recent developments at home and abroad, are woven in a variety of forms into the instruction materials and lecturers' presentations. After the preparatory year, the indoctrination tends to lessen for students going into engineering, technical and medical studies, for most of their time henceforth is necessarily consumed by the exacting subjects of their specialization, which are by their very nature ill-suited for incursions of Marxism-Leninism. To be sure, their communist advisers do encourage such students to "enrich" their professional study programs by registering for some additional courses with Marxist-Leninist content; and many of them evidently do so, often for fear that a refusal might have detrimental effect on their further progress and grades. But except for this, the bulk of their studies seems to be relatively indoctrination-free.

Just the opposite is true, however, of students choosing social sciences, as these are precisely the areas of knowledge most affected and most distorted by Marxism-Leninism in all of the communist countries. Since communist professors and lecturers must deal with social sciences strictly from the Marxist-Leninist viewpoint as the only correct approach, the Third World students enrolled in social sciences (as well as law studies) never actually cease being fed heavy doses of Marxism-Leninism throughout all the years of their studies at communist institutions of higher learning.

Nor is indoctrination limited to the classroom. As bared by both official communist sources and the students themselves, the host regimes do their best to smuggle bits of indoctrination into the students' extra-curricular "cultural life" and leisure as well. Student and youth associations of the host countries organize meetings and forums with foreign students at which communist speakers seek to acquaint them with, and gain their support for, communist standpoints on various international developments.[121] "Committees of Friendship with Foreign Students" have been established at communist universities to see to it that foreign students meet the right kind of people.[122] Not infrequently, foreign students are paired with dependable communist students as room mates. Students of various countries or major regions of the Third World have been organized in each communist country into clubs, associations or federations which serve, under vigilant eyes of communist supervisors, not only as additional media of indoctrination and control, but are also utilized for manifestations and demonstrations in favor of communist-sponsored causes. Thus the various associations of African, Asian, Middle Eastern and, more recently, even Latin American students in the Soviet Union, Czechoslovakia, East Germany and other communist countries have been time and again called upon or encouraged to do such things as:

to demonstrate their "solidarity with the advancing democratic forces in Sudan" (prior to General Numeiry's reprisals against the Sudanese Communists for their participation in the 1971 coup);

to condemn the Iraqi regime (deemed at the time as reactionary) of aggression against the Kurds;

to protest in front of the U.S. and British embassies the Israeli aggression against the Arab countries;

to call for the liquidation of American foreign military bases and protest the U.S. aggression in Vietnam, Laos and Cambodia;

to adopt resolutions against various alleged imperialist transgressions by the U.S. and its associates; etc., etc.[123]

Perhaps the most blatant illustration of such communist-demanded "political activism" on the part of such associations in recent years has been the declaration adopted by the "Third Congress of the Federation of Latin-American Students in Czechoslovakia" which revoked the protest made by the Federation in 1968 against the Soviet invasion of Czechoslovakia, alleging that the said protest "harmed the cause of socialism and the struggle against imperialism and the world reaction."[124] Nor are the communist strategists loath to recruit some of the Third World students studying in communist countries for subversive purposes.[125]

Politics lurks also behind communist educational ventures within the developing countries. As mentioned earlier, all citizens of communist countries sent to the Third World, whatever their primary mission, must serve also as propagators of the communist way of life and culture. But those sent as professors and teachers are in an especially advantageous position in this respect. Provided with captive audiences consisting mostly of young people from whose ranks future leaders of the developing nations will most likely emerge, they are expected by their regimes to take the fullest advantage of such unexcelled opportunities for proselytizing in favor of communism. A classic illustration of just such proselytizing was the Lumumba Institute in Kenya built with Soviet money and staffed by Soviet instructors. Designed to train the officials of KANU, Kenya's ruling party, the Institute became the hotbed of communist and pro-communist political activism so that it had to be closed two years later.[126] Even instructors in such a traditionally apolitical field as sports have been used for political indoctrination purposes. A typical case of this kind was reported in 1967 from Tunisia where the Chinese table-tennis instructors were caught mixing heavy doses of Maoism into their ping-pong lessons.[127]

Political motivation is clearly apparent also in the other aspects of communist cultural diplomacy vis-a-vis the Third World. No special substantiation is certainly necessary to prove the self-evident fact that politics is the guiding rationale behind the massive communist broadcasting to Asia, the Middle East, Africa and Latin America. The same holds true of the services of communist press bureaus offered mostly free to the Third World newspapers and newsgathering agencies.[128] And it applies also to facilities provided in several communist countries, free of charge, for the training of Asian and African journalists as well as the huge quantities of books, brochures and periodicals distributed, mostly free or below cost, among the people of developing nations. All these and other communist operations represent annually a substantial outlay of personnel, materials and money, for the cost of these operations to communist countries exceeds by far whatever material benefits they might expect in return. Nor do the communist countries, as said earlier, obtain from their cultural "exchanges" with the developing countries anything that would come anywhere near to being an equivalent in cultural values. Hence, unless one is willing to credit the communists with sheer altruism, political considerations must be singled out as the basic rationale of the communist cultural diplomacy vis-a-vis the Third World.

This is borne out also by both the geographical pattern and the timing of communist cultural operations.

If cultural considerations were really fundamental to communist cultural relations, one would expect that their magnitude and intensity would be correlated somewhat to the cultural values with which the respective developing countries can reciprocate. But this is not the case. As mentioned earlier, most of the Third World participants in cultural "exchanges" with communist countries have very little *quid-pro-quo,* be it in science, education, literature, creative or performing art, or other segments of culture. Nor are the communist cultural programs governed at all by the principle that communist aid be larger when its Third World recipient has more of its own culture to offer in return. For instance, communist cultural offerings to many countries of

Africa are more substantial, often considerably so, than those to the various countries of South America, even though most of the latter possess more cultural values with which to respond than most of the African beneficiaries of communist cultural assistance. About the only Third World country where the above-mentioned principle seems *prima facie* to operate is India which, after all, has a good deal to offer in some aspects of culture. However, even in this case the magnitude of the communist cultural offensive is due to India's high place in communist strategic designs rather than to her cultural assets.

The timing of communist cultural offerings to the developing nations and their subsequent vicissitudes are just as revelative of its overwhelming political motivation. Until Soviet Russia became aware of the new possibilities and ways of advancing the cause of communism in the Third World in the middle fifties, she and her communist associates displayed very little interest in cultural exchanges with the developing nations. Even thereafter, the decision to offer cultural assistance to a given country at a given time appears invariably to have been guided by the communist judgment regarding the respective country's susceptibility to communist influence. Thus, as had been the case with communist extension of economic aid, the various countries of the Arab Middle East emerged as major targets of communist cultural generosity not because of a sudden communist awareness of Arab culture or Arab cultural needs, but because the flare-up of Israeli-Arab hostilities and the rampant Arab anti-Westernism created propitious conditions for communist penetration of the area. Similarly, communist cultural activities in India were greatly stepped up in the Khrushchev era when the Soviet leaders undertook a massive endeavor to lure India into a Soviet-style non-alignment. Indonesia of the Sokarno regime registered a substantial intensification of communist cultural activities which subsided again when the country had to be written off, at least temporarily, as a promising objective of communist wooing under Suharto. In the same vein, communist cultural relations with the countries of Africa reveal a pattern of substantial fluctuations, increasing and decreasing in intensity in proportion to what communist strategists thought the prospects for the attainment of communist political objectives to be in a given country at a given time. Such have been, for instance, the cases of Ghana, Guinea, Tanzania, Kenya, and, more recently, Nigeria which emerged suddenly as a major target of surging communist "cultural" interest when the Nigerian regime became angry with the West over the Biafran rebellion.

Finally, a classical communist (though in this case mainly Castroite) utilization of culture for political purposes has been the "Tricontinental Cultural Congress" held at Havana on January 4-12, 1968, on the general theme "Colonialism and Neo-colonialism in the Cultural Development of the Peoples" (*Colonialismo y neo-colonialismo en el desarrollo cultural de los pueblos*). Carefully prepared by Cuban communists and attended by 500 delegates from 70 countries and covered by 110 journalists from 40 countries, the Congress became a handy platform for a stream of wanton attacks on "North American imperialism" and "the U.S. policy of cultural colonization."[129] The Declaration adopted by the Congress praised Che Guevara as a "supreme example of a contemporary revolutionary intellectual" and called upon the "writers, scientists, artists and professors, workers and students, peasants, people in general" to follow "the heroic example of Che" and to resort to "armed struggle" and risk death "if it is necessary to make a new and better life possible." Indeed, as *Este y Oeste* correctly points out, the "Cultural" Congress was characterized by "an almost total absence of themes related to the promotion of culture..."[130] Much the same pattern prevailed at the earlier-mentioned Seventh Congress of the *International Organization of Journalists* held in Havana in January 1971.[131]

The Pros and Cons of the Communist Cultural Diplomacy

As has been the case with other devices of communist strategy, communist cultural diplomacy could take advantage of certain factors conducive to its success. At the same time, however, it has run into a number of difficulties and problems.

The Pros

One important advantage that recent history bestowed upon

communist cultural diplomacy in the Third World stems from the fact that Western culture has been the culture of former colonizers. Although culture *per se* had hardly anything to do with the imposition of colonialism (and its predominantly liberal ethos actually helped to prepare the ground for eventual de-colonization in the end), its past association with the one-time colonial masters affords facilities for anti-Western innuendos and insinuations of nefarious political intentions. Since the presentday communist countries have mostly had no part in the colonization of what today constitutes the Third World, the bearers of communist cultural gifts are in a more advantageous position in that respect.

Nor is communist cultural diplomacy inconvenienced by the kind of a racial problem that damages some aspects of the U.S. cultural relations with the Third World, especially its black portion. As shown below, racial bias is by no means absent from the countries of the world socialist system and they have registered some adverse publicity on that account, mainly because of their populace's attitude toward the Third World's non-white students studying at communist institutions of higher learning. But what Gunnar Myrdal called the "American dilemma" is so much larger and so much more publicized throughout the world that the communist bias occasionally displayed toward black students dwindles by comparison.

Another advantage that communist cultural diplomacy has over similar Western endeavors lies in the realm of finances. Since few, if any, ventures of cultural relations with developing nations are financially self-supporting, they must be subsidized. At the first glance, this would seem to favor the United States and its Western partners who are richer than their communist competitors. Indeed, the West's expenditures on cultural aid to the Third World are larger than those of the world socialist system. But there are at least two aspects of financing where the communist countries have an important advantage. First, while Western financial support generally comes from a variety of more or less independent sources, public, semi-public and private, contributions from each communist country are determined by and directed from one all-powerful center. Second, whereas Western contributions are subject to everpresent public scrutiny and criticism, no such considerations apply to communist appropriations and disbursements. Thus, communist strategists are clearly in a better position than their Western counterparts in securing the needed resources even when their purpose has little to do with genuine cultural activities, and in their ability to spend them on such operations as would return the best political dividend irrespective of their cultural worth. A very good illustration of the kind of difficulty plaguing the democratic West but not the communist East in the matter of financing political-cultural activities was provided a few years ago by the quandary of the U.S. National Student Association after it had been revealed that the Association was receiving funds from the C.I.A. For reasons too obvious to be recounted, such a situation would be unthinkable in Soviet Russia or any other communist country where overt and covert government subsidization of such undertakings is a permanent rule of the game.[132]

Yet another factor favoring communist cultural penetration of the Third World is related to the kind of cultural exports to the developing nations. As suggested earlier in this chapter, the cultural goods sent by communist countries are mostly products of socialist realism and as such are more likely to be understood by, and appeal to, the ordinary people of the Third World than the more modernistic and usually more sophisticated cultural offerings of the West.

In a somewhat similar vein, the fundamental difference in the operational pattern of the Western and communist political systems gives communist strategists a distinct edge in their utilization of educational aid for political purposes. The Third World students studying at the U.S. and other Western institutions of higher learning have to meet the standards prescribed for Western students. To lower these standards for students from developing nations in order to make allowance for their inadequate preparation would hardly be feasible in a Western democratic system even if the government would want to do it. As a result, quite a number of Third World students eager to study in the West either do not qualify for admission or fail to complete their studies. Understandably, the disappointed students become no friends of the West.

On the other hand, communist political systems are in a better position to cope with this delicate problem. Enjoying the monopoly of decision-making in all matters of education, the ruling oligarchies of communist states can and do manipulate educational criteria to accomplish the desired political objectives. Naturally, communist leniency toward the Third World students cannot be pushed too far, for that would in the end depreciate even the political value of communist educational aid. However, as documented from various sources, standards for the Third World students are set generally lower than those applicable to native students; and the tendency is to pass as many of the former as possible, especially at special institutions for foreign students, such as the Lumumba University of Moscow and the 17th of November University of Prague. Thus the occurrences of student disgruntlement *because of failures* in their studies are lesser in communist countries than in the West.

Finally, a political advantage of sorts over the West accrues to the Soviet Union and the other communist countries from the lack of temptation on the part of the Third World students to settle in the world socialist system after having completed their studies there. As a result, unlike the West, communist countries can by no means be held responsible for any "brain drain" from the developing countries. On the contrary, they can and do point an accusing finger at the West and, in particular, the United States and blame them for having "imported" thousands of specialists from the developing nations and thus "poaching on the intellectual potential of the Third World."[133]

The Cons

As has been the case with communist economic aid, an important factor impeding communists in the pursuit of their political objectives through cultural diplomacy has been the recipient countries' growing realization of communist motives. This has occurred, in particular, in connection with communist aid to education. Even though the developing nations have been appreciative of communist assistance in this field, above all the educational facilities provided for their students in communist countries, they have become in due course aware of the communist use of education for purposes of political indoctrination. As a matter of fact, reports of the Third World students who have studied in communist countries are replete with complaints about heavy doses and over-doses of Marxist-Leninist indoctrination.[134] Quite a number of students who have cut short their studies in communist countries have listed excessive indoctrination among the reasons why they left.[135] "We don't need fanatical propagandists here," Guinea's Sekou Toure was reported to have said when recalling Guinean students from Moscow in 1962.[136] Undoubtedly, some of the students' complaints about indoctrination have been exaggerated. But their substance appears to be well founded and in accordance with the communists' avowed objective of influencing their student guests in favor of Marxism-Leninism.

Resentment over political indoctrination built into the communist cultural diplomacy, especially its educational component, is further compounded by the gap between the rosy propaganda about cultural freedoms allegedly enjoyed in communist countries and the stark reality of communist cultural and political repression. A visitor to a communist country who spends there only a few days or at most a few weeks, stays at hotels reserved for foreigners and is shown the best the host country has to offer, can be easily made to miss the seamier sides of life under communist rule and leave with an altogether distorted picture of the situation. That is true, in particular, of official guests — writers, journalists, educators or student representatives — given the well-known communist red-carpet treatment. But with foreign students it is different. Their sojourn in communist countries extends to months and years. In due time, most of them learn the language of the host country. They live in student dormitories, eat in student cafeterias, take sometimes even part in the summer work brigades. In this way most of them end by becoming well acquainted with everyday life, the prevalent political climate and conditions in the realm of culture and education as they really are.

The results of this prolonged exposure of the Third World students to the unadorned facts of communist life have been rather disappointing from the communist viewpoint. As borne out by a wealth of evidence and corroborated implicitly by occasional communist statements, it does not take foreign students too long to become aware of the limitations imposed upon political, cultural, and other freedoms by the regimes of their host countries.[137] They have also been quick to note the more or less subtle surveillance over their own activities, including even censorship of their correspondence, restrictions of their movements, and occasional "doctoring" of their radio sets so as to curtail listening to non-communist broadcasts. They have been dismayed by the unavailability of Western noncommunist newspapers and books, including even textbooks other than those approved by their communist teachers. Nor has it escaped their attention that so many citizens of their host countries appeared to be anything but enthusiastic about the system under which they were living and that there was little love left for the Russians in all the other countries of the world socialist system.

Added to the resentment over too much indoctrination and the awareness of the repressive nature of communist systems as factors hampering communist endeavors must be the coolness and often downright hostility toward the Third World students on the part of the local populace as well as the native students. As reported by many of the Third World students, especially Africans, who have studied in communist countries, they are often looked upon by the man-in-the-street as strange and deeply alien characters free-loading at his expense, "eating out" his country and enjoying undeservedly all sorts of privileges.[138] They have experienced ostracism, social rebuffs, humiliations and insults, especially when trying to socialize with local girls. There have been a number of instances of African students being beaten up because of their real or alleged relations with the opposite sex and the girls willing to go out with them have been warned, threatened and vilified.[139] Claiming racial discrimination, several hundreds of African students have time and again responded by cutting short their studies in communist countries and leaving either for home or the West. Collective exoduses of this sort have taken place, for instances, from Soviet Russia in 1963 and 1965, Bulgaria in 1963 and 1965, China and Czechoslovakia in 1962. Moreover, individual departures blamed on racial bias have been occurring fairly regularly.

The Third World students have also lodged over the years

good many protests and resorted to even a number of sitdown strikes and demonstrations against what they considered to be racial prejudice, phenomena of "apartheid" and other iniquities. The largest of these demonstrations have been the two that took place in Moscow in December 1963 and in Sofia in February 1963. The Moscow demonstration, triggered mainly by the African students' conviction that a fellow Ghanaian student was murdered by a Russian for wishing to marry a Russian girl, was staged at the Red Square by some 500 angry Africans swarming through police road blocks and carrying placards with inscriptions such as "Stop Killing Africans" or "Moscow, a Second Alabama."[140] The Sofia demonstration, brought about by the Bulgarian regime's ban of an autonomous African student organization and other student complaints, involved some 200 African students who battled the Bulgarian police on Sofia's Lenin Boulevard and suffered a number of injuries and arrests.[141] Lesser demonstrations for similar reasons occurred in China in 1962 (involving Cameroonian students) and in Czechoslovakia in 1963.[142]

Again, as in the case of student complaints about excessive indoctrination, the overall picture is not as bad as claimed by the foreign students complaining of discrimination and racial prejudice. Moreover, communist regimes involved have shown grave concern in the matter and have striven to remove the causes of friction and misunderstanding. While denying that there has been racial discrimination, they have publicly condemned those insulting foreign students and initiated prosecution of those responsible for assaults on them. In a futile attempt to find a convenient scapegoat, the Soviet regime chose in 1965 and again in 1966 to blame the students' discontent on United States diplomats, alleging that they have been conducting an anti-Soviet campaign among the African students in Moscow and inducing them to leave Soviet Russia for the West. The United States cultural attache in Moscow, Norris D. Garnet, was expelled from Russia on the basis of such allegations and two other members of the U.S. Embassy were similarly attacked by a Soviet paper in 1966.[143] Nonetheless, communist rulers have found it impossible to overcome their subjects' overwhelmingly negative attitude toward the presence of the Third World students, an attitude caused not merely by a residual prejudice of the common man against people of different race and customs, but also, especially in the case of the East Europeans, by the populace's disagreement with their rulers' political motivations behind the educational aid.

Yet another factor contributing to the unhappiness of the Third World students stationed in some of the communist countries stems simply from the climate and the overall living conditions that differ so much from those of Africa, the Middle East and Southeast Asia, the areas supplying the bulk of the Third World students studying in communist countries. Most of these communist countries are situated in a geographical location where winters are quite frigid and thus hard on students coming from much warmer parts of the world. The clothing they bring with them is not suited for such a harsh climate and the allowance the students receive as a supplement to their scholarships to buy winter clothing is insufficient to meet their needs. The food they are served is altogether different from what they have been accustomed to and the daily diet is mostly dull and repetitive, especially in Soviet Russia. The living quarters assigned the students are usually quite crowded. These may be considered as trivial matters. But complaints about them do abound in the students' reports and petitions. Thus the unfamiliar and adverse living conditions in their turn tend to weaken the intended political impact of communist educational aid.

As in most other aspects of communist strategy vis-a-vis the developing nations, the effectiveness of communist cultural diplomacy has suffered also in recent years because of the Sino-Soviet conflict. While being virtually at one in the assessment of the role of cultural diplomacy in communist strategy and employing similar methods of operations, the two communist giants have used their cultural relations with the Third World not only to enhance their own cultural image and to denigrate Western culture, but also to snipe at one another. Thus each of the Third World student groups studying in Soviet Russia and Communist China have been served with a somewhat different version of Marxism-Leninism and made to understand that the other version is either a dogmatist or revisionist distortion. Proceedings of communist-controlled international cultural organizations have been marred by mutual Sino-Soviet re-criminations. Some of them, such as the Afro-Asian Writers' Bureau, divided into separate pro-Soviet and pro-Chinese units and began to condemn each other of "splittism."[144] Events held in communist China and Soviet Russia to honor developing nations, such as the customary Africa Liberation Days, have been utilized for mutual accusations and counter-accusations of bad faith with the Third World.

Finally, communist efforts to score politically through the use of cultural means are sometimes undone by revelations that cultural relations have been used to cover up espionage and subversion. Indeed, in a number of instances, cultural attaches and information officers of communist embassies in several countries of the Third World have been unmasked as working at least part time for intelligence services. So have been the representatives of communist press agencies, such as Soviet Russia's *Novosti*, Communist China's *New China News Agency*, Czechoslovakia's *ČTK*, as well as representatives of communist film services and even members of communist cultural delega-tions. Some of them have been caught red-handed at these "cultural" activities, others have been implicated and their operations exposed by Soviet and other communist defectors, such as Aleksandr Kaznachaev, Vladimir Petrov, Yuri Rastvo-rov, who gave ample testimony about the frequency of such subversive uses of communist diplomacy.[145] Also, as bared by reports of the Third World students who have studied in Soviet Russia and other communist countries, there have been recurrent communist attempts to entice some of them to become commu-nist agents.[146] Similar endeavors have been noted at some of the cultural centers and educational facilities provided with commu-nist help in the developing countries. The most noteworthy examples of this abuse have been the earlier mentioned Lu-mumba Institute of Kenya and Kwame Nkrumah Institute of Economic and Political Science of Ghana, commonly known as the Winneba Ideological Institute.[147]

The Balance Sheet

What have been the overall results of communist cultural

diplomacy vis-a-vis the Third World to-date? What, if anything, have the communists gained politically in Asia, the Middle East, Africa and Latin America from their manifold operations in the realm of education and culture?

Again, as has been the case with their efforts in the economic field, communist strategists invariably use cultural instruments in conjunction with other strategic devices. Hence, what has been said in the preceding chapter about the impossibility of determining to what extent, if any, a communist success or failure is attributable to economic aid applies to the communist use of culture as well. While an accurate overall assessment of the amount of influence secured through communist cultural diplomacy *per se* cannot be made, one can at least venture to draw a tentative list of communist gains and losses resulting from main communist cultural operations.

To begin with, communist cultural offerings could not but break the virtual monopoly that Western culture enjoyed throughout the Third World. Just as the communist economic aid provided the Third World with an alternative source on which to draw, so did communist cultural assistance enable the developing nations to decrease their cultural dependence on the West and make them thereby more susceptible to communist influence. Thus far, however, the degree of communist cultural penetration of the Third World has not been very impressive. Although the monopoly of Western culture influence has been broken, Western culture still appears to be predominant throughout the Third World, and this even in countries that have been stridently anti-Western and have been hailed by the Soviet Union as having embarked, or about to embark, onto the Soviet-recommended non-capitalist and national-democratic path.

A substantial amount of good will toward the communist countries has resulted from the prolific communist use of cultural flattery described earlier in this chapter. "It seems likely," holds Barghoorn, "that the communists reap their richest rewards, particularly in terms of the good will of foreign intellectuals, artists and scientists, not by display of their own achievements but by courteous and sympathetic appreciation of those of other countries."[148]

The continuous barrage of anti-Western political and cultural propaganda aimed at Asia, Africa and Latin America via the spoken and printed word has also attained a measure of success in generating or strengthening attitudes unfavorable to the West and slanted in favor of communist-sponsored causes and interpretations. So have the generous services of communist press bureaus flooding the editorial offices of the Third World periodicals and radio and television newscasters with materials screened and edited by communist censors. In this respect, communist endeavors have been well served by the facilities provided for the training of the Third World's journalists, such as the above mentioned International School of Agency Journalism and Techniques in Prague.

Nor could the communist purpose of gaining sympathies among the populace of the developing countries fail to be furthered by such ventures as the assiduous participation of communist countries in fairs, exhibitions, film festivals, "cultural weeks," sport shows and other such events held in various parts of the Third World. With plenty of money to spend on such things, communist countries tend to perform rather well in these respects, leaving native audiences usually with a very good impression of communist achievements in the fields concerned and enhancing thus the communist image. So do most of the "Friendship Societies" whose diligent activities are calculated to make communist cultural presence in the countries of the Third World a year-round phenomenon.

One aspect of communist diplomacy that is especially difficult to evaluate in terms of its political yields is communist aid to the Third World's education. As noted earlier, there is a wealth of evidence indicating that communist educational offerings to developing countries have not had the impact desired and anticipated by communist donors. That has been true, above all, of students who have attended schools in communist countries. Many hundreds of these students are known to have shed whatever beliefs they may have had in the superiority of the communist system and way of life. Even those of them who have remained grateful for the educational opportunity given them by their communist hosts have returned to their native countries as anything but ardent supporters of communism.

On the other hand, some of the students, though probably not very many, have lived up to communist expectations, becoming friends of communist countries and willing to repay their debt by working for communist-backed causes. Whether most of them have been guided by a genuine conviction about the suitability and desirability of the communist system for their own countries or by a hope that a pro-communist stand would be good for their political fortunes, is impossible to say.

However, the great unknown in this respect has been the attitude of those of the students who have neither been openly critical of communism nor have become active in a communist or pro-communist way. How many of this "silent majority" of the Third World recipients of communist education has their prolonged exposure to the communist reality gained for communism or pro-communism, and how many has it influenced in just the opposite direction? While a fully documented answer to this query cannot be given, it is the conviction of this writer, based on circumstantial evidence gathered in this chapter, that this "silent majority" falls overwhelmingly into the latter category.[149] If the students went to the world socialist system, as most of them undoubtedly did, with a sympathetic mood toward their communist host regimes, most of them have come out with their earlier sympathies more or less cooled. If they went there mentally uncommitted or doubtful, they have most probably come out even more uncommitted to the communist cause.

Thus it would seem that, whatever political gains communist cultural diplomacy may have registered in the developing countries, they have been rather modest. The Third World has certainly become much better acquainted with, and more appreciative of, the culture of the various communist countries than had been the case only fifteen years or so ago. But the political dividends collected thus far on communist cultural investments have most probably been more meager than the communist strategists had hoped.

Footnotes for Chapter XII

[1] Robert Blum, ed., *Cultural Affairs and Foreign Relations*, New York, 1963.

[2] Frederick Barghoorn, *The Soviet Cultural Offensive*, Princeton, 1960, p. 10.

[3] A. Maslin, *"Sotsializm i kul'tura,"* (Socialism and Culture), *Pravda,* July 28, 1970.

[4] Unlike in some other aspects of communist strategy, there appear to be no significant differences in the assessment of the role of cultural diplomacy between the Soviet and Chinese communist version, let alone the East European communist version. Thus, there is no need for a separate treatment of each in this respect.

[5] Chapter VI: The Struggle Against Bourgeois and Reformist Ideology. Ritvo, p. 93. See also, A. Maslin, *op. cit.*, attacking those striving after a "deideologization" of culture.

[6] Maslin, *op. cit.*

[7] p. 610.

[8] pp. 607-613, and 717.

[9] See, for instance, G. G. Karpov, *O Sovetskoi kulture i kulturnoi revoliutsii v SSSR* (On Soviet Culture and Cultural Revolution in the USSR), 1954; the *Soviet Communist Party Program;* the 1960 *Declaration of Eighty-One Communist Parties;* the 1969 *Declaration;* Maslin, *op. cit.* For a Western analysis see Barghoorn, *op. cit.*

[10] The 1969 and 1960 *Declarations.*

[11] 1960 *Declaration.* See also G. E. Skorov, *Razvivaiushchiesia strany: obrazovanie, zaniatost', ekonomicheskii rost,* (The Developing Countries: Education, Employment, Economic Growth), Moscow, 1971.

[12] Karpov. *op. cit.*, cited also in Barghoorn, *op. cit.*, p. 18.

[13] A. F. Yudenkov, *O programme KPSS* (On the Program of the Communist Party of the Soviet Union), Part I, p. 537. cited in Barghoorn, *op. cit.*, p. 176.

[14] *The Soviet Union and the Middle East,* New York, 1959, p. 292.

[15] *op. cit.*, p. 216.

[16] Barghoorn, *op. cit.*, p. 188.

[17] The actual use of this technique will be discussed later in this chapter.

[18] p. 608.

[19] pp. 14-15.

[20] For detailed data and statistics on such activities consult materials issued by the Office of Policy and Research of the U. S. Information Agency on communist activities in various areas of the Third World and the annual Research Studies of the Bureau of Intelligence and Research of the U.S. Department of State on Educational and Cultural Exchanges Between Communist and Non-Communist Countries.

[21] Jaroslav Martinic, *"17.listopad a jeho universita"* (17th November and Its University), *Student,* November 24, 1965, p. 2.

[22] United States Department of State, Bureau of Intelligence and Research, RESS-57, August 31, 1972.

[23] From time to time communist sources publish reports on the number of Third World students enrolled in communist universities. Thus *Express wieczorny* of October 21, 1966, mentioned 511 Africans, 347 Asians and 82 Latin Americans studying in Poland in the academic year 1965/66; *Slowo powszechne* of November 1, 1967, gave the number of students from the Third World in Poland as about 1,000, mostly from Africa; the Bulgarian Press Agency, BTA, singled out in its release of January 8, 1968, 520 Syrians as the largest contingent of foreign students in Bulgaria, with 300 Vietnamese as second largest; according to *Práce,* July 8, 1966, about two thirds of the 3,500 foreign students studying in Czechoslovakia in 1966, came from developing

countries of Asia, Africa and Latin America; *Ceskoslovenský svět* of November 12, 1964, wrote of over 3,000 students from 80 countries of Latin America, Asia and Africa; for an early country-by-country breakdown of Third World students sent to study in communist countries in 1956-62, see Maurice David Simon, *Communist System Interaction with the Developing States, 1954-1962; a Preliminary Analysis,* Research Paper No. 10, Stanford University Studies of the Communist Systems, January 1966, pp. 93-4. Even tiny Albania has had a modest part in the program as a small number of students from Algeria, Iraq and Yemen were reported as studying at Albanian institutions in 1962-63. *Zeri i Popullit,* January 6, 1963.

[24] Third World students in the Soviet Union receive a monthly stipend of 90 rubles, i.e., 3 times the normal stipend awarded to Soviet students. Also, they get a lump sum of 300 rubles for purchases of warm clothing. *New York Times,* June 13, 1965.

[25] See, for instance, an article on Soviet Higher Education written by the USSR Minister of Higher and Specialized Secondary Education in *New Times,* No. 46, November 19, 1969, pp. 5-8. He puts the number of citizens of the developing countries who have "obtained diplomas at Soviet specialized secondary and higher schools" at some 5,000.

[26] U.S. Department of State's *Research Study RSES-34* of August 30, 1971, citing *Kommunist,* No. 15, 1970. *New Times,* No. 9, 1971, cites a figure of "some 13,500 students from developing countries" to be trained "in 170 specialties in higher schools and in 48 in intermediate technical schools." (p. 24.)

[27] *Svobodné slovo,* October 14, 1962.

[28] See *"Universitet druzhby"* (Friendship University), *Pravda,* February 7, 1970, and "Friendship University's Tenth Anniversary," *New Times,* No. 6, 1970, p. 23.

[29] *"Universitet druzhby",* op. cit.; *New Times, op. cit.,* speaks of 43,000 applications in 1960.

[30] *"Universitet druzhby,"* op. cit. See also B. Gafurov, "The Soviet Union and the National Liberation Movement," *International Affairs* (Moscow), No. 7, 1971, pp. 17. ff. In his article "Lumumba University: An Assessment," in *Problems of Communism,* XX, 6, 1971, pp. 64 ff. Alvin Rubinstein estimates the student body to be "about 3,500."

[31] Rubenstein lists the following distribution of the student body in the academic year 1970-71; Preparatory College — about 1,000; Engineering College — 655; Medical College — 501; College of Physics, Mathematics and Natural Sciences — 360; College of Economics and Law — 342; College of Agriculture — 336; College of History and Philology — 286. *Op. cit.*

[32] Decreed by a government ordinance of September 15, 1961, No. 108 of the Collection of the Laws. See also "Foreign Students' University," *Prague News Letter,* 17, 11, 1961, pp. 1 and 4.

[33] *Lidová demokracie,* September 17, 1961.

[34] *Rudé právo,* November 18, 1961.

[35] *"Universita pro 80 zemi"* (A University for 80 Countries). *Československý svět,* No. 23, 1964, p. 7.

[36] 380 in 1966 (Rudé právo, November 18, 1966) and 350 in 1965 *(Rudé právo,* November 18, 1965).

[37] *Rudé právo,* November 18, 1966.

[38] *Rudé právo,* July 4, 1967.

[39] See government ordinance of January 19, 1966, No. 5 of the Collection of the Laws.

[40] An interview with Jaroslav Martinic, President of the University of 17th November, *Večerní Praha,* November 17, 1966.

[41] See, for instance, *Rudé právo,* October 19, 1961.

[42] Prague Radio, February 19, 1962, as monitored by Radio Free Europe.

[43] An interview with Ludmila Hobzová, head of the department in question, in *Kulturní tvorba,* No. 42, October 21, 1965.

[44] Ibid. See also *"17. listopad a jeho universita," op. cit.* and *"Jak na universitě 17. listopadu"* (How Is It at the University of 17th November), *Student,* No. 39, September 27, 1967.

[45] *"Inštitut medzinárodneho práva," Večer,* March 3, 1971.

[46] For a recent illustration see the visit of Chile's Minister of Education and the interview he gave to the *New Times,* No. 12, 1970, p. 15.

[47] "Great Success to First Graduates of University of Friendship," *Pravda,* June 30, 1965, V. S. Sergeyev, "Business Ties with Developing Countries," *New Times,* No. 12, 1966, pp. 5-7. As listed by Vasily Sergeyev in the earlier mentioned interview with *New Times* (No. 3, 1971, pp. 18 ff.) 4.2 percent of Soviet aid to the developing countries has been for "education, culture, public health and sports."

[48] *op. cit., New Times,* No. 46, November 19, 1969.

[49] Cited in note 30 above.

[50] The graduation of the first group of graduates from the Polytechnical Institute of Conakry became an occasion for a self-congratulatory article in *Pravda,* August 10, 1970, p. 4: *"Molodye kadry Gvinei,"* (Young Cadres of Guinea).

[51] *Mizan,* 7, 7, 1965, p. 4.

[52] *Pravda,* December 2, 1965, p. 4.

[53] *Mizan,* Supplement, No. 4, 1966, p. 4 and Research Memo of the U.S. Department of State, RSB-65, May 31, 1968.

[54] Tass release of July 12, 1966, *Mizan,* Supplement A, No. 4, 1966, p. 14, and U. S. Department of State's *Research Study RSES 34.*

[55] V.B. Solodovnikov, "The Soviet Union and Africa," *New Times,* No. 21, 1969, pp. 8-10.

[56] Research Memo RSB-65.

[57] *Ibid.*

[58] *Ibid.*

[59] "Economic Cooperation with India," *New Times,* No. 9, 1970, pp. 23-25.

[60] *Rudé právo,* January 12, 1966. See also Miroslav Novotný, *"ČSSR a Afrika,"* (Czechoslovak Socialist Republic and Africa), *Nová mysl,* No. 7, 1965, pp. 858-67.

[61] *Lidová demokracie,* August 18, 1965.

[62] Radio Mogadishu, February 14, 1961, and Memo RSB-65.

[63] p. 3.

[64] p. 11.

[65] Some data on communist broadcasting to the Third World in the early sixties may be found in John C. Clews, *Communist Propaganda Techniques,* New York, 1964, pp. 118 ff.

[66] Clews, *op. cit.,* table on p. 122.

[67] Michael Nebolieff, "Review of East European and Communist Chinese Foreign Broadcasts," *Radio Free Europe Research,* Bloc/1, June 28, 1971.

[68] Carl T. Rowan's syndicated column, "Anti-U.S. Drive," *Austin States-man*, February 24, 1969; also, Memo RSB-65.

[69] Nebolieff, *op. cit.*

[70] *ibid.*

[71] Memo RSB-65. See also Arthur Stein, *India and the Soviet Union*, Chicago, 1969.

[72] *Ibid.*

[73] See the releases of the U.S. Information Agency: Communist Propaganda Activities in East Asia and Pacific Area, 1967, R-9-68, February 26, 1968; Communist Propaganda Activities in the Near East and South Asia — 1967, R-13-68, March 19, 1968; Communist Propaganda Activities in Latin America — 1967, R-15-68, April 30, 1968.

[74] For a listing of the Third World's indigenous publishing houses, bookstores and other propaganda outlets see the materials of the U.S. Information Agency listed in the preceding footnote.

[75] See, for instance, Antony Buzek, *How the Communist Press Works*, New York, 1964, pp. 206 ff. and Stein, *op. cit.*, especially p. 230. As of 1971, TASS has 21 bureaus in Africa, 14 in North and South America and 26 in Asia. The *New China News Agency* has 13 bureaus in Africa, 5 in the Middle East and 3 in Latin America. See Alan Dean "Red Agents are Fake Journalists," *Austin Statesman*, Aug. 18, 1971, and Mark W. Hopkins, *Mass Media in the Soviet Union*.

[76] Brzezinski, *Africa and the Communist World*, note on p. 236.

[77] Aleksandr Kaznachaev, "Soviet 'Operation Burma'" *New Leader*, January 18, 1970, pp. 13-15, and his *Inside a Soviet Embassy*.

[78] Carl Rowan, "Anti-U. S. Drive", *op. cit.*

[79] For a discussion of typical activities carried out by information officers of Soviet embassies see Aleksandr Kaznachaev, *Inside a Soviet Embassy*, and the same author's article in *New Leader* cited above.

[80] *Soviet Cultural Offensive*, p. 337.

[81] Memo RSB-65.

[82] *The Democratic Journalist*, Nos. 5 and 6-7, 1961.

[83] As reported in Stein, *op. cit.*, p. 235, the pro-Soviet Indian paper *Patriot* could be sold cheaply thanks to outside financial support.

[84] Radio Prague, February 21, 1961 and *Svět v obrazech*, No. 31, July 30, 1966.

[85] *Novinář*, No. 2, 1967.

[86] Jiří Goldschmid, *"Skola pro africké novináře,"* (A School for African Journalists), *Svět v obrazech*, No. 23, June 5, 1965, p. 19.

[87] Jiří Goldschmid in *Novinář*, No. 2, 1967.

[88] P. Naumov, "Journalists' Congress," *New Times*, No. 4, 1971, pp. 11-12. See also G. Skakhnazarov "10 Congress in Havana," *World Marxist Review*, 14, 3, 1971, pp. 126. ff.

[89] For a listing of showings of communist films in the Third World see the materials of the U.S. Information Agency cited above; also, *"Infiltracion comunista en medios culturales, deportivos, etc."* (Communist Infiltration of the Media of Culture, Sports, etc.) in *"El Comunismo en El Uruguay,"* (Communism in Uruguay) *Este y Oeste*, VII, No. 126-127, pp. 32-36.

[90] Solodovnikov, *op. cit.*

[91] See for inst., William F. Buckley, Jr. "Chile and Communism" *The Washington Star*, October 21, 1970.

[92] See listings in the materials of the U.S. Information Agency cited above.

[93] See Solodovnikov, *op. cit.*

[94] *Rudé právo,* March 27, 1967.

[95] A major contest of this sort was organized, for instance, in 1964 by the Czechoslovak-Indian Friendship Society in Bombay. *Rudé právo,* May 3, 1964.

[96] For a description of the activities of Soviet Friendship societies in Africa, see Solodovnikov, *op. cit.*

[97] *Rudé právo,* May 17, 1964.

[98] Solodovnikov, *op. cit.*

[99] Soviet Cultural Centres exist, for instance, in India, U.A.R., Ethiopia, Somalia, Senegal, Brazzaville Congo, and Nigeria. Solodovnikov, *op. cit.* In Chile there is a very active Chilean-Soviet Cultural Institute. Czechoslovak Cultural Centres have been established in Egypt and Iraq.

[100] As claimed by *Rudé právo* on December 25, 1965, tens of Radio Praha Clubs exist in Africa and Latin America. See also *Lidová demokracie,* September 9, 1962, and *Rudé právo,* May 3, 1964.

[101] *Rudé právo,* May 3, 1964.

[102] Shelepin, *op. cit.*

[103] See, for instance, A Dzasokhov, *"Ochistit zemliu ot kolonializma"* (To Clean the Land from Colonialism), *Pravda,* May 24, 1970 *"Po sluchaiu Dnia osvobodzhdeniia Afriki,"* (Concerning the Day of Africa's Liberation), *Pravda,* May 26, 1970. V. Korovikov, *"Edinstvo v bor'be i sozidanii: Den osvobozhdeniia Afriki,"* (Unity in Battle and Building, The Day of Africa's Liberation), *Pravda,* May 25, 1972.

[104] For a good account see "Chou En-lai's Visit to Africa," *Mizan,* 6, 5, 1964, pp. 45-56.

[105] Solodovnikov, *op. cit.*

[106] "Focus on Latin America," *New Times,* No. 7, 1970, p. 25.

[107] "International Congress of Historians," *New Times,* No. 35, 1970, p. 15.

[108] See the introduction to the first volume published in 1970.

[109] Cairo Radio, December 16, 1963, as cited in *Mizan, op. cit.,* p. 52.

[110] Barghoorn, *Soviet Cultural Offensive,* p. 193.

[111] George Liska, "The Politics of 'Cultural Diplomacy'", *World Politics XIV,* 3, 1962, pp. 532-541.

[112] N. Lenin, *Complete Works,* Moscow, 1935, XXV, p. 449.

[113] See, for instance, a study made by the Federation of German Student Organizations based on reports of African students, cited in "The East Block as Host to Students from Developing Countries," *The Bulletin,* Bonn, 11, 9-10, 1963, pp. 3 and 7-8.

[114] For instance, the government-owned *The Zambia Daily Mail* of September 13, 1971, complained that the East German Trade Mission in Zambia, meanwhile expelled, sent a number of Zambian students to East Germany without the government's permission.

[115] "Kenyatta Reappraises Communist Aid," *Free Europe Radio Research Paper,* May 13, 1966.

[116] *Ibid.;* also, George Bennett, "Kenya's 'Little General Election,'" *The World Today,* 22, 8, 1966, pp. 336-43.

[117] *Bulletin,* (Bonn) 11, 9, March 5, 1963, p. 3.

[118] See, for instance, a UPI report from Bonn: "East Germans Entice Africans Failing West German Institutions," *Austin Statesman,* April 26,

1966; *Bulletin* (Bonn), *op. cit.; "Sudanští studenti ze západního Německa v ČSSR"* (Sudanese Students from West Germany in the Czechoslovak Socialist Republic), *Mladá fronta,* August 29, 1963.

[119] Moscow Radio Broadcast, November 17, 1960.

[120] *"Desetiletí..." op. cit.*

[121] See a report on such an "Open Forum on Contemporary International Politics" held in Prague in November 1963, *Mladá fronta,* November 12, 1963.

[122] 35 such committees were reported at Czech universities alone, *Mladá fronta,* February 3, 1963.

[123] See for instance: "Protest studentow Krakowa," (The Protest of Cracow Students), *Trybuna ludu,* June 7, 1968; *Lidová demokracie,* June 7, 1967; *Mladá fronta,* October 31, 1964; *Tass* releases of March 6 and 10, 1964; *Rudé právo,* June 15, 1963; etc.

[124] *"Historie jednoho prohlášení"* (The History of One Declaration), *Rudé právo,* April 8, 1970.

[125] More about this in Chapter XIII.

[126] George Bennett, *op. cit. World Today.*

[127] *Time,* September 29, 1967, p. 40.

[128] See, for inst., Kaznachaev, *Inside A Soviet Embassy,* esp. pp. 101 ff.

[129] See a major report on the Congress, *"Congreso Cultural de la Habana,"* (The Cultural Congress of Havana), *Este y Oeste* VII, No. 123, February 1969, p. 7-27.

[130] *Ibid.,* p. 15.

[132] For the Soviet utilization of CIA's support of the National Student Association see G. Albanov and V. Lyadov, "Secrets of the Intelligence Service," *New Times,* No. 38, 1970, pp. 29-31.

[133] Alexei Vladin, "Poaching Brains from the Third World," *New Times,* No. 27, 1970, pp. 21-22.

[134] See, for instance: *Neue Zürcher Zeitung,* January 16, 1962; *Arbeiterzeitung* (Vienna), February 3, 1963; "The East Bloc as Host to Students from the New Nations." *Bulletin, op. cit.;* "Alien Students See Prague as All Red," *New York Times,* April 11, 1962; Anthony Okotcha, "Moscow Trained me for Revolution in Africa," *Daily Nation* (Nairobi), August 10-12, 1961; Lawrence Fellows, "Kenyans Charge Soviet Brutality," *New York Times,* April 7, 1965; Priscilla Johnson, "Apartheid University," *Harper's Magazine,* December 1960; Andrew Richard Amar, *A Student in Moscow.*

[135] For instance, *Mizan,* 7, 7, 1965, pp. 19-20, reporting on the return of Kenyan students from Moscow; *České slovo* (Munich), March 1962, on the departure of Somali and Guinean students from Prague.

[136] Colin Legum, *"Moskaus Rückschläge in Afrika,"* (Moscow Backslaps in Africa) *Die Zeit* (Hamburg), March 30, 1962, cited in Brzezinski, *Africa and the Communist World,* p. 34.

[137] See various reports by students who have studied in communist countries, cited earlier in this chapter. Also *"S Juanem Fernandezem u zahraničnich studentů,"* (With Juan Fernandez Visiting the Foreign Students), an interview in the Czech student paper *Student* with Third World students studying in Prague, December 1, 1965, and Rubinstein, *op. cit.*

[138] For a sampling of students' reports on the people's attitudes as well as communist admissions see, in addition to sources already mentioned above: *"Doplácíme na to?"* (Are We Losing Money on It?), *Svobodné Slovo,*

November 15, 1967; *"Afrika představ a faktů"* (The Africa in Assumption and Reality), *Literární noviny,* April 1, 1967; Theodore Shabad, "Africans in the Soviet," *New York Times,* December 19, 1963, and "Soviet Warns Students from Africa on Protests," *New York Times,* December 21, 1963, *"O zahraničních studentech a problémech kolem nich"* (On Foreign Students and the Problems Around Them), an interview with the past President of the University of 17th November, Kulturní tvorba, November 14, 1963; *"O zahraničních studentech,"* (About the Foreign Students), *Rudé právo,* January 23, 1966; "An open Letter to All African Governments," *East Europe,* 9, 12, 1960, p. 46; *"Jsou našimi soudruhy,"* (They Are Our Comrades), *Tribuna,* No. 46, November 17, 1971, p. 7.

[139] See for instance: "African Students Beaten in Prague," *New York Times,* May 15, 1963; "Bulgarians Clash with Africans," *East Europe,* 11,10, 1962, pp. 32-33; Seymour Topping, "Africans Complain of Bias in Moscow," *New York Times,* June 4, 1963; Jan Carew, *Moscow is Not My Mecca,* London, 1964; F. Zdobina, *"Nestrpíme chuligánské výtržnosti,"* (We will not Tolerate Hooligan Outbursts), *Rudé právo,* May 16, 1963; UPI report from Vienna of June 28, 1970, reporting a protest march of one hundred African students in Sofia in mid-January 1970.

[140] Henry Tanner, "500 Africans Fight Police in Moscow in Race Protest," *New York Times,* December 19, 1963; *Tass* release of December 29, 1963, admitting the demonstration.

[141] See AP report from Vienna, February 13, 1963; also, *Rudé právo,* February 20, 1963.

[142] *"China a Trzeci Świat,"* (China and the Third World), *Polityka,* June 27, 1970.

[143] Henry Tanner, "Soviet Ousts U.S. Cultural Aide As Inciter of African Students," *New York Times,* May 12, 1965, and *Komsomolskaia Pravda,* July 20 and 21, 1966.

[144] See Chapter IX; also, the New China News Agency release of June 22, 1966.

[145] See Barghoorn, *Soviet Cultural Offensive,* p. 24; Kaznachaev, *Inside a Soviet Embassy,* Alan Dean, *op. cit.,* etc. In 1967 Ghana expelled a correspondent of the Czechoslovak Press Agency, ČTK, as well as a correspondent of *Pravda* and another one of the *Novosti* Agency. Kenya ordered out of the country in 1968 a correspondent of *Novosti* and a representative of Sovexportfilm. In 1966 Kenya expelled a correspondent of ČTK and a year before that a correspondent of *New China News Agency.*

[146] More about this in Chapter XIII.

[147] See on the latter *Nkrumah's Subversion in Africa,* an updated publication of Ghana's Ministry of Information after Nkrumah's ouster.

[148] *Soviet Cultural Offensive,* p. 47.

[149] As for the students of Lumumba University, Western residents of Moscow are said to believe that most of them "come away from their experience with an anti-Soviet bias — notwithstanding the improvements in the University in recent years." Rubinstein, *op. cit.*

CHAPTER XIII

USING NON-PEACEFUL METHODS

Having proclaimed "the abolition of war and establishment of ever-lasting peace on earth" to be "an historical mission of communism" and the principle of peaceful coexistence to be the guiding rationale of communist foreign policy, Soviet communists and their Eastern European and Third World partners have had to de-emphasize quite substantially the role assigned to violence in the communist operational code. At the same time they could not afford to part with violent options altogether, for they fully realize that the ultimate communist goal in the Third World may well prove to be unattainable through peaceful means alone. Moreover, the rather phlegmatic Soviet attitude regarding the role of violence under the conditions presently prevalent in many parts of the Third World has met with varying degrees of skepticism and even outright disapproval on the part of several segments of the world communist movement. As has already been noted in Chapter II, the Chinese communists view the use of violence, especially in the form of armed struggle and guerrilla warfare, as the principal method of anti-imperialist strategy; and so do the pro-Chinese factions that have cropped up in many parts of the Third World following the Sino-Soviet schism in the early sixties. A similar preference for violence characterizes the stand of Castro and his radical-left supporters throughout Latin America. Even some of the Third World Communist parties belonging to the Soviet camp have embraced, at one time or another, armed struggle as the method best suited to the specific conditions of their respective countries.

Hence, it is hardly surprising that current communist pronouncements on the role of violence in communist strategy vis-a-vis the Third World are marked by considerable ambivalence.

The Soviet Version

The prime example of such ambivalence is offered by the current Soviet dicta which bristle with ardent professions of an unshakeable Soviet commitment to the cause of peace and the use of peaceful means to "bury" capitalism, yet all along keep open non-peaceful alternatives should the non-violent approach fail.

While accusing the "imperialist" countries of regarding "wars of aggression as a natural means of settling international issues," the 1961 *Program of the Soviet Communist Party* credits the Soviet Union and other communist countries with having developed *"a new type of international relations"* based on "the principle of peace," "respect for the independence and sovereignty of all countries," and "humane methods of socialist diplomacy,"[1] It underlines that "the working class and its vanguard - the Marxist-Leninist parties - seek to accomplish the socialist revolution by *peaceful means.*"[2] Indeed, "the joining of the efforts of the newly-free peoples and of the peoples of the socialist countries in the struggle against the war danger" is designated as "a cardinal factor of world peace."[3]

In the same vein, the *Fundamentals* lays strong emphasis upon peaceful methods. Discussing the various forms of transition to a socialist revolution, it states that "the working class does not make it its aim to solve social problems by violence."[4] It denounces as a deliberate lie the allegations of "the enemies of communism" claiming that communists indulge in "tactics of 'palace revolutions', *putches* and seizure of power by armed minorities."[5] It devotes many pages to the exposition of the communist "programme for normalising international relations and stabilizing world peace, one which would exclude all use of force to settle disputes between states" and would reduce the struggle between capitalism and socialism to a mere "peaceful competition" waged primarily "in economic, cultural and social fields."[6] And it holds that "the peaceful assumption of power is more in keeping with the whole world outlook of the working class."[7]

Quite understandably, the preference for peaceful ways displayed in the official Party documents has been echoed by Soviet writers specializing in the affairs of the Third World. Without exception, they have dwelt upon the desirability and feasibility of advancing the cause of "scientific socialism" in the non-committed countries of Asia, Africa and Latin America through peaceful means. They have cautioned against "giving Leninist theory on revolution an exceedingly one-sided slant" and laying "particular stress on non-peaceful methods of carrying out a revolution."[8] They have warned their collaborators in the Third World against "adventurism," "blanquism," "revolutionary romanticism," "ultra-leftism." They have reminded them of Lenin's saying that revolutionaries perish when they begin to write the revolution with capital R.[9] They have admonished them that "the concept of violent revolution, which the ultra-left opportunists seek to impose upon the national-liberation movement, has nothing in common with Marxism-Leninism."[10]

The Soviet condemnation of such "anti-Marxist theses" has come to the fore, in particular, in heated polemics with the Chinese communists which have continued ever since the Sino-Soviet conflict broke into the open. While conceding that resort to armed struggle may in some instances be necessary, Soviet strategists have denounced Mao and his associates for "sticking to the old blueprint," "calling for armed struggle in any conditions," and thus following an adventurist and irresponsible "all-or-nothing" slogan.[11] They have ruled as erroneous the Chinese view considering a struggle as "revolutionary only if it takes the form of civil war."[12] They have rejected "the adventurist, pseudo-revolutionary recipes" recommended by Peking to the countries of Asia and Africa.[13] Denouncing "Peking's diplomatic maneuvres in the U. N.," a Soviet analyst cautioned the developing countries to "remember well how the very same men at the helm in Peking instigated certain quarters in Burma, Indonesia, and India to anti-government actions, flouted the sovereignty of Nepal and Ceylon, and tried to interfere in the internal affairs of countries as remote from China as Kenya and Tunisia."[14] In particular, they have lashed out against the Maoist "formula of political power deriving from the gun" as amounting to "declaring armed struggle the only acceptable form of action, to implanting a cult of violence."[15] Similar accusations have been leveled by Soviet specialists on Latin America against various ultra-leftist groups of Latin America (evidently those seeking to emulate Castro's exploits) holding that "armed struggle can be provoked artificially at any time and in any country. . ."[16]

However, the lopsided Soviet emphasis on peaceful methods notwithstanding, all the major Soviet pronouncements on strategy and tactics do contain provisions allowing for the use of non-peaceful means. "Where the exploiting classes resort to violence against the people," prescribes the 1961 *Soviet Communist Party Program*, "the possibility of a *non-peaceful transition to socialism* should be borne in mind."[17] Discussing such a possibility, the *Fundamentals* goes so far as to invoke the American Declaration of Independence in support of the "Leninist thesis" of the people's right to seize power through an armed uprising.[18] While favoring a "peaceful assumption of power" and cautioning against "any adventurism or conspiratorial playing with 'seizure' of power," the Party's Manual does predict that "in a number of capitalist countries the overthrow of bourgeois dictatorships will inevitably take place through an armed class struggle."[19] As bared by Soviet writings on the Third World, this thesis on the use of violence applies to the developing nations as well. "All means, including armed uprising, are employed in a struggle against imperialism aimed at winning national independence and ensuring its security," states a 1970 Soviet authoritative volume.[20] In particular, Soviet spokesmen have felt compelled to give a qualified public endorsement to non-peaceful methods in order to counter the Chinese accusations that the Soviet Union was not earnest in supporting adequately the national-liberation movement. While taking the Chinese to task for "their un-

Marxist thesis of the absolute priority of armed struggle,"[21] Soviet strategists do approve of resorting to armed struggle if and when conditions favoring it exist in the country concerned.

What these conditions are has been discussed time and again in Soviet writings and at various communist gatherings, such as those of the (now defunct) *Communist International* and the presentday international communist conferences.[22] However, guided by the all-embracing desire to endow communist strategy and tactics with maximum flexibility, Soviet statements on the matter are couched in rather general terms.

To begin with, there must exist, of course, what Lenin used to call a "revolutionary situation." As noted in Chapter I, such a situation presumably occurs in a given country only when certain "objective" conditions are present, namely, when the ruling classes can no longer maintain their rule in an unchanged form, when the suffering of the oppressed classes becomes more acute than usual, and when the masses have sharply increased their activities to give vent to their discontent and indignation. Moreover, as the *Fundamentals* hastens to point out, "a revolution does not arise out of every revolutionary situation, but only when *subjective* conditions are added to the necessary objective conditions.[23] One such "subjective" condition is said to be "the ability and readiness of the revolutionary class to carry out decisive action strong enough to smash or impair the existing power". The other one appears to be the presence of a Marxist-Leninist vanguard "which understands the requirement of the historical moment, is closely connected with the masses and can lead the masses."

When the postulated combination of the avove-mentioned "objective" and "subjective" conditions develops, the country in question is deemed to be ready for the type of a revolution visualized in communist writings. Then the question arises as to how to stage such a revolution and how to push it to successful completion. Evidently, as noted above, the Soviet strategists would very much prefer doing it "peacefully" but they insist at the same time on the communist right and duty to use non-peaceful means whenever the resistance of the ruling class makes a peaceful solution impossible. Whether or not non-peaceful means would actually be used is to be decided by a careful

Marxist-Leninist analysis of all the factors involved. "It is not a matter of preferring some one form of struggle, be it even armed revolt," states *The Third World,* "but rather a matter of giving all-round consideration to the situation in a given country, to the relationship of political forces, and to political expediency." [24]

Foremost among the requisites ordained by Soviet dicta for resorting to armed struggle is the participation of masses. Lenin "always thought of an uprising as extensive action of the working people headed by the class-conscious part of the working class," stresses the *Fundamentals.* [25] That the same general rule applies to the developing countries is affirmed by the authors of *The Third World:* "Armed revolts, unless they are assured of the full support of the working people ... may simply lead to a loss of contact between the small armed detachment and the people." [26] It is this involvement of the masses, especially the workers and peasants, that makes the difference. If "the masses" join the vanguard in the venture, resort to armed violence is considered to be a correct and commendable application of Marxist-Leninist strategy and tactics. If they do not, then it is an incorrect and reprehensible manifestation of "adventurism," "blanquism," "putchism," or petty-bourgeois "pseudo-revolutionism."

However, under the thick layer of ideological rhetoric surrounding the delicate issue of the use of peaceful or non-peaceful means one can spot without too much difficulty what undoubtedly is the most decisive criterion for approving or disapproving resort to armed force in the pursuit of the revolution, namely, the chances of its being successful. That is obviously what is implied in the *Third World's* above-quoted reference to "political expediency." To be sure, the active participation of "the masses," provided they side with the communists, is highly desirable as such participation is a major and often decisive element of force in any revolutionary situation. But the failure to mobilize the masses would certainly not be held against a Marxist-Leninist vanguard if and when the latter succeeded in seizing and holding power without the masses' help and in spite of their apathy. After all, resort to armed struggle in Vietnam, Laos and Cambodia, which appeared to offer a good chance of success when begun, gained Soviet approval even though the bulk of Indo-Chinese peasants (who evidently would have preferred to be left alone by both sides), could hardly be said to have rallied in support of the Vietcong.

As for the kind of revolutionary actions that do constitute legitimate uses of non-peaceful means in terms of the Soviet version of the Marxist-Leninist strategy, Soviet theoreticians have not developed any clearcut classification or even adequate definition of the different types of non-peaceful methods. Nor does Soviet terminology relative to such methods reveal any consistent pattern. "Armed struggle," "armed class struggle," "armed revolt," or "armed uprising" are terms mostly used in that respect; and there is little further elaboration about their meaning. Undoubtedly, this is due both to the desire to retain the fullest flexibility of the non-peaceful approach and the understandable reluctance to discuss publicly communist uses of violence at a time when the Soviet Union strains itself to project an image of peace-loving benevolence vis-a-vis the Third World.

One non-peaceful method about which Soviet strategists do talk with fervor and unreserved approbation is the "war of national liberation." Probably the most authoritative exposé of the Soviet stand on the matter was made by Khrushchev in his speech delivered in January 1961 at a joint meeting of the Party organization of the Higher Party School, the Academy of Social Sciences and the Central Committee's Institute of Marxism-Leninism.[27] In the speech he distinguished three types of wars. Two of these he sharply condemned: world wars and local wars. But the Party's First Secretary had nothing but praise for the third type - the national-liberation war. Citing "the armed struggle of the Vietnamese people," the Algerian war against the French and Castro's uprising in Cuba as recent examples of such wars, he expressed "the Marxists' attitude" toward them in no uncertain terms: "These uprisings must not be identified with wars among states, with local wars, because in these uprisings the people are fighting to exercise their right to self-determination and for their social and independent national development; these are uprisings against rotten reactionary regimes and against colonialists. Communists fully and unreservedly support such just wars and march in the van of the peoples fighting wars of liberation."

This commitment to communist participation on the side of

the "people" in national-liberation wars has since been stated and restated by Soviet spokesmen on numerous occasions.[28] Some Soviet writers have also sought to legitimize such wars in terms of international law. Writing in the *Kommunist* in 1965, a Soviet author claimed that such wars are covered by Article 51 of the United Nations Charter recognizing the people's inherent right of individual and collective self-defense."[29]

Of course, to qualify as a national-liberation war worthy of communist support, such a war must be "revolutionary" or "progressive" in the Soviet meaning of the word. It must be a war waged against Western colonialists or, as Khrushchev put it, "against rotten reactionary regimes." Thus the Vietnamese war fits perfectly the Soviet concept of a national-liberation war as it is aimed at overthrowing a regime that Soviet rulers consider as reactionary and, since it has American backing, as a puppet of foreign imperialists. On the other hand, the Biafran rebellion, a massive popular uprising of a people seeking to assert their right of self-determination, failed to qualify as a national-liberation war in Soviet eyes, for it was waged against a regime that the Soviet leaders were hoping to lure into closer cooperation with the Soviet Union. Nor would Soviet theoreticians accept as a "progressive" national-liberation war a popular uprising aimed against an already established communist or pro-communist regime.

A similar ambivalence characterizes the Soviet attitude toward yet another form of violence that has been of frequent occurrence in the Third World, namely, military coups. As explained more fully in Chapter IX, Soviet strategists have modified in recent years quite substantially their erstwhile negative posture toward the military takeovers in the Third World and have become much less selective in condoning and even approving them. While still continuing to be critical of military actions resulting in an overthrow of governments sympathetic to Soviet Russia, such as those that toppled Nkrumah in Ghana and Sokarno in Indonesia, they now tend to put their stamp of approval on military takeovers whenever the new regime is anti-Western and willing to "normalize" relations with the Soviet Union.

On the other hand, Soviet strategists view with jaundiced eyes, at least in the present situation prevailing in the Third World, the various acts of individual and group terrorism perpetrated today in many countries of Asia, Africa and Latin America. Such *coups de force* as rural guerrilla operations à la Che Guevara, hit-and-run urban guerrilla tactics of kidnaping or assassinating government officials and foreign diplomats, robbing banks and throwing bombs, are considered as typical phenomena of irresponsible adventurism. Not that the Soviet leaders are displeased by the problems such terrorism poses for the bourgeois regimes involved. However, since such acts are more often than not blamed, rightly or wrongly, on the communists, they realize that such atrocities tend to undercut the effectiveness of Soviet strategy of peaceful coexistence. Thus, besides being premature because of the absence of some of the Soviet-prescribed conditions necessary to trigger a revolution, such acts of insurgent terrorism are deemed to be detrimental to the overall Soviet strategy in the Third World.

Finally, the Soviet ambivalence regarding the role of violence is further compounded by the semantic licentiousness with which Soviet spokesmen interpret the meaning of the word "peaceful." "Peaceful transition to socialism necessarily involves recourse to revolutionary coercion in relation to the exploiters, though the revolution remains peaceful in as much as it is not attended by bloodshed or civil war," wrote A. Rumiantsev in rebutting the Chinese communists for considering a struggle as revolutionary only if it takes the form of civil war.[30] Even more significantly, a favorite example of a "peaceful" transition to socialism that the Soviet leaders are wont to cite is the 1948 communist takeover of Czechoslovakia, although the communist victory there resulted from an overt threat of a forcible seizure of power with the help of armed communist workers' militia and the backing of the Soviet Union. Nor could the 1939-40 incorporation of the Baltic Republics into the Soviet Union - another Soviet-quoted illustration of the use of a "peaceful" method - qualify as such in the generally understood meaning of the word.

It would thus seem that Soviet interpreters of Marxism-Leninism hold as peaceful many acts that would be considered as non-peaceful by Western students. The Soviet definition of "peaceful" methods is evidently broad enough to include such devices of "revolutionary coercion" as : occupying public build-

ings, radio stations, factories and editorial offices of anti-
communist papers; resorting to "citizens' arrests" and forcible
removals of high-ranking officials of a bourgeois regime; dis-
arming the police and arming the population with weapons seized
from occupied arsenals and armament factories; forming armed
"people's militia" and using them to enforce "the will of the
people." As long as "the exploiters" and their henchmen yield
without too much resistance and no bloodshed occurs, the
transition is deemed to be "peaceful." Only when the regime
decides to fight back and blood is spilled in the process does the
transition become non-peaceful. But the blame for this is
assigned to those who "refuse to take account" of the working
class's preference "to take the power peacefully" and thus "force
on the revolutionary workers the sharpest, most violent forms
and methods of struggle."[31]

The East European Position

As noted in Chapter II, except for Yugoslavia and Albania,
the officially approved East European communist statements
relative to the Third World have faithfully echoed the Soviet line.
And our discussion of the various "peaceful" aspects of communist strategy vis-a-vis the developing countries of Asia, Africa
and Latin America undertaken in the preceding chapters also
reveals the identity of Soviet and official East European communist standpoints. Hence, it should not come as a surprise that this
uniformity applies to the role of violence as well.

The highest official corroboration of the East European
acceptance of the Soviet view on the matter is contained, once
again, in the two afore-mentioned Moscow-drafted documents
designed to prescribe the proper course of action of the world
communist movement, namely, the 1960 *Declaration of 81
Communist Parties* and the *Declaration* adopted by the 1969
International Conference of Communist and Workers' Parties.

While emphasizing the communist commitment to peace and
preference for peaceful means, the 1960 *Declaration* provides for
the use of both armed struggle, including the national-liberation
wars, and peaceful methods as approved devices of communist
anti-imperialist strategy. As do the *Fundamentals* and the Soviet

Communist Party *Program,* it makes the decision whether to rely on peaceful or non-peaceful means contingent "on the concrete historical conditions," especially on "the specific balance of the class forces in the country concerned, on the organization and maturity of the working class and its vanguard, and on the extent of the resistance put up by the ruling classes." It suggests that "in the event of the exploiting classes' resorting to violence against the people, the possibility of non-peaceful transition to socialism should be borne in mind."[32]

In much the same ambivalent language, the 1969 *Declaration* harps on the communist preoccupation with the preservation of peace. But it hastens to add that "the policy of peaceful coexistence does not contradict the right of any oppressed people to fight for its liberation by any means it considers necessary - armed or peaceful." And it refers to "the inalienable right to take up arms in defence against encroachments by imperialist aggressors" as "an integral part of the general anti-imperialist struggle."

Thus, by appending their signatures to the two documents, communist rulers of Eastern Europe (except those of Yugoslavia and Albania), have endorsed the Soviet line on the role of violence, for both documents do no more than paraphrase the Soviet viewpoint.[33]

The Soviet line has been also strictly adhered to on the relatively few occasions when Soviet Russia's East European partners have spoken or written on the matter. They have done so, in particular, when siding with the Soviet leaders and theoreticians in their public polemics against the Maoists. For example, East European communist spokesmen and writers have resolutely condemned the one-sided Chinese emphasis on armed struggle as the best method of promoting the cause of communism in developing countries. They have taken the Chinese to task for "equating social revolution with war."[34] They have labeled as un-Marxian the views, attributed to the Chinese communists as well ás the Castroites and various Latin American leftists, that "the armed form of the revolution is presumably typical for relatively backward countries whereas the peaceful road is characteristic for developed capitalist countries."[35] They have argued that recourse to armed struggle when suitable conditions therefor do not exist "not only does not lead to the achievement of the desired goals but on the contrary leads to the isolation of the revolutionary forces and even to their suppression."[36] Also, in differentiating between various types of wars - just and unjust, revolutionary and counter-revolutionary - they have singled out the national-liberation wars as the prime example of just and revolutionary armed struggle worthy of communist support.[37]

Attitudes of the Third World's Moscow-oriented Communists

Like the ruling communist parties of the member-states of the Warsaw alliance, the leaders of the Moscow-oriented parties of the Third World took part in the above-mentioned Moscow conferences of 1960 and 1969, and signed the two documents adopted there.[38] In so doing, they have subscribed to the Soviet-recommended theses contained in the said *Declarations,* including the line on the uses of peaceful and non-peaceful means.

It should be pointed out, however, that for the Communist parties of the Third World the entire matter of the peaceful versus the non-peaceful approach has been of much more far-reaching significance than for their East European comrades. For the latter it has been an issue of purely academic, and rather abstract, theoretical concern. After all, a defeat of native communists in one or another developing country resulting from a faulty choice of strategy would affect little, if at all, the fortunes of the communist regimes of East Europe. But for the communists of the Third World the selection of the correct method of struggle has been a very concrete and fateful matter, wrapped in controversy and pregnant with grave dilemmas and risks whatever the chosen path. Nor has it been easy for them to resist the more heroic road of the armed struggle over the much less glamorous peaceful approach. Realizing that a combination of all the conditions that the Soviet interpreters of Marxism-Leninism deem necessary for the successful launching of a proletarian revolution would be very slow in materializing in their respective countries, even a good many pro-Soviet communists of the Third World have wondered whether the desired results might not be attained faster via an armed-coup shortcut. Moreover, the temptation could not help being strengthened, especially in Latin America, by Castro's victory in Cuba and by the recourse to armed struggle on the part of the leftist guerrilla extremists which made the Moscow-oriented communists appear as over-cautious, non-revolutionary and even cowardly.

Plagued by such dilemmas, the pro-Soviet leaders of the Communist parties of the Third World have been rather inconsistent in determining whether peaceful or non-peaceful means should be given priority in their respective countries. Up to the early and middle sixties a number of Moscow-oriented parties tended to stress the armed struggle as the main, or at least concurrent and increasingly important, method of the anti-imperialist struggle. That was the case, in particular, of a number of Communist parties of Latin America and Asia, such as those of Venezuela, Guatemala, Colombia, Peru, the Dominican Republic and the Philippines.[39] "...the time of illusions concerning the possibility of achieving revolutionary ends by peaceful means is ended...," proclaimed the Venezuelan communist leader Pompeyo Marquez in 1964, "what the masses are really waiting for is revolutionary action, armed combat."[40] Even as late as November 1967 another prominent Venezuelan communist, Francisco Mieres, writing in the Soviet-sponsored *World Marxist Review,* held that "as regards the general strategic road in Latin America," armed struggle was "the rule" and "the peaceful way the exception."[41]

However, in the last three years of the 1960-70 decade the erstwhile inclination toward the armed struggle began to recede. The defeats and losses that the *guerrilleros* sustained virtually everywhere throughout Latin America, crowned by the failure of Che Guevara's venture in Bolivia in 1967, badly hurt the rationale of the guerrilla tactics and made the protagonists of such approaches more vulnerable to the communist accusations of "adventurism," "blanquism" and "infantile revolutionism." Nor did their critics have to worry any longer as much as previously about being victimized by Castro, for by 1969-70 the *Jefe Maximo* himself has evidently toned down his earlier elation about the guerrilla warfare as the only correct road to victory.[42]

As a result, virtually all the leaders of the Moscow-oriented

Communist parties of the Third World, including most of those having previously gravitated toward armed struggle, became in the late sixties rather critical of it. Rather, they began expressing preference for the peaceful approach consisting mainly of a resolute class struggle, efforts to gain or regain legality and freedom of operations for native communist parties, education of "the masses" in "revolutionary consciousness," organizing workers and peasants, discrediting communism's opponents, and the like.

Probably the most striking example of this about-face occurred in Venezuela where the Communist party decided to replace armed struggle with the use of "all legal avenues" in its fight "for true revolutionary changes, for the abolition of imperialist domination, for democracy and socialism in our country."[43] Similar statements abjuring armed struggle and affirming or reaffirming the peaceful approach have been made by other prominent pro-Soviet communists of Latin America, such as Argentine's Rodolfo Ghioldi and Rubens Iscaro, Uruguay's Rodney Ariśmendi, Brazil's Luis Carlos Prestes, and others.[44] An especially scathing attack on "adventuristic trends" and "putchist ideas" was made in November 1970 by Luis Carlos Prestes. Writing in the *World Marxist Review,* the Brazilian communist leader ridiculed "the ultra-revolutionaries," including even "such active and experienced ex-Party members as Marighela, Mario Alves and others," for advocating "an immediate 'revolutionary offensive' which by a stroke of magic wand would transmute defeat in victory." He condemned them for spreading "various schemes of armed struggle, whether in the form of a peasant guerrilla war, urban 'combat centers,' etc." Comparing them to the Russian Otzovists of 1907-1910, he accused "these would-be 'liberators'" for "contemptuously rejecting all elementary forms of struggle that would help re-establish contact with the masses."[45] Similarly, the docilely pro-Soviet communists of the Arab Middle East have become rather critical of the Palestinian guerrillas for "belittling the organized struggle of the masses" and favoring only "one form of struggle."[46]

This trend toward reliance on peaceful methods of anti-imperialist struggle has been further strengthened, especially as far as Latin America is concerned, by the election of Salvador Allende to Chile's Presidency in 1970 and the ensuing appointment of several communists to his Cabinet. Hailed by pro-Soviet communists of the Third World as a tremendous victory for their cause, it has been cited as an example *par excellence* of a successful use of peaceful means in promoting socialism and as a telling rebuff to those believing that this could not be done without recourse to armed struggle.[47] As pointed out in the Venezuelan communist paper *Tribuna Popular,* "the Chilean Communists have provided corroboration of the Marxist-Leninist theory of revolutionary paths and have thereby dealt a telling blow to the dogmatic and adventurist theories of the ultra-lefts who absolutize armed struggle as the only possible one."[48]

This recent emphasis on the peaceful road to socialism does not mean, of course, that the Moscow-oriented parties of the Third World have dropped resort to violence, including the armed struggle, guerrilla operations or national-liberation wars, from the repertory of their strategy and tactics. In line with the directives. of the 1960 and 1969 *Declarations,* they retain the option to employ non-peaceful methods should peaceful methods fail and should the "right" conditions therefor present themselves. Even so ardent an advocate of peaceful means as Chile's leading communist Luis Corvalan chose to stress, in the wake of the 1970 success, that "the Chilean Communists do not presume to hold up their experience as a model applicable to all countries" and that "only the revolutionaries in each given country can decide whether or not such a non-armed possibility exists, whether it could arise and if so, in what specific form."[49] Indeed, at least three of the Moscow-oriented parties of Latin America, the Guatemalan Party of Labor, the Dominican Communist party and, most recently, the Communist Party of Colombia, have concluded that such a "non-armed possibility" could not arise in their respective countries. While criticizing the "Leftist adventurists" for relying on "spontaneity, improvisation and spectacular action," shunning "painstaking organizational work" and under-estimating the role of the Party and "contact with the masses," the Program of People's Revolution adopted by the Fourth Congress of Guatemala's Communist party held in December 1969 declared the "armed struggle in the form of a people's revolutionary war" to be "the only correct path of the Guatemalan revolution."[50] As for the Dominican Communist party, its preference for armed struggle was once again reaffirmed by the communique that the Party issued in October 1967 and in which it criticized the "waverers" who would use the death of Che Guevara to denounce the guerrillas as adventurists.[51] In much the same vein, the resolution adopted by the Eleventh Congress of the Communist party of Colombia in December 1971 referred the guerrilla movement as the main reserve of the revolutionary movement and "supreme form of man's struggle in Colombia."[52] Discussing the decisions of the Congress in the *World Marxist Review,* Manlio Lafont, member of the Party's Executive Committee, hailed the guerrilla operations as "part of the people's mounting struggle."[53] Furthermore, he claimed that its "kernel," the "Revolutionary Armed Forces," are "directed by the Communist Party and led by a member of its Central Committee, Manuel Marulanda Velez." Yet another Communist party that has recently embraced, not at all surprisingly, armed struggle as the only way how to "overthrow the anti-popular regime and establish a national democratic front government with Communist participation," has been the clandestine Communist party of Indonesia.[54] The fact that such resolutions advocating recourse to armed struggle have been allowed to appear in the Soviet-controlled media, such as the *World Marxist Review* and its *Information Bulletin,* indicates at least a tacit Soviet approval.

The Chinese Communist and Castroite Stand

While the Chinese communists and the Fidelistas do not see eye to eye on some of the aspects of communist strategy in the Third World, their views concerning the role of violence appear to be similar enough to warrant their discussion under one heading.

As pointed out in Chapter II, Mao and his followers have discounted the possibility that the victory over imperialism and transition to socialism in the Third World could be attained through peaceful means. In their "theses" and other statements and articles designed to expose the Soviet "revisionists" for their "brazen betrayal" of Marxism-Leninism by their reliance on peaceful means, the Chinese communists have re-affirmed most emphatically Mao's precept that "the seizure of power by armed force" was "the central task and the highest form of revolution," and a Marxist-Leninist principle valid "universally for China and all other countries."[55] They have proclaimed the armed struggle and wars of national liberation to be the only way to defeat imperialism and the violent revolution to be "a universal law" of the proletarian revolution.[56] They have publicly commended those Communist parties or factions in the Third World who have chosen the path of armed struggle and have criticized those who have opted for the peaceful approach.[57]

Much like Mao and his associates, Castro and the Fidelistas have had nothing but contempt for the "*vía pacifica.*" As shown elsewhere in the present volume,[58] they have continually derided the Latin American communists who have embraced the Moscow-sponsored strategy of peaceful-coexistence. They have succeeded in getting their militant doctrine of more Sierras Maestras for Latin America endorsed by the 1966 Tri-Continental Solidarity Conference, the 1966 Student Conference of the Latin American Continent, and the 1967 Latin American Solidarity Conference.[59] In the introduction he wrote for Guevara's diary published in 1968, Castro attacked the "pseudo-revolutionaries" who viewed Guevara's death as "the swan song of the revolutionary armed rebels in Latin America."[60]

It is true, as has been noted by several students of Latin American affairs, thât since 1968 Castro has reduced his earlier blanket approval of guerrilla warfare. In a speech of April 22, 1970, honoring Lenin's birthday, the Cuban leader conceded that the Cuban support for the Latin American revolutionary movement "does not necessarily have to be expressed "exclusively in favor of guerrilla movements."[61] Also, by saying in the same speech that "there will not be two revolutions that will develop in the same way" and that "new possibilities and new forms appear," he implicitly admitted that the Cuban example was not necessarily applicable everywhere. Similarly, Castro's 1971 visit to Chile and his speeches there have amounted to a concession that *vía pacifica* was O.K. under the specific conditions obtaining in Chile. Nonetheless, it would be incorrect to assume, as had

done some students of Cuban policies, that Castro had shifted all
the way toward the Soviet line on the matter of the armed
struggle.[62] That seems to be borne out by a statement made in
January 1971 by the prominent Cuban communist Carlos Rafael
Rodriguez, sent by Castro to represent Cuba at the inauguration
of President Allende. Speaking at a press conference at Santiago,
Chile, Castro's emissary had this to say: "Categorically, we do
not consider canceled the frequent revolutionary postulation, to
which our country subscribes, that in Latin America the fundamental way toward development of revolution is by means of
arms."[63] Furthermore, and most significantly, Rodriguez referred to Chile herself as being almost "the only possibility at the
moment for the application of the electoral way of access to
government and for the eventual transformation of that government into a revolutionary power."

The Operational Pattern

The ambivalence and flexibility that characterizes communist
teaching on the place and role of violence is reflected also in
actual communist operations. An overview of communist activities undertaken in the Third World in the last two decades reveals
a pattern of fluctuations between peaceful and non-peaceful
approaches from one country to another and from one period to
another. Not infrequently, the same communist parties or
factions that had preached and practised violence have shifted to
peaceful or semi-peaceful methods, and vice-versa. Some of the
communist groupings have followed over the years fairly consistently one and the same path, whether peaceful or non-
peaceful. Others still have engaged simultaneously in both
peaceful and non-peaceful tactics, following thus Lenin's time-
honored precept of meshing legal and illegal work.

In general, but with a certain measure of over-simplification, it
can be said that the recourse to, or abstention from, violence in
actual communist operations has been commensurate to the
degree of emphasis or deemphasis laid upon the matter in the
respective communist pronouncements. In line with their statements, the Soviet communists and their East European Comecon

partners have been relying overwhelmingly on peaceful means (in the Soviet meaning of the term) and have become involved in non-peaceful activities only in relatively few instances. Similarly, oscillations between peaceful and non-peaceful methods that have characterized the strategy and tactics of the Moscow-oriented communists in various parts of the Third World have paralleled their verbal statements. Much the same confluence of words and deeds has marked the tactics of the Castroites who have been doing their best to pursue the armed guerrilla approach they have been advocating so assiduously in their pronouncements.

On the other hand, words have not been always matched by deeds in the case of Communist China. While Chinese communist pronouncements on strategy and tactics bristle with fiery rhetoric urging recourse to violence, actual Chinese participation in violent activities in the Third World has been rather modest. With a few notable exceptions, Communist China has tended to offer little more than verbal assistance to the Third World's revolutionaries engaged in the Peking-recommended armed struggle. That has not been quite true of Peking-oriented communists of the Third World itself. Whereas some of them, such as the pro-Chinese splinter parties in Latin America, have been expressing their approval of violence more in words than deeds, others, particularly in non-communist Asia, have striven hard to translate into reality the Maoist precept of the relentless "people's revolutionary war."

Even though reliance on peaceful means is currently the order of the day for the overwhelming portion of the world communist movement that continues to follow Moscow, recourse to violence in communist strategy and tactics in the Third World has been none-too-rare. Indeed, there has been enough of it to fill a good-sized monograph should one wish to produce a complete recount of communist involvement in various non-peaceful operations undertaken in the Third World in the last two decades. With no ambition to do this, the present chapter purports merely to single out the main types of non-peaceful approaches employed in communist strategy and tactics in the Third World and to offer a few examples of each for purposes of illustration.

1. *Wars of National Liberation.*

The most violent of the types of armed struggle that the communists have used or participated in thus far in the Third World has been what they call the war of national liberation. As pointed out above, the war in Indo-China, the Algerian war against the French, and Castro's take-over in Cuba have been cited by Khrushchev himself as examples of a national liberation war. Added to these can be (from the communist standpoint) the Korean war of 1950, the Egyptian defense against the 1956 Anglo-Franco-Israeli invasion, the civil war in (Kinshasa) Congo in the sixties and possibly the shortlived uprising in the Dominican Republic. Moreover, the operations of groups fighting against the Portuguese in Mozambique and Angola are also considered as incipient stages of a national-liberation war.[64] Except for Cuba (where communist aid came only after Castro took over), communist participation in one form or another has taken place in all these instances. In nearly all of them, however, communist countries have refrained from direct military intervention or commitment of their own citizens to actual fighting. Apart from fiery verbal encouragement, communist support for the wars of national liberation has consisted mostly of shipment of weapons and other needed materials, financial aid, training of native fighters and advising them on the use of weapons and methods of warfare. Thus Soviet Russia, Communist China, Czechoslovakia, East Germany, Bulgaria and other communist countries are known to have delivered weapons of all sorts and other needed equipment and supplies to the Vietcong, Pathet Lao, and North Vietnamese forces fighting in South Vietnam, Laos and Cambodia, the Algerian rebel forces waging war against the French, the Lumumba-Gizenga side in the Congolese civil war as well as the insurgent forces in Portugal's African colonies, and elsewhere.[65] Military training has been provided not only at appropriate institutions in Soviet Russia, Communist China and Castro's Cuba, but also at facilities established by or with the aid of communist countries in some of the developing countries themselves and staffed mostly by Soviet, East European and Chinese instructors. The best documented cases of the latter were the secret camps set up in Ghana (prior to

Nkrumah's ouster) for the training of African "freedom fighters" by Russian and Chinese instructors.[66] Another such camp was reported to have been operated by the Chinese at Gambone in Brazzaville Congo.[67] Somewhat similar facilities have been established in Cuba for the training of revolutionaries for Latin America and, at one time, also Congo.[68]

In at least three instances, though, the involvement of communist countries did amount to direct participation in actual fighting. The most flagrant and the most massive case of this sort was, of course, the entry of the communist "volunteers" into the Korean war. Another such instance has been the prolonged and continuous North Vietnamese participation in the fighting in South Vietnam, Laos and Cambodia. (There is also a reported 18 thousand strong contingent of Chinese troops in Laos). And if the Israeli and western intelligence is correct, yet another such involvement, though on a much smaller scale, has been the use of Soviet pilots to fly missions in the Middle East and Soviet specialists to help operate the Egyptian anti-aircraft missile stations along the Suez canal.[69]

2. *Armed Uprisings and Coups d'Etat*

Closely related to the national liberation wars are what the communists call simply armed uprisings or armed revolts. In fact, while virtually all national-liberation wars have been at the same time armed uprisings, all uprisings are not wars of national liberation. Only those uprisings qualify as wars of national liberation in communist meaning of the word that are conducted against foreign rulers or such native regimes as are considered to be stooges and lackeys of foreign imperialists. Thus a communist-favored uprising staged in a country that had already acquired national independence and whose regime cannot very well be described as lackey of imperialism would be described simply as "people's armed revolt, "class-revolutionary struggle" or even "people's revolutionary war," but not as a national-liberation war. However, communist terminology used in this context is so vague and ambiguous and the predilection for the "national liberation" so compelling that communist spokesmen often tend to refer to an uprising as a national-liberation war even when it has nothing to do with national liberation proper or can hardly be called a war.

Good examples of communist-led or communist-favored uprisings in the Third World have been:

the 1965 abortive revolt aimed at liquidating the top army leadership and establishing a communist-led regime in Indonesia;

the protracted insurrection staged in Burma by the pro-Peking "White-Flag" communists;

similar long-drawn insurgent operations conducted over many years in Thailand, Malaysia, the Philippines, and more recently Oman;

various coups d'etat and attempts at coups d'etat designed to replace "national-bourgeois" regimes with "revolutionary" regimes more likely to behave to communist liking, such as the 1965 overthrow of the moderate socialist government in Brazzaville Congo and the ouster of General Abboud's regime in Sudan in 1964;

the 1971 "Che Guevarist" uprising in Ceylon.

In most of these and other instances, there has been abundant evidence about communist participation in one form or another. Again, as in wars of national liberation, the most common form of involvement on the part of the communist countries has been advising, training, and supplying the needed weapons and other materials. Thus Communist China has been training and arming, and for some time even providing field advisors, for insurgents in Thailand, Malaysia, Burma, Yemen, Oman, Zanzibar, Ceylon, Cameroon and Brazzaville Congo.[70] An especially interesting case of Chinese communist involvement was the 1965 seizure of power in Brazzaville Congo by the One-Party National Revolutionary Movement. Masterminded by Chinese communist advisors operating from the Chinese Embassy at Brazzaville and spearheaded by terrorist bands of the Congolese "Jeunesse" behaving much in the fashion of Mao's Red Guards, the coup was rightly labeled as "a classic communist-style takeover."[71]

Though less overtly than Peking, Moscow has also participated in some of the native uprisings in the Third World, mostly by providing weapons, finances and advisors. Probably the best-known case of this kind was the Soviet and East European support for the Kurdish insurgency against the Iraqi regime at a time when Iraq and the Soviet Union were at loggerheads.[72] A more recent illustration is supplied by the Dhofar rebellion in Oman that has been supported by both Soviet and Chinese arms and supplies.[73] Moreover, Soviet strategists have lately added a new and ironic twist to Russia's involvement in the Third World uprisings by throwing their support behind the established regimes against the rebels rather than the other way round. The most conspicuous instance of active Soviet participation in such counter-insurgency warfare occurred in southern Sudan where Soviet Russia supplied weapons and, as reported by several western correspondents, even pilots and advisors in the field for the Sudanese regime's military operations designed to crush Sudan's rebellious blacks.[74] In a somewhat similar way, Communist China stepped in to help the Algerian regime to fight the anti-regime rebels in Kabylia by supplying weapons to Algeria's "Popular Militia" for that purpose.[75] And in their turn, Castro's instructors were instrumental in helping to suppress the rebellion staged against the regime of President Massamba-Debat in Brazzaville Congo in 1966.[76]

3. *Guerrilla Warfare*

Defined usually as harassment of the enemy by small bands of irregulars, guerrilla warfare is generally an off-and-on-again operation on a considerably smaller scale than a war of national liberation or an uprising. Its main and probably only justification in the context of Marxist-Leninist strategy and tactics is that it may weaken the "reactionary" regime against which it is directed, help the revolutionaries to gain experience in armed struggle and, under certain propitious conditions, contribute toward bringing about the desired "revolutionary situation" in the country involved. However, since resort to guerrilla warfare leads more often than not to increased repression that renders revolutionary activities more difficult, and since it tends to put a question mark behind communist professions of peaceableness, it is rarely favored by orthodox communist strategists.

Nonetheless, despite the official Marxist-Leninist inhibitions, guerrilla warfare has become the most widely used method of armed struggle throughout the Third World, employed not only by various non-communist revolutionary groups, but also by groups claiming to be communist and affiliated with one or another segment of the world communist movement.

As noted earlier in this chapter, most active of all Marxist-Leninist groups in this respect have been Castro's followers in Latin America who have been engaged well-nigh continually in all sorts of guerrilla operations throughout Latin America, both rural and urban.[77] In so doing, they have had the fullest backing of Castro's Cuba, including tactical guidance, training, financial help and weapons supplies.[78] Castro's Cuba was reported also to have trained a number of guerrilla fighters who took part in the revolution in Zanzibar in 1964. In a number of instances there has also been direct Cuban participation in actual guerrilla operations, the most blatant, but by no means the only, examples being the abortive venture of the Guevara group in Bolivia and the participation (admitted by Havana) of a number of Cubans in guerrilla fighting in Venezuela.[79]

Over the years, the Peking-oriented communist parties and factions in Asia have also engaged in substantial guerrilla operations in many parts of Asia, such as Burma, Thailand, Malyasia, Sarawak, Indonesia, and even some parts of India and in Ceylon.[80] In some of these areas they have been able to escalate their guerrilla activities into full-scale uprisings, only to fall back again upon the less ambitious hit-and-run guerrilla tactics when the uprising failed. Thus the Indonesian Communist party, whose armed uprising had been crushed in 1965, was reported as having begun again in 1968 organizing guerrilla detachments and "people's defense schools" in remote areas of the country.[81] The operations of the Asian guerrillas have been supported by Communist China in much the same way as Castro's Cuba has been helping *guerrilleros* in Latin America, namely, with weapons, training in guerrilla tactics, and even Chinese communist field advisors. Moreover, Peking has extended help in a similar way also to such guerrilla groups as Yemeni anti-royalists, the Palestinian commandoes and the Naga and Naxalite rebels in India.[82] Also Chinese guerrilla warfare specialists were sent to Ghana to train the African "freedom fighters" during Nkrumah's rule.[83]

Although the Moscow-oriented communist parties of the

Third World are supposed to refrain from such "adventurist" exploits, quite a few of them have let themselves be drawn, at one time or another, partly or fully into guerrilla operations. As indicated above, that was the case of a number of communist parties of Latin America, such as those of Venezuela, Peru, Colombia and Guatemala, and also of some of the pro-Soviet parties of Asia, such as the Communist party of the Philippines. While most of them have withdrawn from guerrilla operations in the latter sixties, at least three of them, the Communist parties of Guatemala, the Dominican Republic and Colombia, as pointed earlier, have opted to continue in their guerrilla endeavors. Moreover, a growing number of the members of Communist parties that had shifted officially to peaceful means have refused to go along and have continued in guerrilla operations. Such have been, to cite a few outstanding examples, the cases of the Venezuelan communists Luben Petkoff and Douglas Bravo, the Brazilian communist Carlos Marighela, author of the famous "Mini-Manual of the Urban Guerrillas," slain subsequently in a police ambush at Sao Paulo in 1969, and the Filipino communist Joe M. Sison.

As for the Soviet strategists and their East European colleagues, their tendency has been, at least in recent years, to stay out of guerrilla operations as much as they could. Having staked the chances of the advancement of communism in the Third World, at least at the present stage, primarily on the strategy of peaceful coexistence, they had no desire to be caught red-handed in such violent ventures, especially when they were likely to end in failure. Nonetheless, as pointed out earlier in this chapter, both the Soviet Union and its Comecon partners are known to have contributed to the guerrilla cause by providing weapons, financial means and training in armed struggle tactics, subversion and use of weapons and explosives. As reported in *Nkrumah's Subversion,* Soviet vessels based on the Ghanaian port of Tema carried weapons to opposition groups in nearby African countries.[84] *Al Fatah* commando units were reported in 1969 to have obtained, through Czechoslovakia, some of the Soviet-type Katusha ground-to-ground rocket launchers.[85] Probably the best-known illustration of Soviet financial support of guerrilla activities has been the case of an Italian communist courier couple caught in 1965 at the Caracas airport with 150,000 $ intended for the Venezuelan communists who were at that time deeply involved in guerrilla operations against the Venezuelan government.[86] In 1971 the government of Mexico expelled five Soviet diplomats for complicity in violent anti-government riots in Mexico City in 1968 and for Soviet Russia's implication in allowing some of the Mexican students of Moscow's Lumumba University to be trained in urban and rural guerrilla warfare at a training camp in communist North Korea.[87] As estimated by Western observers, some 2,000 terrorists from 25 different countries, mostly African and Latin American, have been trained under a program financed by the Soviet Union, mainly in North Korea.[88]

The kinds of operations comprised in the guerrilla warfare in the Third World need not be recounted here in any detail as they are well-known from numerous reports in the daily and weekly press. Moreover, they have been listed quite explicitly in various manuals of guerrilla warfare, such as Marighela's earlier mentioned "Mini-manual of the Urban Guerrillas." They have included:

attacking police stations, jails, small army posts, arsenals;

occupying, sacking and burning government buildings, radio stations, editorial offices of "reactionary" newspapers;

ambushing, killing and executing the military, policemen and other functionaries of the regime against which guerrilla operations are directed;

kidnapping native high-ranking officials and even foreign diplomats and businessmen to be exchanged for arrested *guerrilleros* or money to be used in fostering the revolutionary cause;

robbing banks for the same purpose;

committing acts of sabotage against railways, airplanes, and other transportation means, pipe lines, refineries and other targets whose destruction harms and disrupts public services and normal life;

and even violent acts perpetrated solely for the sake of terrorizing so that the climate of fear and uncertainty be maintained or stepped up.

4. *Other Non-Peaceful Means*

The three main types of communist-approved armed struggle -

the national-liberation wars, uprisings, and guerrilla warfare - are supplemented by other tactics which, though not as violent as the former, do nonetheless qualify as non-peaceful.

The most commonly used such device has been the communist tactic of converting non-violent confrontations into violent ones. As observed in Chapter IX, this has been accomplished most easily among the students. Exploiting student grievances and impatience (oftentime quite justified) communist agitators, especially of the Castroite and Maoist variety, have succeeded in pushing student demonstrations in many parts of the Third World onto the path of violence. Similarly, there have been numerous communist attempts, some of them successful, to escalate strikes and labor disputes in a number of developing countries into bloody clashes with the police. On a number of occasions even some communist diplomats have played a role in such endeavors.[89] Nor can one consider as peaceful the forcible seizures of land by armed peasants perpetrated with overt or covert communist encouragement and participation in some countries of the Third World, such as the Maoist-sponsored Naxalite land grabs in India and the illegal takeovers of land by native Indian peasants in some countries of Latin America.[90]

Finally, one other approach of communist strategy and tactics vis-a-vis the Third World deserves to be listed under this heading (even though it has thus far been promoted through peaceful means), for it carries with it a not-so-peaceful potential for the future: the Soviet efforts to secure naval bases in several strategically important areas of the Third World. According to various reports, the Soviet Union has already obtained such facilities (in varying phases of development) at the Egyptian harbor of Mersa Matruh, West of the Nile, on the Socotra Islands at the entrace of the Red Sea and in several ports along the African coast, including Somalia's Mogadishu and Berbera, as well as at Trincomalee in Ceylon and on the Island of Mauritius in the Indian Ocean.[91] There have also been indications of Soviet endeavors to gain similar concessions at the Chilean port of Valparaiso. Thus, while issuing ardent calls for the abolition of all foreign military bases, Soviet strategists have at the same time been striving hard to provide such facilities for themselves, albeit in a deftly camouflaged form. To be sure, Soviet naval objectives have so far been pursued solely by peaceful means, as a *quid-pro-quo* of Soviet economic and developmental aid. However, once firmly established, such facilities are admirably suited to double as staging areas and solid bases of support for any type of non-peaceful strategy and tactics on which the Soviet Union might eventually decide.

Problems and Results

As indicated both by the conflicting views on the role of violence in presentday communist strategy in the Third World and by the rambling pattern of actual operations, communist utilization of non-peaceful means has encountered several problems, three of which have been most detrimental to the furthering of the communist cause.

1. First, because of their deep dissension about the usefulness, desirability and viability of non-peaceful methods at the present stage of the anti-imperialist struggle, the various segments of the world communist movement have gone in different, and often diametrically opposed, directions, and this even in one and the same country and in the same period of time. While one group would resort to armed struggle, another one would stay out of it and even condemn it. Thus, instead of joining forces, the different components of the world communist movement have often fought against one another more than against their common enemy.

Probably the most striking examples of such counter-productive behavior have been the cases of the Dominican Republic and India where different brands of communists have been involved in street fights and other forms of violent confrontation with one another.[92] Similarly, the extremist Maoist "People's Liberation Front" (nicknamed also "Che Guevarists") staged in 1971 an overt uprising against the leftist Ceylonese government of Siramo Bandaranaike based on a coalition with the pro-Moscow Communist party of Ceylon.[93] Even where open warfare has been avoided, the inability of the communist faction engaged in armed struggle operations to get help from other factions remaining opposed to such actions has tended to further weaken whatever chances of success there originally may have been.

2. Second, wherever one or another communist group or faction resorted to violence, it has failed to gain the support of

the masses and has thus been denied what true Marxist-Leninists consider to be the *sine qua non* of a successful armed struggle. Especially disappointing in this respect has been the attitude of the Third World's peasants whose overwhelming majority, as explained in Chapter VIII, did not succumb to communist wooing. While some of them could be induced occasionally to participate in forcible land seizures in several developing countries such as India, Brazil, and Chile, the bulk of the Third World's peasantry not only kept away from direct involvement in any communist-sponsored armed struggle, but proved also far from willing to help the *guerrilleros* indirectly by providing shelter and supplies (unless forced to do so). This appears to be true even of Indo-China where the Vietcong have had to resort to all kinds of coercive actions against the peasants to obtain what they needed. Such has also been the experience of rural guerrillas of Latin America whose failures in Venezuela, Colombia, Peru, Bolivia and elsewhere are accountable in part to the non-cooperative stand taken by the local peasantry. Che Guevara's admission concerning his inability to gain the support of Bolivia's *campesinos,* some of whom even betrayed his whereabouts to the authorities, bears a vivid testimony to the extent of peasant negativism in that respect.[94]

3. Third, recourse to armed struggle by some segments of the communist movement has aggravated the quarrel over the revolutionary leadership. The issue (discussed more fully in Chapters VI and VII) of who was entitled to lead the revolutionary forces in developing countries arose, of course, irrespective of the matter of peaceful or non-peaceful methods. But it could not but become even more complicated as a result of communist participation in armed struggle. Claiming that only those were the true revolutionaries who fought the imperialists with weapons in their hands, Castroite and Maoist guerrilla fighters assigned to themselves the leadership of the revolutionary struggle. Thus they clashed head-on with the orthodox communist parties which consider themselves, in line with the traditional Marxist-Leninist thesis, to be the sole legitimate vanguard of the revolution.

Often, it was the frantic desire to capture or recapture the contested leadership of the revolutionary forces and to counter accusations of cowardice leveled at them by Castroites, Maoists

and other radicals of the extreme left that has prompted some of
the orthodox communist parties to take part in the armed
struggle even though the proper conditions for its successful
pursuit did not obtain. However, not only did such a behavior fail
to bring them the coveted leadership, but the defeat of the armed
struggle into which they allowed themselves to be drawn further
weakened their prestige.

What, then, have been the results secured through non-
peaceful methods of the anti-imperialist struggle? What gains
have accrued to, and what losses were sustained by, the communist cause in the Third World through resort to violence in one
form or another?

As for the gains, these are most conspicuous in Indo-China
and the Middle East. Their recourse to armed struggle has
already given the communists control of very substantial portions of Laos and Cambodia (not to speak of South Vietnam
which is not a part of the Third World in the context of the
present volume), and it has placed them under a grave threat of
total engulfment into the world socialist system. The deepening
Soviet involvement in the military operations in the Middle East
has greatly increased Soviet influence in Egypt, Syria and Iraq.
The Soviet and Chinese aid to the communist-favored factions in
Yemen and Oman appears to have been instrumental in enhancing communist stature and in providing Soviet Russia and
Communist China with naval facilities in the area. Outside of
Indo-China and the Middle East, the emergence of a distinctly
pro-Communist regime in Brazzaville Congo through a Peking-
abetted coup also qualifies as a communist gain achieved through
non-peaceful means.

On the other hand, it is doubtful whether the cases of Algeria
and, even less, Sudan should be placed in the column of
communist gains attributable to non-peaceful means. While
communist countries did contribute to the Algerian war effort
against the French, it would seem that communist influence on
Colonel Boumedienne's regime is rather slight, his regime's anti-
Western stand notwithstanding. Nor, as borne out by their
Party's liquidation in 1971, did the Sudanese communists gain
any lasting political leverage through their active participation in

the coup that ousted General Abboud's government in 1964 and in the leftist coup of 1969.

As for the passive ledger of the communist balance, it must include, first of all, the long string of failures of communist and communist-backed uprisings mentioned in preceding pages. With the possible exception of Indo-China, all these resorts to armed struggle have been either crushed or at least contained and weakened. Some of them, such as those of Indonesia, (Kinshasa) Congo, and, most recently, Sudan in 1971, can be characterized as resounding communist fiascos. The communist-sponsored guerrilla operations have so far fared no better and the abandonment of guerrilla warfare by most of the Soviet-oriented communist parties of the Third World speaks for itself. Far from advancing the cause of communism, these terrorist activities have tended to alienate even those who were susceptible to pro-communist sympathies.

Thus the balance sheet of communist gains and losses in the Third World attributable partly or fully to recourse to non-peaceful methods has thus far been mixed, inconclusive and, save for Indo-China and some portions of the Middle East, rather meager. Moreover, it should be noted that about the only meaningful gains have been attained where the communist-led armed struggle could be supported, on a massive scale and over many years, by Soviet Russia and other communist countries, and this not merely by continuous and very substantial supplies of all sorts of weapons, but also by direct and very sizeable participation of outside forces in the actual fighting. Wherever this type of aid was not available, communist use of non-peaceful means appears to have mostly done the communist cause more harm than good.

Notes for Chapter XIII

[1] *Ritvo*, p. 110. Italics in the Program.
[2] *Ibid.*, p. 77. Italics in the Program.
[3] *Ibid.*, p. 92.
[4] p. 498.
[5] p. 17; see also pp. 498-99.

[6] pp. 470-71.

[7] p. 500.

[8] A. Belyaev and F. Burlatsky, "The Leninist Theory of Socialist Revolution and Our Times," *Kommunist*, No. 13, September 1960, p. 10.

[9] Sobolyev at the Cairo Seminar on "Africa - National and Social Revolution," *World Marxist Review*, 9, 10, 1966.

[10] *Third World*, p. 23.

[11] Mirskii in *"Sotsializm, Kapitalizm, Slaborazvitye Strany,"* (Socialism, Capitalism, the Less Developed Countries), *MEIMO*, No. 6, 1964, p. 65.

[12] A. Rumyantsev, "Concerning the Basic Contradiction of Our Time," *World Marxist Review*, 7, 7, 1964, pp. 3 ff. See also "Pseudo-Revolutionaries Unmasked," *Information Bulletin*, No. 11, 1970, pp. 34 ff.

[13] B. Gafurov, *"Internatsionalizm i natsional'no-osvoboditel'naia bor'ba"* (Internationalism and the National-Liberation Struggle), *Pravda*, September 4, 1969.

[14] G. Kochin, "China and the Third World," *New Times*, No. 52, 1971, pp. 23 ff.

[15] V. Shelepin, "Maoist Intrigues and the Third World," *New Times*, No. 26, 1969, pp. 6-8. See also *Third World*, p. 23.

[16] M. Mostovets, *"Boevoi front kommunisticheskogo dvizheniia,"* (The Battle Front of the Communist Movement), *Pravda*, November 20, 1968; also, V. Vol'skii, *"Latinskaia Amerika - Novyi etap bor'by narodov,"* (Latin America - A New Stage of the Struggle of the Peoples), *ibid.*, March 19, 1968.

[17] *Ritvo*, p. 78. Italics in the Program.

[18] p. 498.

[19] p. 303.

[20] *Third World*, p. 22.

[21] *Ibid.*, p. 23.

[22] See, for instance, "The Programme of the Communist International," *International Press Correspondence*, Special, Vienna, December, 1928, 8, 92, especially p. 1767. Cited in *Third World*, p. 24.

[23] p. 496-497, quoting Lenin. Italics in the original.

[24] p. 23.

[25] p. 499.

[26] p. 23.

[27] *The Current Digest of the Soviet Press*, XIII, 4, 1969, pp. 8-9. See also Thomas W. Wolfe, "Communist Outlook on War," in Vernon V. Aspaturian, *Process and Power in Soviet Foreign Policy*, Boston, 1971, pp. 401 ff.

[28] See, for inst., *The Third World*, pp. 22; "Maoist Intrigues in the Third World," *op. cit.*

[29] G. Starushenko, "Fiction and Truth About Wars of National Liberation," *Kommunist*, No. 2, August 1965, pp. 94-97.

[30] "Concerning the Basic Contradiction of Our Time," *op. cit.*

[31] *Fundamentals*, p. 498.

[32] *Jacobs*, p. 40.

[33] The Yugoslav communists did not attend either of the two conferences and did not sign either of the two Declarations. The Albanian communists did attend the 1960 Conference and signed the 1960 Declaration, but they subsequently reneged on it after the outbreak of the Sino-Soviet split; and they did not attend the 1969 Conference.

[34] Todor Zhivkov, "Socialism: Its Role in the World Revolutionary Process," *World Marxist Review*, 7, 8, 1964, pp. 12 ff.

[35] Dr. Jozef Gregor, *"Násilná a pokojná cesta,"* (The Violent and the Peaceful Road), *Predvoj*, July 6, 1967, pp. 6-7; see also, Karel Jezdinský's and Stanislav Budín's articles critical of Castro's and Guevara's emphasis on guerrilla violence in the Czechoslovak journal *Reportér* cited in the *Radio Free Europe Research Paper* (1968, no date): "Castro Strikes at Communist 'Microfaction' in a challenge to Moscow." Cited after "Translations on Latin America," Washington, No. 3, November 24, 1967, pp. 506.

[36] E. Paloncy, "Communism and the Movement for National Liberation," *Nová mysl*, No. 8, August 1963 cited in *Czechoslovak Press Survey*, No. 1308.

[37] See, for inst., Karel Kára, *"Problematika války v současné epoše,"* (The Problem of the War in the Present Epoch), *Dějiny a současnost*, No. 2, 1966, pp. 1-4; also, G. Kalmar, "Side by Side Without Illusions," *Nepszabadsag*, February 2, 1966. Cited in the *Hungarian Press Survey*, No. 1689, March 3, 1966, a classical example of ambivalence on the matter of peaceful and nonpeaceful methods.

[38] Of the Third World's Communists attending the 1969 Conference only the delegates of the Dominican Communist party declined to sign the Declaration.

[39] See, for instance, B. Alvarado Monson, "Some Problems of the Guatemalan Revolution," *World Marxist Review*, 9, 10, 1966, pp. 39-47; Alvaro Vasquez, "Combining All Forms of Revolutionary Struggle in Colombia," *ibid*, 9, 4, 1966, pp. 54 ff.; Cesare Levano, "Lessons of the Guerrilla Struggle in Peru," *ibid.*, 9, 9, 1966, pp. 44-51; Jorge Maravilla, "Philippines: Results, Difficulties, Prospects," *ibid.*, 13, 12, 1970, pp. 37-43; Prof. S. Gonionsky, "What is Happening in Colombia," *New Times*, No. 11, 1966, pp. 14-16.

[40] Marquez's statement published in the Chilean communist paper *El Siglo*. Cited in Luis E. Aguilar, "Fragmentation of the Marxist Left," *Problems of Communism*, XIX, 4, 1970, pp. 1-12; see also Robert J. Alexander, "The Communist Parties of Latin America," *Problems of Communism, ibid.*, pp. 37-46.

[41] *World Marxist Review*, 11, 11, 1967, p. 80.

[42] See more about this below.

[43] Juan Rodriguez, "Venezuela: Communist Party Regains Its Legality," *World Marxist Review*, 12, 5, 1969, pp. 41-42.

[44] See Rodolfo Ghioldi, *"No puede haber una revolucion en la revolucion,* (There Cannot be a Revolution in a Revolution), Buenos Aires, 1967, cited in Aguilar, *op. cit.;* Cheddi Jagan, "Lenin and Our Time" *World Marxist Review*, 13, 4, 1970, pp. 54-59; Rubens Iscaro, "Peaceful Coexistence and Revolutionary Struggle," *ibid.*, 13, 10, pp. 34-37; Luis Carlos Prestes, "Political Line and Tactics of Brazilian Communists in the New Conditions," *ibid.*, 11, 6, 1968, pp. 31-38; O. Vargas, "Peaceful Way of Achieving Democracy and Social Progress in Costa-Rica," *ibid.*, 9, 7, 1966, p. 56. ff.

[45] "Lenin's Heritage and Fight Against Opportunism in the Brazilian Communist Party," *World Marxist Review*, 13, 11, 1970, pp. 10-17, and "Battle of Brazil's Communists," *ibid.*, 15, 2, 1972, pp. 16-23.

[46] *Ila Al Aman* (Beirut), October 6, 1968, citing the Jordanian Communist party paper *Al-Taquadum*. Reported in the *Radio Free Europe Research* paper: "Arab CPS Criticize Guerrillas, Urge 'Just Peace,'" December 23, 1968.

[47] See, for instance, "Important Landmark on the Way to Democracy and Independence," *World Marxist Review*, 13, 11, 1970, pp. 75-77, and Luis Corvalan, "Chile; the People Take Over," *ibid.*, 13, 12, 1970, pp. 5-12.

[48] "Important Landmark on the Way to Democracy and Independence," *op. cit.*, p. 77.

[49] Corvalan, *op. cit.*

[50] Antonio Carillo Giles, "Fourth Congress of the Guatemalan Party of Labor," *World Marxist Review*, 13, 10, 1970, pp. 34-37; see also Huberto Alvarado, "The Guatemalan Revolution and Lenin's Ideas," *ibid.*, 13, 12, 1970, pp. 26-30.

[51] *Communism in Latin America*, November 1967.

[52] See "Communist Party of Colombia: Political Resolution of 11th Congress, *Information Bulletin*, 1-2, 1972, pp. 18 ff.

[53] "Unity of Working Class and People - Earnest of Victory," *World Marxist Review*, 15, 2, 1972, pp. 54 ff.

[54] "Advancing Under the Banner of Marxism-Leninism," *Information Bulletin*, 4-5, 1972, pp. 65 ff. See also Tomas Sinuraja, "Indonesian Communists Continue Struggle," *World Marxist Review*, 15, 6, 1972, pp. 64 ff.

[55] "The Proletarian Revolution and Khrushchev's Revisionism. Comment on the Open Letter of the C. C. of CPSU (8)," *Peking Review*, 14, April 3, 1964. Their reference is to Mao's "Problems of War and Strategy," *Selected Military Writings*, Peking, 1963, p. 267.

[56] The Chinese letter of June 14, 1963, and "The Proletarian Revolution" *op. cit.*

[57] See, for instance, "Political Report and Resolution of the Peruvian Communist Party," *Peking Review*, IX, No. 2, January 7, 1966, 20-22, praising the Peruvian Communist party for adopting a resolution stressing the necessity of using violence (a position meanwhile abandoned); on the other hand, see the Chinese communist letter indicting the Communist party of Chile for advocating a peaceful road.

[58] See Chapter VI.

[59] See more about it in Chapter VI; also, "Reds Plan More 'Vietnams'" *U. S. News and World Report*, January 31, 1966, p. 27.

[60] Leroy T. Aarons, "Castro Blasts Fellow Reds," *Washington Post*, July 3, 1968.

[61] *Granma*, May 3, 1970, pp. 2-5. Some of the Latin America's leftists began even to accuse Castro of abandoning the Latin American guerrilla fighers. See, for instance, Douglas Bravo's declaration published in *El Nacional*, Caracas, January 13, 1970, and in London *Times*, January 17, 1970.

[62] See Edward Gonzales, "Castro: the Limits of Charisma," *Problems of Communism*, XIX, 4, 1970, pp. 12-14; the author claims that "Havana seems to have swung back into line behind Moscow since 1968, fully endorsing the Soviet Union's domestic and foreign policies."

[63] David E. Belnap, "Castro Goal Retold," *Austin Statesman*, January 4, 1971. The citation is said to be taken from the complete stenographic transcript of the conference published in *Punto Final*, a magazine of leftist news and comment.

[64] See, for instance, *"Za polnoe osvobozhdenie"* (For a Full Liberation), *Pravda*, February 1ł, 1971.

[65] According to an AP report Soviet aircraft were used to fly military equipment and supplies to Sudan for transshipment to the Congolese rebels in

1964. Also, Egypt and Algeria were reportedly told at the same time that the weapons they would send to the Congolese rebels would be immediately replaced by the Soviet Union. A Czechoslovak ship was also involved in a clandestine shipment of guns for "Gizenga forces." See *Newsweek,* November 22, 1971, p. 37.

[66] See *Nkrumah's Subversion,* pp. 6 ff.

[67] *Radio Free Europe Release* of July 14, 1966: "Outlines of the Congo."

[68] Such a facility, dubbed "Academy of Terror," has been reported as being located at Minas del Frio in the Sierra Maestra mountains. See also C. L. Sulzberger, "Fidel Castro Balked," *New York Times New Service release, Austin Statesman,* September 27, 1967.

[69] See, for instance, Paul Scott, "Red Star in Mideast," *Austin Statesman,* December 28, 1967, and Joseph Alsop's many columns on the Middle Eastern war. See also, William King, "Castro and the Kremlin," *To the Point,* 1, 10, 1972, pp. 40-41.

[70] See "Peking: A Center of Subversion in S. E. Asia," *Radio Free Europe Research paper,* January 17 and 18, 1966; "Reds' Penetration Into Thailand," *U. S. News and World Report,* July 18, 1966; "Strategic Straits at Stake in Oman Guerrilla Struggle," *Austin American,* January 4, 1971; "Red Chinese Beef Up Insurgency Drive in Thailand" a report by Jack Foise of *Los Angeles Times, Austin Statesman,* May 7, 1970; Robert Conley's report "Red-Trained Africans Consolidate Hold After Zanzibar Revolt," *New York Times,* January 20, 1964; Robert S. Allen and John Goldsmith, "Ceylon Choice," *Austin Statesman,* May 26, 1970, (on a Colombo police report about the training of communist extremists in China); in an address before the United Nations General Assembly on October 5, 1962, the Foreign Minister of Cameroon accused Communist China of training and arming Cameroonian terrorists trying to overthrow the government of his country; "Ceylon. The 'Che Guevarist' Uprising," *Time,* April 19, 1971, p. 21; Ray Cromley's Washington report "China's Thai Role," *Austin Statesman,* January 14, 1972; "UK Troops Fighting Rebels in Oman," *Manchester Guardian Weekly,* 106, 2, January 8, 1972; Eric Rouleau, "South Yemen After Independence: A Hard Friendless Road to Socialism," *Manchester Guardian Weekly,* 106, 25, June 17, 1972.

[71] Lloyd Garrison's reports from Brazzaville, "A Red Takeover in 'Classic' Style," *New York Times News Service, Austin Statesman,* March 8, 1965, and "The Chinese Foothold in West Africa," *Austin Statesman,* March 5, 1965, Subsequently, Cuban instructors were reported as having replaced most of the advisers from other countries. See "Castro Gets a 'Satellite' in Africa," *U. S. News and World Report,* August 8, 1966, p. 44.

[72] Czechoslovakia was also involved at that time in supplying weapons to the Kurds.

[73] "Strategic Straits at Stake in Oman Guerrilla Struggle", *op. cit.;* Andrew Wilson "Russian, Chinese Weapons Used to Stop Sultan of Oman," *Austin Statesman,* August 20, 1970. See also A. Vasilyev, "Rebels Against Slavery," *New Times,* No. 38, 1971, pp. 27 ff., which is full of praise for Dhofar rebels and their "lively interest in Marxism-Leninism."

[74] See "Africa: Rumblings on a Fault Line," *Time,* March 1, 1971, p. 30; Rowland Evans and Robert Novak, "Soviet Thrust in Africa," *Austin Statesman,* January 6, 1971; "Reds Join Arab War on Blacks," a report from London *Observer,* published in *Austin American,* March 31, 1971. A vitriolic refutation of the above-mentioned report of the *Time* by a "Sudanese

Diplomat" was published in *New Times,* No. 12, 1971, p. 13, under the title "Reply to 'Time' Magazine."

[75] "Algeria Signs Pact for Red China Arms," *New York Times,* February 13, 1965.

[76] "Castro Gets a 'Satellite' in Africa," *op. cit.*

[77] See on this, for instance, Robert Alexander, "The Communist Parties of Latin America," *Problems of Communism, op. cit.*

[78] See, C. L. Sulzberger's revealing interview with the Cuban Army captain Manuel Espinoza Diaz captured in Venezuela in 1967: "Fidel Castro Balked," *op. cit.;* "Cuban Aggression Against Venezuela Confirmed," *Venezuela Up-To-Date,* Washington, Vol. XI, No. 7, Spring 1964, p. 11; in 1967 the second secretary of the Cuban Embassy in Mexico City was caught passing money to agents of the Guatemalan communist rebels, as reported by James Reston, "The Real Danger in Latin America," New *York Times News Service, Austin American,* April 6, 1967: "Peru's Chief Says Reds Stir Unrest," *New York Times,* July 22, 1965.

[79] AP report from Havana: "Cuba Tells of Helping Guerrillas," *Austin Statesman,* May 18, 1967, and "Latin America: Castro's Targets," *Time,* May 19, 1967, p. 36.

[80] Dilip Mukerjee's report to Washington Post from New Delhi: "West Bengal Hurt by Internal Strife," *Austin Statesman,* February 3, 1971. Anthony Short, "The Communist Party of Malaya: in Search of Revolutionary Situations," *The World Today,* 26, 12, Dec. 1970, pp. 529-35; An AP report from Ceylon: "Ceylonese Battle Extremists," *Austin American,* April 12, 1971.

[81] Ray Cromley, "Indonesia Lesson," *Austin Statesman,* October 23, 1968.

[82] Colin Legum, "China Challenge," *Austin Statesman,* May 22, 1969; Robert S. Allen and John A. Goldsmith, "Mideast Talks Periled," *American Statesman,* January 8, 1971, (on Peking giving money and training to Arab commandoes); Frank N. Hawkin's AP report from New Delhi: "Naga Rebels Losing Out," *Austin American,* November 12, 1969; "India: The Land Grab War," *Newsweek,* August 3, 1970, p. 31; "Peking and the Palestine Guerrilla Movement," *Radio Free Europe Research paper* of September 1, 1970. See also Yasser Arafat's acknowledgement of Chinese aid at a banquet given in the honor of the Palestinian National-Liberation Movement at Peking on March 21, 1970. NCNA release of March 21, 1970.

[83] *Nkrumah's Subversion,* pp. 7 ff.

[84] pp. 2, 39.

[85] John K. Cooley's report from Beirut to the *Christian Science Monitor,* January 25, 1969.

[86] "Communists; New Strategy," *Time,* April 13, 1965.

[87] AP report from Mexico City "Guerrilla Plot Stirs Mexicans," *Austin Statesman,* March 20, 1971, and Rowland Evans and Robert Novak, "Mexican Backfire. Russians Caught Redhanded in Latin Plotting," *Ibid.,* March 26, 1971. "Mexico, Troubles on the Via Pacifica," *Time,* April 19, 1971, pp. 23-24; "Students Renew Mexican Protest," *New York Times,* April 3, 1971.

[88] Alan Dean, "Russians Increasing Terrorists," A Copley News Service report from London, *Austin Statesman,* August 18, 1971.

[89] For instance, four members of the Soviet embassy in Mexico City were ordered out of the country for such activities in October 1966.

[90] Some of the forcible land seizures that occurred in Chile in 1970 and 1971 appear also to have been at least tacitly condoned by extremist segments among

Chilean communists. But the official leadership of the communist party of Chile disapproved such actions.

[91] See Joseph Alsop's report "Soviet World Strategy," *Austin American,* January 11, 1971. However, Cairo's Voice of the Arabs reported on December 5, 1970, a denial by the People's Republic of Yemen that there was a Soviet base on Socotra, *USSR and Third World* I, 1, 1971, p. 25.

[92] William Ryan, "Reds in Dominica Fight Each Other," *Austin Statesman,* March 5, 1971: Francis B. Kent's report to *Los Angeles Times:* "Left Battles Left in Santo Domingo," *Austin Statesman,* January 8, 1971; Dilip Mukerjee's report to *Washington Post* "West Bengal Hurt by Internal Strife," *Austin Statesman,* February 3, 1971.

[93] See, for instance, "Ceylon's Pro-Red Premier Fights pro-Red Rebels," *National Observer,* April 12, 1971, p. 3.

[94] See an analysis by Robert F. Lamberg, "Che in Bolivia: the 'Revolution' that Failed," *Problems of Communism,* XIX, 4, 1970, pp. 25-37.

CHAPTER XIV

CONCLUSIONS AND PROSPECTS

For almost two decades the developing nations of the Middle East, Asia and Africa have been the prime target of Soviet Russia's strategy of "peaceful coexistence." More recently, Latin America has been added to the roster and assigned a high priority in the Soviet design for the communization of the world. By choice or otherwise, the Soviet Union's East European partners have followed the Soviet lead. Communist China has also focused her attention on the Third World, especially non-communist Asia, the Middle East and some parts of Africa. Castro's Cuba, the latest entrant into the world socialist system, has been pushing the Fidelista brand of communism throughout Latin America while Yugoslavia's Tito has kept busy selling his concept of "active non-alignment" to as many countries of the Third World as possible.

Thus, the whole world socialist system, including even tiny Albania, has come to participate in the ambitious multi-stage project designed to substitute communist for Western influence throughout Asia, Africa and Latin America, pave the way for their gradual communization and thereby contribute toward the hoped-for victory of communism in the entire world.

As is invariably the case with any major communist under-taking, the increased emphasis on the Third World as a desirable target of communist strategy had to be explained in terms of the Marxist-Leninist world outlook. Hence, ever since the middle fifties when the current communist pre-occupation with the Third World began, the interpreters of Marxism-Leninism have been busy delving into Lenin's prolific writings in search for appropri-ate dicta designed to prove that the recent thrust into "im-perialism's preserve" in Asia, Africa and Latin America is precisely what the Master would have done. By laying excessive emphasis on those of Lenin's statements fitting the postulates of presentday situation, such as the thesis on the by-passing of capitalism by developing nations, and by tacking onto them new or renovated constructs, such as the concepts of national democracy and non-alignment, they have produced an updated neo-Leninist version that they consider to be a satisfactory ideological justification of current operations in the developing areas of the world.

However, the basic rationale underlying this recent shift of emphasis from the advanced industrialized countries of Europe to the less developed areas of Asia, Africa and Latin America lies in considerations of strategic and tactical rather than purely ideological nature. Whereas the growing economic and political consolidation of non-communist Europe of the post-1947 era, coupled with the firm United States commitment to defend it, nipped in the bud any chance of meaningful communist gains (let alone a repetition of the process that had led to the communist takeover of Eastern Europe in the latter forties), "the vigorous process of disintegration of the colonial system" occurring in many parts of the world seemed to offer too good an opportunity for the advancement of communism to be passed over. The rampant anti-Westernism, chaotic political and economic condi-tions, preference for socialism over capitalism and other such factors attendant upon what the Soviet Communist Party Program called the "period of stormy national-liberation revolu-tions" looked indeed like creating the most favorable locale for a successful unfolding of the communist strategy.

To take advantage of the new opportunities, communist strategists have resorted to a variety of devices, methods and techniques ranging all the way from innuendos and seemingly innocuous calls for united fronts of all "progressive" and "patriotic" forces to outright subversion and recourse to armed struggle. Most of the traditional tools of communist strategy and tactics could be made to serve the present needs in much the same forms in which they had been used in the past. Others had to be adjusted, refashioned or updated to fit the conditions prevalent in one or another portion of the Third World.

Thus economic aid, used only sparingly and in a rather different manner prior to the middle fifties, has become a major instrument of communist strategy in the Third World at the current state of the anti-imperialist struggle. Taking advantage of their increased industrial potential in the capital goods production, Soviet Russia and the countries of communist East Europe have launched a substantial program of economic and technical assistance aimed at making as many developing nations as possible economically dependent on the world socialist system. The timing of the aid, the way of selecting the recipients and the entire handling of the program leaves no doubt that political rather than purely economic considerations have been the main determinants. Although Communist China does not approve of the Soviet emphasis on, and handling of, economic aid, she has not been loath to employ economic instruments, though on a much smaller scale, to foster her influence in some parts of the Third World.

Another device that has been assigned a prominent role in today's communist strategy and tactics vis-a-vis the Third World has been cultural penetration. Linked to the world socialist system through a massive interlocking network of agreements on cultural, educational and scientific cooperation, much of the Third World has become a favorite target of communist cultural beneficence designed to persuade the developing nations how much better off they would be if they turned their backs on the "decadent" and "depraved" culture of the "capitalist money-bags" and embraced the superior "truly spiritual culture" presumably flourishing in communist countries. All sorts of approaches have been used for this purpose, including the greatly stepped-up broadcasting in all major native languages of the Third World, generous distribution of books, pamphlets, periodicals, free news services by communist press agencies, establishment of a vast network of Friendship societies, an almost incessant stream of mutual visits by various cultural, scientific, artistic and sport groups, provisions of training facilities for the African and Asian communications media workers and flattering the ego of the developing nations by repetitive and excessive praise of their cultural and other achievements.

But the most novel of the various devices of communist cultural diplomacy vis-a-vis the Third World have been the present offerings in the field of education. Although Soviet Russia and the Comintern did provide in the past educational and other training facilities for foreigners, among them also for Asians, Latin Americans and a few Africans, such offerings were mostly reserved for *bona fide* Communist party members and were meant mainly to train and instruct Party functionaries and communist agents. (About the only non-communists educated in the Soviet Union in earlier days were a small number of nationalist revolutionary soldiers, such as Chiang-kaishek, who were admitted to special training at Soviet military institutions). On the other hand, presentday Soviet, East European and Chinese educational offerings are intended primarily for the "progressive" non-communist segment of the Third World's youth yet to be converted to the cause of "scientific socialism." Moreover, today's operations are on a much larger scale, involving as they do tens of thousands of students, full-fledged higher studies curricula, the creation in the world socialist system of special universities and other educational facilities to serve the needs of the developing nations, the establishment of educational institutions in the Third World itself and loans of many hundreds of teachers and professors.

Another time-honored Leninist thesis that has had to be "creatively" reinterpreted to make it fit better the conditions obtaining in most of the Third World has been the postulate of the leadership of the proletariat and its conscious vanguard, the Communist parties. The imperative necessity of such a leadership has always been one of the most fundamental tenets of the Marxist-Leninist ideology and strategy. While temporary leadership by one or another non-proletarian stratum and party could, if absolutely unavoidable, be tolerated at the bourgeois-

democratic or national-democratic stage of the revolution, especially at its initial phase, the assumption of hegemony by
communist-led industrial working class has been viewed as a *sine
qua non* for a successful transition to genuine socialism in the
Marxist-Leninist meaning of the word.

However, realizing that both the proletariat and the communist parties of most of the developing nations were too weak,
numerically as well as ideologically and organizationally, to be
able to assume their "historical" leadership mission, some of the
communist ideologues and strategists have begun dropping
occasional hints suggesting interim alternatives. Pending the
emergence of a proletariat and a communist vanguard capable of
taking over, some of the Soviet spokesmen appear to be willing
to concede such a leadership to "the international working
class," the trade unions, or even to "elements close to the
working class," such as the "revolutionary democrats." But
these suggestions seem not to have found favor with most of the
native communists of the Third World who have continued to
cling stubbornly to the original Leninist thesis that no transition
to socialism can be effectively carried out and brought to its
completion except under communist leadership. Nor have the
impatient Chinese communists gone along with the Soviet-
recommended alternatives. Their emphasis has remained unequivocally upon the immediate seizure of leadership by the
working class and its communist vanguard. Moreover, since the
Chinese notion of the working class revolves mainly around the
rural and agricultural proletariat rather than urban-industrial
proletariat, the Chinese leadership formula differs somewhat
from that of their Soviet comrades. The Fidelistas also have
turned thumbs down on the leadership claims of the traditional
communist parties and assigned the leadership of the revolution
at all its phases to fighting Castroite *guerrilleros*. Thus the all-
important issue of who should lead whom in the Third World has
become a major bone of contention among the various segments
of the world communist movement.

So also has the question of the desirability or non-desirability
of using armed struggle. Both the Maoists and the Fidelistas view
armed struggle, especially guerrilla warfare and the wars of
national-liberation, as the principal methods of anti-imperialist

strategy. Indeed, they appear to consider recourse to armed struggle to be virtually the only way how to defeat imperialism and pave the way for communist victory. Also, their deeds have matched for the most part their words as they have participated in various forms of armed violence in a number of developing countries, especially in Asia and Latin America. Even some of the Communist parties of the Third World belonging to the Soviet camp have opted for and taken part in armed struggle at one time or another. On the other hand, Soviet and East European communists have displayed a preference for a non-violent approach at this stage of the East-West struggle. They have persisted in accusing the Maoists and other "ultra-revolutionaries" advocating use of indiscriminate violence of irresponsible and self-defeating adventurism. Also, with the exceptions of Indo-China and Egypt, Soviet and East European communists have mostly refrained from participation in violent confrontations in the Third World.

The communist penetration of the Third World has been facilitated by several important factors.

Foremost among them had been the rampant anti-colonialism and nationalism whose tide has risen to unprecedented heights throughout Asia, Africa and Latin America in the postwar era. Since it was the West that had colonized and ruled most of what constitutes today the Third World, it is hardly surprising that the African, Arab, Asian and Latin American anti-colonialism and nationalism has become so stridently anti-Western. Nor is it too difficult to understand why it has zeroed on the United States just as much as, or often even more on main ex-colonial powers, such as Britain and France. Even though the United States was in fact the first colony to stage what amounted to the national-liberation revolution and its subsequent participation in traditional colonialism of the 19th and early 20th century was negligible, its association with the ex-colonial powers of Western Europe and its economic penetration of many areas of the Third World has made the United States a convenient target of whipped up anti-Western resentment. So has the United States' stand on Vietnam and the American support of Israel which can be easily distorted to portray America as the sworn enemy of the legitimate national aspirations of the emerging nations. On the other hand, having been mostly uninvolved in the colonization of Africa, Latin America, Southeast Asia and the Middle East, Russia and the other countries of the world socialist system have managed to escape the colonizers' opprobrium, at least in the eyes of the great majority of the Third World's masses.

The massive American economic involvement in so many developing nations has made the United States especially vulnerable to charges of neo-colonialism which presumably strives to keep the developing nations in subjection by dominating them economically rather than through the old-fashioned military-political methods. Besides allegedly depriving the emerging nations of their economic independence, without which political independence is little more than an empty shell, these neo-colonialist endeavors are said to perpetuate the perennial economic despoliation that has already cost the countries of the Third World billions upon billions of dollars siphoned off over the years into the pockets of Western monopolists. Hence, the communist-suggested solution of the problem, consisting in the ejection of such Western exploiters and in the nationalization of their enterprises, sounds rather appealing, especially to those eager to find a convenient scapegoat for their countries' economic backwardness, poverty and mismanagement. Since such anti-Western actions are bound to exacerbate the Third World's relations with the Western countries concerned, they play invariably into communist hands and afford openings for communist incursions. Also, by ridding the native-bourgeois entrepreneurs of foreign competition, nationalization of foreign companies and the various restrictions imposed upon those allowed to remain have tended to facilitate communist efforts aimed at gaining cooperation of the national bourgeoisie at the initial phases of communist penetration.

These anti-Western trends have been further strengthened by the strong anti-capitalist and pro-socialist bias that prevails throughout the Third World. Socialism is, of course, a Western product and several Western countries could serve as better examples of what true socialism is all about than the perverted forms of socialism practised today in the communist countries governed under the aegis of Marxism-Leninism. Nevertheless, communist propaganda has managed to sell a number of

developing countries on the notion that, in constructing socialism, they ought to look toward the world socialist system and its
"rich experience" with socialism rather than the West which is
alleged to at best offer only an ineffective reformist potpourri.

Nor could the communist cause in the Third World but benefit
from the impatience displayed by the leaders and the masses of
most of the developing nations in their search for some sort of a
miraculous shortcut from poverty to prosperity following their
liberation from the colonial rule. As explained more fully in
previous chapters, this "revolution of rising expectations" could
be exploited much more easily by communist strategists and
propagandists than by their democratic equivalents. Working at
all times under the constant scrutiny of the public, the opposition
and the free communications media, Western democratic regimes could hardly afford making lavish promises of early and
significant betterment as a sure reward for those following the
Western way. On the other hand, unrestrained by such limitations of democratic accountability, their communist competitors
could and did attempt to lure the developing nations into closer
cooperation with the world socialist system by assuring them
that, with communist help and guidance, they would be able to
advance speedily from backwardness to modernity and would
achieve in one generation what otherwise would take them
centuries.

In a somewhat similar vein, communist endeavors in the Third
World have been aided also by the fact that most of the
developing nations were not and are not yet ready for Western-
type democracy, but can operate better, at their present stage of
development, under one or another form of authoritarianism. As
a result, such countries of the Third World as are governed in an
authoritarian manner, especially as one-party states headed by
strong men or *juntas*, often find at least some aspects of the
communist dictatorial patterns and practices more relevant for
their own needs than the democratic ways of the West.

Another important factor conducive to the rise of communist
and a corresponding decrease of Western influence in the Third
World has been the natural desire of most of the developing
nations to lessen their traditionally heavy economic and cultural
dependence on the West and, even more so, to stay out of the

politics of the cold war. The striving for lesser dependence on the West has meant in many instances more willingness on the part of the developing nations to increase economic and cultural relations with the countries of the world socialist system and to create thus, willy-nilly, additional facilities for communist penetration. The wish to stay out of the East-West tug-of-war has induced most of the nations of the Third World to opt for non-alignment. Since a number of the developing countries remained, even after attaining political independence, tied to the West by various commitments of political, economic and even military nature, their choice of non-alignment was bound to lead, sooner or later, to the annulment of such commitments, which could not but weaken the position of the West and provide at least a relative advantage for its Eastern rivals.

Yet another advantage that communist strategists enjoy over their Western competitors derives from the belief, widespread in the Third World, that the West, and particularly the United States, is primarily interested in the preservation of the *status quo* whereas the communists presumably stand for a radical revolutionary transformation of the society that alone is deemed capable of effecting a meaningful improvement. True or not, such an impression tends to enhance the appeal of communism, especially for the Third World's radically-minded intelligentsia, students and youth. This pro-communist bias is further strengthened by the slow pace of economic and social reforms undertaken by some of the Third World's regimes, for this slowness is often blamed upon an unholy conspiracy of Western and local vested interests.

Finally, the United States' racial dilemma and the bitter inner strife over the war in Vietnam could not but tarnish the American image throughout much of the Third World and raise doubts about America's will and ability to render effective aid to future victims of communist designs in the Third World. This fits, of course, neatly into the communist line that seeks to portray the United States as a racist, sick and strife-torn country that cannot and should not be trusted.

While the communist strategy vis-a-vis the Third World has been aided by the above-mentioned factors, it has also run into a number of impediments.

Undoubtedly, what has hurt the communist cause most has been the Third World's growing awareness of real communist motives and ulterior intentions. Desirous as they have been to lessen their countries' dependence on the West, to secure communist economic aid, political support and, if needed, military hardware, the regimes of most of the developing nations have assumed and striven to maintain a friendly pose toward the communist countries, especially the Soviet Union. They have appended their signatures to a host of communist-sponsored communiques and declarations denouncing Western imperialism and subscribing to various communist themes. Their spokesmen at the United Nations and other international forums have gone a great length to avoid any statements or actions likely to antagonize the Soviet Union. All the same, as has been indicated throughout the present volume, the leaders of most of the developing nations do seem to realize full well what the ultimate communist objective really is. Nor would it be easy for them to forget it, for they keep being reminded of it by such displays of communist behavior as the 1968 invasion of Czechoslovakia, the ominous implications of the "Brezhnev doctrine," the Soviet off-and-on pressures against Rumania and Yugoslavia and, most of all, the none-too-infrequent recourse to subversion, sabotage, conspiracy and other acts of bad faith committed time and again by native communists in one or another part of the Third World, oftentime with covert or overt Soviet, Chinese or Castroite backing.

Another factor that has adversely affected communist operations in the Third World has been the major schism that has developed in the world communist movement in the sixties, mainly (though not solely) as a result of the Sino-Soviet split and, as far as Latin America is concerned, the Fidelista deviationism. The vicious accusations and counter-accusations hurled against one another by the different segments of the communist movement and their bitter public controversies over strategy, tactics and ideology have torn asunder the much-acclaimed unity of the world communist movement which had been one of the most important assets of its power.

Nor has the appeal of Marxism-Leninism fared well in competing with the notions of native socialism prevalent in many areas of Asia, Africa, the Middle East and Latin America. To be sure, the preference for socialism over capitalism displayed by most of the leaders of the Third World has made them interested in Soviet Russia's and communist East Europe's experience and has even prompted them to utilize some of it in their experimentation. But the more they learned about the Marxist-Leninist *modus operandi*, the more they seemed to realize that an updated or "restructured" form of their own native socialism with its rejection of the concepts of the class struggle and the dictatorship of the proletariat was more desirable than the Marxist-Leninist model, whether of the Soviet or Chinese variety.

One particular aspect of Marxism-Leninism that has lessened its attractiveness for the nations of the Third World has been its identification with atheism. Since religion plays a major role in the life of the peoples of Asia, Africa, the Middle East and Latin America, be they Christians, Moslems, Buddhists, Hindus or other, any teaching that denies the existence of God inevitably saddles itself with a fairly heavy burden. Although Marxian communism's atheist connotation does not necessarily preclude the adoption of some of the communist economic and social prescriptions even by believers in God, it makes it virtually certain that any such adoption will fall far short of an acceptance of the Marxist-Leninist "scientific socialism" in its entirety. As clearly indicated by their eagerness in promoting various "dialogues" between the Marxists and the believers in God, communist strategists are well aware of their problem in this respect. However, the rigidity of the orthodox version of Marxism-Leninism has so far prevented them from abandoning the thesis of the incompatibility of "scientific socialism" with religious belief as West European socialists had done a long time ago.

Sobering second thoughts about the suitability of the Marxist-Leninist model have also cropped up in several other respects. The appreciation of economic aid has in good many instances been undercut by such things as the low quality of communist goods, delays and interruptions in deliveries, and the restrictive disadvantages of the bilateralism that is so strictly adhered to in communist economic dealings with developing nations. Also, because of their aloofness and their overall behavior, considered peculiar by local population, most of the many thousands of

Soviet technicians and advisers sent to the Third World could not have helped becoming actually counter-productive as propagandists for the communist way of life. Nor did the prolonged exposure of the Third World's students sent to study in communist countries to the stark realities of everyday life under communism appear to have been instrumental in converting them into pro-communist sympathizers. While they may have remained grateful for the educational opportunities given them by their communist hosts, most of the students have returned home convinced that Marxism-Leninism had much less to commend it than they had been led to believe.

Also, many Third World revolutionaries have become disillusioned with the subvervience of most communists of the Third World to Moscow, their doctrinal rigidity and bureaucratization. This disillusionment, particularly among the intelligentsia and the younger generation, has greatly weakened communist appeal in many developing countries and all but destroyed the native communists' chance of ever fulfilling the revolutionary leadership mission assigned to them in Marxist-Leninist strategy. The native communists' position is further undermined by Soviet Russia's courting of the very national-bourgeois or "revolutionary democratic" regimes which were making life difficult for them.

What, then, have been the results obtained so far? To what extent has communist strategy succeeded or failed to achieve its objectives? With a number of factors helping and a number of other factors impeding the communist endeavors in the Third World, it is hardly surprising that an overall evolution should yield a mixed and often rather perplexed picture of successes, failures and inclusive draws.

It would seem that communist strategists have registered a good measure of success in the pursuit of their initial and intermediate goals. Thus they have certainly contributed to the weakening, in some instances quite substantial weakening, of Western influence in the Third World. Political ties between the West and many developing nations have been loosened and in some instances strained. Progressive nationalization of major Western enterprises and ever stiffening restrictions imposed on those still left in private hands have impaired the West's economic position. The abandonment of several Western military facilities in response to adverse reaction (zealously encouraged and exploited by communist propagandists) has tended to complicate Western defense in several strategically important areas.

The weakening of Western influence has been paralleled by a corresponding strengthening of communist influence. A number of developing nations selected as especially desirable targets for massive communist economic penetration have become strongly dependent upon their communist benefactors; and the dependence has been further compounded when the countries concerned were in need of communist military hardware and Soviet political backing. The stepped-up cultural diplomacy of the communist countries, aided by various communist-controlled Front organizations, has managed to expose developing nations to a steady stream of communist propaganda. New communist parties have been set up where none existed prior to the unfolding of the Soviet offensive in the Third World. Soviet-recommended national democratic fronts with overt or covert communist participation have been created in a number of countries of the Third World. In a few instances native communists have even succeeded in realizing their long-sought goal of gaining entry into the ruling coalitions and securing cabinet-level positions. Communist-controlled labor unions and student organizations have been organized in various parts of Asia, Africa and Latin America and thus provided communist strategists with important tools in their never ceasing efforts to gain the support of the Third World's working class and intelligentsia. In the international arena a substantial number of developing nations have acquired the habit of lending verbal support to Soviet-sponsored causes or at least refraining from speaking up when expressing approval would be too much to ask.

There is, of course, no sure way of determining how much of the decrease of Western influence in the Third World is attributable to communist policies and actions and how much of it has been caused by factors and circumstances that have nothing to do with communism and the world socialist system. On the basis of the evidence gathered in the present volume, this writer has come to the conclusion that most of the postwar decline in the West's stature in the Third World has to be attributed to factors unrelated to communism, such as nationalism, anti-colonialism, resentment of Western economic and cultural superiority, Western collaboration with upopular regimes and, in the Arab case, Western support for Israel. Thus Western influence would have declined even if Soviet Russia and the world socialist system did not exist. What communist strategy has mainly done has been to exploit the above-mentioned factors and make it easier for the countries of the Third World to turn against the West by compensating them, at least partially, for the losses sustained in the process. In this sense, communist strategists are correct in claiming credit for speeding up and deepening anti-Westernism in the Third World by their readiness to lend a helping hand.

While making good headway toward the attainment of their intermediate goals, communist strategists have fared rather poorly in the pursuit of their main objective òf pushing the Third World unto the road leading toward "scientific socialism" (in the Marxist-Leninist meaning of the term) and the establishment of "the dictatorship of the proletariat," the well-known Marxist-Leninist euphemism for communist seizure of power. Not only have the communists failed so far to gain control of any country of the Third World, but in most of them they seem to be farther away from their main goal than when the communist offensive in the Third World began in earnest in the middle fifties.[1]

To be sure, many of the developing nations have opted for what communist theoreticians like to call the "non-capitalist path" and, as noted above, have expressed preference for socialism over capitalism. But it has gradually become ever more obvious that what they have in mind is a kind of socialism that is far different from the Marxist-Leninist variety. Not even those among the leaders of the developing nations who have been most anti-Western and most vocal in their commitments to socialism have displayed any desire to go all the way toward a wholesale collectivization of their economy along Soviet lines. Rather, they appear to favor a mixed system combining public ownership of basic resources and major industries, especially in the extractive industry and capital goods production, with private enterprises in the remainder of the economy. Nor is there any indication that they intend to follow the Soviet example in agricultural collectivization. On the contrary, their agrarian reforms seem to envisage retention of private farming on an individual and cooperative basis as a predominant and *lasting* feature of the operative pattern of the agriculture.

These meager results of communist endeavors to "marx-leninize" the economic foundations of the developing nations have been paralleled by a similar lack of meaningful progress in bringing about communist-desired changes in the Third World's political and cultural "superstructure." Of all the developing nations of Asia, Africa, the Middle East and Latin America, as of 1972 only five — Chile, Ceylon, Iraq, Syria and Southern Yemen — have government coalitions with communist participation; and in all these cases the few communist incumbents have been wisely kept away from such key cabinet posts as control the armed forces and the police. Most of the Third World's national democratic fronts, so ardently recommended by Soviet strategists, have also proved to be something of a disappointment for their communist advocates. With the exception of Chile, where the communists do have a good deal of political leverage in Allende's popular-unity front, and two or three states of India, the influence of native communists in such fronts ranges from negligible to modest. In many instances, being outlawed, local communists are barred from participation in legitimate national fronts and similar groupings on a party basis and can at best join them only as individuals. Thus "the Marxist-Leninist parties" of the Third World are still very far from becoming, as the 1961 *Program of the Soviet Communist Party* would have it, "a universally recognized national force enjoying ever greater prestige and followed by large sections of the working people." Nor has any country of the Third World as yet reached the status of "national democracy", the Soviet devised transitional stage of development through which developing nations are supposed to progress toward a "higher form" of Marxist-Leninist statehood. At various times, Soviet writers did refer to several developing nations, such as the United Arab Republic, Algeria, Burma, Brazzaville Congo, Guinea and Ghana, as being close to becoming states of national democracy. Yet none of them has thus far been deemed worthy of that designation, mainly, no doubt, because they have not given native communists the full freedom of operations that is considered to be the most essential ingredient of national democratic statehood in the Soviet definition of the term. (At the moment, Chile is the only country of the Third World that appears to meet the criteria prescribed by the 1960 *Declaration of 81 Communist Parties* for a state of national democracy.)

The various segments of the Asian, African and Latin American population have also failed thus far to live up to communist expectations. The "new contingent of the world proletariat — the young, working-class movement of the newly-free, dependent and colonial countries of Asia, Africa and Latin America —" still appears to be lacking in the kind of Marxist-Leninist class consciousness, organizational ability and other characteristics deemed necessary for a class assigned the "historical mission" of revolutionary leadership. As mentioned above, communist organizers have attained a measure of success in being able to set up pro-communist labor unions and even some trade union centres in a number of developing countries, especially in Latin America, and in persuading additional labor unions not to join the pro-Western *International Confederation of Free Trade Unions*. But they have not been quite as successful in their endeavors to recruit the labor unions of the developing nations for the communist-controlled *World Federation of Trade Unions*, especially in Africa. The Third World's peasantry has remained stubbornly disinterested in the worker-peasant alliances that communist strategists consider so crucially important for the success of their cause. Whenever and wherever one or another peasant group did embark upon the revolutionary action, it was almost always in the form of forcible land seizures (such as occurred in Chile, India and Brazil) considered as "adventurist" by Soviet and other orthodox communist parties.

The "national bourgeoisie", the primary target of communist wooing at the early phases of the national-liberation process, has been losing steadily its "revolutionary potential" and has by now been virtually written off in but a few countries as a "progressive" force. Nor have communist strategists derived as much satisfaction as they had hoped from the behavior of the "revolutionary democrats" and "patriotic officers" who have now replaced the national bourgeoisie as the Third World's most promising non-proletarian stratum in communist calculations. Not one of them has as yet moved to the positions of Marxism-Leninism as some Soviet theoreticians had confidently predicted. Worse still, most of them have been anything but kind toward their own native communists as revealed time and again by actions of such "revolutionary democrats" and/or "patriotic officers" as Algeria's Boumedienne, Burma's Ne Win, Egypt's Nasser and Sadat or Sudan's Numeiry.

Finally, the Soviet strategists and their native collaborators have recently been encountering increasing difficulties in their operations among the Third World's youth, especially its student segment. Although most of the young Asians, Africans and Latin Americans are anti-Western in their political leanings and pro-socialist in their economic thinking, many of those among them who had initially gravitated toward communism, have been lately losing faith in the rigidly doctrinal gospel of orthodox Marxism-Leninism. Dissatisfied with the meager yields of the Soviet-recommended strategy of "peaceful coexistence" and eager to speed up the course of the revolution, they have been leaning increasingly toward what Soviet theoreticians and pro-Soviet communists call anarchism, ultra-leftism and adventurism. This and their unwillingness to endorse the orthodox communist principle of proletarian leadership have further compounded the present disarray in the world communist movement.

Turning to the field of cultural relations, communist cultural diplomacy should certainly be credited with having broken the virtual cultural monopoly that the West had once enjoyed throughout what is today called the Third World. It has made the intellectual circles and even the broad masses in many parts of the Third World aware of communist scientific and cultural achievements. It has succeeded in creating an impression that the peoples of the Soviet Union and other communist countries are more interested in, and appreciative of, the native culture of Asia, Africa and Latin America than the public of Western Europe and the United States. Nonetheless, in spite of all the communist efforts to the contrary, cultural, scientific and educational orientation of the overwhelming majority of the developing nations has remained predominantly Western. Clearly, thanks to long-standing traditions, the widespread knowledge of

English, French and Spanish, and other factors, the attractive force of Western science, education, literature and art throughout most of the Third World continues to be vastly superior to that of corresponding communist offerings.

Thus, viewed in terms of the main communist objectives, the overall results of the communist involvement in the Third World can qualify only as very mediocre. But what about the prospects for the future? Will the continued pursuit of the strategy of "peaceful coexistence" lead eventually to the hoped-for "overgrowth" of the national democratic revolutions into the proletarian socialist revolutions of the Marxist-Leninist type? While anything could happen in the unstable situation and highly emotional atmosphere that continues to prevail in much of the Third World, the odds seem to be overwhelmingly against such an eventuality. In venturing such a prediction this writer relies primarily on his estimate that the importance of certain factors that have helped the communist cause in the Third World in the past is likely to wane (and has already begun waning) whereas the impact of some of the factors that have hampered communist endeavors is likely to remain and might even become more pronounced.

As the Third World's memories of Western colonialism inevitably keep growing ever dimmer and more irrelevant with the passage of time, communist exploitation of anti-colonialism against the West is bound to become less and less effective. Once completed, the nationalization of major Western-owned enterprises will *ipso facto* weaken and eventually destroy the bogey of neo-colonialism and deprive thereby communist strategists of a major means of anti-Western propaganda Also, as the leaders and subsequently even the masses of the Third World come gradually to realize that nationalization and the "ejection of foreign monopolies" has by no means been the panacea they have been led to believe, the thesis blaming the United States and Western imperialism for virtually all the economic ills plaguing the ex-colonial nations will become less and less credible. This will pave the way for better relations with the West. Western investment and knowhow will again seem more desirable and will be treated as a valuable asset rather than an attempt at economic domination.

Finally, the United States' position in the Third World cannot fail to improve when the Vietnamese war is ended and if and when some sort of a settlement is reached in the Arab-Israeli strife. Rightly or wrongly, much of the Third World has deemed America rather than North Vietnam or the Vietcong to be the villain of the Vietnamese war. As for the Arab conflict, a substantial majority of the developing countries have sided with the Arabs against the Israelis, and therefore also against the United States which is considered to be Israel's main backer. Hence, when the two conflicts are resolved, and resolved in a manner that cannot be construed as America's defeat, communist strategists stand to lose two powerful weapons of their propaganda arsenal.

On the other hand, most of the factors that have impeded communist penetration of the Third World in the past do not show any sign of receding. If anything, the Third World's leaders, including the "revolutionary democrats" and "patriotic officers", seem today to be more aware of the real communist, and especially Soviet, intentions than they have been in earlier years. Thus the thrust of native nationalism, the Third World's most potent and most pervasive ideology, is likely to become gradually less anti-Western and more anti-Soviet and anti-communist. Nor will Marxism-Leninism's identification with atheism be less prejudicial for the communist cause in the future than it has been in the past. The disarray inflicted upon the world communist movement by the Sino-Soviet split and the relentless inroads of revisionism continues unabated and may increase rather than decrease in the future, especially in so far as revisionism is concerned. The erstwhile belief in the suitability of the communist economic model for the developing countries that was fairly widespread throughout the Third World in the late fifties and early sixties, has been losing ground steadily in recent years. Since the well-known difficulties that the rigidly centralized Soviet-style economic systems have been encountering can hardly be resolved unless the system itself is radically changed, there is little chance that the erosion of faith in the Marxist-Leninist economic formula could be arrested, let alone reversed.

If the above assumptions are correct, then communist expectations that the continued deployment of the Marxist-Leninist strategy of "peaceful coexistence" in the Third World would eventually culminate in a successive series of proletarian revolutions and the establishment, in one developing country after another, of governments based on the "dictatorship of the proletariat" in the Marxist-Leninist meaning of the term are doomed. This does not mean, of course, that no communist seizure of power could take place in any part of the Third World. Should a set of cirumstances develop that is especially favorable for communist operations, a possibility of a communist take-over cannot be ruled out. Especially vulnerable in this respect would be a developing country, particularly a small one, where instability and chaos would be further compounded by a protracted civil war or a sharp power struggle in which one of the feuding factions would be in dire need of substantial communist help in order to win. Such a confluence of circumstances has developed in Indo-China and it might occur, at onetime or another, in other parts of the Third World. Should this happen, however, it would afflict only one, two or in any case very few of the developing nations rather than becoming a continental or transcontinental phenomenon envisaged by communist strategists. Nor does it appear likely that a communist takeover in a given developing country would trigger a pro-communist stampede or a chain reaction of communist take overs throughout the Third World.

Thus the only way in which the communists could possibly succeed in attaining their ultimate objective of communizing the Third World would be a resort to large-scale armed uprisings supported, not merely politically and economically but also militarily, by the Soviet Union and/or Communist China. To be fully effective, such a support would have to amount in most instances to a direct intervention of outside communist forces in one form or another. Such an intervention in any part of the Third World would be, of course, a flagrant violation of the Marxist-Leninist operational code as prescribed by the *Fundamentals of Marxism-Leninism*, the 1960 and 1969 *Declarations* and a host of other authoritative statements on presentday communist strategy, Soviet as well as Chinese. But this would certainly not be an obstacle should a military intervention seem to be the only way to communist seizure of power. After all, as amply reconfirmed by the "Brezhnev doctrine," the principle of proletarian internationalism can be stretched to justify ideologically almost any kind of communist intervention.

Moreover, as communist strategists will realize more and more that their ultimate objective in the Third World is unattainable by "peaceful means" alone, their temptation to resort to armed struggle and intervention is bound to become stronger. Whether or not they will eventually yield to the temptation will depend primarily on the communist assessment of what would be the probable Western, especially American, response. Should communist strategy-makers conclude that the United States and the West might take effective counter-measures that would make a communist intervention counter-productive, the chances are good that they would stop short of launching it. But should they ever come to believe that the United States and the West have grown so weak, so tired of acting as "the policeman of the world" and so fearful of a danger of possible armed confrontation with the Soviet Union and/or Communist China that they would respond with little more than verbal protestations, then the likelihood of an escalation of communist strategy from "peaceful means" to ever more daring recourse to armed struggle and intervention would be greatly enhanced.

Notes for Chapter XIV

[1] As noted earlier in this volume, Cuba is not considered as a part of the Third World as she is now a member of the world socialist system.

BIBLIOGRAPHY

Books and Monographs

Abid, Ali, *The Indian Communists Exposed*, New Delhi, 1965.

Adzhubei, A. ed., *Vstrecha s Afrikoi* (Meeting with Africa) Moscow, 1964.

African Communists Speak. Moscow, 1970.

Agrarno-krest'ianskii vopros v stranakh yugo-vostochnoi Azii (The Agrarian-Peasant Question in the Countries of South-East Asia), Moscow, 1963.

Agrarno-krest'ianskii vopros na sovremennom etape natsional'no-osvoboditel'nogo dvizheniia v stranakh Azii, Afriki i Latinskoi Ameriki (The Agrarian-Peasant Question at the Present State of the National-Liberation Movement in the Countries of Asia, Africa and Latin America), Moscow, 1965.

Agrarnyi vopros v natsional'no-osvoboditel'nom dvizhenii (The Agrarian-Peasant Question in the National-Liberation Movement), Moscow, 1962.

Aguilar, Luis E., *Marxism in Latin America*, New York, 1968

Agwani, M. S., *Communism in the Arab East*, London, 1970.

Akhundov, V. Iu., ed., *Velikaia oktiabr'skaia revoliutsiia i natsional'no-osvoboditel'noe dvizhenie narodov Azii, Afriki i Latinskoi Ameriki* (The Great October Revolution and the National-Liberation Movement of the Peoples of Asia, Africa and Latin America), Moscow, 1969.

Alexander, Robert J., *The Communist Party of Venezuela*, Stanford, 1969.

Alexander, Robert J., *Communism in Latin America*, New Brunswick, 1957.

Alitovskii, S. N., *Agrarnyi vopros v sovremennom Irake* (The Agrarian Question in Contemporary Iraq), Moscow, 1966.

Allen, Robert L., *Soviet Influence in Latin America: the Role of Economic Relations*, Washington, 1959.

Allen, Robert L., *Middle Eastern Economic Relations with the Soviet Union, Eastern Europe and Mainland China*, Charlottesville, 1958.

Allen, Robert L., *Soviet Economic Warfare*, Washington, 1960.

Almond, Gabriel A., *The Appeals of Communism*, Princeton, 1954.

Altman, Gavro, *Standing Clear of Blocs*, Belgrade, no date.

Anderson, George L., *Of Cultural Diplomacy in Asia*, Lawrence, 1959.

Ansprenger, Franz, *Politik im Schwarzen Afrika, Die modernen politischen Bewegungen im Afrika französischer Prägung* (The Politics in Black Africa. Modern Political Movements in ex-French Africa) Köln, 1961.

Apeland, Nils H., *Communist Front Youth Organizations*, Bombay, 1959.

Apeland, Nils H., *World Youth and the Communists,* London, 1958.

Arabadzhian, A. X., et al., eds, *Ekonomicheskoe polozhenie stran Azii i Afriki v 1960 g.* (The Economic Position of the Countries of Asia and Africa in the Year 1960), Moscow, 1962.

Arismendi, Rodney, *Lenin, la revolución y America Latina* (Lenin, the Revolution and Latin America), Montevideo, 1970.

Arzumanian, A. A., *Krizis mirovogo kapitalizma na sovremennom etape* (The Crisis of World Capitalism at the Contemporary Stage), Moscow, 1962. Boston, 1971.

Astaf'ev, G. V., et al., *Vneshniaia politika KNR* (The Foreign Policy of PRC), Moscow, 1971.

Atkinson, James D., *Politics of Struggle: The Communist Front and Political Warfare,* Chicago, 1966.

Aspaturian, Vernon V., ed., *Process and Power in Soviet Foreign Policy,*

Atsamba, F. M., and L. A. Fridman, *Rabochii klass stran Azii i Afriki* (The Working Class of the Countries of Asia and Africa), Moscow, 1966.

Aubrey, Henry G., *Coexistence: Economic Challenge and Response,* Washington, 1961.

Avarin, V. Ia., *Problemy industrializatsii suverennykh slaborazvitykh stran Azii* (The Problems of the Industrialization of Sovereign Less Developed Countries of Asia), Moscow, 1960.

Avarin, V. Ia.. and M. V. Danilevich, *Natsional'no-osvoboditel'noe dvizhenie Latinskoi Ameriki na sovremennom etape* (The National Liberation Movement of Latin America at the Contemporary Stage) Moscow, 1961.

Badi, Sh. M., et al., *Formirovanie rabochego klassa stran Azii i Afriki* (The Formation of the Working Class of the Countries of Asia and Africa), Moscow, 1971.

Bandyopadhyaya, Jayantanuja, *Indian Nationalism versus International Communism, Role of Ideology in International Politics,* Calcutta, 1966.

Baratashvili, D. I., *Novye gosudarstva Azii i Afriki i mezhdunarodnoe pravo,* (New States of Asia and Africa and International Law), Moscow, 1968.

Barghoorn, Frederick C., *Soviet Foreign Propaganda,* Princeton, 1964.

Barghoorn, Frederick C., *The Soviet Cultural Offensive,* Princeton, 1960.

Barnett, Doak A., *Communist Strategies in Asia,* New York, 1963.

Baskin, V. S., et al, eds., *Ekonomicheskoe sotrudnichestvo SSSR so stranami Afriki* (Economic Cooperation of the USSR with the Countries of Africa), Moscow, 1968.

Belaev, V. P., et al., *Politicheskie partii Latinskoi Ameriki* (Political Parties of Latin America), Moscow, 1965.

Belousov, A. A., *Krizis i raspad kolonial'noi sistemy imperializma. Osobennosti ekonomiki razvivaiushchikhsia stran* (The Crisis and Disintegration of the Colonial System of Imperialism. The Particularities of the Economic of Developing Countries), Moscow, 1970.

Bendik, A. K., and A. M. Grishina, eds., *Literatura o stranakh Azii i Afriki* (The Literature About the Countries of Asia and Africa), Moscow, 1967.

Benham, Frederick C., *Economic Aid to Underdeveloped Countries,* New York, 1961.

Benz, Ernst, *Buddhism or Communism?* Garden City, 1966.

Berliner, Joseph, *Soviet Economic Aid: the New Aid and Trade Policy in Underdeveloped Countries,* New York, 1958.

Berton Peter, and Alvin Z. Rubinstein, *Soviet Works on Southeast Asia: A Bibliography of Non-periodical Literature, 1946-1965,* Los Angeles, 1967.

Berzin, E. O., *Katolicheskaia tser'kov v Yugo-vostochnoi Azii* (Catholic Church in Southeast Asia), Moscow, 1966.

Bessmertnaia, E. Ia., ed., *Govoriat kommunisty Afriki* (The African Communists Speak), Moscow, 1970.

Biskup, Reinhold, *Sowjetpolitik und Entwicklungsländer. Ideologie und Strategie in der Sovjetischen Politik gegenüber den Entwicklungsländern.* (The Soviet Policy and the Developing Countries. Ideology and Strategy in the Soviet Policy Toward the Developing Countries), Freiburg, 1970.

Black, Cyril, and Th. P. Thornton, *Communism and Revolution. The Strategic Uses of Political Violence,* Princeton, 1964.

Black, Lloyd D., *The Strategy of Foreign Aid,* Princeton, 1968.

Blackstock, Paul W., *Agents of Deceit, Frauds, Forgeries and Political Intrigue Among Nations,* Chicago, 1966.

Blackstock, Paul W., *The Strategy of Subversion: the Politics of Other Nations,* Chicago, 1964.

Blum, Robert, ed., *Cultural Affairs and Foreign Relations,* Princeton, 1963.

Bochenski, Joseph, and Gerhardt Niemeyer, eds., *Handbook on Communism,* New York, 1962.

Bodianskii, V. L., et al., *Prosveshchenie i podgotovka natsional'-nykh kadrov v stranakh vostoka* (The Education and Training of National Cadres in the Countries of the East), Moscow, 1971.

Boersner, Demetrio, *The Bolsheviks and the National and Colonial Question, 1917-1928,* Geneva, 1957.

Bognar, Joszef, *Obstacles to Economic Development and the Political Power,* Budapest, 1967.

Bognar, Joszef, *The Perspectives of Our Relations with the Developing Countries,* Budapest, 1968.

Bogush, Evgenii Iu., *Mif o 'eksporte revoliutsii' i sovetskaia vneshniaia politika* (The Myth About 'the Export of the Revolution' and the Soviet Foreign Policy), Moscow, 1965.

Bogush, Evgenii Iu., *Maoizm i politika raskola v natsional'no-osvoboditel'nom dvizhenii* (Maoism and the Policy of Schism in the National-Liberation Movement), Moscow, 1969.

Bonifat'eva, L. I., et al., eds., *Problems of Economic Regionalization in the Developing Countries.* Moscow, 1968.

Bouscaren, Anthony T., *Soviet Foreign Policy: a Pattern of Persistence,* Bronx, 1962.

Boyd, R. G., *Communist China's Foreign Policy,* New York, 1962.

Brackman, Arnold C., *The Communist Collapse in Indonesia,* New York, 1969.

Bragina, E. A., et al., *Problemy industrializatsii razvivaiushchikhsia stran,* (The Problems of the Industrialization of the Developing Countries), Moscow, 1971.

Braginskii, Moseiev I., *Osvobozhdenie Afriki* (The Liberation of Africa), Moscow, 1962.

Brimmel, J. H., *Communism in Southeast Asia,* New York, 1959.

Brutens, K. N., *Protiv ideologii sovremennogo kolonializma* (Against the Ideology of Contemporary Colonialism), Moscow, 1961.

Brutens, K. N., *Politika imperializma SSHA v razvivaiushchikhsia stranakh* (The Policy of Imperialism of the USA in the Developing Countries), Moscow, 1969.

Brutens, K. N., *Novaia forma poraboshcheniia narodov. (Neokolonializm. sushchnost' i metody)* (A New Form of the Enslavement of Peoples. (The Neocolonialism: Essence and Methods), Moscow, 1969.

Brutens, K. N., ed., *Kolonializm segodnia* (Colonialism Today), Moscow, 1967.

Brutens, K. N., et al., *Antiimperialisticheskaia revoliutsiia v Afrika*, (The Anti-Imperialist Revolution in Africa), Moscow, 1967.

Brzezinski, Zbigniew, *Ideology and Power in Soviet Politics*, New York, 1962.

Brzezinski, Zbigniew, ed., *Africa and the Communist World*, Stanford, 1963.

Burlatskii, F., *Maoizm ili Marksizm?* (Maoism or Marxism?), Moscow, 1967.

Buzek, Antonin, *How the Communist Press Works, Domestic and International Operations*, New York, 1964.

Čapek, Mikuláš, *Državstevnictví v rozvojových zemích* (Cooperativism in Developing Countries), Praha, 1965.

Carew, Ian, *Moscow is Not My Mecca*, London, 1964.

Carlton, Robert G., ed., *Soviet Image of Contemporary Latin America: A Documentary History, 1960-1968*, Austin, 1970.

Carter, James R., *The Net Cost of Soviet Foreign Aid*, New York, 1971.

Clark, Ronald J., *Latin American Economic Relations with the Soviet Bloc, 1954-1961*, Bloomington, 1963.

Clews, John C., *Communist Propaganda Techniques*, New York, 1964.

Clissold, Stephen, ed., *Soviet Relations with Latin America, 1918-1968, A Documentary Survey*, New York, 1970.

Cohen, Arthur A., *The Communism of Mao*, Chicago, 1964.

Cohn, Joel G., *The Role of the Third World in Marxist-Leninist Theory as Viewed During the Khrushchev Leadership, 1959-1964*, An unpublished dissertation, Notre Dame University, 1971.

Communism in Latin America, Los Angeles, 1962.

Coombs, Philip H. *Education and Foreign Aid*, Cambridge, 1965.

Cornell, Richard, *Youth and Communism: an Historical Analysis of International Communist Youth Movements*, New York, 1965.

Cox, I., *Socialist Ideas in Africa*, London, 1966.

Crozier, Brian, *The Struggle for the Third World*, London, 1966.

Dallin, Alexander, and Thomas B. Larson, eds., *Soviet Politics Since Khrushchev*, Englewood Cliffs, 1968.

Daniels, Robert V., *The Nature of Communism*, New York, 1962.

Danilevich, M., *Rabochii klass v osvoboditel'nom dvizhenii Latinskoi Ameriki* (The Working Class in the Liberation Movement of Latin America), Moscow, 1962.

Dantsig, B. M., *Ekonomicheskoe polozhenie stran Azii, Afriki i Latinskoi Ameriki* (The Economic Position of the Countries of Asia, Africa and Latin America), Moscow, 1959.

Dantsig, B. M., ed., *Politika Frantsii v Azii i Afrike, 1945-1964* (The Policy of France in Asia and Africa, 1945-1964), Moscow, 1965.

Davidson, A. B., et al., *Russia and Africa*, Moscow, 1966.

Davies, Joan, *African Trade Unions*, Baltimore, 1966.

Delavignette, Robert, *Du bon usage de la décolonization* (Putting Decolonization to Good Use), Paris, 1968.

Dementev, I. A., and I. V. Milovanov, eds., *Strany blizhnego i srednego vostoka,* (The Countries of the Near and Middle East), Moscow, 1964.

D'Encaussé, Helen C, and Stuart Schramm, *Le Marxisme et l'Asie* (Marxism and Asia), Paris, 1965.

Der Ostblock un die Entwicklungsländer (The Eastern Bloc and the Developing Countries), Hanover, 1964.

Dinerstein, Herbert, *Soviet Policy in Latin America,* Santa Monica, 1966.

Dinerstein, Herbert, *Castro's Latin American Comintern,* Santa Monica, 1967.

Dinkevich, A. I., ed., *Aktual'nye problemy ekonomiki stran Azii* (Urgent Problems of the Economy of the Countries of Asia), Moscow, 1965.

Doka, Charles, *Les relations culturelles sur le plan international* (Cultural Relations on International Level), Neuchâtel, 1959.

Donovan, John, *Red Machete: Communist Infiltration in the Americas,* Indianapolis, 1962.

Dowse, Robert E., *Modernization in Ghana and the USSR: a Comparative Study,* New York and London, 1969.

Dubois, Jules, Operation America: the Communist Conspiracy in Latin America, New York, 1963.

Duff, Vidya P., *China and the World: an Analysis of Communist China's Foreign Policy,* New York, 1966.

Dumoga, John, *Africa Between East and West,* London, 1969.

Dvatsatyi siezd kommunisticheskoi partii Sovetskego Soiuza (The Twentieth Congress of the Communist Party of the Soviet Union), Moscow, 1956.

Dvozhak, L., *Ekonomicheskie osnovy neo-kolonializma* (The Economic Bases of Neo-Colonialism), Moscow, 1969.

Dzhumisov, M. S., *O nekapitalitisticheskom puti razvitiia* (About the Non-Capitalist Path of Development), Moscow, 1963.

Ekonomicheskoe sotrudnichestvo SSSR so stranami Afriki (Economic cooperation of the USSR with the Countries of Africa), Moscow, 1968.

Elegant, Robert S., *The Center of the World; Communism and the Mind of China,* New York, 1968.

Ermolaiev, V. I., and A. F. Shul'govskii, *Rabochee i kommunisticheskoe dvizhenie v Latinskoi Amerike (s oktiabria do nashikh dnei)* (The Workers' and Communist Movement in Latin America (from October to Our Days)), Moscow, 1970.

Etinger, Ia, and O. Milikian, *Neitralizm i Mir* (Neutralism and Peace), Moscow, 1964.

Etinger, Ia, *Politicheskie problemy afrikanskogo edinstva* (Political Problems of African Unity), Moscow, 1967.

Evans, F. Bowen, *Worldwide Communist Propaganda Activities,* New York, 1955.

Fairbairn, Geoffrey, *Revolutionary Warfare and Communist Strategy,* London, 1968.

Fairhall, David, *Russia Looks to the Sea: A Study of the Expansion of Soviet Maritime Power,* London, 1971.

Falkowski, Mieczyslaw, *Contribution Socialiste à l'étude de la croissance économique des pays en voie de dévéloppement,* (Socialist Contribution to the Study of the Economic Growth of Developing Countries), Warsaw, 1966.

Fanon, Frantz, *Les Damnés de la terre* (The Wretched of the Earth), Paris, 1968.

Fanton, Frantz, *Toward the African Revolution: Political Essays*, New York, 1967.

Fedchenko, A. F., *Irak v bor'be za nezavisimost', 1917-1969* (Iraq in the Struggle for Independence, 1917-1969), Moscow, 1970.

Fetov, V., *Dollarom, mechom, durmanom* (With Dollar, Sword and Dope), Moscow, 1969.

Fituni, L. A., and V. D. Shchetinin, *Problemy pomoshchi ekonomicheski slaborazvitym stranam* (Problem of the Aid to Economically Less Developed Countries), Moscow, 1961.

Floyd, David, *Mao Against Khrushchev: A Short History of the Sino-Soviet Conflict*, New York, 1964.

Fokeev, German V., *Uneshniaia politika stran Afriki* (The Foreign Policy of the Countries of Africa), Moscow, 1968.

Fournial, Georges, and Roland Labarre, *De Monro à Johnson. La politique des Etats-Unis en Amérique Latine* (From Monroe to Johnson. The Policy of the United States in Latin America), Paris, 1966.

Frankel, Charles, *The Neglected Aspect of Foreign Affairs*, Washington, 1965.

Friedland, William, and Carl G. Rosberg, *African Socialism*, Stanford, 1964.

Friedländer, Paul, and Haramut Schilling, *Kolonialmacht Westdeutschland* (The Colonial Power West Germany), Berlin, 1962.

Fundamentals of Marxism-Leninism, Moscow, 1963.

Furtak, Robert K., *Kuba und der Weltkommunismus* (Cuba and World Communism), Köln, 1966.

Gafurov, B. G., et al., eds., *Natsional'no-osvoboditel'noe dvizhenie v Azii i Afrike* (The National-Liberation Movement in Asia and Africa), Moscow, 1967-68.

Gafurov, B. G., et al., eds., *Marksizm i strany vostoka* (Marxism and the Countries of the East), Moscow, 1970.

Gafurov, B. G., *Neutralism and the National Liberation Movement*, Moscow, 1966.

Gafurov, B. G., et al., *Politika SShA v stranakh iuzhnoi Azii: India, Burma, Indoneziia* (The Policy of the USA in the Countries of South Asia: India, Burma, Indonesia), Moscow, 1961.

Gafurov, B. G., *Politika SShA na blizhnem i srednem vostoke* (The Policy of the USA in the Near and Middle East), Moscow, 1960.

Gafurov, B. G., ed., *Asia in Soviet Studies*, Moscow, 1969.

Gafurov, B. G., *Oktiabr'skaia revoliutsiia i natsional'no-osvoboditel'noe dvizhenie* (The October Revolution and the National Liberation Movement), Moscow, 1967.

Gafurov, B. G., et al., *Lenin i natsional'no-osvoboditel'noe dvizhenie v stranakh vostoka* (Lenin and the National-Liberation Movement in the Countries of the East), Moscow, 1970.

Galenson, Walter, *Labor in Developing Economies*, Berkeley, 1962.

Gankovskii, Iu. V., ed., *SSSR i strany vostoka* (The USSR and the Countries of the East), Moscow, 1961.

Gankovskii, Iu. V., et al., eds., *Velikaia oktiabr'skaia sotsialisticheskaia revoliutsiia i natsional'no-osvoboditel'noe dvizhenie narodov Azii, Afriki i Latinskoi Ameriki* (The Great October Socialist Revolution and the National-Liberation Movement of the Peoples of Asia, Africa and Latin America), Moscow, 1969.

Gavrilov, Iu, N., et al., eds., *Afrika, 1961-65* (Africa, 1961-65), Moscow, 1967.

Gavrilov, Iu. N., and Iu. N. Chubarov, eds., *Tropicheskaia Afrika: problemy razvitiia* (Tropical Africa: Problems of Development), Moscow, 1970.

Gavrilov, Iu. N., *Nezavisimye strany Afriki: ekonomicheskie i sotsial'nye problemy* (Independent Countries of Africa: Economic and Social Problems), Moscow, 1965.

Ghioldi, Rodolfo, *No puede haber una revolución en la revolución* (There Cannot Be A Revolution in The Revolution), Buenos Aires, 1967.

Ghose, Subratesh, *Trade Unionism in the Underdeveloped Countries,* Calcutta, 1960.

Gittings, John, *Survey of the Sino-Soviet Dispute: A Commentary and Extracts from the Recent Polemics, 1963-1967,* London, 1968.

Goh, King S., *Communism in Non-Communist Asian Countries,* Singapore, 1967.

Goldenburg, Boris, *The Cuban Revolution and Latin America,* New York, 1965.

Goldman, Marshall, *Soviet Foreign Aid,* New York, 1967.

Goncharov, L. V., *Ekonomika Afriki* (The Economy of Africa), Moscow, 1965.

Goncharov, L. V., et al., eds., *Stroitel'stvo natsional'noi ekonomiki v stranakh Afriki* (The Construction of National Economy in the Countries of Africa), Moscow, 1968.

Gonzales, Luis, and Gustavo A. Sanchez Salazar, *The Great Rebel: Che Guevara in Bolivia,* New York, 1969.

Gott, Richard, *Guerrilla Movement in Latin America,* New York, 1971.

Great Strategic Concept, Peking, 1967.

Griffith, Samuel B., *Peking and People's Wars: An Analysis of Statements by Official Spokesmen of the Chinese Communist Party on the Subject of Revolutionary Strategy,* New York, 1966.

Griffith, William, *Sino-Soviet Rift,* Cambridge, 1964.

Grigorian, S. N., ed., *Nekotorye voprosy ideologicheskoi bor'by v stranakh Azii i Afriki* (Some Problems of the Ideological Struggle in the Countries of Asia and Africa), Moscow, 1971.

Grigorian, S. N., ed., *Sovremennye ideologicheskie problemy v stranakh Azii i Afriki* (Contemporary Ideological Problems in the Countries of Asia and Africa), Moscow, 1970.

Gromyko, A. A., ed., *Afrika v mezhdunarodnykh otnosheniiakh* (Africa in International Relations), Moscow, 1970.

Guber, A. A., *Politika evropeiskikh derzhav i natsional'no-osvoboditel'noe dvizhenie v yugovostochnoi Azii* (The Policy of European Powers and the National-Liberation Movement in Southeast Asia), Moscow, 1967.

Guber, A. A., and Iu. N. Chubarov, eds., *Natsional no-osvoboditel'naia bor'ba narodov na sovremennom etape* (The National-Liberation Struggle of the Peoples at the Contemporary Stage), Moscow, 1966.

Guernier, Maurice, *La dernière chance du tiers monde* (The Last Chance of the Third World), Paris, 1968.

Guevara, Ernesto, *Che Guevara on Guerrilla Warfare,* New York, 1961.

Halperin, Ernst, *The Sino-Cuban and Chilean Communist Road to Power; A Latin American Debate,* Cambridge, 1963.

Halperin, Ernst, *Communism in Mexico,* Cambridge, 1963.

Halperin, Ernst, *Nationalism and Communism in Chile,* Cambridge, 1965.

Hammond, Thomas T., *Lenin on Trade Unions and Revolution, 1893-1917,* New York, 1957.

Hamrell, Sven, and C. G. Widstrand, *The Soviet Bloc, China and Africa,* London, 1964.

Hesse, Kurt, *Entwicklungsländer und Entwicklungshilfe.* (The Developing Countries and Development Aid), Berlin, 1962.

Hevi, Emmanuel J., *The Dragon's Embrace: The Chinese Communists in Africa,* New York, 1967.

Hevi, Emmanuel J., *A Student in Peking,* New Delhi, 1963.

Hindley, Donald, *The Communist Party of Indonesia, 1951-1963,* Berkeley, 1964.

Hinton, Harold C., *Communist China in World Politics,* New York, 1966.

History of the Communist Party of the Soviet Union, Moscow, 1939 and 1960.

Holdsworth, Mary, *Soviet African Studies,* London, 1961.

Hopkins, Mark W., *Mass Media in the Soviet Union,* New York, 1970.

Horecky, Paul, ed., *Russia and the Soviet Union,* Chicago, 1965.

Hsieh, Alice L., *Communist China's Military Policies, Doctrine and Strategy,* Santa Monica, 1968.

Hughes, John, *Indonesian Upheaval,* New York, 1967.

Hughes, John, *The End of Sukarno: A Coup That Misfired: A Purge That Ran Wild,* London, 1968.

Hurewith, J. C., ed., *Soviet-American Rivalry in the Middle East,* New York, 1969.

Hyde, Douglas, *The Roots of Guerrilla Warfare,* Chester Springs, 1968.

Iablochkov, L. D., and K. S. Kremen, eds., *Ideinye techeniia v tropicheckoi Afrike* (Ideological Trends in Tropical Africa), Moscow, 1969.

Iastrebova, I. P., ed., *Rabochii klass Afriki* (The Working Class of Africa), Moscow, 1966.

Iegorov, Iu., ed., *Natsional'no-osvoboditel'noe dvizhenie* (The National Liberation Movement), Moscow, 1967.

Inozemtsev, N. N., ed., *Uchenie V. I. Lenina ob imperializme i sovremennost'* (Lenin's Teaching on Imperialism and the Present Time), Moscow, 1967.

Institute for International Politics and Economics (Belgrade), *The Policy of Non-Alignment in the Contemporary World,* Belgrade, 1969.

Iordanskii, V. B., *Strategiia bor'by za nezavisimost'* (The Strategy of the Struggle for Independence), Moscow, 1968.

Iordanskii, V. B., *Tupiki i perspektivy tropicheskoi Afriki* (Blind Alleys and Perspectives of Tropical Africa), Moscow, 1970.

Isenberg, Irwin, ed., *The Russian-Chinese Rift: Its Impact on World Affairs,* New York, 1966.

Ishwer, C. Ojha, *Chinese Foreign Policy in an Age of Transition. The Diplomacy of Cultural Despair,* Boston, 1969.

Iskenderov, A. A., *Molodye gosudarstva Azii i Afriki,* (The Young States of Asia and Africa), Moscow, 1969.

Iskenderov, A. A., ed., *Polozhenie rabochego klassa i rabochee dvizhenie v stranakh Azii i Afriki, 1959-1961* (The Position of the Working Class and the Workers' Movement in the Countries of Asia and Africa, 1959-1961), Moscow, 1962.

Iskenderov, A. A., et al. *Mezhdunarodnoe rabochee dvizhenie* (The International Workers' Movement), Moscow, 1971.

Iskenderov, A. A., et al., eds., *Rabochii class stran Azii i Afriki,* (The Working Class of Asia and Africa), Moscow, 1964.

Iskenderov, A. A., *Natsional'no-osvoboditel'noe dvizhenie* (The National-Liberation Movement), Moscow, 1970.

Iskenderov, A. A., et al. *Rabochee dvizhenie v stranakh Azii i severnoi Afriki na sovremennom etape* (The Workers' Movement in the Countries of Asia and North Africa at the Present Time), Moscow, 1969.

Ivanova, I. P., *Sel'skoe khoziaistvo ob'iedinennoi Arabskoi Respubliki* (Agriculture of the United Arab Republic), Moscow, 1970.

Jackson, D. Bruce, *Castro, the Kremlin and Communism in Latin America,* Baltimore, 1969.

Jacobs, Dan N., ed., *The New Communist Manifesto and Related Documents,* Evanston, 1961.

Johnson, Cecil, *Communist China and Latin America, 1959-1967,* New York, 1970.

Johnson, John J., ed., *The Role of the Military in Underdeveloped Countries,* Princeton, 1962.

Kanaev, G. Ie., *Profsoiuznoe dvizhenie v Marokko* (The Trade Union Movement in Morocco), Moscow, 1962.

Karpov, G. G., *O sovetskoi kul'turnoi revoliutsii v SSSR* (The Soviet Cultural Revolution in the USSR), Moscow, 1954.

Kaufman, A. S., *Rabochii klass i natsional'no-osvoboditel'noe dvizhenie v Birme* (The Working Class and the National-Liberation Movement in Burma), Moscow, 1961.

Kaufman, A. S., and N. A. Simoniia, eds., *Agrarno-krest'ianskii vopros v stranakh iugo-vostochnoi Azii,* (The Agrarian-Peasant Question in the Countries of Southeast Asia), Moscow, 1961.

Kautsky, John H., *Communism and the Politics of Development,* New York, 1968.

Kautsky, John H., *Political Change in Underdeveloped Countries,* New York, 1962.

Kay, David A., *The New Nations in the United Nations, 1960-1967,* New York, 1970.

Kazakevich, I. S., ed., *Strany dal'nego vostoka i iugo-vostochnoi Azii* (The Countries of the Far East and Southeast Asia), Moscow, 1970.

Kaznachaev, Aleksandr. Iu., *Inside a Soviet Embassy; Experiences of a Russian Diplomat in Burma,* New York, 1962.

Kemenes, Egon, *The Reform of the International Monetary System and the Developing Countries,* Budapest, 1968.

Khan, G., *Nekotorye voprosy nekapitalisticheskogo puti razvitiia* (Some Questions of the Non-Capitalist Path of Development), Alma-Ata, 1971.

Khrushchev, Nikita S., *For Victory in Peaceful Competition with Capitalism,* New York, 1960.

Khvoinik, P. I., *Mirovoi rynok: prepiatstvie ili soiuznik?* (The World Market: Obstacle or Ally?), Moscow, 1971.

Kim, G., and A. Kaufman, *Leninizm i natsional'no-osvoboditel'noe dvizhenie,* (Leninism and the National-Liberation Movement), Moscow, 1969.

Kim, G., *Razvitie kooperatsii v stranakh tropicheskoi Afriki* (The Development of Cooperation in the Countries of Tropical Africa), Moscow, 1969.

Kirkpatrick, Evron M., ed., *Target the World: Communist Propaganda Activities in 1955,* New York, 1956.

Kleer, Jerzy, *"Trzeciswiat" a socjalizm* (The "Third World" and Socialism), Warsaw, 1964.

Kleer, Jerzy, *"Traeci swiat" a socjalizm* (The "Third World" and Socialism), Warsaw, 1964.

Klesmet, O. G., *Problemy industrializatsii Latinskoi Ameriki* (The Problems of Industralization in Latin America), Moscow, 1966.

Klieman, S. Aaron, *Soviet Russia and the Middle East,* Baltimore, 1971.

Klinghoffer, Arthur J., *Soviet Perspectives on African Socialism,* Rutherford, 1969.

Klochkovskii, L. L., *Ekonomicheskaia ekspansiia SShA v iugo-vostochnoi Azii* (The Economic Expansion of the USA in Southeast Asia), Moscow, 1965.

Kočandrle, Jaromír, *Nová Afrika* (The New Africa), Praha, 1961.

Kochetov, A. N., *Buddizm* (Buddhism), Moscow, 1968.

Kodachenko, A. S., *Ekonomicheskoe sotrudnichestvo razvivaiushchikhsia stran, Problemy i perspektivy.* (The Economic Cooperation of Developing Countries, Problems and Prospects), Moscow, 1968.

Kolarz, Walter, *Communism and Colonialism,* New York, 1964.

Komarov S. N., and A. D. Litman, eds., *Ideologicheskie problemy sovremennoi Indii* (Ideological Problems of Contemporary India), Moscow, 1970.

Koptev M., and M. S. Ochkov, *Imperializm i razvivaiushchiesia strany* (Imperialism and the Developing Countries), Moscow, 1970.

Korendiasov, E. N., *Kollektivnyi kolonializm v deistvii. Ekonomicheskie aspekty assotsiatsii afrikanskikh stran s evropeiskim ekonomicheskim obshchestvom* (Collective Colonialism in Action. Economic Aspects of the Association of African Countries with the European Economic Community), Moscow, 1969.

Korneev, S. G., *Nauchnye sviazi Akademii nauk SSSR so stranaim Azii i Afriki* (Scholarly Ties of the Academy of Sciences of the USSR with the Countries of Asia and Africa), Moscow, 1969.

Korotkova, Ie. N., *Ekonomicheskoe sotrudnichestvo nezavisimykh stran Afriki.* (Economic Cooperation of the Independent Countries of Africa), Moscow, 1966.

Kosukhin, N. D., *Vostochnaia Afrika: bor'ba protiv kolonializma i ego posledstvii* (East Africa: the Struggle Against Colonialism and Its Consequences), Moscow, 1970.

Kotovskii, G. G., ed., *Agrarnyi vopros v stranakh Azii i severnoi Afriki* (The Agrarian Question in the Countries of Asia and North Africa), Moscow, 1968.

Kotovskii, G. G., *Sotsial'no-ekonomicheskie posledstviia agrarnykh reform i sotsial'naia struktura derevni v razvivaushchikhsia stranakh* (The Social-Economic Consequences of Agrarian Reforms and the Social Structure of the village in Developing Countries), Moscow, 1966.

Kotovskii, G. G. and I. A. Svanidze, eds., *Sel'sko-khoziaistvennye rabochie v stranakh Azii i Afriki* (Agrarian Workers in the Countries of Asia and Africa), Moscow, 1966.

Kotovskii, G. G., ed., *Agrarnye otnosheniia v stranakh iugo-vostochnoi Azii* (Agrarian Relations in the Countries of Southeast Asia), Moscow, 1968.

Koval', B. I., et al. *Proletariat Latinskoi Ameriki* (The Proletariat of Latin America), Moscow, 1968.

Kovner, Milton, *The Challenge of Coexistence. A Study of Soviet Economic Diplomacy,* Washington, 1961.

Kulagina, L. M., et al., eds., *Aktual'nye problemy stran blizhnego i srednego vostoka* (Urgent Problems of the Countries of Near and Middle East), Moscow, 1970.

Kulagina, L. M., et al., eds., *Strany Blizhnego i Srednego Vostoka* (The Countries of the Near and Middle East), Moscow, 1969.

Kutsenkov, A. A., et al., eds., *Rabochii klass i anti-imperialisticheskaia revoliutsia v Azii, Afrike i Latinskoi Amerike,* (The Working Class and the Anti-Imperialist Revolution in Asia, Africa and Latin America), Moscow, 1969.

Kuznetsova, N. A., and L. M. Kulagina, *Iz istorii sovetskogo vostokovedenia* (From the History of Soviet Oriental Studies), Moscow, 1970.

Labarca, Goddard Ed., *Chile Invadido: Reportaje a la Intromision Extranjera* (Chile Invaded: A report on External Involvement), Santiago de Chile, 1969.

Labin, Suzanne, *Embassies of Subversion,* New York, 1965.

Lambers, Robert F., *Prag und die Dritte Welt* (Prague and the Third World), Hanover, 1966.

Lapina, S. N., *Leninskaia teoriia perekhoda otstalykh stran k sotsializmu* (The Leninist Theory on the Transition of Backward Countries to Socialism), Moscow, 1969.

Laqueur, Walter, *The Soviet Union and the Middle East,* New York, 1959.

Laqueur, Walter, *Communism and Nationalism in the Middle East,* Melbourne, 1956.

Larichenko, M. V., *Ekonimicheskoe sotrudnichestvo SSSR so stranami Azii, Afriki i Latinskoi Ameriki* (Economic Cooperation of the USSR with the Countries of Asia, Africa and Latin America), Moscow, 1961.

Larkin, Bruce D., *China and Africa, 1949-1970. The Foreign Policy of the People's Republic of China,* Berkeley, 1971.

Lar'kov, A. M., *Natsional'no-osvoboditel'noe dvizhenie na sovremennom etape* (The National-Liberation Movement at the Present Stage), Moscow, 1968.

Lasky, Victor, *The Ugly Russian,* New York, 1965.

Lauerhass, Ludwig, *Communism in Latin America, a bibliography; the postwar years (1945-1960),* Los Angeles, 1962.

Lavretskii, A., *Ten' Vatikana nad Latinskoi Amerikoi* (The Shadow of the Vatican over Latin America), Moscow, 1961.

Lavrishchev, A. A., et al., eds., *Razvivaiushchiesia strany v mirovoi politike* (The Developing Nations in World Politics), Moscow, 1970.

Lebedev, V. Z., *O sovremennoi sovetskoi diplomatii* (Contemporary Soviet Diplomacy), Moscow, 1963.

Legum, Colin, *Pan-Africanism: A Short Political Guide,* New York, 1965.

Legvold, Robert, *Soviet Policy in West Africa,* Cambridge, 1970.

Lenin, Vladimir I., *Against Revisionism,* Moscow, 1959.

Lenin, Vladimir I., *Collected Works,* Moscow, 1927, London 1960.

Lenin, Vladimir I., *Imperialism, the Highest Stage of Capitalism,* New York, 1939.

Lenin, Vladimir I., *Leftwing Communism, An Infantile Disorder,* Moscow, 1952.

Lenin, Vladimir I., *Marx-Engels Marxism,* Moscow, 1953.

Lenin, Vladimir I., *On the International Working Class and Communist Movement,* Moscow, 1961.

Lenin, Vladimir I., *Selected Works,* New York, no date: London, 1936-39.

Lenin, Vladimir I., *Sochineniia* (Works), Moscow, 1934-1935, 1941-50 and 1964.

Lenin, Vladimir I., *The Awakening of Asia,* New York, 1971.

Lenin, Vladimir I., *The National Liberation Movement in the East,* Moscow, 1957.

Lenin, Vladimir I., *The Preliminary Draft of Theses on the Agrarian Question, Alliance of the Working Class and the Peasantry,* Moscow, 1959.

Lenin i vostok. Sbornik statei (Lenin and the East. A Symposium), Moscow, 1925.

Lenin o druzhbe s narodami vostoka (Lenin on Friendship with the Peoples of the East), Moscow, 1961.

Letoch, T., ed., *Polityka zagraniczna panstw afrykanskich. Zbior dokumentow* (Foreign Policy of African Countries. A collection of Documents), Warsaw, 1970.

Levkovskii, A. T., and I. N. Rozaliev, eds., *Krupnyi kapital i monopolii stran Azii* (Big Capital and Monopolies of the Countries of Asia), Moscow, 1970.

Levkovskii, A. I., *Tretii mir v sovremennom mire* (The Third World in the Present-day World), Moscow, 1970.

Lewis, John W., ed., *Major Doctrines of Communist China,* New York, 1964.

Li, Vladimir F., *Strategiia i politika neokolonializma SShA* (The Strategy and Policy of the Neo-colonialism of the U. S. A.), Moscow, 1971.

Liska, George, *The New Statecraft: Foreign Aid in American Foreign Policy,* Chicago, 1960.

London, Kurt, ed., *New Nations in a Divided World,* New York, 1963.

Long Live Leninism, Peking, 1960.

Losada, Ramon Aldana, *Dialectica del subdesarrollo* (The Dialectics of Inderdevelopment), Caracas, 1967.

Löwenthal, Richard, *World Communism. The Disintegration of a Secular Faith,* New York 1964.

Löwenthal, Richard, ed., *Issues in the Future of Asia: Communist and Non-Communist Alternatives,* New York, 1969.

Loziuk, N. I., and G. H. Bykov, *Problemy industrializatsii razvivaiushchikhsia stran* (Problems of the Industrialization of Developing Countries), Kiev, 1970.

Madariaga, Salvador de, *Latin America Between Eagle and Bear,* New York, 1962.

Mallin, Jay, ed., *"Che" Guevara on Revolution: A Documentary Overview,* Miami, 1969.

Manchkha, P. I., *Avangardnye otriady revoliutsionnoi bor'by v Afrike* (The Vanguard Detachments of the Revolutionary Struggle in Africa), Moscow, 1971.

Mander, John, The Unrevolutionary Society, New York, 1969.

Mandi, Peter, *Quantity and Quality in the Educational Policies of Developing Nations,* Budapest, 1969.

Mandi, Peter, *The Development of Education in Africa and its Problems,* Budapest, 1966.

Mao, Tse-tung, *On Revolution and War,* Garden City, 1969.

Mao, Tse-tung, *People of the World Unite and Defeat the U. S. Aggressors and All Their Running Dogs,* Peking, 1971.

Mao, Tse-tung, *Selected Works of Mao Tse-tung,* London, 1954.

Mao, Tse-tung, *The Question of Independence and Autonomy Within United Front,* Peking, 1954.

Mao Tse-tung on People's War, Peking, 1971.
Maoizm glazami kommunistov (Maoism Through Communist Eyes), Moscow, 1969.
Martin, Lawrence, ed., *Neutralism and Non-Alignment: The New States in World Affairs,* New York, 1962.
Marvin, David K., *Emerging Africa in World Affairs,* San Francisco, 1965.
Marx and Engels, Selected Works, Moscow, 1958.
Mavliutov, R. R., *Islam,* Moscow, 1969.
Mayer, Peter, *Cohesion and Conflict in International Communism,* The Hague, 1968.
Mayorov, V. V., *U. S. Aid: Weapon of the Monopolies,* Moscow, 1971.
McCabe, Robert K., *Storm over Asia: China and Southeast Asia; Thrust and Response,* New York, 1967.
McKenzie, Kermit E., *Comintern and World Revolution, 1928-1943,* New York, 1964.
McLane, Charles, *Soviet Strategies in Southeast Asia,* Princeton, 1966.
McVey, Ruth T., *The Rise of Indonesian Communism,* Ithaca, 1965.
McVey, Ruth T., *The Soviet View of the Indonesian Revolution,* Ithaca, 1962.
Mehnert, Klaus, *Peking and the New Left At Home and Abroad,* Berkeley, 1969.
Mehnert, Klaus, *Peking und Moskau* (Peking and Moscow), Stuttgart, 1962.
Melikian, O. N., *Neitralizm gosudarstv Afriki* (The Neutralism of African States), Moscow, 1966.
Mertens, Pierre, and Paul F. Smets, *L' Afrique du Pékin* (Peking's Africa), Brussels, 1966.
Mikhailov, S. S., ed., *Osvoboditel'noe dvizhenie v Latinskoi Amerike* (The Liberation Movement in Latin America), Moscow, 1964.
Millen, Bruce M., *The Political Role of Labor in Developing Countries,* Washington, 1963.
Miller, Donald L., *Strategy for Conquest: A Study of Communist Propaganda Techniques,* Washington, 1966.
Milovanov, I. V., et al., eds., *Rabochii klass i rabochee dvizhenie v stranakh Azii i Afriki,* (The Working Class and the Workers' Movement in the Countries of Asia and Africa), Moscow, 1965.
Mirovoi sotsializm i razvivaiushchiesia strany (World Socialism and Developing Countries), Moscow, 1968.
Mirskii, G. I., *Armiia i politika v stranakh Azii i Afriki* (The Army and Politics in the Countries of Asia and Africa), Moscow, 1970.
Modzhorian, L. A., *Kolonializm: vchera i segodniia* (Colonialism: Yesterday and Today), Moscow, 1967.
Mogutin, V. B., *Kapitalisticheskii kredit - orudie vneshne-ekonomicheskoi ekspansii* (Capitalist Credit - A Weapon of External Economic Expansion), Moscow, 1969.
Morrison, David, *USSR and Africa,* New York, 1964.
Mozengo, Abdul H., *Sino-Indonesian Relations, An Overview 1955-1965,* Santa Monica, 1965.
Muller, Kurt, *The Foreign Aid Programs of the Soviet Bloc and Communist China,* New York, 1967.
Mutagirov, D. Z., *Strategiia i taktika mezhdunarodnogo kommunisticheskogo dvizheniia* (The Strategy and Tactics of the International Communist Movement), Leningrad, 1969.

Naborov, V. B., and V. G. Kur'erov, *Vneshneekonomi cheskaia politika SShA i razvivaiushchiesia strany* (The Foreign Economic Policy of the USA and Developing Countries), Moscow, 1968.

Naik, J. A., *Soviet Policy Toward India: from Stalin to Brezhnev*, New Delhi, 1970.

National Liberation Movement, Vital Problems, Moscow, no-date.

Natsional'no-osvobodite'noe dvizhenie v Indonezii, 1942-1965, (The National-Liberation Movement in Indonesia, 1942-1965), Moscow, 1969.

Natsional'nye protsesy v stranakh srednego vostoka (National Processes in the Countries of the Middle East), Moscow, 1970.

Nekrasov, A. Ia., *SSSR i razvivaiushchiesia strany v OON* (The USSR and the Developing Nations in the UNO), Moscow, 1970.

Neuhauser, Charles, *Third World Politics: China and the Afro-Asian People's Solidarity Organization, 1957-1967*, Cambridge, 1968.

North, Robert, *Chinese Communism*, New York, 1966.

North, Robert, *The Foreign Relations of China*, Belmont, 1969.

Nove, Alec, *Communist Economic Strategy*, Washington, 1959.

Nove, Alec, and J. A. Newth, *The Soviet Middle East: A Communist Model for Development*, London, 1967.

Novosel'tseva, A. A., *Vlianie dvukh mirovykh sistem na ekonomiku razvivaiushchikhsia stran* (The Influence of Two World Systems On the Economy of Developing Countries), Moscow, 1969.

Nyerere, Julius K., *Freedom and Socialism*, New York, 1968.

Obminskii, E. Ie., *Torgovaia politika razvivaiushchikhsia stran* (Trading Policy of Developing Countries), Moscow, 1967.

Okello, John, *Revolution in Zanzibar*, Nairobi, 1967.

Oman, E. E., *Ideologicheskaia deiatel'nost' nezavisimykh stran Afriki* (Ideological Activity of Independent States of Africa), Moscow, 1971.

Orleanskaia, L. K., *Sel'sko-khoziaistvennaia kooperatsiia v nezavisimoi Indii* (Agrarian-Economic Cooperation in Independent India), Moscow, 1969.

Osipov, Iu. M., *Finansovye metody mobilizatsii nakopleniia v razvivaiushchikhsia stranakh* (Financial Methods of Mobilizing Capital Accumulation in Developing Countries), Moscow, 1969.

Oswald, J. Gregory, and Anthony J. Strover, eds., *The Soviet Union and Latin America*, London, 1970.

Oswald, J. Gregory, ed., *Soviet Image of Contemporary Latin America. A Documentary History, 1960-1968*, Austin, 1970.

Overstreet, Gene, and Marshall Windmiller, *Communism in India*, Berkeley, 1959.

Padmore, George, *Pan-Africanism or Communism*, London, 1956.

Page, Stanley W., *Lenin and World Revolution*, New York, 1959.

Page, Stephen, *The USSR and Arabia*, London, 1971.

Pauker, Guy J., *The Rise and Fall of the Communist Party of Indonesia*, Santa Monica, 1969.

Pennock, Roland D., ed., *Self-government in Modernizing Nations*, Englewood Cliffs, 1964.

Pentony, DeVere, E., ed., *Soviet Behavior in World Affairs*, San Francisco, 1962.

Peters, Geoffrey, *Yugoslav Foreign Policy Toward the Non-Aligned Countries*. An unpublished dissertation, American University, 1970.

Petersen, William, ed., *The Realities of World Communism*, Englewood Cliffs, 1963.

Petkoff, Teodoro, *Socialismo para Venezuela* (Socialism for Venezuela), Caracas, 1970.

Petkoff, Teodoro, *Checoeslovaquia: El Socialismo Como Problema* (Czechoslovakia: Socialism as A Problem), Caracas, 1969.

Pipes, Richard, *The Formation of the Soviet Union: Communism and Nationalism, 1917-1921*, Cambridge, 1954.

Politika SShA v stranakh iuzhnoi Azii (The Policy of the USA in the Countries of Southern Asia), Moscow, 1961.

Pomeroy, William J., ed., *Guerrilla Warfare and Marxism*, New York, 1968.

Ponomarev, B. N., *World Revolutionary Movement of the Working Class*, Moscow, 1967.

Ponomarev, B. N., et al., *Istoriia vneshnei politiki SSSR, I. 1917-1945, II. 1945-1970*. (History of the Foreign Policy of the USSR. I. 1917-1945, II. 1945-1970), Moscow, 1966 and 1971.

Popov, K. M., eds., *Kolonializm - zleishii vrag narodov vostoka* (Colonialism - the Worst Enemy of the Peoples of the East), Moscow, 1962.

Poppino, Rollie E., *Communism in Latin America: a History of the Movement, 1917-1963*, New York, 1964.

Potekhin, I. K., *African Problems, Analysis of An Eminent Soviet Scientist*, Moscow, 1969.

Potekhin, I. I., *Afrika smotrit v budushchee* (Africa Looks Toward the Future), Moscow, 1960.

Potekhin, I. I., *Narody Afriki* (The Peoples of Africa), Moscow, 1954.

Potemkin, Iu. V., *Alzhirskii narod v bor'be za nezavisimost'* (The Algerian People in the Struggle for Independence), Moscow, 1962.

Pozdniakov, E. A., *Molodye gosudarstva Azii i Afriki v OON* (Young States of Asia and Africa in the UNO), Moscow, 1971.

Problemy ekonomicheskoi nezavisimosti stran iugo-vostochnoi Azii (The Problems of Economic Independence of the Countries of Southeast Asia) Moscow, 1970.

Problemy industrializatsii razvivaiushchikhsia stran (Problems of Industrialization of Developing Countries), Moscow, 1971.

Prokhorov, G. M., *Problemy sotrudnichestva sotsialisticheskikh i razvivaiushchikhsia stran* (Problems of Cooperation of Socialist and Developing Countries), Moscow, 1966.

Pryor, Fred, *The Communist Foreign Trade System*, Cambridge, 1963.

Profsoiuzy stran zapadnoi Afriki (The Trade Unions of West Africa), Moscow, 1962.

Pye, Lucian W., *Guerrilla Communism in Malaya*, Princeton, 1956.

Ra'anan, Uri, *The USSR Arms the Third World*, Cambridge, 1969.

Rabochee dvizhenie v stranakh Azii i severnoi Afriki na sovremennom etape (The Workers' Movement in the Countries of Asia and North Africa at the Present Stage), Moscow, 1969.

Rabochii klass i antiimperialisticheskaia revoliutsiia v Azii, Afrike i Latinskoi Amerike (The Working Class and the Anti-Imperialist Revolution in Asia, Africa and Latin America), Moscow, 1969.

Rastiannikov, V. G., *Razvivaiushchiesia strany: prodovol'stvie i politika* (The Developing Countries: Food and Politics), Moscow, 1968.

Ratliff, William E., *Yearbook on Latin American Communist Affairs:* 1971, Stanford, 1972.

Revolutionary Movement in the Colonies. (Theses of the Sixth Comintern Congress), New York, 1932.

Ritvo, Herbert, *The New Soviet Society,* New York, 1962.

Romanova, Z. I., *Ekonomicheskaia ekspansiia SShA v Latinskoi Amerike* (Economic Expansion of the USA in Latin America), Moscow, 1963.

Romanovskii, S. K., *Mezhdunarodnye kul'turnye i nauchnye.ṣviazi SSSR* (International Cultural and Scholarly Ties of the USSR), Moscow, 1966.

Rossi, Mario, *The Third World: the Unaligned Countries and the World Revolution,* New York, 1963.

Rostovskii, S. N., *Rabochee i natsional'no-osvoboditel'noe dvizhenie v stranakh iugo-vostochnoi Azii posle vtoroi mirovoi voiny* (The Workers' and National-Liberation Movement in the Countries of Southeast Asia after the Second World War), Moscow, 1959.

Rothermund, Dietmar, *Indien und die Sowjetunion* (India and the Soviet Union), Köln, 1968.

Rubinstein, Alvin Z., *The Foreign Policy of the Soviet Union,* New York, 1966.

Rubinstein, Alvin Z., *Yugoslavia and the Non-Aligned World,* Princeton, 1970.

Rubinstein, Alvin Z., and George Ginsburgs, *Soviet and American Policies in the United Nations,* New York, 1971.

Rubinstein, Alvin, Z., *The Soviets in International Organizations; Changing Policy Toward Developing Countries, 1953-1963,* Princeton, 1964.

Rumiantsev, A., ed., *Puti razvitiia stran zavoievavshikh natsional'nuiu nezavisimost' i mirovoi sotsializm* (The Paths of Development of the Countries That Have Won National Independence and World Socialism), Moscow, 1964.

Russia Looks at Africa, London, 1960.

Rybakov, V. B., and L. V. Stepanov, *Pomoshch osvobodivshimsia stranam v politike i strategii imperializma* (The Aid to the Liberated Countries in the Policy and Strategy of Imperialism), Moscow, 1964.

Sable, Martin H., *Communism in Latin America, An International Bibliography: 1900-1945, 1960-1967,* Los Angeles, 1968.

Sager, Peter, *Moscow's Hand in India: An Analysis of Soviet Propaganda,* Berne, 1967.

Samuel, Albert, *Castrisme, Communisme, Démocratie Chrétienne en Amérique Latine* (Castroism, Communism, Christian Democracy in Latin America), Paris, 1966.

Sardesai, S. G., *India's Path to Socialism,* New Delhi, 1966.

Saunders, J. Roscoe, *The Challenge of World Communism in Asia,* Grand Rapids, 1964.

Savel'ev, N. A., *Natsional'naia burzhuaziia v stranakh Azii* (National Bourgeoisie in the Countries of Asia), Moscow, 1968.

Sawyer, Carole, *Communist Trade with Developing Countries, 1955-65,* New York, 1966.

Scalapino, Robert A., ed., *The Communist Revolution in Asia, Tactics, Goals and Achievements,* Englewood Cliffs, 1965 and 1969.

Schatten Fritz, *Communism in Africa,* New York, 1966.

Schmitt, Karl, *Communism in Mexico: a Study in Political Frustration,* Austin, 1965.

Schmidt, Dana A., *Yemen: the Unknown War,* New York, 1969.

Schramm, Stuart R., ed., *The Political Thought of Mao Tse-tung,* New York, 1969.

Seleznev, G. K., et al., *Strany Latinskoi Ameriki v sovremennykh mezhdunarodnykh otnosheniiakh* (The Countries of Latin America in Contemporary International Relations), Moscow, 1967.

Selezneva, Ie. I., *Politika neprisoiedineniia molodykh suverennykh gosudarstv Azii i Afriki* (The Policy of Non-Alignment of the Young Sovereign States of Asia and Africa), Moscow, 1966.

Sel'skokhoziaistvennye rabochie v stranakh Azii i Severnoi Afriki (Agricultural Workers in the Countries of Asia and North Africa), Moscow, 1969.

Semin, N. S., *Strany SEV i Afrika. Voprosy ekonomicheskogo sotrudnichestva* (The Comecon Countries and Africa. Questions of Economic Cooperation), Moscow, 1968.

Seven Letters Exchanged Between the Central Committee of the Communist Party of China and the Communist Party of the Soviet Union, Peking, 1964.

Shabal'ev, B. A., *Rabochii klass stran Magreba* (The Working Class of Maghreb), Moscow, 1968.

Sheinin, E. Ia., *Ekonomicheskaia ekspansia gosudarstv-chlenov EEE v Latinskoi Amerike* (The Economic Expansion of the States-Members of the EEC in Latin America), Moscow, 1969.

Shmelev, N. I., *Problemy ekonomicheskogo rosta razvivaiushchikhsia stran* (Problems of the Economic Growth of Developing Countries), Moscow, 1970.

Shpazhnikov, G. A., *Religii stran Afriki* (The Religions of African Countries), Moscow, 1967.

Shpirt, A. Iu., *Nauchno-tekhnicheskaia revoliutsiia i razvivaiushchiesia strany Azii i Afriki* (The Scientific-Technical Revolution and Developing Countries), Moscow, 1970.

Shpirt, A. Iu., *Ekspansiia inostrannogo gosudarstvennogo-monopolisticheskogo kapitala v Afrike* (The Expansion of Foreign State-Monopoly Capital in Africa), Moscow, 1966.

Sigmund, Paul E., ed., *The Ideologies of Developing Nations,* New York, 1972.

Simon, Maurice D., *Communist System Interaction with the Developing States, 1954-1962. A Preliminary Analysis,* Stanford, 1966.

Simon, Sheldon W., *The Broken Triangle: Peking, Djakarta and the PKI,* Baltimore, 1969.

Simoniia, N. A., *Ob osobennostiakh natsional'no-osvoboditel'nykh revoliutsii* (Special Features of National-Liberation Revolutions), Moscow, 1968.

Singh, Baljit, *A Planned Market Economy: India's Model,* Budapest, 1967.

Sinha, Viveka B., *The Red Rebel in India: A Study of Communist Strategy and Tactics,* New Delhi, 1968.

Sivovolov, A. M., *Ekonomicheskie problemy soiuza rabochego klassa i krest'ianstva v Latinskoi Amerike,* (The Economic Problems of the Union of the Working Class and the Peasantry in Latin America), Moscow, 1963.

Sivovolov, A. M., *Natsional'no-osvoboditel'noe dvizhenie v Afrike* (The National-Liberation Movement in Africa), Moscow, 1961.

Skorov, G. E., *Razvivaiushchiesia strany: obrazovanie, zaniatost', ekonomicheskii rost* (The Developing Countries: Education, Employment, Economic Growth), Moscow, 1971.

Slovenská akademie vied, *Z najnovšich dejin československo-sovietských vztahov po roku 1945* (From the most recent history of Czechoslovak-Soviet Relations after 1945), Bratislava, 1962.

Smelev, N. P., *Ideologiia imperializma i problemy slaborazvitykh stran,* (The Ideology of Imperialism and the Problems of Less-developed Countries), Moscow, 1962.

Smirnov, G. V., et al., eds., *Planirovanie v razvivaiushchikhsia stranakh Afriki* (Planning in Developing Countries of Africa), Moscow, 1970.

Solodovnikov, V. G., *Afrika vybiraet put'* (Africa Chooses the Way), Moscow, 1970.

Solodovnikov, V. G., et al., eds., *Politicheskie partii Afriki* (The Political Parties of Africa), Moscow, 1970.

Solodovnikov, V. G., *Africa Fights for Independence,* Moscow, 1970.

Solodovnikov, V. G., et al., eds., *Africa in Soviet Studies,* Moscow, 1969.

Solodovnikov, V. G., and V. P. Rumiantsev, eds., *Strany Afriki* (The Countries of Africa), Moscow, 1969.

Solonitskii, A. S., *Eksport kapitala v neokolonialistskoi strategii byvshikh metropolii* (The Export of Capital in the Neo-Colonialist Strategy of Former Metropolitan Countries), Moscow, 1971.

Sorokin, G., et al, eds., *Mirovoi sotsializm i razvivaiushchiesia strany* (World Socialism and Developing Countries), Moscow, 1969.

Sotsialreformizm i kolonial'nyi vopros (Social Reformism and the Colonial Question), Moscow, 1961.

Sovremennye ideologicheskie problemy razvivaiushchikhsia stran Asii i Afriki (Contemporary Ideological Problems of the Developing Countries of Asia and Africa), Moscow, 1969.

Spector, Ivan, *The Soviet Union and the Muslim World, 1917-1958,* Seattle, 1959.

Spirkin, Aleksandr G., *Theoretical Questions of Communist Strategy and Tactics,* Moscow, 1966.

SShA i razvivaiushchiesia strany, (USA and Developing Countries), Moscow, 1969.

Staley, Eugene, *The Future of Underdeveloped Countries: Political Implications of Economic Development,* New York, 1961.

Stahn, Eberhard, *Kommunistische Modelle für Afrika? Ghana and Guinea,* (Communist Models for Africa? Ghana and Guinea), Hanover, 1967.

Starushenko, G. B., *Natsiia i gosudarstvo v osvobozhdaiushichikhsia stranakh* (Nation and State in Emerging Countries), Moscow, 1967.

Stauber, Leland, *Recent Soviet Policy in the Underdeveloped Countries. The Significance of the "National Democracy" Doctrine.* Unpublished Dissertation, Harvard University, 1964.

Stein, Arthur, *India and the Soviet Union,* Chicago, 1969.

Štěpanovský, Jiří, ed., *Dokumenty k národně-osvobozeneckému hnuti, 1955-1961,* (Documents Concerning the National-Liberation Movement, 1955-1961), Praha, 1963.

Stokke, Beard R., *Soviet and East European Trade and Aid in Africa,* New York, 1967.

Strausz-Hupé, Robert, *Protracted Conflict,* New York, 1959.

Sufrin, Sidney C., *Unions in Emerging Societies,* Syracuse, 1964.

Svanidze, I. A., *Problemy razvitiia sel'skogo khoziaistva Afriki* (The Problems of Development of Agrarian Economy of Africa), Moscow, 1969.

Sworakowski, Witold S., *The Communist International and Its Front Organizations,* Stanford, 1965.

Szentes, Tamas, *Economic and Social Disintegration and Some Questions of Self-Help in the Developing Countries,* Budapest, 1969.

Tachau, Frank, *The Developing Nations. What Path to Modernization?* New York, 1972.

Tang, Peter S. H., *The Nature of Communist Strategy in the Areas of Emerging Nations,* Washington, 1962.

Tang, Peter S. H., *Communist China as a Developmental Model for Underdeveloped Countries,* Washington, 1960.

Tarabrin, Ie. A., *Strategiia i taktika neokolonializma Anglii* (The Strategy and Tactics of English Neo-Colonialism), Moscow, 1969.

Tarasov, K. S., ed., *Strany Latinskoi Ameriki. Politiko-ekonomicheskii spravochnik* (The Countries of Latin America. A Political-Economic Manual), Moscow, 1969.

Tatarovskaia, I. M., *Razvivaiushchiesia strany v bor'be za mir* (Developing Countries in the Struggle for Peace), Moscow, 1970.

Taufer, Otakar, *Význam hospodářské spolupráce s africkými zeměmi* (The Importance of Economic Cooperation with African Countries), Praha, 1964.

Ten Glorious Years 1949-1959, Peking, 1960.

Teoriia ekonomicheskogo razvitiia osvobodivshikhsia stran Azii (The Theory of the Economic Development of Liberated Countries), Moscow, 1970.

The USSR and Developing Countries. (Economic Cooperation). Moscow, no-date.

Thomas, L. V., *Le socialisme et l' Afrique* (Socialism and Africa), Paris, 1966.

Thornton, Thomas P., ed., *The Third World in Soviet Perspective,* Princeton, 1964.

Tiagunenko, V. L., *Bypassing Capitalism,* Moscow, 1966.

Tiagunenko, V. L., *Problemy sovremennykh natsional'no-osvoboditel'nykh revoliutsii* (Problems of Contemporary National-Liberation Revolutions), Moscow, 1969.

Tiagunenko, V. L., et al., eds., *Klassy i klassovaia bor'ba v razvivaiushchikhsia stranakh* (Classes and Class Struggle in Developing Countries), Moscow, 1967-1968.

Trager, Frank, and William Henderson, eds., *Communist China 1949-1969. A Twenty-Year Appraisal,* New York, 1971.

Treadgold, Donald W., ed., *Soviet and Chinese Communism. Similarities and Differences,* Seattle, 1967.

Triska, Jan F., and David D. Finley, *Soviet Foreign Policy,* New York, 1968.

Tropkin, N. V., *Ob osnovakh strategii i taktiki Leninizma* (The Bases of the Strategy and Tactics of Leninism), Moscow, 1955.

Trukhanovsky, V. G., *Leninskim vneshnepoliticheskim kursom* (Following the Leninist Course of Foreign Policy), Moscow, 1971.

Tuchkin, G. M., *Ekonomicheskaia effektivnost' vneshnei torgovli* (The Economic Effectiveness of Foreign Trade), Moscow, 1969.

Tuganova, O. E., *Mezhdunarodnye otnosheniia na blizhnem i srednem vostoke,* (International Relations in the Near and Middle East), Moscow, 1967.

Tumanova, L. K., *Formirovanie afrikanskoi burzhuazii* (The Forming of the African Bourgeoisie), Moscow, 1969.

Ulam, Adam B., *The Unfinished Revolution,* New York, 1960.

Ul'ianovskii, R. A., *The Dollar and Asia. U. S. Neo-Colonialist Policy in Action,* Moscow, 1965.

Ul'ianovskii, R. A., *Neokolonializm SShA i slaborazvitye strany Azii* (The U. S. Neo-Colonialism and the Less Developed Countries of Asia), Moscow, 1963.

Ul'ianovskii, R. A., *Sotsializm in osvobodivshiesia strany* (Socialism and the Liberated Countries), Moscow, 1972.

Ul'ianovskii, R. A., ed., *Nekapitalisticheskii put' razvitiia stran Afriki* (The Non-Capitalist Path of Development of the Countries of Africa), Moscow, 1967.

U. S. Congress, *Communist Conspiracy. Strategy and Tactics of World Communism.* House Report No 2240- , 1956-

U. S. Department of State, *Intervention of International Communism In Guatemala,* Publication No 5556,

U. S. Department of State, *The Threat of Soviet Economic Policy,* Publication No 7234, 1961.

U. S. Department of State, *The Sino-Soviet Economic Offensive Through June 30, 1962,* Research Memorandum RSB-145, 1962.

U. S. Department of State, *Communist Governments and Developing Nations: Aid and Trade,* Research Memorandum RSB-50, 1966.

U. S. Department of State, *Communist Governments and Developing Nations: Economic Aid and Trade,* Research Memorandum RSB-80, 1967.

U. S. Department of State, *Communist Governments and Developing Nations: Aid and Trade in 1967,* Research Memorandum RSE-120, 1968.

U. S. Department of State, *Communist Governments and Developing Nations: Aid and Trade in 1968,* Research Memorandum RSE-65, 1969.

U. S. Department of State, *Communist States and Developing Countries: Aid and Trade in 1969,* Research Study RECS-5, 1970.

U. S. Department of State, *Communist States and Developing Countries: Aid and Trade in 1970,* Research Study RECS-15, 1971.

U. S. Department of State, *Communist States and Developing Countries: Aid and Trade in 1971,* Research Study RECS-3, 1972.

U. S. Department of State, *World Strength of the Communist Party Organizations,* 23rd Annual Report, 1971 Edition.

U. S. Department of State, *World Strength of the Communist Party Organizations,* 24th Annual Report, 1972 Edition.

U. S. Department of State, *Educational and Cultural Exchanges between Communist and Non-Communist Countries in 1969,* Research Study RSES-35, 1970.

U. S. Department of State, *Educational and Cultural Exchanges between Communist and Noncommunist Countries in 1970,* Research Study RSES-34, 1971.

U. S. Department of State, *Educational and Cultural Exchanges between Communist and Noncommunist Countries in 1971,* Research Study RESS-57, 1972.

U. S. Information Agency, *Communist Propaganda Organizations and Activities in the Near East and South Asia During 1966,* R-23-67, 1967.

U. S. Information Agency, *Communist Propaganda in Africa, 1966-1967,* R-16-68, 1968.

U. S. Information Agency, *Communist Propaganda Activities in the East Asia and Pacific Area-1967,* R-9-68, 1968.

U. S. Information Agency, *Communist Propaganda Activities in Latin America - 1967*, R-15-68, 1968.

U. S. Information Agency, *Communist Propaganda Organizations and Activities in Latin America During 1966*, R-17-67, 1967.

U. S. Information Agency, *Communist Propaganda Activities in The Near East and South Asia-1967*, R-13-68, 1968.

U. S. Information Agency, *Communist Propaganda Activities in The East and Pacific Area, 1966*, R-22-67, 1967.

Usneseni a dokumenty U. V. KSČ od celostátní konference KSČ 1960 do XII sjezdu KSČ (Resolutions and Documents of the C. C. of the Communist Party of Czechoslovakia from the All-state conference of the CPC 1960 to the xii. Congress of the CPC), Praha, 1962.

Utkin, E. A., *Problemy ekonomicheskogo razvitiia osvobodivshikhsia stran* (The Problems of the Economic Development of the Liberated Countries), Moscow, 1968.

V zashchitu bortsov protiv reaktsii i imperializma. K sobytiiam v Indonezii (For the Defense of The Fighters Against Reaction and Imperialism. Concerning the Events in Indonesia), Moscow, 1967.

Vakhrushev, V. V., *Neokolonializm i mezhdunarodnye organizatsii* (Neo-Colonialism and International Organizations), Moscow, 1968.

Van der Kroef, Justus, *Communism in Malaysia and Singapore: A Contemporary Survey*, The Hague, 1967.

Van der Kroef, Justus, *The Communist Party of Indonesia. Its History, Program and Tactics*, Vancouver, 1965.

Van Ness, Peter, *Revolution and China's Foreign Policy: Peking's Support for Wars of National Liberation*, Berkeley, 1970.

Vaněk, Jan, *Afrika na prahu samostatného politického a ekonomického rozvoje* (Africa on the Threshold of An Independent Political and Economic Development), Praha, 1963.

Velikaia okt'iabrskaia sotsialisticheskaia revoliutsiia i nátsional'no-osvoboditel'noe dvizhenie narodov Azii, Afriki i Latinskoi Ameriki. Mezhdunarodnaia nauchnaia konferentsiia, Baku, (The Great October Socialist Revolution and the National-Liberation Movement of the Peoples of Asia, Africa and Latin America. The International Scholarly Conference, Baku), Moscow, 1969.

Venys, Ladislav, *African Policies of the Socialist World, the Case of East Africa*, Syracuse, 1968.

Verin, V. P., *Prezidentskie respubliki v Afrike* (Presidential Republics in Africa), Moscow, 1963.

Vinogradova, L. V., *Afrika: voprosy integratsii ekonomiki* (Africa: Questions of Economic Integration), Moscow, 1968.

Višváder, František, *Latinská Amerika - nepokojný kontinent* (Latin America - a Tumultuous Continent), Bratislava, 1963.

Vol'skii, V. V., *Latinskaia Amerika: neft' i nezavisimost'* (Latin America: Petroleum and Independence), Moscow, 1964.

Vol'skii, V. V., ed., *SSSR i Latinskaia Amerika, 1917-1967*, (The USSR and Latin America, 1917-1967), Moscow, 1967.

Vyshinskii, A. J., and S. A. Lozovskii, *Diplomaticheskii slovar'* (Diplomatic Dictionary), Moscow, 1948.

Wallerstein, Immanuel M., *Africa, the Politics of Independence*, New York, 1961.

Walters, Robert S., *American and Soviet Aid: A Comparative Analysis,* Pittsburgh, 1970.

Whelan, Joseph G., *World Communism, 1967-1969: Soviet Efforts to Re-establish Control,* U. S. Senate, Washington, 1970.

Whiting, Allen, *Soviet Politics in China, 1917-1924,* New York, 1954.

Wilber, Charles K., *The Soviet Model and Underdeveloped Countries,* Chapel Hill, 1969.

Wiles, P. J. D., *Communist International Economics,* New York, 1969.

Wint, Guy, *Communist China's Crusade; Mao's Road to Power and the New Campaign for World Revolution,* New York, 1965.

Woddis, Jack, *Africa, the Roots of Revolt,* London, 1960.

Woddis, Jack, *Africa, the Lion Awakens,* London, 1961.

Woddis, Jack, *Africa, the Way Ahead,* New York, 1964.

Woddis, Jack, *An Introduction to Neo-Colonialism,* London, 1967.

Wolfe, Charles, *Foreign Aid: Theory and Practice in Southern Asia,* Princeton, 1960.

Worsley, Peter, *The Third World,* Chicago, 1964.

Yakemtchouk, R., *Assistance économique et pénétration industrielle des pays de l' Est en Afrique* (Economic Assistance and Industrial Penetration of Eastern Countries in Africa), Paris, 1966.

Yakovlev, A., *World Socialist System and National-Liberation Movement,* Moscow, no date.

Yearbook of International Communist Affairs, 1966 and following years, Stanford, 1966 and following years.

Zabih, Sepehr, *The Communist Movement in Iran,* Berkeley, 1966.

Zablocki, Clement J., ed., *Sino-Soviet Rivalry: Implications for U. S. Policy,* New York, 1966.

Zagladin, V. V., ed., *Mezhdunarodnoie kommunisticheskoe dvizhenie* (The International Communist Movement), Moscow, 1970.

Zagoria, Donald, *The Sino-Soviet Conflict, 1956-1961,* Princeton, 1962.

Zevin, L. Z., *Novye tendentsii v ekonomicheskom sotrudnichestve sotsialisti-cheskikh i razvivaiushchikhsia stran* (New Trends in Economic Cooperation of Socialist and Developing Countries), Moscow, 1970.

Zhukov, E. M., ed., *Sovremennye teorii sotsializma "natsional'nogo" tipa* (Contemporary Theories of Socialism of "National" Type), Moscow, 1967.

Zhukov Iu., et al., *The Third World: Problems and Prospects,* Moscow, 1970.

Zhukov, Ie. M., et al. eds., *Problemy natsional'no-osvoboditel'nogo dvizheniia* (Problems of the National-Liberation Movement), Moscow, 1970.

Zimmerman, William, *Soviet Perspectives on International Relations,* Princeton, 1969.

Periodicals

Africa in Soviet Studies
African Affairs
African Digest
Al- Ahram (Cairo)
Al Jumhuriyya (Cairo)
American Political Science Review
American Statesman

Arbeiterzeitung (Vienna)
Argumenty (Warsaw)
Asian Survey
Austin American
Austin Statesman
Avanti (Rome)
Aziia i Afrika Segodnia

Borba (Belgrade)
Buenos Aires Herald
Bulgarian Press Survey (New York)
The Bulletin (Bonn)
České slovo (Munich)
Československý svět (Prague)
Christian Science Monitor
Current Digest of the Soviet Press
Czechoslovak Foreign Trade (Prague)
Czechoslovak Press Survey
   (New York)
Daedalus
Daily Nation (Nairobi)
Dějiny a současnost (Prague)
The Democratic Journalist
Department of State Bulletin
Die Zeit (Hamburg)
Družstevník (Prague)
East Europe
Ekonomicheskaia gazeta
Ekonomska politika (Belgrade)
Este y Oeste
Filosofický časopis (Prague)
Foreign Affairs
Free Labour World
Granma (Havana)
Glos Pracy (Warsaw)
Harper's Magazine
Hospodářské noviny (Prague)
Hungarian Press Survey (New Yor
Ila Al Aman (Beirut)
Information Bulletin
   (of the World Marxist Review)
International Affairs (London)
International Affairs -
   Mezhdunarodnaia zhizn' (Mosco
International Journal
Izvestiia
Journal of Inter-American Studies
Kommunist (Moscow)
Komsomolskaia pravda
Krasnaia zvezda
Kulkereskedelem (Budapest)
Kulturní tvorba (Prague)
L'Unità (Rome)
Labour Monthly
Latinskaia Amerika
Lidová demokracie (Prague)
Literární noviny (Prague)
Manchester Guardian -
   Le Monde Weekly

Mezinárodní politika (Prague)
Mirovaia ekonomika i
   mezhdunarodnye otnosheniia
Mizan
Mladá fronta (Prague)
Narody Azii i Afriki
The National Observer
Nedeljne informativne novine
   (Belgrade)
Nepszabadsag (Budapest)
Neue Zürcher Zeitung
Neues Deutschland (Berlin)
New Leader
New Times (Novoe Vremia)
New York Times
Newsweek
Nová mysl (Prague)
Novinář (Prague)
Novo vreme (Sofia)
Nowe drogi (Warsaw)
Odborář (Prague)
Orbis
Ost-Probleme
Partelet (Budapest)
Peking Review
People's Daily (Peking)
Polish Press Survey (New York)
Politicheskoe samoobrazovanie
Politika (Belgrade)
Politique étrangère
Politique Hebdo (Paris)
Polityka (Warsaw)
Práce (Prague)
Prague News Letter
Praha-Moskva (Prague)
Pravda (Bratislava)
Pravda (Moscow)
Pravda (Plzeň)
Predvoj (Bratislava)
Problems of Communism '
Rabotnichesko Delo (Sofia)
Red Flag (Peking)
Review of International Affairs
Review of Politics
Rudé právo (Prague)
Rumanian Press Survey (New York)
Saturday Review
Slowo powszechne (Warsaw)
Social Science Quarterly
Socialist Thought and Practice
   (Belgrade)

Sovetskoe gosudarstvo i pravo
Student (Prague)
Survey
Svět v obrazech (Prague)
Svobodné slovo (Prague)
Sztandar mlodych (Warsaw)
Tarsadalmi Szemle (Budapest)
Terzo Mondo
Time
To The Point
Tribuna (Prague)
Trybuna (Warsaw)
U. S. News and World Report
USSR and Third World
Večerní Praha (Prague)
Voprosy ekonomiki

Voprosy filosofii
Voz proletaria (Bogota)
The Washington Post
World Marxist Review
World Politics
The World Today
Yugoslav Facts and Views
Yugoslav Life
Yugoslav Survey
Zahraniční obchod (Prague)
Zemědělské noviny (Prague)
Zeri i Popullit (Tirana)
Život strany (Prague)
Żolnierz wolnośći (Warsaw)
Życie Warszawy (Warsaw)

Index

Abarka, Alfredo, 180
Abboud, Ibrahim, General, 135, 430, 439
adventurism, see blanquism and dogmatism
Afghanistan, 9, 283, 287, 292, 303, 304, 308, 311, 316, 326, 352, 374
African Party of Independence, 130
African Trade Union Confederation, 106
Afro-Asian Solidarity (conference and committee), 115, 370
Afro-Asian Permanent Writers' Bureau, 239-40, 398
Afro-Shirazi Party, 130
Afro-Shirazis, 185
agrarian reforms, 17, 76, 154, 177-183, 191, 193, 218, 252, 274, 460
agriculture, 273, 274-76, 277, 296, 459-60
Aidit, 106, 187
Al Fatah, 433
Albania, 41, 55, 68, 113, 279, 296, 369, 418, 419, 446
Algeria, 52, 136, 137, 146, 159, 160, 162, 180, 212, 237, 246, 248, 252, 253, 294, 306, 311, 312, 313, 327, 352, 368, 374, 375, 376, 415, 428, 431, 438, 460, 461
Ali-Yata, 105, 136
All-African Trade Union Center, 106
All-African Trade Union Federation, 105
All-India Kisam Sabba, 185

All-India Student Federation, 237
All-India Trade Union Congress, 106, 115
Allen, Robert L., 305, 309
Allende, Salvador, 79, 109, 156, 157, 180, 184, 192, 241, 423, 426, 460
Altman, Gavro, 45
Alves, Mario, 422
anarcho-syndicalism, 96
Angola, 428
anti-yanquismo, 110
Arab Socialist Rebirth Party, 131
Arab Socialist Union, 130, 162, 253
Arbenz, Jacobo Guzman, 134
Argentina, 104, 134, 138, 141, 148, 185, 234, 240, 242, 308, 323, 422
Arismendi, Rodney, 151, 422
armed struggle (see also guerrillas and wars of national liberation), 43, 54, 56, 77, 84, 149, 150, 239, 390, 409, 410, 418-28 passim, 431, 433, 434, 436-39 passim, 448, 450-51, 466
army officers, 19, 51, 219, 224, 225, 244-47, 248, 461-62, 464
Arzumanian, A. A., 23, 74, 90
Aspaturian, Vernon, 7
Aubrey, Henry G., 318, 320, 328
Australia, 304
Avakov, R. 90
Avant-Garde Socialist Party, 237

Bagdash, Khaled, 91, 136, 137, 143, 161, 198, 251
Baltic Republics, 417